Musical!

A GRAND TOUR

THE RISE, GLORY, AND FALL OF AN AMERICAN INSTITUTION

Denny Martin Flinn

Schirmer Books
An Imprint of Simon & Schuster Macmillan
New York

Prentice Hall International
London Mexico City New Delhi Singapore Sydney Toronto

Schirmer Books
An Imprint of Simon & Schuster Macmillan
1633 Broadway
New York, NY 10019

Library of Congress Catalog Number: 96-46030

Printed in the United States of America

Printing number

1 2 3 4 5 6 7 8 9 10

Library of Congress Cataloging-in-Publication Data

Flinn, Denny Martin.
Musical! : a grand tour / by Denny Martin Flinn.
p. cm.
Includes index.
ISBN 0-02-864610-X (alk. Paper)
1. Musicals—United States—History and criticism. I. Title.
ML1711.F57 1997
782.1'4'0973—dc20 96-46030
CIP
MN

This paper meets the requirements of ANSI/NISO Z39.48–1992 (Permanence of Paper).

Musical!
A GRAND TOUR

For Brook and Dylan,

and all the children

who missed it

Musical Comedy, the most glorious words in the English language.

—JULIAN MARSH IN *42ND STREET*

When I was twelve years old, I was taken to see a road company of *How to Succeed in Business Without Really Trying,* and the pre-Broadway tour of *Oliver!* (although I didn't know what a pre-Broadway tour was, or a road company). I was mesmerized. There I saw worlds of such boundless energy, humor, joy, eccentricity, oddity, and passion that I wanted to live there. I didn't know then they were artificial, manufactured. I didn't even know there was a backstage. I only knew it was musical comedy.

Somehow I found my way inside. And although I spent the next two decades deconstructing the illusions, to this day, whenever I am in an audience, when the house lights go down, I get goose bumps waiting those interminable seconds for a new world, a singing and dancing world, to invite me in.

I don't know why everyone doesn't feel the same way. I've actually heard several (eccentric) people say, "I don't like musicals." I feel sorry for them. Unwilling or unable to suspend their disbelief for the most theatrical of all arts, or perhaps unaware that they have yet to attend a first-class production of a good musical, they are missing one of the great cultural achievements of twentieth-century America—one a long time coming, and one that will one day be a long time gone.

This book is about the art and craft of the American musical. Part 1 is an overview of those theatres in world history from which certain ideas derived, ideas that ended up as a fundamental part of the American musical theatre. It isn't very well acknowledged, for example, that Shakespeare included many songs and dances in his comedies, nor that Molière virtually wrote musicals. In those days—as too often in this one—musical sequences were considered to be something less than literature, and often were quickly forgotten.

Part 2 traces the American musical via the landmark productions, with a few side trips to include progress made not so much one stunning opening night, but over a number of shows. It begins with *The Black Crook* in 1866, because that spectacle is generally acknowledged as the first American musical comedy. Don't look, however, for anything really exciting to happen until the turn of the century.

The American musical began with *Little Johnny Jones* in 1904, because its creator George M. Cohan, growing up in vaudeville, infused his outsider's assault on Broadway with the slick show biz and Americana he had learned there. The musical got serious with *Show Boat* in 1927 and *Porgy and Bess* in 1935. Both undertook astoundingly literate, realistic stories, a huge leap forward from the princess-of-Bavaria-in-disguise-as-chimney-sweep-meets-dashing-young-man-in-Long-Island-drawing-room musicals of the twenties. Both boasted genius composers of American music who sculpted their melodies to illustrate the dramatic intentions of the book.

Dance, long the most entertaining part of the American musical, came of age when Agnes de Mille choreographed *Oklahoma!* in 1943, not only because she brought state-of-the-art American character ballet onto a stage that had seen only classical ballet and Rockette-style tap dancing, but because she insisted on a theme for her dances, extending our understanding of the principal characters with a vivid psychological "dream" ballet. With that, the golden age was well underway.

The year 1957 brought *West Side Story,* not only a greatly entertaining show and a leap forward in the use of dance as plot and song as character, but a smoothly integrated show that virtually defined the structure of a perfect musical. It inaugurated an era during which musicals were *staged.* Not just the dances choreographed, not just the songs set carefully in spotlights, not just efficient entrances and exits, but a whole flow of scene-song-dance structure devised by a director-choreographer for maximum fluidity.

If *Oklahoma!* defines the beginning of the golden age, *A Chorus Line* (1975) marks its peak. Here the integration of singing, acting, and dancing came into full flower, with every idea put forth to the audience not in song, dance, *or* dialogue but in song, dance, *and* dialogue virtually simultaneously; a show composed and choreographed to within an inch of its life in a cinematic and aural fluidity moving so swiftly from idea to idea that it brooked no set, but took place on an empty stage.

That was the essence of the American musical. We invented the actor who can sing, the singer who can dance, the dancer who can act. We invented the people who can do all three. We created the shows that demanded those talents.

When *A Chorus Line* gave its final Broadway performance fifteen years after it opened, the last great American musical went dark, and the epoch was over.

That year critic Jonathan Yardley wrote, "When a cultural phenomenon has run its course, there's little to do except go on to other things. That no doubt is what Sondheim has been trying to do in his solemn musicals . . . and Lloyd Webber in his overpadded spectaculars; but whatever these things may be, they aren't Broadway musicals as we once knew and loved them."

The musical is an art form like any other, destined to change, and ultimately, like the sock that is darned so many times there isn't a single original thread left, metamorphose completely.

And one day you wonder, "What happened to that great old sock I used to wear?" To find out, we have to begin long ago and far away . . .

"The pestilence lasted during both this and the following year, the consulship of Gaius Sulpicius Peticus and Gaius Licinius Stolo. In the latter year (364 B.C.) nothing memorable occurred, except that with the object of appeasing the divine displeasure they made a banquet to the Gods, being the third in the history of the city; and when neither human wisdom nor the help of Heaven was found to mitigate the scourge, men gave way to superstitious fears, and, amongst other efforts to disarm the wrath of the Gods, are said also to have instituted scenic entertainments. This was a new departure for a warlike people, whose only exhibitions had been those of the circus; but indeed it began in a small way, as most things do, and even so was imported from abroad. Without any singing, without imitating the action of singers, players who had been brought in from Etruria danced to the strains of the flautist and performed not ungraceful evolutions in the Tuscan fashion. Next the young Romans began to imitate them, at the same time exchanging jests in uncouth verses, and bringing their movements into a certain harmony with the words. And so the amusement was adopted, and frequent use kept it alive."

—LIVY (59 B.C.–17 A.D.)

Part One
EUROPEAN INFLUENCES

ANTIQUITIES

The city needs its playwrights.

—ARISTOPHANES

GREEK COMEDY

In the fourth and fifth centuries B.C., the great Greek city-state of Athens sponsored dramatic festivals twice a year (without censorship or political interference), *and* paid the two-obol entry charge to the theatre for those too poor to pay it themselves. (In *Frogs* Aristophanes has Dionysus say of the fare for transportation to the underworld, "Two obols seems the entry everywhere in the world!")

Athenian society felt that competition, in both sport and art, was the surest way to stimulate achievement. Officials were appointed annually by lot six or seven months prior to the festivals. Dramatists supplied this board with their scripts. Since these officials were unlikely to possess any special qualifications as literary or theatrical critics, the opportunity lay (much as it does today) more with those playwrights who were well known and established by previous festival productions of their work than with newcomers.

Posterity has been an even harsher critic, for of fifty Athenian comic playwrights whose careers overlapped, only Aristophanes' plays have survived (and only 11 out of 40 he wrote).

There is no evidence to support the idea that politics ever interfered with this process. Aristophanes' comedies are replete with examples of attacks on the men in power, the respected social, educational, legal, and political institutions, and the reigning political viewpoints. No playwright in Broadway history has ever been so direct in his or her critical attacks, except Gore Vidal in his 1972 play *An Evening with Richard Nixon and....* Vidal's use of masks, staging, debate, and frontal assault on the subject matter closely resembled Aristophanic comedy. Aristophanes' position was generally conservative, for it was to new ideas that he most often took exception. Not only could he have expected some of his victims to be in the audience, on occasion he would harangue the crowd itself for their taste and judgement. His parodies were so exact, his lyrics and imagery so elegiac, his buffoonery so comic, that audiences adored him. As for public sponsorship of his plays and the lack of censorship or interference in the process, Aristophanes had been born into the first and finest democracy the world had ever known.

For each of those plays that was selected a producer came forward to support the effort. Aristophanes wrote for three to five actors who were supplied by the state, indicating that they were on some sort of fixed yearly salary. The production values of a play, including the elaborate masks and costumes and the training of the twenty-four chorus members, was the fiscal responsibility of the benefactor. As this was considered an honor, especially if the play were to take first prize and the producer's name were inscribed on a monument (erected at his own expense), there seems to have been much the same inducement as is held out to philanthropists today—the public glory of being known for one's taste and charity. The producer was also responsible for a feast (or opening night party) following the performance. Aristophanes followed the ancient wisdom, "never put up your own money." Five of his plays were produced by Calistratus, two by Philonides, and two by the playwright Ararus, one of Aristophanes' three sons. One he did produce himself which, born of a wealthy father, he would have had the resources to do.

The producer also had the obligation of staging the production. It is not known how often the producer felt capable of mounting the play or how much of the direction and choreography Aristophanes himself participated in. Though little is known about the physical movements of the chorus, they were a unit organized independently ("Do you think we could get the Acropolis Balladeers?") and probably provided much of their own choreography.

The direction was very creative work, for the profusion of effects available could be used in a variety of ways. Few stage directions other than entrances and exits are recorded in the manuscripts ("Enter Iris, from above") and translators often have difficulty not only deciding who is speaking but exactly who is on stage at any given time. Because only three or four actors were employed, some doubling and tripling of roles was required, with the actors exchanging masks off stage.

Choreography concerned the improvisatory movements of actors when singing ribald songs, as well as the more formal dancing of the chorus, who represented wasps, animals, clouds, birds, men, and women. The all-male chorus acted not only as women, but distinguished between country women, city women, and slaves.

At the finale of *Wasps,* the chorus leader exhorts the audience to

> *. . . come if you like, dance with me,*
> *Join with the chorus, no one before*
> *Has danced, danced out a comedy!*

(Involving the audience would remain in vogue through the age of Molière, when aristocratic ballets were devised for royal participation.)

Greek Old Comedy was divided into seven sections, and Aristophanes and his fellow playwrights always employed the same structure. There were variations, and the form succumbed to periodic changes, but the greatest flexibility was generally employed within, rather than outside, this format. The greatest achievements were in the best use of an established criteria.

In structure and concept, the nearest form to Greek Old Comedy is vaudeville, where the audience, which did not expect a logical or sequential connection between the various acts, was entertained by song and dance, monologue, chorus girls, topical satire, trained animal acts, magicians, and jugglers. What the audience did expect, in both Aristophanes and vaudeville, was a specific number and type of acts, certain types of jokes, and satirical allusions to current affairs.

The earliest theatres consisted of a broad flat playing area facing the concave slope of a hill. By Aristophanes' time, the back of the playing area had been fitted with a building two stories high, with working doors and windows and a flat roof. Windows in the upstage building were functional and characters are seen climbing in and out of them, as well as passing overhead as Gods, clouds or birds. *Birds* takes place in the lyrical and imaginative "Cloudcookooland," and the possible stagings are full of exhilarating beauty. The building housed at least one and probably two doors during Aristophanes' early comedies, and before he was through a standard of three doors had been established. Most of the physical property was meant for the tragedies, and it was felt that comic playwrights could make do with the same.

The area immediately in front of this building became the stage for the principal actors, and the larger area in front of that became the playing area for the chorus, which came to be known as the orchestra. One or two steps separated the stage from the orchestra because the principal characters had many interactions with the chorus and needed to step back and forth easily. There were entrances on both sides of the orchestra near the stage, and because the theatre in Athens faced south, with the town and harbor to audience right and the open country to the left, it became a convention that those who made their entrance from the right (stage left) came from the town or the sea, and those who entered from audience left (stage right) came a long distance by land.

There were several mechanical devices in use. One was a platform on which interior scenes could be played and various props rolled out onto the stage. Another was a machine that could help an actor appear in or fly through the air, which was probably operated from the roof of the house. Other devices could suspend an actor in midair, imitate thunder, and allow an actor to appear from underground, the latter a trap through which an actor could be pushed. There was no stage lighting; all performances were carried out in daylight. Eventually painted drops were available for scenes, and playwrights, producers, and directors went to spectacular lengths. An ancient Medicean manuscript indicates that Aeschylus "adorned his settings, and astounded the eyes of his spectators with their brilliance—with paintings and stage devices, altars and tombs, trumpets, ghosts, Furies." Aristotle attributes the invention of painted scenery to the playwright Sophocles, so it is clear that, despite the help they had, the authors took an overall interest in the production of their plays. Each actor and the twenty-four chorus members wore masks and costumes, and the costumes for the chorus were elaborate. In Aristophanes' *Birds,* each chorus member dressed to look like a different bird known to inhabit Athens at the time. (It appears that feathers were as early a part of musical comedy as any other element in its repertoire.)

Seldom in the history of theatre does a period of great playwrighting coincide with a period of great acting, but when it does, as it did in Athens, on the Elizabethan stage, and in America from the 1930s to the 1950s, the effect is always one of a greatly significant, yet popular, theatre. Method acting did not originate in twentieth-century New York. The Greek actor Polus is said to have used an urn containing the ashes of his real-life son when he was playing Electra mourning over her dead brother's ashes, in order to achieve the proper mood.

The golden age of Greece revered the actor's profession. Callipides, Nicostratus, Aristodemus, Neoptolemus, Athenodorus, Phyrynichus, Polus, Myniscus, Cleander, Tiepolemus, and Cleidimides are among the renowned actors of ancient Athens. Their union, the Artists of Dionysus, governed working conditions both at home and on the road. Young men who qualified were exempted from military duty and trained in the proper techniques, which consisted primarily of vocal production and a wide range of meaningful physical gestures that were recognized and expected in performance.

The actor was trained to project his voice in all postures, and three separate techniques were necessary; for dialogue, a declamatory style with special emphasis on enunciation; for recitative, the passages were intoned to a musical accompaniment; third, the actor had to sing lyric sections solo, in duet, in trio, or with the chorus, though harmony was as yet unknown. Additionally, the actor was expected to be a dancer. Tragedy required a slow and graceful movement known as the *emmeleia,* and comedy called for a fast and bawdy dance known as the *kordax.* The satyr plays employed the *sikinnis,* a vulgar parody of the tragic dance.

Actors were typecast. By the time the writer Sophocles had added a third actor to the two from the theatre of Aeschylus and only one prior to that, the roles, and all the actors, were neatly divided into the protagonist (a tenor), the deuteragonist (a baritone), and the tritagonist (bass). Nonspeaking parts and the chorus were filled with those younger, less experienced performers who went out in the chorus but undoubtedly hoped to come back a star. Actors specialized in only one of the three role categories and in either tragedy or comedy. The protagonist was an actor of supreme reputation, often acting as contractor for the remaining company of players much the way the actor-manager did from Elizabethan to Victorian times. They received splendid salaries, while the lower ranks suffered a hand-to-mouth existence.

Nor were actors protected from criticism. When Callipides demanded praise from King Agesilaus for his ability to "sing like a nightingale," the King replied sarcastically, "I have heard the bird itself."

Though women did not appear on the stage until centuries later, this did nothing to hinder early playwrights. There is hardly a well known play in the entire early history of drama or comedy before the appearance of the actress in which a reader could discover that women players were not meant to be included. The preponderance of male roles and the proclivity for the author to put a female character into pants is one hint in the Shakespearean canon, but this could just as easily reflect the fact that men controlled society, and thus the concerns of a plot that could interest an audience naturally employed more men than women. Within this body of work exists some of the finest female roles in theatrical history. When reading *Romeo and Juliet* it is almost impossible to believe that Shakespeare wrote Juliet for a young man whose voice had not yet deepened.

Aristophanes' existing body of eleven plays include three—*Thesmophoriazusai* ("Women Taking Part in an All Female Festival"), *Ecclesiazusai* ("Women Attending the Assembly") and *Lysistrata*—that were peopled mostly by women characters, and concerned their inclusion in society. However, fewer manuscripts of these plays exist than of the others, and the "Women Plays," were left out of the collected works of Aristophanes for nearly nineteen centuries before they were taken as seriously. Today *Lysistrata*—in which the women end war by withholding their sexual gifts until they dominate the men in bed and politics—is the most commonly known of all Aristophanes' work.

As a noun, "burlesque" is defined twice in *Webster's*—as a "literary, dramatic, or other imitation which makes a travesty of that which it represents," and as a "type of theatrical entertainment . . . characterized by broad humor and slapstick." Aristophanes' plays boasted both the form and the style. He employed the burlesque form in several comedies, most notably *Frogs,* where actors portraying Aeschylus and Euripides engage in a literary contest, matching verse for verse. The scene is underscored with music, bracketed by a singing chorus, and consists of lyrics sung and then weighed on scales for their potential. (In the Spring of 1975, Burt Shevelove directed a musical version with songs by Stephen Sondheim in which that scene took place between William Shakespeare and George Bernard Shaw. The musical took place at the Yale swimming pool and included a chorus of swimmers.)*

Aristophanes' work also features satire, and offers a comprehensive indictment of Athenian life. *The Birds* caricatures the schemes and ambitions of his fellow Athenians; *The Clouds* attacks Socrates' theories where right and wrong take a back seat to argument; in *The Wasps* Aristophanes attempts to alter the judicial system through an exposure of a corrupt alliance; and *Lysistrata* points out the governmental chaos caused by the long Peloponnesian War. Aristophanes took the theatre that preceded him and did much to elevate comedy from mere horseplay and rude personal satire to a thoughtful criticism of governmental policies and current tendencies in philosophy and literature.

As for off-color humor, it did not begin with Minsky's burlesque.

SOCRATES: GOT A GRIP ON ANYTHING?

STREPSIADES I'VE GOT MY COCK IN MY RIGHT HAND!

(CLOUDS)

This acting style, in which one can never stoop too low to secure a laugh, carried the comedies of Aristophanes into the hearts of his countrymen and made palpable his themes, which consistently recommended changes in political or social behavior.

The audience for Greek comedy was dominated by male citizens. Only their opinions and concerns were considered important (a fact that Aristophanes takes to task in the "Women Plays"). Places in the amphitheatre unfilled by men, however, could be taken by boys and women, and although it may have been difficult for them to get a close look at the proceedings, they were certainly part of the audience. Probably the segregation

* This was not the first musical to feature swimming. Ziegfeld had used underwater scenes, and for *Wish You Were Here* producers Leland Hayward and Joshua Logan built a swimming pool in the floor of the Imperial Theatre.

of men and women in this way encouraged the proliferation of off-color humor. It is hard to imagine that anywhere else in Greek society, except possibly the baths, was there such a profusion of sexual humor, and the proceedings were not hindered by the appearance of male actors in female roles. The audience was quick to recognize the difference, in the exaggerated leather phalluses worn for male roles and tights with pubic hair painted on the crotch for female ones. The masks that each actor wore would have been painted to resemble the character and could have effectively hidden the beard which every man wore at the time.

The comic musical theatre of Aristophanes is filled with innuendoes and titillation. In *Wasps,* an old man is leading a slave girl, and as he steps up onto the stage from the orchestra area he turns to the girl and offers her his leather penis:

> Come up this way my little golden beetle, put your hand round this rope. Hold on to it, but be careful, because the rope's pretty old. All the same, it doesn't mind a bit of friction.

When *Lysistrata* is coaching the women in abstention, she exhorts them to wear sweet smelling scents, flimsy nightgowns, and to "shave down below to a nice triangle." Another scene concerns a wife who literally does a striptease for her husband, brings a mattress and blankets, and at the last minute runs off. The poor husband complains that "she's left me *standing,*" and for his "old cock . . . these pangs of unemployment are more than a body can bear." In the final scene a naked slave girl is brought forward as the character of Reconciliation and exhorted to

> . . . fetch those Spartans. Don't tug them in the boorish way our husbands do us; be thoroughly feminine—but if they won't give you their hands, take them and tow them, politely, by their . . . life lines. Then fetch the Athenians too, and if they won't take your hand, grab hold of whatever they offer . . .

In *Acharnians* one man has disguised his daughters as pigs and is trying to sell them. Aristophanes exploits the ambiguities of the Greek word *khoîros,* which means "young pig" and at the same time, in slang, "cunt." When the second man suspects that he is not buying a pig, the first responds:

> What an idea! Such a mistrustful man! He says this isn't a *khoîros.* All right, if you're willing, I'll bet you a bag of thyme-salt that this (pointing between the girls' legs) is what every Greek calls *khoîros.*

He later explains that "the flesh of these *khoîros* is absolutely delicious when it's skewered on a spit."

Homosexual humor was not lacking either, although it is less common and is used to ridicule certain characters. Some Greek words for penetration refer equally to the heterosexual and homosexual; one is translated here as "fuck," in a passage between Euripides and Mnesilochos just prior to the entrance of Agathon, an effeminate playwright.

EURIPIDES	THAT'S WHERE THE FAMOUS DRAMATURGE AGATHON'S LIVING, OR PARTLY LIVING . . .
MNESILOCHOS	THIS AGATHON?
EURIPIDES	*THE* AGATHON!
MNESILOCHOS	THE CREPUSCULAR MUSCULAR DARK TOUGH?
EURIPIDES	NOT THAT AT ALL. HAVE YOU SEEN HIM?
MNESILOCHOS	THE ONE WITH THE GREAT BUSH BEARD?
EURIPIDES	DEPENDS *WHERE.* HAVE YOU SEEN HIS *FACE?*
MNESILOCHOS	NOT SO FAR AS I KNOW.
EURIPIDES	WELL, YOU'VE FUCKED HIM! BUT MAYBE YOU DON'T KNOW HIM! LET'S GET TO ONE SIDE, HE'S COMING OUT.

The humor is earthy, vulgar, and to the Athenians, enormously funny and entertaining. Their delight in it is paralleled by the painted vases that formed a part of their culture, on which artists felt free to depict scenes of sexual intercourse, male and female masturbation, and bondage. In *Acharnians,* the character Dikaiopolis celebrates the delight of peace with this song. (Phales is the personification of the penis, and its worship is part of the fertility rites.)

O Phales, Phales,
How much nicer
To find your neighbor's pretty Thracian slave
Collecting wood, pinching it from your slopes,
And seize her round the waist and lift her up
And lay her down
And pick her fruit
O Phales, Phales!

Phallic props and nudity, off-color humor, coarse vulgarity, ass jokes, farting jokes, excrement comedy, ribald sons, transvestite humor, buggery and fucking . . . surely the most direct descendant of Aristophanes is the American burlesque show, that wonderful institution of baggy-pants comedians, "Girls Terrific Girls," pig bladders and strippers, that boomed in the United States until it was closed by puritans, and the comics refined their sketches and headed uptown to join forces with the Shubert Alley crowd. Acting in the American burlesque show became again what it had been at its Greek roots: a celebration of fertility.

Aristophanes attempted to eliminate the element of indecency which his audience had become accustomed to.

> Now comes my comedy . . . how modest and pure she is! She doesn't come on waving a property phallus to get a laugh from the coarse children; she doesn't poke fun at bald heads, or flaunt her sex in an indecent dance; there's no old man literally doing slap-stick to bolster his rotten jokes. Nobody wildly rushes on brandishing torches, there's no comical wailing—This play relies on nothing but its merit! *(Clouds)*

However, he found that he had gone too far. He was rewarded with last place at the great Dionysus festival in the spring of 423 B.C., losing to a play by Cratinus, which scholars believe was much more obscene. In his next attempt, *Wasps,* he has his chorus harangue the audience for failing to appreciate his last effort, then returns to the obscenities to which they were accustomed.

The Peloponnesian War, which Aristophanes had criticized in his plays for its corruption and mismanagement, ended in defeat for Athens.

Aristophanes lived to see his city lose its power, stripped of a Navy that once had ruled the Mediterranean, the grape and olive orchards which had been the center of her commerce torn down. Democracy was replaced by a series of oligarchies less hospitable to invective, and comedy lost its pointed attacks. As the Greek state declined, so did the state of Greek drama. Burlesque, parody, and satire were not popular among playwrights who knew they could be burnt at the stake should their opinions contradict those of a dictator. Perhaps even the audience, in the midst of gloomy days, lost its appetite for what had once been a riot of language and actions. Before Aristophanes died the democracy was restored and Athens found some of its former glory, but the age of Old Comedy had given way to Middle and then New Comedy, which were milder in both tone and approach. An interest in romantic love blossomed. (How Aristophanes would have lampooned that!)

Music and lyrics were a vital part of Greek theatre, though historical analysis is difficult because music notation was not yet known. Some lyrics are not part of the manuscripts of Aristophanes' plays, as the chorus was trained separately for the performance, and songs and dances not authored by the playwright were interpolated. Some playwrights wrote their own music (Aeschylus and Sophocles) and others did not (Euripides). Whether Aristophanes did or not is unknown. At any rate, stanzas of lyric poetry were sung to music at various points throughout Aristophanes' work, sometimes by a leading character, more often by the chorus.

In Athens during the fifth century B.C., in the midst of the golden age of a remarkable society, Aristophanes became one of the first creators of musical comedy. He utilized the tumblers, jugglers, and ballad singers that had wandered in to his amphitheatre from an ancient age by turning them into chorus singers and dancers. He wrote in high wit and style of subject matters close to the hearts of his audience, driving them to consider the current issues, and dazzled them with entertainment both humorous and emotional in its words and music. They left both satisfied and enlightened. The comic musical theatre of Aristophanes has left a legacy of burlesque and burlycue, parody and satire, vaudeville and light opera, tits and ass and feathers, grand beauty, mechanical devices, subsidized theatre, songs of lyric beauty and high wit, and dances of character and vulgarity. It will be twenty-four centuries later and half way around the world before all these elements appear together again.

BRING ON THE LOVERS, LIARS, AND CLOWNS

As Greek Old Comedy metamorphosed, musical sequences became less important, and in his last plays Aristophanes indicated where chorus songs would occur but did not record them. When Old Comedy had given way to New Comedy the singing chorus lost its relevance to the play and eventually disappeared altogether. When the ribald, fantastic, burlesque satires of Greek Old Comedy gave way to the complicated plots of mistaken identity and thwarted lovers of Middle and New Comedy, the political and intellectually oriented material, with its personal attacks on public figures, was replaced by socially oriented domestic stories and a host of stock comic characters.

From the middle transition period, though fifty names of playwrights are left to us, no complete manuscripts exist. From New Comedy only one exists, *The Dyskolos (The Grouch)* by Menander. Considered the greatest of all New Comedy authors, Menander produced over one hundred plays for an Athens that had lost its once great democracy and was under the dictatorship of Macedonian successors to Alexander the Great. Such a political system didn't allow for the criticism, invective, and personal satire that marked Aristophanes and the democracy, but Menander, employing a new format that had crippled the talent of Aristophanes, rose to new heights. Quintilian, Rome's first professor of literature, insisted that one could become a good orator by studying Menander alone. Plutarch asks: "For what other reason, truly, would an educated man go to the theatre except to see Menander! Oh, life! Which one of you imitated the other?" Not a bad review.

Menander turned the formula plots, nearly always involving stock characters and a thwarted love that works itself right in the end, to his own good use in a philosophic kind of comedy that abounded in aphorisms.

The most complete and characteristic plot of the New Comedy is this one for *The Epitrepontes (The Arbitrators)*, the manuscript of which is not in existence. From many fragments, Professor Cedric H. Whitman has recreated the story:

> In the darkness of a night festival Charisius had raped Pamphlia and given her a ring. A few months later, without knowing each other, they marry and live happily, until Pamphlia has a baby, somewhat too soon. She manages to conceal the fact and abandons the infant with tokens, including the ring, but the slave Onesimus tells Charisius, not out of

> malice but the inability to keep a secret. Charisius goes to live at a friend's house, where he carouses with friends and a harp girl, Abrotonon. Pamphlia's father, Smicrines, hears of it and tries to take back Pamphlia and the dowry, but Pamphlia will not agree. Meanwhile, the baby has been found by a Shepherd and given to a Charcoal Burner, but without the tokens. The Charcoal Burner wants the tokens so that the child may discover his identity, but the Shepherd, who intends to sell them, refuses to give them. In accordance with Greek customs in minor disputes, they refer the matter to the first passer-by for arbitration. Smicrines, who is passing, decides that the tokens go with the baby. After a series of complications and intrigues, in which Onesimus and Abrotonon are chiefly instrumental, the truth is revealed, husband and wife are reunited, Smicrines subsides, and Abrotonon and Onesimus are given their liberty.

All of the typical themes arise: intrigue, chance, a lost baby, the tokens, the thwarted love, and the characters of New Comedy, which may include old men ill-tempered or kindly, young men from the country or city, light-minded or honest, often father and son; courtesans, with or without a heart of gold; old women irascible or good-natured; cunning slaves; parasitic relatives; dishonest matchmakers; swaggering soldiers; a cook; and young women, of which fourteen types were recorded. All were distinct, fixed types, within which the playwright had to draw a relevant social picture of contemporary society. The primary fluctuation consisted of the author's new and increasingly devious variations in plot.

The use of music and dance became increasingly disconnected to the play after Aristophanes, and the dramatic importance of the chorus decreased. It merely entertains the audience at prescribed intervals without relevance to the plot—a description just as apt to the Broadway musical comedy of the 1920s.

ROMAN THEATRE—BATTLES, BARBAROUS AND BLOODY

In the early centuries of its existence, the Roman republic had no recorded theatre and hardly any literature. Too busy with the work of their empire, and too stoic and warlike to embrace theatricals, entertainment consisted of several casual forms: *fescennine* verses, which were recited on holidays and festival days and were abusive and obscene; *satura,* consisting of songs, dances, and short sketches, and resembling a variety show; and a dramatic form known as *fabula atellana,* short plays with stock characters indicated by masks. The characters included *Maccus,* the stupid clown, *Bucco,* the glutton or braggart, *Poppus,* the foolish old man, and *Dossennus,* the hunchback or trickster. These plays dealt with trickery and obscenity in short farcical situations that were handed down by the actors, unrecorded, probably traditional, and at least partly improvised. There were also dancing, imported from Etruria, which influenced other forms, and mime, in which the performers, without masks, acted out situations and stories to the music of a flute and sometimes a sung verse.

These last two forms were extraordinarily popular, not least because they were the first to employ women. Dancing girls, made to perform their numbers on top of the tables of noblemen, were a hit with the wealthy classes. They wore extremely flimsy costumes, and often nothing at all. What these performances led to is not recorded, but it is likely that the best little whorehouse in Texas had nothing on the holy Roman Empire. Dancing was popular enough to find its way into all other theatrical forms, and outlasted the literate Roman drama to come and the empire itself.

By 240 B.C. the Romans came into closer contact with the Greeks of southern Italy and Sicily and realized how inadequate their own cultural growth had been. A demand for more elaborate entertainment led Livius Andronicus, a slave and tutor in a Roman family, to adapt a Greek comedy and a Greek tragedy into Latin, and that performance was the first scripted production for the Roman Empire. Although they never developed an original theatre of their own, adaptations by Plautus and Terence of Greek comedies and by Seneca of Greek tragedies reached new heights in prose and poetry, elaborating on the Greek New Comedy and tragedy forms from which they chose their material almost exclusively.

The written comedies that have survived the Roman Empire—twenty by Plautus and six by Terence—are primarily an elaboration of the Greek New Comedy form, portraying local characters, customs, and comedies of error and mistaken identity in which confusion results from both accident and deliberate deceit, and comedies of trickery in which the misunderstanding is deliberately created by, usually, a clever slave, either to earn money for his freedom or to help his master gain a young lover. The panoply of roles includes the old men, old women, young men, courtesans, cooks, soldiers, and parasites of the Greek form. Plautus' contribution is reflected in more elaborate plots, extension of the characters to original and grotesque degrees, and a more robust and farcical approach that included jokes, puns, word play, and convoluted comic names. He utilized song and dance much more, and though the Greek chorus disappeared, as did the five interludes of choral song and dance, he gave this material directly to the characters, integrating such numbers both during the plays and as festival conclusions, to the extent that we can once again recognize the modern musical comedy form in his work. By including the pre-literary farces and dancing popular at the time, he successfully broadened his comedies to a fuller, deeper style, returning some of the exuberance, inanity, and burlesque to the stage. Such integration led to an early use of the musical scene.

The Greek theatre, while using both song and dance extensively, did so by character but seldom in plot. But this scene from *Pseudolus,* for example, in which the clever slave who plays the leading role is drunk, was carefully developed by Plautus to utilize song, dance, and acting:

> *(Very drunk, with garland on his head, singing tipsily)* O feet, feet, wha's a matter now? Is this any way to behave? Stand up, stand up, won't you? Ya' want me to fall, and have someone pick me up here? If I fall down, it'll be all your fault. *(Staggering wildly)* Still at it, eh? Ha! Wanna make me lose my temper? *(To the audience, confidentially)* That's the trouble with drinking: goes right to your . . . feet; trips you up, like a tricky wrestler. Oh boy, oh boy! What a swell bender I'm having: choice food, everything so nice—fit for the Gods; such a jolly place—and such a jolly party. I'd better come right out with it, and tell you: this is what makes a fellow in love with life. Here's every pleasure—everything charming. It's just next to being a God, I think. When a chap's in love—and is hugging his sweetie—when he presses lip to lip—when they snatch each other's tongues with kisses—don't hide it—when tender breasts are pressed, and when the fancy takes you—bodies joined together—and a fair white hand with a sweet tankard—drinking healths to love; and no one there to annoy you or pester you—no silly twaddle; perfumed oil, incense, ribbons, lots of flowers,

> no expense spared—as for the rest of the banquet, don't ask me! That's the way young master and I have merrily spent the day, after I put across my job, just as I wished, and put the enemy to flight. I left 'em lying there, still drinking and petting with their wenches—left my own wench there too—all of 'em giving themselves a swell time. But when I got up to go, they all begged me to dance. I showed off for 'em with a few fancy steps—like this. *(Staggers drunkenly around the stage)* I've had pretty good teaching, you see—I'm an honor graduate of the Ionic School of Dance. Then I draped myself in my cloak—like this—strutted around like this *(With a few suggestive movements)* all in fun, ya' understand. Got a big hand; they yelled "Encore!" so I'd come back again. I started up again—with this step. *(Illustrating)* Didn't like it—still, I wanted to show off to my sweetie, so she'd love me. I was whirling around when—down I went: That killed the show!

In the original Greek this scene would have been in lyric form, probably six meter, and more easily fitted to the music than it appears in translation. Still, we can see that the leading comic actor has everything he needs in this scene to perform a hilarious musical number, singing most or all of the dialogue while dancing drunkenly around the stage. His accompaniment was at least a flute, possibly a harp, and percussion instruments as well.

The variety of metric form employed by Plautus leads us to believe that he utilized the integration of song and dialogue to a greater extent than either his literary predecessors or his contemporary Terence. Although the development of Greek comedy from Old to New lessened the integration of song and dance, Plautus reversed the process and combined the high wit and style of the Menandrian New Comedy with the songs and dances of Italian entertainments into a Roman musical farce that marked the high point of that society's theatre. His great popularity was due at least in part to the musical elements in his work.

Plautus also made particularly good use of the aside, in which an actor steps out of character to address the audience for comic effect, such as this remark from *Pseudolus:*

CALIDORUS: TELL ME, WHAT ARE YOU GOING TO DO?

PSEUDOLUS: YOU'LL LEARN IN GOOD TIME. *(TO THE AUDIENCE)* I DON'T WANT TO TELL IT TWICE, THESE COMEDIES ARE LONG ENOUGH AS IT IS.

Plautus was also the first to put his hero and heroine on equal footing. The love interest occurred between a boy and a girl of equal stations in life. Until his comedies, men played the dominant roles, and sex and love was a one-sided affair in which the man pursued slave girls and courtesans, their use similar to the buxom beauties who stood around American burlesque sketches for the comic use and abuse of male actors. In Greek and Roman society a woman had no rights at all. She was married at the whim of her father and divorced without consultation by her husband. While the Greek woman lived at home in virtual seclusion, Roman women enjoyed a much greater physical freedom to move about society but remained politically subservient. That Plautus wrote comedies allowing a woman to marry the young man of her own dreams was an instance of theatre improving upon life. This is reflected in the comedies, and by the time of Terence, who wrote in a polished style that greatly pleased the aristocracy and followed Plautus closely in popularity, women characters enjoyed a much greater role in theatrical plots. (Actresses themselves, however, were still confined to naked and near-naked dancing in mimes and entertainments, and their roles were portrayed by men.)

The golden age of acting died with the Greek democracy, and for centuries to come performers were treated as rogues and vagabonds, thieves and prostitutes. Roman actors were all slaves. Classified as *infami,* their profession was despised while their art was admired. The Senate decreed that no Roman citizen could be an actor, and should one appear on the stage he lost all of his civil rights. No actor was buried in holy ground. The church was against the theatre completely and forbade their followers to even attend a performance. Should a soldier, that most noble of all Roman characters, become an actor, he could be put to death.

Divided into tragedians, comedians, and pantomimists, an actor's income ranged from nothing to the equivalent of $20,000 for a performance. No union protected them, and working conditions included realistic performances of adultery and crucifixion—certainly the end of a career—acted out on the mime stage.

If the contribution of the literature of Roman theatre remained secondary to that of the Greek age, the Roman contribution to musical comedy makes it an era of some importance: the increasingly accessible language of the playwrights, their ability to humanize the great themes for their audiences, and the introduction of adaptation. Its direct legacy includes *A Funny Thing Happened on the Way to the Forum* (from the plays of Plautus generally, three in particular, and featuring the comic slave Pseudolus), and *The Boys from Syracuse* (from Shakespeare's *The Comedy of Errors,* which derives from Plautus' *The Twin Menaechmi* and is indebted also to his *Amphitryon*). Additionally, dramatists in subsequent ages have adapted these plays, including Molière, whose theatre closely resembles the work of Plautus and many of whose plays are Plautine adaptations.

But theatre performances were dwarfed by the spectacles, circuses for the masses that best characterize the Roman civilization. They were not festivals but a palliative for the civic abuses of a conservative government. These elaborate productions included wild animal fights, contests to the death between men and beasts and men and men, chariot races, and elaborate sea battles for which the arena was flooded and slave ships fought to the death. Greater and greater extravaganzas were arranged to titillate the audience—one performance lists six hundred mules among its props. These gladiatorial spectacles were paid for by a politician in the course of a campaign, by the state, or by a wealthy individual citizen.

From a directorial standpoint, the Roman spectacle theatre actually provides numerous inventions, for the Romans were a meticulous and scientific people with enormous engineering skills. If the Greeks left us great literature, it was played out in an amphitheatre carved into the side of a hill with only rudimentary practical application, the most significant of which was its acoustics. The Romans were builders, and their theatres reflected the needs of their entertainments much more directly.

The Roman theatre was an elaboration of the Greek theatre. The stage was raised to five feet and the orchestra pit was filled with seats for the Senators. The building behind the stage became much more elaborate, with at least three doors, alleyways between the houses for characters to eavesdrop on conversations, and a forestage representing a street, running as long as 180 feet in length. A wooden roof was erected over the stage and a linen roof over the audience provided protection from the elements while allowing the performance to be illuminated from the sunlight that filtered in between. Lamps and torches added artificial light to the theatre for the first time. Because the Romans disdained luxury, for some time the playhouses included no seats at all, and the law required spectators to stand. Later, backless benches served as theatre seats.

Only three permanent theatres were ever built in Rome. The entertainments were considered too frivolous to warrant permanent structures, but the temporary buildings, thanks to the enormous skill of the architects and engineers, were ornamentally elaborate and architecturally magnificent. With names like Circus Maximus and the Coliseum, seating 15,000, 40,000, and in one case 80,000 spectators, these structures were often torn down two or three days after they were completed and used. To one theatre is credited the first arched passageways underneath the seating for the entrance and exit of the audience, because Roman theatres were often freestanding and not dug into the side of a hill like their forebears. To another theatre goes the distinction of the first flexible auditorium arrangement. It consisted of two wooden structures, each with a half circle of seats, built back to back, for the presentation of two plays simultaneously. At the conclusion of this performance the two huge units were pivoted around to face each other for the presentation of athletic and gladiatorial contests in the center.

In addition, Roman ingenuity contributed a wide range of innovations to the practical theatre, including:

- The first front curtain, which was raised from a trough downstage to conceal the set and dropped into it to begin the performance.
- The first air conditioning, which consisted of cool running water built into special passageways for circulation. In some cases, fine sprays of water mingled with perfume were blown over an audience to make them more comfortable.
- The first tap shoes. A hard piece of metal, called a *scabilla,* was attached to the dancer's shoes for percussive effect in dancing.
- The first extended orchestrations. The Romans added lyre, pipe, cymbals, and trumpets to the flute and harp of the Greeks.

- The first reserved seats. Coins were marked with different configurations that indicated which section of the theatre the spectator was entitled to sit in.
- The first claques. Actors paid people to sit throughout the audience and applaud vigorously. (Gone from the theatre, this odious practice still continues in some of the world's great opera houses.)
- The first ushers. Soldiers with sticks were stationed in the aisles to control rowdyism.
- The first lip-synched performance. Livius Andronicus, the translator and adaptor of Greek tragedies, was also an actor. When his voice gave out, he arranged the speaking lines to be done offstage by another actor while he mimed and danced the part.

If the Roman theatre contributed little to the Greek literature that today's dramatic theatre rests on, musical comedy inherited spectacle and numerous technical achievements from this austere, mechanical, and jaded society.

THE DARK AGES

A troupe of strolling players are we . . .

Following the decline and fall of the Roman Empire, the great poets and playwrights of Greece and Rome disappeared, governments and producers withdrew their sponsorship, and the Christian Church—which dominated the moral and intellectual life of the citizenry in the Middle Ages—informed the people that the theatre was a root of evil and issued edicts forbidding theatrical production.

Performers took to the streets, roaming the towns and villages of Europe and England. The skills of the singer, dancer, tumbler, juggler, mime, magician, and actor were kept alive sans script. Entertaining in the marketplace and crossroads, the itinerant performers were often beaten, arrested, and driven out of town. In order to appease audiences and avoid persecution from the church, many took to bringing news, gossip and rumor from other places. The most popular of these traveling minstrels put their stories and news into song.

This use of song and drama ceased when print came into use, but from 1935 to 1939 the federal theatre arm of the Works Progress Administration (W.P.A.) developed on Broadway a "living newspaper" production which consisted of editorials on current issues, in the form of staged documentaries, and utilized the hundreds of reporters, editors, directors, choreographers, actors, singers and dancers available to the W.P.A.

The power of the church was not enough to suppress dramatic activity. So anxious were the people for entertainment that the church soon found itself using theatrics in the presentation of biblical stories, Christian myths, and religious ceremonies for the edification of its congregation. Ignoring the glorious history of script and spectacle from the Greek and Roman theatre, the church developed its own unique and original theatre.

By the sixth century A.D., the fixed ritual of the Mass, with prayers, reading, chanting, and singing, was nearly a drama in itself. One portion of the Easter Mass, with which church drama began, was the singing of "Alleluia" by the choir at certain intervals. Some time around the turn of the ninth century an anonymous monk-musician began to hold the last syllable of "Alleluia" and sing it to more music. In time these tunes became more elaborate and were particularized for individual ceremonies. They became immensely popular, were long and numerous, and had to be memorized by the monks, as there were no hymn books at the time.

Then an unknown monk had an idea to put words to these long wordless passages, and a famous musician, Notker Balbulus, who had had a difficult time learning the wordless sequences as a choirboy, used passages from the Bible suited to the special significance of the particular Mass. For the first time words and music were parallel, one note for one syllable. Because much of the material was already in dialogue form, the chorus divided the material and passed the lines back and forth, often in the form of questions and answers.

Because the parishioners were illiterate and listening to the Mass in Latin, a language that few understood, a dumb show was devised, with painting and statues representing the figures of importance, and monks demonstrating the stories. By the tenth century, impersonation had entered the service, with men and choir boys singing their parts and dressing in the roles. Several biblical episodes were combined, and the Easter play of some twenty or thirty minutes began to be imitated at other festival days, notably Christmas. More and more stories were acted out for the instruction of the laity. This became the most popular of the church's activities, and on feast days the people crowded in. Thus, the second beginning of drama—developed by the church in complete ignorance of, and disdain for, the first—was equally steeped in music, if not dance. In fact, the form could best be defined as operatic, since at first the entire play was sung: it was the performance of the choir and soloists, and the brilliance of the entrancing musical sequences, that attracted the attention of the crowd.

Before long the church found this to be the most effective method of teaching the history of religion. It wasn't long before the sung Latin was dropped in favor of the popular dialogue, and singing disappeared almost completely from the plays it had inspired. The stories became more complex and the casts became larger. The drama moved outside into the church courtyard, and from there to the front of the church gates, to accommodate the greater number of actors and the spectacles. For the increased size of the cast it was necessary to employ the help of the congregation.

In time the church withdrew altogether from the productions, which moved to the market squares and the courtyards of aristocratic mansions, and the clergy no longer acted in, produced, or directed the plays. The eleventh century brought the first play in the local vernacular, and the first play that was meant to be played outdoors. This secularization allowed the plays to recombine with the mimes, dancers, and entertainers who were waiting in the marketplace.

These plays remained enormously popular through the sixteenth century. Grouped roughly in four categories, they ran in length from an ordinary performance to several days. Mystery or cycle plays were based on biblical stories (*Godspell, Joseph and the Amazing Technicolor Dreamcoat,* and *Jesus Christ Superstar* are modern equivalents). Miracle plays employed non-biblical plots involving popular saints as heroes or heroines. Morality plays were allegories originating in the Lord's prayer and seen to combat the seven deadly sins (*Everyman* was the most popular).

Folk plays, the only one of the four not originating with the church service, were based on popular myths and heroes and performed at rural festivals. The legend of Robin Hood was extremely popular in both England and France. The great significance of the folk play was that its purpose was pure entertainment, as opposed to the teachings of the church, and at last the theatre can be seen again as a popular one, having returned to the people.

Throughout the Middle Ages there was not a single permanent theatre building in use. Rumors of a theatre still operating in Rome in 467 A.D., another in Barcelona early in the seventh century, and a third somewhere in the eastern portion of the Empire in 692 A.D., remain scholastically unconfirmed due to the underground nature of the enterprise at the time. For the mystery plays, each scene, with its own cast, was mounted on a wagon that moved into place, played out its serial, and then moved to another location as it was followed by the succeeding scene. In this way the play was given at several locations around the town during the day—the citizens would choose in advance the most convenient location from an announcement posted a month before the performance.

Like every theatre age that does not have playwrights, there developed extensive production values in scenery, costumes and lighting. A great deal of time and money, and the talent of some of the finest architects of the age, went into elaborate settings and special effects, including heavenly beings descending from on high surrounded by the lights of stars, trap doors opening to swallow up buildings and persons, dragons spouting fire, trees and flowers springing from the earth to indicate the creation of the world, grapevines bearing fruit immediately upon watering, water for the deluge piped over the rooftops of the surrounding marketplace to fall in a downpour, descending clouds, the turning of water into wine (a simple conjuror's trick), thunder, lightning, and fire. All this was under the supervision of a "master of machines" who employed a construction crew to build and operate the effects, and who went to great lengths for a single visual wonder. The costuming was rich and fairly standardized, as were the draperies of silk and satin used in the set designs. Horns, cloven feet, and forked tails adorned Lucifer, while Mary wore white and gold.

The Middle Ages were the heyday of the amateur. By far the greatest number of parts went to local townspeople who earned their living in other ways. Plays were rehearsed for several weeks, then trumpeters and heralds were sent out to neighboring towns to make announcements. Coordinating the pageants was the director, or *régisseur,* who strode around the stage *during the performance* with a baton in one hand and a promptbook in the other, guiding the actors through their roles and whispering dialogue in their ears. When a play could last several days, no actor could remember all his lines.

Working with amateurs was a trying situation. One contemporary spectator left this record of an attempt by a director—onstage among his actors at the time—to get an actor to step further downstage.

> Quoth the director, "Go forth, man, and show thyself." The gentleman steps out upon the stage, and, cleaving more to the

> letter than the scene, pronounced the words aloud. "Oh," (says the director in his ear), "You marred the scene." And with this his passion, the actor makes the audience in like sort acquainted. Herein the prompter falls to flat railing and cursing in the bitterest terms he could devise; which the gentleman with a set gesture and countenance still soberly related, until the director, driven at last into a mad rage, was faine to give over all. Which action, though it broke off the Interlude, yet defrauded not the beholders, but dismissed them with a great deal more sport and laughter than twenty such plays could afford.

By the twelfth century the guilds were politically powerful units in England, where the craft unions took over management and presentation of the plays. They took great pride in the work and although amateurs, always endeavored to meet high standards. The town council assigned episodes of a play to each guild: to the plasterers and carpenters went the Creation; to the shipwrights went the Noah episode; to the goldsmiths, the Magi; to the cooks, the Harrowing of Hell; to the bakers, the Feeding of the Five Thousand or the Last Supper; and to the Scriveners, the Disputation in the temple.

The guild prepared the sets and costumes, hired and rehearsed the actors, and presented its portion of the play. The necessary funds were taken from the town or guild treasury, or were created for the occasion by special taxes.

If the Middle Ages left little in the way of theatrical heritage for plays and musicals, it kept alive the skills that would soon enough find great plays to employ them. The need to be entertained with spectacle and laughter, music and mime, is so basic that it would survive a thousand years in the dark.

Yet even the medieval theatre had one outstanding legacy for the actors and actresses of today's musical stage. A large, highly polished basin was held up to reflect the sunlight into a narrow shaft of light beamed at the leading player . . . the world's first spotlight.

Alvin Theatre

PLAYBILL MAGAZINE

Three

THE RENAISSANCE

Send in the clowns . . .

By the end of the church's ten-century grip on theatre and the decline in sacred drama, the art of comic acting, audience interest in secular plays, and the popular desire to be entertained for sheer pleasure, had set the stage for the greatest flowering of cultural activity and acceptance in the history of humankind—the Renaissance, which, appropriately, means "rebirth" in French.

The Renaissance reawakened interest in all the arts. Though the skills never coalesced around a musical comedy format, the pursuit of painting, sculpture, music, literature, and drama brought advancements in set, costume and light design, acting, and playwriting. From a good and varied theatre in Spain, Italy, and Germany came the greatest age in French (Molière) and English (Elizabethan) theatre, the codification and development of opera and ballet, and the finest achievements in comic acting, the commedia dell'arte. Without the advances made on these artistic fronts, the contemporary musical theatre would not exist today.

THE COMMEDIA DELL'ARTE

The many famed commedia dell'arte troupes that toured Europe throughout the Renaissance permanently influenced the popular stage. Never again would the theatre be anything less than an actor's theatre. To the performances of the great Harlequins, Pulcinellas, and Scaramouches, and all the stock characters so familiar to audiences, theatergoers thrilled in anticipation and delight.

There are over eight hundred scenarios employed by the commedia companies. No real scripts existed. The actors were required to know the various stories in their repertoire by heart. The scenarios, freely lifted from novels, old plays, remembered incidents, and current gossip, were explained by the head of the company, who would indicate the line of action, the situation, and the cast of characters. As in the Roman *fabula atellana* from which it is vaguely descended and the American burlesque show to which it bequeathed its standardized scenarios, the commedia consisted of stock characters whose characteristics and reactions the audience could depend on. Each actor specialized in one character and developed his talents accordingly.

Scapino, sometimes called Brighella or Pulcinello (from whom Punch of Punch and Judy is descended), was the top banana. He was always stirring up complicated intrigues, breaking up or arranging marriages, and duping other characters with flattery, chicanery, and impersonation, for which he often assumed momentarily the role of soldier, tavern keeper, hangman, or fortune teller.

Harlequin, the second banana, took little part in the plot, but was counted on to keep the rhythm of the performance intact. He needed acrobatic skills, including the ability to walk on stilts and on his hands, and to make stunt falls, sometimes from high places.

Pantalone was a ridiculous old man who played duped husbands, old lovers, irate fathers, and Venetian merchants. Avaricious and miserly, his greatest vice was lust, for he was always chasing after a young woman, sometimes in competition with his own son.

The Dottore (doctor of law) was a graduate of many academies, a busybody, and a presumptuous meddler. His twin joys were love, which he always failed to find, being cuckolded often, and lecturing, from which it is nearly impossible to keep him quiet. His part is either a crony or a rival of Pantalone.

The Captain is a braggart soldier directly descended from Plautus' Miles Gloriosus. He is usually attended by a servant who constantly prompts him to recall his daring exploits and brave feats, which he does with gusto. He's exceedingly well mannered, and is under the illusion that he can have any woman he wants.

Scaramouche was so well performed by Tiberio Fiorilli (1602–1694) that scarcely any literature of the time exists without referring to him. Dressed in black and white, he typified that aspect of the theatre that is universally appreciated and endlessly useful—the logical synthesis of laughter and pathos. In the phrase of a Giordano Bruno, "in tristitia hilaris, in hilaritate tristis" (in sadness, laughter, in laughter, sadness). Molière was one of his greatest fans, and modeled after him the role of Sganarelle in his *Le Cocu Magnifique.*

All the characters wore certain identifying outfits—Harlequin in diamond shaped patches of many colors; Scapino in shirt and baggy trousers of white ("because I have carte blanche to do whatever I like") and green ("because I can always keep the desires of my clients green with the many tricks of my devising"); Pantalone predominantly in reds; the Dottore in black except for a broad white collar, white cuffs and a white handkerchief; and the Captain, elegant and pompous with colored beads, ribbons, braids, a huge hat with feathers and plume, shining buttons, garters, riding boots, and a scarlet mantle lined with another bright color. Thus costumed, the characters were instantly recognizable by their audience. The commedia, in fact, was often performed in dialects unknown to those listening, who knew from the acting what was going on and from the costumes who was who.

There were female versions of the same characters, and though young men still performed female roles as well, the first professional women on stage came from the commedia. The family orientation of the troupes virtually ensured that the theatre would not be without women much longer. By the middle of the sixteenth century, Marie Fairet had visited Paris with her company, and become the first woman to appear on the professional stage in France. Apparently Italian troupes also incorporated women by that time.

The female servants and maids were noted for quick wit, rhythmic gaiety, and gossipy demeanor. They rarely failed to help the lovers get together and often ended by marrying the male servants themselves. Specializing in quick changes and disguises, the maid was often useful to her opposite number, the cunning, plot-thickening servant, in carrying out his deceits for the good of their mistress.

The *lovers*—who always used their own names—had to be young and attractive because, unlike most of the others, they played without masks. They were experts at scenes of courtship, jealousy, and love.

Perhaps never before or since has the theatre been so solely devoted to the skills of the actor. Throughout the sixteenth, seventeenth, and early eighteenth century companies of actors roamed Europe. They were professional, highly skilled, and traveled constantly, and they were built largely around a family. They were run by an actor-manager who made the arrangements, collected and divided the money, ran the rehearsals, and allocated the roles.

Though enormously respected for their performances, the actors were under constant criticism, particularly from the Puritans in England and the Church in Spain. They had no civil rights and could not be buried in consecrated ground. The records of litigation and imprisonment for debt contain the names of many actors and managers, for commedia players had no patrons and were dependent for subsistence on what they could earn from the public. Though often unsuccessful at supporting themselves adequately, these troupes were nevertheless the first commercial theatres. They ranged from a single player to full companies.

In addition to its theatre, the commedia contributed the first written contract. On February 25, 1545 a group of Venetian actors signed and had notarized a legal document that is the earliest extant actors' contract:

> The undersigned colleagues, Ser Maphio known as Zanini from Padua, Vicentio from Venice, Francesco Moneybags, Hieronimo from San Lucax, Zuandomengo known as Rizo, Auane from Treviso, Thogano de Bastian and Francesco Moschini, being desirous to form a brotherly company which is to continue in being until the first day of Quadregesima next, that is to say in the year 1546 and which is to begin in the octave of next Easter, have together concluded and resolved that said time without hatred, rancor or dissolution and shall make and observe amongst them with every goodwill, as is the custom of good faithful comrades, all the articles hereunder written and promise

> to keep and observe them without quibbling, under penalty of loss of the monies written hereunder . . .

Contracts included such items as health insurance (anyone ill would be taken care of by the company) and an equal division of profits at the end of the tour. Some contracts even stipulated that "the said comrades should not play together at cards or in any way save it be for foodstuffs."

From Italy these players spread to every corner of Europe—to England, France, Spain, Germany, Austria, and Poland. One troupe made several trips to Russia. Their influence was felt in every theatre community for generations and they permanently altered the shape of theatre. Their plot devices—mistaken identity; one or more characters in disguise; young people of unknown origin who turn out to be brother and sister of high birth; a friend torn between love and loyalty to his comrade; a lover posing as a servant to be near the girl he adores and to save her from marriage to a rich old man; a girl dressed as a man; the use of twins, sometimes two sets; and a variety of standard comic bits—have been exploited continuously since.

As for shtick, here called *lazzi,* that hallmark of silent films, American burlesque, and the early musical comedy, it was taken to extreme heights by the famous *zanni,* or comics, of the commedia. From 1729 there is a print of comics squirting water—possibly the first seltzer bottle routine—and an engraving of one actor smashing a painting over the head of Pantalone, his face popping up through the frame.

One of the most popular bits performed by Scapino was the moment he would forget that he was in the comedy, often to the extent of relieving himself onstage, until another actor reminded him and he returned to the comedy. The comic actor with one foot in the play and another in his own performance has been refined by such musical theatre actors as Bobby Clark, Bert Lahr, Zero Mostel, and Robert Morse. Though few musicals have directly adapted commedias,* many have benefited from the commedia dell'arte legacy.

* The musical *Tricks* (1973) was an eight-performance flop, but it featured René Auberjonois and Christopher Murney, two outstanding comic actors working in the commedia style (right down to the pissing on stage).

HUMANIST THEATRE

If the Renaissance had brought only the art of comic acting to its zenith, its place in the history of musical theatre would be secure, but a second, equally popular theatre was part of the cultural life of Europeans from the middle of the fifteenth century on.

The commedia was a professional theatre, playing in outdoor marketplaces, temporary stages, and courtyards with few props, minimal sets, and no lights, and supporting itself from the admission it would charge. But meanwhile, an amateur, indoor, well-subsidized theatre, lavishly fixed with brilliant designs, intricate props and machinery and the first system of lights illuminating scripted performances was taking shape in the ballrooms, courts, and eventually the specially constructed theatres of the nobility.

Except for Spain's Lope de Vega, no significant dramatic literature arose out of the Renaissance, yet the presentation of plays in theatre productions as we know them today began with the indoor productions of the intelligentsia and nobility of the Renaissance. Using the Greek and Roman plays as models, playwrights built pictures of their society in *humanist* plays, investing stock characters and situations with a native flavor. Sensational and vigorous, these dramas often dealt with marital infidelity and lust. Though the names of comic authors are meaningless to us today, two have some significance. Pietro Aretino introduced the idea of a principal character dominated by a single chief characteristic, such as misogyny or hypocrisy, a writing gimmick later developed in the plays of Molière and Ben Jonson. And Machiavelli introduced the concept of character development: in *Mandragola,* considered the one good play of the period, the virtuous, chaste wife is changed into a cynical, disillusioned mistress.

If the written comedies of the period were of little value, the tragic theatre was of even less. Bloody, tedious and overly romantic, filled with ghosts, maxims, prolonged oratory and the revenge motive, declamatory acting and the substitution of horror for tragedy and narration for acting, this literature is almost useless to us today. Still, Cinthio, not so much through his long-forgotten plays as through his *Discourse on Comedy and Tragedy* (1543), held the theatre to certain concepts of interest. A five-act division of the play, with each act given a specific purpose, existed into the nineteenth century and continued in many three-act plays, where boy-meets-girl, boy-loses-girl, boy-gets-girl plots gave audiences a new development with each new act. He also continued the unities of time and place that now have only a specialized use.

But if literature was not the contribution of the humanist theatre, production was. Wealthy patrons spared their playwrights no expense, and the first magnificent indoor theatre, including dozens of mechanical inventions, is the second great legacy of the Renaissance.

Until the theatre became respectable enough to warrant its own designers, it required artists from other disciplines to outfit the plays for presentation. Thanks to the multifaceted interests of the Renaissance artists, painters, sculptors, tailors, and architects fastened upon the theatre and brought it their best efforts.

The early humanists built temporary platforms in halls, then decorated them in an increasingly elaborate manner. Various designs—recreating a classic theatre from their research on the Greeks and Romans—appeared in designers' manuscripts. In Paris, the famed Hôtel de Bourgogne, built in 1548, was the first public playhouse built since the fall of Rome, and the first theatre to be moved indoors, thus placing theatre on a new footing. The indoor theatre gave focus to the play rather than the event, and drama was set on the road to respectability. In 1580 the Olympic Academy of Vicenza commissioned Andrea Palladio to design and construct a theatre according to the best classical ideas of the time, and the Teatro Olympico became the first permanent theatre building of the Italian Renaissance. By the time this magnificent theatre was constructed, Madrid had two permanent theatres, London three, and Paris one.

It was an Italian architect who constructed the splendid theatres and set designs that presaged the modern theatre. In 1616, in Parma, the Prince commissioned the Teatro Farnese. The architect Aleotti gave this theatre a proscenium arch with wings behind it, parallel to the proscenium, a design which became a permanent part of indoor theatre.

Tremendous interest in the art of perspective painting came into set design at this time, and revolutionized the audience viewpoint. The extreme to which artists went—sometimes the entire design focused to a single point in the far distance—is seldom duplicated, but today the use of forced perspective is common. In 1545 Sebastiano Serlio, to augment the sense of perspective, used the raked stage for the first time, with the stage floor rising to the back wall.*

These stages featured a front curtain, which had been used in the

* Though difficult to dance on, the sets of *Pippin* and *Chicago* (by Tony Walton) featured raked stages, and Jo Mielziner's *1776* set used it to great effect.

Middle Ages to mask the preliminary preparations of actors who had no dressing rooms and little back stage area on makeshift wagons. Joseph Furttenbach, who spent ten years in Italy before returning to his native Germany, painted these curtains with a scene relating to the play, inventing the Act Curtain.

The Renaissance curtain was not lowered again until the end of the performance. All scene changes were engineered to flow smoothly as part of the performance, and were usually accompanied by music. This method remained predominant until the 19th century, when reliance on the drop—used both to cover scene changes and to back up a performance—increased. In vaudeville, the practice of alternating numbers "in one" (on the forestage with a curtain behind the act) with the full stage enabled the more cumbersome acts (dogs, acrobats, magicians, chorus lines) to set up. In Burlesque, sketch drops covered the set-up and striking of nude tableaux, since undressed girls were at first not allowed to move. The Broadway musical of the first half of the twentieth century often used the drop to cover major set changes.

By the late 1940s designers began to return to what had been practiced during the Renaissance: incorporating set changes into a smooth, flowing performance. When orchestrators filled the time with music the reversal was complete. Today clever director-choreographers integrate even the dances and movement into the changes, and seamless musical comedy has become the standard to aim for, just as it once was in the courts of the Medicis.

Renaissance actors had to sing, dance, and play an instrument as well. While musical sequences were not integral to the plays as they had been in Aristophanes' day, they were nevertheless a vital part of the presentation. Musical interludes filled the four intermissions of the five-act dramas. In Spain a ballad preceded the play and a dance followed it.

Underscoring these sequences were musicians sitting in yet another invention of the Renaissance master builder—the pit. In 1662, Lodovico Burnacini designed a proscenium arch for a production in Vienna that incorporated a pit for the musicians in front of the stage, thus legitimizing the placement of those musicians who had, from the Greeks through the Middle Ages, stood or sat near the front of the stage for optimum aural effect.

Costumes had not as yet become realistic. Actors wanted to look their best whether playing a prince or a pauper, and the designers and seamstresses of the humanist theatre used fine fabrics to ensure a magnificent appearance. Though the costumes of the characters were not representative of any time, place, or station, an attempt was made to dress the characters in proportion to the overall alignment of the cast. Thus, if a servant might be magnificently garbed, his master was sure to have an even finer array of trims, brocades, and threads.

It was in the field of lighting design, however, that the indoor theatre took on a striking new look. The strategic placement of oil lamps provided illumination for this first-ever artificially lit theatre. Colored water or wine in glass vessels placed in front of the lamps, and reflectors placed behind, multiplied the quality and color of available light. Mirrors strategically placed and hidden on the set itself could reflect this light, making the set look bright and joyful. Di Soma invented the practice of a darkened auditorium:

> As you know, it is natural that a man in the dark sees an object shining in the distance much better than if he were in a lighted place, because the glance goes more directly to the object. . . . And for this reason I place only very few lights of the hall behind the listeners' backs, so that no interposed lights will interfere with their view, and above them, as you see, I have also made openings, so that they will not cause any harm anywhere by their smoke. . . . [S]till another useful thing results from this, namely, that it saves the Duke fifty ducats' worth of additional torches he usually puts in this hall.

The actors who benefited from the technical effects were, unlike their outdoor counterparts, largely unheralded. All were amateurs, and hardly any of their names are recorded. Commedia actors were used on occasion to augment the necessary talents until, late in the Renaissance, the best aspects of both theatres were combined.

Acting style has, throughout history, swung back and forth between the declamatory and the natural. Following the great oratorios of the ancients, by the time of the Renaissance, the actor

> . . . must avoid that mode of delivery which seems a sing-song learned by heart. And he must, above all, make an effort to bring it about that what he says be spoken with effectiveness

and seem to be nothing more than a familiar discourse which comes about spontaneously. (Di Soma, *On Actors and Acting*)

Moving indoors gave a more natural stage demeanor greater emphasis, since the more intimate the setting, the increasingly subtle the actor could be. Thus the humanist theatre—indoors, elite, amateur, subsidized, lacking a great literature of its own—contributed a serious pursuit of the visual arts, and an increased naturalism in acting. The commedia dell'arte—outdoors, public, professional, commercial, lacking the visual elements too cumbersome to travel with and too expensive to afford—raised comic acting to virtuosic levels. That two such distinct theatres could exist side by side was remarkable.

The cultural spirit of the Renaissance provoked a magnificent two-and-a-half-century quest for new artistic achievements. Since no theatre in modern history has depended on production technique to dazzle its audience as heavily as the contemporary musical theatre of Broadway, and no literature has required the smooth engineering of numerous sets, props, virtuoso lighting, and costumes within the libretto of the musical, the debt owed by the American musical theatre to the architects, directors, and patrons of the humanist theatre is enormous. The great halls and patronage of the nobles encouraged architects and designers to construct the first really extravagant settings and effects. Modern musical theatre is still three centuries away, but in its all-encompassing use of the various art forms, it will be the primary beneficiary of advances in painting, sculpture, acting, theatre construction, set design, and lighting design. The spectacles of shifting scenery, special effects, and mechanical tricks within the proscenium arch would forever after enhance the audience's enjoyment.

As the cultural achievements of the Renaissance came to a climax, new freedoms in philosophical and political thought allowed the arts to focus on contemporary life and away from religion. The stage was becoming increasingly popular with and accessible to all the classes. The public found the theatre a great release, a social gathering point, and a superb entertainment. Increased transportation and communication allowed cross-pollenization of theatrical achievements, particularly between England, France, and Italy. The artist's response to broadening interest in the theatre arts was magnificent. These developments created a golden age of drama for the Elizabethans, of comedy and ballet for the France of Louis XIV, of ballet and opera for Renaissance Italy. Marked by singular achievements in drama by William Shakespeare, in comedy by Molière, in ballet by Lully, and in opera by Lully, Monteverdi, and Cavalli, this age, immortalized by a hundred other creators and a thousand great works for the stage, caused, for the first time, a soaring of the human spirit that showed humankind what it was to be a cultural animal. His soul would never again go underfed.

ELIZABETHAN DRAMA

The court of Henry VIII was the center of the new humanist learning in England, and the scene of lavish productions. When Elizabeth succeeded him in 1547 she cut down severely the royal budget for spectacle. Nevertheless, at the same time the schools began to stage productions of the classics they had been studying from the surviving Greek and Roman manuscripts. Their boys were trained in music and singing. Concurrently, the professional theatre companies performed in commercial theatres and were influenced by Henry's spectacles, the scholarship of the learning institutions, and popular drama from the Middle Ages from which they were descended. Though Latin was the international language of scholarship, works in the vernacular by Chaucer (1340?–1400) gained in popularity and more and more literary productions were staged in the native tongue. This obviously made the work much more accessible to the population.

Public theatre became a full-time operation. Writers found their work in abundant demand. Actors earned a fair living and pursued their craft full-time. A grudging admiration was awarded their profession, and if they still suffered the indignities of excommunication and low-class standing, it was largely because of the continued opposition of the church, which had a decreasing influence on the people.

In England, domination of the seas and strength in world trade gave the English fierce pride in their homeland and a swelling belief in the Renaissance ideal of the heroic proportions of the individual man. A strong optimism for the quality of life pervaded. Infinite possibilities for the good life stretched before the English people. This robust attitude was well reflected in the theatre, where performances were given daily by many companies and, judging from some records of receipts and the affluence of the better troupes, were well attended.

The popularity of the stage in the age of Queen Elizabeth enabled artists to carry on a more or less stable existence for the first time in their history. Prior to the building of the first playhouses, companies would rent, at either a flat rate or a percentage, an inn, making London innkeepers the first commercial theatre owners (with the majority of their profits from the sale of beverages).

The Puritans elected one of their own as mayor and dominated the Board of Aldermen and the Town Council. Their opposition to the plays greatly restricted the inns and theatrical activity; finally, to avoid their jurisdiction, James Burbage built his own playhouse in one of the few areas outside civil authority. By virtue of their status as former Roman Catholic Church holdings, the new premises were subject only to the crown. In the fall of 1576 the Theatre, as it was simply called, opened and became the first public playhouse of Renaissance England. It was an enormous success and soon another was built by Henry Lanman. (By 1585 Burbage gained control of this second theatre and became, briefly, the first owner of a chain in history.) Several more theatres were built before the turn of the century, including the Globe, and a rush of theatrical activity ensued. Some twenty-three acting companies were represented in London at the height of its theatrical activity, providing continual performances of ever-changing plays to a population of only two hundred thousand.

The financial arrangement for the companies was as close to a profit-sharing plan as the theatre has ever known. In companies all over England as well as on the continent, actors were considered shareholders, and took a pre-arranged portion of the theatre's income, depending on seniority. Authors, most of whom were actors as well, including Shakespeare and Molière, usually took the receipts from a single performance designated as Authors' Night, in addition to their regular income as members of the company. The theatre became, for the first time in history, an efficient business enterprise as well as an art form.

Women were already appearing on the stage in Europe, but were still unknown on the public stages of England, and for this reason there is a minimum of physical contact between the sexes. Shakespeare's most famous love scene is played with Juliet on the balcony and Romeo below in the garden.

As for musical comedy, England as yet had none and wouldn't for fifty more years. Still, various interludes of instrumental music, dancing, and singing were interspersed throughout the plays. Shakespeare speaks of twelve different dance forms and writes fifty times of dancing in his plays and poems. As many as fifteen of his plays require a dance as part of their dramatic structure. Since travelers from the continent frequented theatre without understanding the language, these entertainments were included specially to attract them. Playwrights took the talents of their actors for granted, and simply indicated "dance" in their scripts. An actor's versatility included many dance forms, as well as mime, fencing, acrobatics, and instrumental music. This approach demanded study, and almost every accomplished actor took on an apprentice and provided his training and education.

Although the Elizabethans, like the Greeks, are known for a great body of literature, in reality, just as in the Greek theatre, their productions were highly theatrical, rough, common, popular, and musical, using every artifice available to entertain broad audiences. The great works of Shakespeare, Christopher Marlowe, and Ben Jonson were written, sometimes hastily, to provide acting companies with fresh material and satisfy a demanding (and often loud and impolite) audience.

Only a portion of the Elizabethan plays were published and many were lost, since they were closely guarded by the acting companies whose sole success rested on their ability to produce new material frequently. These plays nearly always reflected the optimism, pride, and nationalism of England, the spirit of a growing people who saw themselves at the ever-expanding borders of cultural, scientific, and political frontiers. If Shakespeare wrote of Denmark, it was an "English" Denmark; if he wrote of Verona, it was an anglicized Verona. Here can be drawn a strong parallel between this golden age and the great age of musical theatre in the 1940s, 1950s, and early 1960s, for when Tin Pan Alley composers and American directors and choreographers created their version of the South Pacific or the Far East or anywhere else, it was translated into Broadwayese, and every musical reflected the spirit of America.

As drama took greater steps forward, ballet became increasingly sophisticated and opera more complex. Inevitably, each form used the others to promote and vary its own purpose. Many productions were designed utilizing all three.

THE MASQUE

Inside the royal courts an even greater spectacle, if less literary, was taking place: the court masques. Dancing was a great passion all over Europe.

Elizabethan London was full of dancing schools frequented by the nobility as much as by the citizens. It was said that Queen Elizabeth's greatest passion was for dancing. Productions of the masques ranged from the London citizenry to the lower nobility to the courts of Elizabeth and then the Stuart kings, from a modest scale to lavish spectaculars that lasted all day, were rehearsed for many weeks in advance, and included hundreds of musicians, singers, and dancers, all supporting the nobility who danced the leading roles and around whom the choreographers created the piece.

The most famous and successful collaboration of the time was between Ben Jonson, a poet and playwright, and Inigo Jones, a scene designer.

Inigo Jones had traveled through Europe and seen the virtuosity of the Italian stage mechanics and the beauty of the lavish French court productions. He attempted to translate both into the English idiom. He brought the proscenium stage back with him, decorated each new production with a frame designed specifically to enhance it, and mounted the first theatrically effective group scenes. He delighted in scene changes and stage images, and produced the finest technical achievements England had yet seen.

Jonson, first an actor, then a dramatist, had been imprisoned for appearing in and coauthoring a scandalous satire in 1596 that resulted in the temporary closing of London's theatres. He was imprisoned a second time for killing an actor, and a third time for another satire in 1605. He created *Volpone,* a comedy in which the leading character is drenched in a single greedy caricature, but his contribution to the musical came with his spectacles.

Jonson provided plots that were meant as political propaganda to display the power of the throne and the richness of the realm. For Jonson, undoubtedly the first librettist to write specifically for the musical theatre, the masque provided an opportunity to further his poetic vision using all the virtuosic techniques at hand: song, dance, drama, and spectacle. Writing specifically to integrate the various portions, Jonson had stumbled upon the essence of musical theatre as a synthesis of all the arts. In addition, Jonson and Jones developed the principle of contrast. Because the purpose of the masque was to emphasize the richness of the realm, there developed a sameness in scene after scene of splendor. Jonson and Jones used sequences called the "anti-masque," which employed witches and hags given comic dialogue, and increased the splendor of the royal roles by contrast.

Jonson eventually realized that the visual splendor of his productions was overwhelming his own work, and in 1631 ended his collaboration with Jones. English masques were already having trouble keeping up with certain standards. One critic wrote of a Jonson-Jones masque in 1618, "spoiled as we are by the graceful and harmonious music of Italy, the composition did not strike us as very fine."

In Italy, extraordinary things had developed in the musical world.

WE OPEN IN VENICE . . .

Combining music with drama had been popular in both the tragedies and comedies of the Greeks and the liturgical drama of the Middle Ages. In sixteenth-century Florence, instrumental music was a lively art. Young radical intellectuals began to combine music with plots based on Greek tragedy, in the belief (brilliantly conceived and forevermore an axiom of every sort of musical stage) that *music would intensify the emotional impact of the drama.* Then they wrote the first arias. Feeling the need for a type of song that would *move the action forward,* they then created the recitative, which preceded the longer musical sequences.

Opera began around 1600 A.D. when a society of scholars, philosophers, and amateur musicians in Italy promoted the *dramma per musica* (drama through music)—a single line of melody and lyric with musical accompaniment. In 1594 two young Florentines, Jacop Peri and Giulio Caccini, collaborated on *Dafne,* creating the first opera. Then they split up and each composed an opera titled *Eurydice.* In 1607 a professional organist and singer, Claudio Monteverdi, created his first opera, *Orfeo,* and followed it a year later with *Arianna.* Instead of a simple accompaniment on a keyboard instrument, Monteverdi for the first time specified which instruments were to play which notes. His recitatives not only imitated the ordinary inflections of speech, but also carried much greater emotional impact and musical complexity. Monteverdi used his music to reflect the drama of the librettos. In 1637 the world's first public opera house opened in Venice. By 1700, hundreds of operas were being produced in sixteen theatres there.

FRENCH MUSICAL COMEDY

Italy began the development of opera and gave European theatre the technical virtuosity of its stage designs, and England brought the art of commedia dell'arte into the playhouses and literature of its theatre. France, principally through the talents of one actor-manager-playwright, brought the art of comedy to its zenith. Jean Baptiste Poqueline, under the stage name Molière, raised comedy to the stature of tragedy.

The greatest influence on Molière's career was the art of the commedia dell'arte. He studied acting with Tiberio Fiorillo, the most famous Scaramouche of his day. He constantly attended the performances of commedia troupes appearing in Paris, and is known to have loved their virtuosic acting style. After a difficult beginning—he was in and out of debtor's prison twice and barnstormed the provinces for twelve years—Molière finally became a success in Paris, where he enjoyed the royal favor of the king. In Paris Molière's troupe shared a theatre with a commedia troupe, alternating performances.

Molière added two significant improvements to the commedia style. First, he wrote his plays in such a way as to allow, indeed require, a broad, farcical acting style. For the first time, there was a scripted performance that called upon the talents of the commedia. Second, he added satire. It was readily apparent to audiences that the central character of *Le Misanthrope* was the well known Duc de Montausier, and that the four doctors held up to ridicule in *L'Amour Médecin* were easily recognizable as the leading physicians of the court of Louis XIV. Satire had disappeared with the decline of Greek democracy over two thousand years earlier. Scholarship existed in the Greek and Latin theatre, and Molière would have encountered it during his education. A cynical bent in his personality would have appreciated it.

The need to write plays incorporating the singing, dancing, and spectacle the court was so fond of would turn three of his plays—*The Bores* (1661), *Monsieur de Pourgeaugnac* (1669), and *The Would-Be Gentleman* (1670)—into authentic musical comedies. In his translation, Morris Bishop writes "there is no doubt that in 1670 *Le Bourgeois Gentilhomme* was regarded as primarily a song and dance show; as in any musical comedy, the librettist was the servant of the composer."

The composer Molière collaborated with was Jean Baptiste Lully, who would become renowned throughout Europe for his work in ballet and opera, as a choreographer and composer, the first in a line of musical theatre directors whose concepts were the focal point of their productions. He wrote for all of Molière's plays with the exception of *The Imaginary Invalid.* The music was based on harpsichord; the player was generally the leader and could fill in additional notes at his discretion. There were five stringed instruments to which flutes, oboes, and bassoons were often added. For major court appearances, orchestras of twenty or more were used.

If the court performances were carried out in an atmosphere of polite attention and cultivated taste, the public theatres were not nearly so refined. This paragraph from *La Pratique du Théâtre* by Francois Hedelin, Abbot of Aubignac, was written at the time:

> As for the disorders of the spectators, we may consider that nothing was more safe and quiet than the ancient theatres, the magistrates being always present, and everything being done by their orders; but amongst us there is no order at all, but any sorts of people wear swords in the pit, and other places, and therewith attack very often many respectable spectators, who have no other defence than the authority of the laws. Among the Greeks and Romans, the women were so safe in the public theatres that they often brought their children with them; but with us a company of young débauches come in, and commit a hundred insolences, frightening the women, and often killing those who take their protection.

Doorkeepers could be wounded or killed trying to collect admission. The first act of Edmond Rostand's *Cyrano De Bergerac,* if read from the point of view of the poor actor, gives a good account of what it must have been like to perform. The practice of arriving late and talking loudly throughout the performance was begun by the arrogant nobility of the period (and continued today by attendees of Broadway's matinées), many of whom felt that their seat should be right on the stage, where occasionally it became so crowded that the audience could hardly separate the players from the onlookers.

If the church did not yet condone the theatre, the crown not only did, but manipulated plays and playwrights to express its own glory. The king himself was godfather to Molière's child and interceded with the church to allow Molière to be buried in sacred ground. (The ceremony was carried out in secret and after dark to avoid scandal.) Women also were realizing an equal footing, and while they were not yet on the English public stage they appeared on the French stage in all the youthful female roles.

Character men continued to portray older women, as female actresses refused to admit to their age.

The first press agent came along at this time. Known as the company "orator," it was his job to announce the play for the following week at the conclusion of the performance and to spread handbills and posters throughout the city to herald a new production.

Actors had to provide their own costumes, which were rich and colorful and generally mirrored the dress of the times, though directors were beginning to balance the stage and catch some semblance of suitability to character. A Paris merchant, Monsieur Bourgeois, opened the first costume rental house, enabling actors to wear costumes for their performances costing much more than they could afford in real life.

During a performance as his famous hypochondriac, the imaginary invalid, Molière took sick. He finished the performance, went home, and died within hours, leaving a number of masterpieces and having raised comedy to a new plateau. In his last year he had lost the royal charter and performances had become increasingly difficult to arrange. This was due to the influence of his former collaborator Lully, who had become, through elevation of the arts of ballet and opera and his own extraordinary ability at court politics, the first powerful director-choreographer in history. His story, which plays a large part in the development of the musical, begins with the origins of ballet.

THE ORIGINS OF STAGE DANCING

Folk dances will always be a powerful source of material for the theatrical choreographer. However, stage dancing began with ballet, the origin of which dates to the Renaissance and a man who "exceeded all men in the dance," Guglielmo Ebreo di Pesaro (William, Hebrew of Pesaro).

Traveling throughout Italy, Guglielmo wrote extensively about dance, codifying the steps and outlining the basic requirements. He created many ballets—the word is French and did not come into common use until years later—for royal patrons. His most significant achievement was a ballet created for Vittoria Colonna which personified her personal purity. It was the beginning of the regal posturing that characterized ballet, replacing the lusty folk dance vocabulary. His work elevated the dance, and courts and dancing masters copied it.

When Catherine de Medici, the daughter of one of the greatest houses of Italy, went to France to marry Henry II, she brought with her a company of musicians and dancers to supervise her artistic presentations. At first these ballets were pageants, made up of parades and social dances interspersed with long speeches honoring a royal marriage, birth, the ending of a war, or other occasion. They were long, magnificent, expensive and had no plot to speak of (shades of the early American musical!). Also, there was never any question about the endings. Everyone suitable—usually royalty, hosts, and the honored guest—were installed on Mount Olympus accompanied by great lighting effects and much splendor.

In 1581, on the occasion of the marriage of the queen's sister, Catherine commissioned her chief violinist and dancing master, Balthasar de Beaujoyeulx, to produce the entertainment. (Baldassari de Belgiojoso had changed his name when he came to France from his native Italy.) The entertainment he worked out was known as *Le Ballet Comique de la Reine.* He explained the terms "ballet" and "comique" in an introduction to the printed edition of the libretto, saying that "comique" stood for the "lovely, tranquil and happy conclusion by which it ends," and that "ballet" meant "a geometric combination of several persons dancing together." The work cost 400,000 crowns, a great deal more than the most expensive Broadway musicals of today. It was based on the story of a Greek hero who was enchanted by Circe and at last freed by the intervention of the gods.

For the first time, a court spectacle of this sort confined itself to a consistent dramatic subject throughout, and all its verses, music, and dancing were appropriate to the development of the theme. It was, in addition, the beginning of concern with geometric patterns which could be the chief landmark in the transition from country folk dancing to ballroom dances to stage dancing. It took the Renaissance man, with his eye always seeking beauty, to look for the patterns that would mark ballet, and the release of the church's power would turn the motivation of art away from religion and toward the architecture of beauty in nature and humanity.

The experiment was enormously successful. Thousands of common people attempted to obtain admission to the palace to see it. Eventually ten thousand did. Copies of the work were printed and sent to all the courts of Europe, and Catherine's political ambitions were achieved, as well as Beaujoyeulux's artistic ones. From then on the French court was established as the center of ballet's development, and the artistic principles which

Beaujoyeulx had established were practiced, though usually on a far more modest scale.

The ballet, however, did not yet take on the theatrical aspect which characterizes it today. At first it was only danced by royalty, in ballrooms, at celebratory events. In 1653 Louis XIV, at the age of fifteen, appeared in *Ballet de la Nuit* as the sun, and derived his famous nickname, *le Roi Soleil* (the Sun King) from that role. The performance lasted thirteen hours and was notable for the fact that the twenty-one-year-old Lully danced with the king, and began his career not only as a dancer but as the artistic dictator at the focal point of European culture.

Louis XIV was the greatest of all royal patrons of the dance, and during his reign the court ballet reached new heights. He was an excellent dancer and loved to prove it to his court, which led him to engage and encourage the most brilliant of his composers, painters, and poets to collaborate on ballets. In time Louis became too old to display his once shapely physique. Gradually the nobility gave way to the professionals. The artists Louis had gathered were still together to see that the art of musical theatre was not lost, and chief among them was Lully.

A youth of tremendous agility and many musical talents, Lully began his career in the household staff of the cousin of the king of France. Not the least of his talents was the ability to ingratiate himself with the right people. He soon was given a post with the house orchestra. After calling attention to himself as both a musician and a dancer, he left the house and danced in *Ballet de la Nuit* with Louis XIV, who appointed him conductor of a twenty-four-string orchestra.

Lully was an Italian-born artist and an able if not too scrupulous politician. In 1672, by devious means and through the bankruptcy of the founders, he obtained the charter of the Académie Royale de Musique, and absorbed it into the Academy of Dance. During his career he wrote many operas and ballets that were performed not only in Paris under his direction but all over the continent. Influenced by Italian opera, he nevertheless sensed the mood of French chauvinism and created an operatic theatre with a lighter, more French touch.

He elevated ballet to professional levels and moved it from the tennis courts and ballrooms of the nobility to a proscenium stage, where he could perfect the art of "line" by limiting the angles from which the audience could view the performer. He always sensed the public's taste and created, with Molière, a number of musical comedies. His operas always included dancing, and his ballets often had singing. His sense of musical theatre was superb, and with him the integration of the great arts of drama, song, and dance began. In 1681 he created "The Triumph of Love," using trained women for the first time. Until then, all female roles had been performed by men in wigs and masks. The year 1708 saw the first ballet commissioned for a public performance; until then the ballet was a court spectacle for the nobility only. It wasn't until 1773 that choreographer Noverre abolished masks, and dancers were free to use their own expressions.

• • •

In England, on September 2, 1642, Parliament, by now firmly controlled by the Puritans, closed the playhouses. Between 1644 and 1649 they were torn down and the theatre was driven temporarily underground. But the Puritans never succeeded. Theatre was too successful, and the English theatre continued. In France, the death of the Sun King drew the curtain on a dazzling society, but not before the establishment of the Comédie Française, the world's first national theatre, which King Louis personally chartered. In Italy, the Renaissance was played out against a background of almost constant bickering between families and city-states, yet both comic acting and opera continued to develop. It was the greatest of all ages for playwright, actor, and audience.

Shakespeare and his fellow Elizabethans produced, as Polonius said in *Hamlet,* "tragedy, comedy, history, pastoral, pastoral-comical, historical-comical, tragical-historical, tragical-comical-historical-comical, scene individable and poem unlimited." Molière polished the art of farce comedy in both writing and acting to its brightest hue. Song and dance were integral parts of nearly every play. Opera was born and developed in both Italian and French forms. Ballet was born and codified and raised to a spectator art. Lully touched the pulse of the Parisians, all the French, and ultimately all Europeans, with his combinations of opera, ballet, and drama in light, comical-musical productions.

Aria and recitative, ballet, instrumental music, drama, comedy, social and political satire, acrobatics and tumbling, magical scene design, and everywhere a popular, successful, commercial theatre. The stage was set for the first musical comedy in the English language.

GREENWICH VILLAGE THEATRE

Management FRANK CONROY and HAROLD MELTZER

Arthur Hopkins

Presents

Mr. Nigel Playfair's London Production of

THE BEGGAR'S OPERA

By MR. GAY

New Settings of the Airs and additional Music by

Frederic Austin

THE CAST

PEACHUM	*Arthur Wynn*
LOCKIT	*Charles Magrath*
MACHEATH	*Percy Heming*
FILCH	*Alfred Heather*
THE BEGGAR	*William Eville*
DRAWER	*C. C. Lewis*
MRS. PEACHUM	*Lena Maitland*
POLLY PEACHUM	*Sylvia Nelis*
LUCY LOCKIT	*Dora Roselli*
JENNY DIVER	*Nonny Lock*
DIANA TRAPES	*Edith Bartlett*

Member of Macheath's Gang:

Charles Tobin, Edward Ciannelli, James Wolff, Walton Macafee, Mario Carboni, S. Rossmussen

Women of the Town:

Miss Meg Mellors, Clytie Hine, Gladies Johnson, Julie Meo, Vera Hurst, Enid Lindsay

PERIOD 1728

ACT I. - - Peachum's House

ACT II. Sc. 1 A Tavern. Near Newgate
Sc. 2 Newgate

ACT III. Sc. 1 A Street
Sc. 2 Newgate
Sc. 3 The Condemn'd Hold

In this version of Mr. Gay's famous *English* Ballad Opera every possible effort has been made to recapture the spirit of the original work, much of which was "improved away" in the representations of the early nineteenth century. Unfortunately in an age which lacks the leisure of the eighteenth century the opera cannot be given in its entirety; in the work of curtailment and selection the producer has been much helped by Mr. Arnold Bennett.

New settings have been provided for the Songs, and the music in general has been re-arranged and supplemented where necessary by Mr. Frederic Austin. The versions of the tunes used have been taken from contemporary eighteenth-century editions, and many beautiful and characteristic numbers omitted in later times have been restored.

THE ORCHESTRA

consisting of String Instruments, Oboe, Flute and Harpsicord (Special Engagement of Miss Pelton - Jones)

Conductor: JOHN MUNDY

Scenery and Costumes designed by C. Lovat Fraser

Scenery made by Edgar Brickel and painted by Victor Hembrow

Costumes executed by Charles Wilson & Co., Great Tichfield St., W.

Wigs by Clarkson

Dances arranged by Marian Wilson

THE BEGGAR'S OPERA

There is in it such a labefactation of all principles as may be injurious to morality.

—DR. JOHNSON ON *THE BEGGAR'S OPERA*

The Restoration period in English history (1660–1700) saw a reopening of the theatres that had been closed since 1642. The theatres produced weak tragedies that are rarely read today and practically never revived. Moreover, the great works of the Elizabethans were reviled and rewritten.

In the field of comedy, however, George Etherage, William Wycherly, William Congreve, John Dryden, and George Farquhar produced brilliant, well-crafted plays, broad satire in a stylish, drawing-room style licentious enough to torture the Puritans. These comedies of manners had a strong influence on the young John Gay.

Gay was born to a prominent family in Barnstable, Devonshire, England in 1685, and was educated at the local grammar school. At the age of seventeen he was apprenticed to a silk merchant in London for four years. After a brief return to Barnstable, he went back to London to work as secretary to poet and playwright Aaron Hill, a schoolmate from Barnstable. Hill introduced him to the literary circles of London.

At the age of twenty-one Gay published his first poem, a burlesque entitled *Wine,* and by the age of twenty-six, in 1711, he had met and become a member of a celebrated circle of Tory wits, including Alexander Pope, Jonathan Swift, and Dr. John Arbuthnot. A year later he completed his first play, which was never produced. In 1713 he published two poems and had his play, *The Wife of Bath,* produced at the Drury Lane Theatre. In 1714 he wrote *The Shepherd's Week,* his first real success. The next year his *The What D'Ye Call It,* also had a successful run at Drury Lane.

He published more poems, and had other plays acted, but was frustrated in his attempt to receive a lucrative court appointment, the primary means of income for writers and artists of the period. In 1727 George II succeeded to the throne and Gay was offered a menial post, far less than he had expected from his acquaintance with Queen Caroline. He refused the appointment, feeling cheated and slighted, and set out to share his opinion of the hypocrisy and double dealing at St. James Palace and Whitehall with the general public.

He took for his source a poem, "Newgate's Garland," that he had written two years earlier, celebrating the trial of three highwaymen at the Old Bailey. (Jonathan Wild, London's notorious master criminal, had turned king's evidence against the others, Jack Shepherd and Jonathan Blake, refuting the old adage of honor among thieves.) In Newgate Gay found his metaphoric key for a story of corruption in high places, and *The Beggar's Opera (a Newgate Pastorale)* became both social and political satire.

In his script, the thieves and whores of Newgate often act with overly elaborate courtesy, and the men claim an integrity and honor that is not theirs. Their leader Macheath addresses his gang as "gentlemen." The message was that affected manners and elaborate trappings do not disguise a blackguard. In the opening number, Peachum sings:

Through all the employments of life
Each neighbor abuses his brother;
Whore and Rogue they call husband and wife:
All professions be-rogue one another.
The priest calls the lawyer a cheat,
The lawyer be-knaves the divine;
And the statesman, because he's so great,
Thinks his trade as honest as mine.

The specifics of Gay's political attack were immediately clear to his audience, for the term "great" in the second to last line, when referring to a statesman, was an expression often applied in sarcasm to the current Whig prime minister, Sir Robert Walpole. Walpole had used his office to put together a considerable personal fortune, and his belief that "every man has his price" was well known. These traits were deftly mirrored in the character of Peachum. If there was any doubt about his intentions, Gay assigned this speech to the beggar near the end:

> Throughout the whole piece, you may observe such a similitude of manners in high and low life, that it is difficult to determine whether (in the fashionable vices) the fine gentlemen imitate the gentlemen of the road, or the gentlemen of the road the fine gentlemen.

In exactly what style *The Beggar's Opera* was written must have been hard to define at the time, for it combined the elements of political satire (on the Whig government and the prime minister in particular) and social satire (on corruption in royal circles with which Gay had recent negative experiences), with a burlesque of the Italian opera entertainment that had dominated the English stage for years. Gay set his own lyrics to folk songs and inserted them in his play. (The audience surely left the theatre humming the tunes, since the melodies were familiar to them before they arrived.)

Most of the songs came from a six-volume songbook of popular ballads published ten years earlier. Some music was by Handel, whose Italian operas had been all the rage at The Queen's Theatre since 1705. The score had been arranged by John Pepusch and was a direct reaction to Handelian and Italian opera, with their noble themes, exalted personages, and elaborate baroque music. The burlesque of the form paralleled Gay's satire on the subject matter. Thus was ballad opera born—the text of a burlesque farce interspersed with songs written to popular tunes.

Gay's friends all agreed that *The Beggar's Opera* would either be a great success or a large failure. It seemed so unusual to Pope and Swift, to his friend and patron the Duke of Queensberry, and to William Congreve, who was respected as the elder statesman of the stage, that none would hazard a guess as to its future. The Duke remarked to Gay, "This is a very odd thing." Indeed, it was the beginning of musical theatre.

Theatre managers were no more enthusiastic than Gay's friends. Colley Gibber, the manager of London's most reputable theatre, Drury Lane, rejected the play, not fully understanding the degree of satire. John Rich, manager of the Theatre Royal at Lincoln's Inn Fields and Gibber's chief rival, agreed reluctantly to produce the play upon the prodding of the Duchess of Queensberry. In January of 1728 he put the play into rehearsal. It opened on the 29th to an audience that, by coincidence, included one of the targets of Gay's satire, Sir Robert Walpole. Apparently the ballad opera form Gay had employed—in fact, nearly invented—took an act to catch on. By the beginning of the second act, both the satire and the style were clear. And the audience loved it.

The commercial success of *The Beggar's Opera* was astonishing. In the English theatre of the late Restoration period, many moderately successful plays gave only a single performance, and very successful plays ran four or five nights. By the end of its run *The Beggar's Opera* had played an unprecedented sixty-two performances and established a new long-run record, which it held for nearly a hundred years. Lavinia Fenton, the actress who portrayed Polly Peachum, until then entirely unknown, became the toast of London, with multitudes of admirers sending poems and doing her likeness in sculpture, painting, and engraving. Thomas Walker, also virtually unknown, was transformed overnight into the hero of the town's young gallants with his portrayal of Macheath. "Polly Peachum fans" were sold throughout England.

The era of the commercial theatre manager had just begun. After trying very hard to overlook the project altogether, John Rich found himself to be the producer of what was the most popular musical ever to appear on the English stage. It made him wealthy.

Gay himself became a celebrity overnight, both as the author of the most popular play of the century and as a spokesman for the Tory cause. He came to his position as a leader of the Tory attack on the incumbent Whig government reluctantly, however. He was never as politically opinionated as his friends, and the success of his play was unexpected. The quality of similar satire had been, up to that point, hackwork. The only source of previous editorial attacks had been ineffectual essays distributed in pamphlets that didn't bother the prime minister or his party in the slightest. But Gay had come upon a formula that, *because of its entertainment value,* had found an enormous audience. In the next quarter century there were hundreds of imi-

Hogarth etching of *The Beggar's Opera*
Photofest

tators to Gay's piece. Gilbert and Sullivan operettas are direct descendants of the form Gay had founded.

If every plateau in art is motivated by rejection of a prior form, this letter by Gay to Swift, five years before *The Beggar's Opera,* clearly indicates his opinion of Italian opera:

> As for the reigning amusement of the town . . . [t]here's nobody allowed to say "I sing" but a eunuch and an Italian woman. Everybody is grown now as great a judge of music as they were in your time of poetry, and folks that could not distinguish one tune from another now daily dispute about the different styles of Handel, Bononcini, and Atillio [composers of Italian opera]. People have now forgot Homer and Virgil and Caesar, or at least they have lost their ranks, for in London and Westminster in all polite conversations, Senesino [a leading singer in Italian opera], is daily voted to be the greatest man that ever lived.

Gay's reference to eunuchs and Italian women refer to castrati and prima donnas, whose virtuosic singing had so caught on that many of the arias had literally nothing whatever to do with the story and were only for the demonstration of the performer's voice.

In the enormous success and acceptance of Gay's production was a dramatic achievement so important that its discovery alone begins the history of the musical comedy—the musical numbers were woven into the plot. Gay was the first librettist-lyricist to integrate song and story. The songs are motivated more by the dramatic situation from which they arise than by the characteristics of the singer. Gay's comic opera made the current favorite, Italian opera, seem somewhat absurd, leading to an astounding development—the public's appreciation changed literally overnight from the Italian opera form to the comic opera form.

That *The Beggar's Opera* was in English made it available as drama as well as music. Nearly everyone in London from royalty to the poorest apprentice saw it, or wanted to. It swept the populace because it appealed to them on a number of levels, the most significant being dramatic. The technical aspects of the Italian opera, however great, were appreciated only by those who had the experience to understand the achievement. In fact opera became, from that time on in the English-speaking world, a separate art form with a fanatical but small audience. Musical comedy took over and has ever since commanded a much larger portion of the public's attention.

It had taken over two thousand years for the farcical, satirical, musical theatre that had been so popular in Aristophanes' Athens to resurface. In 1728 John Gay had combined nearly all of the arts to produce a musical comedy that, considering the proportions of theatre activity to date, might well be considered the most successful production of all time.

In 1946 John LaTouche (book and lyrics) and Duke Ellington translated *The Beggar's Opera* into contemporary terms, making Mack the Knife an American gangster (portrayed by Alfred Drake). But an eclectic if talented cast (Zero Mostel as Mr. Peachum, Avon Long as Filch, Libby Holman as Jenny) and three directors (John Houseman, Nicholas Ray, George Abbott) couldn't focus the weak material, and *Beggar's Holiday* flopped on Broadway. In 1948 Benjamin Britten turned it into an opera. In 1953 a motion picture version was made, starring Laurence Olivier. But its most successful offspring came in Germany in 1928 when Bertolt Brecht wrote his own version, with original music by Kurt Weill. They called their version *The Threepenny Opera.*

Curiously enough, *The Beggar's Opera* not only began musical comedy in England, but nearly marked its highest point as well. A year later Gay wrote a sequel, but by then both the government and the court recognized the power of satire to affect their status, and *Polly* was suppressed. In the preface to *Polly,* Gay wrote that his work meant to "lash in general the reigning and fashionable vices and recommend and set virtue in as amiable a light as possible." Ballad opera would be succeeded by sentimental opera that would look at life not as it was, but as a romanticist would like it to be. One popular author was Isaac Bickerstaffe (1735–1812), whose most successful works were *Love in a Village* and *The Maid of the Mill.* The titles alone indicate the pastoral direction the English musical stage would follow.

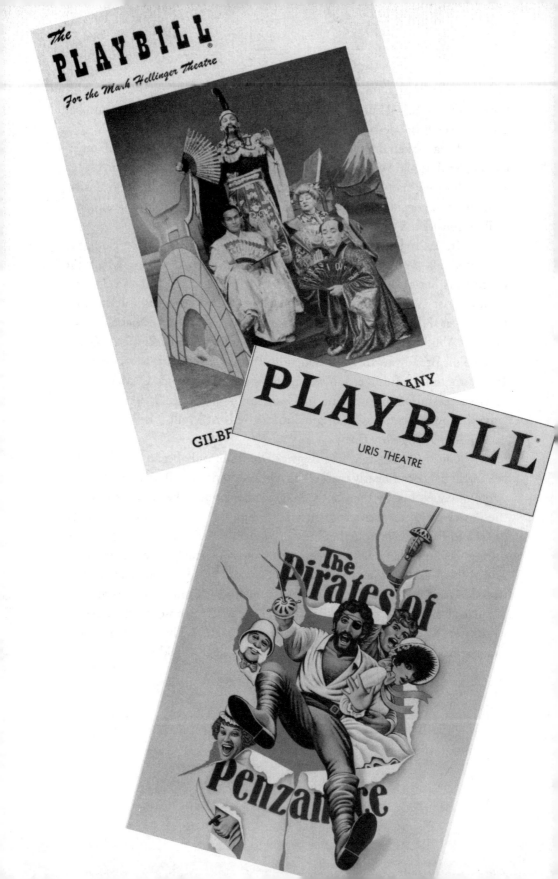

The PLAYBILL

For the Mark Hellinger Theatre

Five

Comic Operas

Several sources name Mozart as the originator of the term *operetta,* meaning "little opera." Operetta represents a link between grand opera and musical theatre, and came about through the direct efforts of nineteenth-century writers and producers to cater to the public with comedy, melody, and girls. It's a toss-up whether the definition of operetta as "opera for the common man" is more insulting to the opera or operetta fan.

The roots of operetta lie in England's ballad opera *The Beggar's Opera*—because it was popular and funny and dealt with contemporary society—and an *opera buffa* in Italy in 1733 titled *La Serva Padrona,* an entertainment known as an *intermezzo,* performed between the acts of opera. But the birth of the form might be traced to . . .

FRANCE, 1858

It is fitting that some of the roots of musical theatre are embedded in the romantic, pleasure-loving city of Paris, where Molière made his success, where girls first danced the can-can, and where theatres of all kinds crowded the boulevards. In that year licensing restrictions previously confining *opéra bouffes* to one act and two characters were lifted, allowing composers Hervé (Florimond Ronger), at the Folies-Concertantes, a small theatre on the Boulevard du Temple, and Jacques Offenbach, with his Bouffes-Parisiens company, to expand the size and length of the comic, satirical, musical entertainments that were so successful with audiences.

Hervé first created short musical plays to be performed as therapy by the inmates of the Hôpital Bicêtre in Paris. They were so successful he was given the position of conductor at the Théâtre du Palais-Royal. From there he went on to compose larger works. Hervé not only composed, but wrote the libretti, sang and acted in, and directed and conducted his work. The risqué jokes and scantily clad female chorus (for 1860) in Hervé's works would certainly identify his operettas as an American musical antecedent, even if the topical references and slapdash staging did not.*

Hervé's principal works—*Les Chevaliers de la Table Ronde* (1866), *L'Oeil Crevé* (1867, with a ten-month run), *Chilpéric* (1868), *Le Petit Faust* (1869), *Mam'zelle Nitouche* (1883)—have long been forgotten, for although Hervé was well established, his music was quickly overshadowed by the greater melodies of Jacques Offenbach (whose real name was Jacob Ernest, son of a music teacher and cantor.) It was Offenbach who first wrote a full three-act work in the emerging style, prompting Hervé to copy Offenbach (who had originally expanded on Hervé).

Offenbach's first two-acter, *Orphée aux Enfers* (Orpheus in the Underworld), based on the Orpheus legend (but with the gods going to Paris), was greeted warmly, but it was a subsequent notice in the newspaper referring to the play as a "profanation" that increased business to the level of a sellout hit. Offenbach's *La Grande-Duchesse* was mounted for the Paris Exposition of 1866, and was the hottest ticket on the continent, thanks in part to a battle with censors over its political parody.

Offenbach's own company first inhabited a theatre so small and steep that its intimacy surely prefigures the influence of New York's Princess Theatre musicals and the de-emphasis of spectacle. His collaborators Henri

* Additionally, Hervé may have been the first composer to be killed—literally—by a critic. Supposedly his asthma was aggravated by a cruel review of *Bacchanale* in the newspaper *Le Figaro* in 1892, and he died a few days later at the age of sixty-seven.

Meilhac (1831–1897) and Ludovic Halévy (1834–1908) deserve a stronger mention in any history of the American musical than they have yet received. They were the first legitimate librettists. The composer has long been the favored star in the universe of musical theatre. But the best shows always boast fine books, of which these two wrote many for Offenbach and others. They also wrote a number of internationally successful plays. They wrote the libretti for *Orphée* and the play *Le Réveillon,* which became Johann Strauss's *Die Fledermaus,* a cornerstone of Viennese operetta. They authored Offenbach's *La Vie Parisienne,* about the (mis)adventures of tourists visiting the city, which is probably the French operetta that most resembles the American musical, primarily because it was in modern dress, dealt with current subjects and recognizable characters, and featured a can-can. They also provided the words for Bizet's *Carmen.*

Because of the topical—often politically or socially satirical—nature of the libretti of early operettas, words and music were equally important. This is what sets operetta off from grand opera, and what led to the increasing popularity of musical entertainment. It led also to dramatic tenets becoming a principle value, and thus paved the way for the musical as total theatre. Unfortunately for writers of the words, over the years their contribution is less appreciated than the more universal music. As time passes, their topicality—the very hallmark of popular entertainment beginning with operetta—is no longer understood, and translations are often feeble.

In addition to creating entertaining libretti, Meilhac, Halévy, and their contemporaries knew what the form required. They provided solos, duets, trios, quartets, chorus scenes, and dances, allowing the composer to strut his stuff. Their characters were prefigured to include appropriate types of voices—sopranos and tenors for heroines and heroes, baritones and basses for villains.

In twenty-five years Offenbach wrote more than ninety operettas. His work, however, with plots comic, satiric, and political, was eventually supplanted by a more romantic operetta, best exemplified by French composer Charles Lecocq (*La Fille de Madame Angot, Giroflé-Girofla, Le Petit Duc*). Eventually French audiences no longer enthused over political satire on the musical stage, and more romantic stories became the rage. (Perhaps the constant upheavals of the French government tired the people.) One successful operetta of Lecocq's—*Miss Helyett* (*Miss Elliot*)—drew its success from the opening incident, in which an American girl on vacation in France fell off a cliff, and was saved by a branch that caught her dress, turning her upside down and exposing her underwear. The reigning French operetta star, Hortense Schneider, apparently had a pair of legs that caused remarks of admiration that have come down to us via historians.

All operas in Paris had to begin Act 2 with a ballet, because the Jockey Club, a group of influential French aristocrats, dined at eight o'clock and did not bother to arrive at the theatre until the second act. Primarily, they wanted to see an exhibition of the ballerinas whom they expected to "sample" after the performance—clearly, the principal feature of operetta was not the music.

Offenbach's and Lecocq's music was often based on infectious rhythms, if not specific dances—the waltz, for one—that were currently popular. This brings us to the second great European influence on the operetta form, which was developing almost concurrently in . . .

VIENNA, 1860

The Theater an der Wien, under the direction of Alois Pokorny, did not have enough money to purchase the German rights to Offenbach, so they created a local imitation, which eventually became Viennese operetta. The form enjoyed an equal popularity abroad and had an even greater influence on American theatre.

In November of 1860, *The Boarding School* by Franz von Suppé premiered as the first Viennese operetta. The city responded, and von Suppé wrote more operettas and lived the life of a successful composer. Nevertheless, his work is utterly forgotten except by historians. His successors were not, however.

The waltz, a dance in three-quarter time descended from a traditional German dance called the *Ländler,* had an effect on dancers and audiences that is almost impossible to understand today. Compared to popular American music of the twentieth century, the romantic, stately waltz is virtually antique, useful primarily for sentimental ballads. In the nineteenth century, however, the truncated 4/4 time signature, the rushing ahead to the beginning of the next measure one beat sooner than expected, and the dance that was designed around it, was so exciting, so heady, as to be almost libidinous. It spoke to an emerging attitude in Europe's middle nineteenth century as clearly as ragtime and jazz did to America in the early twentieth.

There were both medical and moral objections when it was first popularized. A 1797 German pamphlet called the whirling speed "proof that waltzing is a main source of the weakness of the body and mind of our generation." Perhaps it was. A traveler in 1799 described what he saw on the continent:

> The dancers grasped the long dress of their partners so that it would not drag and be trodden upon, and lifted it high, holding them in this cloak which brought both bodies under one cover, as closely as possible against them and in this way the whirling continued in the most indecent positions; the supporting hand lay firmly on the breasts, at each movement making little lustful pressures; the girls went wild and looked as if they would drop. When waltzing on the darker side of the room there were bolder embraces and kisses.

An 1813 painting by Edward Francis Burney is entitled "The Waltz" and illustrates a virtual orgy.

By the 1830s it was a craze in the dancehalls of Vienna, and Johann Strauss, Sr., toured the continent playing his compositions. When he used the concert waltz in the operetta he was opening up possibilities as exciting as George M. Cohan had when he later crowded it out with ragtime.

Johann Strauss, Jr., a second-generation composer, had already earned the title of "waltz king" as a concert and dance band conductor. He was encouraged by his wife, a singer, and another theatre manager to match the Offenbach operettas. Almost all of Strauss's operettas connived to have a ballroom scene for which a waltz could be composed and danced. In 1841 Strauss composed *Indigo and the Forty Thieves,* the first of eleven productions which would make him the king of the Viennese operetta. His greatest and most influential operetta premiered in Vienna in 1874 and gained fame gradually. *Die Fledermaus* ran for sixty-eight performances in Vienna and two hundred in Berlin, and eventually enraptured London and New York. The libretto was by Haffner and Genée, based on a French play by Meilhac and Halévy (who had used a German play by Roderick Bendix). *Die Fledermaus* had a convoluted and coincidental plot of mistaken identity and passionate flirtation and was hugely popular for its contemporary story in modern dress, as well as its enchanting musical score. Broadway saw translations in 1912 (as *The Merry Countess*), 1929 (*A Wonderful Night*), 1933

(*Champagne Sec*), 1950 at the Metropolitan Opera (with a new English libretto by Howard Dietz), and 1942 (*Rosalinda*), each with increasing success.

The Viennese operettas were invariably written in three, rather than two, acts, because theatre managers paid librettists by the act. Their subject matter differed greatly from the French in that it was almost exclusively romantic, and plots, which now seem to us complex, contrived and downright silly, invariably revolved around the barriers, compromises, intrigues, and destinies of romantic love.

Vienna's second great epoch in operetta, known as the silver period (Strauss was the gold), is exemplified by Franz Lehár, whose most notable work, *Die Lustige Witwe* (1905), is still performed. It is thought to have had more productions than any musical work ever written. It was produced in London as *The Merry Widow* in English translation, and that production came to Broadway in 1907, where it ran for a year and was revived constantly. Curiously, a mild first reception was countered with publicity created when its composer played the score in concert everywhere he could. Eventually its success swept the comic opera off the stage and led to a decade-long love affair with romantic operetta. Broadway was subsequently swamped with translations of Viennese operetta, including Emmerich Kalman's *The Gay Hussars, The Gypsy Princess,* and *The Countess Maritza;* Oscar Straus's *The Chocolate Soldier* and *The Waltz Dream;* as well as *The Dollar Princess, The Slim Princess, The Balkan Princess, The Spring Maid, The Doll Girl, The Peasant Girl,* and more. You get the idea.

As a testament to the vagaries of commercial theatre, *The Merry Widow*'s equal in success at the time—Ivan Caryll's *The Pink Lady*—is neither performed nor remembered today.

Meanwhile, on the English stage, the comic opera reigned supreme. But before we follow the trail to England, we have to visit Germany, and, of all things, grand opera, to meet a man of extraordinary interest in all things theatrical . . .

RICHARD WAGNER

In truth, it all started deep in the heart of opera country, literally and metaphysically, with a composer who felt that the romanticism of Beethoven could take the art of music no further. Between 1849 and 1851 composer Richard Wagner wrote three essays: "Art and Revolution," "The Artwork of the Future," and "Opera and Drama." In them he proposed the "music drama," a form of theatre that would combine all the arts: dance, music, poetry, architecture, sculpture, and painting. Such combination had been a hallmark of the Greek theatre, and Wagner was not the first to propose returning to it, but he was certainly the most famous and the most successful. He called his drama *Gesamtkunstwerk,* a "total work of art,"—in this concept lies the true greatness of the American musical, though the Broadway stage would not fully embrace the principles until the second half of the twentieth century. Wagner felt that only by combining the arts could each rise to its fullest potential, that the best theatre was a synthesis of all the arts, and that drama was the backbone of music.

Wagner's egocentric, showy personality and intellectual arrogance, combined with a childhood fascination with the theatre, made for a theatrical imagination that may be unequaled before or since. He wrote his own libretti, and directed his premiere productions, demonstrating for his singers by throwing himself into every part. For his first opera, *The Fairies,* completed at the age of twenty-one, Wagner argued strenuously with management over the costumes—he wanted authentic knightly apparel of the early Middle Ages, but the management used inappropriate turbans and kaftans.

With *Rienzi* in 1842 he began to show a remarkable ability as his own producer. Although the opera was his first great success, Wagner, ever the showman, worried by its inordinate length, tried to cut it, but the chorus master restored cuts Wagner had given to the copyist. In 1843 his *Flying Dutchman* made the first use of the musical idea he would come to call leitmotif, a short musical phrase associated with a character, object, emotion, or concept that would return throughout the work. By 1850, with *Lohengrin*, Wagner was writing detailed instructions for the production in the libretto. For a French production of *Tannhäuser* in 1861, 164 rehearsals and a quarter of a million francs were required. Wagner added a bacchanal, as an opera without a ballet was unheard of in Paris at the time. He refused, however, to include a ballet in the second act. The dancers, robbed of their traditional interlude, mobilized their friends in the Jockey Club to sabotage the production. The result was pandemonium, derision, and booing at the premiere. Wagner withdrew the work after the third performance. It had a number of champions, however. "This handful of nit-wits," Baudelaire wrote, "is bringing us all into disrepute."

But it is *Der Ring des Nibelungen* that most adheres to Wagner's stated principles. Begun in 1853 and completed in 1874 (he had stopped writing because he saw no hope of it being performed), the cycle of four operas on a mythic Norse theme eventually became his most enduring, magisterial, and theatrical work.

It was patronage that saved Wagner. The nineteen-year-old King Ludwig II of Bavaria had become enamored with the fifty-one-year-old Wagner and his work, and in 1864 they became the closest of friends. Ludwig not only took Wagner out of a cycle of poverty and debt, which had even led to a short imprisonment, but financed the building of a theatre to Wagner's specifications in Bayreuth. In 1876 *Das Festspielhaus* premiered the Ring Cycle. The theatre had been designed by Wagner and was devoted to the presentation rather than the social aspect of theatregoing. Eliminating the significant stratifications that kept the classes separate—balconies, rings, and boxes—he put every seat where it could view not the rest of the audience but the stage to best advantage. Its auditorium was less ostentatious than other theatres of the time. Even the seats were uniformly bare wood.

Wagner covered the orchestra pit so that the musicians would be heard but not seen, and he insisted on turning out the lights in the auditorium and closing the doors during the performance. In short, he demanded that his audience attend the theatre in order to see the opera—a revolutionary concept. He was always a capable and visionary producer, and many of his demands were impossible in the theatres of the time, but Herculean efforts were made to fly the Valkyries, show the Rhine maidens swimming, and authenticate the Viking helmets and shields.

Opposition to Wagner's ideas was enormous during his lifetime, but they became accepted and dominated opera in succeeding generations. Today *Das Festspielhaus* still performs Wagnerian music dramas, and theatre, opera, and musical theatre directors everywhere adhere to his belief that in the unity of all the arts lies the greatest theatre.

If the stage arts of the future American musical owe allegiance to Wagner's principles, it was still operetta that entertained the vast majority of theatregoers. And before operetta traveled to America, it made extraordinary progress in . . .

NINETEENTH-CENTURY LONDON

To Victorians in the mid-1800s, the theatre was a den of iniquity; consequently it was enormously popular.

In 1857 Offenbach's Bouffes-Parisiens company traveled to London and performed their one-act operettas in French at the St. James Theatre. English-language productions by local impresarios of his full-length work followed—in 1865, *Orpheus in the Underworld* (which became *Orpheus in the Haymarket*); in 1866, *Bluebeard Repaired* and *Helen*; in 1867, *La Grande-Duchesse de Gérolstein*. Hervé played in London as well, where his female chorus girls often stuffed their costumes with newspapers in certain places they needed endowments with which nature had not gifted them.

These productions, and many more from the continent including the romantic, Viennese school, were undoubtedly seen by two men whose work would—in the comic opera avenue of the operetta form—become the benchmark against which all things musical and comic would forevermore be judged. Without these two men, the subsequent history of musical comedy would be substantially different if it existed at all. In the audience at a good many London productions of Offenbach and Hervé, and probably Strauss and Lehár, almost assuredly sat . . .

GILBERT AND SULLIVAN

When William Schwenk Gilbert and Arthur Seymour Sullivan teamed up, their subsequent work together defined the comic opera. It comprises the most notorious single body of work for the musical stage. Their productions virtually drove French operetta out of the West End. English comic opera and the romantic operettas from the Viennese school are the two formidable parents of the American musical.

Gilbert was the first star lyricist. If the romantic melodies of the Viennese composers rose above clunky and silly lyrics, the Gilbert and Sullivan comic operas were admired as much for their lyrics as for their music. Though Gilbert's plotting was farcical and often absurd, as in operetta, the lyrics were deft, witty, and barbed, lampooning contemporary Victorian life and recognizable characters. They took the musical entertainment descended from Gay's *Beggar's Opera* to a new plateau. The Gilbert and Sullivan stage was the origin of a literate musical theatre.

Gilbert was always enamored of the theatre. He was a public-servant clerk, obtained a commission in the Army without ever seeing action, passed the bar, and set up in London as a lawyer. But he was always devoted to writing. In his teen years he created entertainments for his school chums which he wrote, produced, designed, directed, and sometimes acted in. He wrote everything—essays, dramatic criticisms, burlesques (travesties of grand opera), and musical extravaganza. His first success was "Bab Ballads," satiric verses for a *Punch* magazine imitator called *Fun,* which were eventually collected and published in book form. All the comic operas he was to write had foundational ideas in "Bab Ballads." Gilbert's father was an inveterate writer of unproduced plays and unpublished novels, while Sullivan's father was a clarinetist and bandmaster.

Sullivan was raised on band music, and learned to play all the wind instruments. A child prodigy, he received a scholarship to study in Leipzig, Germany. His first concert upon returning was music for *The Tempest.* It was an overnight success, and he went on to write just about everything, including "The Lost Chord," (emotionally written at his brother Fred's deathbed) which remained among England's most popular songs for half a century.

John Hollingshead was the first to produce Gilbert and Sullivan on the same bill. Founder and manager of the Gaiety theatre in London, purveyor of stage entertainments, "licensed dealer in legs, short skirts, French adaptations, Shakespeare, Taste, and the musical glasses," in 1869 he produced a one-act burlesque by Gilbert (with composer Frederick Clay) entitled *No Cards,* alongside a one-act comic opera that Sullivan had written (with librettist Frank Burand) entitled *Cox and Box.* Two years later, Hollingshead brought Gilbert and Sullivan together as librettist and composer to create a ninety-minute afterpiece entitled *Thespis,* wherein a troupe of actors takes the place of the gods on Mount Olympus and, while the gods in turn are enjoying the actors' disguises on earth, bungle things. The piece was successful and ran a month.

Between *Thespis* and their next work together, both were separately successful, the toast of the British musical world and stage. Yet none of the work from their pre-Savoy period is now interesting to the nonacademic.

When Gilbert wrote the libretto for *Trial by Jury* he offered it to another composer, who wanted to score it but dropped out when his wife died. Gilbert then showed it to Richard D'Oyly Carte, a popular theatrical manager, a composer of some operatic music himself, and the manager of the Royalty Theatre in Soho. Carte commissioned it for the Royal as a curtain raiser for Offenbach's *La Perichole.* Gilbert then read it to Sullivan in, as described by Sullivan, "indignation and unhappiness," while Sullivan "screamed with laughter." Sullivan agreed to write the music. *Trial by Jury* contains no dialogue, is forty-five minutes long, and was performed on a very realistic set of a courtroom in which Gilbert had once practiced. It opened in 1875 and was an enormous success, running more than a year to standing room audiences, and putting Offenbach in the shade. The Gilbert and Sullivan comic operas were born.

Sullivan had a talent for setting complicated words comfortably to music, without upstaging them. This was perhaps due as much to the ease, speed, and prolificacy with which he worked (often without a piano) as it was to his understanding of comic opera, in which the comedy—and thus the lyrics—was paramount.

When *Trial by Jury* became a huge success, D'Oyly Carte decided to create a company devoted to English composers and writers. Carte found investors—Sullivan's music publisher, a piano maker, and a wealthy man who owned the local street sprinkler monopoly—and in 1876 the Comedy Opera Company was formed, partially as a reaction against the tide of French imports in the field. Gilbert and Sullivan wrote their first full-length work for Carte.

Carte and Gilbert recognized the need for unusual performers—light comedians without heavy voices—and went outside the traditional London theatre circle of the time for singers who could act. They collected among others, George Grossmith (who would turn up again after the centennial as the producer and bookwriter of *Primrose,* with music by George Gershwin and lyrics by Desmond Carter). Their search was inspired by a sometime practice in English operetta for leading men to talk their songs. (When *The Merry Widow* was in rehearsal in London, the producer told the composer Franz Lehár that the leading man had a sore throat; it was not until the final dress rehearsal that Lehár realized that an American song-and-dance artist with no singing voice to speak of had been hired to play the lead.)

In 1877, Gilbert, Sullivan, and Carte opened their new enterprise with *The Sorcerer,* "An Entirely Original Modern Comic Opera." They created a comedy (lampooning the clergy) based not so much on stock comedy or broad farcical gestures, but on high style and mannerisms. It ran for 175 performances, and the success of the new theatre and the trio of Gilbert, Sullivan, and D'Oyly Carte was firmly established. So too was the form, which included youthful lovers, an elderly lady and gentleman, a robust, comic character, and a native-to-the-scene chorus.

Their second full-length production for the theatre elaborated significantly on their earlier work. In 1878, *H.M.S. Pinafore (or The Lass That Loved a Sailor),* "An Entirely Original Nautical Comic Opera in Two Acts," did not immediately attract an audience. It was a hot summer and audiences were very slow to attend. The second night's receipts were only fourteen pounds, and the theatre almost went into bankruptcy. But the cast took a cut in salary, and Sullivan played *Pinafore* tunes at Covent Garden Theatre concerts where he was the conductor. This helped to promote the production.

But, in fact, it was with their American productions that acclaim came to the trio and their theatre at home became famous throughout the world. While *Pinafore* was floundering in London, Carte sailed to America and discovered that a number of sloppy productions of Gilbert and Sullivan were already taking place. American copyright law was in complete disarray, and it was possible to produce anything that was published. Due to an absurd U.S. court decision, it was possible for awhile to produce anything that one had seen and could remember!

The first American Gilbert and Sullivan production opened in 1875, but *Trial by Jury* was a flop. Then, during "the 14th week of the 36th regular dramatic season" (in 1878), the Boston Museum Dramatic Company presented the "famous new musical absurdity," *H.M.S. Pinafore,* and it was hugely successful. San Francisco and Philadelphia saw it before it went to Broadway, since New York was not yet the center of American theatre.

Carte discovered all this on a visit to America, and sent for Gilbert and Sullivan and some of the original artists. The first sanctioned U.S. production took place at the Fifth Avenue Theatre in New York on December 1, 1879. Later in 1879 and 1880 the D'Oyly Carte company itself came to America, bringing a first-rate English production of *Pinafore* and the world premiere of *The Pirates of Penzance.* Carte tried to circumvent copyright problems by arranging simultaneous productions of *Pirates* in New York and London. Gilbert and Sullivan wrote *Pirates,* at least partially, while they were in America with *Pinafore,* and it was their third full-length success.

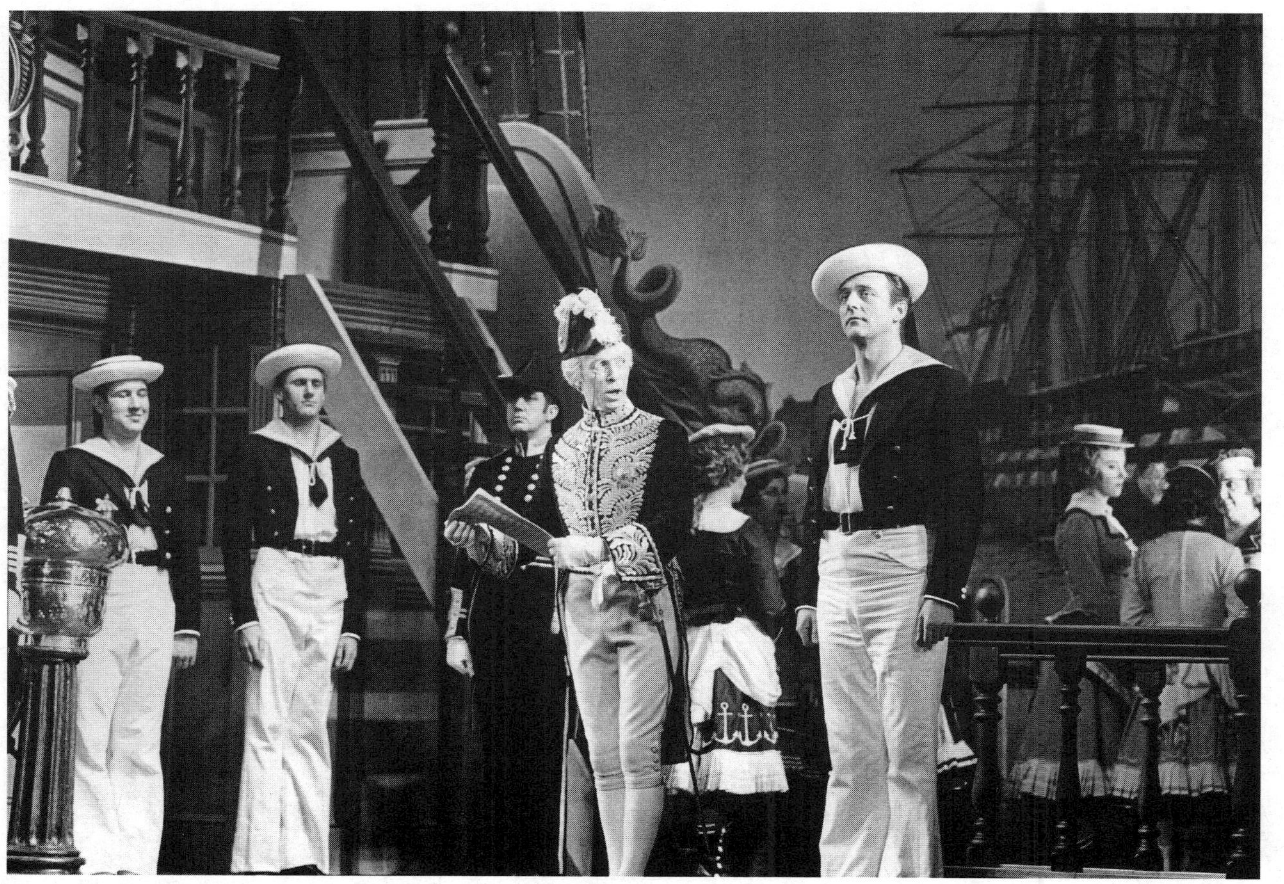

His Majesty's Ship the *Pinafore*
Photofest/John Blomfield

D'Oyly Carte then bought land in the heart of London and built the Savoy Theatre. It was the first theatre to be lit throughout by electricity and held 1,292 seats. When the house was full, half the income would be profit. The theatre was ready for the October 10, 1881 opening of the team's next comic opera, *Patience,* for which Gilbert chose the cult of aestheticism, particularly Oscar Wilde, to lampoon. *Patience* thus became the first of the "Savoy operas" and established the soon-to-be-world-famous "Savoyards," the actors and actresses who presented the comic musicals so well.

Three days after *Patience* closed in 1882, *Iolanthe* was ready. On opening night Sullivan discovered that he was penniless, due to the bankruptcy of a firm in which he had invested all his savings. He nevertheless conducted opening night, as had become his habit. That same night Gilbert discovered that one of the young ladies of the chorus had received a "note" from someone in a box. Gilbert had the offending gentlemen thrown out of the theatre. In spite of all these backstage goings on, the comic opera was a success.

When *Iolanthe* closed in 1884, their next, *Princess Ida,* was not quite ready; meanwhile, Carte revived *Trial by Jury* and *The Sorcerer.* The theatre also mounted *Pirates* with a cast of children for matinées. The trio's popularity was building to epic proportions, and early in 1884 Gilbert and Sullivan signed a five-year agreement with Carte, clearly excited about their future in the comic opera form.

Less than a year later Sullivan attempted to end the association. The split, which was amicable, began over Sullivan's eagerness to write more serious music—a grand opera—and his dislike of a libretto Gilbert had in mind for their next collaboration. "I have been continually keeping down the music in order that not one word should be lost," he wrote. "The music is never allowed to rise and speak for itself." However, in 1885 Gilbert delivered the libretto which became *The Mikado,* Sullivan accepted it, and their partnership resumed. Ironically, *The Mikado* is considered their greatest comic opera. It ran at the Savoy for 672 performances.

With the copyright situation still in a muddle and America filled with producing pirates, Carte executed a brilliant coup. He brought the entire *Mikado* company to America secretly—a difficult feat, considering they had to sail the Atlantic unidentified—and on August 20, 1885 opened in New York, whereupon the copyright of the entire production, orchestrations and all, was secured.

Three little maids of *The Mikado*

Photofest/David Cooper

Although Sullivan was rapidly losing interest in comic operas, frustrated in his intentions to be known as a serious composer, in a great deal of pain from kidney stones that would haunt him from his forties until his death, and running out of patience for his irascible, arrogant, high-handed partner (who once remarked that comic opera "would be all right if it were not for the music"), he continued working. From childhood Sullivan had been a beloved favorite, while Gilbert seems to have been born with "a genius for petulance, for hostility, for dissidence." Gilbert was never popular, and always domineering. The two were passionate collaborators but lived in different social milieus—perhaps they functioned well creatively as opposites. Sullivan received from Gilbert the perfect librettos for his talents as a composer, and Sullivan had a strong instinct for characters on the stage. The team opened the dark *Ruddigore* in 1887, *The Yeoman of the Guard* in 1888 (which, like *Oklahoma!* to come, flaunts convention by getting underway not with the chorus but with a single soprano onstage), and *The Gondoliers* in 1889 (a return to utter wit).

Sullivan then attempted outright revolt. Tired of the numerous rhymes, long verses, and farcical stories, he wanted to write serious music that was not subordinate to the lyrics. Gilbert, wisely knowing he was at his best with Sullivan, attempted to preserve the relationship. The situation came to a head with the famous carpet story.

Carte had purchased an expensive carpet for *The Gondoliers*, which was thus the expense of all three as partners. Gilbert refused to pay for it, claiming that it was used for Carte's office. (Probably it later was—not a few producer's offices are furnished with the detritus of past shows.) Gilbert may have been especially peeved because in that office Carte was conducting outside business for himself as well as the business of the Savoy. Gilbert and Carte were equally famous for their tempers and exchanged hot words. Sullivan—usually noncommittal and out of his league with men who were ungracious and uncivil—was pressed to take sides and did so. With Carte. This was a mistake. Artists should never take the side of management against their collaborators, no matter the issue. The quarrel caused such a rift that Gilbert refused to come to the premiere of Sullivan's beloved, finally grand, opera *Ivanhoe.*

Ivanhoe was the work Sullivan had long hoped to write. Gilbert had refused to write the libretto for it, feeling that an opera libretto did not reflect well on the librettist. Julian Sturgis did the lyrics, from the novel by

Sir Walter Scott. D'Oyly Carte bet the bank on it when he opened his new theatre, the English Royal Opera House, in 1891, expressly for the purpose of doing for grand opera what he and Gilbert and Sullivan had done for comic opera. Although it ran only 160 performances, insignificant by Gilbert and Sullivan standards, no grand opera had ever run that long, and England had seen nothing like it.

Three years later a reunion was effected. The team created *Utopia, Unlimited* and Carte gave it the most expensive mounting of all their operas. Sullivan, displeased with the finale, rewrote it entirely four days after the opening. Gilbert allowed the critics to see the piece during a dress rehearsal as well as on opening night, the better to understand it. Nevertheless, it closed unexpectedly after 245 performances, leaving Carte without a successor at the Savoy, whereupon he continued the practice of revivals between premieres. In 1896 *The Grand Duke* played only 123 performances. Neither work ranks with Gilbert and Sullivan's best. The fire was out.

Perhaps Sullivan was in declining health. Perhaps he held a disregard for Gilbert and his lyrics which led him to set them cavalierly, for he now chaffed at the strictures of light opera. Thus the brilliant collaboration of twenty years ended in bitterness and with two failures.

In *The Beggar's Opera* and the works of Gilbert and Sullivan we see the beginning of musical theatre as a parody of opera. It was so successful that it blew Italian opera right off the London stage. More importantly, however, the songs grow naturally out of the text, due to the satiric nature of the content and to the fact that both Gay and Gilbert authored the story as well as the lyrics.

Sullivan's success in addition to the comic operas—with songs, a number of orchestral works, and his one grand opera—made him England's premiere composer. This always galled Gilbert, and the knighthood Sullivan was offered in 1883 didn't help. Curiously, the fact that Gilbert was not simultaneously knighted was part of a snub of lighter musical entertainment on the part of society, for it was thus made clear that Sullivan was knighted for his more "serious" music. One periodical went so far as to opine that, henceforth, a "Sir" should no longer write comic operettas, but only grand opera. But then, snobs have always circled like vultures around musical comedy. Anyway, Gilbert eventually got his knighthood as well.

Though numerous productions in the decades since would surely pirouette Carte, Gilbert, and Sullivan in their graves—America alone has seen "Hot" and "Swing" *Mikados,* as well as modern costuming and numerous other production inventions—it is a tribute to the magnificent creations of Gilbert and Sullivan that they have stood the test of time so well, and can be entertaining in a variety of forms.

Never a creator of soaring, florid melodies, Sullivan's music was eminently singable, and ideally suited to the comic librettos of the caustic, character-oriented Gilbert. A year after Gilbert was born, Queen Victoria began her reign, and she was still on the throne when Gilbert and Sullivan's last collaboration ended. If their work now seems Victorian, it was the very essence of the musical comedy stage in the late nineteenth century.

Regarding how Gilbert and Sullivan were trying to change the existing formula for comic opera, Gilbert said:

> We resolved that our plots, however ridiculous, should be coherent, that our dialogue should be void of offence; on artistic principles, no man should play a woman's part and no woman a man's. Finally, we agreed that no lady of the company should be required to wear a dress that she could not wear with absolute propriety at a private fancy ball; and I believe I may say that we proved our case.

They did, with the exception of the ladies dresses. They would never prove as popular as tights.

Crucial to an understanding of the metamorphosis from opera to musical theatre via comic opera is the Gilbert notion that the words—and thus the drama—came first. It was Sullivan's great talent to write inspiring music that supported the words clearly. Rhythms matched the sentences, vowels and consonants fell in the correct places, and melody never distorted vowels or meaning.

The quality of the lyrics causes Gilbert and Sullivan to lose a great deal in translation. There simply are no lyricists in other languages capable of rising to the cleverness, wit, rhyme, satire, and tongue-tripping semantics of Gilbert. But in English there is probably no more popular body of work on the musical stage. Fans proliferate throughout the world. Amateur productions and professional revivals have been continuous for more than a century. In 1980 the New York Shakespeare Festival produced a slightly spoofed, commercially successful revival of *Pirates* starring Kevin Kline,

George Rose, and pop star Linda Ronstadt that opened at the outdoor Delacorte Theatre, then moved to Broadway and ran for 772 performances. The universal appeal of the Gilbert and Sullivan canon can never be understated. The works are entertaining, comic, and, above all, great theatre. They were (and still are) internationally successful, especially on the other side of the Atlantic Ocean, where a budding theatre spoke the same language.

• • •

From Aristophanes to Gilbert and Sullivan, musical entertainment had enthralled audiences. All the techniques—the singing, the dancing, the stagecraft—would next come together in a single theatre. They would all find a home in . . .

Part Two

THE AMERICAN MUSICAL

JOSIE: WHAT IS BROADWAY?

JONES: BROADWAY?

JOSIE: A STREET?

JONES: SURE, IT'S THE GREATEST STREET IN THE WORLD.

JOSIE: SOME PEOPLE SAY IT'S TERRIBLE.

JONES: PHILADELPHIA PEOPLE.

JOSIE: AND SOME PEOPLE SAY IT'S WONDERFUL.

JONES: THAT'S JUST IT. IT'S TERRIBLY WONDERFUL.

JOSIE: I DON'T UNDERSTAND.

JONES: NOBODY UNDERSTANDS BROADWAY. PEOPLE HATE IT AND DON'T KNOW WHY. PEOPLE LOVE IT AND DON'T KNOW WHY. IT'S JUST BECAUSE IT'S BROADWAY.

JOSIE: THAT'S A MYSTERY, ISN'T IT?

JONES: THAT'S JUST WHAT IT IS, A MYSTERY.

—GEORGE M. COHAN, FROM *BROADWAY JONES*

NIBLO'S GARDEN

LESSEE AND MANAGER . . . . WM. WHEATLEY.
STAGE MANAGER . . . . L. J. VINCENT.

Doors open at Seven. Curtain rises quarter before Eight.

September 12 1866 – First Night –

EVERY EVENING

AND

SATURDAY AFTERNOON

AT TWO,

Will be presented, after a preparation of several months, and

AN ACTUAL OUTLAY OF OVER

FIFTY THOUSAND DOLLARS

The Original, Grand, Romantic, Magical and Spectacular Drama in Four Acts, by CHAS. M. BARRAS, Esq., entitled The

BLACK CROOK

The SOLE RIGHT of which production in New York and its vicinity has been purchased by MR. WHEATLEY; who has also entered into an agreement with

MESSRS. JARRETT & PALMER

For the introduction of their Great

PARISIENNE BALLET TROUPE,

Under the direction of the renowned Maître de Ballet

SIGNOR DAVID COSTA,

(Of the Grand Opera, Paris,) who will appear in the

MOST COSTLY AND MAGNIFICENT DRAMATIC SPECTACLE

EVER PRESENTED IN AMERICA.

The Black Crook

All I need now is the girl . . .

In 1866 Harry Palmer and Henry Jarret had booked a French ballet company to perform *La Biche aux Bois* at the Academy of Music on Fourteenth Street in New York City. Fortunately for the future of the American musical, the theatre burned down before the premiere, and the company of one hundred female dancers, having already arrived on American shores, was stranded.

At the same time, William Wheatley, the manager of Niblo's Garden at Broadway and Prince Streets, had on his hands a flop melodrama by Charles M. Barras entitled *The Black Crook.* Described as "incredibly ridiculous," it was based loosely on the legend of Faust: an alchemist had to deliver one soul every year in order to extend his own life. The idea arose to combine forces, forming, over author Barras's objections, an extravaganza of music, song, and dance. Put simply, whenever the melodrama began to drag, the girls rushed on and danced.

The music was arranged by Groseppi Operti, who wrote some incidental music and gathered the songs from local music shops, utilizing the work of several currently popular composers. Dances included the "Grand Ballet of Gems" and the "Pas de Demons." The songs "The March of the Amazons" and "You Naughty, Naughty, Men" were commissioned to fit the dancers in. "Naughty Men" was a popular success, as sung by Millie Cavendish, and thus became the first hit song to be driven by a musical. Special effects included the "hurricane in the Harz mountains." Wheatley spent between $25,000 and $55,000 by various accounts, considered to be an enormous sum for the time.

The combination of music, dance, specialty acts, elaborate fairyland scenery, and the plot (which by now no one but its original author cared about) ran for five and a half hours on opening night, September 12, 1866. (This length was not so unusual for an evening's entertainment at the time, except in that it encompassed a single show.)

Although there was little attempt to integrate the musical numbers into the plot (the word "hodgepodge" appears in almost every contemporary account of this musical) the evening is generally considered to be the beginning of musical theatre in America for two good reasons. One, the musical spectacle did, thanks to the intermittent intrusion of the Faust adaptation, have a beginning, middle, and end. Two, there was the eye-popping sight of one hundred bare-limbed beautiful girls in an outrageously scandalous new costume: flesh-colored silk tights.

The production was hugely successful. It ran continuously for sixteen months, playing 474 performances, a record at the time. It was revived in New York at least fifteen times, and toured throughout the United States for the next *forty years.*

More important, the genre, whether for the music, spectacle, plot, or shapely legs, was so successful that it encouraged numerous imitations. Subsequent productions included *The Black Crook Jr., The White Crook, The Red Crook,* and *The Golden Crook.* (An account of the making of *The Black Crook* was the plot of the 1954 musical *The Girl in Pink Tights.*)

The production gained considerable notoriety from outraged clergymen and blue-nosed citizens who called publicly for censorship of the scanty costumes of the dancers. Customers sometimes came in disguise to avoid being identified by their neighbors. One clergyman forced himself to see the show so he could report back to his flock about

> . . . the immodest dress of the girls; the short skirts, undergarments of thin material allowing the form of the figure to be discernible; the flesh colored tights, imitating nature so well that the illusion is complete; with the exceedingly short drawers, most tight-fitting, extending very little below the hips; arms and neck apparently bare, and bodice so cut as to make their undergarments spring up, exposing the figure beneath from the waist to the toe, except for such coverings as we have described.

Miss Olive Logan, an actress who felt upstaged by the competition, published her reaction to the show:

> When *The Black Crook* first presented its nude woman to the gaze of the crowded auditory, she was met with a gasp of astonishment at the effrontery, which dared so much. Men actually grew pale at the boldness of the thing; a deathlike silence fell over the house, broken only by the clapping of a band of claquers [sic] around the outer aisles; but it passed; and, in view of the fact that these women were French ballet dancers after all, they were tolerated.

What made *The Black Crook* so successful was the simple expedient of showing the female leg to its best advantage. Nudity as a selling point had already appeared at the very inception of dancing, when female dancers and mimes performed naked at Roman entertainments. In America in the last half of the nineteenth century the very whisper of even the most minimal advance in eroticism was enough to affect the box office substantially.

In 1833 Mademoiselle Francisquay, appearing in a legitimate play, *The Ice Witch,* at the Bowery Theatre in New York, was hissed off the stage by patrons in orchestra seats for wearing a dress that was showing too much cleavage. (Those in the balcony and gallery seats, however, went wild with delight.)

On June 7, 1861, in Albany, the actress Adah Isaacs Menken appeared in the title role—actually a pants part—of a dramatization of a Byron poem, entitled *Mazeppa,* or *The Wild Horse.* In the finale she was strapped—appearing nude though actually wearing tights—to a horse that galloped up a ramp. A week later the triumphant production played New

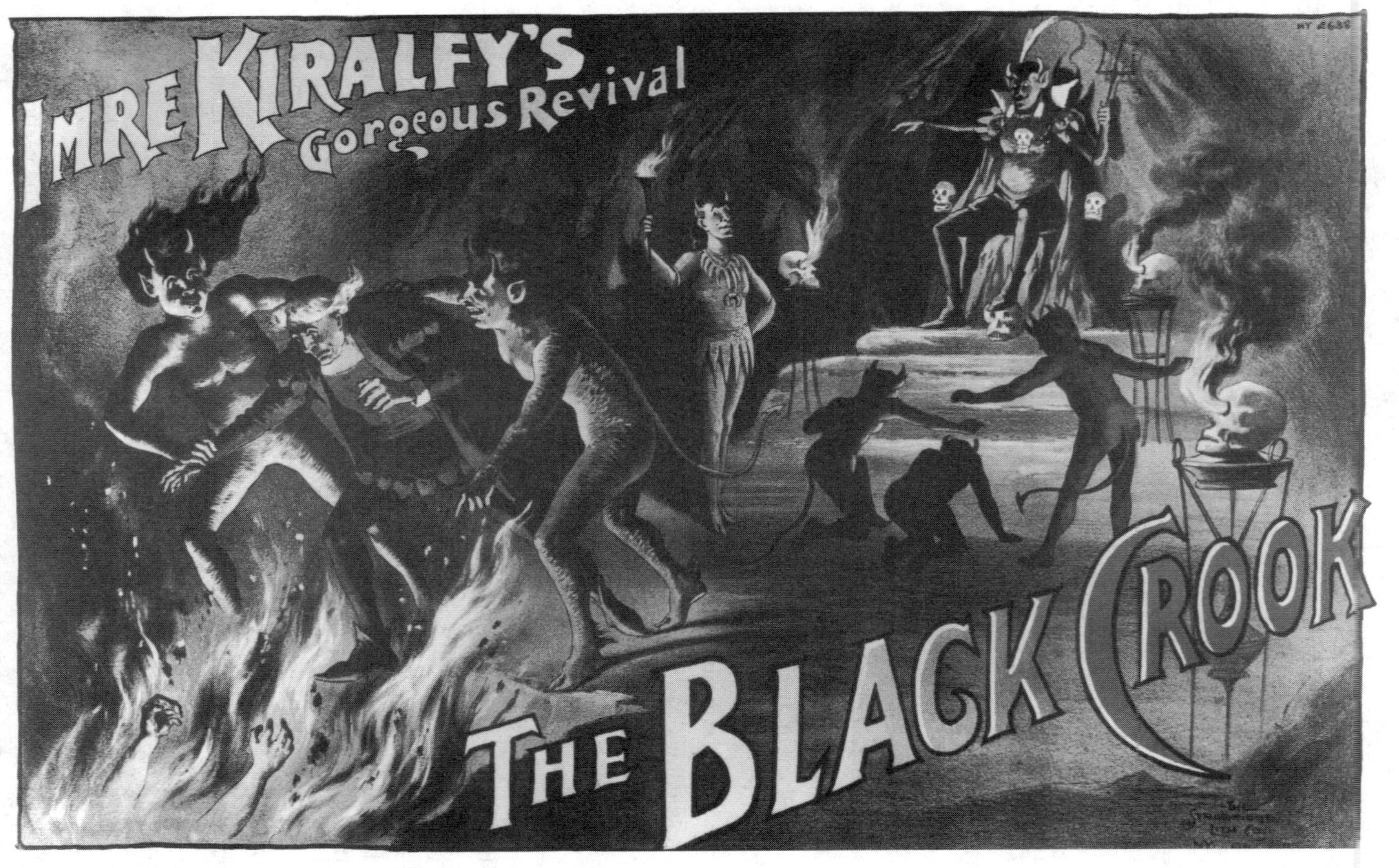

The first American musical featured devils and tights

Museum of the City of New York, J. G. Strowbridge Collection

York, and her career was made. Menken toured throughout the United States in the play, and became one of the earliest female stars, appearing also in an early American musical titled *Three Fast Women.* Her career included five husbands and one hundred performances in Paris.

When the actress Olga Nethersole, portraying the title role in *Sappho* (1900), allowed her leading man to carry her, fully clothed, upstairs and into an *offstage* bedroom, the mere suggestion of lascivious behavior was enough to have Miss Nethersole arrested. (She was acquitted and the play was an enormous success.)

These events took place within an environment of stuffy morality, thereby marking them as all the more popular. By taking a bold, sexual step forward, almost any producer could assure himself of a stampede at the box office, and should representatives of a puritanical viewpoint voice any objection, whether in the newspapers, the pulpit, or the courts, the press agent knew immediately that his job would be considerably easier.

Appeals to prurient interest mark the beginning of the American burlesque show as well as the introduction of female pulchritude to musical comedy. If shortly burlesque and the musical will develop along different lines, they will have so much in common that only the death of burlesque will end the constant exchange of talents and techniques between uptown and down. Burlesque gave Bert Lahr, Hal Skelly, Montgomery and Stone, Lewis and Dody, Gallagher and Shean, Clark and McCullough, James Barton, Gus Edwards, Phil Silvers, Joey Faye, and Abbott and Costello to vaudeville and Broadway. The cooch dancing of burlesque fell to the choreographers Jack Cole and Bob Fosse, and found a theatricalized version in the performances of Gwen Verdon in *Damn Yankees* and *Sweet Charity.* In 1979 the Broadway musical revue *Sugar Babies* recalled these sketches, though not the stripping.

Burlesque followed a rocky road, treading a fine line between irregular censorship and harassment on one side and popular success with audiences on the other. The defection of the best comics to vaudeville and Broadway and the chronic problem of finding good-looking women willing to take their clothes off for a poor salary did not help. Burlesque began in 1869, when Lydia Thompson and her British Blondes invaded America and showed the colonies their legs in tights. (Standing up for the dignity of the actress, Thompson and one of her girls once horse-whipped a *Chicago Times* writer who impugned their morals.) It ended in the mid-1930s, when it was banned. Success had led to competition, which had led to an increasing rawness and nudity. After a few years of court battles and a case settled in favor of New York City in 1937, Mayor Fiorello La Guardia (himself the subject of the 1959 musical *Fiorello!*), and License Commissioner Paul Moss (a former theatrical producer) closed down the burlesque theatres by censorship of the key attraction that kept the customers satisfied—the striptease.

Musical comedy fared better. *The Black Crook*'s combination of book, chorus line, songs, and dances enchanted American audiences, and producers from then on saw to it that theatregoers never lacked product. Niblo's Garden followed *Crook* with *The White Fawn,* another long musical spectacular which had comparatively less success (150 performances) but which introduced the can-can to American audiences. In 1874 another big success was *Evangeline.* First labeled "an American opéra bouffe" (in tribute to the current popularity of Offenbach), then as "an American extravaganza," it was really a musical spoof of Longfellow's poem of the same name, with much less decor and no ballet company, but with the same scantily-clad chorus girls. It also featured a hugely popular dancing cow, and numerous songs and dances by Edward E. Rice and J. Chever Goodwin, this time written *intentionally* on the same subject as the book, a very significant step forward. First produced in Boston and enjoying only a two-week run at Niblo's Garden in New York, *Evangeline* became the most-beloved American musical theatre piece of the era, returning in revival after revival for years.

In 1879 a production written by Nate Salisbury called *The Brook* was the first to actually label itself "a musical comedy." The title became affixed to the genre and, by coincidence, the show emphasized American locales and characters, marking a significant though not absolutely necessary part of the musical's definition: that it exploit a home-grown milieu.

In October, 1882 the Casino Theatre at Broadway and Thirty-ninth, built by Rudolph Aronson, opened with a production of Johann Strauss's *The Queen's Lace Handkerchief.* The theatre was unfinished, cold, and damp, and the audience was forced to wear overcoats, but it was the first theatre constructed specifically to house musical shows.

In 1900 a successful British musical extravaganza that had run 455 performances in London was thought not good enough for Broadway, and all the established managements rejected it. A new team chose to produce it, however, and *Florodora* became a huge hit. "Tell Me, Pretty Maiden," a chorus number featuring six lovely ladies swinging on flower-festooned swings toward the audience, was the first hit song from a Broadway musical introduced by the chorus and not a principal. It became the second musical in

New York history to run more than 500 performances, more even than its London original. Many legends surround the original sextet, including that they sometimes didn't wear underwear and that each married a millionaire stage-door Johnny. Evelyn Nesbitt, the young beauty whose millionaire husband Harry K. Thaw murdered her lover, architect Stanford White, in one of the great scandals of the day, eventually appeared on the swings.

Wolf Mankowitz, Adah Isaacs Menken's biographer, wrote:

> The new free Protean mixed bag of female pulchritude, melodrama, music, dancing, bad jokes, circus act, and anything else an enterprising showman could dream up, was the most rapidly evolving vital theatrical form of the nineteenth century, till now an endless doldrum of boring old melodramas, heavy comedies and poorly performed classics. The American musical had been born. Bastard it might be, . . . it was lusty enough to survive its strange and confused origins, to grow up to become the American theatre's specific, irreplaceable, and inimitable contribution to the arts of modern urban entertainment."

Thus *The Black Crook* was the beginning of a new era in theatre. Shortly after it opened, fourteen of New York City's sixteen legitimate playhouses were presenting the same formula, which became the musical theatre. No theatre industry anywhere outside of Broadway, even within the United States, has ever been able to duplicate it consistently, and by the time *Show Boat* was presented in 1927, the form became uniquely, permanently, extravagantly American.

Until then, however, three separate and distinct styles effervesced side by side on Broadway: the operetta, the revue, and the productions of a dynamo from vaudeville named George M. Cohan.

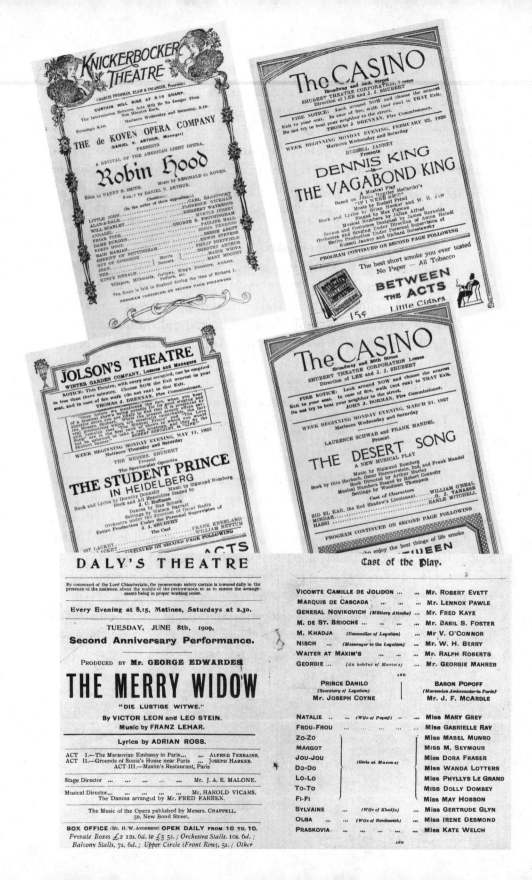

KNICKERBOCKER THEATRE
CHARLES FROHMAN, KLAW & ERLANGER, Proprietors
CURTAIN WILL RISE AT 8.10 SHARP.
The Intermission Between Acts Will Be No Longer Than Ten Minutes Each.
Evenings, 8.10. Matinees Wednesday and Saturday, 2.10.

THE de KOVEN OPERA COMPANY
(DANIEL V. ARTHUR, Manager)
PRESENTS
A REVIVAL OF THE AMERICAN LIGHT OPERA,
Robin Hood
Book by HARRY B. SMITH. Music by REGINALD de KOVEN.
Staged by DANIEL V. ARTHUR.
Characters
(In the order of their appearance)

LITTLE JOHN........CARL GANTVOORT
ALAN-A-DALE........FLORENCE WICKHAM
WILL SCARLET........HERBERT WATEROUS
ANNABEL........MYRTLE JERSEY
FRIAR TUCK........GEORGE B. FROTHINGHAM
DAME DURDEN........PAULINE HALL
ROBIN HOOD........MISHA FERENZO
MAID MARIAN........BESSIE ABOTT
SHERIFF OF NOTTINGHAM........EDWIN STEVENS
GUY OF GISBORNE........PHILIP SHEFFIELD
JOAN........ } Morris } ....DOROTHY ARTHUR
NED........ } Dancers } ....MARIE WIOVA
KING'S HERALD........MARY MOONEY

Villagers, Milkmaids, Outlaws, King's Foresters, Archers, Pedlars, etc.
The Scene is laid in England during the time of Richard I.
PROGRAM CONTINUED ON SECOND PAGE FOLLOWING

The CASINO
Broadway and 39th Street
SHUBERT THEATRE CORPORATION, Lessee
Direction of LEE and J. J. SHUBERT
FIRE NOTICE: Look around NOW and choose the nearest Exit to your seat. In case of fire, walk (not run) to THAT Exit. Do not try to beat your neighbor to the street.
THOMAS J. DRENNAN, Fire Commissioner.
WEEK BEGINNING MONDAY EVENING, FEBRUARY 22, 1926
Matinees Wednesday and Saturday
RUSSELL JANNEY
Presents
DENNIS KING
in
THE VAGABOND KING
A Musical Play
Based on Justin Huntley McCarthy's
"IF I WERE KING"
Music by Rudolf Friml
Book and Lyrics by Brian Hooker and W. H. Post
Staged by Max Figman
Musical Numbers by Julian Alfred
Scenes and Costumes Designed by James Reynolds
Orchestra and Singing Under Direction of Anton Heindl
Entire Production Under Personal Supervision of
Russell Janney and Richard Boleslawsky
PROGRAM CONTINUED ON SECOND PAGE FOLLOWING

JOLSON'S THEATRE
WINTER GARDEN COMPANY, Lessees and Managers
NOTICE: This Theatre, with every seat occupied, can be emptied in less than three minutes. Choose NOW the Exit nearest to your seat, and in case of fire walk (do not run) to that Exit.
THOMAS J. DRENNAN, Fire Commissioner.

"Once before we mentioned the fact, when you hear of a musical show's being notable for its good singing and superior score you are likely to find that it is presented by the Messrs. Shubert. While the present season offers several productions which are musically remarkable, the fact still remains that "The Student Prince" and "The Love Song" are in the first rank of shows to which you would not be ashamed to take a real musician, and they fly the Shubert banner."
ROBERT BENCHLEY, in "LIFE."

WEEK BEGINNING MONDAY EVENING, MAY 11, 1925
Matinees Thursday and Saturday
THE MESSRS. SHUBERT
Present
The Spectacular Operetta
THE STUDENT PRINCE
IN HEIDELBERG
Book and Lyrics by Dorothy Donnelly Music by Sigmund Romberg
Book and All Ensembles Staged by
J. C. Huffman
Dances by Max Scheck
Settings by Watson Barratt
Orchestra under the direction of Oscar Radin
Entire Production Under the Personal Supervision of
J. J. SHUBERT
The Cast
1ST LACKEY........FRANK KNEELAND
LACKEY........WILLIAM NETTUM
PROGRAM CONTINUED ON SECOND PAGE FOLLOWING

The CASINO
Broadway and 39th Street
SHUBERT THEATRE CORPORATION Lessee
Direction of LEE and J. J. SHUBERT
FIRE NOTICE: Look around NOW and choose the nearest Exit to your seat. In case of fire, walk (not run) to THAT Exit. Do not try to beat your neighbor to the street.
JOHN J. DORMAN, Fire Commissioner.
WEEK BEGINNING MONDAY EVENING, MARCH 21, 1927
Matinees Wednesday and Saturday
LAURENCE SCHWAB and FRANK MANDEL
Present
THE DESERT SONG
A NEW MUSICAL PLAY
Music by Sigmund Romberg
Book by Otto Harbach, Oscar Hammerstein, 2nd, and Frank Mandel
Book Directed by Arthur Hurley
Musical Numbers Staged by Robert Connolly
Settings by Woodman Thompson
Cast of Characters
SID EL KAR, the Red Shadow's Lieutenant......WILLIAM O'NEAL
MINDAR........O. J. VANASSE
HASSI........EARLE MITCHELL
PROGRAM CONTINUED ON SECOND PAGE FOLLOWING

DALY'S THEATRE

By command of the Lord Chamberlain, the proscenium safety curtain is lowered daily in the presence of the audience, about the middle of the performance, so as to ensure the arrangements being in proper working order.

Every Evening at 8.15, Matinee, Saturdays at 2.30.

TUESDAY, JUNE 8th, 1909,

Second Anniversary Performance.

PRODUCED BY **Mr. GEORGE EDWARDES**

THE MERRY WIDOW

"DIE LUSTIGE WITWE."

By VICTOR LEON and LEO STEIN.

Music by FRANZ LEHAR.

Lyrics by ADRIAN ROSS.

ACT I.—The Marsovian Embassy in Paris... ... ALFRED TERRAINE.
ACT II.—Grounds of Sonia's House near Paris ... JOSEPH HARKER.
ACT III.—Maxim's Restaurant, Paris

Stage Director ... ... Mr. J. A. E. MALONE.

Musical Director... ... ... Mr. HAROLD VICARS.
The Dances arranged by Mr. FRED FARREN.

The Music of the Opera published by Messrs. CHAPPELL, 50, New Bond Street.

BOX OFFICE (Mr. H. W. ANDERSON) OPEN DAILY FROM 10 TO 10.
Private Boxes £2 12s. 6d. to £5 5s.; Orchestra Stalls, 10s. 6d.; Balcony Stalls, 7s. 6d.; Upper Circle (Front Row), 5s.; Other

Cast of the Play.

VICOMTE CAMILLE DE JOLIDON ... ... Mr. ROBERT EVETT
MARQUIS DE CASCADA ... ... Mr. LENNOX PAWLE
GENERAL NOVIKOVICH (*Military Attaché*) ... Mr. FRED KAYE
M. DE ST. BRIOCHE ... ... Mr. BASIL S. FOSTER
M. KHADJA (*Counsellor of Legation*) ... Mr V. O'CONNOR
NISCH ... (*Messenger to the Legation*) ... Mr. W. H. BERRY
WAITER AT MAXIM'S ... ... Mr. RALPH ROBERTS
GEORGIE ... (*An habitué of Maxim's*) ... Mr. GEORGIE MAHRER

AND

PRINCE DANILO (*Secretary of Legation*) Mr. JOSEPH COYNE | BARON POPOFF (*Marsovian Ambassador in Paris*) Mr. J. F. MCARDLE

NATALIE ... ... (*Wife of Popoff*) ... ... Miss MARY GREY
FROU-FROU ... ... Miss GABRIELLE RAY
ZO-ZO } (*Girls at Maxim's*) { Miss MABEL MUNRO
MARGOT Miss M. SEYMOUR
JOU-JOU Miss DORA FRASER
DO-DO Miss WANDA LOTTERS
LO-LO Miss PHYLLYS LE GRAND
TO-TO Miss DOLLY DOMBEY
FI-FI Miss MAY HOBSON
SYLVAINE ... (*Wife of Khadja*) ... Miss GERTRUDE GLYN
OLGA ... ... (*Wife of Novikovich*) ... Miss IRENE DESMOND
PRASKOVIA ... ... Miss KATE WELCH

AND

Seven

Operettas (or The Thin Lady Sings)

Jacques Offenbach's *La Grande Duchesse de Gérolstein* was hugely successful in French in New York City in 1867. Four years later, in 1871, his *The Princess of Trébizonde* was performed in English and was condemned as lewd. American conservatives only caught on to the risqué nature of the early operetta libretti when they understood the language.

In 1879, America saw one hundred productions of *H.M.S. Pinafore,* including an all-black company, an all-children's company, and a Yiddish company. Of twelve Broadway theatres, three were playing *Pinafore.* More even than *The Black Crook, Pinafore* stirred the American public's interest in musical theatre. Though there were a dozen or fewer musicals on the boards in any given season prior to *Pinafore,* the seasons thereafter boasted twenty to thirty. In 1907 Lehár's Viennese operetta *The Merry Widow* premiered in New York, and took the town. Its principals became stars, its music was played everywhere, merry widow hats became the rage, and six road companies swept across the country.

American operettas were written in response to the success of these imported Viennese and British works. Reginald De Koven's *Robin Hood* (1890) was one of the first to succeed. The first performance was given at the Chicago Opera House on June 9, 1890 by an opera company, the Bostonians. Its book and lyrics were written by Harry B. Smith, who reports that

> Owing to lack of confidence in the piece, no money was spent on costumes, and the curtain rose on the opening night disclosing a production which had cost $105.50. The tenor sang Robin Hood in his "Il Trovatore" costume, and the dresses of all the principals had seen service in "Martha," "The Bohemian Girl," and other operas of their repertoire. The company had been so inadequately rehearsed that it was necessary to revive that antique auxiliary, the prompter's hood, and I was delegated to serve as prompter, standing under the stage with my head through a trap concealed from the audience by the canvas hood. . . . It was a very hot night and after I had stood for nearly four hours close to the footlights, with my head in a canvas box, the fate of the opera was a matter of comparative indifference. As I had to read most of the dialogue to the actors, the performance, dramatically, was slow and depressing. The musical numbers went well. The press criticisms were friendly, more favorable than such a performance deserved; but the consensus of opinion was that "Robin Hood" was not as good as its predecessor, "Don Quixote."

Nevertheless, the Bostonians added five thousand dollars for sets and costumes, opened in New York in September of 1891, and succeeded. Broadway's first really successful American operetta ran continuously for five years, and was frequently revived.

John Philip Sousa's *El Capitán* (1896) ran for 112 performances, then toured the country for four years. Ziegfeld produced *Papa's Wife* in New York in 1899, an English-language amalgamation of Hervé's *La Femme à Papa* and *Mam'zelle Nitouche,* with additional music by De Koven.

The operetta featured extremely complex love stories with lots of hurdles and complications before the (usually contrived and unbelievable) resolution. There was little dramatic conflict for the characters, conflict arising almost solely from the circumstances of the (standard) plots: lovers from different social classes, mistaken identity, disguises, aversion to a prearranged marriage, and poor-little-girl-makes-good stories. As the principal thrust of these entertainments evolved from comedy to romance, the comic opera became the operetta and plots increasingly revolved around European royalty and Cinderella characters. European-trained composers held the most influence over the form.

Victor Herbert, the first great American theatre composer, was born in Dublin and educated in Germany. He came to the United States to play cello with the Metropolitan Opera orchestra, accompanied by his soprano wife, who was hired to sing. Ambitious to compose—his first composition, not unnaturally, was *Suite for Cello and Orchestra*—he was attracted to popular music and hoped to write songs for variety shows. But his classical background suited him for operettas. His first score is reputed to have been *La Vivandiere* for Lillian Russel, but it was never produced. This probably soured him on star vehicles, for he always disliked writing them. His first produced work was *Prince Ananias,* which toured for two years. In 1895 *The Wizard of the Nile* succeeded on Broadway.

A prolific composer of forty-six Broadway scores, his most renowned were *Babes in Toyland* (1903), *Mlle. Modiste* (1905), *The Red Mill* (1906) for comedians Montgomery and Stone (at 274 performances the longest run of any Herbert operetta, featuring the first moving electric sign on Broadway), *Naughty Marietta* (1910), *Sweethearts* (1913), and several *Ziegfeld Follies.* For the 1899–1900 season he wrote four operettas at once. One of his lesser shows—*Old Dutch* (1909)—featured a nine-year-old Helen Hayes in her Broadway debut.

In 1916 Herbert was an organizing member of the American Society of Composers and Publishers (ASCAP) and brought the test case that went all the way to the Supreme Court to establish the rights of songwriters to receive royalties for performances of their work.

Herbert wrote ballads, comic songs, waltzes, and marches during an industrious and prodigious career. If none of his shows survive, it is due not to his sumptuous music but to the weak libretti and the eventual collapse of the operetta form. Before his influence waned, however, he passed it on to other European-trained composers.

Rudolf Friml and Sigmund Romberg inherited the Herbert mantle. The leading composers of the late teens and early twenties, they imitated Herbert at first, then grew increasingly romantic. They were influenced by a fast-rising new entertainment, the silent screen, for which music—composed and sent along with films for local orchestras and organists to play as accompaniment—had to be richly evocative and lush. Both Friml and Romberg grew up in Europe, had classical music training, and were intrigued by the popular theatre.

When soprano Emma Trentini, starring in Herbert's *Naughty Marietta,* refused to sing an encore of his "Italian Street Song" he stormed out of the theatre and refused to write her next vehicle. Producer Arthur Hammerstein gave the assignment to young Rudolph Friml, and in 1912 *The Firefly* launched his career. (Friml's relationship with the soprano was more cordial—his wife divorced him over their affair.) He eventually wrote twenty-two scores, among them *Rose-Marie* (1924), *The Vagabond King* (1925), *The Three Musketeers* (1928) and a score for *The Ziegfeld Follies.*

Romberg had intended to write popular songs. In love with the new country the moment he arrived, he worked as a restaurant pianist and then bandleader and composer. His first assignment consisted of songs for a forgotten Shubert revue at the Winter Garden Theatre that featured the advertisement, "Wherever you look, just girls!" As a Shubert staff composer he turned out songs for revues, spectaculars, and operettas, and many interpolations, at one point writing for fourteen musicals in two years. Altogether he wrote fifty-five scores in a variety of styles, including *Maytime* (1917)—which was so successful that two companies played at once across the street from each other—*Blossom Time* (1921), *The Student Prince of Heidelberg* (1924)—at 628 performances his longest run—*The Desert Song* (1926), *The New Moon* (1928), *Up in Central Park* (1945), and *The Passing Shows* of 1914, 1916, 1918, 1919, 1923, and 1924. His last score, *The Girl in Pink Tights* (1954), was finished after his death by Don Walker, managed 115 performances, was appreciated only for its star performer Jeanmaire, and is notable only for its choreographer, Agnes de Mille, and subject matter, the making of *The Black Crook.*

Among Herbert, Friml, and Romberg an epoch on the Broadway stage came and passed. Their music was popular in restaurants, cafes, and concerts. Their European-influenced music, written for the finest voices on the lyric theatre stage of the time, brought lush orchestrations, Viennese waltzes, and sophisticated harmonics to Broadway. Additionally, the variety and minstrel shows that formed the bulk of musical productions on the American stage at the time were peopled almost entirely by men. The operetta afforded women great roles as singers for the first time on the American stage.

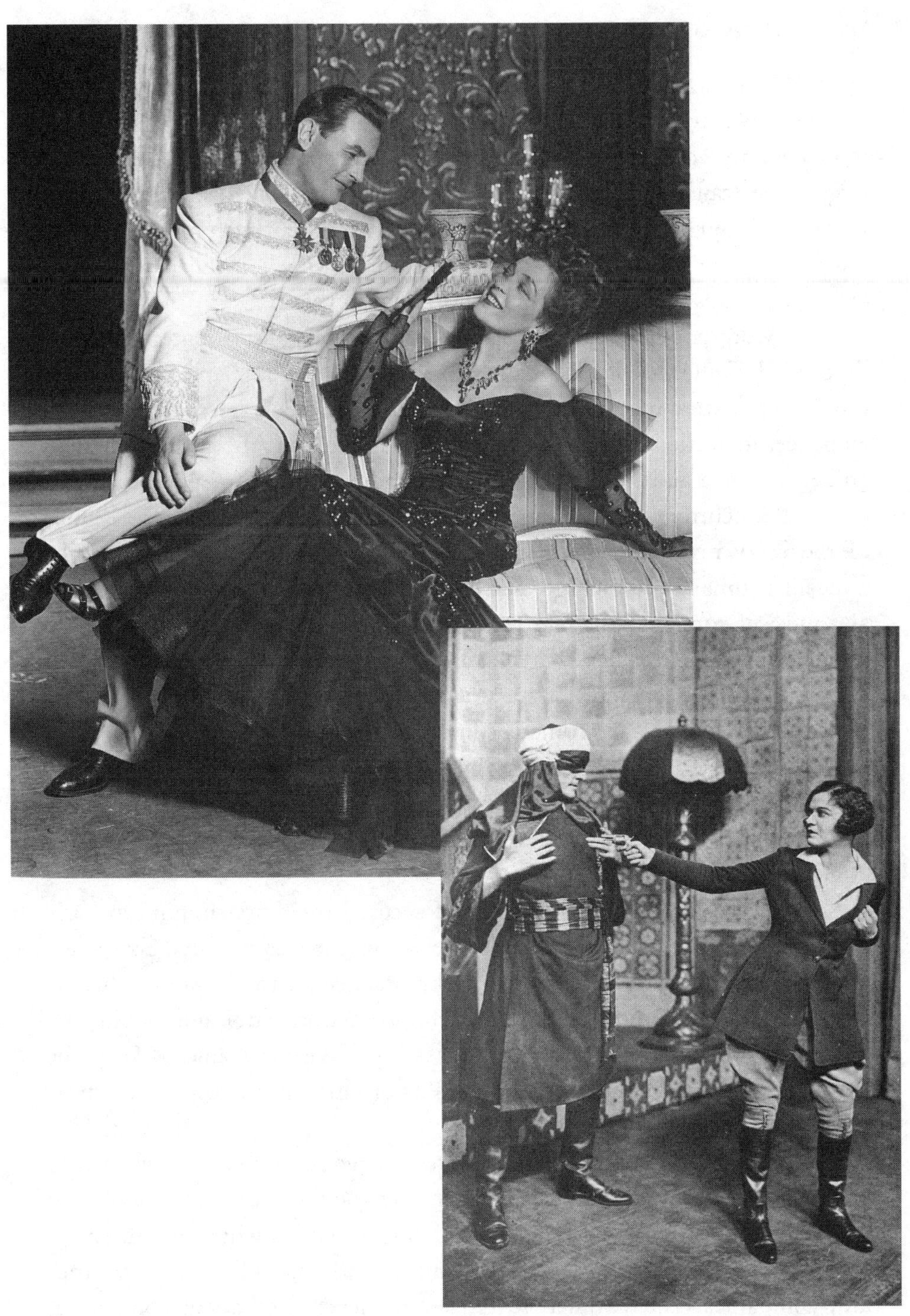

Romantic heroes and heroines from the age of operetta
Photofest/Alfredo Valente
Photofest

Not only were American operettas overshadowed by English and Viennese works produced here, but the form itself was increasingly less interesting to Americans. The imported operettas proved to be too heavy for large American audiences, and disappointing in their sheet music sales. Operettas, though beloved by their followers, would not even have been produced as often as they were had not J. J. Shubert, who controlled many theatres on Broadway and across the country, loved them.

More popular than the operettas were two musical entertainments descended from *The Black Crook: Adonis* (1884) and *A Trip to Chinatown* (1890). They were written in a popular vernacular, a character jargon, which audiences identified with, and their music was Tin Pan Alley, which charged and entertained audiences better than the more classical operetta scores.

Concurrent with the operetta's heyday on Broadway was the heyday of the jazzy musical comedy, the revues, and the rise of composers like Vincent Youmans and George Gershwin. Throughout the twenties, operetta and musical comedy struggled for preeminence. Ultimately the two forms merged in such shows as *Show Boat* and *Porgy and Bess.*

That the operetta score was doomed from the beginning to be replaced with the musical comedy song was apparent early on with the practice of inserting additional songs by American composers into imported scores, a dreadful attack on the unity of style and tone created by the original composer, but to the producer a necessary supplement to entertain his American audiences.

In 1927 the Dramatist's Guild secured their first minimum basic agreement, and thereafter the composer's consent was required for "alterations." Because of the Guild's work, the practice swiftly began to change. In the mid-1960s producer Ray Stark hoped Barbra Streisand would sing "My Man" in *Funny Girl,* but composer Jule Styne was able to keep the Fanny Brice-associated material out of his original score for the Broadway (though not the film) version.

None of the operettas are revived frequently today, and when they are—generally by opera and light-opera companies—the result is often a pale and stolid imitation of the original. The directors who stage them are far too timid, too reverent, and usually limited by budgets (in the case of theatre companies) and cavalier attitudes (in the case of opera companies) toward the material.

Because operetta's drama is of no interest to contemporary audiences, its music has disappeared, too. Though the music was superb in some cases, it was not dramatically inspired and its revival is often unsuccessful. In 1973, the operetta-smitten producer Moe Septee mounted a credible production of *The Desert Song* on Broadway, but audiences could have cared less and it closed after fifteen performances.

Operetta needs the huge chorus of singers, lavish sets, and large orchestras it boasted in its heyday. In old photographs of the chorus numbers you can count over sixty singers, and sometimes as many as a hundred (usually standing in long lines). This kind of production is no longer economically viable. The entire chorus of the 1973 *Desert Song* revival numbered only thirty-one.

Another problem is that composers of fuller scores, freed from the tenets of writing for specific characters and a time and place, tended to take the opportunity to throw in everything but the kitchen sink (always including the necessary waltz and march). Consequently some scores are appreciated even while they contribute to a director's inability to give the production a cohesiveness of style.

In the theatre, *story* engages audiences. The elaborate display of the human voice and the wide-ranging melodies the composers supplied it served the music well, but not the story, for that kind of singing is unnatural, and undercuts the actor-singer's ability to portray character believably.

Nonetheless, the Italian, French, German, English, and American versions of operetta all had in common their desire to steer clear of the complexity, histrionics, and stilted mannerisms of grand opera, and the mythic-sized plots and characters of that form. Instead, they presented romantic, comical plots, usually of farce-like complexity, in a gay, light, and popular form, which took occasional respites from melody to present dialogue and dance as well.

Operetta had a long and varied history which precedes and overlaps the musical comedy to such an extent that its impact can be seen, in lesser or greater degree, to both positive and negative effect, in nearly every extant musical theatre piece. Though much of operetta's basic tenets are anathema to the fundamentals of musical theatre, its history looms large over all Broadway musicals. *Show Boat, Carousel,* and *On the Twentieth Century* were heavily influenced by the operetta form, and two later American musicals that most closely and successfully attempted to follow it were *She Loves Me* and *Candide. She Loves Me* is based on the 1937 Hungarian comedy

Parfumerie by Miklos Laslo and the 1940 Ernst Lubitsch film *The Shop Around the Corner.* The story provided the kind of period romance that operettas thrived on, and allowed Jerry Bock and Sheldon Harnick to create their most romantic score. Nevertheless, a small chorus replaces the huge battalions of yore, the music is appropriately stylish to the place and period and characters, and the roles are best played by fine actors and actresses who can sing the score, as they were in the original—from Barbara Cook, Broadway's greatest singing-ingenue of her generation, to Jack Cassidy, one of its finest comic actors ever, to the handsome, charming, but mild-voiced Daniel Massey.

Candide is "a comic operetta." Voices in the original production were superb—Cook again—and, unleashed by a story with nonrealistic settings, Leonard Bernstein was able to create a wonderful score of complexity and soaring musicianship. On the other hand, the musical failed to catch on until it was given a thoroughly musical comedy staging in the 1973 Harold Prince revival.

As for operetta's often maudlin sentiment, popular entertainment has been and always will be shameless. Sentiment offers the composer a great opportunity, and musicals will always benefit from romantic stories, big ideas, and tear-inducing emotions.

Offenbach, Strauss, and England's Arthur Sullivan had in common a yearning to write grand opera. Musical snobbery at the time put operetta in an incorrect light, as if it were the stepchild of opera. In fact it stands on its own as a form whose golden age lasted longer than that of the American musical. It provided the American theatre with the musical seriousness that the musical, at its best, would eventually embrace. The composers took their musicianship seriously, almost always orchestrating their own melodies and creating overtures—some of which are concertized today—and even dance music.

Whether or not the training and seriousness of the operetta composers influenced many in Tin Pan Alley is difficult to judge. Victor Herbert clearly did what he could to shame them into it:

> Some composers think in terms of the piano, but pay little attention to it. I consider all the resources of orchestra and voice given to me to work with. If I did not work out my own orchestrations, it would be as if a painter conceived the idea of a picture and then had someone else paint it.

If George M. Cohan and Irving Berlin knew little of music, George Gershwin studied it all his life. Eventually the best Broadway musicals were written with both the sophistication and complexity of the classically trained operetta composers and the native syncopation and American flavor of Tin Pan Alley.

Romberg left an accurate description of the operetta by listing what it was he appreciated most about them:

> When I write for the theatre, I like books with charm to them. And charm suggests the old things—the finest things that were done long ago. I like a full-blooded libretto with luscious melody, rousing choruses and romantic passions.

Operetta impressed these characteristics on the emerging spirit of musical comedy, and if it died out, it was only because it was overshadowed by a louder if less beautiful, faster if less sophisticated, native if less classical, form of entertainment.

• • •

The romanticism and the richly melodic settings of the operetta were obviously appreciated by audiences, who supported the form for decades. That in the end operetta came to be a form outside of the mainstream is more a reflection of the mood of America at the time, a mood that less sophisticated composers like George M. Cohan were able to put their finger squarely on.

By the 1920s American audiences were impatient with the waltz and wanted the rippling syncopations of ragtime. They were less and less interested in Graustarkian principalities and wanted to see contemporary settings. The characters they increasingly identified with were not princes, princesses, or upper-class ne'er-do-wells, but middle-class Americans. The Irish, German, and Jewish immigrants that frequented the theatre liked to laugh at themselves, in the guise of dialect comedians. The electricity Americans wanted didn't come in chandeliers. America was growing up and finding its own identity, and there was a format as old as entertainment itself that was flexible enough to change as America did.

New Amsterdam Theatre

42nd Street, West of Broadway

ERLANGER, DILLINGHAM & ZIEGFELD............Managers

THIS THEATRE, UNDER NORMAL CONDITIONS, WITH EVERY SEAT OCCUPIED, CAN BE EMPTIED IN LESS THAN THREE MINUTES. LOOK AROUND NOW, CHOOSE THE NEAREST EXIT TO YOUR SEAT, AND IN CASE OF DISTURBANCE OF ANY KIND, TO AVOID THE DANGERS OF PANIC, WALK (DO NOT RUN) TO THAT EXIT.
THOMAS J. DRENNAN, Fire Commissioner

WEEK BEGINNING MONDAY EVENING, OCTOBER 6, 1919
Matinees Wednesday and Saturday

FLORENZ ZIEGFELD, JR., Offers His
Thirteenth Edition

ZIEGFELD FOLLIE

Staged by NED WAYBURN
Words and Music by
IRVING BERLIN, GENE BUCK, RENNOLD WOLF and DAVE
Ballet Composed by VICTOR HERBERT
Scenes by JOSEPH URBAN
Produced under the Personal Direction of F. ZIEGFEL

PROGRAM

This entertainment, absolutely intact as pre nightly, may be witnessed at the Wednesda Saturday matinees at the popular scale of $2.0 $1.00, 75c. and 50c.—no seat higher than $2.00

ACT I.

EARL CARROLL THEATRE
Seventh Avenue at Fiftieth Street
New York City

NOTICE: This Theatre, with every seat occupied, can be emptied in less than three minutes. Choose NOW the Exit nearest to your seat, and in case of fire walk (do not run) to that Exit.
THOMAS J. DRENNAN, Fire Commissioner.

THIS THEATRE IS ABSOLUTELY FIREPROOF

WEEK BEGINNING MONDAY EVENING, JULY 30, 1923
Matinees Thursday and Saturday

EARL CARROLL'S
"VANITIES OF 1923"
Lyrics and Music by Earl Carroll
Dialogue staged by Wm. Collier Designs by R. Reid Macguire
Dances by Sammy Lee Dresses by Paul Arlington, Inc.
Ballet by F. Renoff
Orchestra under the direction of William Daly

ACT I.

Overture.
Scene 1—The Birth of a New Revue—
The Composer........................Roy Giusti
The New-Born........................Alice Weaver
The Cohan Revue........................Polly Lux
The Winter Garden........................Thelma DeLorez
White's Scandals........................Ruth Hargraves

Winter Garden
The Winter Garden Company
Lessees & Managers

FIRE NOTICE
Look around NOW and choose the nearest Exit to your seat. In case of fire walk (not run) to THAT Exit. Do not try to beat your neighbor to the street.
ROBERT ADAMSON, Fire Commissioner.

WEEK BEGINNING MONDAY EVENING, JUNE 15, 1914.
Matinees Tuesday, Thursday and Saturday.

THE WINTER GARDEN COMPANY Presents
THE THIRD ANNUAL REVUE
THE PASSING SHOW OF 19

Dialogue and Lyrics by HAROLD ATTERIDGE.
Music by SIGMUND ROMBERG and HARRY CARROLL.
Incidental ballet music selected and arranged by MELVILLE
Production staged by J. C. HUFFMAN.
Dances and Numbers arranged by JACK MASON.
Costumes designed by MELVILLE ELLIS.

Cast.

Deuce Baggot
Mary Packard
A Camera Man
Miss High Jinks
The Midnight Girl
Rip Van Winkle Roosevelt
Little Buttercup, the Queen of th
Huerta
Sari
A Gypsy Fiddler
Lady Windermere
The Misleading Nut
First Attendant
Second Attendant
Jarrold McGee
Panthea
Kitty MacKay
Baron Criquet
Billie Burke
Leonora
Mr. Varenka
Mr. Manhattan
Pierrot
Prunella
Omar Khayyam
Shireen

PROGRAM CONTIN

GLOBE THEATRE
CHARLES DILLINGHAM, Proprietor and Manager
Broadway and 46th Street, New York City

THIS THEATRE, UNDER NORMAL CONDITIONS, WITH EVERY SEAT OCCUPIED, CAN BE EMPTIED IN LESS THAN THREE MINUTES. LOOK AROUND NOW, CHOOSE THE NEAREST EXIT TO YOUR SEAT, AND IN CASE OF DISTURBANCE OF ANY KIND, TO AVOID THE DANGERS OF PANIC, WALK (DO NOT RUN) TO THAT EXIT.
THOMAS J. DRENNAN, Fire Commissioner

WEEK BEGINNING MONDAY EVENING, JUNE 14, 1920
Matinees Wednesday and Saturday

SECOND ANNUAL EVENT
GEORGE WHITE'S SCANDALS OF 1920
A MODERN MUSICAL REVUE
Book by Andy Rice and George White
Music by George Gershwin Lyrics by Arthur Jackson
Staged by George White
Book Directed by William Collier
Scenes by Law Studios Herbert Ward, Art Director

THE PRINCIPALS IN THE CAST
ANN PENNINGTON
LA SYLPHE
ETHEL DELMAR
FRANCES ARMS
CHRISTINE WELES
GEORGE WHITE
LOU HOLTZ
LESTER ALLEN
GEORGE BICKEL
GEORGE ROCKWELL
LLOYD GARRETT
JAMES MILLER
YERKES JAZZY SIX
LESTER O'KEEFE
JAMES STEIGER

PAGE FOLLOWING

NEW AMSTERDAM THEATRE

ERLANGER, DILLINGHAM & ZIEGFELD..................MANAGING DIRECTORS

THE NEW AMSTERDAM THEATRE PLANNED AND DESIGNED BY
F. RICHARD ANDERSON AND A. L. ERLANGER

PROGRAM · PUBLISHED · BY · THE · NEW · YORK · THEATRE · PROGRAM · CORPORATION

FIRE NOTICE: Look around now and choose the nearest exit to your seat. In case of fire, walk (not run) to that exit. Do not try to beat your neighbor to the street.
JOHN J. DORMAN, Fire Commissioner.

BEGINNING MONDAY EVENING, JUNE 15, 1931

MATINEES WEDNESDAY AND SATURDAY

MAX GORDON
PRESENTS
FRED and ADELE ASTAIRE
FRANK MORGAN
HELEN BRODERICK
TILLY LOSCH
IN
"THE BAND WAGON"
A REVUE
By GEORGE S. KAUFMAN and HOWARD DIETZ
Music by ARTHUR SCHWARTZ

Eight

Revues

Something for everybawdy . . .

From the beginning, the American musical theatre was aided and abetted by a plethora of revues. For that matter, the difference between revues and musical comedies was almost invisible for some time, since many revues featured a thread of a story and many musical comedies featured paper-thin books. The ostensible difference was that musical comedies had character-driven plots, and one could follow a character from first scene to last.

In 1894 the revue *The Passing Show* at the Casino Theatre featured a slim story, and something else which was already a landmark of the musical theatre. The *New York Sun* wrote:

> The skirts were made of gauze so thin that the upper halves of their legs and lower halves of their bodies were plainly exposed in skin-tight, flesh-colored silk webbings . . . a flagrant and shameful exploit in nudity. . . . [W]omen averted their eyes and men were ashamed to look.

(I bet.)

The Passing Show (produced by George Lederer) contained a nationally known chorus line of beauties, and was a sumptuous production with a forgettable score noted for its topical comedy. Subsequent editions were *The Merry World* and *In Gay New York,* the latter the most successful of all three and probably the first musical production in which some of the sets were purposefully changed in front of the audience.

Ned Harrigan and Tony Hart teamed up in vaudeveille and held forth on Broadway from 1873 to 1896 with variety shows and full musicals that featured caricatures of Irish and German immigrants and black Americans. Harrigan wrote the material, and Hart often played in drag. In September of 1896 Joe Weber and Lew Fields opened their Music Hall and produced shows through 1903. Their productions featured one musical comedy and one burlesque of a current Broadway hit on a double bill. Their spoofs were so popular that Broadway producers bribed them to mock their plays. The Music Hall was a small theatre, sumptuous, and known for the "superior" beauty of its chorus line. Harrigan and Hart, with their Irish caricatures, and Weber and Fields, with their German ones, brought poor immigrant characters to the stage for the first time, and thus created a popular theatre for a middle- and lower-class audience who loved seeing themselves in all their accents and old-world foibles reflected on the stage. It made them feel they now belonged to America.

But it was the impresario Florenz Ziegfeld who created a series of revues so successful that their name will always be synonymous with the form: *The Ziegfeld Follies.* Ziegfeld was born in Chicago in 1867, and his first act as an impresario came when he was 22 years old. He promoted a dancing duck in a tent set up in Chicago Park. When it was discovered that an arrangement not unlike a barbecue was hidden under the small table, and that the duck danced only when an assistant turned up the heat, the police closed Ziegfeld down.

Because his father was director of musical events for the 1893 Chicago Fair, it became young Ziegfeld's job to book musical entertainments for the Exposition. He was sent to Europe to find classical music acts, but instead he booked a series of third-rate vaudeville performers who failed to attract much of an audience and almost bankrupted his father. When he publicized a strongman act he had seen at New York's Casino Theatre, however, his fortunes changed.

With his first act (not counting the duck), Ziegfeld created a pattern for his future. He promoted the The Great Sandow with inspiration,

A Ziegfeld cast
Museum of the City of New York

ensuring that posters appeared everywhere in the city, dressing him only in tight silk shorts—less than strongman acts had ever worn before—inviting society ladies from the audience to feel the man's bulging biceps, and manipulating light and inventing props to create a theatrically dazzling act. After the Exposition he and Sandow toured for more than two years. Before the turn of the century Ziegfeld had made more than $250,000 promoting Sandow. And gambled it all away.

Ziegfeld's second promotion was Anna Held, with whom the enthusiastic 29-year-old fell in love when he saw her on stage in London. He brought her to New York with much fanfare, and produced the play *A Parlor Match.* Though this was already a much-revived comedy, the appearance of the diminutive beauty with the eighteen-inch waist singing "Come Play With Me" in the second act caused a sensation. So did Ziegfeld's publicity machinations, which included the famous milk-bath hoax, in which the press—even the staid *New York Times*—was convinced that Miss Held took daily baths in fresh milk, and they were allowed to take pictures to prove it. Ziegfeld managed to keep the story on the front pages for days.

For several years "the Ziegfelds"—he and Anna Held had announced that they were married, but they were not—toured the country in a succession of productions, all chosen to flatter Anna. They led a lavish life, traveling by private railroad car amid Ziegfeld's ceaseless publicity. In 1899 he produced *Papa's Wife* with sixteen ravishing chorus girls—the beginning of the famous "Ziegfeld girls." In 1901 it was *The Little Duchess,* with a libretto by Harry B. Smith.

The next year the program for the return engagement read, "Owing to the length of the performance the plot has been eliminated," indicating that Ziegfeld was already leaning toward the revue format in his presentations. And then in 1906 a musical came along which started it all.

The Parisian Model, book and lyrics by Harry B. Smith, Julian Mitchell staging, featured not only Held but sixteen dancing girls who, in one scene, lay on a revolving stage kicking their legs in the air, and in another, roller-skated. The choreography was criticized as libidinous. When six girls entered wearing neck-to-floor capes, stood behind painter's easels that only covered them from shoulder to thigh, and disrobed, suggesting that they were standing naked behind the easels, the audience was aghast. Shocked patrons kept the play running thirty-three weeks in New York, and "The Beauty Trust"—a nickname given to all pretty girls in Broadway shows—had arrived.

But the relationship between Held and Ziegfeld was deteriorating. While they were on tour with *Parisian Model,* a fortune in jewels was stolen from Held, and ransom money was also lost. Held always suspected Ziegfeld, as did the police. Still gambling, he had almost bankrupted the immensely wealthy Held. Fortunately they had never been legally married—the Roman Catholic Church would not give Held and her first husband a divorce—or Held would have been responsible for Ziegfeld's debts. At this propitious moment, Marc Klaw and Abe Erlanger hired Ziegfeld (at a lowly salary) to stage a show for them.

It was actually Harry Smith, librettist and lyricist for Ziegfeld's first *Follies* (and four of the next five) who gave the productions their title. He called it *Follies of the Year,* based on his newspaper column "Follies of the Day." Ziegfeld, who meddled in every aspect of his productions, changed it to *Follies of 1907.* This first *Follies* cost $13,000, had one director and three choreographers, notably Julian Mitchell, and was successful enough to warrant a tour as well as future editions.

Early revues, aping vaudeville and variety shows, often changed their material and their cast during the run. Ziegfeld's publicity for the 1907 edition boasted weekly changes, and his star, Nora Bayes, left after half the run. Consistent, however, was a chorus line of fifty "Anna Held Girls," named in deference to Ziegfeld's wife. The influence of the early Paris revues, as well as the Eurocentric cultural leaning of the period, can be seen in the fact that its title may have intentionally conjured up the famous *Folies Bergère,* and the roof of the New York Theatre was rechristened the Jardin de Paris for the production.

But the first *Follies* were only mildly successful, and Ziegfeld hadn't yet embraced them completely. That same season he produced a much more glamorous musical, *Miss Innocence,* for Held. His relationship with her finally ended when he and a drunken doctor physically forced an abortion on her—it was his child—so that she could appear in a production on which he had lavished his attention (and on which his fortunes, as usual, wavered). She recovered and opened in the production. It was a great success, but she never again loved him.

His private life became increasingly hectic as his shows became increasingly lavish. He lived at the Ansonia Hotel with Anna and installed Lillian Lorraine, his mistress, upstairs. Both ladies were in several *Follies* and *Miss Innocence* together, and the entire city knew of Ziegfeld's affair. In 1912

Anna finally sued him for divorce, needing first to find a court in Paris that would consider them married by common law.

But the *Follies* were off and running. The 1908 edition boasted the song "Shine on Harvest Moon," considered the first good piece of music, certainly the first real hit, in a revue. Although Ziegfeld's outstanding taste and his lifelong commitment to quality were the basis of the *Follies'* artistic success, he wasn't known for his musical ear. Fortuitously, the more successful he became the more he pursued successful collaborators, and his *Follies* benefited from their age, one in which a host of great young composers and lyricists were bursting forth—both European immigrants with classical musical training and young American-born Tin Pan Alley enthusiasts. In his career he produced songs and scores by Gene Buck—one of the composing stalwarts of the *Follies*—Victor Herbert, Jerome Kern, George Gershwin, Sigmund Romberg, Irving Berlin, and Noël Coward.

For the 1910 production he signed Bert Williams, the already famous black entertainer, and broke the color barrier of the Broadway show. Williams, in fact, appeared in comic sketches with white comedian Leon Errol, and the long tradition of separatist entertainment received its first tiny crack. Ziegfeld had to browbeat some members of the company and fire others when they refused to appear with Williams.

For the 1911 edition he added his name to the title, and the *Ziegfeld Follies* insured that his name would forever be synonymous with the idea of a great revue. In the 1915 production Ziegfeld hired the designer who would help him mark the *Follies* as the most artistic theatrical presentations of the twentieth century. Joseph Urban, Austrian-born architect, set designer, and children's book illustrator, eventually designed sixteen Ziegfeld musicals (and fifty-four productions for the Metropolitan Opera, thirty films, the Ziegfeld Theatre, the New School for Social Research, hotels in Palm Beach, and interiors for nightclubs). Urban not only created a series of sumptuous and tasteful sets, but also revolutionized scene design in the theatre. His exquisite designs brought to the musical revues—and by imitation to theatre in general—a new level in production design. The artistry of the sets and costumes reached heights that had not been seen since the Renaissance. Urban used a George Seurat-like painting style—careful spots of paint, shadings, layerings, and the now-common technique known as spackling—instead of the traditional broad washes of paint. He followed trends such as art nouveau and later art deco. He painstakingly conceived and executed breathtaking settings. In a first for set design, Urban's sets were

A Ziegfeld production number
Photofest

color-coordinated, with each new scene boasting its own palette. The 1915 edition was designed around blue, the favorite color of both Urban and Ziegfeld. The look of the shows was not only organized around specific colors and designs but originally intended to flow in a certain pattern that enhanced the momentum of the evening. Unfortunately for this last idea, productions at the time, especially revues, often underwent a rearrangement of numbers and sketches during writing, rehearsing, and tryouts—thus, Urban's overall design concepts were never truly presented in the order in which they were meant to be seen.

Like all great artists, Urban affected his collaborators too; for Ziegfeld saw and understood, then upgraded his costumes as a consequence. If the big revues were the first ones to benefit from Urban's influence, book musicals eventually began to use more artistic designs as well.

The 1915 *Follies* began the Urban era, but ended the era of Julian Mitchell, though Mitchell returned for one more edition nine years later. Ned Wayburn took over the staging, a man 29 years younger than Mitchell who reflected new tastes, styles, and tempos. The *Follies* then graduated from the ponderous, largo pacing of all the big musical shows since *The Black Crook,* to the modern tempo of the George M. Cohan-inspired entertainments. Wayburn is sometimes credited with inventing tap dancing, which in fact developed as an amalgam of Irish clog dancing and black minstrel-show dancing, and was already well in vogue in vaudeville. But perhaps Wayburn canonized the form on Broadway with better organized and more frequent use. Wayburn also brought careful auditions to the *Follies,* where in the past Ziegfeld had hired and fired more casually. Urban had already learned that a show shouldn't have to wait for long scene changes, and Ziegfeld and Wayburn insisted that the *Follies* must flow more rapidly than ever before, and that something must always be happening.

At their height, between 1915 and 1922, the *Ziegfeld Follies* were the most lavish musical productions in Broadway history. Notoriously, the thirteenth edition of 1919 was the best, featuring Bert Williams, Eddie Cantor, Marilyn Miller, and songs by Irving Berlin. The 1919 *Follies* cost $150,000 (the same season, *Irene* cost $40,000). The 1921 *Follies* were the first to cost over a quarter of a million dollars at a time when the average musical could still be mounted for $50,000. The 1927 edition was scored entirely by Irving Berlin, including "Shakin' the Blues Away," and reputedly cost $289,035.35 (when *Good News* cost $75,000).* The show featured the beautiful Marion Davies, who was discovered by Ziegfeld and became the notorious mistress of newspaper baron William Randolph Hearst.

It should also be noted that Busby Berkeley's work did not flower in a vacuum. The 1927 *Follies* boasted nineteen girls playing nineteen white pianos. Ziegfeld used sixty to seventy-five girls, exquisitely dressed and undressed, the magnificent designs of Urban, and, of course . . .

Stars. W. C. Fields portrayed his snarling, curmudgeonly character, performed his famous pool-table routine, and, when Ed Wynn attempted to improvise his way into the sketch, knocked Wynn unconscious with a pool cue. In the 1909 *Follies,* Nora Bayes got newcomer Sophie Tucker fired from the show for stopping it. When told that her one number would be cut from the 1910 edition, Fanny Brice desperately improvised comedy shtick, the audience went wild, and she became a star. In the 1921 edition she sang "I Was a Florodora Baby" ("Five little dumbbells got married for money, and I got married for love") as well as "Second Hand Rose" and "My Man." This latter number was all the more poignant because of her notorious ne'er-do-well husband, the gambler-gangster Nick Arnstein. (Capitalizing on the publicity, Ziegfeld took this number away from French chanteuse Mistinguett and assigned it to Brice during rehearsal.) Eddie Cantor was the centerpiece of the 1927 *Follies,* but walked out after a fight with Ziegfeld, ending the edition prematurely. Will Rogers was too homespun for Ziegfeld, but after he convulsed his first audience at Ziegfeld's roof-garden *Frolics*—a more intimate, late-night revue—he was promoted to the *Follies* and became a close friend and confidant.

During this great era Ziegfeld added the tableaux of Ben Ali Haggin, a society painter he engaged to pose the girls in exotic settings. Apparently, girls could move around with very little on, but if they were entirely naked they had to stand still. Ziegfeld's invention of the tableau led the Shuberts to create *Artists and Models* for obvious reasons. Characteristically less tasteful and a little cheaper, the Shubert versions of the revue (six between 1923 and 1943) provided many beautiful girls with drafty work, but little else.

* It seems only fair to conjecture, however, that Ziegfeld may have overreported his capitalizations for obvious reasons. Contemporary publicity reports—taken at face value by some of Ziegfeld's biographers—list stage props like "authentic gold plates," and "the finest silk from china for the girls' unseen underwear." These extravagances are suspect, if only because any good designer knows that the real thing doesn't always look as good on the stage as the faux.

A Ziegfeld girl

Museum of the City of New York, The F. Fox Collection

These spectacularly visual revues were beginning to compete with themselves, and Ziegfeld's fortunes declined. Ziegfeld had an erratic personality. Smith called him "Napoleonic, even in trifles." He was probably manic-depressive and obsessive-compulsive as well. He grew increasingly ill and mentally unstable, behaving more and more erratically. Surrounded by process servers and litigation, estranged from his loyal wife Billie Burke, and terrified that he was losing his sexual prowess—thus, he frantically urged himself on to more and more chorus girls—he spun nearly out of control. Then, in a period that astonishes the chroniclers of his career, he came back with four book musical hits. Between 1927 and 1928 he produced *Rio Rita, Show Boat, Rosalie,* and *Whoopee.* After that, just when he'd managed to cobble together $2 million in savings for his young daughter, an only child to whom he was devoted, the stock market crash wiped him out.

The 1931 *Follies,* his last personal edition, was a behemoth that couldn't survive the waning interest in the lavish shows (in that respect Ziegfeld was a victim of his own success, for he couldn't top himself) or the depression. The crash had also hurt, or at least scared, the millionaires who financed his shows, and by 1931 he could no longer raise the large sums of money he needed.

He died, with the American twenties, in 1932. On his death the Shuberts licensed his name from his widow Billie Burke, who was trying to pay off mountainous debts, because the great Ziggy always spent every penny he earned and more. The Shuberts produced more editions with less taste, and the era of the spectacular musical revue was over.

Ziegfeld left his imprint on the American theatre. He was the first producer-star, his name alone a guarantee of audience interest. Only producer David Merrick would ever rival him. The Shubert Brothers lasted longer and produced more shows—five hundred on Broadway in the first forty-five years of the twentieth century, owning thirty-one playhouses in New York and sixty more nationwide—but never made an artistic mark on the theatre. They produced popular entertainments, reducing the theatre to comedies and musicals, primarily operettas, and according to their friend and associate Donald Flamm, "were constantly criticized, ridiculed and satirized by columnists and drama desk writers" for their lowbrow taste.

Show Boat—for all the work of Jerome Kern and Oscar Hammerstein—was known at the time as a Ziegfeld show. And the success of the *Follies* inspired many other productions during the heyday of the great revues, including . . .

The Passing Shows. The young Shuberts battled the Theatrical Trust (controlled by Klaw and Erlanger, with whom Ziegfeld was aligned) and won, bringing their own brand of monopolistic, untrustworthy practices to Broadway. They took the name of the earlier revue and mounted more *Passing Shows*—less expensive imitations of the *Follies*—from 1912–1922. Theatrical historian Cecil Smith credits the 1914 edition with the death of the buxom beauty prototype:

> Gone forever were the Amazonian marches and drills . . . girls' legs, which had been emerging from their tights inch by inch for several seasons were now presented unadorned and au naturel. . . . Skirts were short and arms were bare, and at one point the glittering spangles were dispensed with, revealing bare midriffs on the upper-class New York stage for the first time.

Actually it's unlikely that the change occurred so suddenly, because films were already promoting a thinner version of feminine beauty.

Hitchy Koo began four editions in 1917, of which Jerome Kern and Cole Porter each wrote one. George M. Cohan authored three revues: *Hello, Broadway!* (1914, 123 performances), *The Cohan Revue of 1916* (165) and *The Cohan Revue of 1918* (96). Among his other achievements, Cohan Americanized something in *Hello, Broadway!* that had been vaguely old-world, for the form had begun in Paris, drifted to England, and been brought here by well-traveled producers like Ziegfeld. Heretofore the lavish Broadway spectacles had generally featured at least the semblance of a plot. But Cohan didn't have a plot of any sort for *Hello, Broadway.* According to the performers he had a hat box that contained it. In the final moments of the show the hat box is at last opened, but it is empty. "What became of the plot?" one character says, to which the answer is, "There never was a plot." From then on even a thin excuse for a show was no longer necessary, and the modern American revue was born.

John Murray Anderson, a ballroom dancer and nightclub master of ceremonies created the *Greenwich Village Follies* (1919–1928). Ziegfeld brought a lawsuit but the courts chastised him for thinking he had a patent on the word "follies." There were eight editions, two in the Village and the rest on Broadway, marked by the great Erté's costume designs. These *Follies* were known for their "ballet ballads" and dance songs like "When My Baby Smiles at Me." Another Anderson revue, *What's in a Name?*, was the first to use drapes and curtains instead of painted scenery, thus speeding up the pace of the American revue. Two editions of *John Murray Anderson's Almanac* (1929 and 1953) tried to carry on the tradition, but failed.

The George White Scandals began in 1919. They were paced by the ex-*Ziegfeld Follies* hoofer George White, with lighter if harder-edged sets and costumes, and introduced a jazz-age sensibility. They were filled with fast dancing just as the ballroom craze for wild dances was getting underway, using the Charleston and introducing the Black Bottom. Their scores were correspondingly superior. George White hired popular bandleader Paul Whiteman to conduct, and Gershwin introduced dozens of songs and the opera *Blue Monday* in White's *Scandals*. The best edition is reputed to have been mounted in June of 1926, with a score by DeSylva, Brown and Henderson that included "The Birth of the Blues." There was an equal mix of hoofing, comics, and songs, and a new high price of $5.50 for the best seats. The last edition was produced in 1939, by which time the *Scandals* had begun the transition to the faster, material-oriented revues.

The Music Box Revues, produced by Sam Harris and Irving Berlin and written by Berlin, issued only four editions (1921–1924) but left behind the Music Box Theatre for which they were conceived—one of the finest theatres ever designed for Broadway. Berlin had already created his World War I revue *Yip, Yip, Yaphank,* and during World War II he wrote *This is the Army.* Both editions featured him singing "Oh, How I Hate to Get Up in the Morning," and both ended with soldiers marching off to end war for the last time.

The Earl Carrol Vanities and *Sketchbook* (1923–1940) featured tasteless nudity, and the shows were sometimes attacked by courts on the basis of morality. But H. L. Mencken said, "You'll never go broke underestimating the taste of the American public." Carroll and his principal backer, a rich Texas oil man, never did. They featured primarily girls and comedy. Harold Arlen's "I Gotta Right to Sing the Blues" is the only song still remembered from these lackluster scores. The final edition ran in 1940 for only three weeks, but marked the first use of microphones and amplification in Broadway theatre history. This technical device was lambasted by the critics.

With the waning of the revue format, several producers tried to combine the book musical and the revue. Ziegfeld's *Sally* (1920) is about a dishwasher who dreams of being in the *Follies;* Earl Carrol's *Murder at the*

Vanities (1933) limns the backstage murder of a chorus girl by the mother of a dancer who hopes to take her place; and in *Manhattan Mary* (1927) Ed Wynn helps a girl get a job in George White's *Scandals*.

As the lavish, showgirl-studded revues became too expensive and old hat, their place was gradually taken by smaller, more sophisticated revues, based on good material and talent.

The 49ers (1922) introduced the verbal, literary revue, featuring a number of witty sketches by members of the Algonquin Round Table.

Charlot's Revue (1924) featured the material of Noël Coward—then unknown—and performers Bea Lillie, Gertrude Lawrence, and Jack Buchanan from England. It was hugely successful, intimate, and witty, with a good balance between songs and sketches. It was imitated in America by . . .

The Garrick Gaieties (1925, 1926, and 1930). This was performed by the junior members of the Theatre Guild. It began as a benefit, then went on to a regular run. Richard Rodgers and Lorenz Hart contributed seven songs to the original edition, launching their career.

The Little Show opened at the Music Box Theatre at the end of 1929, featured great material performed by new stars Fred Allen, Clifton Webb, and Libby Holman, and launched an era for witty sketches and better music. It didn't rely on nudity or design, but on the quality of its writing. The score was written by Howard Dietz (lyrics) and Arthur Schwartz, (music).

Dietz, who had gone to school with Ira Gershwin, began his career as a copywriter with an advertising agency and then became a publicist for Samuel Goldwyn. Eventually he headed publicity at MGM, a post he never gave up (and where he was credited with devising the famous lion logo), even as his lyric writing career advanced. Schwartz, a self-taught piano player, taught English and practiced law, but gave up both professions when his songs found their way into Broadway shows. After writing with other partners, they collaborated on the songs for *The Little Show*. This intimate revue ran for 321 performances. One of their songs, "I Guess I'll Have to Change My Plan," became a hit, and their careers were underway.

A year later, *The Second Little Show* ran only sixty-three performances, but *Three's a Crowd* (1930), produced by Max Gordon and directed by Hassard Short, and featuring the stars from *The Little Show*, played 272 performances.

But *The Band Wagon* (1931), featuring Fred and Adele Astaire and running 262 performances, was the finest of the new, nonspectacular but sophisticated Broadway revues. Hassard Short directed, and Dietz and Schwartz provided a full score (without interpolation from others). The show featured "Dancing in the Dark," and was the all-time greatest of the smart, fast, Broadway revues, a style by then in full swing. It was exquisitely designed and staged. Notably, *The Band Wagon* cut its footlights and hung lighting lamps from the balcony rail instead, an extraordinary innovation in light design. This gave lighting designers far more flexibility and altered forever the ghostly, ghastly look of traditional theatre. Neither did the show feature a front curtain—instead, the company came in, sat on chairs, and mirrored the audience. They looked at their programs and demanded that they witness something "good"—a unique and original opening.

The following year's entry by Dietz and Schwartz, *Flying Colors,* earned 181 performances and several more hit songs, but the bloom was off the rose. *Revenge With Music* (1934) was their first book show together. Although it ran only 158 performances, it featured "You and the Night and the Music." They returned to the revue with *At Home Abroad* with Bea Lillie (1935, 198 performances), and became a bit more experimental with *Between the Devil* (1937, 93 performances). *Inside U.S.A.* (1948, 399 performances) did especially well, but by then television was becoming popular. By the early fifties television variety shows replaced the Broadway revues, and there was never to be another production in the league of *The Band Wagon.*

Though neither Dietz nor Schwartz wrote substantial hits with other collaborators, Dietz was applauded for his English lyrics to *Die Fledermaus* and *La Bohème,* which he wrote for the Metropolitan Opera, and Schwartz wrote the charming *A Tree Grows in Brooklyn* with lyricist Dorothy Fields.

• • •

The stock market crash of 1929 and the subsequent depression sped the transition from spectacle to material as the principal dramatic value of the revue, but also ushered in songs and sketches of increasing social significance. A modern descendant of the medieval guild shows was remarkably successful on Broadway. In 1937, after rehearsing for a year and a half at night, members of the International Ladies Garment Workers Union presented Harold Rome's original revue *Pins and Needles* at the Princess Theatre, renamed the Labor Stage. Performed completely by men and women who worked all day in New York's garment district, the topical, satirical, union show ran for 1,108 performances in three versions: *Pins and Needles*, *Pins and Needles 1939*, and *New Pins and Needles*. The sketches and songs poked fun at both the labor movement and management.) We might not find the show very radical today, but during the Great Depression, in light of the growing schism between management and employees, it was radically left-wing. This inexpensive show eventually ran for three years—an extraordinary accomplishment, though one that ought to be compared with off-Broadway rather than Broadway musicals. Uptown, political satire in revues seldom played as well. When Harold Rome wrote songs for *Sing Out the News* (1938), with sketches by George Kaufman and Moss Hart, it didn't hang on long, nor did *One for the Money* (1939), *Two for the Show* (1940), or *Three To Make Ready* (1946)—three politically right-wing revues that all had difficulty attracting audiences.

Leave it to Irving Berlin (songs), Moss Hart (sketches), and Hassard Short (direction) to create *As Thousands Cheer* (1933), one of the greatest of all revues, rivaling *The Band Wagon* for sheer craft and bridging the gap to the socially conscious 1930s. Most of the show's material was topical if not radical. It even featured a concept—all of its songs and sketches grew out of newspaper headlines. The weather provided Ethel Waters's sizzling "Heat Wave," but the most haunting number was Water's singing "Supper Time" to the newspaper report of her husband having been lynched, and wondering what to tell her children. This verseless song, which reaches a climax when the singer shouts "Lord!" was an early piece of anti-racist writing, and probably then the most powerful ever created for the Broadway musical stage. "No where else in American song have I heard a single note and a single word combined so shatteringly," wrote Alec Wilder.

The leftist leanings of the thirties, however, are best seen in the travails of a book musical—*The Cradle Will Rock* by Marc Blitzstein tells the story of workers attempting to organize a union in Steeltown. Staged by Orson Welles and John Houseman for the WPA Theatre Project, it was canceled when its "Communist sympathies" were suspected. The intrepid impresarios went ahead anyway, whereupon a legal injunction was placed against the work.

On opening night, the company found themselves locked out of the theatre. They marched the cast *and audience* twenty blocks uptown to another theatre. There Blitzstein sat at a piano on stage while the cast—having bought tickets to circumvent an Actor's Equity decree that they couldn't perform—rose in their seats to perform their roles. The notoriety

"Dancing in the Dark" in the ultra-elegant revue *The Band Wagon*

Museum of the City of New York/Vandamm

alone pushed the production to 108 performances. Censorship invariably causes the opposite effect that the censors are hoping to achieve.

Snug in the "new material, new performers" category sits *Leonard Sillman's New Faces,* a series of editions featuring just that. These editions were always well reviewed, witty, and chic, but curiously enough left nothing of consequence behind. Surely they deserve some sort of never-give-up record for the greatest span, featuring editions in 1934, 1936, 1942, 1952, 1956, 1962, and 1968. (The unquestionable champion was 1952.)

By the end of the thirties the revue's only contribution was the introduction of talent. In 1939 *The Straw Hat Revue* featured rising talents Imogene Coca, Alfred Drake, Danny Kaye, and Jerome Robbins (as a performer). Scores for revues lost their hold on audiences, who began to favor the dramatically connected songs of the modern book musical. Sid Caesar, who as a relative unknown had starred in the inconsequential revue *Make Mine Manhattan,* quickly moved to the new medium of television, where the revue format could be seen in the comfort of a living room. With his success there, the Broadway revue was finished.

By the fifties, revues had left Broadway altogether for off-Broadway and cabarets, where they happily carry on today.

Martin Charnin unearthed some wonderful performers and songwriters when he mounted *Upstairs at O'Neals* (1982), the hysterical highlight of which was the song "Something,"—the acting teacher Mr. Karp's answer to Morales's complaint that he taught her "Nothing" in *A Chorus Line. Forbidden Broadway* (1982), the first successful "annual" since the days of the great revues, harks back to the burlesque/parody form popularized decades earlier by Joe Weber and Lew Fields while keeping up with the latest hits by spoofing them. *Niteclub Confidential* (1984) used a pulp/film noir plot to link some original and some authentic songs of the forties and fifties. *Forever Plaid* both spoofed and revered the close harmony talents of groups like the Four Freshmen.

Today the kind of show the theatregoer thinks of when he hears the word revue is a compendium of old songs with something in common—a time period (*Tintypes*, 1980), a single composer (*By Bernstein,* 1975, *By Strouse,* 1978), a lyricist (*A Party with Comden and Green*), a songwriter (*The Decline and Fall of the Entire World as Seen Through the Eyes of Cole Porter,* 1965; *Jacques Brel is Alive and Well and Living in Paris,* 1966), or a songwriting team (Kander and Ebb, *The World Goes Round,* 1991; Rodgers and

Hammerstein, *A Grand Night for Singing*). David Shire and Richard Maltby took their best songs from five unproduced Broadway musicals to create an off-Broadway revue of their trunk, *Starting Here, Starting Now* (1977). Maltby directed Fats Wallers' raucous songs in the joyful *Ain't Misbehavin'* (1978), which successfully moved to Broadway. But when Broadway tries to rev up its own revues, it usually fails. Rodgers and Hart's *In Celebration* (1975) was a lackluster beige songfest without concept, and *Smokey Joe's Cafe* (1995), featuring the songs of rock-and-roll composers Jerry Lieber and Mike Stoller, was eight terrific performers and thirty-six wonderful numbers in search of a show. These productions say a good deal for our history, but not much for our future.

In their heyday, and without competition from radio, film, or television, the revues captured large American audiences. The half- to all-naked girls, the comedians, and the American scores held their own against the operetta. The music of Tin Pan Alley was fast becoming society's anthem. Rhythmic, jazzy, careening from phrase to phrase and scene to scene, it was as American as the operetta was European.

This kind of theatre began in vaudeville, and no one personified it more, or worked harder to transfuse Broadway with it, than George M. Cohan.

LIBERTY THEATRE

42d Street, West of Broadway.

THE KLAW & ERLANGER AMUSEMENT CO., - Owners
KLAW & ERLANGER, - - - - - - - Managers

WEEK BEGINNING MONDAY EVENING, DEC. 5, 1904

Matinee Saturday Only.

SAM H. HARRIS Presents

THE YANKEE DOODLE COMEDIAN,

GEO. M. COHAN

And His Singing and Dancing Company, In His Latest Musical Play,

Little Johnny Jones

(THE AMERICAN JOCKEY)

ANTHONY ANSTEY, an American gambler........................JERRY J. COHAN
SING SONG, editor of the Pekin Gazette........................J. BERNARD DYLLYN
TIMOTHY D. McGEE, a New York politician and horse owner..........SAM J. RYAN
HENRY HAPGOOD, who also makes the trip........................DONALD BRIAN
THE UNKNOWN..TOM LEWIS
JENKINS, starter at the Cecil.......................}
CAPTAIN SQUIRVY, of the St. Hurrah................} ....C. J. HARRINGTON
BELL BOY..WM. SEYMOUR
INSPECTOR PERKINS..CHARLES BACHMANN
STEVENS, a waiter..JOSEPH LESLIE
CHUNG FOW...CHARLES STEVENS
HUNG CHUNG..FRED WILLIAMS
JOHNNY JONES, the American Jockey..........................GEO. M. COHAN
MRS. ANDREW KENWORTH, a fanatic on the subject of reform..HELEN F. COHAN
FLORABELLE FLY, of the San Francisco Searcher..............TRULY SHATTUCK
BESSIE, an American girl..EDITH TYLER

—AND—

GOLDIE GATES.............}
ROSARIO FAUCHETTE......} ....ETHEL LEVEY
EARL OF BLOOMSBURY.....}

Female Reformers, American Girls, English Policemen, Life Guards, Sailors, etc.

The Play and Songs Written by GEO. M. COHAN.
Produced by GEO. M. COHAN, assisted by JAMES GORMAN.

Programme continued on second page following.

Nine

George M. Cohan

That famous American stride, full of musical comedy pride.

There is no better definition of the vaudeville stage than the first paragraph of Douglas Gilbert's 1940 volume, *American Vaudeville, Its Life and Times*:

> Vaudeville was American in motley, the national relaxation. To the Palace, the Colonial, the Alhambra, the Orpheum, the Keith Circuit and chain variety houses, N.Y. to L.A. we flocked, vicariously to don the false face, let down our back hair, and forget. Vaudeville was the theater of the people, its brassy assurance a dig in the nation's ribs, its simplicity as naive as a circus. The two-a-day variety show all of us knew and many of us loved was a complete characterization of a pleasantly gullible, clowning America, physically bestirring itself, sunnily unsophisticated. Its social implications, reflected in the response of the audiences, are pronounced because its enter-

tainment was largely topical fun. The trend of its humor was the march of those times. Thus, vaudeville is an important chapter, not only of the stage, but of America."

It was a time when the nation was confident of its superiority, its moral values, and its happy isolation from the intrigues of the old country, from which many of our parents and grandparents had emigrated.

Vaudeville was destined to leave a greater mark on the musical stage in America than operetta. It had a history just as brief—fifty or so years at most, beginning on October 24, 1881 when Tony Pastor opened his Fourteenth Street house in New York, the first clean show for an audience of men, women, and children. Vaudeville began to wane through the twenties, and ended in 1932 with the changeover at the Palace Theatre from two performances a day to five. Writers were unable to keep the pace and the audience grew tired of the material. E. F. Albee spruced up the acts he booked, and the low comedy and slapstick farce that was a staple of vaudeville disappeared—with it went some of the delight of the customers. The lack of unionization—the organization of vaudeville performers known as the White Rats had failed in their attempt to organize the field—created oppressive conditions for the performers, and as the best ones deserted for more lucrative media, so did their audiences. The nail in vaudeville's coffin was knocked in by the appearance of radio and film.

But in vaudeville's brief heyday, some of the greatest performers of all time had come into their own, and the musical comedy is nothing if not a vehicle for great performers. Comedy grew more and more sophisticated. Music and lyrics were turned out for specialty acts, comedy acts, dance acts, and soubrettes. Pacing for the hectic shows became all-important. And this peculiarly American form of stage entertainment influenced a young boy who would go on to shape the first really good American musicals.

During the gilded age the Broadway musical stage featured three different categories of shows: these included comic operas and operettas, whose American versions began with *Robin Hood* in 1890 and by the 1920s became too ponderous, and revues, nonbook productions whose heyday began with *The Passing Show* in 1894, climaxed with *The Band Wagon* and *As Thousands Cheer* in 1931 and 1933, and then retreated to off-Broadway.

The third category—and the most influential on subsequent American musical theatre—was the creation of one man: George Michael

Cohan. His career dominated Broadway from 1904 until 1920 and ran on until 1928.

Full-grown, Cohan was five feet six inches tall and weighed 140 pounds. He had blue eyes and a pugnacious jaw, and, in the words of Oscar Hammerstein II, "never was a plant more indigenous to a particular part of the earth than was George M. Cohan to the United States."

Hammerstein might as well have been talking about Broadway, for Cohan had fought hard to get there from vaudeville, had truly owned it in his day, and did not let his influence wane without a terrible struggle.

Cohan was born on July 4, 1878 (more likely the day before) and spent his formative years on the road with his mother Nellie, father Jerry, and sister Josie in a vaudeville act. Little Georgie's first star part came at age thirteen in the title role of *Peck's Bad Boy.* It was a role for which the egotistical, arrogant young Georgie was admirably suited, for he was already the scourge of the circuit, responsible for the family's eviction from more than one theatre by stage managers who wouldn't listen to his explanation of how the show business (as it was referred to in those days) should be run. On the road with his family, he made loud demands of management for better lighting, better placement on the bill, and more rehearsal time. His arrogance probably marks the beginning of a trait in the personality of the American theatre director-choreographer that survives to this day.

George ended the family's association with B. F. Keith, the dictator of booking, when he stormed into Keith's office, told him off, and promised that no member of his family would ever work for him again. None ever did.

At the age of fifteen, George told his father that the family ought to head for New York and the big time. His father declined, so George decided to leave the family act and conquer Broadway as a songwriter, playwright, and performer by himself. While he was packing, his father walked in (having learned from the ticket agent at the bus station that George had bought a one-way ticket). He announced that he had changed his mind, and that the family would take George's advice after all and make their assault on the big city. At that moment a subtle change in their relationship occurred, and George took over management of the act from his genial, easygoing father.

The first year in New York was difficult, and the Four Cohans did not find work. Josie, however, was successful as a single, making more money that season as a singer and dancer than the whole family ever had. But she chose not to break up the family act, and after a long, hard climb the family

Book, music, lyrics, production, direction, choreography and starring George Michael Cohan
Archive Photos

began playing the best circuits for top money. By the end of the century the Four Cohans were the top act in American vaudeville.

Cohan was musically illiterate and had no formal education, but he had written songs and sketches for the family act since the age of seventeen. Cohan carried most of the ambition for the family, and it was his constant desire to conquer Broadway. In 1901 he set out to do just that.

His first full-length musical was *The Governor's Son* (book, music, lyrics, direction, and choreography by George M. Cohan). It was an expanded version of one of the family's vaudeville sketches, and it accommodated a fifth Cohan—George's new wife Ethel. The show lasted at Broadway's Savoy Theatre for thirty-two performances. George was twenty-two, and already managers in New York were calling him Mr. Cohan. His second attempt, *Running for Office,* ran forty-eight performances in 1903. It was rewritten as *The Honeymooners* in 1907 and ran for seventy-two more.)

Both shows played short Broadway runs but were hugely successful on tour due to the fame of the Four Cohans, giving George the valuable opportunity of rewriting and redirecting his productions as they played to large audiences across the country. If George M. Cohan was not the first to invent the road tryout, he was the first to make good use of it. His work constantly attempted to entertain the audience, and it was their collaboration (and theirs alone) that he relied on throughout his career.

Perusing the sports news one day, Cohan realized that a jockey was an ideal role, tailor-made both for his own talents—the cocky jockey was a brash and flamboyant character—and for success, representing an American pride that never failed to draw applause. ("What makes the Americans so proud of their country?" someone asks in *Little Johnny Jones.* "Other countries" is the reply.)

Where his first two productions had been vaudeville sketches lengthened for Broadway, *Little Johnny Jones* was written specifically as a full-length musical comedy. He planned to give himself the principal role because his sister, heretofore the most talented of the four, had married—George realized that he could not depend on her for much longer. In fact, Josie and her new husband, also in the business, accepted roles in another Broadway musical that season.

Jones opened in Hartford, Connecticut on October 10, 1904, and the out-of-town audience was enthralled. The most notable ingredient of the show was a flag-waving sentiment that became a hallmark of Cohan productions. A chauvinistic bias permeated this story of an American jockey in

Little Georgie, and the family he would lead to glory
Archive Photos

London. One song in particular, heard for the first time in this musical, electrified the audience:

I'm a Yankee Doodle Dandy,
A Yankee Doodle do or die;
A real live nephew of my Uncle Sam,
Born on the Fourth of July . . .

The musical also featured the early show-biz anthem "Give My Regards to Broadway."

When *Little Johnny Jones* arrived in New York, it was not the unanimous success it had been on the road, though it had a respectable run of 52 performances. However, four Cohans (George's first wife Ethel Levey replaced sister Josie) took it back out on the road. George worked it over and brought it back to Broadway twice—in 1905 for a five-month run, and again in 1907—ultimately earning a good deal of money and acclaim. By then he was without peer in the art of writing and staging a popular musical. He had virtually invented the melodramatic* musical, and had also become one of Broadway's first great stars.

Little Johnny Jones captured the cold commercial eye of Abraham Lincoln Erlanger, the leading figure in The Syndicate, an organization that held a virtual monopoly over the theatre business both in New York and on the road. Erlanger believed that *Little Johnny Jones* had, as much as anything he had yet seen, captured the spirit of the American middle class, and that its lively rhythms, brash performing, and exuberantly American patriotism was the box-office bonanza of the future. He approached Cohan and asked, "Do you think you could write a play without a flag?" Cohan promptly replied, "I could write a play without anything but a pencil."

Erlanger had stars Fay Templeton and Victor Moore under contract at the time, and Cohan fashioned a production specifically for their talents—the first musical he had written for someone other than himself and his family. A road tryout preceded the New York critics' first glimpse.

Erlanger was responsible for the title, on which he insisted after hearing the song that sported it. He was less enthusiastic about almost everything else connected with the production. With a minimum of sets, an unusually tiny chorus (for the time) of only eight girls in calico dresses, he

* The original meaning of "melodrama" was "play with musical accompaniment."

The Four Cohans

Museum of the City of New York

was certain that the musical lacked the bright, decorous quality that audiences wanted.

But Cohan sensed something that Erlanger had not. While audiences might like to watch the rich and dashing, they also like to see themselves on stage, and the world of an ordinary home was just right for them. *Forty Five Minutes From Broadway* opened at the New Amsterdam Theatre on Forty-second Street on January 1, 1906. The musical boasted three acts, with songs—including "So Long, Mary," "Mary's a Grand Old Name," and the title song—featured in only the first and third acts. Cohan reserved the second act to speed the plot along. The story was a melodramatic tearjerker, a shameless play on emotions which audiences responded to if critics did not.

Cohan solidified his success with his fourth show, *George Washington, Jr.*, the third production starring four Cohans. He secured his reputation for patriotism with the song "You're a Grand Old Flag." (Originally it was "Rag" but Cohan altered it when a critic complained that calling the American flag a "rag" was profane.)

By the age of thirty-one, George was crowned with a theatrical dinner—virtually a roast—to which all of Broadway's elite came and applauded.

During a productive career, Cohan wrote a number of plays, including *Broadway Jones* (1912, 176 performances), a straight play that featured him and his parents; *The Song and Dance Man* (1923, 96 performances), in which he played the title role;* *Seven Keys to Baldpate,* in which he turned a successful mystery novel into great stage melodrama (its central character a playwright successful with audiences, but not critics); and *The Tavern.*

The Tavern was based on a bad but intriguing play written by a forty-year-old typist. Cohan reworked it, put it into rehearsal, and was dissatisfied. While the actors waited, he rewrote the play entirely, going back into rehearsal and supplying pages virtually a day ahead of their needs. Finally it was an enormous success.

The Tavern was more than a melodrama. It was a satire on melodrama, the be-all and end-all of melodramas. It begins with a thunderclap, a pistol shot, and a howling wind. Its densely complicated plot features a mysterious stranger, murder, and mayhem. People came out of the rain dry, the thunder was meant to sound like a sound effect, the costuming spanned

* At one point in this show the "song-and-dance-man" says, "Don't ever leave the theatre. There's no happiness for people of the theatre outside the theatre. Take it from me."

George Cohan as Little Johnny Jones
Museum of the City of New York

several centuries within a single character's wardrobe, and the dialogue often referred to the theatricality of it all. "Damned silly, my pretended bravado, but I loved the drama of the thing," one character says.

Atlantic City got it, but New York did not. The opening-night audience sat through much of the play in ignorance of the put-on, and the overnight critics lambasted the show. Then three magazine critics, Robert E. Sherwood (later a playwright himself), Dorothy Parker, and Robert Benchley—the same three who could be heard laughing uproariously in the otherwise silent audience on opening night—wrote accurately and glowingly about the send-up. Future audiences apparently picked up on the tongue-in-cheek humor, and the play grew to become Cohan's greatest success. He took over the lead role and played it in New York and on the road, later revived it, and eventually wrote a sequel (which misfired).

Alone or with partner Sam H. Harris, Cohan produced over seventy-five shows, often "Cohanizing" scripts by others. He proudly claimed that not a single play produced by Cohan and Harris had been untouched by his pencil. Not all of the authors were appreciative—in particular, the original author of *The Tavern,* Cora Dick Gantt, never liked Cohan's version. (Then again, she spent the last fourteen years of her life in a mental institution.)

In Cohan's long career he authored the book, music, and lyrics, and directed and choreographed (or tightly supervised the direction and choreography of) twenty-one musical plays, including . . .

The Talk of New York (1907, 157 performances) began his long association with coproducer Sam Harris.

Fifty Miles from Boston (1908, 32 performances) featured the hit song "Harrigan."

The Yankee Prince (1908, 28 performances) brought the original Four Cohans back together.

The Man Who Owns Broadway (1909, 128 performances) didn't star George, but it gave him the moniker he deserved by then.

The Little Millionaire (1911, 192 performances), a musical without music in the second act, featured George and his parents. His cavalier combination of a play with a musical, which often resulted in long stretches of dialogue without songs in severe defiance of a musical's pacing, never misfired—Cohan always kept the plot moving.

The Royal Vagabond (1919, 208 performances) satirized Cohan's competition by staging a takeoff on operetta, exploding the form much as he had done with melodrama in *Baldpate* and *The Tavern.* As a favor to Isidore Witmark, who had published his first song, he read a yet-to-be produced operetta titled *Cherry Blossoms,* and found it bad, but not quite bad enough. Almost as a joke, and confidently aware that his version would be eminently more entertaining, he rewrote it. Then he and Harris produced it. The opening lyric indicates his attitude toward the operetta form.

Tra la la la, tra la la la
The villagers sing tra la la
In every comic opera it's got to be sung
The villagers, the hes and hers
Are there when the tra la la occurs
The lyric would make you laugh, ha ha!
For that we pay the royalties
They sing in 50 different keys
Here comes the Chefchik, the keeper of the inn
There's got to be an inn
Or a comic opera can't begin

Little Nellie Kelly (1922) was Cohan's most successful run, with 248 performances.

The Rise of Rosie O'Grady (1923, 87 performances) cast a young Ruby Keeler.

Billie (1928, 112 performances) was his last score for Broadway, a musicalization of his own play *Broadway Jones.* By this time Cohan's prestige, if not yet his success with the public, had waned, though one critic still accurately called him "an American institution."

Cohan was a consummate man of the theatre. A close friend and fellow performer said, "George is not the best actor or author or composer or dancer or playwright. But he can dance better than any author, write better than any actor, compose better than any manager, and manage better than any playwright. That makes him a very great man."

A child actor was on the road in one of Cohan's productions when the leading man was replaced with an actor who couldn't dance well enough to perform one number. Cohan asked the child if he could do it. "Maybe," the boy replied. Cohan chastised the boy for not replying in the affirmative at once. "If a director, if a producer, if an author, ever asks you if you can do something—I don't care if he asks you at your present age if you can play Shylock in *The Merchant of Venice*—you tell him yes," Cohan lectured him.

The classic theatre director's line is attributed to Cohan. Returning from a tour, he made a surprise visit to one of his New York productions and assembled the cast. "Rehearsal tomorrow morning at ten to take out all the improvements," he announced. Cohan's biographer is certain that Cohan coined the phrase, "I don't care what you write about me . . . as long as you spell my name right."

James Metcalfe, the drama critic for *Life* magazine wrote about Cohan:

> [I]t is not unusual for a Hebrew to exchange a patronymic which betrays his race for one which will conceal it, but for anyone bearing a good old mouth-filling Irish name as Costigan for a distinctively Hebrew appellation is strange indeed . . .

In addition to exposing his anti-Semitism, Metcalfe got it wrong. He was assuming that Cohan had changed his name from Costigan (his mother's maiden name), and that Cohan was a variant of Cohen. In fact, Cohan's ancestors had changed their name from O'Caomhan when they came to America from Ireland. It was the Irish jig that most influenced Jerry Cohan's tap dancing style, and in turn George's.

Metcalfe went on to describe Cohan's shows accurately, if grudgingly, when he wrote of their "mawkish appeals to the cheapest kind of patriotism" and the use of "chorus and show girls now indispensable to the success of anything on the American stage."

Cohan's musical creations became the epitome of one of the two extremes of American musical comedy at the turn of the century. In the end, Cohan's style triumphed over operetta. These Cohan lyrics clearly expressed his feelings about the Broadway he had wanted to conquer (and change) since he was a teenager:

Same old songs about the same old moon,
Few new words but the same old tune;
Dashing on before us,
We see the merry chorus
And everything they do, you know's been done;
You hear the same old joke,
That make the same old hit,
The scenery's just the same
But its been painted up a bit;
You can ask most any showman,
Inquire of Charley Frohman,
And he'll say there's nothing new beneath the sun.

Cohan wrote book musical entertainments he was convinced audiences wanted, and he was proved correct. Although critics throughout his career refused to praise him and found his brand of theatre cheap, vulgar, and popular, audiences supported him for two decades.

Augustus Thomas, a prominent playwright of the time who was unable to contain his disapproval of the new, nonformalistic approach and the popular vulgarity of the Cohan entertainments, one day asked him archly, "On what lines do you construct your plays, Mr. Cohan?"

"Principally on the New York, New Haven and Hartford—and once in a while on the Pennsylvania," Cohan replied.

Cohan is probably the twentieth century's earliest example of an artist who so satisfied the populace that critical reviews couldn't stop his juggernaut. Academics have long maligned Broadway for its emphasis on crass entertainment over edifying art. The whole twentieth-century history of Broadway contradicts this belief. The very idea that entertainment isn't art, can't be art, or that art shouldn't be entertaining misunderstands the meaning of art itself.

Cohan's work forms the link between nineteenth century musical entertainments—spectacle, burlesque, minstrel shows, and vaudeville—and the American musical. More succinctly, Cohan *modernized* the American musical. He was the champion and principal creator of the form that battled operetta for transcendence, and he won. He *Americanized* the form as well, for all the great operetta composers had been born and trained in Europe.

But it was Cohan's staging more than his writing which left a lasting impression. He defined it himself when he said, "Speed! Speed! And lots of it! That's the idea of the thing. Perpetual motion!"

Cecil Smith wrote:

> Whatever the merits of their content, Cohan's musical comedies introduced a wholly new conception of delivery, tempo and subject matter into a form of entertainment that was rapidly dying for want of new ideas of any kind. Brushing aside the artificial elegances based on English and German models, he reproduced successfully the hardness, the compensating sentimentality, and the swift movement of New York life, which, except for surface sophistications, has not changed much between then and now.

Until Cohan, characters on the legitimate stage spoke well, no matter who they were. Cohan used slang to the delight of his audiences, if not the critics. Irving Berlin gave Cohan credit for bringing ragtime to the Broadway musical score. He popularized dancing by a male lead, identified the audience's hunger for home-grown stories, and brought slick stagecraft to the musical.

On January 31, 1914, during curtain calls for *Broadway Jones,* Cohan's parents Jerry and Nellie announced their retirement. In 1916 Cohan's sister Josie died; a 1973 biography insisted that the cause of death was heart disease due to a lifetime of "strenuous dancing"—an absurd idea. In 1917, his father Jerry died.

This double tragedy sent George into a tailspin of grief. His family had been the bedrock of his early life, and George's father was his greatest influence—he carried his father's opinions for life. The sturdiness of the Cohan family pervaded George's writing. It also gave him the confidence to deal with an ungainly profession, and probably it allowed him to do without a wide circle of intimate friends. His family had been his only world beyond the theatre. In later years he sometimes thought he saw his deceased father watching him from the wings.

The most dramatic period of George Cohan's life centered on the formation of Actors' Equity Association, several years later. Cohan always treated his actors well. He paid them for rehearsal, he was solicitous of the conditions in which they worked, and—like his father—his word was his bond, and it was always honored. But other managers were not as loyal to their employees. In those pre-union days, actors were not paid for rehearsals, which lasted as long as the managers deemed appropriate. (Sometimes producers were still raising money during rehearsals.) Actors were often fired at a moment's notice, sometimes simply because they had already garnered excellent notices for the show and another, less expensive actor could be put in their place. Their salary could be reduced randomly. They were often stranded out of town when a show closed, and they paid for their own wardrobe. As a producer, Cohan imposed none of these conditions, but he was unwilling to let go of the idea that conditions should be dictated by his prerogatives.

In 1919, the recently formed Actors' Equity Association struck Broadway for better working conditions. It was during a summer when more than forty productions were making money for their producers and theatre owners hand over fist. Other managers capitulated.

Cohan was not disposed toward unions. (He had been angered earlier when *Seven Keys to Baldpate* had moved from the Astor Theatre at Forty-fifth Street to the Gaiety Theatre at Forty-sixth Street—the stagehands' union had insisted that the move made the production a road show, and required three additional stagehands.) Cohan refused to consider the proposal for a standard Equity contract. Because of his fame, he became a kind of lightning rod for actors' dissatisfaction. The man who had treated actors so well now found himself having to stand in as the symbol for their enmity. Gunshots were fired at his house, which only sealed Cohan's opposition.

Sam Harris, his partner and friend at the time, was more pragmatic and less stubborn and accepted the union, but Cohan never did. They dissolved their partnership, and agreed never to disclose the reason. Cohan was greatly saddened by the whole affair. He was the only actor who never joined Equity, and he never performed under their contract.

By 1940, Cohan felt badly that the theatre had passed him by. Intransigent in his style and interests, his scripts were more and more old-fashioned, and his performing depended on his scripts. He disliked performing in those of others, though he had been successful in the musical *I'd Rather Be Right* as President Franklin Roosevelt, and in Eugene O'Neill's play *Ah, Wilderness!* Cohan's last play—and his last performance—was an unsuccessful sequel to *The Tavern* titled *The Return of the Vagabond.* He died in the fall of 1942.

Monuments to his talent include a bronze statue on the island where Broadway and Seventh Avenue cross Forty-seventh street; "Over There," the song he composed for American servicemen in World War I; the 1968 Broadway musical *George M,* written by Mike Stewart and John and Fran Pascal around the songs of Cohan, featuring Joel Grey as Cohan, directed and choreographed by Joe Layton; and the 1943 biographical film *Yankee Doodle Dandy.* James Cagney's impersonation of Cohan is probably the image most people carry in their minds of the inimitable Cohan verve. Cagney had seen him perform, and copied his dancing style.

Neither the tenets of Victor Herbert's operettas nor the pacing of George M. Cohan's musical comedies were lost on the emerging form of the American musical. The beauty of a romantically-scored, lushly-designed musical was first brought to Broadway by Herbert, Friml, and Romberg. The core of the American musical, however, is descended from vaudeville and the writing and directing of George M. Cohan. He was the father of the American musical in its heyday.

Within the immense complexity of the modern American musical lies a valuable inheritance from these two vastly different forms that dominated musicals in the first two decades of the twentieth century. They were the formidable parents of the modern musical, and the stage was set for the first great work in the emerging musical theatre—a work that would not only be a commercial success and an artistic triumph, but would live to become an enduring American classic.

Before *Show Boat* graced the Broadway stage with its unique combination of operetta and Cohan entertainment, however, the "princess musicals" would revolutionize the American musical stage and create the format within which both styles could coexist.

The Princess Theatre

F. RAY COMSTOCK, Manager

"NEW YORK'S SMARTEST PLAYHOUSE"

FIRE NOTICE

LOOK AROUND NOW AND CHOOSE THE NEAREST EXIT TO YOUR SEAT. IN CASE OF FIRE WALK, (NOT RUN) TO THAT EXIT. DO NOT TRY TO BEAT YOUR NEIGHBOR TO THE STREET.

ROBERT ADAMSON, Fire Commissioner.

WEEK BEGINNING MONDAY, MARCH 6, 1916

MATINEES WEDNESDAY AND SATURDAY

THE MARBURY-COMSTOCK COMPANY Presents

VERY GOOD EDDIE

Book by Philip Bartholomae and Guy Bolton

Lyrics by Schuyler Greene — Music by Jerome Kern

Founded on the Farce "Over-Night"

CAST OF CHARACTERS

(In the order of appearance)

STEWARD on "The Catskill" .... Benjamin F. Wright
MONSIEUR DE ROUGEMENT .... Mr. James Lounsbery
PURSER on "The Catskill" .... Lew Fullerton
DICK RIVERS .... Oscar Shaw
MME. MATROPPO .... Ada Lewis
ELSIE LILLY .... Anna Orr
EDDIE KETTLE .... Ernest Truex
GEORGINA KETTLE, his wife .... Helon Raymor
MAGAZINE GIRL .... Genevia Sinc

(Program Continued on Page 4)

MAXINE ELLIOTT'S THEATRE

FIRE NOTICE

Look around NOW and choose the nearest Exit to your seat. In case of fire walk (not run) to THAT Exit. Do not try to beat your neighbor to the street.

ROBERT ADAMSON, Fire Commissioner.

This theatre does not advertise in the "New York Times."

TENTH WEEK—BEGINNING MONDAY, JUNE 21, 1915, Matinees Wednesday and Saturday.

F. RAY COMSTOCK Presents

NOBODY HOME

By GUY BOLTEN and PAUL RUBENS.

Music by JEROME KERN and Others.

(The Marbury-Comstock Co., Proprietors)

Note—Students of American slang, and the numerous authors claiming priority in the use of the phrase, "Nobody Home," may be interested in knowing that Charles Dickens makes use of the expression in "Nicholas Nickleby." Squeers, in presenting Smike to a visitor, indicates the poor imbecile's lack of balance by tapping his forehead significantly with the remark "Nobody home, no matter how hard you knock." Dickens himself unquestionably took the expression from an epigram by Alexander Pope, who died in 1744 and whose saying was paraphrased by William Cowper, as follows:
"You beat your pate, and fancy wit will come;
Knock as you please, there's Nobody at Home."

Characters

(Named in the order of their appearance)

Maurice, assistant manager, Hotel Blitz .... Tom Graves
Bell Boy, at the Blitz .... Quentin Tod

PROGRAM CONTINUED ON SECOND PAGE FOLLOWING.

F. RAY COMSTOCK'S

PRINCESS THEATRE

104 West 39th Street, New York City.

NEW YORK'S SMARTEST PLAYHOUSE

F. RAY COMSTOCK .... Manager

HARRY BROWN, JR. .... Business Manager

FIRE NOTICE

Look around NOW and choose the nearest Exit to your seat. In case of fire walk (not run) to THAT Exit. Do not try to beat your neighbor to the street.

ROBERT ADAMSON, Fire Commissioner.

WEEK BEGINNING MONDAY EVENING, MARCH 26, 1917.

Matinees Wednesday and Saturday.

THE COMSTOCK-ELLIOTT COMPANY Presents

The Fourth New York Princess Theatre Musical Production

"OH, BOY!"

Book and Lyrics by Guy Bolton and P. G. Wodehouse

Music by Jerome Kern

Staged by Edward Royce

Cast of Characters

(In the order of their appearance)

FULTON THEATRE

46th Street, Just West of Broadway

DILLER THEATRE CORPORATION, Lessee

C. B. Dillingham, President — A. L. Erlanger, Vice-President

NOTICE: This Theatre, with every seat occupied, can be emptied in less than three minutes. Choose NOW the Exit nearest to your seat, and in case of fire walk (do not run) to that Exit.

THOMAS J. DRENNAN, Fire Commissioner.

WEEK BEGINNING MONDAY EVENING, MAY 12, 1924

Matinees Wednesday and Saturday

F. RAY COMSTOCK AND MORRIS GEST Present

SITTING PRETTY

A Musical Comedy by BOLTON, WODEHOUSE and KERN

—with—

QUEENIE SMITH

LIBERTY THEATRE

42nd STREET West of BROADWAY

KLAW & ERLANGER Managers

The Klaw & Erlanger Amusement Co., Owners.

THIS THEATRE, UNDER NORMAL CONDITIONS, WITH EVERY SEAT OCCUPIED, CAN BE EMPTIED IN LESS THAN THREE MINUTES. LOOK AROUND NOW, CHOOSE THE NEAREST EXIT TO YOUR SEAT, AND IN CASE OF DISTURBANCE OF ANY KIND, TO AVOID THE DANGERS OF PANIC, WALK (DO NOT RUN) TO THAT EXIT.

WEEK BEGINNING MONDAY EVENING, JANUARY 15, 1917.

Matinees Wednesday and Saturday.

HENRY W. SAVAGE Offers

The New Musical Comedy

HAVE A HEART

Book and Lyrics by Guy Bolton and P. G. Wodehouse

Music by Jerome Kern

Staged by Edward Royce

Characters

(In the order of their appearance)

Henry, the elevator boy at Schoonmaker's .... Billy B. Van
Ted Sheldon .... Donald Macdonald
Lizzie O'Brien .... Marjorie Gateson
Detective Baker, of the Blueport Police .... Eugene Keith
Rutherford Schoonmaker, proprietor of the Schoonmaker Department Store .... Thurston Hall
Captain Charles Owen .... Roy Gordon
Peggy Schoonmaker .... Eileen Van Biene
Mrs. Pyne, Peggy's aunt .... Flavia Arcaro
Matthew Pyne .... James Bradbury
Dolly Brabazon .... Louise Dresser
Yussuf, the entertainer .... Joseph del Puente
Maitre d'Hotel .... Eugene Revere
Georgia .... Peggy Fears

PROGRAM CONTINUED ON SECOND PAGE FOLLOWING

F. RAY COMSTOCK'S

PRINCESS THEATRE

104 West 39th Street, New York City.

NEW YORK'S SMARTEST PLAYHOUSE

F. RAY COMSTOCK .... Manager

HARRY BROWN, JR. .... Business Manager and Treasurer

FIRE NOTICE

Look around NOW and choose the nearest Exit to your seat. In case of fire walk (not run) to THAT Exit. Do not try to beat your neighbor to the street.

THOMAS J. DRENNAN, Fire Commissioner.

WEEK BEGINNING MONDAY EVENING, JUNE 3, 1918.

Regular Matinees Wednesday and Saturday.

F. RAY COMSTOCK and WILLIAM ELLIOTT Present

The Fifth New York Princess Theatre Musical Production

OH, LADY! LADY!!

Book and Lyrics by Guy Bolton and P. G. Wodehouse

Music by Jerome Kern

Staged by Robert Milton and Edward Royce

Cast of Characters

(In the order of their appearance)

Parker .... Constance Binney
Mollie Farringdon .... Vivienne Segal
Mrs. Farringdon .... Margaret Dale
Willoughby French .... Carl Randall
Hale Underwood .... Harry C. Browne
Spike Hudgins, Willoughby Finch's valet .... Edward Abeles
Fanny Welch .... Florence Shirley
May Barber .... Carroll McComas
Cyril Twombley .... Reginald Mason
William Watty .... Harry Fisher
Miss Lettice Romayne .... Gladys Dore
Miss Lotta Pommery .... Bobby Brewster
Miss Della Catesson .... May Elsie
Miss Hallie Butt .... Patricia Clarke
Miss Sal Munn .... Dorothy Allan
Miss Marie Schino .... Jane Carroll

PROGRAM CONTINUED ON SECOND PAGE FOLLOWING

THE PRINCESS MUSICALS

The whole growth of our musical comedy can be seen through the growth of integration.

—LEONARD BERNSTEIN

World War I took away many young composers, and the quality of the great light operas of Europe began to suffer. The Central Powers—nationalities popular in the romantic plots—were increasingly seen as the enemy. Operettas became unpatriotic. When America entered the war, the epoch of European imports ended quickly. World War I ushered in the American era of the great theatre musicals because it gave an opportunity to so many young American writers who were ready, willing, and able to take over. These writers, like America itself, were tired of the classically-based European music and yearned for melodies and rhythms more expressive of the American character.

Irving Berlin was already at the top by 1915, but George Gershwin was only twenty years old when he wrote his first show, *La, La, Lucille,* in 1919. Oscar Hammerstein II was twenty-four in 1920 when he wrote his, *Always You.* Richard Rodgers and Lorenz Hart, eighteen and twenty-five years old, wrote their first show, *Poor Little Ritz Girl,* in 1920. Vincent Youmans was twenty-one years old in 1921 when he and the twenty-five-year-old Ira Gershwin (under the pseudonym Arthur Francis) wrote *Two Little Girls in Blue.* Cole Porter had gotten an earlier start, and hit his stride at the ripe old age of thirty-one with the *Greenwich Village Follies of 1924.* But the first and most influential on the form and art of the American musical was Jerome Kern.

Kern was born in New York and learned the piano from his mother. He studied piano and harmony for a year at the New York College of Music, then theory and composition in London. Like many great melodists, he had been writing songs all along, starting with school plays, and playing them for anyone who would listen.

In London in 1903 or 1904 he wrote songs for Alfred Butt, the assistant manager of the Palace Music Hall, and for Seymour Hicks and George Edwardes, musical comedy producers. He also obtained a curious job from West End producer Charles Frohman. English audiences at the turn of the century arrived fashionably late to the theatre, and Kern was hired to compose songs unrelated to the evening's presentation that could be performed while people were still being seated.

At the Gaiety Theatre, Kern provided songs for musical comedy star and producer George Grossmith, Jr. (himself the son of a principal Gilbert and Sullivan comedian), who had a special reason for needing them. He was Gertie Millar's leading man, and in real life Ms. Millar was Mrs. Lionel Monckton, principal melodist of the Edwardian musical. Her husband saw to it that she had the best songs, so Grossmith had to look elsewhere for material. He found

> a penniless little Jewish song writer who hailed from America, but made his home in London. I knew him as Jerry Kern and liked him immediately. He came often to my house and played to us. He played divinely, like nearly all his kind, with a tremendous gift of 'tune.' He was the only one I could detect in a barren field likely to fill the shoes of Monckton, Paul Rubens and Leslie Stuart.

Kern returned to Broadway and worked as a song plugger for the Lyceum Publishing Company, then as a salesman for the famous Max

Dreyfuss of T. B. Harms. Since Harms was deeply involved with the theatre scene through the publishing of show scores, Kern began to meet many people involved in Broadway musicals and soon proved his value as a rehearsal pianist. Not shy about his own compositions, he would play his songs during lunch and rehearsal breaks for anyone who would listen. (One of the secrets of interpolation is that, when compared to material that has been heard over and over during rehearsal, new songs are bound to seem fresh.) This accounts for Kern's popularity as a rehearsal pianist among producers. Writing this way for the theatre, he developed a keen eye for plot and character requirements and the placement of material, skills which would show up in his later work on full scores.

Soon Kern was a respected young songwriter, contributing interpolations to many operettas and revues. Because Kern was interpolating songs in so many shows, he digested both the florid, openly romantic, wider-ranged songs of the Viennese school and the English musicals, all imitating Gilbert and Sullivan shows, and usually written for weak-voiced leads.

Kern's earliest critical notice came from Alan Dale (Alfred Cohen), who said of *Mr. Wix of Wickham* (1904), for which the nineteen-year-old Kern wrote five songs:

> [I]ts music, by Jerome D. Kern, towers in such an Eiffel way, above the average hurdy-gurdy, penny-in-the-slot, primitive accompaniment to the musical show that criticism is disarmed and Herbert Karnley's weak and foolish 'book' sterilized.

The Eiffel Tower remark followed Kern throughout his career, as did Dale, one of his earliest and staunchest supporters.

Kern hit his musical comedy stride with two songs in 1914: *The Laughing Husband* contained "You're Here and I'm Here," which became a hugely successful dance song, and "They Didn't Believe Me," interpolated into *The Girl From Utah,* for which Kern also served as rehearsal pianist. "They Didn't Believe Me" is now considered by many musicologists as the father of great musical comedy songs, a graceful, unhackneyed melody ("as natural as walking," said Alec Wilder), unusual harmonies, and a climactic key change all set a new, modern style. Its 4/4 meter effectively pushed aside forever the 3/4 waltz meter for Broadway's favorite ballads. Kern was also partially responsible for the first saxophones in a Broadway pit when for *Oh,*

I Say! (1913) with orchestrations by Frank Saddler, and he began to incorporate jazz into his Broadway scores.

Soon Kern was looking to write musicals that were less of a patched-together nature. The Shubert brothers were the first producers to champion Kern as the principal composer of a new show. His score for the first Western musical comedy, *The Red Petticoat* (1912), suffered no interpolations by other composers, an extraordinary occurrence for the higgledy-piggledy approach of the times. It journeyed to three Broadway theatres but ran only sixty-one performances.

That same year the Princess Theatre was built at 104 West Thirty-ninth Street, somewhat south of the principal theatre district, whose southern boundary had been established as Forty-second Street with the construction of the glamorous New Amsterdam Theatre in 1903. The Princess contained only 299 seats. A single aisle ran down the middle of fourteen rows, and there was a small balcony with two rows. There were also two boxes on each side, one above the other.

This little jewel of a theatre opened with a program of one-act plays adapted from gory paperback thrillers and produced in the Grand Guignol style. These productions did not succeed. F. Ray Comstock was an ambitious manager who shortly afterward bought out two of the three owners (not the Shuberts, who may have never sold a theatre in their lives). By 1915 he was having difficulty finding attractions for his theatre.

At that point Elizabeth "Bessie" Marbury suggested to Comstock a series of small musicals with the idea that

> . . . everyone is reforming the drama. Various societies are doing their best to elevate it. It seems to me that now is the time for someone to do the same thing for musical comedy. (as recorded by Stanley Green in *The World of Musical Comedy*)

Comstock not only accepted the idea—he took on Marbury as his co-producer.

Marbury was a successful literary and actor's agent, already credited with convincing writers to demand a percentage of gross instead of accepting a flat fee, who managed and promoted the famous dancers Irene and Vernon Castle. She was well read, had a deep voice and a large figure, and dressed mannishly. Guy Bolton called her a "charming and benign elephant," and P. G. Wodehouse labeled her "dear, kindly, voluminous, Bessie Marbury." Though she had sued Comstock in 1913 for plagiarism on behalf of a client (Wodehouse said she once went "nose to bosom" with Comstock), apparently this did not deter them from working together.

Comstock and Marbury could not afford a big Broadway name—Marbury suggested Jerome Kern. Comstock knew Kern because Comstock had coproduced *Fascinating Flora* (1907) at the Casino Theatre, for which Kern had written a number of songs, though only one ended up in the show.

"Costume" musicals were still the biggest draw. The theatre industry was decidedly wary of the new concept and the venture itself was risky. On the other hand, by the time their first musical was announced, "Barnes's South African Moving Pictures" were being shown at the Princess Theatre, so Comstock didn't have much to lose.

For their first show at the Princess Theatre, Comstock and Marbury asked Paul Rubens to adapt his successful English play *Mr. Popple (of Ippleton).* They changed the name to *Nobody Home,* from Dickens's *Nicholas Nickleby,* in which Squeers hits Smike on the head and says, "Nobody home!" At a total capitalization of $7,500, there was no money for an out-of-town tryout, so friends were invited to a dress rehearsal.

It was a disaster.

The producers wanted to doctor it and closed the show for two weeks. This was the chance Kern had been waiting for. He convinced the producers to replace bookwriter Rubens with Guy Bolton.

St. George Guy Reginald Bolton's childhood had been lonely. His mother died of alcoholism and his father retreated into depression. Extreme shyness kept him from making friends, and he relied on his older sister for companionship. Bolton studied engineering and embarked on a career as an architect, but wrote stories at night. In 1904 he sold his first story to *Smart Set* magazine. In 1910 an acquaintance asked him to collaborate on a play. Although their play was performed only once (as a benefit for the Bide-A-Wee Society for stray cats and dogs), Bolton thereafter focused exclusively on theatre writing (with the exception of a few trips to Hollywood to write screenplays). Throughout his life he threw himself into prodigious amounts of work while fumbling through four marriages, chasing chorus girls, and ignoring his children.

Bolton had met Jerome Kern when they worked on *Ninety in the Shade. Shade* had lyrics by Harry B. Smith. Staged by Robert Milton, starring Marie Cahill, and produced by Cahill's husband, it was tried out in

Syracuse. Kern and Bolton had worked hard to integrate the songs into the book, featuring smooth lead-ins as well as character and plot choices that would soon revolutionize American musical entertainment. Stars Cahill and Richard Carle, however, used the out-of-town tryout to return the work to a more traditional format. When the show arrived on Broadway on January 25, 1915, it flopped. Miss Cahill filed for bankruptcy and had to go back to vaudeville to recoup. Never one to give up a melody easily, Kern eventually reused most of what he wrote for *Shade* in future shows.

But Kern and Bolton had planted the seed of a musical style that would shortly revolutionize the American musical. For one thing, because of the dance craze sweeping the ballrooms of America—which began in 1911 with Irving Berlin's "Alexander's Ragtime Band"—almost all of Kern's melodies were designed for dancing.

Nobody Home had two sets instead of the dozen or more typical of the operettas; a chorus of eight to twelve, all dancers (operettas often employed ninety); eleven musicians (operettas used forty-five); young, inexpensive performers; and writers not so well known. Since box office income (at $1.50 per seat, the potential gross was only $3,588 a week) could not sustain the kind of extravagant operetta that was the norm on Broadway at the time, the authors were called upon to create a fast-moving story with musical numbers for the principals growing easily out of the book.

Together Bolton and Kern made substantial changes on the uneven *Nobody Home.* They discarded all the music, reset the story in America, rewrote all night, and rehearsed all day. A potpourri of lyricists and composers worked on the new show, yet one senses (primarily from his own personality) that Kern was the driving force behind it all, and he was devoted to the sharpness and integration that Bolton was providing.

To Kern and Bolton, the limited resources of the producer and the small theatre gave them just the opportunity they were looking for. With less distraction from production elements, their songs and comedy, in addition to standing on their own, had to carry the action forward consistently, and thus had to be *an integral part of the plot* in order to keep the audience interested. Thus, Kern and Bolton stumbled upon another important concept for the developing musical form: trite and banal books will destroy a score. When Kern was interpolating his tunes into the revues and operettas, the audience was content to appreciate the melodies on their own, but as the musical numbers became more integrated within the show, they depended increasingly on the quality of the book for ultimate effect.

Since the new songs were carrying their own responsibilities regarding the dramatic action, their effectiveness depended not just on the melody, but on how well they told their part of the story. The degree to which the writers succeeded in capturing the emotional content of the scene in music and lyrics became as important as the quality of the song itself.

The revised version of *Nobody Home* opened on April 20, 1915, two weeks late, and was a hit. It played 135 performances in New York, moving from the Princess to a larger theatre after two months in order to increase the potential gross. Eventually there were three road companies. The musical was probably the fastest-paced show on Broadway, Cohan's work excepted, and featured smooth lead-ins to the songs—a previously unheard-of technique. Additionally, the show's sophisticated decor and dresses—done inexpensively by cast member Elsie DeWolfe, Marbury's lover—became popular in an era when society looked to the theatre for cultural guidance.

Before the next Princess Theatre musical was created, one small event may (or may not) have taken place which has since become part of theatrical legend. Kern was still writing songs for insertion into London musicals, and had booked a transatlantic voyage. He stayed up all night playing poker or composing, slept late and missed his intended departure on the *Lusitania.* When the ship was sunk by a German U-boat, producer Charles Frohman went down with it. Harry B. Smith also claims to have been invited for the crossing, but declined.

• • •

For their next show, Comstock and Marbury chose *Over Night,* a successful farce by Philip Bartholomew, a young, handsome millionaire who had abandoned his family business for the theatre. Bartholomew adapted his play into a musical, Schuyler Greene was enlisted to write the lyrics, and Kern composed the majority of the songs. There was a tryout in Schenectady, New York, whereupon the production closed. It was rewritten and recast. The choreographer was replaced. New lyrics were written by Herbert Reynolds (a.k.a. M. E. Rourke). And once more, Guy Bolton came in and doctored the book.

A second tryout took place in Cincinnati, then the musical opened at the Princess Theatre on December 23, 1915. The title was changed to match the last line of Batholomew's original script, so the show was called *Very Good, Eddie* and ended with that line. (Comedian Fred Stone had made this phrase popular when he spoke it to his dummy in the previous season's *Chin Chin.*)

Very Good, Eddie was an instant hit. As with *Nobody Home,* the producers abandoned the Princess Theatre for a larger venue (and income), moving to the Casino Theatre and then the 1,200-seat Lyceum. They returned the show to the Princess before its 341-performance run ended, after which it spawned two road companies. It was revived in 1976 by the Goodspeed Opera house, then transferred to Broadway by David Merrick, where it ran a season and toured.

The new American musical form was thus a complete success within two productions. If the first was somewhat of a compromise, being a bold, if not complete, step in the right direction, the second was a more finished product in the new structure.

Eddie's book was even tighter than the book of *Nobody Home.* The score supported the book, and songs grew out of the drama. Bolton's writing had improved overall, and the traditional musical comedy jokes were replaced with humor that grew out of character and situation.

• • •

During *Eddie*'s opening night performance, Jerry Kern came over to where Bolton stood leaning on the back-rail, his face pale, his lips moving as if in prayer.

"How do you think it's going?" he asked.

Guy came out of his trance.

"I'm too numb to tell. There's a man in large spectacles over there in the tenth row who seems to be enjoying it."

Jerry glanced in the direction indicated.

"Wodehouse," he said.

"I suppose it is," said Guy, "but that's only to be expected on an opening night. The question is, what's it going to be like tomorrow?"

"What on earth are you talking about?"

"You said it's a good house."

"I didn't. I said Wodehouse."

"Oh, you mean his *name* is Woodhouse?"

(For the benefit of the uninitiated, that is the way it is pronounced.)

"That's right. Plum Wodehouse."

A gentleman in the last row, down whose neck Jerry was breathing, turned.

"I've no doubt what you two are saying is a lot funnier than what's going on on the stage," he said, "but I can't follow the two plots at once."

"Sorry," said Guy, cringing, "Actually what's going on on the stage is very funny indeed."

"Sez you," said the man in the last row morosely.

The team-mates withdrew to the balcony stairs and sat down on them. A decent five or six feet now separated them from the audience.

Any old night is a wonderful night
If you're there with a wonderful girl . . .

sang Oscar Shaw.

"Lousy lyric," said Kern.

A standee turned to them.

"Look," he said, "if you don't like this show, why don't you get out?"

The pair withdrew to the lobby. If you applied an eye to the crack of the folding doors, the stage could still be seen. The doorman, who had been using this vantage-point to watch the proceedings, obligingly made way for them. Guy squinted through the crack.

"What has Ada Lewis done to her face?" he muttered anxiously. "She looks most peculiar."

"That isn't her face," said the doorman. "She's walking on her hands. Saving her face for the last act."

Guy eyed the honest fellow with displeasure.

"We should have come to you for some gags," he said coldly.

"Why didn't you?" said the doorman. "I'd have been glad to help out if I'd known the show was supposed to be funny."

"How's it going?" Jerry asked Guy.

"It seems to be going all right."

"What's happening in there?" said Jerry. "Have the customers rushed the stage yet?"

"Not yet," Bolton replied. "And that chap with the spectacles is laughing again."

The lights on the stage dimmed for the "Babes in the Wood" number.

Give me your hand:
You'll understand

We're off to slumberland . . .sang Ernie Truex in a cracked voice.

"God!" said Jerry. "You never know what words are going to sound like till you hear them with a first-night audience. Why don't you get Plum to do your lyrics?"

"Does he write lyrics?"

"He certainly does. I did half a dozen numbers with him for a thing in London called *The Beauty of Bath.* One of them—'Mister Chamberlain'—used to get ten encores every night. As a lyric writer he's the cat's pyjamas."

"Rather a dated expression," said Guy coldly.

The audience began to stream into the tiny lobby. The man with the spectacles came up to them.

"Oh, hullo, Jerry," he said.

"Hello," said Kern. "This is Bolton. You two fellows ought to know each other."

Guy and Plum shook hands.

"I hope you liked the show," said Guy.

"Best thing I ever saw in my life."

"I wonder," said Guy, "if you would mind stepping over behind that man with the crumpled shirt-front and the rumpled hair? He is the *Tribune* critic."

They moved to where Heywood Broun was chatting with Alexander Woollcott.

"What did you think of our little entertainment, Mr. Wodehouse?" asked Guy in a clear, carrying voice.

"Not bad," said Plum.

After the final curtain Jerry took them to his apartment on West 68th Street. There they were joined by a group of English friends who were appearing at Dillingham's Globe Theatre in *Tonight's the Night.* Fay Compton was there, and Lawrie Grossmith and his brother George, also Lawrie's brother-in-law, Vernon Castle, with his wife and dancing partner, Irene. They were all eager for news of *Very Good, Eddie.*

The two interested parties had decided they would wait up for the notices. They were glad to have company for part of the night. Jerry took his place at the piano, Fay stood beside it and sang. Two or three of the girls were working away in the kitchen making sandwiches.

Plum and Guy gravitated to a corner. "Do you think *Eddie* got over?" said Guy.

"I think it's a smash. I was listening to the audience as they came out. The woman ahead of me said it was the cat's pyjamas."

"Really?" said Guy, beaming. "The cat's pyjamas—one of my favorite expressions. Very clever and original. By the way Jerry Kern used it about you."

"Me?"

"Yes, as a writer. He says you write good lyrics. Have you done any over here?"

"Not yet. But only the other day I missed landing a big job by a hair-breadth. Somebody gave me an introduction to Lee Shubert, and I raced round to his office. 'Good morning, Mr. Shubert,' I said. 'I write lyrics. Can I do some for you?' 'No,' said Lee Shubert. Just imagine if he had said 'Yes.' It was as near as that."

"Would you like to join Jerry and Me?"

"I'd love it."

"Then let's get together."

The Bolton diary of this date has the following entry:

> "*Eddie* opened. Excellent reception. All say hit. To Kerns for supper. Talked with P. G. Wodehouse, apparently known as Plum. Never heard of him, but Jerry says he writes lyrics, so, being slightly tight, suggested we team up. W. so overcome couldn't answer for a minute, then grabbed my hand and stammered out his thanks."

Turning to the Wodehouse diary, we find:

> "Went to opening of *Very Good, Eddie.* Enjoyed it in spite of lamentable lyrics. Bolton, evidently conscious of this weakness, offered partnership. Tried to hold back and weight the suggestion, but his eagerness so pathetic that consented. Mem: Am I too impulsive? Fight against this tendency."

• • •

I ought to tell you now that the preceding section was written by Guy Bolton and P. G. Wodehouse for their book *Bring on the Girls,* one of the funniest theatre memoirs ever penned. Its veracity is highly suspect, since both Bolton and Wodehouse were humorous fiction writers with extraordinary imaginations. One diligent historian has tracked down the startling news that *Tonight's the Night* had already closed and the cast gone to London by the time of the opening-night party for *Eddie.* On the other hand, the very tone of the writing probably tells us more about the Princess musicals than could any academic prose.

So Bolton, Wodehouse, and Kern agreed to write musicals together, and they wrote a great many. "Musicals," Wodehouse wrote later, "are like salted almonds. You can always write one more." They were a potent and interesting triumvirate. The tall Wodehouse towered over the very short Bolton and Kern, and in publicity photos they invariably made him sit down.

Pelham Grenville "Plum" Wodehouse was born in Guilford, England in 1881, and narrowly avoided an unsuitable career in banking by writing numerous short stories and sending them out in large quantities. He first began to succeed when he returned from a trip to New York, which gave him something to write about that London's editors found original. But America's bright energy seduced the young man, and he returned, never to live full-time in England again. He found success with short stories and novels written for the *Saturday Evening Post* and dramatic criticism for *Vanity Fair,* which explains his presence—in a good and complimentary seat—at the opening night of *Very Good, Eddie.*

The first full show the three wrote together was not, however, for Ray Comstock or the Princess Theatre. Marc Klaw and Abe Erlanger, who ran the New Amsterdam Theatre, commissioned the trio to rewrite a Viennese operetta. The music was written by Emmerich Kalman, with interpolations by Jerome Kern, a new book by Bolton, and lyrics by Wodehouse. *Miss Springtime* (originally *Little Miss Springtime,* until Erlanger decreed that nothing little would ever play his theatres) opened on September 25, 1916, succeeded, and ran approximately 230 performances at the New Amsterdam.

It was Comstock who stalled the trio's arrival at the Princess. He called them in for a meeting, and pitched a play for adaptation that the writers did not see as a musical. They pitched him two ideas of their own, but he stuck with his project, and proved them right. The play was called *Go To It,* featured a corpse, had little song-and-dance justification, and flopped when lesser, obviously hungrier, writers took up Comstock's assignment, and the Princess Theatre musicals almost came to a premature end.

The Princess Theatre trio—Bolton and Kern always made Wodehouse sit for publicity photos
Museum of the City of New York/Vanity Fair

Bolton, Wodehouse, and Kern next created *Have a Heart* for producer Colonel Henry Savage. Marbury had arranged to use Savage, and presumably Comstock considered her disloyal and eliminated her as his coproducer from all future productions at the Princess.

Have a Heart tried out in Atlantic City, Reading, Pennsylvania, and Wilmington, Delaware; underwent some recasting and rewriting on the road; and opened on January 11, 1917 at the Liberty Theatre, where it ran for only seventy-six performances. Of all the critics, only young George S. Kaufman, writing for *The New York Times* (one of a dozen influential newspapers at the time), gave it a negative review. Savage kept it on the road successfully for six years.

It was with *Have a Heart* that Bolton, Wodehouse, and Kern reached their stride. Due to the addition of the witty, sophisticated, and intelligent lyrics of P. G. Wodehouse and the special collaboration between Bolton and Wodehouse, the trio's work now featured effortless transitions between book and song. One wonders how hard Bolton and Wodehouse had to work to keep faithful to the text, since musical productions of the day featured the constant moving, removing, and reworking of songs and material during rehearsals and tryouts.

Shortly after *Have a Heart,* Comstock needed another show quickly, as his own project had left the theatre empty. "What about that thing you mentioned?" he must have said, and they were delighted to receive a commission to write up Bolton's idea, entitled *Oh, Boy!*

When it opened on February 20, 1917 at the Princess—after a smooth out-of-town tryout in Schenectady (only two cast changes and some plot rewrites)—*Oh, Boy!* marked their most successful production. Ticket prices were raised to an astonishing $3.50 due to a high capital cost of $29,000. Nevertheless, partly because of the trio's rising reputation, it had the largest box office advance in theatre history. Perhaps the show's success was also influenced by its cast, which included eighteen-year-old Marion Davies and nineteen-year-old Justine Johnstone, two of Ziegfeld's reigning beauties whom Comstock had stolen away by promising them speaking parts. It eventually ran 463 performances and put five separate companies out on the road. It also ran 167 performances in London under the title *Oh, Joy!*

Soon after that, Comstock bought George Ade's play *The College Widow.* Bolton, Wodehouse, and Kern turned it into *Leave It to Jane,* tried the musical out in Atlantic City, then opened it on Broadway at the uptown Longacre Theatre (*Oh, Boy!* was still in residence at the Princess) on August

28, 1917. This was a highly unusual opening date, since theatres at that time did not have air conditioning and generally closed for the dog days of summer. In fact, of the seven shows that might legitimately be called "the Princess musicals," only four actually played the Princess Theatre. *Jane* has the distinction of being the first musical to list the "ladies and gentlemen of the ensemble" in its program. Until then, singers and dancers either went uncredited or were given character names. Although *Jane* didn't run as long as *Oh, Boy!*—167 performances—it spawned three companies. Due to a successful 1959 off-Broadway revival (928 performances) and accompanying cast album, it is the best known of the Princess musicals today.

The trio's next musical was *Miss 1917* (also known as *The Second Century Show* because it was the second show in the big Century Theatre), an extravaganza coproduced by Ziegfeld and Dillingham—usually archrivals—that was so lavish it was said to lose several thousand dollars a week even if it sold out. Fortunately, it flopped. *Miss 1917* was basically a revue with music by Jerome Kern and Victor Herbert for which Bolton and Wodehouse fashioned a slight plot. To end the show, the hero says to the heroine, "I've followed you through two acts and an intermission." The heroine says, "You've really followed me through all that maze of dancers and specialty people?" and falls into the hero's arms. The show's most extravagant boast is that a nineteen-year-old George Gershwin was the rehearsal pianist.

Comstock again called upon Bolton, Wodehouse, and Kern, and they wrote *Oh, Lady! Lady!!* from a Bolton idea. *Lady* ran 219 performances at the Princess beginning February 1, 1918 after three weeks on the road and multiple changes, which included dropping the song "Bill." The title came from a popular expression in minstrel shows of a generation earlier, and continued the Princess tradition, established by *Very Good, Eddie,* of using the title as the final curtain line. Although the show was another gem for its creators, audiences might have felt they had seen it before, and it didn't have the longevity of *Oh! Boy!* It did have a plot so strong that Wodehouse used it for a subsequent novel entitled *The Small Bachelor.*

In 1924 Sam Harris arranged for Wodehouse, Bolton and Irving Berlin to write a musical for the Duncan Sisters, who were stars of vaudeville. When the sisters suddenly became unavailable due to their appearance in the Chicago success of *Topsy and Eva* (a musical version of *Uncle Tom's Cabin*), Berlin and Harris dropped out, feeling that the story would not work without the special charm of the sisters. Ray Comstock took up the project, and Jerome Kern stepped in and wrote the score, reuniting the

The ladies of the ensemble of *Oh, Lady! Lady!!*

Museum of the City of New York/White Studio

Bolton-Wodehouse-Kern trio after four years. *Sitting Pretty* opened on April 8, 1924 at the Fulton Theatre, not the Princess, because Comstock wanted a theatre with a larger gross potential.

But probably Berlin had been right—the show did not work well without its intended stars. In addition, Kern withheld the score from recordings because he claimed that the jazz orchestrations used on recordings—"original" cast albums not having yet come into vogue—mutilated his songs. The strong-minded, often irascible Kern wrote:

> None of our music now reaches the public as we wrote it except in the theatre. It is so distorted by jazz orchestras as to be almost unrecognizable . . . [T]he trouble with the current popular musical rendition is that it runs everything into the same mold, utterly heedless of the original score and of the right of the composer, whether living or dead. Increasingly in the course of the last five years I have noted . . . that this debasement of all music at the hands of cabaret orchestras has grown by leaps and bounds.

Without song recordings, *Sitting Pretty* got a good deal less publicity than other hit shows and ran only ninety-five performances. Thus the seventh and last Princess musical was a flop, and an era was over.

But *Sitting Pretty* is not without merit. Kern was beginning to abandon the all-dance-tune musical in favor of ballads. He used extended melody lines. He wove some of his melodies elsewhere into the fabric of the show (as in Richard Wagner's *Leitmotif*), hinting at his interest in the conceptual, dramatic use of music that he would use so successfully in years to come. Kern's overture for *Pretty* was not the usual collection of the show's tunes, but a unique seven-minute symphony ("A Journey Southward") evoking a train ride from New York to Florida. In future productions, the piece might be profitably choreographed as an entr'acte, since act one takes place in New Jersey and act two in Florida.

• • •

It is something of a mystery why the trio of Bolton, Wodehouse, and Kern broke up. History has given (too much) credence to a small rift that came between the self-effacing, mild-mannered Wodehouse and the arrogant, often impossible Kern. Ziegfeld had asked the three to write a vehicle for his dancing star Marilyn Miller. They apparently agreed, and they had an idea from their Princess days that Comstock had declined. But Wodehouse had to abandon the project when he traveled to England, and eventually most of the lyrics were created by others. In a letter to his wife dated November 28, 1920, Wodehouse wrote:

> I forgot to tell you in my last letter the tale of the laughable imbroglio or mix-up—which has occurred with Jerry Kern. You remember I sent my lyrics over and then read in *Variety* that some other cove was doing the lyrics and wrote to everybody in New York to retrieve my lyrics. Then that cable came asking me if I would let them have "Joan of Arc" and "Church Round the Corner," which, after a family consultation, I answered in the affir. Well, just after I had cabled saying all right, I got a furious cable from Jerry—the sort of cable the Kaiser might have sent to an underling—saying my letter withdrawing the lyrics was "extremely offensive" and ending "You have offended me for the last time!" Upon which the manly spirit of the Wodehouses (descended from the sister of Anne Boleyn) boiled in my veins—when you get back I'll show you the very veins it boiled in—and I cabled over "Cancel permission to use lyrics." I now hear that Jerry is bringing an action against me for royalties on *Miss Springtime* and *Riviera Girl,* to which he contributed tunes. The loony seems to think that a lyricist is responsible for the composer's royalties. Of course, he hasn't an earthly . . . but doesn't it show how blighted some blighters can be when they decide to be blighters . . .

This show eventually became the hugely successful *Sally,* one of their best and most unusual, and also the one over which they suffered the most aggravation. Because Wodehouse was in London, three other lyric writers were brought in (Buddy DeSylva, Anne Caldwell, and Clifford Grey), and Ziegfeld brought in Victor Herbert to write the ballet finale for Miller. (This show is notable, by the way, as the *second* score from which "Bill" was dropped, since Marilyn Miller didn't like it.) *Sally* is the story of an orphan girl who begins as a dishwasher and ends up as the star of a *Follies* (along the way finding, losing, and finding love). Miller's first entrance was the talk of Broadway, and Bolton fought for it over Ziegfeld's objections. Instead of a dazzling entrance she appeared quietly at the end of a line of ragged orphans, surprising the audience. It was the first attack on the star entrance in musicals, and established the maxim that a *dramatic* entrance is worth twice as much as a spectacular one.

After success in Baltimore and Atlantic City, *Sally* opened on Broadway in December of 1920 to great acclaim. Called an "epochal entertainment" by one critic, it ran 570 performances at the New Amsterdam Theatre—almost four years including touring—and 383 performances in London the following season. It featured Kern's "Look for the Silver Lining." If Ziegfeld's constant interference and Marilyn Miller's ego—Ziegfeld's daughter remembers Miller throwing an ashtray at her retreating father—weren't enough to aggravate the volatile Kern, seeing Herbert, during the third act of the opening night performance, walk down the aisle and climb into the pit to take the baton from the musical director and conduct his ballet music would have clinched it. *Sally* was the trio's biggest commercial hit, but their least favorite experience.

The idea that Wodehouse would object to having other writers' lyrics interpolated among his own is absurd, since he himself had engaged in that practice for years. In those days of song interpolation more than one composer and more than one lyricist were often asked to write tunes for a project. Sometimes new lyrics were set to an already used melody. Sometimes new songs were put into a show after it had opened successfully, to keep it fresh and topical, or just to showcase a new potential hit. There are even instances where one composer wrote the verse and another the chorus. Given such a climate, it's hardly likely that Wodehouse would suddenly object to this practice.

But for whatever reasons, Kern did not write the next two Bolton-Wodehouse shows. Bolton and Wodehouse wrote *Oh, My Dear!* with music by Louis Hirsch (189 performances at the Princess Theatre in 1918), and *The Rose of China,* with music by Armand Vecsey (47 performances at the Lyric Theatre in 1919). The trio that had created the *integrated* American musical comedy never wrote together again, but their seamless welding of book, music, and lyrics left a mark on the American musical forever.

Another possible explanation for the breakup is Kern's ego, for Comstock had turned down three of their suggestions for a Princess show. (One, a story called *The Little Thing,* which they had been flogging for years, became *Sally.*) Comstock's taste for larger (and more profitable) shows probably contributed to the end of the Princess commissions as well.

Moreover, Bolton, Wodehouse, and Kern were never perfectly matched. Wodehouse and Bolton spent the rest of their lives in happy communion as the best of friends, occasional collaborators, and eventually neighbors. However, Kern and Bolton had considerable egos and tempers. Kern had all along arranged for Wodehouse and Bolton to get a royalty of two percent respectively for lyrics and book, while he collected three percent for his music. Bolton talked the low-keyed, never worldly, go-along Wodehouse into giving him half of Wodehouse's royalties, partially on the odd grounds that the lyrics were easier to write than the book. Wodehouse agreed to this absurd arrangement until he died, when his widow finally shut off the Wodehouse largesse from a still greedy Bolton.

Yet probably there is no mystery at all. Composers, lyricists, and librettists in those days worked with anyone and everyone. The immortal songwriting teams about which later generations would boast did not yet exist. During the period of the Princess musicals, in fact, all three authors were involved in numerous other projects simultaneously—Kern worked with other lyricists, and Bolton and Wodehouse, separately and together, worked with other composers.

The hectic activity of the period must have been artistically invigorating. Between September 1916 and December 1917, for example, the three were involved in *Have a Heart; Miss Springtime; Oh, Boy!; Leave It to Jane; Kitty Darlin'* (Bolton and Wodehouse with Rudolf Friml, a flop in Buffalo); *The Riviera Girl* (Bolton and Wodehouse, with music by Jerome Kern and Emmerich Kalman); and *Miss 1917.* The last five were all playing on Broadway at the same time! By today's standards, the trio had done a lifetime of work during one brief era, itself a fraction of their individual career achievements.

Kern did write one more time with Wodehouse after their *Sally* contretemps—they collaborated on *The Cabaret Girl,* which ran 462 performances at London's Winter Garden Theatre in 1922. Also, Kern and Bolton collaborated on *Zip Goes a Million* (based on *Brewster's Millions*) in 1919, the only Kern musical to close out of town. Finally, Bolton and Wodehouse collaborated on their memoirs in 1954.

• • •

If all three did not work as a team after *Sitting Pretty*, it was almost surely a question of circumstances. The fact that they didn't may not have marked the end of the revolution we call the Princess musicals so much as the rapidly changing musical theatre of the twenties. For one thing, an intimate, small-cast, two-set musical in a 299-seat house would have an economic profile that would not appeal to producers. For another, the Princess principles were soon being incorporated into the dramatic fabric of larger musicals.

To fully understand the Princess contribution, we need to look at the theatre of the time. Because the standard model allowed for good songs to be jammed into the book willy-nilly, elaborate song cues had to be devised by bookwriters, who thus wandered further and further from their stories.

Reality came late to the musical stage, partly because musical entertainment had not been treated with the same deference as dramas of social realism, but also because sets, costumes, makeup, and lights were still devoted to a macabre theatrical style. Here's a paragraph on the look of the early musicals from Gerald Bordman's biography of Jerome Kern:

> To some extent the elaborateness of sets and costumes was necessary to soften the rather harsh effects of turn-of-the-century lighting. Gas and calcium lights were fast giving way to electricity, but dimmers were extremely primitive and within reach of only the best houses. Nor could filters be changed with ease. Except for one or two spotlights controlled from a booth in the furthest heights of a house, all lighting came directly from the stage, especially from footlights, which lit the stage and performers from underneath and at close range. The subtleties of modern lighting were at best far-fetched dreams. Partly as a result of these lighting problems and partly as a carryover from days of even less workable lighting and larger theatres, make-up could often be grotesquely artificial, not merely for patently

grotesque comedians but even for young leading men and ingénues. Juveniles made up with what was called "five and nine," a pale yellow base topped with a nutty brown. The mouth was customarily outlined in black and the eyes with blue, dotted with red. Ingénues "hot-blacked" their eyelashes, utilizing a wax-like mascara that was melted in a spoon over a candle flame. The wax, applied with a hairpin, extended the lashes preposterously.

The Princess shows were hugely successful, almost beloved. Both Dorothy Parker and George S. Kaufman have been credited with a poem that still stands as a critical monument to their succession of hit musicals:

This is the trio of musical fame,
Bolton and Wodehouse and Kern;
Better than anyone else you can name,
Bolton and Wodehouse and Kern;
Nobody knows what on earth they've been bitten by,
All I can say is I mean to get lit and buy,
Orchestra seats for the next one that's written by,
Bolton and Wodehouse and Kern.

Apropos of the quality of the new American musical, it became increasingly literary. By this time it was very much a part of the literary world, authors and audiences flowing naturally from plays and musicals to newspapers, magazines, and comic novels.

Here is a summation of the Princess plots. Young man loves young woman, but her guardian aunt looks down on him because he's a "society dancer" (*Nobody Home*). We witness the machinations of three couples on a cruise (act 1) and at a honeymoon hotel (act 2) (*Very Good, Eddie*). Young couple goes on second honeymoon and husband encounters his old flame (*Have a Heart*). Young man is determined to marry his sweetheart without alienating his rich guardian aunt (*Oh, Boy!*). Young girl lures a football star away from her school's archrival, and eventually they fall in love (*Leave It To Jane*). Young woman marries young man despite her mother's objections (*Oh, Lady! Lady!*). Crooks and young women are in love with men to whom their guardians are opposed (*Sitting Pretty*).

If these shows all ran along the same lines and were generally set in a fantasy world to which the audience was gratefully admitted, the plots were a transition between the European operetta stories and the contemporary, more realistic stories to come. It was the way in which the musicals stuck to their plots—and didn't make fun of themselves—that characterized the shows more than their content.

Perhaps some of the stories from the early generation of musicals were not so fanciful after all, since nearly all the writers were part of the moneyed, heady upper-class. During rehearsals for *Daffy Dill* (1922), with music by Herbert Stothart, lyrics by Oscar Hammerstein II, and book by Guy Bolton, Bolton had an affair with Hammerstein's wife. Though the liaison had a shorter run than the show—nine weeks—it eventually ended Hammerstein's marriage, and marked the first and last collaboration between Bolton and Hammerstein. This was not Bolton's only transgression. Long after the heyday of early American musicals, George Middleton, one of Bolton's many collaborators, wrote to him, "You've made quite a career with your pen and your penis, haven't you?"

Hammerstein met his second wife while each was still on their first marriage. And while preparing for the out-of-town premiere of *Rose-Marie,* composer Herbert Stothart's wife arrived at the hotel to surprise him, and found him in bed with her sister, whereupon she leaped out of the window to her death.

Wodehouse was born in England to English parents; Bolton was born in England to American parents; and Kern, an ardent Anglophile, made three working trips to the West End before he was twenty-one years old. On one trip he found himself an English wife. No mystery, then, that the Gilbert and Sullivan comic operas and the musical comedies of the West End during the first decade of the twentieth century had an influence on the Princess musicals. *Oh, Boy!* and *Leave It To Jane* prompted one critic to recall "the delicate texture which once distinguished the George Edwardes musical comedies." Bolton, Wodehouse, and Kern had all worked for Edwardes.

Bolton and Wodehouse later called the Princess shows "midget musical comedy." They were intimate musicals usually without star parts, "interest being distributed among a number of characters," according to the authors' memoirs. Because of the small orchestra pit, a celeste took the place of the woodwinds. Each of the two acts featured a single set, which greatly enhanced the efficiency of the staging. The books had a consistency of style and tone more sophisticated than the puns and gags that littered previous musical librettos. The characters spoke like the audience in a dialogue that approached the colloquial, as opposed to the theatrical dialogue that had held the stage until then.

The Princess musicals are particularly noted for a significant jump forward in lyrics because Wodehouse was probably the first arch-literate lyricist of the American musical theatre. His work lay so comfortably on the tongues of the characters that the actors were virtually forced to remain in character. His words rolled like Bolton's dialogue, and thus the songs were not only dramatically integrated, but stylistically integrated as well.

Probably the Kern-Wodehouse song that still stands in sharp relief today is "Bill." It is a magnificent ballad that has stood the test of time, and it was eventually used in *Show Boat.* "Bill" is a good example of the tremendous contribution of the Princess style. It's the first conversational torch song. The lyrics avoid poetic metaphor, overt romanticism, and attention-calling meter; and the words fall easily on the melody, the important ones landing on the strongest notes—Wodehouse always wrote to an existing melody, insisting that was the best way. Ordinary, character-driven language could grows easily out of dialogue in this Wodehouse lyric (prior to minor alterations made by Hammerstein for *Show Boat*):

> *I used to dream that I would discover the perfect lover some day; I knew I'd recognize him, if ever he came round my way. I always used to fancy then, he'd be one of the godlike kind of men, with a giant brain and a noble head, like the heroes bold in the books I'd read.*
>
> *But along came Bill, who's quite the opposite of all the men in story books. In grace and looks I know that Apollo would beat him all hollow. And I can't explain, it's surely not his brain that makes me thrill. I love him because he's just my Bill.*
>
> *He's just my Bill, he has no gifts at all: a motor car he cannot steer.* And it seems clear whenever he dances, his partner takes*

* Wodehouse bought his first car from the producer Seymour Hicks, who gave him one hasty lesson. An hour later he drove it into a hedge, got out, took a train back to London, and never got behind the wheel of an automobile again.

> *chances. Oh I can't explain, it's surely not his brain that makes me thrill. I love him, because he's—I don't know—because he's just my Bill.*

This number still stands as one of the best blendings of words and music in realistic form written for the American theatre, especially when compared to the croon-and-spoon-in-June-under-the-moon lyrics that characterized prior musicals.

All the Princess shows were created as intimate productions, and all strove for fully integrated book, music, and lyrics. Bolton wrote of *Very Good, Eddie:*

> It was the first of its kind to rely on situation and character laughs instead of clowning and Weberfieldian* cross-talk, with which the large scale musicals filled in between the romantic scenes.

He remarked of *Oh! Boy!* that "every song and lyric contributed to the action," and that "the humor was based on situation, not interjected by the comedians."

And he said to a journalist:

> Our musical comedies depend as much upon plot and the development of their characters for success as upon their music, and because they deal with subjects and people near to the audiences. . . . Every line, funny or serious, is supposed to help the plot continue to hold. . . . If the songs are going to count at all in any plot, the plot has to build more or less around, or at least, with them.

Jerome Kern spoke of the structure by pointing out that "the musical numbers should carry on the action of the play and should be representative of the personalities of the characters who sing them. Songs must be suited to the action and the mood of the play." And Dorothy Parker liked "the way the action slides casually into songs."

* Referring to the vaudeville team of Joe Weber and Lew Fields.

The Dramatic Mirror wrote that *Have a Heart* "has a plot upon which Mr. Kern's music always has a direct bearing."

Wodehouse, characteristically modest, wrote the following for *Vanity Fair* under a pseudonym:

> The public has at last awakened to the fact that it is possible for the book of a musical comedy to be coherent, sensible, and legitimately amusing, and now it demands these qualities before it consents to allow the box office man to withdraw the two dollar bill from its grasp.
>
> The man who is responsible for this state of affairs, who has revolutionized musical comedy to such an extent that all the other authors will either have to improve their stuff or go back to box stenciling, is Guy Bolton . . .

These comments, and the work they refer to, were all made between 1915 and 1917. They spell out clearly the modern musical comedy format—the American musical would never be the same old hodgepodge. It was firmly and forever launched on its way toward integration. Thanks to George M. Cohan and the Princess trio, it was fast, clever, and dramatically efficient. In 1918 the *New York Evening World* made the pronouncement that "New York sets the pace for musical comedy. London is no longer in the running, Vienna is on its last leg, and Paris has lagged behind the procession for years." It was the beginning of a dynasty that would last more than half a century.

Detail-oriented historians do not credit the Princess shows exclusively with the seminal achievement their reputation claims. Other musicals before them integrated musical numbers, relied on small budgets, and featured American plots and characters. But let us use the phrase "Princess shows" and the hard work and quality results of Bolton, Wodehouse, and Kern to illustrate a step forward in the art of the American musical that was taken just after the turn of the century. Although that step was by no means complete by the 1920s, more than one teenage admirer of Kern's shows had a better idea of how to write a good theatre score. George Gershwin heard a Kern song at the age of sixteen and resolved to emulate it. Irving Berlin admired Kern's music, loath though he was to admit it. At the age of fourteen, Richard Rodgers went to see *Very Good, Eddie* a dozen times in order to study the invigorating new style. He later remarked that Kern "had his musical roots in the fertile middle ground of European and English school of operetta writing, and amalgamated it with everything that was fresh in the American scene to give us something wonderfully new and clear in music writing."

George Gershwin and Richard Rodgers would put their own marks on the musical, though Rodgers's early work is extremely imitative of Kern. All composers to come owed a good deal to the groundbreaking Princess musicals of Bolton, Wodehouse, and Kern.

• • •

Guy Bolton went on to do yeoman's work on plays and musicals in New York and London, though after the Princess era he never again achieved the success he experienced in those heady days. His talent for skilled comedy, dialogue, and the new musical form limited him to collaborations, often on other authors' stories. His last years were a combination of semi-retirement and frustration.

P. G. Wodehouse wrote a number of successful plays, including an adaptation of a Ferenc Molnár play called *The Play's The Thing* (1926, 326 performances). Wodehouse and Bolton were two of the four librettists on *Anything Goes* (1934), with a score by Cole Porter. Wodehouse continued writing hugely successful comic novels, and was working on his ninety-sixth when he died peacefully at the age of ninety-three.

Jerome Kern had yet another significant achievement in his future . . .

ZIEGFELD THEATRE

SIXTH AVENUE AT 54TH STREET

DAN C. CURRY - - - - *Resident Manager*

FIRE NOTICE—Look around NOW and choose the exit nearest to your seat. In case of fire walk, (not run) to THAT EXIT. Do not try to beat your neighbor to the street.—JOHN J. DORMAN, Fire Commissioner.

Week Beginning Monday, December 3rd, 1928

AN ALL AMERICAN MUSICAL COMEDY

Adapted from Edna Ferber's novel of the same name
Produced by

FLORENZ ZIEGFELD

Music by JEROME KERN
Book and Lyrics by OSCAR HAMMERSTEIN, II
Dances and Ensembles arranged by SAMMY LEE

Scenes by JOSEPH URBAN
Dialogue staged by ZEKE COLVAN
Costumes Designed by JOHN HARKRIDER

ALFRED CHENEY JOHNSTON, *Exclusive Photographer for Ziegfeld Theatre*
VICTOR BARAVALLE, *Musical Director*

NOW PLAYING

LYRIC THEATRE—Ziegfeld Production — DENNIS KING in "THE THREE MUSKETEERS"

"RIO RITA" On Tour

CAST OF CHARACTERS
(In the order of their appearance)

Windy	Allan Campbell
Steve	Charles Ellis
Pete	Bert Chapman
QUEENIE	AUNT JEMIMA
PARTHY ANN HAWKS	EDNA MAY OLIVER
CAP'N ANDY	CHARLES WINNINGER

Eleven

Show Boat

You never seen a show like this before . . .

With his intimate Princess musicals, Jerome Kern established a reputation equal to the top composers on Broadway. Yet he found that producers sought him to write the very kind of songs, for the very kind of shows, that he had turned away from in revolutionizing the form. Uptown producers were not interested in large Broadway musicals based on the formula Bolton, Wodehouse, and Kern had worked out so successfully—Kern was once again forced into the kind of bookless songwriting he thought he had forsaken. For almost ten years he worked on more than a dozen now-forgotten musicals, including two big commercial successes, *Sally* (1920, 570 performances) and Sunny (1925, 517 performances).

For *Dear Sir* (1924) Kern composed the first score, which stretched his own musical interests. Several of the songs have extremely long choruses (eighty-five and seventy-five bars as opposed to the standard thirty-two) and unusually wide ranges. Kern was so frustrated by the orchestra's inability to phrase the longer, more complex melodies that he replaced the conductor in tryouts. The show, nevertheless, could not sustain the score—not even the critics recognized Kern's attempt—and it closed quickly. But Kern did not turn back.

On *Sunny* he worked for the first time with Oscar Hammerstein II, a man who, like Kern, was increasingly frustrated with the work he found himself doing for the stage. Kern and Hammerstein were a mismatched pair. Kern had always been an arrogant and imperious man, arranging to take more and more credit and publicity as he became successful. *Lucky* (1927) was a lavish show produced by Dillingham with several Kern songs. When the show was in trouble out of town and its producer was in the hospital, Kern took over the production and locked bookwriter partner Otto Harbach out of the theatre. Once when he went to see a notoriously difficult producer, he introduced himself with, "I hear you're a son-of-a-bitch. Well, so am I!"

Hammerstein, on the other hand, was gentle, courteous, erudite, well-educated, and able to get along with a variety of collaborators. Hammerstein came from a theatrical background verging on royalty. His grandfather Oscar was an eccentric man who made his money in real estate from apartment houses and theatres—he built the Victoria Theatre, a popular home of vaudeville. He poured considerable money into his great passion, the opera. He built gigantic opera houses in Manhattan and Philadelphia, presented grand opera on a lavish scale, sponsored new and nontraditional works, and created an opera company that went head to head with the Metropolitan. He was continually involved in lawsuits and always verged on bankruptcy as he poured profits from the Victoria into grand opera. His son William ably managed the Victoria Theatre for his father and became one of the most respected presenters in the vaudeville field, and his son Arthur was a successful producer of plays and operettas on Broadway.

William's son Oscar II was the third generation to be smitten by the musical theatre. His first show was *Home, James,* the Columbia University varsity musical for 1917. Oscar collaborated on the book and the lyrics, but he gained college fame as the show's leading comedian. The following year he wrote and directed the varsity show *Ten For Five.*

In spite of young Oscar's passion for theatre and writing, he expected to become a lawyer as he had promised his father before he died at the youthful age of forty. William simply did not want his children going into the theatre. William—staid and successful at least in part because of a far more reasonable personality than Oscar I—attempted all his life to keep his family away from the theatre altogether.

He was not successful. Dissatisfied with law school and his part-time job in a law firm, and finding himself too thin to enlist for World War I, Oscar II defied his promise to his deceased father, dropped out of school, and headed for Uncle Arthur's office. The persuasive Oscar overcame his uncle's objections—which included an awareness of his brother's desires and his agreement that show business was no place for the third generation of Hammersteins—and was given a job as the assistant stage manager on Arthur's hit musical *You're in Love* (score by Rudolf Friml).

The next period in young Oscar's life gave him the education that would lay the foundation of his brilliant work in the future. He read plays for his uncle, worked as an office boy, stage-managed shows, and hung around rehearsals, both in official and unofficial capacities. On occasion he was even assigned to write a lyric. Refusing to return to the law (despite the advice of young Mae West while she appeared in Arthur's *Sometime* in 1918) and not anxious to be a performer or stage manager, Oscar turned increasingly to writing.

Arthur produced Oscar's first straight play, *The Light,* which closed out of town in seven performances (" . . . that failed"). At the Saturday matinée, attended by all of twenty people, Oscar left the theatre, went to a park bench, and began work on his second script.

During the Actors' Equity strike of 1919, Oscar was relieved from supervising the various activities of his uncle's office and could not attend other plays and musicals (he never missed one in those days). At this time, Hammerstein wrote the book and lyrics for *Always You,* and in December, 1919 the first professional musical by Oscar Hammerstein II began out-of-town tryouts. In January, 1920 it opened on Broadway.

It was not too unsuccessful—sixty-six performances and an extensive road tour. Although "the plot of a 1919 musical comedy did not matter a great deal" according to Brooks Atkinson ("an especially good thing for this particular production"), Hammerstein credits the experience with a change in his beliefs, a change that would ultimately affect the history of the

American musical. The prevailing theatrical wisdom had taught Oscar that what mattered were the girls, the jokes, the dancing, and the sets, but while sitting in the audience and listening to their response to his own dialogue, he came to believe in the unusual dictum that the playgoer actually follows the plot—thus, *the plot supports everything else.* He spent the rest of his career working from that tenet, which permanently focused the course of the American musical.

The score of *Always You* was published by Max Dreyfuss of T. B. Harms. Hammerstein had arrived squarely in the middle of the influential players of the Broadway musical in the heady days before the Great Depression.

Uncle Arthur produced a huge number of his nephew's first efforts; he was a talented producer who invented many effective theatrical devices to enhance Oscar's shows. Oscar teamed up with Otto Harbach for the book and lyrics of *Tickle Me, Jimmie* (both produced in 1920, with music by Herbert Stothart), *Wildflower, Mary Jane McKane* (both produced in 1923, with music by Vincent Youmans), *Rose-Marie* (1924, music by Rudolf Friml and Stothart), *Sunny* (music by Kern), and *The Desert Song* (1926, music by Friml). *Desert Song* was a great success, and ran 465 performances. There were five road tours and productions in England, France, and Australia. MGM Studios eventually made three film versions.

Oscar and his various collaborators had been working increasingly on the idea of integrating their songs into their books, a technique that had finally begun to reach big Broadway productions via the pioneering work of the Princess musicals. The new concept reached an apotheosis with *Rose-Marie* in 1924, when they wrote in the program: "The musical numbers of this play are such an integral part of the action that we do not think we should list them as separate episodes." In hindsight, this was as much wishful thinking as anything else, but the lush Rudolf Friml score was extensive, popular, and written for the story.

When Hammerstein first worked with Kern on *Sunny,* a vehicle Dillingham engaged them to create for Marilyn Miller (whom he had stolen away from Florenz Ziegfeld), the musical featured forty chorus girls, twenty-eight chorus boys, a circus motif, real animals, an ocean liner, a ballroom, and a fox hunt. Kern and Hammerstein had little chance to work on the integrated kind of score they both had flirted with in the past. Yet both men were intelligent and sensitive, and they spent much time discussing the musical theatre. Eventually they agreed to look for a story upon which they could build the adult musical they both envisioned.

• • •

Edna Ferber's *Show Boat* first appeared in serial form in *Woman's Home Companion* from April through September, 1926, and was subsequently published as a novel. Kern telephoned Hammerstein one evening and suggested that *Show Boat* was the story they had been waiting for. Hammerstein took to the material just as quickly, and they agreed to collaborate on a Broadway musical version. Kern must have had great faith in the younger Hammerstein, because it was to be Oscar's first solo effort at book and lyrics. Oscar had previously collaborated with Otto Harbach on his books, and Kern was convinced that his thirty-one-year old partner was ready to write a libretto on his own.

Anxious to secure the rights, Kern asked Alexander Woollcott to arrange an introduction to the author. Woollcott promised he would. On October 12, 1926, in the lobby of the Globe Theatre during the intermission of the opening of Kern's *Criss Cross* (a Fred Stone and Dorothy Stone vehicle Kern had composed), Kern ran into Woollcott and reminded him of his promise. Woollcott bellowed across the lobby, "Ferber! Hi, Ferber! Come on over here a minute!" and introduced the diminutive lady novelist to Kern.

Ferber thought a musical version of her novel was a terrible idea, and considering the form and content of the popular Broadway musicals of the time, she was certainly justified. Nevertheless, she gave them the rights in exchange for a small advance and a royalty of one and one-half percent of the gross weekly box office receipts.

As soon as he heard about the project, Ziegfeld expressed his desire to become the show's producer. Although Hammerstein's uncle Arthur felt he should produce it, the authors gave it to Ziegfeld. *Show Boat* was a marked contrast in possibilities to the lavish revues featuring the half-dressed beauties and great comedians Ziegfeld was famous for. To his eternal credit, Ziegfeld recognized the possibilities at once.

Kern and Hammerstein visited a real show boat for verisimilitude (as Ferber had done), the first hint that they intended to create something more realistic than the musicals of the day. The subsequent process of writ-

Hammerstein and Kern rehearse the first modern musical
Museum of the City of New York

ing and producing, short by today's standards, was by no means straightforward.

Early script drafts indicate that Hammerstein suffered too much respect for Ferber's novel and too little experience of his own. The final result, however, indicates that writing the musical educated him. *Show Boat* marks a clear turning point in the craft of Oscar Hammerstein II. Yet Kern and Hammerstein were so certain about their theories and their work, they staged the production themselves. Ziegfeld never bothered to engage a director.

Ziegfeld scheduled the production within months of the day he signed his contract, indicating that he was unaware of the attention that the authors were expecting to lavish on the show and on their new theories of dramatic musical construction. Ziegfeld was accustomed to authors who could turn out a second (albeit absurd) act in a hotel room overnight. He had not been getting along with Marc Klaw and Abe Erlanger, with whom he was partnered in the New Amsterdam Theatre on Forty-second street.

With financial backing from newspapermen William Randolph Hearst and Arthur Brisbane, he built the Ziegfeld Theatre on the northwest corner of Sixth Avenue and Fifty-fourth street. It was designed by Joseph Urban, who had designed many of Ziegfeld's gorgeous *Follies* sets, and it held 1,632 seats. Urban designed the sprawling show as well.

History does not adequately record Ziegfeld's opinion of the Kern-Hammerstein project. Some sources say that he worried because *Show Boat* was not the kind of show with which he had been successful; others say that he loved the show in all its seriousness from the beginning. It is likely that Kern and Hammerstein's careful approach to the first draft caused most of the delay—they were working on an unusually large and complex musical with theories that had only been used in the far smaller Princess musicals. Eventually *Rio Rita* (with book by Fred Thompson and Guy Bolton, Kern's collaborator from the Princess days) opened the new Ziegfeld Theatre on February 2, 1927, and *Show Boat* was scheduled for the Lyric Theatre on Forty-second street somewhat later. Ziegfeld postponed the production even after he had signed three stars for the leads, whom he lost in order to give Kern and Hammerstein the time they required to prepare the text and music.

If Kern wasn't worried that *Show Boat* was Hammerstein's first solo effort, Ziegfeld was. He never understood the sprawling story—production, not drama, was Ziegfeld's strong suit—and after seeing early drafts he tried to get Hammerstein to take on a collaborator. Hammerstein and Kern refused.

Nevertheless, Ziegfeld lavished all the care and taste on the production that he had on his extravagant revues. The Ziegfeldian largesse, though operetta-inspired, complimented the scope and sweep of the story. The show boasted thirty-six white chorus girls, sixteen white chorus boys, sixteen black male singers, sixteen black female singers, and twelve black female dancers.

Kern had seen the twenty-six-year-old Helen Morgan sitting on top of an upright piano in a small revue, *Americana,* the year before, and was satisfied he had found his Julie. (When she was eighteen, though, Ziegfeld had hired her for, and fired her from, the chorus of *Sally.*) Legend has it that Ring Lardner gave Morgan her trademark pose. Worried that the diminutive singer couldn't be seen at Billy Rose's speakeasy, he got up from his seat and lifted her onto the piano. In fact, she kept singing at the speakeasy, and went there after her *Show Boat* performances. On the fourth night of *Show Boat*'s Broadway run, the speakeasy was raided for selling bootleg liquor, and Ziegfeld had to get Morgan out of jail to continue with the musical.

Hammerstein directed the book scenes and most likely the principal songs. Sammy Lee was engaged to direct the dances, but he was not allowed to use the specialty numbers or chorus girl routines that were so popular in the Broadway musicals of the time—Lee had to keep to authentic dances necessitated by the plot. The result was a perfect combination of the beautiful, lavishly appealing old musicals and the powerful, serious, and effective book, music, and lyrics of the authors.

The show was first billed as "An All American Musical Comedy," but the opening night program eventually read "An American Musical Play." Critics called it an operetta, a term which continued to cling to lavish, spectacular musicals for some time.

The first public performance took place at the National Theatre in Washington, D.C. on November 25, 1927, and ran for four and a half hours. The *Washington Times* said, "It was 12:50 by the post office clock when a cheered, but slightly enervated, audience emerged into the night."

Fifty minutes of cuts were made that night, rehearsed the next morning, and excised at that day's matinée; forty more minutes were cut the next day; the now famous "Why Do I Love You" was written during tryouts; a second act ballet was cut, further indicating that dance was no longer useful unless it advanced the plot; and seven songs were cut (but not Kern's wonderful "Bill," for which Hammerstein adapted Wodehouse's original lyric).

It is almost axiomatic that musicals have second-act troubles, and *Show Boat* was not an exception. Many of the changes that the authors made out-of-town were in the second act, in which a story that has a virtual begin-

Helen Morgan in her traditional position atop a piano
Museum of the City of New York/White Studio

ning, middle, and end in the first act goes on for some time longer (and even longer in the book than in Hammerstein's adaptation).

While work on the production continued daily, the show traveled along the East Coast. Its tour gives a strong indication of the efficiency of stagehands. On November 21 it opened in Pittsburgh; on November 28 it opened in Cleveland; and on December 5 it opened in Philadelphia, where it settled in for three weeks. By this time Ziegfeld had decided to move it into his own theatre instead of the Lyric, which meant moving the already-opened *Rio Rita* to the Lyric instead. Although the Broadway premiere was planned for the December 26, the double move took an extra day and *Show Boat* opened at the Ziegfeld on December 27, 1927. By then it was only three hours and ten minutes long.

A total of 268 shows opened on Broadway during the 1927–28 season—eighteen the same week as *Show Boat,* and eleven on the previous Monday. On Tuesday, many of the first-string critics attended Philip Barry's play *Paris Bound* rather than *Show Boat.* This period represented a peak of theatrical activity in the United States, so there's more than one reason to divide the history of American musical theatre into "before and after *Show Boat,*" as historian Miles Krueger has done.

The season had already seen *Good News,* the DeSylva, Brown and Henderson college football musical, as well as Rodgers and Hart's *A Connecticut Yankee.* Sigmund Romberg wrote three musicals that fall: *My Maryland, My Princess,* and *The Love Call* (and he checked in with *Rosalie* later that season). George M. Cohan was represented by *The Merry Malones,* and Irving Caesar had tried unsuccessfully to reprise the success of *No, No, Nanette* with *Yes, Yes, Yvette.* Guy Bolton and Fred Thompson had written *The Five O'Clock Girl* with a score by Kalmar and Ruby, and the Astaires were appearing in *Funny Face,* singing George Gershwin tunes. Hammerstein's *Golden Dawn,* in fact, had opened only a month earlier, and Ziegfeld had opened *Follies of 1927* that August.

The theatrical establishment was skeptical. Unhappy marriages, miscegenation, slavery . . . Ferber's novel was filled with downbeat subjects for a musical. There was so little applause on opening night that the creators were alarmed, and Ziegfeld, fighting for a personal comeback in his career, was deeply depressed. In fact the audience was stunned, for they had never seen anything like it. The great sweep and scope of the story, the lush, powerful music, the black chorus—it was a success of enormous proportions.

Whether you call it the greatest American operetta or the first serious American musical, its humanity shook audiences and its craft startled the theatrical community.

"There isn't a drop of treacle in its makeup," wrote Alan Dale, Kern's earliest critical fan. "It never falls into the customary mawkish channels that mistake bathos for pathos," Arthur Waters wrote in the *Public Ledger*. Another reviewer said that *Show Boat* "has many of the finer attributes of musical comedy, operetta, even of revue, with a definite suggestion of legitimate drama." (*Variety* panned it as a "leviathan of a show" and singled out the song "Bill" for particular disapproval.)

Some critics did not fully understand *Show Boat*'s achievement until the first successful tour and the first revival, but many were delighted with the serious nature of the work. The public responded at once, and it ran over 570 performances. Audiences were offered not a silly, mindless unreality, but a look at life as it really is for part of the American population. The serious adult themes presented with a newly sophisticated technique had, overnight, antiquated the musical comedies of the 1920s.

In the future, writers like the Gershwins, Rodgers and Hart, and Cole Porter would draw on the rhythm of American life and new jazz influences, and would return to the sophistication of well-heeled Manhattanites for their subject matter. Kern and Hammerstein (and the future team of Rodgers and Hammerstein), on the other hand, would continue to rely on more rural, sentimental material. But all of them would be working in a format that could no longer be described as sheer entertainment—a theatre newly defined by the unique collaboration of Kern, Hammerstein, and Ziegfeld in 1927, wherein the libretto, the lyrics, the music, and even the décor would be faithful to the requirements of the plot and characters of a serious show.

• • •

The plot of the show with the "million dollar title" (Kern) begins in 1870 and continues to 1926. It is a sweeping, epic story, romantic yet real, that incorporates several generations of a Show Boat family as well as themes of racism, gambling, miscegenation, mismatched but great love, and American characters black and white. This is no Long-Island-drawing-room, boy-meets-girl story.

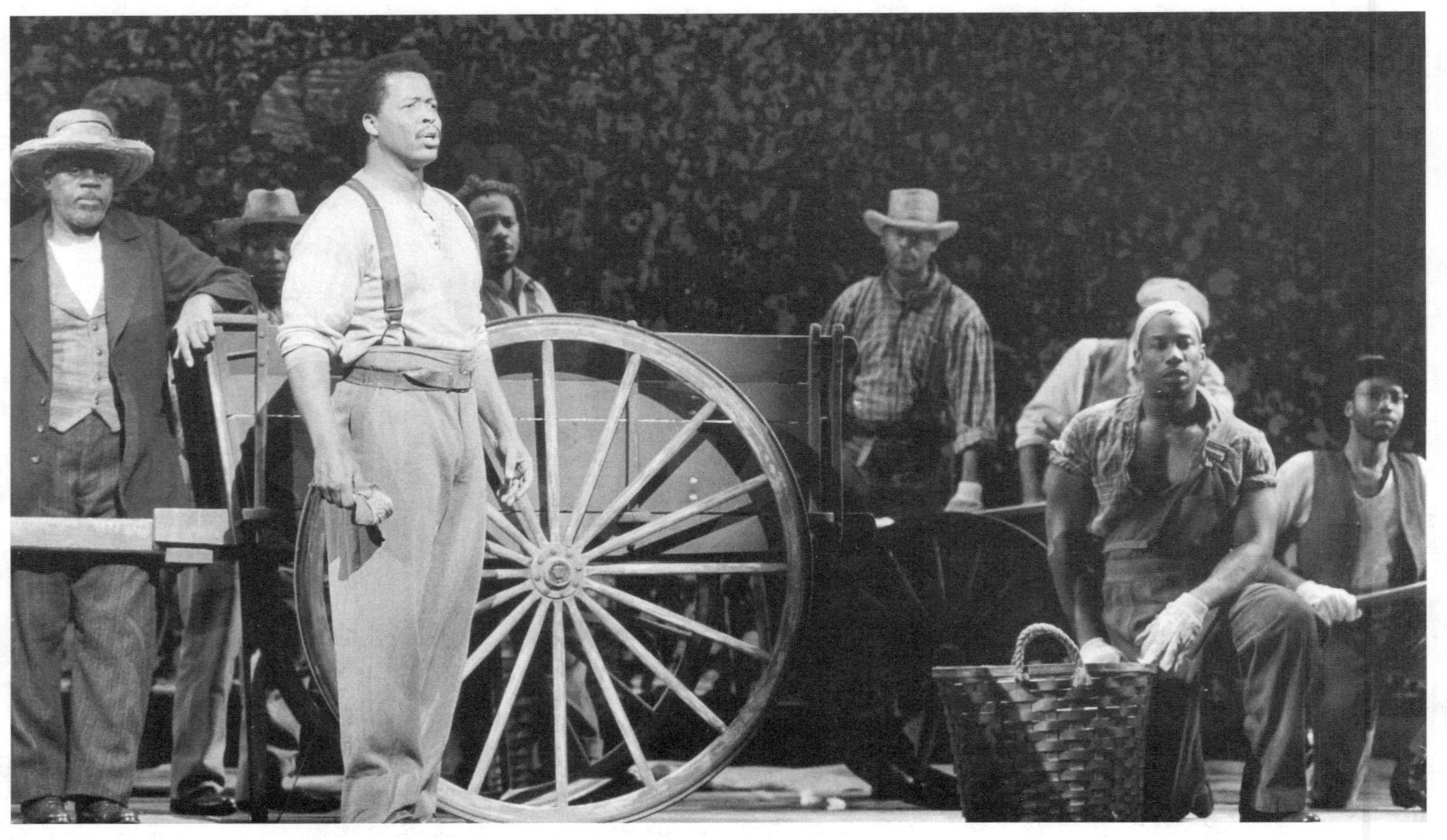

The evocative leitmotif "Old Man River"

Livent Production/Catherine Ashmore

One conflict dramatized in *Show Boat* is racial prejudice. Because miscegenation was strictly against the law, and because black and white performers were not allowed on the same stage at the same time, *Show Boat*'s Julie (half black) and Steve (white) become outcasts. Although the unfolding story is more concerned with Magnolia's love for a riverboat gambler and the soap-opera machinations that ensue, one never forgets Julie, the mulatto (and one is reminded again at the end). And, of course, "Ol' Man River" reverberates throughout the musical. *Show Boat* was a modern American romantic spectacle operetta, but its art was the towering precursor of the modern American musical theatre. The story is as rooted in Americana as any in dramatic literature. The strengths of *Show Boat* are its historical sweep and broad humanity, and the most effective productions are those which emphasize that Old Man River just keeps rolling along.

Although Kern raided not only his trunk but his published songs for melodies (as was his custom), the *Show Boat* score is a remarkable piece, the more so because it is such an enormous canvas. Themes are quoted throughout the show, used to underscore the emotionality of a scene or to foreshadow coming events. *Show Boat* was the first musical to use underscoring so successfully, and thus to draw so much of the show together. Remember that musicals of the time were rarely the work of one songwriter—in fact, the original production of *Show Boat* contained all or part of ten songs by other writers. Remarkably, in every case these were inserted by Hammerstein and Kern for realism, not by the producer to pump the show with hits. The Trocadero nightclub scene contained the "Washington Post March" by John Philip Sousa, Jacques Offenbach's "Valse des Rayons" from his ballet *Le Papillon,* a cakewalk using Joseph Howard's "Goodbye, Ma Lady Love," and Kerry Mills's "At a Georgia Camp Meeting." Magnolia sang "After the Ball" by Charles Harris, as well as Theodore Metz's "A Hot Time in the Old Town Tonight."

Prior to *Show Boat,* plots were merely excuses for entertainment. Musical numbers were haphazardly fitted into the action, and often the action was tailored to available musical material—material that had been written to show off the particular talents of a cast that had been put together in advance of both book and songs. In his review of *The Desert Song* (which Hammerstein had worked on) for the *Herald Tribune,* Richard Watts, Jr. wrote that "[t]he question of how simple-minded the book of a musical comedy can be was debated last night, and the verdict arrived at was 'no end.'"

The original production of *Show Boat* changed American musicals boldly, radically, and suddenly. *Show Boat* is reminiscent of operetta in the ambition behind its score and the exotic setting of life on the Mississippi, and even in its cross-class relationships—riverboat gambler and showboat captain's daughter; mulatto woman and white man—but it's pure musical theatre in every other aspect. It was written by American-born writers, featured an American setting, and used a vernacular in its libretto and lyric vocabulary, and very little of the score was in 3/4 time. Most importantly, the score was built on rhythm, harmonies, and intervals suggested by the setting. Content dictated form.

In 1849 Richard Wagner wrote that "[t]he error in the art of opera consists in the fact that a means of expression (music) has been made the object, while the expression itself (the drama) has been made the means." In opera, music had tried and failed to establish itself as the dramatic focus, and Wagner claimed that its resurrection lay in an equal collaboration with the libretto. No characters should be onstage for the sake of their sound—only those characters essential to the plot. Melodies should be written with as much attention to the demands of the lyrics as to the composer's particular inspiration.

Seventy-five years later Jerome Kern and Oscar Hammerstein would put the same simple theory to work on the musical stage: all the tools previously used as a means of *entertainment* would henceforth be employed as a means of *expression,* subservient to the story. Kern and Hammerstein discovered what Wagner had found so useful—that when music is properly applied to the plot and characters of the play, it takes on so much additional depth that its artistry (and Kern's talent for melody was considerable) gets magnified. Until both dialogue and music were made to serve the plot, the slapdash alternation of comedy and music was an insurmountable barrier to the emotional momentum of the evening. Additionally, the epic grandeur of *Show Boat,* its glorious and romantic score, and its sweeping Americana almost obscured the fact that, for the first time in the history of the American musical theatre, its subject matter was essentially downbeat.

It was the beginning of the serious musical, the point at which the all-encompassing "musical theatre" would replace "musical comedy," marked by the supreme achievement of the integration of book, music, and lyrics. From *Show Boat* on, no score for the musical stage would be considered first-rate unless it amplified the mood, plot, and character requirements of the

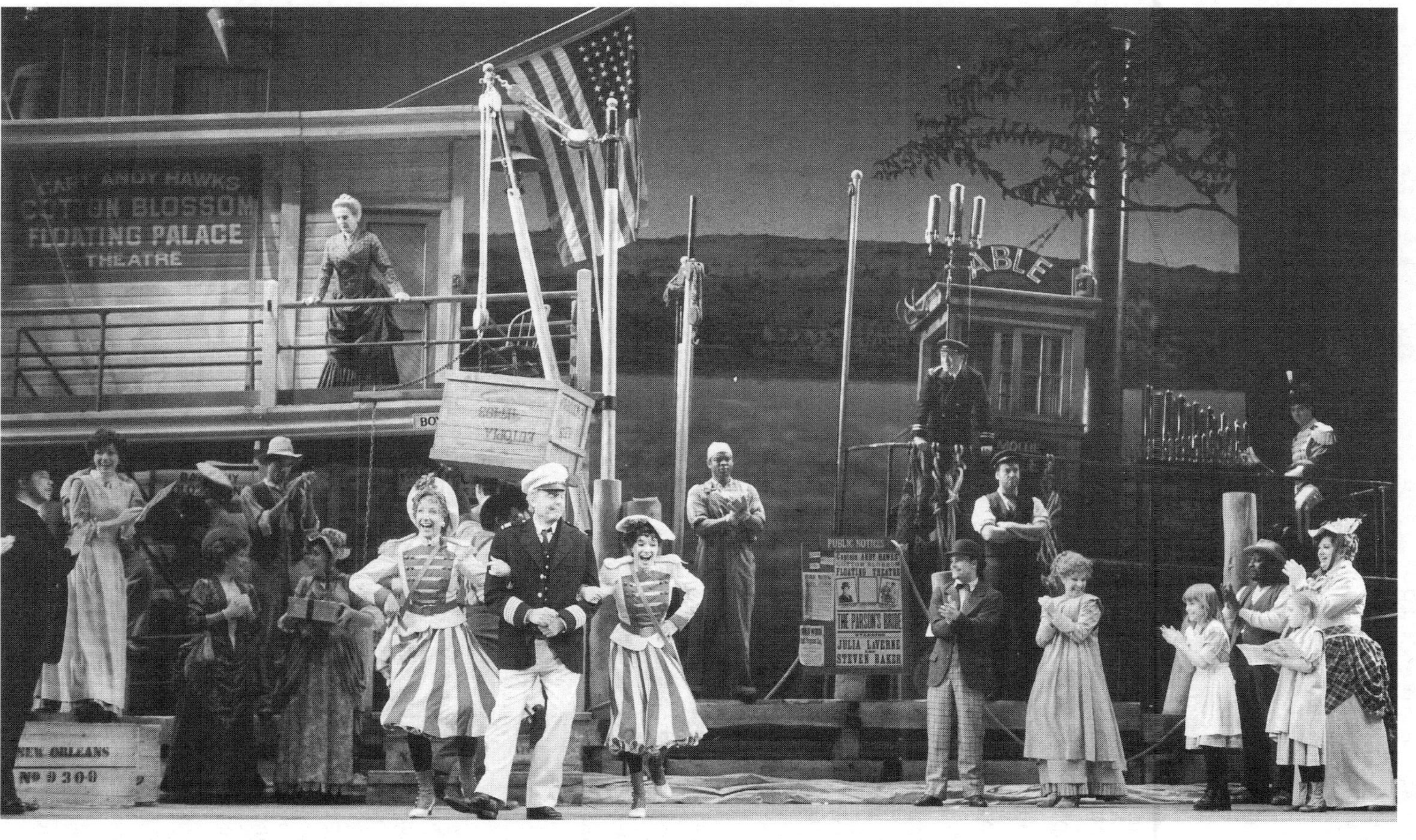

The cotton blossom docks, from the Harold Prince revival. Capt. Andy gives locals a preview of the show
Livent Production/Catharine Ashmore

story. From *Show Boat* on, weak, silly librettos would not only be unacceptable on their own, they would trivialize the accompanying music as well. Kern became the first composer to write specifically for an American musical theatre, and *Show Boat* created the pattern from which all modern musicals are cut.

To use the power of a serious story and to complement Kern's music most effectively, Hammerstein had to invent a further axiom: the highest emotional point of the scene would be the portion to be musicalized. When simple comedy exploitation scenes were artificially linked to songs, the arrangement mattered little—it was primarily a job of proper pacing. When the scene and the song became linked through emotional action, arrangement became more delicate. Hammerstein arranged his libretto and lyrics to alternate so that when a character reached a point of emotional commitment that dialogue could no longer properly illustrate, he or she broke into the more subtly expressive, more emotional, less intellectual mode of music. If the Princess musicals worked hard to smooth the integration of scene and song, *Show Boat* now gave that integration additional responsibilities—those of emotional pacing.

Critics described Kern as having left musical comedy behind for something they variously described as opera or light opera composing. In fact, it was pure musical *theatre.* Thanks to Kern and Hammerstein, the American musical was on its way to greatness as an art form.

• • •

The first London production of *Show Boat* opened at the Drury Lane Theatre on May 3, 1928 and ran for 350 performances. Ziegfeld revived it on Broadway in 1932, just three years after it had closed, with much of the original cast; it was a careful and sumptuous production. Ziegfeld died during that run. Rodgers and Hammerstein revived *Show Boat* in 1946, by which time theatre craft had improved considerably, and Hammerstein cut three scenes that had been written solely to cover slow set changes.

For the 1946 revival, on the heels of a rise in the popularity of dance due to *Oklahoma!* two years earlier, choreographer Helen Tamiris was given considerable latitude. But her additional choreography served only to distract from the musical's original cohesiveness, for Hammerstein had used dance only when it added drama to the libretto.

The 910-performance run of the 1971 British revival was the longest, in spite of that production's eccentric nature. This revival featured a hodgepodge of accents and performances, as well as new orchestrations that attempted to echo primitive recordings of the 1920s in the mistaken belief that this fairly represented the score. (In fact, recordings were not then made as "original cast albums," but as dance records.)

However, in 1994, New York experienced a remarkable revival of *Show Boat,* especially significant considering the feeble state of American musical theatre by then. The word "revival" doesn't do justice to this lush reworking of the sixty-seven-year-old material. Directed by Harold Prince and produced by Garth Drabinsky the production restored the sweeping grandeur of the original, though in a grittier, more realistic design style. The huge Gershwin Theatre on Fifty-second street had never before run a production that filled it with sixty-eight performers, more than five hundred costumes, and mechanized scenery that Hammerstein could only have dreamed of.

Show Boat had never been given such careful and successful thought. Although the powerful "Niggers All Work on the Mississippi" was altered to "Colored Folk . . .," the majority of the dialogue was authentic, the word "nigger" wasn't buried, and the "colored only/whites only" water barrels on the set stood starkly as an accurate expression of the racial attitudes of the time and place. The powerful anthem "Mis'ry's Comin' 'Round" was included, and the song "I Have the Room Above Her," written for the 1936 film, was used. Even some new dances were used to good effect, as the sweep of time from 1900 to 1927 was montaged through a series of period social dances, further underlining the epic nature of the production. Although the New York version was twenty minutes shorter than the Toronto debut—probably due to union costs as much as a tightening of the show—the greatness of *Show Boat* was all in evidence. Hammerstein himself would have loved the technical and artistic innovations that allowed the story to flow uninterrupted. This production reminds us that no musical will ever represent American romanticism as well as *Show Boat.*

• • •

Even as the original production of *Show Boat* was running, the theatre was starting to be affected by the Depression, sound films, and audience interest in lighter, more escapist fare. Although Kern and Hammerstein announced two projects with American settings, neither came to fruition. The economy, combined with Kern's desire to cease turning out three or four scores a season and concentrate on writing really fine shows like *Show Boat,* threw Kern's once prolific career into a tailspin.

Hammerstein's *Golden Dawn,* with book by Hammerstein and Otto Harbach, music by Emmerich Kalman, Herbert Stothart, and Robert Stoltz, codirected by Reginald Hammerstein, and produced by Arthur Hammerstein, had opened while *Show Boat* was in preproduction, but *Golden Dawn* would close in several months. It was a Viennese operetta set in Africa, with white performers in blackface playing Africans. Walter Winchell called it the "golden yawn."*

Next, Kern and Hammerstein created *Sweet Adeline* (1929) for Helen Morgan. Its cast featured a Jewish impresario, and Kern—always involved in every aspect of his musicals—insisted that the exaggerated characteristics and mannerisms (stemming from the vaudeville stage) that Jewish comedians still used should be eliminated in favor of a more realistic performance. The show received good reviews, including one in *Theatre* magazine indicating that Hammerstein and Kern were still attempting to avoid the clichés of the current musical stage: "It was a relief to sit through a musical evening without having long lines of mechanized dancing preempting the stage from time to time for no good reason at all." The show also contained an overture not composed by Kern—a medley of songs from the gay nineties, to set the period. Unfortunately the stock market crash abruptly ended its success.**

For *The Cat and the Fiddle* (1931) Kern composed an extremely ambitious score, using underscoring and long melody lines and taking verses seriously; however, the musical simply did not have the impact of *Show Boat.* It was well reviewed, but the Depression affected its run. Then, too, Dillingham, who owned the theatre in which Max Gordon had produced

* The show is noted, however, for the first topless girl in a legitimate musical and an actor named Archie Leach in the second male lead. Leach's spectacular good looks and acrobat's body—he had started in English music hall as a stilt-walker and clown—were not matched with an adequate singing voice. In *A Wonderful Night* (1929), Leach lip-synched to a voice provided by a real singer behind a curtain. No critic noticed this appalling deceit, and he was told that his vocal abilities had improved since his earlier appearances. Leach later changed his name to Cary Grant and tried films.

** In another blow to serious musicals, during those years it seemed as if sillier and happier musicals were less likely to be affected by the Depression.

the show, absconded with a week's box office receipts. But the real reason *The Cat and the Fiddle* has not come down to us with the authority of *Show Boat* is the story, which was simply not original, or American, enough. (A high-brow Romanian composer and a female American tunesmith have a relationship in Brussels.)

Music in the Air (1932) was another Kern gem. It was produced by Peggy Fears (with Elizabeth Marbury, one of the first female producers on Broadway), a former Ziegfeld girl bankrolled by her husband. It played for 342 performances, in spite of its eccentric history. Oscar had wanted to set a show in the office of a Tin Pan Alley music publisher—an outstanding idea and probably, in Hammerstein's career, the one that got away—but Kern suggested a mellower, more romantic setting: Bavaria. Unfortunately, critics and audiences alike were rapidly giving up any lingering interest in Bavarian operetta. Its initial title was *Karl and Sieglinde,* and it featured a plot from the operetta era—a music teacher and a schoolmaster from a Bavarian village compose a song based on a bird call (Kern had in fact transcribed a bird's song he had heard for "I've Told Every Little Star"), and they undergo trials and tribulations in the big city of Munich. The story would likely have been far more effective on Tin Pan Alley. Still, Hammerstein began experimenting with dialogue in the rhythm of an upcoming song to promote smoother transitions. While an actor sang, other actors would continue acting behind him, another example of Hammerstein's constant attempt to keep a musical moving.

In 1934 only two book musicals were produced on the Great White Way. No wonder many established writers like Kern and Hammerstein fled Broadway's depression and accepted lucrative offers to write for pictures.

Following a series of desultory shows in London, Hammerstein accepted a contract with MGM and relocated to Hollywood. As with many of Broadway's emigrés, his time in Hollywood yielded little, partly because of Hollywood and partly out of ennui. They had no creative control over their material and no financial stake in its success or failure, and they had to put up with Hollywood executives—a breed of businesspeople with an uncanny knack for knocking the artistic spirit out of any project. Most of the talented writers who entrained for Los Angeles found themselves pursuing an endless round of parties, gambling, games, dinners, and elaborate practical jokes. They wiled away their time, phoned in their work, and collected enormous paychecks. Film executives promised Hammerstein that he could produce and direct his own features, but that promise never materialized.

Nevertheless, the demands of a cinematic score sometimes gave Hammerstein more freedom than he would have on stage. "When I Grow Too Old To Dream" became a substantial hit for Hammerstein and Sigmund Romberg (Hammerstein was still writing with a number of partners, including Kern) after it appeared in a modest film called *The Night is Young* (1934), in which a European archduke loves a ballerina. Hammerstein never felt the lyrics made sense, but he liked the imagery so much he never changed it. Thus it was probably his first successful "pop" lyric, and he came to accept the usefulness of words *as* music in addition to words *for* music, which enriched his work. Hammerstein and Kern's only interesting film musical was *High, Wide and Handsome* (1937).

Hammerstein returned to New York and wrote *May Wine* (1935) with Romberg, which had a reasonably satisfying seven-month run but did not approach *Show Boat* in quality or commercial success.

Very Warm for May (1939) was the result of Kern's idea to do a Princess-inspired musical on Broadway. He and Hammerstein concocted a plot that included a summer stock playhouse owned by a Ray Comstock prototype, with Eve Arden playing Bessie Marbury. By eyewitness accounts, *May* was a wonderful show, but producer Max Gordon didn't like it. He replaced the director and demanded rewrite after rewrite, turning the ebullient and successful out-of-town premiere into a frustrating tryout tour. When the show finally opened on Broadway on November 17 at the Alvin Theatre, it was purportedly much worse ("*Very Warm For May* not so hot for November") and ran for only fifty-nine performances.* (Max Gordon was also the man who rid himself of an investment in *Oklahoma!* at the intermission of that musical's premiere performance.) The score featured "All the Things You Are," a song Kern thought too complex to be a popular hit at the time—it is now considered one of Kern's all-time gems.

• • •

In spite of *Show Boat*'s almost continuous appearance somewhere in the world, Kern and Hammerstein entered a prolonged period of failure and frustration. In 1945 Jerome Kern came to New York for a revival of *Show*

* The inexperienced reader may find it difficult to understand how something good can actually be reworked into something bad at the prodding of a producer—unfortunately this is not an unusual story.

Boat and to write the score for *Annie Get Your Gun*, but he collapsed of a cerebral hemorrhage three days later.

Show Boat notwithstanding, Jerome Kern had one foot in the past, for his musical adolescence had been in the world of operetta. He hardly realized what his Princess shows and *Show Boat* had wrought, and many of his post-*Show Boat* scores were European-influenced. The next composer to tackle the Broadway musical with an equally serious approach grew up in the raucous America of New York's Lower East Side, and roller-skated around a tumultuous Manhattan that was growing up fast. Through its growing pains, George Gershwin's retentive ear heard the emerging, original sound of America.

Otto Kahn, chairman of the Metropolitan Opera, asked several prominent composers to write an American opera, a jazz opera in the (new) native American style. He approached Irving Berlin, Jerome Kern and George Gershwin. Berlin and Kern both realized that they did not have the technical proficiency, and declined, though both championed the idea. Gershwin accepted the challenge.

BEGINNING
MONDAY EVENING,
OCTOBER 21, 1935

(THIRD PRODUCTION OF THE EIGHTEE

THE THEATRE GUILD

Presents

PORGY AND BESS

An American Folk Opera

(Founded on the play "PORGY" by DuBose and Dorothy Heyward)

Music by GEORGE GERSHWIN

Libretto by DUBOSE HEYWARD

Lyrics by DUBOSE HEYWARD and IRA GERSHWIN

Production Directed by ROUBEN MAMOULIAN

Settings Designed by SERGEI SOUDEIKINE

Orchestra Conducted by ALEXANDER SMALLENS

CAST

(In the order of appearance)

MINGO .... *Played by* .... FORD L. BUCK
CLARA .... " " .... ABBIE MITCHELL
SPORTIN' LIFE .... " " .... JOHN W. BUBBLES

Twelve

Porgy and Bess

We are living in an age of staccato, not legato.

—George Gershwin

Broadway wasn't quiet between *Show Boat* and *Porgy and Bess,* but there was hardly a murmur of serious, integrated theatre. There were numerous romantic musical comedies based on French farces (*Lovely Lady, The Madcap, Luckee Girl, Sunny Days*), a much-mined source. Most of these featured peppy music and groups like the Chester Hale dancers, the Tiller Girls, and the Albertina Rausch dancers in precision tap-and-kick routines. Richard Rodgers and Lorenz Hart supplied the best of those scores for *She's My Baby, Present Arms, Chee-Chee,* and *Heads Up.* Florenz Ziegfeld mounted *Rosalie* for Marilyn Miller, supporting her with material from Guy Bolton, P. G. Wodehouse, Sigmund Romberg, and the Gershwin brothers, but it was primarily an extravaganza, a Ziegfeld specialty best defined as spectacle with caution thrown to the winds.

Rudolf Friml's adaptation of Alexandre Dumas's *The Three Musketeers* featured both the Tiller girls and the Albertina Rausch girls in

France. Bessie Marbury produced *Say When* with the Princess formula, a sound idea in the presence of a reaction to overblown musicals, but without Bolton, Wodehouse, and Jerome Kern the quality simply wasn't there.

The Shuberts continued their love affair with foreign operetta styles, and mounted *White Lilacs,* a biography of Chopin. Hammerstein and Romberg wrote *The New Moon,* and they had a hit after closing out of town and rewriting the show entirely. Hammerstein and Kern wrote *Sweet Adeline* and *Music in the Air.* George M. Cohan mounted his last musical, *Billie. Paris* introduced Cole Porter and his inimitable style ("Let's Do It"), after which Porter wrote *Gay Divorce* for Fred Astaire. Meanwhile, Noël Coward offered his equally witty songs in *Bitter Sweet.*

The Marx Brothers pounded their material in *Animal Crackers.* (Bookwriter George S. Kaufman once turned to someone as they were standing in the back of a theatre and said, "Just a minute, I think I heard one of my original lines.") Vincent Youmans's *Rainbow* had parallels to *Show Boat* in its American story and epic scope and ambition. Eddie Cantor dazzled audiences in Ziegfeld's *Whoopee.* DeSylva, Brown, and Henderson produced their last New York show, *Flying High.* Ethel Merman belted out "I've Got Rhythm" for the Gershwin brothers' *Girl Crazy* and began her Broadway legend as the "golden foghorn" (Cole Porter's anointment).

There were three unusual political satires—*Strike Up the Band, Of Thee I Sing,* and *Let 'Em Eat Cake,* about which more later. Broadway audiences were introduced to Kurt Weill's distinctive music in *The Threepenny Opera,* and Jerome Kern went back to musical comedy with *Roberta,* which included "Smoke Gets In Your Eyes."

The quintessential thirties musical was *Anything Goes* (1934) featuring the writing talents of Bolton, Wodehouse, Howard Lindsay, and Russell Crouse; the songs of Cole Porter; and the voice of Ethel Merman ("You're the Top," "Blow, Gabriel, Blow"). (The musical was still effervescent in 1987 when director Jerry Zaks, designer Tony Walton, and musical director Edward Strauss recreated it with slick contemporary craft for the awkward Vivian Beaumont Theatre.) And of course there were the revues, the best of which was *The Band Wagon,* and any number of *Follies, Scandals, Vanities, Gaieties,* and the like.

But in 1935 a musical came along that would push the boundaries beyond even *Show Boat.* Jerome Kern and George Gershwin had nearly identical careers during their early years. Both dropped out of high school and worked Tin Pan Alley in their late teens. Both song-plugged for Max

Dreyfuss at T. B. Harms, both worked as rehearsal pianists—of all the apprenticeships for writing great Broadway tunes, that of rehearsal pianist seems the most productive—and both accompanied female singers on tour.

Dreyfuss discovered Gershwin's songs and signed him to a $35-a-week contract. Gershwin's first Broadway song, "Making of a Girl," appeared in the Shuberts' *Passing Show of 1916.* At the age of twenty-five, Gershwin wrote "Swanee" to a lyric by Irving Caesar. Al Jolson sang it on tour in *Sinbad* and recorded it (1920), whereupon the song sold a million copies of sheet music and two million records. George Gershwin was introduced to fame and success, both of which he took to comfortably and eagerly.

From 1920 to 1924 Gershwin wrote forty-five songs for various editions of George White's *Scandals.* He also composed *Blue Monday,* a fifteen-minute one-act opera (lyrics by Buddy DeSylva) in the new jazz idiom. *Blue Monday* takes place in a Harlem nightclub and features a Frankie-and-Johnny plot. It premiered as part of the *Scandals of 1922* but was dropped after opening night. White thought it too serious, and too long, for his revue. But one prescient reviewer wrote, "[I]n it we see the first gleam of a new American musical art."

But the arrival of that new art was still a decade away. In the 1920s most Broadway musicals were built on the same conventions: already-cast stars and comedians, dance turns, a girl chorus, and complex comic plots of boy-meets-girl and mistaken identity. Critics' remarks invariably contained lines like "a barely serviceable book" (that was a compliment), with careful consideration reserved for the songs and the performances. For these shows George Gershwin and his older brother Ira created a plethora of good songs unconnected to the book, usually tunes George had already written up in his notebook which Ira would recall and put words to. Even as the shows varied wildly in effectiveness, the Gershwins' songwriting matured through a number of shows . . .

Primrose was done in London (1924) and included "Boy Wanted," its score (lyrics by Ira Gershwin and Desmond Carter) far better integrated than the average musical of the period, probably because it featured a strong book for which the numerous songs and one ballet were created.

Ira and George reached their stride with *Lady, Be Good!* (1924), which included the fresh and extremely syncopated "Fascinating Rhythm." The show had a rhythmic complexity, matched by Ira's lyrics, that had never before been attempted on Broadway. Producer Alex Aarons had the idea that by combining Fred and Adele Astaire (a brother/sister team that had been a hit for him in London) with songs exclusively by George and Ira Gershwin (their first full score together), he could do for the American musical what Paul Whiteman had done for concert music—that is, speed its emergence as an American art form. Aarons instinctively felt that the Astaires' dancing and the Gershwins' songs would be a good match, and all of them wanted to do something in the Princess Theatre mode—the Kern-Bolton-Wodehouse musicals had been an admired revelation to the Gershwins, as they had been to Rodgers, Hart, and nearly every youth dreaming of Broadway at the time. Aarons enlisted Guy Bolton, and later Fred Thompson, to do the book. From early on, George had trusted little to his arrangers, writing a detailed piano part to form the basis of the orchestrations, and later the full orchestrations. He also wrote transition music, dance music, and overtures, all of which no other Broadway composer did. For *Lady, Be Good!* he put a two-piano team—Ohman and Arden—into the pit, because Whiteman (who conducted) had used two pianos in his concert "jazz" band. They were inordinately successful, and playgoers sometimes stayed in their seats at intermission to listen to the two improvise on a Gershwin tune. They also played a post-show jam session that Fred Astaire later said was very popular and contributed to the success of the show. In the end, Alex Aarons's instincts were golden, and the careers of both the Gershwins and the Astaires took off. Out-of-town critic Linton Martin, identifying the typical 1920s musical, wrote, "If any one brand of show can be counted upon to run true to type, it is the ever-unostentatious musical comedy, with its $1500 a week comedians, its insipid ingénues, piping prima donnas, heart-breaking humor, range of two plots (Cinderella or Go-Getters) and its tinkly-twinkle tunes." Martin went on to describe the leap that Alex Aarons and company had made: "But here if you please, and even if you don't, we have in *Lady, Be Good!* a Vital Contribution to American Music. Indeed, nothing less than a Musical Milepost." Calling Gershwin's music "tonal Jiu-jitsu," he characterized it as "music that one may listen to time and again . . . it is elusive, subtle, individual, piquant and plaintive."

Curiously, the best example is a song that didn't make the cut. "The Man I Love" had been written on its own during a Gershwin work session, inserted into *Lady,* and helped to convince Otto Kahn to invest in the show. The song was cut during the out of town run, unheard again when the second musical to use it closed out of town, and lost a third time when it was dropped in rehearsal from *Rosalie.* In the end, "The Man I Love" was never actually performed in a musical, yet it is considered by Gershwin musicologist Deena Rosenberg to be the "first great song written for a new genre—the American musical." George had brought blue notes—the flatted third or seventh in a major key that projects a sad feeling—into theatre music with *Blue Monday* and "Stairway to Paradise." Ira, with his plaintive lyric for "The Man I Love," ("Someday he'll come along . . ."), matched the feeling well and released something in his own soul that the quiet, contemplative wordsmith hadn't yet plumbed. The Gershwin brothers' symbiotic talent was confirmed, and the true Gershwin song was born. Just as Irving Berlin had brought black ragtime into white theatre, George brought black blues and Jewish music into the theatre. (Writing of the melody of "My One and Only," George's first biographer said that it "begins Yiddish and ends up black.")

Tell Me More (1925) was a big hit in London and an equally big failure on Broadway. This show will go down in musical theatre history for giving up its original title, *My Fair Lady.*

Tip Toes (1925) featured "Looking for a Boy."

Oh, Kay! (1926) boasted "Do-Do-Do," "Someone To Watch Over Me," and Gertrude Lawrence in her first Broadway starring role.

Funny Face (1927) featured "S'Wonderful" and the Astaires. Fred's rhythmic ability would perfectly compliment George's complex syncopations on Broadway and later in Hollywood.

The last and best of the silly Gershwin musicals, *Girl Crazy* (1930), marked the fifth time the brothers had worked with a book by Guy Bolton (good thing Gershwin wasn't married), which rippled with "Bidin' My Time" and "Embraceable You." *Girl Crazy* also introduced an eighteen-year-old Ethel Merman, singing "I Got Rhythm." Ginger Rogers, then nineteen, played the lead. When the producers asked Fred Astaire to choreograph a dance they were having trouble with, Astaire was introduced to Rogers and they worked together informally in the lobby of a theatre for the first time.

The orchestra for *Girl Crazy* included Red Nichols, Benny Goodman, Jimmy Dorsey, Glenn Miller, Gene Krupa, and Jack Teagarden—if ever there was a chance to imagine the rollicking sounds of the Broadway musicals of the twenties, it is with that list of pit musicians. The rich Gershwin songs deepened the characters they wrote for and, bolstered by talents like Gertrude Lawrence and Ethel Merman, the American musical heroine became a stronger emotional character.

But by the late twenties, George and Ira sensed that the formula needed to change. Ira wondered if he could come up with any more songs in the old formula without repeating himself. Together they ventured on to a more integrated type of song that grew out of the plot and expressed something more than happy-go-lucky romance. They accomplished this over seven years with three political satires written by playwrights George S. Kaufman and Morrie Ryskind. Crafting their songs to follow an already extant book, George and Ira wrote comic operetta and parody songs for those characters that were meant to satirize American institutions, and jazz-inflected, modern American theatre songs for the average man and woman caught up in the madness.

Strike Up the Band was a satire on war and war profiteers with a score that referred deliberately to Gilbert and Sullivan. The show closed in Philadelphia in 1927, but its biting satire was softened and given a happy ending for another try in 1930, when it became a Broadway hit. It featured "I've Got a Crush On You," and its title has since become a rousing football song but was in fact a biting antiwar profiteer satire. The Stock Market Crash of 1929 had given American audiences a bit more backbone, and Ryskind's revised book met them halfway.

Of Thee I Sing (1931) was the longest-running Gershwin musical at 441 performances. It won the first Pulitzer Prize in drama ever awarded to a musical, though Gershwin didn't receive recognition because the committee was unaware of how integral music is to a musical. It was a satire on politicians, offended only politicians, and featured a happy ending, testified to in "Love is Sweeping the Country." The rest of the score was so integrated in the Gilbert and Sullivan style—including rhymed recitative set to music—that it doesn't boast typical Gershwin tunes.

Let 'Em Eat Cake (1933) was a sequel to *Sing*. The book predicts an American dictator created by politicians, industrialists, and the military, and features long musical sequences far beyond the simple song form. It was the Gershwins' most ambitiously integrated score, due largely to Ira, who based many of his lyrics on the book, before the music was written. This last—and probably best—attempt by Kaufman, Ryskind, and the Gershwins to use the traditional musical comedy form in a significant way was a "satire on practically everything." But the political climate—the Depression, Hitler and

Mussolini on the rise, Japan invading China—encouraged the writers to become darker when audiences sought the escape offered by lighter fare.

All three satires marked an increase in the integration of book, music, and lyrics. Thus the scores have fewer songs that can be extracted and promoted as a popular hits. Nevertheless, the success of two of these unusual musicals—albeit the happiest and least controversial—encouraged the Gershwins' ambitions. George had been enamored with *Show Boat* since he saw it, believing it to be "the finest light opera achievement in the history of American music." Concurrent with his songwriting, he had created three hugely successful "serious" musical works for the concert hall: *Rhapsody in Blue* (1924), *Concerto in F* (1925), and *An American in Paris* (1928). All three had been influenced less by Tin Pan Alley music than by one of the earliest forms of music that had evolved from American Negro spirituals, which had begun in New Orleans, come up the Mississippi River to Chicago and Kansas City, and evolved into ragtime in St. Louis. It was popularized by Scott Joplin and brought to New York around the turn of the century by Ben Harney. By then you could call it "jazz," and it fascinated George Gershwin.

A curious and continual student of music, Gershwin had done his own orchestrations for all his concert work after *Rhapsody.* He had even signed a contract with the Metropolitan Opera to create an opera out of the Jewish folk tale *The Dybbuk,* using a Yiddish version that had been presented at the Neighborhood Playhouse in 1926. He started collecting ideas in his tune book until it was discovered that the rights were unavailable. During rehearsals for *Oh, Kay!* he read the novel *Porgy* and wanted to turn it into an opera.

• • •

The long odyssey of the drama about the black denizens of Catfish Row in Charleston, South Carolina began in the mind of DuBose Heyward, a white, genteel Southerner who lived nearby. Poor, orphaned, and self-educated (two years with polio left him with a crippled right arm and a love of books), Heyward dropped out of high school. He began a career in insurance, then turned to writing, first poetry and then the novel *Porgy,* which was published in 1925. He caught the flavor of an American subculture, using a unique southern dialect known as Gullah, and he fashioned a story (suggested by a newspaper article about a cripple in a goat cart who had twice been arrested for assault) that was rich with melodrama. The novel made many bestseller lists.

By 1926 the artistically restless George Gershwin was impressed with *Porgy*'s possibilities as a libretto for his latest ambition: a full-length jazz opera. But Dorothy Heyward, the author's wife and a failed playwright, was the first to recognize the novel's dramatic possibilities, and she had been secretly drafting a play based on her husband's novel. When Gershwin wrote to DuBose of his desire, Dorothy told her husband about her work. Loyal to his wife, Heyward informed Gershwin that Dorothy's version had to come first. However, this was not a problem because George was busy writing Broadway musicals, wanted to study serious music for a few more years, and realized that a play would provide a stronger structure as a base for his eventual opera.

The Theatre Guild, dedicated to expanding the American drama, agreed at once to produce the Heywards' play on Broadway. Their first director, however, made only a halfhearted attempt to cast the play—which was difficult, as there were very few experienced black performers involved in the professional theatre at the time—and soon he abandoned the production, leaving the Heywards frustrated. But the Theatre Guild tried again, and this time they stumbled upon a young man whose eventual career would encompass not only a number of Broadway hits and several wonderful Hollywood films, but two of the eight shows that revolutionized the American musical.

His name was Rouben Mamoulian, and he was known at the time among Theatre Guild personnel as "that mad Armenian." Mamoulian was born in Tiflis, Russia in 1898 (the same year George Gershwin was born in Brooklyn), where his mother was president of the Armenian Theatre. He studied with the studio theatre arm of the Moscow Art Theatre, wrote dramatic criticism, and founded a drama studio in Tiflis. When the revolution came he moved to London, where he formed a Russian repertory theatre and directed a West End success in the style of utter realism pioneered by Konstantin Stanislavsky. George Eastman then invited Mamoulian to direct the new American Opera Company in Rochester, which brought him to America. From there he was invited to run the Theatre Guild's drama school in New York City.

Mamoulian was feverishly ambitious. He staged a student production

Ira Gershwin, George Gershwin, and DuBose Heyward create the first folk opera for the American musical theatre

Archive Photos

of George Cohan's *Seven Keys to Baldpate* to which he dragged the Guild's board of directors. It was a spellbinding production, and the timing was fortuitous for the future of the American musical. The Guild invited him to take over their floundering production of *Porgy.* The play, which included authentic spirituals, opened in 1927 (three months prior to *Show Boat*), and was a success. Mamoulian was hailed as a brilliant theatre director and his career skyrocketed.

Meanwhile, DuBose Heyward had met George Gershwin in person. Gershwin, enthusiastic as ever about the potential opera, had waited for the production of the play—now he was ready.

Although history has glossed over Dorothy and Dubose Heyward's contribution to the libretto in favor of Ira Gershwin, in fact it was DuBose who wrote a good deal of the lyrics (including "Summertime"). By all accounts the collaboration was a comfortable one: DuBose provided the first drafts, and Ira altered some—but not all—of the words to fit George's music.

George's music filled the piece. Not only did George write the songs (which he sometimes referred to as arias) and not only did he labor mightily to write his own orchestrations (which few Broadway composers did), but he scored the spoken dialogue as well, creating the "recitative" sections which would eventually prove central to arguments over *Porgy*'s form.

Producers Theresa Helburn and Lawrence Langner of the Theatre Guild took on the production, and Rouben Mamoulian—by now well-established on Broadway as well as in Hollywood, thanks to his film of the original play version—directed this triangular story of love and death.

A cast was difficult to find. Talented black singers and actors were used to delivering lines directly to the audience in musical revues and vaudeville. They were not accustomed to extensive rehearsals, and they had little experience in taking dramatic direction. Under Mamoulian, rehearsals were as painstaking as any in the modern era of the perfectionist director-choreographer. Though he was not a dancer, he staged the entire show, including chorus and principal movement well in excess of what opera performers are expected to do. He was an imaginative and innovative director whose eye for theatrical effects, for stage pictures that augmented the drama, and for the canvas as a whole, informed the production.

With his background in realism, Mamoulian was unwilling to let the singers think of themselves as less than actors—in this, he was a forerunner of the men who would transform American musical theatre staging

Rouben Mamoulian directs a large cast
Museum of the City of New York/Vandamm

and direction in the future. He was meticulous in his instructions and slavish in his devotion to the tenets of theatre. He broke the cast of the operatic habit of keeping their eyes on the conductor. He was indestructibly patient, for a good many of his cast members had little theatre experience. The majority of the principals had strong musical backgrounds, but John Bubbles (of the vaudeville team Buck and Bubbles), who played Sportin' Life, had little understanding of what Mamoulian was trying to do. Bubbles drove the musical director to distraction with his inability to repeat his songs properly.

The tryout at Boston's Colonial Theatre was a huge success with the audience, who cheered for fifteen minutes. The production ran three and a half hours. The participants—Broadway showmakers all—agreed that it was too long, and the running time was abbreviated by almost an hour for the sake of showmanship. By the time it reached New York, the show was not the work that had been acclaimed in Boston.

• • •

On October 10, 1935 at the Alvin Theatre,* *Porgy and Bess* opened before a glittering audience, filled with celebrities as well as theatre and music critics. When it was over, they cheered for half an hour. Four hundred people were invited to the opening night party, a Latin band was engaged, and bandleader Paul Whiteman (who had premiered Gershwin's *Rhapsody in Blue* several years earlier) brought along his orchestra. Gershwin settled at the piano—his customary place at any party—and he and the cast sang through most of the opera once again. The extravagant gathering continued until dawn. It had all taken place in the private penthouse apartment of magazine magnate Condé Nast.

In the morning the mood changed—criticism was decidedly mixed. Music critics tended to begrudge the work, principally for its jazz foundation, while theatre critics tended to praise it. One critic called it the "first authentic American opera," but another labeled it an "aggrandized musical show." Virgil Thompson (whose avant-garde opera with Gertrude Stein,

* "Alvin" was derived from the names Alex A. Aarons and Vinton Freedley, two Broadway producers who had long championed the Gershwin brothers. They brought us *La La Lucille; Lady, Be Good; Tip Toes; Oh, Kay!; Funny Face; Girl Crazy;* and *The Band Wagon.* Sadly, their halcyon days have been forgotten with the renaming of their West Forty-seventh Street theatre to the Neil Simon.

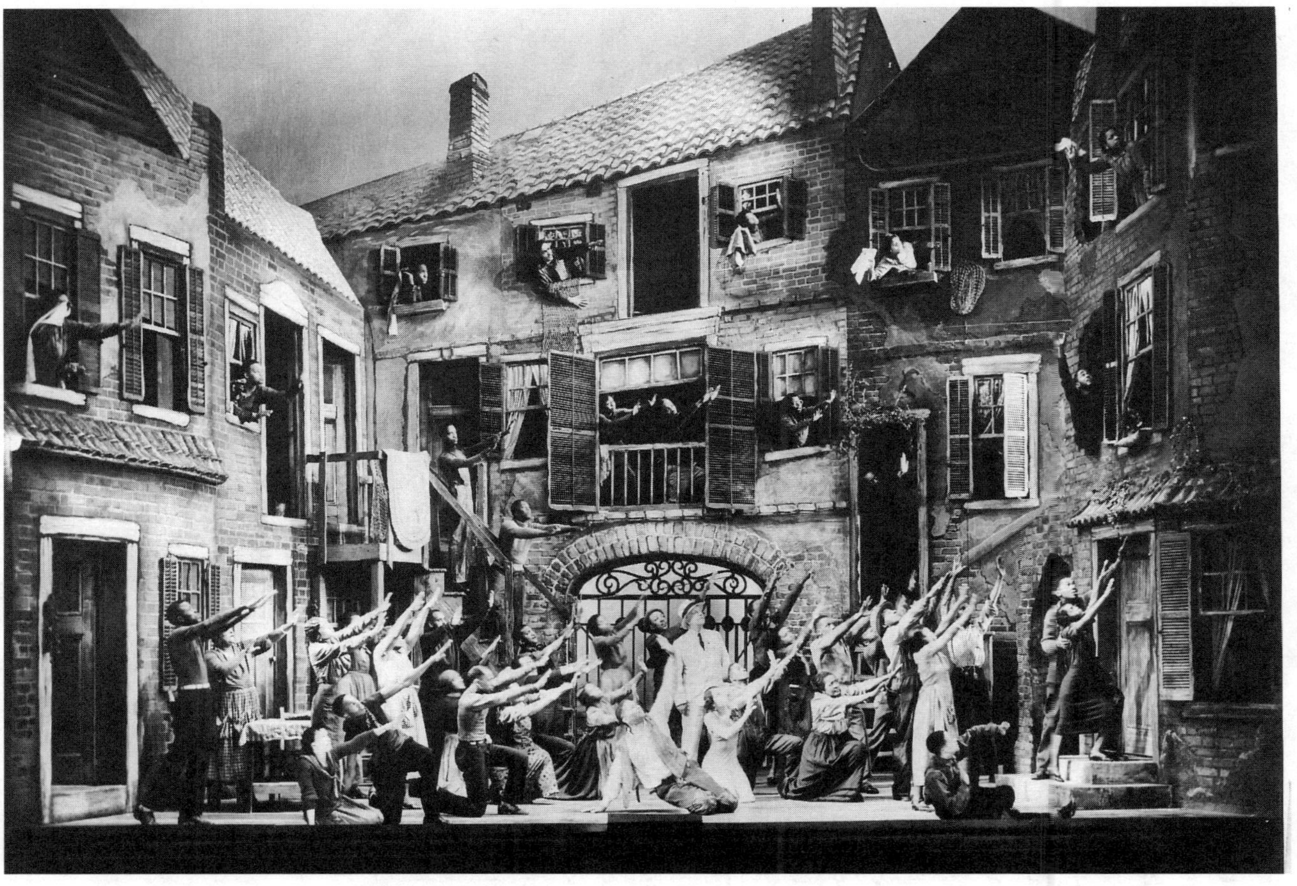

Catfish Row and Mamoulian's surreal staging

Photofest

Four Saints in Three Acts, had featured an all-black cast a few years earlier) wrote a primarily negative review. He knew virtually nothing of George Gershwin's previous work, even his serious compositions, and several errors in the review gave away his ignorance.

George Gershwin had long been good box office. He had appeared on the cover of *Time* magazine as early as 1925. There had been detractors since the time Gershwin broke out of the musical comedy mold, all from the high-minded, serious school of classical composition, all of whom lacked the success, fame, and fortune of Gershwin, and whose own compositions have not stood up to time well. In many cases, their envy was transparent. Others were just staunchly conservative. Daniel Gregory Mason wrote that American music was "corrupted by black jazz," and the "insidiousness of the Jewish menace to our artistic integrity."

The show floundered because of these reviews, and because it was an extremely costly production (with an orchestra twice as large as that for a traditional Broadway musical) that virtually required sold-out houses in order to break even. And it opened in the middle of the Depression. The ticket price was dropped from $4.40 to $3.30, to no avail. The musicians sunk a plan for all parties to take salary and royalty cuts by refusing to participate, and when the weekly running costs could not be lowered, *Porgy* was forced to close after only fifteen weeks.

A four-city tour followed, but the entire investment—including $5,000 each from George, Ira, and Dubose—was lost. *Porgy and Bess* is a one-of-a-kind work of art that cannot be judged against anything else in the history of the American stage. That is its achievement, and its bête noire.

In subsequent decades *Porgy and Bess* has been praised by critics and attended by large audiences all over the world. Its history illustrates a great deal of the controversy over the proper staging of an American musical.

Cheryl Crawford—who had been assistant stage manager for the Theatre Guild's production of the play *Porgy*—ran a summer stock theatre in a converted movie house in Maplewood, New Jersey. In 1942 she reproduced *Porgy and Bess* under extraordinary conditions: in order to scale back the enormous costs that had forced the original production to close, she reduced the size of the large chorus. And she asked the original musical director, Alexander Smallens, to reduce the size of the orchestra.

Interestingly, Smallens had from the very beginning been against the recitatives that George Gershwin—anxious to put his years of musical study to work, and equally anxious, because of his voracious ego, to write a grand opera—had created. Although the weekly operating cost was a factor, Crawford, Smallens (and Brooks Atkinson in his original review) were convinced that the power of *Porgy and Bess* lay not in the tenets of grand opera, but in theatre. With George Gershwin deceased, they converted the recitatives to straight dialogue.

Behind-the-scenes opinions of Crawford's production ranged from "bargain basement" (Ira Gershwin and Dorothy Heyward) to "scaled down" to "theatricalized." The production, notably, was more accessible to audiences. It eventually played on Broadway for twice as many performances as the original production, and successfully toured forty-seven cities in the United States. It was this production much more than the original that established *Porgy and Bess* in the theatrical firmament.

Next, Robert Breen, who was not enamored with operatic acting and was convinced that the proper way to produce *Porgy and Bess* was the Crawford way, produced a European tour. He transposed some scenes and combined the ten scenes into two, rather than three, acts. His desire was to make it good theatre, "to wring from it every legitimate value and illusion of the theatre." He designed and staged it without waiting for lengthy set changes, making it much more fluid and saving enough time to restore three songs that had been eliminated. One of these was "The Buzzard Song," which Gershwin had cut because otherwise Todd Duncan, the original Porgy, would have had to sing three arias in a row, eight times a week. A gifted director and obsessive man, Breen worked hard with the cast to achieve a theatrical production. Still, he reinstalled the recitatives.

The tour started in Dallas summer stock and played some American cities, including Washington, D.C. They headed for Europe under sponsorship from the State Department. In a maze of red tape and on the verge of financial collapse week after week, they played Vienna, Berlin, London, and Paris, then returned to America to play New York's Ziegfeld Theatre for Billy Rose. They then toured nineteen American cities and went back overseas, eventually playing forty cities from Athens to Zagreb, Alexandria to Zurich, in South America, Europe, and the Soviet Union. In all, the show was on the road for nearly four years from 1952 to 1956, and it was enormously successful as a representation of American theatre. However, the show once again closed in the red.

By the middle of the 1950s, twenty years after the original production, *Porgy and Bess* was fully established internationally as a great American opera. Theatres and opera houses all over the world began to mount their own productions.

In 1975 philanthropist Sherwin M. Goldman—enamored with *Porgy* and with opera—decided it was necessary to restage the "full score." He restored *all* the cuts (including many that Gershwin himself had made in Boston), restored the dialogue to recitative, and mounted a production under the direction of Jack O'Brien. This version played at the Mark Hellinger Theatre and then the Uris (now the Gershwin) Theatre, a great cold barn of an auditorium and the largest on Broadway. The success of the musical startled Broadway. Goldman's production finally played the five-thousand-seat Radio City Music Hall.

Next, the Metropolitan Opera produced it in 1985. James Levine said, "It is probably the first time this opera is played in an opera house with opera singers, without cuts and without microphones, as close to the original operatic conception as possible." This was not true, nor did the original production ever boast an "operatic conception," but Levine did dig up and play every last note Gershwin wrote.

Olin Downes, music critic for the *New York Times,* wrote of Levine's production, "If the Metropolitan chorus could ever put one half the action into the riot scene in the second act of *Meistersinger* that the Negro cast put into the fight that followed the crap game, it would be not merely refreshing but miraculous." Clearly, opera audiences were not accustomed to anything so rambunctious.

With the Met's production of *Porgy and Bess,* the work that the Theatre Guild and George Gershwin had called a "folk opera," that Gershwin had thought of as a "grand opera," that historians came to call the first American opera, was finally canonized. Unfortunately, it grew larger and larger during its long journey. The Met production featured ninety singers on stage—they added dancers that were not even called for in the original—gargantuan sets, and scene change music that was no longer necessary. Thus, *Porgy* lost a good deal of its theatrical drama and its magical ability to touch audiences. The "Jazzbo" opening that Goldman's production restored was cut even before the show began performances because George had been satisfied to begin with his lullaby "Summertime." And filler music Gershwin had written "in case of need,"—which contemporary production techniques do not require—was insistently restored by Levine. Where Catfish Row had once been a small, claustrophobic place, poverty-stricken, hot, often tense, by 1985 it was a huge, open-air spectacle, merely a pedestal upon which great black American voices could display their virtuosity. (One of Gershwin's earliest conceptions was that none of the few white roles was a singing part.)

But it isn't the size or length of a production that defines it. The Stanislavsky Players did *Porgy* in Moscow with only piano and drums. It's the treatment—whether or not you use the recitatives, whether you insist on realistic performances or concentrate on highbrow vocalizing, how well the audience can hear and see. In the 1975 Goldman-O'Brien production, the audience could not understand the words to "Summertime," a song by then as popular as any ever written, because of the vowel-heavy enunciation and operatic vocalizing of the singer. In the Los Angeles Opera's 1995 version of a second Houston Grand Opera production, American opera singers, singing in English, required subtitles over the entire show!

Even in the original production Brooks Atkinson didn't favor the recitatives, and he mused, "Why commonplace remarks that carry no emotion have to be made in a chanting monotone is a problem in art [I] cannot fathom." Atkinson's comment articulates the central difference between opera and theatre. Since recitatives have invaded Broadway lately, one assumes that some composers and directors have willingly traded the dramatic ineffectuality of the practice for the impressiveness of curtain-to-curtain music. But the latter, technically exciting as it might be to audiences, doesn't strike at the heart of great musical theatre because it puts some of the drama at a remove and thus overlooks what musical theatre history has striven so hard to achieve—the fullest integration of the various techniques in presenting the story.

That *Porgy and Bess* deserves better treatment is supported by the fact that Rouben Mamoulian's staging of the first production was Herculean in its attempts to create acting performances, and realistic ones at that. In rehearsing the crap game sequence, Mamoulian told the cast to move closer to the principals "not because I tell you, but because you want to hear what they're saying."

As for the music, the question isn't what George Gershwin wanted—it is how best to present such a great musical work. There is no single answer. The largest productions have their values, notably spectacle and sound, with the audience overwhelmed by it all. The smaller productions—Trevor Nunn directed one in the six-hundred-seat Glynbourne Festival Theatre in England—allow the audience to get closer to the drama, and allow the actors to act in a more realistic style.

If Gershwin created the recitatives, he did so because he was a man of great ambition, and even greater talent, who set himself the task of creating an American grand opera in the jazz idiom. He was well aware that this combination was nontraditional and daring. Nevertheless, it was not in his mind to present the work in an opera house, but on Broadway. As for a cast, since there were no black singers at the Met and few in the operatic world at all, he had no choice but to search for newcomers. His was a career that already had a foot planted firmly in both the Broadway musical and the concert hall. His entry into opera was as innocent, headstrong, and unique as the rest of his career. *Porgy and Bess* suited his quest perfectly because of its native subject, and the characters' inherent comfort with the musical idiom he wanted to write in. For the same reason, however, it was a musical often overshadowed by its split profile in both theatre and opera.

And it was overshadowed by another subject that caused even more controversy. The word "nigger" was already drifting into disfavor when the play was in rehearsal, and although it was in constant use in the actual locale of the play—as heard by Dubose and Dorothy Heyward—the New York actors were against it. It stayed in the play, but Ira later eliminated it when the musical libretto was being written.

It was at the Heywards' insistence that the Theatre Guild use black actors to play black roles. The producers were seriously considering having white actors perform in blackface, which had been done for Gershwin's *Blue Monday.* At one time Heyward had been approached about the rights for a musical *Porgy* starring Al Jolson in blackface.

When the original *Porgy and Bess* went to the National Theatre in Washington, D.C., a controversy arose because blacks had never been allowed in the theatre with whites. Todd Duncan refused to perform unless they were—he stood firm against management and eventually the theatre consented to sell tickets to blacks, whereupon they came, sat side by side with whites at every performance. There was never any trouble, nor did a single white customer ask for a refund.

The subject of race is an inseparable part of the *Porgy* phenomenon. Some critics chastised the opera for exploiting blacks, and others took it for a white misrepresentation of black life. Still others applauded the play's representation as not only accurate but fundamentally positive. It could be argued that the influence of black-invented blues and jazz on white composers is a form of plagiarism. White composers' love of black music—from George Cohan to Irving Berlin to George Gershwin to Harold Arlen—was uncompromisingly respectful, and it was the work of these composers that brought the wonderful influences of black-originated music into the mainstream, where it stays to this day. Black composers, unfortunately, did not get their fair share of the limelight.

The production itself broke open many opportunities for black talent on Broadway and on operatic stages. The creators of *Porgy and Bess* were truly colorblind (as much as it was possible to be in those days) in their attempt to put on an impressive Broadway musical.

Just as any argument that *Porgy* is racist because its creators are white is nonsense, arguing over whether *Porgy* is a musical or an opera is an academic exercise. The work stands up to both forms—the music is great enough on its own, and its drama is strong enough to engage. What *Porgy* offers is the possibility of great theatre. If the maxims of theatre are not embraced, the result is a poor production, in any house, at any length. Many operas boast music that is written more to show off the composer's ingenuity and the singer's voice than to support the drama of the libretto, and thus do not provide the opportunity for great theatre. Porgy's music never deviates from the drama.

A larger issue in the history of the American musical is the once-and-for-all effect of George Gershwin's work. He created a completely American score for a serious drama. He relied heavily, as he did in all his writing, on ragtime, blues, and jazz—thoroughly American music.

• • •

Porgy did little that *Show Boat* didn't do eight years earlier. Both productions took on serious subjects. Both were big, dramatic, American stories that eschewed irrelevant dances and comic turns and featured sumptuous but honest productions. Both sets of lyrics grew out of their books naturally, and both scores grew out of their settings. Songs illuminated plot and character, and musical sequences went far beyond the thirty-two-bar forms of then-current musicals.

Both grew out of American soil—Kern's score was rich in ragtime idioms, and Gershwin's featured jazz music and Gullah rhythms and language. Both were staged brilliantly with a theatrical combination of realism and entertainment that left out tricks, gimmicks, or show-biz shtick. If *Porgy* was another giant leap forward, it's due primarily to the fact that Kern's roots were in operetta, and much of *Show Boat* still had one foot in that European form. Gershwin, thirteen years younger than Kern, virtually oblivious to operetta, interested in only the most modern of classical music, influenced by Irving Berlin and Tin Pan Alley, wrote a purely American score that substituted jazz for operetta.

Robert Breen, who by all accounts directed the best and most theatrical of all the productions after the original—certainly the one that finally brought *Porgy and Bess* international fame—was pushed aside. His assistant on the international tour, Ella Gerber, was engaged to direct the dozens of subsequent stage productions. Breen's theatrical talent and great vision were not complemented by a business sense, and he spent the rest of his life wandering aimlessly from one unfulfilled project to another. His wife—the woman who had been the large company's principal morale booster during the long years of touring—had to take odd jobs as a typist to support them in their final years.

Dispirited by the financial failure and mixed criticism of the original *Porgy and Bess,* George and Ira Gershwin accepted an offer to work in film. They traveled west and wrote songs for *Shall We Dance* (1937), *A Damsel in Distress* (1937), and *The Goldwyn Follies* (1938). But soon thereafter George was struck by a brain tumor at the age of 38. He died on the operating table at Cedar-Sinai Hospital.

At the time, Kern was recuperating from his first heart attack in the same hospital. No one told him that George had died, but a month later he heard a radio announcer talking about George in the past tense. John O'Hara wrote the famous line, "George died on July 11, 1937, but I don't have to believe that if I don't want to."

Neither George Gershwin nor Dubose Heyward lived to see universal acceptance of *Porgy.* Nevertheless, Ira Gershwin later said, "To the end of my days I shall never forget the exciting and thrilling period of *Porgy and Bess.*"

The Gershwins' one enormous contribution to the American theatre overshadowed their earlier work, yet it was Gershwin music that had launched American theatre music. Mass migration from Europe to Ellis Island, and from our farms to our cities, was turning America into an urban culture by the 1920s, and the Gershwins expressed it best. In 1925 a critic wrote,

> The two collaborated in working out words and music in a manner that is typically American, using American expressions and phrases that are so much better than the stilted artificiality of the pseudo-English songs of the musical comedy period between Gilbert and Sullivan and Gershwin.

(Let's not forget that Kern and P. G. Wodehouse bridged the gap nicely.) The Gershwins' close personal relationship aided their careers—they constantly spoke and advised each other, writing, even when they were separated, about books, business, shows, and life.

Although Ira continued to work and created a number of wonderful songs ("The Man That Got Away" for Judy Garland in *A Star is Born*) and shows (*Lady in the Dark* with Kurt Weill) with other composers, the incendiary blaze of talent that marked their era on Broadway ended prematurely, and with it any hope that George would add to *Porgy and Bess* with other ambitious shows that might glorify the American musical.

A contemporary diarist labeled George a "wonderful friend and companion, ever reliable, sympathetic and unshakably well-tempered." Gershwin's notorious (and apparently endearing) self-confidence labeled the opera a classic even as it was being written. It was a momentous occasion and a significant link in the evolution of the American musical. On Broadway, a folk opera (was ever there a better definition of musical theatre?) had been created that used serious music to support the drama, its score grown out of American jazz, blues, ragtime, spirituals, and the inherent life-rhythms of its characters.

• • •

In the developing art of the American musical, only one more item was left to serve the story: dancing. Sixteen years after *Show Boat,* nine years after *Porgy and Bess,* the choreographer Agnes de Mille would bring dancers into the fold, and the total integration of the musical would be complete. She would do it for a musical directed by *Porgy*'s Rouben Mamoulian and written by *Show Boat*'s Oscar Hammerstein II, with his new collaborator—Jerome Kern's old fan—Richard Rodgers.

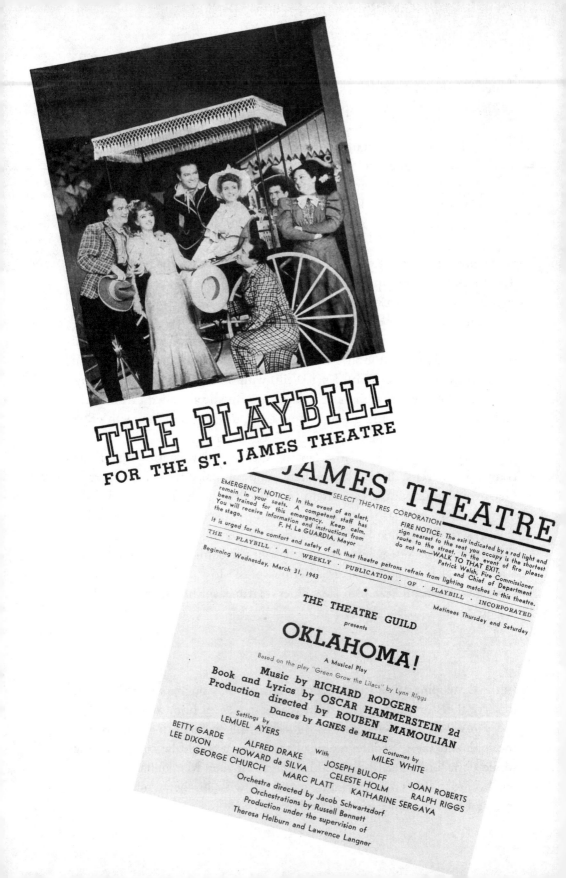

THE PLAYBILL
FOR THE ST. JAMES THEATRE

[ST.] JAMES THEATRE

SELECT THEATRES CORPORATION

EMERGENCY NOTICE: In the event of an alert, remain in your seats. A competent staff has been trained for this emergency. Keep calm. You will receive information and instructions from the stage.
F. H. La GUARDIA, Mayor

FIRE NOTICE: The exit indicated by a red light and sign nearest to the seat you occupy is the shortest route to the street. In the event of fire please do not run—WALK TO THAT EXIT.
Patrick Walsh, Fire Commissioner and Chief of Department

It is urged for the comfort and safety of all, that theatre patrons refrain from lighting matches in this theatre.

THE · PLAYBILL · A · WEEKLY · PUBLICATION · OF · PLAYBILL · INCORPORATED

Beginning Wednesday, March 31, 1943

Matinees Thursday and Saturday

THE THEATRE GUILD

presents

OKLAHOMA!

A Musical Play

Based on the play "Green Grow the Lilacs" by Lynn Riggs

Music by RICHARD RODGERS
Book and Lyrics by OSCAR HAMMERSTEIN 2d
Production directed by ROUBEN MAMOULIAN
Dances by AGNES de MILLE

Settings by
LEMUEL AYERS

Costumes by
MILES WHITE

With

BETTY GARDE
LEE DIXON
ALFRED DRAKE
HOWARD da SILVA
GEORGE CHURCH
JOSEPH BULOFF
CELESTE HOLM
MARC PLATT
JOAN ROBERTS
RALPH RIGGS
KATHARINE SERGAVA

Orchestra directed by Jacob Schwartzdorf
Orchestrations by Russell Bennett
Production under the supervision of
Theresa Helburn and Lawrence Langner

Thirteen

AGNES DE MILLE AND *OKLAHOMA!*

It has long been a subject of some remark that the arts attract the curious, the crotchety and the quirked. But dancing seems to be practiced largely by the downright perverted and deranged.

—AGNES DE MILLE

The year was 1943 and, once again, Broadway was skeptical. The Theatre Guild had recently presented a series of not-very-commercial productions. They had barely $30,000 in the bank and fewer and fewer investors to whom they could turn. Their new musical was based on *Green Grow the Lilacs* by Lynn Riggs, which had been a failure when they first presented it in 1931, running only the minimum sixty-four performances guaranteed by the subscription audience. Numerous backers' auditions were needed to raise the $100,000 capital. There was a death in the plot, something extremely unusual for a musical comedy up until then, even for a villain. The curtain went up on a lone woman churning butter, the first song began offstage—a laconic baritone singing about a beautiful morning—and the chorus girls didn't make their first appearance for forty-five minutes (in long dresses, yet). The Theatre Guild producers were Lawrence Langner and Theresa Helburn, and Broadwayites began dubbing the new musical "Helburn's Folly."

To see how the American musical came to this ignominious turning point, we need to go back several decades.

• • •

By the age of five Richard Rodgers evidenced an extraordinary ear for music. He was able to play songs he had heard, including operatic arias, and it wasn't long before he was making up his own. His greatest interest was the theatre music which his mother and father sang and played at the piano.

As a not-very-scholarly high school student, Rodgers went to many shows and enjoyed none more than the Princess musicals, which he revisited many times. He liked them in particular because, according to his autobiography, they were

> intimate and uncluttered and tried to deal in a humorous way with modern, everyday characters. They were certainly different—and far more appealing to me—from the overblown operettas, mostly imported, that dominated the Broadway scene.

Rodgers especially appreciated the arrangements by Frank Sadler. Fewer musicians created a chamber-music sound, lyrics were heard with greater clarity, and light humor and charm replaced the lush romanticism of previous Broadway orchestrations.

By the time Rodgers decided that he wanted to write for this new musical idiom, Kern was by far his favorite composer. As a high school student, Rodgers wrote three amateur musicals: *One Minute, Please; Up Stage and Down;* and *You'd Be Surprised.* (Aren't the titles of amateur musicals fun?)

One afternoon when Rodgers was sixteen years old, he met Lorenz Hart,* who was then twenty-three. Hart was already an experienced hand, having gotten jobs translating German operettas for the Shuberts. That afternoon they talked about the musical theatre at great length, and agreed

* The man who introduced Rodgers to Hart deserves a footnote in history. He was Philip Leavitt, a classmate of Rodgers's brother at Columbia University.

upon the excellence of the Guy Bolton-P. G. Wodehouse-Jerome Kern formula. Hart wanted to write lyrics that were smarter and more adult than the typical work on Broadway at the time. After meeting Hart that day, Rodgers said, "I left Hart's house having acquired in one afternoon a career, a partner, a best friend, and a source of permanent irritation."

The precocious Rodgers grew tired of high school before he graduated, and he took extension classes at Columbia University while still a high school senior. This qualified him as a "freshman." He and Hart, who had graduated three years earlier, auditioned a musical for the Columbia judges. *Fly With Me* was chosen to become the varsity show of 1920. (The Triangle shows at Princeton, the Hasty Pudding shows at Harvard, and the varsity shows at Columbia probably contributed more alumni to professional show business than any other institution short of the hotels in the Catskills and the Poconos in the 1950s.)

In June of 1919 Lew Fields (originally half of a hugely successful vaudeville duo with Joe Weber, as well as a successful Broadway comedian and producer) wrote and produced *A Lonely Romeo.* Several months after it opened he inserted the first professional Rodgers and Hart song in a Broadway show, "Any Old Place With You." Next Fields went to see the varsity show *Fly With Me* (his son Herb was in it) and promptly offered Rodgers and Hart the opportunity to write the entire score for a Broadway musical he had already booked. (Fields had a score already, but he didn't like it.) They wrote songs for it at once, and *Poor Little Ritz Girl* (1920) headed for out-of-town tryouts.

Having written the songs, Rodgers and Hart were no longer needed and Rodgers took a job as a summer camp counselor. When he returned to visit the show on opening night in New York, he found that eight of his songs had been replaced with the work of Sigmund Romberg. He was startled and mortified—his parents attended the opening with him—but nevertheless a number of Rodgers and Hart numbers had made the final cut, and they had written their first Broadway songs. The following year they wrote again for the Columbia varsity show *You'll Never Know.*

Rodgers then dropped out of Columbia ("wrote two Varsity shows and considered myself eligible for graduation") and entered the music school that later became Juilliard. Surrounded by students of classical music, Rodgers was hell-bent to write for the Broadway stage. He and Hart wrote a series of amateur musicals. The last one, *Garrick Gaieties* (1925), was a revue put on by the bit players of the Theatre Guild to raise money to purchase draperies for the Guild's theatre. It featured "(I'll Take) Manhattan" and was successful enough to transfer to Broadway for a regular run, whereupon their careers began in earnest.

In 1925 they wrote *Dearest Enemy,* eager to prove they could write for plots and characters. Satisfyingly, Frank Vreeland's review in the *New York Telegram* compared the creators of *Dearest Enemy* to the Princess people. "We have a glimmering notion," he wrote, "that someday they [librettist Herbert Fields, Hart, and Rodgers] will form the American counterpart of that once-great triumvirate of Bolton, Wodehouse and Kern." While this comment was flattering to Rodgers and Hart, it contained an inaccuracy: despite their antecedents, the Princess musicals were as American as Broadway.)

Off and running, Rodgers and Hart became the first really well-known Broadway songwriting team, and the first to leapfrog the traditional Tin Pan Alley songwriting apprenticeship. They worked exclusively with each other, creating more than thirty Broadway musicals between 1920 and 1942 . . .

Peggy-Ann (1926) featured fifteen minutes of spoken dialogue before its first song.

A Connecticut Yankee (1927) was based on the Mark Twain story "A Connecticut Yankee in King Arthur's Court." Busby Berkeley staged the dances. Although the Mark Twain story was a strong departure from the simplistic romantic plots that flooded Broadway in the twenties, the haphazard use of good songs here and there indicate that period, place, and character were not yet influencing composition.

Chee-Chee (1928) was based on a novel called *The Son of the Grand Eunuch.* It was known as the castration musical, featured an oriental setting, and required an oriental flavor to the music. This marked the first time Rodgers's music was influenced by anything other than smart Manhattan. *Chee-Chee* was also an early attempt to meld book and lyrics, and the following note appeared in the program: "The musical numbers, some of them very short, are so interwoven with the story that it would be confusing for the audience to peruse a complete list." (Shades of the program note in Oscar Hammerstein's *Rose-Marie!*)

Jumbo (1935) was produced by the short, flamboyant Billy Rose.

Although John Murray Anderson, (of the elegant revues) staged the production, he concerned himself solely with the production values. Rodgers credits George Abbott, hired as book director, with pulling the huge circus musical together. It was the first musical Abbott directed.

I'd Rather Be Right (1937) was a political satire with a book by George Kaufman and Moss Hart. It was the first time the character of a current U.S. president (Franklin D. Roosevelt) was the hero of a musical.

The Boys from Syracuse (1938) was based on *The Comedy of Errors,* and it was the first musical adaptation of William Shakespeare. (Subsequent musicals based on Shakespeare include *Kiss Me Kate* (1948) from *The Taming of the Shrew; West Side Story* (1957) from *Romeo and Juliet; Your Own Thing* (1968) and *Music Is* (1976) from *Twelfth Night; Rockabye, Hamlet* (1976); *Two Gentlemen of Verona* (1971); *Catch My Soul* (Los Angeles, 1968 and London, 1970) from *Othello;* and *Oh! Brother!* (1981) from *The Comedy of Errors.*)

Of greatest interest in the Rodgers and Hart canon, however, are the dance musicals . . .

On Your Toes opened in 1936. Abbott wrote the book, then went to Palm Beach for the winter (for golf and womanizing, at which Abbott was reputed to be an expert). But the director bumbled it, Rodgers sent Abbott a "help" telegram, and Abbott returned and saved the show. In addition to putting things back the way he had written them, Abbott was particularly supportive of the choreographer—then and later in his career.

The term "choreography" was new—before the days of George Balanchine and Agnes de Mille, who were both from the ballet worlds, it was usual on Broadway to see "Dances by" or "Dance Director" above the choreographer's name. For *On Your Toes* George Balanchine choreographed "Slaughter on Tenth Avenue" and "Princess Zenobia," probably the earliest ballets to communicate a significant portion of the plot solely in dance terms. (Albertina Rasch had previously created self-contained ballets for revues.) Rodgers wrote an original score for Balanchine to use rather than allowing a dance arranger to recycle other tunes from the show.

Pal Joey opened in 1940. Writer John O'Hara had written to Richard Rodgers:

> Dear Dick: I don't know whether you happened to see any of a series of pieces I've been doing for *The New Yorker*. . . . They're

> about a guy who is master of ceremonies in cheap night clubs. . . . Anyway, I got the idea that the pieces, or at least the character and the life in general, could be made into a book show . . .

Pal Joey was a musical about the seamy side of life. The actions and motives of its leading character were immoral. The story of a liaison between an older woman and a gigolo was way ahead of its time (the revival a decade later was more successful). In order not to turn the audience off completely, the gigolo character was irresistibly charming, especially as played by Gene Kelly in the original stage version, Harold Lang in the revival, and Frank Sinatra in the film (in which the dancer became a singer).

Pal Joey was George Abbott's most unusual musical, and he had little faith in it. Brooks Atkinson asked, "Can you draw sweet water from a foul well?" Hart burst into tears at the opening night party when this line was read to him. But ironically, Atkinson was impressed and summarized the show by saying, "If it is possible to make an entertaining musical comedy out of an odious story, *Pal Joey* is it."

At 374 performances it was only partly possible. For the 1952 revival Atkinson had the advantage of hindsight, and wrote that the musical "was a pioneer in the moving back of musical frontiers." The audience was better prepared as well. The revival ran 542 performances and bolstered the show's reputation in theatre history.

Rodgers himself wrote:

> It was a weird sort of enterprise to be trying to put on a musical show in which none of the characters (with the exception of one) had even a bowing acquaintance with decency. Even that one didn't have a brain in her head; she was the ingenue. It seemed time to us, however, that musical comedy get out of its cradle and start standing on its own feet, looking at the facts of life.

Pal Joey's strong book came out of John O'Hara's dark, cynical vision of humanity, and though it suffers from his inexperience with stage dialogue, the great script doctor Abbott himself hesitated to rewrite, preferring that O'Hara do it. "The idea of equipping a song-and-dance production with a few living, three-dimensional figures, talking and behaving like human beings," wrote Wolcott Gibbs in *The New Yorker,* "may no longer strike the boys in the business as merely fantastic." Other critics, and some audience members, hated the idea of a loathsome central character, but Richard Watts stood up for the idea when he wrote that it was "a novel fault in a musical show when a too strikingly drawn character is to be held against it." In subsequent musicals such as *What Makes Sammy Run?*, *I Can Get it For You Wholesale,* and even *How to Succeed in Business Without Really Trying* and *The Music Man,* a leading character's self-serving schemes were made palatable by charm, but also by the fact that Joey had paved the way.

Pal Joey's structure was half-mired in the past, with several "specialty" numbers and a "let's-rehearse-that-new-number!" lead-in to a couple of nightclub production sequences. The book appears somewhat dated now, with archaic dialogue and song titles like "Plant You Now, Dig You Later!" But there was probably as much dance on stage as had ever taken place in a book musical, save perhaps Rodgers and Hart's *On Your Toes.*

Another contribution to *Pal Joey*'s novelty was made by the musical's dance director, Robert Alton. Though no critics mentioned it at the time, the now-famous choreographer Jerome Robbins, who was a youth when Alton was the leading dance director on Broadway, recalls a vivid picture of the chorus girls. Alton had employed a unique combination of tall, short, thin, fat, blonde, and dark types who, together, could not be mistaken for a typical chorus line. Starting from the dramatic proposition that Mike's Nightclub, in which much of the show takes place, is a low-class joint, Alton created the first *character* chorus in the evolving history of the musical. If his dancers performed the leg-kicking and tap-dancing that was so popular with pre-*Oklahoma!* musicals, this time it made sense, for the characters were the leg-kicking, tap-dancing, gum-chewing chorines of the Chicago nightclubs.

This contribution remains significant. More and more elements were contributing to the drama and moving the musical away from the one-dimensional idea of sheer entertainment, and dancing was bringing up the rear. In fact, O'Hara assigned several lines to individual chorus girls, giving them an opportunity to establish individual characters. *Pal Joey* also contained a dream ballet sequence as a first-act finale, predating *Oklahoma!*'s dream ballet.

Rodgers and Hart did have some flop shows—*Higher and Higher* (1940) was stolen by a trained seal—but altogether theirs was an extraordinary repertoire of American popular songs for musicals, several of which broke new ground. These include "Mountain Greenery," "With a Song in My Heart," "Ten Cents a Dance," "My Romance," "Where or When,"

"My Funny Valentine," "The Lady Is a Tramp," "Isn't It Romantic?" and "This Can't Be Love."

It was an extraordinary time. After the heady days of the twenties, Broadway stumbled financially along with the rest of the country, but it was one of the first institutions to recover from the Depression. After almost five desultory years, the seasons of 1935–36 and 1936–37 boasted a musical revue by Howard Dietz and Arthur Schwartz called *At Home Abroad* (starring Beatrice Lillie and Ethel Waters); the Gershwin brothers' *Porgy and Bess;* Moss Hart and Cole Porter's *Jubilee;* Oscar Hammerstein and Sigmund Romberg's *May Wine;* an edition of *George White's Scandals;* a Ziegfeld *Follies;* Porter's *Red, Hot and Blue* with Ethel Merman, Jimmy Durante and Bob Hope; the Kurt Weill antiwar musical *Johnny Johnson; Forbidden Melody,* an operetta by Otto Harbach and Sigmund Romberg; Noël Coward's *Tonight at 8:30;* a Vincente Minnelli-directed revue called *The Show Is On,* with Beatrice Lillie and Bert Lahr; and *On Your Toes, Babes in Arms,* and *Jumbo,* all by Rodgers and Hart.

Yet by this time the Rodgers and Hart partnership was beginning to strain. Hart was a severe alcoholic. He failed to show up for the out-of-town tryouts of *The Boys from Syracuse* (how this must have annoyed such by-the-clock workaholics as Rodgers and George Abbott). For the next Abbott, Rodgers, and Hart show, *Too Many Girls* (1939), Rodgers had to start writing lyrics himself because Hart would disappear for longer and longer periods. By the end of *Pal Joey* (for which Hart wrote wonderful lyrics, including the haunting and knowing "Bewitched, Bothered and Bewildered") Hart was unable to write at all.

The alcoholic John O'Hara turned out to be as unreliable as Hart. In a case of the blind leading the blind, Hart would go to O'Hara's apartment before rehearsals, bang on the door, and say "Get up, Baby. Come on, come on. You're hurting George's feelings.," When Rodgers began *By Jupiter* (1942), Hart was found unconscious in his apartment and taken to a hospital. Rodgers rented a room next door, had a piano installed, and wrote with Hart there. Fearful that Hart would disappear again, Rodgers made arrangements with the doctor to keep Hart in the hospital until the work was completed.

By Jupiter was their last work together, and it ran longer than any of their previous shows. The production was tailored for Ray Bolger, who played the tap dancer who had to keep dancing or get shot by gangsters in "Slaughter on Tenth Avenue." By now it was clear that Rodgers was comfortable with dance in musicals.

When Theresa Helburn first suggested a musical version of *Green Grow the Lilacs,* the authors were enthusiastic. *Which* authors, however, is questionable. Some historians claim that Oscar Hammerstein II first approached Jerome Kern with the assignment and Kern turned it down. Others record that Richard Rodgers went to his longtime partner Lorenz Hart and Hart bowed out.* In any case, since 1934 Jerome Kern had made his home in Hollywood, where he was writing film musicals; when Hammerstein first broached *Lilacs* to him, Kern felt the play was insufficient. Hammerstein dropped the subject, but not his feelings about the play's possibilities.

Lorenz Hart was increasingly ill and erratic. A tortured man who could not reconcile his homosexuality with his nice Jewish upbringing, he had descended deeply into alcoholism. Richard Rodgers was a priggish man who disliked his partner's way of life (a disapproval considered by some to be part of Hart's insecurities).

By 1942, Rodgers worried that Hart would not be able to complete the necessary lyrics, for he could no longer be relied on to keep an appointment or deliver work. From the beginning, Rodgers's methodical working habits contrasted with Hart's insomnia and an erratic commitment to work. To his credit, however, Rodgers nursed Hart's unreliability as long as he could, handling all of the business details and working whenever Hart appeared, for in the end Hart could not work alone at all.

Helburn took Rodgers to see a Westport Playhouse revival of *Green Grow the Lilacs* (for which Gene Kelly staged some folk dances), and Rodgers was enthusiastic. When Rodgers accepted the Theatre Guild's offer to write the score for a musical version, he met with Hart, but it was clear that Hart could not do it. They left separately from a conference room in the offices of music publisher Chappell and Co., and one of the greatest partnerships in songwriting history dissolved.

Richard Rodgers and Oscar Hammerstein had been passing acquaintances for years. Twenty-one-year-old Hammerstein had met fourteen-year-old Rodgers at the Saturday matinée of a Columbia University varsity show. They were introduced backstage by Richard's older brother Morty, a member of Oscar's fraternity. Rodgers and Hammerstein wrote

* This historical confusion probably arose because the Theatre Guild used a timeless producers' ploy—they went to Hammerstein and Kern *and* Rodgers and Hart at the same time, telling both teams, "You're our first choice!"

their first songs together, "Can It" and "Weaknesses," for the amateur musical *Up Stage and Down* in 1919. In 1920 Rodgers and Hart submitted their first Columbia varsity show. Oscar Hammerstein was on the play selection committee that chose it, and he collaborated with Rodgers on one song called "Only Room for One More."

In 1921 Hammerstein codirected the second Rodgers and Hart varsity show, *You'll Never Know.* Rodgers had once asked Hammerstein to write the book for a musical he and Hart wanted to do from the Edna Ferber novel *Saratoga Trunk.* The project didn't materialize, though it appeared in 1959 as Harold Arlen's *Saratoga.* Rodgers had once approached Hammerstein for a musical version of *Hotel Splendide,* but that project failed to materialize as well. (In yet another connection, Richard's father, an obstetrician, delivered Oscar's two children.)

Already Hammerstein had collaborated with Herbert Stothart, Rudolf Friml, Jerome Kern, George Gershwin, Sigmund Romberg, Vincent Youmans, and Richard Whiting. But he had not had a hit in a decade. Hammerstein's hiatus from success was principally due, in retrospect, to one thing: audiences had deserted the operetta form in which he had primarily written. Hammerstein had grown up surrounded by operettas and operas his grandfather, his father, and ultimately he himself had worked on, and it took a long time to abandon them completely.

So when Rodgers approached him, he was passing through a lackluster decade in the middle of his career. His successful *Music in the Air* with Jerome Kern (1932, 342 performances) was followed by a number of failures Hammerstein suffered as producer, director, and writer. By the early forties the once super-successful Hammerstein had inspired the odd line "He can't write his hat" in Hollywood's ever-cynical community.

In 1942 Rodgers invited Hammerstein to lunch and asked him if he would like to musicalize *Green Grow the Lilacs.* Hammerstein didn't even have to read it. In a seminal and inevitable event (in hindsight), Richard Rodgers and Oscar Hammerstein II formed a partnership.

• • •

Work began immediately, first with weeks of discussion and planning of musical possibilities. (This indicates just how much the musical theatre had changed since the hectic days of writing whole shows in a matter of weeks.) The very first song they wrote together was the opening. The curtain rises on a lone woman churning butter, and a male baritone—offstage—begins, "Oh, What a Beautiful Morning." How they came to write it, as recorded by Hammerstein himself, illuminates just how big a step the American musical was about to take.

> [T]he first serious problem that faced us involved a conflict of dramaturgy with showmanship. As we planned our version, the story we had to tell in the first part of the first act did not call for the use of a female ensemble. The traditions of musical comedy, however, demand that not too long after the rise of the curtain the audience should be treated to one of musical comedy's most attractive assets—the sight of pretty girls in pretty clothes moving about the stage, the sound of their vital young voices supporting the principals in their songs. Dick and I, for several days, sought ways and means of logically introducing a group of girls into the early action of the play. The boys were no problem. Here was a farm in Oklahoma with ranches nearby. Farmers and cowboys belonged there, but girls in groups? No. Strawberry festivals? Quilting parties? Corny devices! After trying everything we could think of, and rejecting each other's ideas as fast as they were submitted, after passing through phases during which we would stare silently at each other unable to think of anything at all, we came finally to an extraordinary decision. We agreed to start our story in the real and natural way in which it seemed to want to be told! This decision meant that the first act would be half over before a female chorus would make its entrance. We realized that such a course was experimental, amounting almost to the breach of an implied contract with a musical comedy audience. I cannot say truthfully that we were worried by the risk. Once we had made the decision, everything seemed to work right and we had that inner confidence people feel when they have adopted the direct and honest approach to a problem.

Thus the American musical began to take another giant step away from the twenties formula, due to the confidence Rodgers and Hammerstein had in the story they wanted to tell.

It took Hammerstein three weeks to write the opening—Curly's buoyant enthusiasm for a beautiful Midwestern day—but the words were so elegant and euphonic it took Rodgers little more than ten minutes to set them to music. They set the tone by writing the opening first, and they never deviated from their desire to present *Oklahoma*'s rural, homespun material honestly.

It was fate. Kismet. With the union of Rodgers and Hammerstein the twin arms of the Broadway musical merged once and for all, Hammerstein being a descendent of the romantic operetta school, and Rodgers of the jazzy American musicals.

When Rodgers worked with Hammerstein for the first time, the substance of his songs changed drastically. Hart was wry and satiric, with an always-unique perception of humanity, and he wrote in the Broadway vernacular that characterized most of the genre. Where Hart had been brittle, sophisticated, and often arch, Hammerstein was lyrical and poetic. Where Hart used clever polysyllabic and interior rhymes, Hammerstein wrote lyrics as natural dialogue, without drawing attention to them. Hart wrote to fit a pre-existing melody, and did so almost as fast as he could move his pencil, whereas Hammerstein carefully created his lyrics out of the story and characters, then submitted them to the composer. Where Hart had written the musical comedies of the twenties and thirties, Hammerstein had worked in the operettas. With Hart, Rodgers had provided the melodies *prior to the ideas.* The richer, more romantic ideas that Hammerstein provided Rodgers unleashed a deeper, more romantic vein of melody in the composer.

As the production began to take shape, Rodgers, Hammerstein, and the Theatre Guild looked for a director and a choreographer. Joshua Logan went into the Army, and Brentagne Windust and Elia Kazan turned down the property. There wasn't anything Kismetian about hiring director Rouben Mamoulian. He had staged both the play and the musical *Porgy and Bess* brilliantly, and he was an A-list director in both film and theatre. Both Rodgers with Hart (*Love Me Tonight*) and Hammerstein with Kern (*High, Wide and Handsome*) had worked with him already on Hollywood musicals. He had an "exuberant manner" (Rodgers) and probably the strongest hand and richest creative imagination of any director yet involved with American musicals. It was with the choreographer, however, that Lady Fortune really smiled upon the production.

The contributor to the long history of achievements that became the great American musical who suffered the most in her inexorable rise to prominence is surely Agnes de Mille. She grew up in a gracious house in early Hollywood, the daughter of William de Mille, a Broadway playwright and Hollywood film director, and the niece of the great Cecil B. de Mille. She grew up in a loving household where she was stifled with structure imposed by a mother who made Mama Rose look like a shrinking violet. Until she was an adult both her parents were resistant to her interest in dancing. Her father wanted her to have nothing to do it, and her mother thought that self-instruction was the proper course.

When Agnes was fourteen her sister's arches fell, and a doctor told the family that ballet lessons were the only solution. What one child had the other had too, and Agnes was finally allowed to enter the Theodore Kosloff School of Imperial Russian Ballet in Hollywood for two lessons a week.

In fact, she had begun choreographing dances before her first lesson. The course of self-training she embarked upon—watching performances, looking at pictures, reading books, improvising on the lawn—may have ignited her abilities to make up her own original and groundbreaking dances. As a young adult with little training and no opportunities, de Mille set out to create a concert of her own dancing. Not unlike most young choreographers, she choreographed for herself because no one else would. An instinct for the dramatic (abetted by coaching from a young actor friend, Douglass Montgomery) and an uncrushable ambition led her forward. When her parents divorced, Agnes's career became her mother's passion, and they spent years sewing costumes and paying for their own concerts, putting a small divorce allowance into their expenses.

In London de Mille began to study seriously with Marie Rambert. She landed a job on the West End choreographing *Nymph Errant* (1933), a Cole Porter musical starring Gertrude Lawrence, but it didn't lead to more work. There were more seasons in London—six all told—then a return to New York, where de Mille settled into a cycle of unrewarded effort and poverty. (It was not broken by *Oklahoma!*, since choreographers were underpaid and their work was not copyrightable.) She devoted herself to ballet at a time when there was virtually no profitable employment for concert dancers in the United States at all, outside of vaudeville.

But her concerts had been noted, and when Lucia Chase and Richard Pleasant formed the American Ballet Theatre (ABT) they invited her to be one of ten founding choreographers. The ABT had one of the longest and most curious histories in the infant ballet world. Chase had been one of forty-seven dancers in a company headed by the tempestuous and not very talented choreographer Mikhail Mordkin. She had used her family fortune to support the company anonymously.*

Until the late 1930s all great ballet companies—there were none in the United States but several in Europe, including Sergei Diaghilev's revolutionary Ballets Russes—had been run by a single choreographer. Apparently Richard Pleasant, an administrator who had begun as the director of Mordkin's school, had the idea of creating a world-class company virtually overnight by inviting not one, but a dozen great choreographers to work with the new group.

Chase supported Pleasant, and gradually Mordkin was moved aside. Several young Americans, including Agnes de Mille, were invited to be part of the first group. These young Americans took the company's name more literally than it had ever been taken before (or, sadly, since) and began to create ballets in a uniquely American idiom.

Agnes de Mille's first work—an incredibly brave piece called *Black Ritual* set for black amateur dancers to the music of Darius Milhaud—failed. She went out on her own again, putting up her own money in pursuit of concert performing and choreography. She had a personal success in Chicago, and Pleasant invited her back to ABT. She next choreographed *Three Virgins and a Devil* (in which Jerome Robbins had his first solo), at which the audience laughed. Not for the first time. Never an elegant dancer herself, de Mille had developed an unusual capacity for humor in her choreography.

But ABT was *still* cool to de Mille, who is reported in more than one memoir to have been a prickly personality—her own memoirs recount, in extraordinarily beautiful prose and with keen insight, her appreciation for those who labored alongside her—and she was set adrift once again. The down-at-the-heels Ballet Russe de Monte Carlo offered her an opportunity. She asked for a score from Aaron Copeland, and created a new ballet out of themes and movements she had been working with for years. It was to be

* Later, in 1948, her story was used as the plot of the George Abbott-Jerome Robbins musical *Look Ma, I'm Dancing,* featuring Nancy Walker as Lily Malloy, a brewery heiress who underwrites and dances in a ballet company.

a cowboy ballet—although Eugene Loring's *Billy the Kid* came first, de Mille had been planning hers all along—and it was called *Rodeo.*

• • •

For *Rodeo,* de Mille used the best male dancers from world-class companies, and she worked hard to get them to avoid the eighteenth-century classical technique and act like cowboys. At the first rehearsal several of the Russian-trained dandies walked out. But de Mille was working from *character,* not vocabulary. Because she had been allowed few ballet lessons as a child and because she had not been a brilliant technician, de Mille had devised her own style out of a yearning simply to *do*—she was the outsider not forged in the classic tradition of this or that company. Her ballets were very American, and when she began there was no American ballet. She was one of its creators, along with Anthony Tudor (*Pillar of Fire*), Eugene Loring (*Billy the Kid*), Jerome Robbins (*Fancy Free*), Michael Kidd (*On Stage!*), and William Christianson (*Gas Station*).

Rodeo premiered with Ballet Russe at the Metropolitan Opera House on October 16, 1942. The ballet was brilliant, comedic, American, and caught the imagination of audiences, who gave it twenty-two curtain calls on opening night. And Theresa Helburn was in the audience. She telegrammed de Mille, asking her to come to the Theatre Guild offices the following Monday.

Since 1930 de Mille had put in an apprenticeship of heroic hardship. She had danced alone in cold and dusty venues to unappreciative audiences throughout America and Europe, and had created dances in small rooms under very rough conditions. She had paid her own way, without critical or commercial support. But she had also been a part of the invention of a new vocabulary in dance. It was brilliant on the concert stage, but it found a home in the American musical theatre.

The production team was not entirely enthusiastic. Richard Rodgers was the last holdout. Helburn took Rodgers and Hammerstein to see the Met production of de Mille's Western ballet, and finally all agreed to hire her.

It wasn't de Mille's first shot at a Broadway show. As an inauspicious beginning, de Mille had been fired as choreographer from her first Broadway musical (*Flying Colors* by Howard Dietz and Arthur Schwartz,

1932) and was replaced by Albertina Rasch. Her second chance was *Hooray for What* (1937), with book by Howard Lindsay and Russel Crouse, score by Harold Arlen and E. Y. Harburg, starring Ed Wynn, and directed by Vincente Minnelli, who until then had only designed sets and costumes. It was a disaster of epic proportions. She was replaced by Robert Alton, but this time at least she wasn't the only person fired.

For her third assault on musical comedy de Mille insisted on choosing all the dancers herself. This had seldom been done before, since producers, directors, and writers traditionally had girlfriends and favorites to fill the chorus. Yet her demand was met with understanding because Rodgers and Hammerstein and the Theatre Guild were serious about their work.

All the dances were staged in two weeks, and the ballet was put together entirely on a Sunday while the rest of the cast was off. So prodigious was de Mille's output that half the material she invented was eventually cut, still leaving enough to fill the musical with dance.

Actors, singers, and dancers all rehearsed in separate rooms, with dancers consigned to the basement of the theatre. At one point someone came up to director Rouben Mamoulian and said, "You'd better come down to the basement. Agnes is doing some pretty strange things." Agnes de Mille, whose word on her ballets had gone unquestioned and who had spent a lifetime learning to stand up for herself and her dancers, was constantly at odds with the director and the management.

Rodgers was the first to understand what she was doing, and he supported her. Still, de Mille had to be dragged off the stage several times, and once dancer Marc Platt was forced to douse her with cold water. By all accounts, rehearsals were chaotic, featuring the temperamental Mamoulian and de Mille, the frenetic Helburn, the serene Hammerstein, and the nervous Rodgers, all uncomfortably aware of the unusual nature of the production.

Chaos, confusion, unhappiness, complaints, and tantrums preceded the company's departure for out-of-town tryouts. German measles swept through the company, the second act was rewritten on the train to Boston, and entire numbers were restaged. The actors, never having worked with real dancers (only the Broadway variety), were amazed at their stamina and sturdiness. At one tumultuous rehearsal everyone sat on the stage at midnight and Rodgers said, "Do you know what I think is wrong? Almost nothing. Now why don't you all quiet down?"

But the temperamental de Mille and autocratic Mamoulian were not the only source of rehearsal tensions. Underlying the work was a severe dichotomy between traditional musical comedy and the gradual shaping of a very unusual new theatre. Both Rodgers and Hammerstein had experimented frequently in their earlier careers, but never with an entire show. Honing their vision was not easy. Joseph Buloff, playing the comic supporting character Ali Hakim (the peddler), wanted to ham it up like the Yiddish theatre actor he was, but Mamoulian stopped him. The director wanted more spectacle and more realism, both of which had been fundamental to his earlier successes, but the Theatre Guild refused to hire animals and actor Alfred Drake wouldn't sit still for rope tricks. Mamoulian even wanted the ballet cut, because he felt it gave away the plot of the second act. (To some extent it does, but it works well as a Freudian foreshadowing.)

There were Western musicals before *Oklahoma!*—Jerome Kern's *The Red Petticoat,* Harry Tierney and Joseph McCarthy's *Rio Rita,* Vincent Youman's *Rainbow,* Walter Donaldson's *Whoopee*—all long before David Merrick advertised *Destry Rides Again* as the first. But none of the scores had been infused with such a Western sound, and none had been a success. The Theatre Guild was nearly bankrupt. Hammerstein had not had a hit in over a decade. Mamoulian had been in Hollywood a long time. Agnes de Mille was new to Broadway and had been fired from two musicals. Rodgers was not writing with his lifelong partner. Moreover, Rodgers and Hammerstein (rather brilliantly as it turned out) dared to avoid star names the Guild thought would be useful (Shirley Temple as Laurie, Groucho Marx as the peddler) and insisted on casting talented unknowns instead.

The musical version of *Green Grow the Lilacs* opened as *Away We Go!* at the Shubert Theatre in New Haven in March of 1943, the title taken from a square dance call. When the show opened, Walter Winchell published in his column a remark variously attributed to his secretary Rose, the scourge of out-of-town shows whom he had sent to see the musical ("no legs, no jokes, no chance"), and to impresario Mike Todd ("no girls, no gags, no chance"), both of whom had left at intermission. (Todd later claimed he left early because he had to bail a friend out of jail in New York.)

Out of town, the stylistic schism was again an issue. Still attempting to seek traditional forms, the producers tried to bring in George Abbott to doctor the show. However, under the influence of Rodgers and Hammerstein, they decided to be true to the dramatic material.

Specialty numbers were all cut. Anything that didn't advance the action was cut. And there, in spite of a saccharine story that practically stopped the advancing sophistication of the American musical in its tracks, was the production's great contribution to history. By today's standards, no major conceptual reworking was done—there was no recasting, and there were no replacements on the staff. But many small changes were implemented. Finally the title song—written in Boston but first staged as a duet for characters Laury and Curly—was staged for the entire company as a finale. That staging and the broad, rich harmonies that rang down the curtain completed the show's metamorphosis into a hit. In Boston the show's title was changed from *Away We Go!* to *Oklahoma!*

When the show returned to New York, there was little competition. The musical season to date had been dismal: Mike Todd's burlesque revue *Star and Garter,* Irving Berlin's World War II edition of *This Is the Army,* a revival of *Die Fledermaus,* a not-very-inspired edition of Leonard Sillman's *New Faces,* and—the only real success—*Something for the Boys,* a Cole Porter-Ethel Merman musical. Twenty-four musicals had opened that season, of which one was an ice show, one was a Yiddish musical, seven were revivals, and eleven were revues. Curiously, the long run of Rodgers and Hart's *By Jupiter* was probably the best show still on the boards. The sad finale of the season was a *Ziegfeld Follies* without Ziegfeld, which proved conclusively that the Shuberts were no Ziggy. Fortunately, the season included the first Rodgers and Hammerstein musical.

The world was at war and had more important concerns than which cowboy a farm girl would take to the box social. The music and lyrics of the time were sophisticated—Cole Porter, Rodgers and Hart, the Gershwin brothers, and Noël Coward had been the giants of the previous era. American music was increasingly influenced by jazz, and the American musical was still devoted to dancing girls and jokes. In this environment, the American musical took a step into the future and ignored the conventions of the past, although the future was shaped by figures who were steeped in those very traditions.

Oklahoma! opened at the St. James Theatre on West Forty-fourth Street on March 31, 1943, although the event didn't sell out. According to first-nighters, the audience, upon hearing the opening strains of "Oh, What a Beautiful Morning" sung by Alfred Drake amid the rustic beauty of Lemuel Ayers's setting, breathed a great sigh of happiness and were captured completely. A more perfect opening could not have been written, for if the exposition of a play should delineate plot and character, the exposition of a musical must demonstrate style as well. The final curtain rang down to thunderous applause. Even the critics approved.

Eventually the production broke every record, playing five years and nine weeks in New York (2,212 performances, as well as forty-four special matinées for service personnel) and spending ten years on the road in 250 cities. A USO troupe played to soldiers in the Pacific, and the London run was the longest in the 287-year history of the Drury Lane Theatre. The musical was awarded a special citation for drama by the Pulitzer Prize committee. The Antoinette Perry (Tony) Awards had not yet been invented, but at the 1993 ceremony an articulate, wheelchair-bound Agnes de Mille was presented with a special Tony for the show. The company's 2,500-percent payoff to investors must have galled hundreds of angels who were begged to invest but had refused when they heard the material.

The best story of how hot a ticket *Oklahoma!* became is told by Hammerstein himself. A farmer working on Hammerstein's estate asked him for tickets for his son as a wedding present.

"Sure," said Oscar. "When is the wedding?"

"When you can get the tickets," the farmer replied.

The Decca cast album recording—the first-ever cast album of a book musical with a full orchestra—sold over a million copies. Because of this and because of the drama inherent in the music and lyrics—you could listen to the record and *know the story*—the *Oklahoma!* album launched the craze for cast albums. And people all over the country sat at home and imagined the show on stage, which was a significant factor in the launching of Broadway's golden age.

A great many more musicals were available for public consumption in those days, and a great many of them must have seemed alike. Thus, the very reasons the Broadway establishment underestimated *Oklahoma!*'s chances were the same reasons audiences responded so positively. In contrast to the usual star vehicles, the roles of *Oklahoma!* had been carefully filled with talented new actors. Instead of the usual Long Island or Manhattan setting, the audience was transported to the sun-drenched plains of the Midwest. Ignoring the crackling wit and benign sophistication of the current musicals, Hammerstein introduced earthy, sincere characters. Instead of a high-kicking, tap-dancing chorus, de Mille presented American folk ballet.

What no one could predict was that American audiences were indeed ready for a shift in tone, and the nifty, jazzy, Manhattan melody musicals were on their way out on two counts. First, the American musical form was becoming more sophisticated, and second, Americans were anxious to see the dreamy, bucolic heart and soul they had lost to the Depression and the war. *Oklahoma!* captured a spirit of American optimism just when it was sorely needed.

Cole Porter defined the most important change in the musical theatre as, simply, "Rodgers and Hammerstein." And he said it while *Kiss Me Kate* was running against *South Pacific*. What Rodgers and Hammerstein brought to the stage with *Oklahoma!*—and established as the principal métier with all their shows thereafter—was romance, sentiment, great tunes, dancing, a perky heroine, and a sometimes tyrannical, immoral (or at least stubborn) hero. Their scores supported the drama by portraying the time and place. "Surrey with the Fringe on Top" has a clip-clop rhythm; "The Farmer and the Cowhand" is a hoedown; "Kansas City" is a two-step. "Beautiful Morning" and "Out of My Dreams" are written in the more romantic 3/4 time. Rodgers didn't write country and western music—Broadway had to wait for *A Joyful Noise* and *The Best Little Whorehouse in Texas* for that. He wrote something better: theatre music.

Hammerstein worked with Rodgers on *Oklahoma!* the same way he had worked on *Show Boat* with Jerome Kern: he never let the conventions of traditional musical comedy interfere with the best and most direct method of telling the story. This is evident at the outset, for no musical comedy had ever gotten underway with such a simple opening.

Rodgers' graceful melodies are unlike any of his previous tunes, a testament to the powerful effect lyrics can have on a composer's work. *Oklahoma!* launched Rodgers on a career which—however successful he had been with Hart during the twenties and thirties—would harness romanticism to the evolving American musical and confirm the musical's course toward music that was dramatic even more than entertaining.

Something in Hammerstein's writing—and his character—brought to the new partnership a beauty, lyricism, and sentimentality that allowed Rodgers's music to soar to a higher plane of emotion. He gave Rodgers what he needed to write more directly for the human spirit, to strike at the soul and touch his audience not with virtuosity, but with the power of good, pure melody. In addition, Hammerstein's interests ranged to more fundamental stories, American locales, and richly emotional fabrics that sparked Rodgers's writing.

In the heady, prewar days of musicals, the composer almost always provided the melody first. This method was traditional because many operettas were imported, and American lyricists had learned to fit their words to existing scores. Additionally, little thought was given to songs arising out of the text. Rather, the text was fitted to the songs (as well as to the performers, the comedian's trunkful of jokes, and the need for the chorus girls to dance at regular intervals) and first place of importance was given to the melody.

Rodgers had written this way with Hart for twenty years, and Hammerstein had done it with many of his numerous collaborators. But Hammerstein reversed this practice with *Oklahoma!*—thereafter, Rodgers always set his music to Hammerstein's lyrics, which Hammerstein developed in concert with his book. This new method was as large a step as any other toward the greatness of the American musical, for it codified the increasing emphasis on the drama and the ideas.

Rodgers and Hammerstein never forgot the contribution that dance made to their initial success, and they continued to write dance sequences *whenever it made dramatic sense* as they created other shows. They continued to employ Agnes de Mille, and they continued to take extraordinary chances in developing unusual material.

Their next project, *Carousel* (1945), exposed far deeper and darker human emotions than the lighthearted *Oklahoma!* The score of *Carousel*—Rodgers's favorite of his own—would soar to even greater emotional heights. Here the introduction of a soliloquy attached one of the theatre's best and most ancient devices—the inner monologue—to the American musical for all time.

Rodgers and Hammerstein also continued to cast nonstars—they discovered John Raitt for *Carousel* and put him in the Chicago company of *Oklahoma!* to keep him on ice until the new play could go into rehearsal. Mamoulian directed again, and de Mille created a second-act ballet that probed the psychology of the characters and added to the plot. And *Carousel* further developed the song/scene, best exemplified by "If I Loved You." Since music can move a story along quickly because of its ability to limn emotions, more (not less) drama can be packed into a musical, provided one follows the form that Rodgers and Hammerstein had perfected—smooth integration of the song and the scene, and exploration of the psychological fabric of the characters in lyrics.

After brilliantly integrating dance into *Oklahoma!* and *Carousel,* Rodgers and Hammerstein—who by now were their own producers—decided not to have any dancing at all in *South Pacific* (1949), and director Joshua Logan took it upon himself to stage the musical numbers. Logan and Hammerstein had sketched a book that didn't require choreography. Indeed, the sailors who formed the ensemble were a rich and varied character chorus. By this time any musical that simply "brought on the girls" would be a museum piece.

Logan's decision to do the show without a choreographer paid off, and all the staging was natural and realistic. Even "Honey Bun," a show within the show, had the realistic amateurishness of a local entertainment. The Seabees (sailors) were individuals, not chorus boys, and in their ensemble songs ("Nothing Like a Dame") the authors divided up many lines into solos (just as Rodgers and Hart and O'Hara had given the *Pal Joey* chorus girls dialogue to identify them as individuals).

The most important thing about *South Pacific* is the through-action that Logan and (principally) Hammerstein devised. Instead of blacking out, the lights dissolved from one scene to another; changes were made smoothly, and neither scenes nor songs stopped the show in any cumbersome way. It's a device Hammerstein must have been flirting with for years as he tried to smooth the Broadway musical, in both scene/song transitions as librettist-lyricist and scene-to-scene transitions as librettist-director. Here are the stage directions between the first and second scenes of South Pacific:

> (The lights fade out and a transparent curtain closes in on them. Before they are out of sight, the characters of the next scene have entered downstage in front of the curtain. All transitions from one scene to another in the play are achieved in this manner so that the effect is of one picture dissolving into the next.)

South Pacific was less romanticized (operetta-ish) and more realistic than *Oklahoma!*, drawn as it was from James Michener's writings about his experiences in the South Pacific during World War II. Both the lead and supporting actors sang—unusual for a theatre which dictated that if the leads sang, the supporting players danced or were funny. It boasted no dancers or dream ballets, since once again Rodgers and Hammerstein were hewing to the story, not the formula. Because it featured navy personnel, it was as gritty and American as musical settings could be in those days. Because of its antiracist theme, it's surely the most serious of the Rodgers and Hammerstein musicals. (For Oscar Hammerstein it was the culmination of a lifelong devotion to combating anti-Semitism and promoting interracial tolerance, which he had championed through the thirties and forties when it was least popular.)

For *South Pacific,* Rodgers and Hammerstein were awarded the Pulitzer Prize for drama (not just a "special citation," as they had won for *Oklahoma!*). This marked the first time the composer of a musical was so honored. (Gershwin was left out of the citation for *Of Thee I Sing.*) In *South Pacific,* musical comedy's Mary Martin was paired with opera's Ezio Pinza, a neat symbolism for the marriage of Rodgers and Hammerstein.

Rodgers and Hammerstein returned to dance for *The King and I* (1951), another unusual musical whose only love story takes place between two minor characters. Jerome Robbins, who had followed de Mille into ABT, choreographed a set piece, "The Small House of Uncle Thomas." He eschewed a balletic vocabulary altogether in favor of authentic, Thai-based pantomimic movement. The simplicity, eloquence, and exotic vocabulary fit the ballet into the drama far more seamlessly than the dream sequences of de Mille in *Oklahoma!* and *Carousel.* If de Mille's psychological dramas had done the musical theatre of the time a world of good by leaving the mindless entertainment of vaudeville tap and high-kick behind, it was Robbins who finally abandoned the classical vocabulary repertoire entirely, in favor of true invention—movement that sprang from the very same realism that produced the characters.

Although *The King and I* was written for the luminous theatre star Gertrude Lawrence, it was the unknown Yul Brynner whose career exploded, and the king's role forever after dominated the proceedings. Rodgers wrote a limited-range score for Gertrude Lawrence, who had limited vocal capabilities and a tendency to sing flat.

It is unlikely that any writers in the history of American culture created so many classics in their career, or even, as in the case of Rodgers and Hammerstein, the second half of their respective careers. Yet among their shows are also failures that boasted even more experimentation than their hits.

Agnes de Mille rehearses the dream ballet
Archive Photos

Me and Juliet (1953) was an original libretto by Hammerstein about backstage theatre, and was intended to be a fun musical comedy (about fun musical comedy lives). But neither Hammerstein nor Rodgers was capable of writing fun musical comedies any more—this was the team that had retired the musical formula of the twenties altogether—and it ended up as a second-rate work. It has a mediocre score that lacks any particular ambience—Rodgers and Hart could have written it better in their day—and a second-rate book: as a librettist, Hammerstein, the great genius of the formula for the modern American musical, was a craftsman more than an artist, and was at his weakest when fashioning an original book. The staging was imaginative, however. The musical numbers moved around the theatre world—onstage, offstage, above stage, dressing rooms, hangouts—showing Hammerstein's effort to make the show glide. There is a unique number featuring the audience in a "show within a show" ("Intermission Talk") and one strong ballad ("No Other Love Have I"). Due largely to the Rodgers and Hammerstein name, *Me and Juliet* managed a ten-month run.

• • •

The most imaginative failure Rodgers and Hammerstein created was *Allegro.* In the fall of 1947 *Oklahoma!* and three other shows produced by Rodgers and Hammerstein (two plays and the Irving Berlin musical *Annie Get Your Gun*) were playing on Broadway. *Oklahoma!, Carousel,* and *Annie Get Your Gun* were also on tour, and *Oklahoma!* and *Annie* were in London. A road company of *Show Boat* produced by the team was in rehearsal.

And *Allegro* opened at the Majestic Theatre with a huge amount of publicity and the largest box-office advance to date. *Allegro* had eighteen principal actors, twenty-one supporting players, twenty-two dancers, thirty-eight singers, thirty-five musicians, and forty stagehands—an unusually large company even for musicals of the period. Perhaps that was part of the problem, since it had been conceived as an intimate show.

Rodgers was convinced that "a single guiding hand should be in charge of every element of the production," and the producers asked Agnes de Mille to direct as well as choreograph. She may have been the first legitimate director-choreographer in the American musical since George M. Cohan. Certainly she was the first woman to direct a major musical. Some sources say that Rodgers and Hammerstein were unhappy with de Mille's work, but Ethan Mordden, perhaps the most careful auditor of their history, points out that the production faced an unusual amount of problems out of town, and de Mille did not have time to address them all. In any case, Hammerstein took over the direction of the scenes, and Rodgers took a hand in staging the songs.

The show did have problems. Rodgers and Hammerstein had rushed the show into production knowing that the second act wasn't satisfactory. Their many producing commitments diluted Hammerstein's writing attention (subsequently they gave up producing any work other than their own). The New Haven tryout was legendary for its mishaps, including a fire, dancers hurt on Jo Mielziner's mechanical tracks in the stage floor, and Lisa Kirk's fall into the pit while singing, "A clumsy Joe who wouldn't know a rhumba from a waltz," from "The Gentleman Is a Dope."*

But *Allegro* was, in fact, the show most crucial to postmodern (post-Rodgers and Hammerstein) musical comedy history. It set the course for Harold Prince and Stephen Sondheim, for presentational numbers, for fluidity, for concept, for de-emphasizing traditional roles (its leads didn't sing much), and for, more than anything, *experimentation.*

Allegro represented a significant attempt to play with the form of the musical, and took inspiration from Thornton Wilder's *Our Town,* staged nine years earlier. The show used narrative devices, a Greek chorus, an abstract multimedia set, and a minimalist approach to the design that allowed the show to flow over many years and places (like *Our Town,* it was set in uncomplicated, memory-sweetened, small-town America). The songs were shared among a number of characters.

One of the biggest problems with the show was that the Greek chorus idea—the comment song—is fundamentally undramatic, innovative as it might be and no matter how clever its lyrics. It *tells* the audience something instead of *showing* them something, and thus has a limited use.

Allegro's form also put Hammerstein's work into the vein of "preachy," a criticism of the show, and thus moved it slightly away from the engrossing drama of their hit musicals. Whenever a musical becomes didac-

* Kirk was helped up by the musicians, and did not stop singing. She wasn't hurt, because the New Haven theatre, legendary for its tryouts, had no real pit, and the orchestra was on the house floor. The actress apparently regarded this as a *coup de théâtre* and tried it on purpose the next evening. The producers warned her to stick to the blocking.

tic, the audience loses interest. Moralizing is possible only when it is disguised well, and essays aren't theatrical.

Also, allegory can dull the color in the setting, detracting from a score rich with time and place—precisely what Rodgers had pioneered so well. And allegory does not provide characters with enough specificity to make their drama interesting. It is not the form alone, but the characters of *Our Town* that have stood the test of time. However, the design was revolutionary and freed the American theatre from realism.

Finally, on the grounds that death was a downbeat ending, Hammerstein gave up his original story form—cradle to grave of everyman—and the show ended in the hero's mid-thirties, thus suffering from plotus interruptus.

The show had a capitalization of $750,000 when $100,000 was considered large. The top ticket price at the time was $4.50, so the project was a larger-than-usual risk. Its one-season run was not so bad, but the show lost money. In spite of its problems, *Allegro* ran 315 performances and left its mark. Hammerstein pushed the use of song into increasing integration with the dialogue.

Where early musicals began with a scene that was followed by a song, applause, and then a resumption of the routine, Hammerstein began to write more complicated introductions in order to segue smoothly from dialogue to song, as in *Show Boat.* Then he began to go back and forth between dialogue and singing (as in the bench scene from *Carousel*), and he did a great deal more of this in *Allegro.*

Allegro is considered the first play in which lighting served as an integral a part of the staging—something that would reach full fruition in *A Chorus Line*—a necessity because the sets were nonrealistic. But Jo Mielziner's sets and lights ended up being too complex. What was supposed to be a simple set turned out to be a complicated system of treadmills, moving platforms, and projections that overshadowed the drama.

Failure or no, *Allegro* was the first concept musical. Later, Bert Fink of the Rodgers and Hammerstein organization said:

> Reverberations of *Allegro* resound to this day: from a fragmented score (*Grand Hotel*) and seamless staging (*Dreamgirls*), to the introspective use of dance (*West Side Story*) and chorus (*A Little Night Music*), from the thematic (*Company*) to the metaphoric (*A Chorus Line*).

Allegro was "the first really good experimental show," in the words of its young production assistant Stephen Sondheim. Of all the Rodgers and Hammerstein shows that Sondheim studied, he found *Allegro* to be the most instructive. Years later, Sondheim's groundbreaking musical *Company* featured many of the same theatrical devices—an abstract, multimedia set; a Greek chorus;, musical numbers shared by many principal characters; and the commentary song.

Hammerstein worked on a television version in 1960, the possibilities of which were spectacular. He reworked the show after the original experience and looked forward to replacing a cumbersome production with the possibilities of film. Sadly, he died while in the midst of this project.

• • •

As many of his musicals demonstrate, most notably *Show Boat* and *Oklahoma!,* Oscar Hammerstein was an innovative genius. He could easily have taken the American musical to a third plateau, just as he had taken it to a second one with the musicals he wrote with Rodgers. However, partnered with the more traditional Rodgers, for whose music the Rodgers and Hammerstein type of show was a perfect forum, Hammerstein did not have time and energy to push the musical theatre form into a new epoch. He never again attempted anything so rash, experimental, or unique as the noble failure *Allegro.* Instead he returned to the form they had so successfully created, contenting himself with experiments within the idiom.

One of these shows was *Pipe Dream,* with a book based on John Steinbeck's *Cannery Row* characters and setting, but with a new plot that Steinbeck developed simultaneously as another novel, *Sweet Thursday.* The musical did not retain Steinbeck's edge, and was unable to recreate his poetic, dreamy, literature. Helen Traubel was apparently somewhat lost in her role, and Rodgers was in the hospital throughout production; audiences were not happy with its dark plot, and the focus was lost when an attempt was made to soften it. Yet the love story between two fringe kooks—one a hooker—had the earmarks of a great Rodgers and Hammerstein show. This was the one that got away.

Flower Drum Song, with book by Hammerstein and Joseph Fields, seems to have lost potency over time, perhaps because it succumbed to the musical comedy format. Was Hammerstein becoming exhausted with the enormous creative effort his great musicals required? The show was directed by Gene Kelly, who was out of his element in Rodgers and Hammerstein work and hesitated somewhat to attempt the full reach of C. Y. Lee's novel. Bolstered by an outstanding cast and a cheerful score, *Flower Drum Song* managed a success. But a far greater success waited around the corner—a true story that actress Mary Martin and director Vincent J. Donehue wanted as a showcase for her.

Rodgers and Hammerstein married musical comedy's brazen style of entertainment (Rodgers and Hart) with operetta's romantic sentimentality (Hammerstein and Kern), producing entertainment with a great heart. In their last show they went back to the exotic settings that had powered their early masterpieces, and, with the worldwide success of the film version of *The Sound of Music,* the duo became known for the sentimentality of their work. But this was an inaccurate perception that strayed far from the central achievement of their collaboration. *Oklahoma!, Carousel, South Pacific,* and *The King and I* are musical plays as dramatic as anything by William Inge or Eugene O'Neill, while *Allegro* would long be remembered by theatre people as the first truly experimental *concept musical.* The formula that Rodgers and Hammerstein created not only bestrode the times themselves, but influenced all future musicals. Cole Porter, master of a previous era, attributed his later, more theatre-oriented scores (*Silk Stockings, Can-Can, Kiss Me Kate,* and *Out of this World*) to the influence of Rodgers and Hammerstein. ("I think they're great if it takes two men to write a song," he said.) Hammerstein was Stephen Sondheim's principal teacher, mentor, and inspiration.

The haunting "Edelweiss"—so authentic that many people think it's an Austrian folk song—was the last song the duo ever wrote together. In 1960 Hammerstein was diagnosed with an incurable cancer, and he died with the same dignity he wrote with.

It was the end of an era. Rodgers went on to write more shows, including *No Strings* (1962), which featured the musical theatre's first unremarked interracial romance between Diahann Carroll and Richard Kiley. (In *Jamaica* (1957) audiences hadn't noticed that Lena Horne and Ricardo Montalbán were a biracial couple.) Director-choreographer Joe Layton put the musicians right on stage, and choreographed dancers moved the scenery, increasing the fluidity that Hammerstein had spent his life pursuing. It ran seventeen months and made Layton's career, though it has not stood the test of time well. Rodgers wrote his own lyrics for *No Strings* (having had plenty of experience during Lorenz Hart's disappearances). Later, he wrote with

Sondheim (*Do I Hear a Waltz?* 1965) and Martin Charnin (*Two by Two,* 1970), but the theatre was changing and his own career was winding down. He had inaugurated a new era with Hammerstein and *Oklahoma!* and had even been part of some extraordinary steps (*Allegro* and *No Strings*) toward integration. He had altered the use of the overture, replacing it in *Carousel* with the pantomime scene and in *The Sound of Music* with a liturgical hymn, and dropping it altogether for *No Strings.*

Rodgers and Hammerstein had virtually created the second great era of the American musical score. In the first (dominated by George Cohan, Irving Berlin, Cole Porter, Rodgers and Hart) the score was meant to be popular and had no other requirements. But with the second age the American musical became more dramatic, and the musical form lifted itself to a greater plateau. The inclusion of dramatic dance completed the revolution that the Princess shows had begun.

When *Oklahoma!* opened, critic George Jean Nathan, who had supported the plays of Eugene O'Neill and William Saroyan, complained that the traditional chorus line of female beauty had been subverted by the talent of real dancers. He wrote,

> The best musical comedies . . . are those in which sense is reduced to a minimum, the worst, those which aim at rationality. What we want is a return to the old time absurdity, the old-time refusal to reflect life and reality in any way, the old time razzle and dazzle and the incredible.

Fortunately, he never got it.

Ethan Mordden observed that "*Oklahoma!* did not invent the artistically organic musical. What *Oklahoma!* did was to popularize it." And, moreover, it brought all the elements together. Sure, *On Your Toes* had a ballet, but it also had a less dramatically driven score. There had been nonstar shows before, but they were born of necessity, not artistic integrity. Shows had opened in quiet, even odd ways before, but never because it was so dramatically right, and never with mood as a pervasive value. *Show Boat* and *Porgy and Bess* had dramatically-driven scores but no significant dancing.

Agnes de Mille's choreography might have been confined to ballet stages were it not for fortuitous timing. Still, de Mille could just as easily

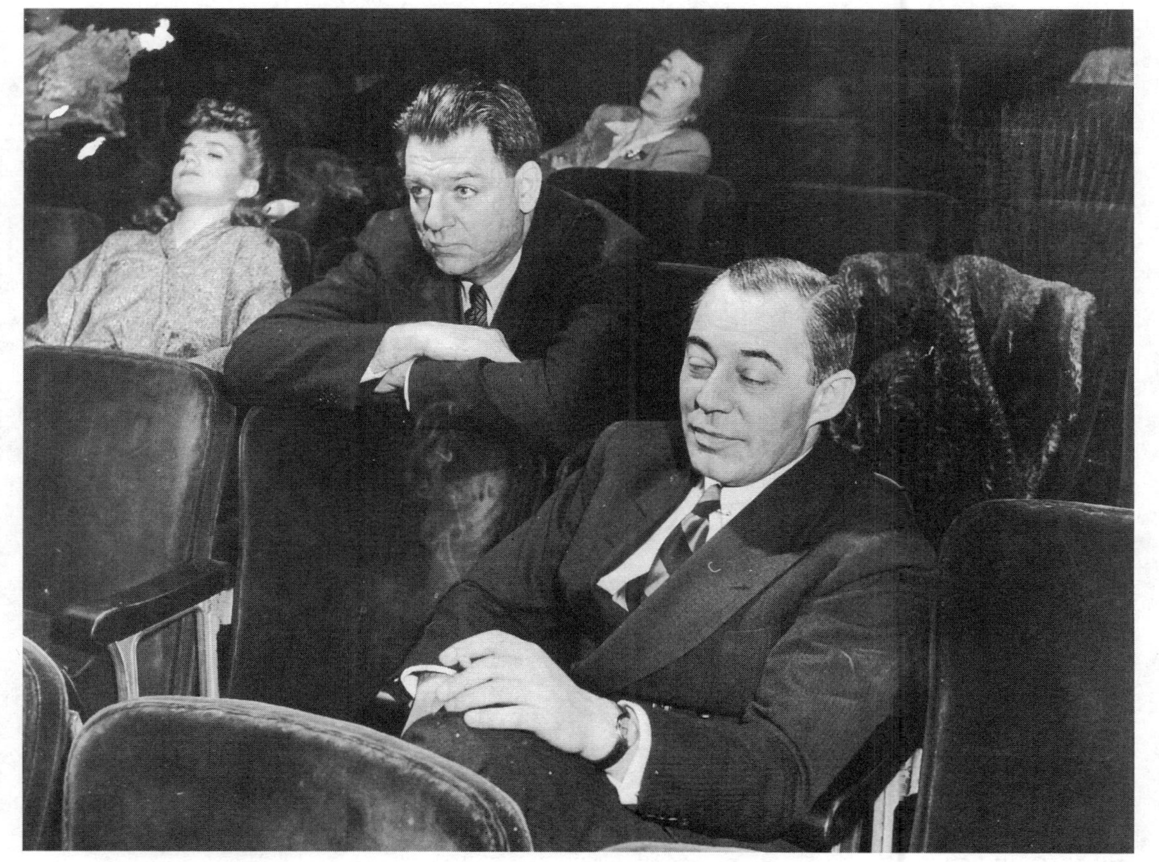

Tired chorus girls wait for Oscar Hammerstein II and Richard Rodgers to settle on the form of the modern American musical
Archive Photos

have made her musical comedy debut in another style, because the special quality of her work that revolutionized musical theatre dancing is the combination of ballet and theatre she used, not the coincidental choice of a Western theme seen only weeks before *Oklahoma!* was looking for a choreographer.

When de Mille arrived in New York with the intention of pursuing a dance career, she found the scene deplorable. Dancers were not respected, and there was very little work on the concert scene. American dance, as with the American musical, was the last of the native arts to gain respectability. Not until George Balanchine and Lincoln Kirstein grubbed the New York City Ballet out of hard soil did New York take notice. But dance had long been a big part of Broadway. The way in which dance was used changed gradually, and it came to a head with *Oklahoma!*

Here is de Mille's description of the position of dance and the choreographer in musicals before *Oklahoma!*:

> In this medium the dance director was no longer boss or anything like. By tradition the composer was tyrant although Oscar Hammerstein was to prove shortly that the author of the book might be equally important. The director has some say and also the producer, but the dance director not much. The designers were never charged to protect the dancing. They were told only to fill the stage with color, see that the girls looked lovely whether they could move or not, to favor the star, and to do something sufficiently splashy to get more shows to design. If the dancing was hobbled or overweighted, it never reflected on anyone but the choreographer. The duration of the numbers would be strictly limited—because of course for every minute of dancing there would be one less minute of singing or acting, something the composer, author and director never forgot.

Before *Oklahoma!*, audiences claimed they could tell whether or not they would like a musical before the curtain was halfway up, a reference to the quality of the leggy chorines. But de Mille took her new assignment seriously. Prior to her work, real dancing had made only limited and sporadic forays into the musical theatre, principally "Slaughter on Tenth Avenue" in *On Your*

Will Parker demonstrates the dazzling dances of the big city to fellow Oklahomans in two different productions of the first Rodgers and Hammerstein musical
Photofest/Vandamm
Photofest

Toes, and none of it had caught on. Partly because of *Oklahoma!*'s success, partly because the achievement was followed with several other long-running de Mille shows, and partly because earlier attempts had been insufficiently complete and integrated, *Oklahoma!* became the landmark case.

Agnes de Mille's choreography for the ballet stage had always been theatrical, spirited, and noted for comic invention (not a prerequisite for the ballet, but invaluable on the musical comedy stage). In extending the frontiers of ballet, her motivation was the same as that of composers like Kern, Berlin and Gershwin, who turned theatre music away from European influences. She was an original artist and an American.

Ballet sequences in Broadway musicals as early as *The Black Crook* had made small attempts to focus on plot. The real contribution by de Mille's dances came from the Western-influenced nature of the dance vocabulary de Mille used to execute the various sequences, particularly dream sequences. Exposure of the Freudian motivations and fears of the characters gave a dimension to the choreography that was original and startling. She wrote:

> The younger choreographers believed that every gesture must be proper to a particular character under particular circumstances . . . the new choreographer does not arrange old steps into new patterns; the emotion evolves steps, gestures, and rhythms . . . the line between dancing and acting is no longer clearly marked.

After *Oklahoma!* too many musicals copied de Mille's ideas, and for years ballets in musicals were hastily conceived and not fully integrated into the style and tone of the overall production.

The less glamorous dancers took heart, for until the de Mille era most of the requirements for employment in a Broadway chorus line consisted of acquaintanceship with production staff or good looks, for men as well as women. Auditions were "cattle calls" because the singing and dancing (and standing around and posing) were not technically difficult in those days. When de Mille employed a trained chorus of exceptional dancers for *Oklahoma!,* the transition was complete. After *Oklahoma!,* musical comedy dancers would require the same rigorous training and classical foundation that concert dancers did. This talent provided Broadway choreographers what they had previously been denied. Instead of being limited to the tap and ballroom steps and kick lines that had been the mainstay of musicals, de Mille was able to use every facet of a real dancer's vocabulary, allowing the choreographer greater versatility. By twisting the classical vocabulary (which had not changed since the court of King Louis XIV) into movements that recalled the cowboys and girls of the Old West, she gave her dances greater theatrical expression, and at the same time gave to the theatre the heightened expression of serious dance. Dance now made the same contributions to musical theatre that serious book writing, lyric writing, and composing had. Emotions that were not easy to communicate in song or scene would now become possible—fighting, for example, as in the upcoming *West Side Story*.

Her achievement was a major turning point in the use of dance in the American musical, as well as a principal factor in the success of *Oklahoma!* She marks the beginning of the new era with a music rehearsal in New York, in which one of her dancers winced when an orchestra member played a wrong note. Richard Rodgers happened to notice her expression, and he was dumbfounded. "How is it that a chorus girl could tell," he thought, "or care?"

Agnes de Mille continued to pursue Broadway dances with imagination. *One Touch of Venus* (1943) contained two outstanding ballets, one in which Venus, recently a marble statue and now a mere mortal, samples life in Manhattan, and a second-act dream ballet in which de Mille exotically imitates pagan rituals. Surely *Bloomer Girl* (1944) appealed to de Mille—its leading character was an early abolitionist and advocated bloomers over hoop skirts. She created a Civil War ballet, a timely, heart-wrenching evocation of the concurrent World War and its widows. For *Brigadoon* (1947), de Mille created a plot-driven chase ballet that used Scottish dancing. She tried her hand at jazzier dancing for *Gentlemen Prefer Blondes* (1949), and for *Kwamina* (1961) she created some riveting African dances.

Other great choreographers followed de Mille from American ballet to American musical theatre, notably Herbert Ross, Michael Kidd, and Jerome Robbins. Robbins, in particular, had a special gift to bring along. His perception of the stage arts, his talent, and his vision of the musical were more all-embracing than anyone before him. Thanks to de Mille, Robbins would have every technique at his disposal in creating his musicals, and what he would do would mark the beginning of yet another new form—not only a successful amalgamation of song, scene, and dance, but also a seamless, unique, and fluid, production.

PLAYBILL
a weekly magazine for theatregoers

Winter Garden
1958

WEST

WINTER GARDEN

ROBERT E. GRIFFITH and HAROLD S. PRINCE
(By arrangement with Roger L. Stevens)
present
A New Musical
WEST SIDE STORY
Based on a conception of Jerome Robbins
Book by
ARTHUR LAURENTS
Music by
LEONARD BERNSTEIN
Lyrics by
STEPHEN SONDHEIM
with
CAROL LAWRENCE
LARRY KERT
ART SMITH
CHITA RIVERA
MICKEY CALIN
Lee Becker
Eddie Roll
David Winters
Tony Mordente
KEN LE ROY
Arch Johnson
Grover Dale

Entire Production Directed and Choreographed by
JEROME ROBBINS

Scenic Production by
OLIVER SMITH
Costumes Designed by
IRENE SHARAFF
Lighting by
JEAN ROSENTHAL
Co-Choreographer
Production Associate

Fourteen

JEROME ROBBINS AND *WEST SIDE STORY*

You're the top . . .

Jerome Robbins came to dancing as a freshman at New York University, where he was studying chemistry. In 1939 he was a chorus boy in *Great Lady* and *Stars in Your Eyes* and a featured performer in *The Straw Hat Revue*. By 1940 he was good enough to join the American Ballet Theatre as a dancer in the corps, moving up to soloist quickly. When Agnes de Mille was looking for a soloist to perform a rhythmically intricate routine within a ballet, the young Jerry Robbins was described to her as a dancer "who could count anything."

In April of 1944, two years after de Mille premiered *Rodeo* with the Ballets Russes, Robbins premiered his own choreography for the American Ballet Theatre, *Fancy Free,* at the Metropolitan Opera House. It was the story of three sailors on leave in New York. Leonard Bernstein, who had recently made a startlingly sudden name for himself as a young conductor with the New York Philharmonic, provided the original score. Oliver Smith, then a relatively unknown designer, did the setting. The morning after the premiere of *Fancy Free,* Robbins, Bernstein, and Smith woke up to find themselves internationally famous.

Robbins wanted to turn the ballet into a full-fledged Broadway musical. Bernstein enlisted two young performers from a four-person Greenwich Village nightclub group called The Revuers* to write the libretto and lyrics. Betty Comden and Adolph Green had been writing their own material throughout the 1930s, finding that if they used other people's material they'd have to pay for it, and they "only had enough money for a pencil." When Comden, Green, and director George Abbott came onto the project, they rejected a number of songs Bernstein pulled from his trunk, and in the end *On the Town* featured all new songs, new music, and a lighthearted but endearing and very realistic wartime plot (including roles that Comden and Green wrote for themselves).

That plot is the first of three notable characteristics that makes *On the Town* one of the great American musicals. Although it was written within the style of musical comedy of the period, its story concerns three sailors looking for sex. At least one of them succeeds with a satisfying, if offstage, matinée. His soul mate ("I Get Carried Away") is an anthropology student, a subtle reminder that we're dealing with primitive relationships. A second lucky gob gets to hear one of the great Comden-Green-Bernstein blasters, and the girl who sings "I Can Cook Too" isn't singing about the culinary arts. (The third intrepid mariner spends too long looking for the girl of his dreams, and doesn't have time to consummate the relationship.)

These three sailors are on leave for only twenty-four hours, giving the plot a wonderful urgency, but underscoring the fact that the audience isn't going to see long-term relationships blossom. The modernity and authenticity of these events—plenty of young men were going off to war, worried they would not return, and plenty of young women wanted to give them a great sendoff—places *On the Town* in a category that isn't all that evident within Comden and Green's polite and bubbly musical comedy style. In fact, the musical was original and risqué, nearly anti-Hammerstein in its sophistication, and one of the first to suggest that sex might take its place beside romance as a worthy human endeavor.

* The other two were Judy Holliday and Alvin Hammer. Holliday went on to stardom on Broadway (*Bells Are Ringing*) and in Hollywood (*Born Yesterday*).

The second characteristic that illuminates *On the Town* is Leonard Bernstein's music, which also startled Broadway ears. His first Broadway score is a direct musical descendent of George Gershwin's efforts to combine American musical idioms—blues, jazz, and ragtime—with a classical structure. The result is one of the truly great Broadway scores. But audiences and critics lagged far behind. None of the tunes became hits. Moreover, when MGM made the film they dumped most of the music in favor of banal and unoriginal songs by Roger Edens. This gap between Bernstein's work and mainstream commercial success always hurt him, but fortunately never curbed his musical ambitions.

The *On the Town* score soared to even greater heights during the dances, the third extraordinary characteristic of this show. Even *Oklahoma!*'s dances featured only regurgitated song melodies reworked by a dance arranger. But twenty-one months after *Oklahoma!* the young talents behind *On the Town* conceived six plot-forwarding dances that Bernstein wrote as *original symphonic suites,* and Jerome Robbins choreographed with a vocabulary that at once thrust de Mille's modern ballet work into ancient history. Using the natural exuberance of sailors, and the jazzy rhythms and syncopations of Bernstein's music, Robbins fashioned dances that not only were comfortable within the show's dramatic fabric, but grew out of it organically. In one startling night (December 28, 1944) and 436 subsequent performances, *On the Town* created and established the greatest of all American contributions to the stage arts: American theatre dance.

In their musical theatre debut, Robbins and Bernstein brought the discipline of serious music and serious dance to the musical comedy. While Richard Rodgers and Jerome Kern wrote popular tunes and Gershwin went to the opera form to exercise his ambitions, Bernstein lavished a more complex song form, more complex harmonies, and less accessible, more intricate melodies on a musical comedy score. Agnes de Mille had created ballets for musicals, but Robbins created musical comedy ballets. If *Oklahoma!* captured the ebullience of a nation growing up in sunshine, *On the Town*'s sunshine was darkened with the urgency of a twenty-four-hour leave prior to impending doom. It's one of the American theatre's greatest works. Because it's extremely hard to do well—witness the miserable 1971 Broadway revival by Ron Field—it isn't often attempted. Robbins's original choreography is an integral part of the show's creativity, and without it the show doesn't fly.

With the success of *On the Town,* Bernstein and Robbins achieved a good deal of mobility in their respective careers. An actor friend of Robbins was cast in a production of *Romeo and Juliet* and asked for his help. Robbins studied the script and became fascinated. In 1949 he conceived the idea of a Broadway musical based on the play. He enlisted his friend Arthur Laurents as librettist and Bernstein as composer, and they began discussions of a musical to be entitled *East Side Story,* with a plot fitted for a Catholic girl and a Jewish boy. Other projects forced the work aside for six years. When they returned to it, times had changed. The idea became *West Side Story* (another early title possibility was *Gangway!*) and the Montague-Capulet enmity was translated into gang warfare between white and Puerto Rican teenage gangs, based on then-current fighting for the turf of Manhattan's West Side, also known as Hell's Kitchen. (Robert Ardrey, playwright and anthropologist, called *West Side Story* the "territorial imperative musical.")

This new translation came to be an important factor in writing the musical. The hostile tensions that infected the urban poor translated well into a number of dance sequences. Robbins found the teenager's natural slouch, violent quixotic energy, and herd instinct useful ideas for his choreography. The battle for control of Manhattan's West Side gave the dancing more specific motivation, which Robbins capitalized on. The Latin-American rhythms gave Bernstein an infectious musical base, and the whole score was infused with a jazzy Manhattan idiom, which he inherited from Gershwin, as well as the romantic Americana of Copland.

The concept was built upon the greatest of all love stories and filled with the explosive energy of very real characters, and it drove what turned out to be one of the most original and authentic American musicals of all time. Eight weeks of rehearsals (two to four more than was customary at the time) were dominated by the autocratic Robbins, who had spent a year looking for talented young dancers to play all the parts.

Final casting for the characters Tony and Maria came down to two couples. Anna Maria Alberghetti and Frank Poretta were two opera-trained legitimate voices, and Larry Kert and Carol Lawrence were two young unknowns with primarily dance backgrounds. Robbins wanted to hire the dancers, but everyone else wanted the experienced singers. Robbins won, as always. He was the first auteur-director-choreographer, and *West Side Story* was the first musical "conceived, directed, and choreographed" by one man (who, in this case, insisted on a box around his name in the billing.)

Rodgers and Hammerstein had usually insisted on strong voices,

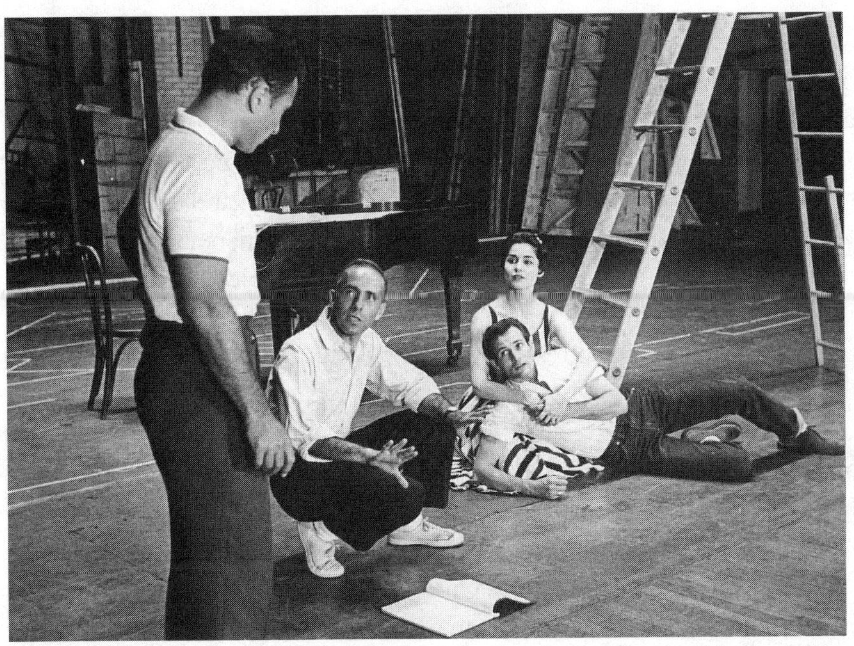

Jerome Robbins and Stephen Sondheim rehearse Larry Kert and Carol Lawrence
Photofest/Freidman-Abeles

When Robbins rehearsed, every step was "full out"
Museum of the City of New York

and it was left to the next generation of innovators to emphasize the acting. In fact, the angel-voiced Larry Kert, who had been a Jack Cole dancer and gymnast, auditioned a number of times thinking he was up for a role in the chorus, and was shocked when he was cast as Tony and sent for voice lessons. Robbins was after a level of realism that had never before been attempted on the stage, and this was reflected in his choice of actors. During rehearsals he separated the Jets and the Sharks, forbidding them to socialize and refusing to allow the actress playing Anybodys to eat lunch with anyone at all.

After a relatively crisis-free tryout, the show opened on Broadway on September 16, 1957. In first reviews, most critics were unable to fully comprehend the magnitude of the achievement, but Brooks Atkinson wrote that the ballets "convey the things that Laurents is inhibited from saying because the characters are so inarticulate."

By settling on the milieu of inarticulate teenagers, the authors were forced into a gut-level emotional approach, perfect for musical theatre, which allowed them to tread the very fine line between reality and impressionism. In the film version it seems a bit awkward for teenagers to be dancing down the street, but on stage the illusion is readily acceptable.

As they had for *On the Town,* Bernstein and Robbins created original symphonic suites and dances to carry forward large chunks of the story. This time they were able to do that with principal characters. For the first time, the structure allowed dance to wander in and out of all the scenes, whereas previously only specific moments were set aside for full dance numbers or ballets.

During the creation of *Oklahoma!* de Mille had rehearsed her dancers separately. All the dances were performed by the chorus. Principal actors had their own songs and, with the exception of Will Parker's "Kansas City," the principals and the chorus seldom interacted. For *West Side Story* there really was no chorus. Each dancer was assigned specific characters to play. All of them sang and danced and spoke. A century earlier, Richard Wagner had dictated that drama should be the content and music the means of expression, which was echoed when Richard Rodgers's music reached new heights of expression in conjunction with the less intellectual, more emotional vocabulary of Oscar Hammerstein. In the 1950s, Robbins knew that by assigning dancers such an important part of the story, he automatically gained dramatic importance for his dances. That strength underscores every dance sequence in *West Side Story*—each one is deeply rooted in the dramatic

The Jets versus the Sharks
Museum of the City of New York

Baby John (David Winters) in front
Museum of the City of New York

action. Thereafter, no matter how quick their tempo, dances that lacked dramatic substance would slow a show down.

The plot and characters of early American musicals were insubstantial—the purpose of the evening was sheer entertainment, and dancing could easily hold its own. After thematic intent was introduced to song and scene, dancing fell behind. Agnes de Mille brought dance back into the fold with both a new approach to the dance vocabulary and an increased contribution to the dramatics of a production. Yet the use of song, dance, and scene still fell short of a cumulative effect for lack of a smooth integration. What the dancers could contribute to the whole was limited to what part they played. In *West Side Story,* the whole show was theirs.

This also allowed for the total integration of all the techniques that had been evolving since the days of Aristophanes. *West Side Story* was one of the first productions to use such a complete range of techniques in support of the drama, and it was a textbook example of how they could be melded. For fight sequences, dance was the primary tool ("Prologue," "The Rumble"). For more emotional moments, such as expressions of love, song was used ("One Hand, One Heart," "Maria"). And when the adults were on stage, the inability of the principals to communicate across the generation gap was presented in dialogue. As in *Porgy and Bess,* in which the white characters do not sing, none of the adults in *West Side Story* sing or dance, thus they are stylistically alienated from the group. And with the "Tonight Quintet," Leonard Bernstein stretched the standard song form into a musical fabric complex enough for opera. Robbins, Bernstein, Laurents and Stephen Sondheim (in his legitimate theatre debut here as a lyricist) had accomplished nothing less than the perfect musical. Only the advent of the choreographer-as-director enabled the musical theatre to take this last, significant step.

Jerome Robbins took directing seriously from the beginning, and became a member of the first director's lab of the Actors' Studio. This dual capacity, which he was the first to popularize, enabled his shows to achieve a seamless integration of song, dance, and scene. As an added bonus, the elements in *West Side Story* appear in nearly equal proportion.

Robbins made another important contribution to the musical theatre with his production of *West Side Story.* In spite of his ballet background, he reorganized the use of vocabulary for his dancers. While Agnes de Mille had used a classic ballet vocabulary and stretched, bent, and stylized it to

West Side Story stunned audiences with a first full look at American jazz dance
Museum of the City of New York/Fred Fehl

Riff and Anybodys dance at the gym
Museum of the City of New York

accommodate her characters (with steps still grounded in ballet), Robbins reversed the process. He abandoned the classic ballet vocabulary altogether, and gave the natural movements of the characters theatrical shape. Theatre dance moved into its third, and greatest, stage. After the tap-dancing and kick-lines of the musicals of the twenties and thirties, and after the ballet of the forties, theatre dance began to draw on a combination of ethnic dances and jazz dances. For *West Side Story* Robbins drew his vocabulary directly from the teenage slouch—the fighting and the arrogant, confident strut—and presented the characters in simple, natural versions, expanding on them until he had created full-fledged musical numbers. Earlier, for *The King and I,* he had gone to the Far East to study dancing. Later, for *Fiddler on the Roof* he would investigate the dances at Jewish weddings on Manhattan's culturally rich Lower East Side. His research led to a more realistic vocabulary, making the dances more itegral to the story.

The audience for a Robbins musical could not see precisely where the action ended and the dancing began. Beginnings and endings of musical numbers were equally fluid, and song and dance blended smoothly back into the book. Thus, the techniques that made up the musical were no longer making their individual contributions episodically, and were seen to be of a single piece. This too had the effect of increasing the audience's involvement in the story. In addition, Robbins eliminated the use of static, pretty pictures in staging that had been traditional from Florenz Ziegfeld's girls to Rouben Mamoulian's painstaking tableaux—instead he kept the cast in constant flux and movement.

Thanks to Robbins's technical ability to integrate all the performing skills into a seamless and cohesive whole, and thanks to the author's ability to write for such fluidity, the theatre musical achieved a new level of dramatic excitement. The American musical reached its next plateau with *West Side Story,* best defined by *synergy,* wherein the whole is greater than the sum of the parts.

Not all the critics thought so. Several clung to the George Jean Nathan school of musical comedy and pronounced the subject matter unsuitable for a musical. Some theatregoers felt that "Gee, Officer Krupke," which makes fun of the police, was in poor taste. Others thought the language was tasteless. The U.S. government canceled *West Side Story*'s booking at the Brussels World's Fair on the grounds that it was bad publicity for America. The Antoinette Perry (Tony) Award for Best Musical of the 1957–58 season went to Meredith Wilson's *The Music Man.*

West Side Story takes to the air . . . the girl in the middle, Lee Becker Theodore, later founded the American Dance Machine, which has tried to preserve the great theatre dances . . . the boy with the hat later wrote lyrics for and directed *Annie*
Museum of the City of New York/Eileen Darby

The Jets try to keep cool
Photofest/Fred Fehl

The Broadway production of *West Side Story* ran for 732 performances. Following a successful national tour, the musical returned to Broadway, where it received more uniformly ecstatic notices and played for 249 additional performances. Apparently the critics had digested the work in the interim.

Today *West Side Story*'s grace as a technically innovative musical, its original and authoritative dancing, and its soaring score still have the power to entertain. In the world of the late fifties it was also emotionally powerful. *Time* magazine called it "a profoundly moving show that is as ugly as the city jungles."

As early as 1913 *The Dramatic Mirror* said of the music for musicals, "The stuff that can be whistled after one hearing is for whistlers, and whistling is a practice avoided in good society." At first, audiences and critics did not recognize the quality of *West Side Story*'s score because they couldn't leave the theatre humming it. Due to the popularity of the film, the score eventually became hummable.

With the Broadway career of Leonard Bernstein, theatregoers and critics were forced to realize that good music, like all art, is often too complex to be digested in a single hearing. Like George Gershwin before him, Bernstein never wrote down to popular taste; and like Gershwin, he led a double life of concert and popular composing, refusing to be limited to either genre. With *West Side Story,* Bernstein and Robbins pushed the envelope of the American musical theatre in both content (a tragic story) and form (a brief book, rich and integrated dances performed by principal characters, and a somber, finger-snapping opening).

Robbins went on to become, if he wasn't already, the leading artist of the musical stage. Having done dances for *On the Town, High Button Shoes, Miss Liberty, Call Me Madam, The King and I,* and *Billion Dollar Baby,* he took over and probably saved *Funny Girl.* He directed and choreographed *Peter Pan* and *Bells Are Ringing.* After *West Side Story* he went on to conceive, direct, and choreograph two more masterpieces—*Gypsy,* the quintessential show-biz musical, and *Fiddler on the Roof,* a work so steeped in artistry and humanity that many consider it to be the finest musical ever created. By directing as well as choreographing, Robbins freed the theatre from its divisional aspects and allowed actors, especially those with dual or triple talents, to create a performance at once realistic and entertaining.

Robbins spent two tumultuous decades in the musical theatre then returned to the more rarefied world of classical ballet. He spent most of his remaining career creating a variety of ballets for the New York City Ballet. There he joined artistic director George Balanchine, who had also spent productive time away from ballet to further the quality of the American musical theatre.

In 1989, Robbins wanted to recreate some of his early show dances for the Lincoln Center Library collection. This desire blossomed into the stunning Broadway entertainment *Jerome Robbins' Broadway,* which encapsulated not only the work of the American theatre's greatest choreographer but many of its scores as well. The production ran for 634 performances but an excessive budget limited its ability to continue, and the musical sequences were not connected to a book. Modern audiences unfamiliar with the great American musicals couldn't truly understand what they were seeing. But theatregoers over forty years old were transported.

Robbins had increased the stature of both the director and the choreographer by combining them successfully. The rise of the director-choreographer would increase the art of the musical and make it attractive on its own. It was no longer a medium in which to go slumming, nor one from which simply to graduate to plays, film, or ballet. A good number of *West Side Story* alumni went on to teach, choreograph, and direct, most notably David Winters (in the burgeoning medium of rock and roll, inventing for Ann-Margret the first Las Vegas act-as-spectacle), Grover Dale, Eddie Roll, Tony Mordente, and Martin Charnin. Eliot Feld later appeared in the show and the film, then founded his own ballet company.

But for one young dancer who apprenticed under Robbins in the European cast of *West Side Story,* the musical theatre was worth a lifetime of commitment.

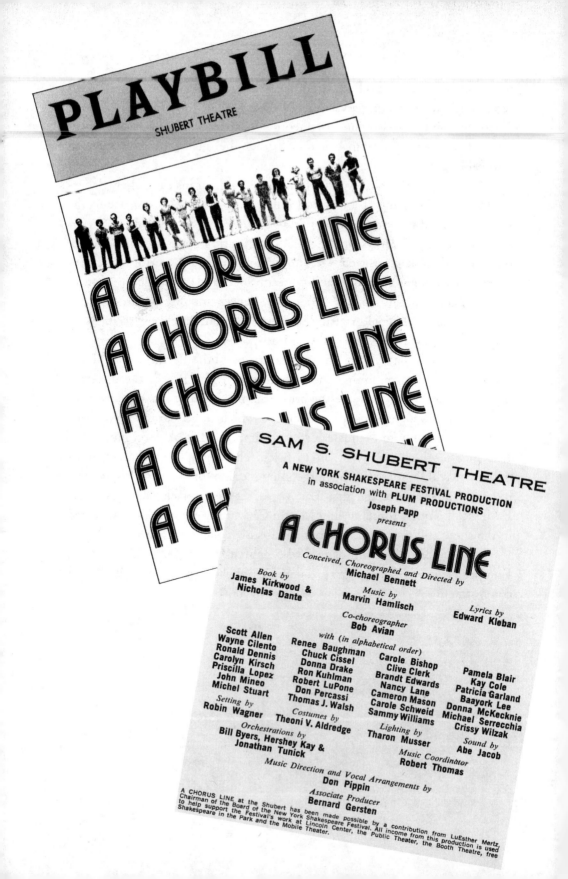

PLAYBILL

SHUBERT THEATRE

A CHORUS LINE
A CHORUS LINE
A CHORUS LINE
A CHORUS LINE
A CHORUS LINE
A CH
A CH

SAM S. SHUBERT THEATRE

A NEW YORK SHAKESPEARE FESTIVAL PRODUCTION
in association with **PLUM PRODUCTIONS**
Joseph Papp
presents

A CHORUS LINE

Conceived, Choreographed and Directed by
Michael Bennett

Book by
James Kirkwood & Nicholas Dante

Music by
Marvin Hamlisch

Lyrics by
Edward Kleban

Co-choreographer
Bob Avian

with (in alphabetical order)

Scott Allen
Wayne Cilento
Ronald Dennis
Carolyn Kirsch
Priscilla Lopez
John Mineo
Michel Stuart
Renee Baughman
Chuck Cissel
Donna Drake
Ron Kuhlman
Robert LuPone
Don Percassi
Thomas J. Walsh
Carole Bishop
Clive Clerk
Brandt Edwards
Nancy Lane
Cameron Mason
Carole Schweid
Sammy Williams
Pamela Blair
Kay Cole
Patricia Garland
Baayork Lee
Donna McKecknie
Michael Serrecchia
Crissy Wilzak

Setting by
Robin Wagner

Costumes by
Theoni V. Aldredge

Lighting by
Tharon Musser

Sound by
Abe Jacob

Orchestrations by
Bill Byers, Hershey Kay & Jonathan Tunick

Music Coordinator
Robert Thomas

Music Direction and Vocal Arrangements by
Don Pippin

Associate Producer
Bernard Gersten

A CHORUS LINE at the Shubert has been made possible by a contribution from LuEsther Mertz, Chairman of the Board of the New York Shakespeare Festival. All income from this production is used to help support the Festival's work at Lincoln Center, the Public Theater, the Booth Theatre, free Shakespeare in the Park and the Mobile Theater.

Fifteen

MICHAEL BENNETT AND *A CHORUS LINE*

Dance remains the essence of the Broadway musical.

—*NEWSWEEK*, 1971

Michael Bennett was nothing if not ambitious. He began staging musical spectacles in high school. Using a short career as a Broadway chorus boy as a stepping stone (*Here's Love, Bajour*), he moved quickly into choreography. He choreographed a number of summer-stock musicals that caught the attention of Broadway producers, managers, and agents. At the age of twenty-three, Bennett choreographed the original Broadway musical *A Joyful Noise* (1966). Although it was a quick failure, he had created several show-stopping dances and earned a Tony nomination for his choreography.

Bennett staged *Henry Sweet Henry* (1967) and three Milliken Industrial shows when they were as lavish and complex as any Broadway musical, and he operated as an unbilled doctor on several musicals, including *How Now Dow Jones* (1967). His first hit was *Promises, Promises* in 1968.

It was well deserved. *Promises* had a funny book by Neil Simon based on *The Apartment* by Billy Wilder and I. A. L. Diamond; a strong score by Burt Bacharach and Hal David at the top of their pop form; taut, sensible direction by Robert Moore; a handsome, fluid set by Robin Wagner; terrific orchestrations by Jonathan Tunick, including the first pit singers to augment onstage voices; charming performances by Jerry Orbach and a host of male character actors; a Tony-winning one-scene knockout by Marian Mercer; and the support of Broadway's best producer, David Merrick. It opened at the jewel of Broadway theatres, the Shubert.

But if there was one really remarkable contribution, it was the musical staging of Michael Bennett. Remember the character chorus of *Pal Joey?* Bennett, as much as possible, pursued that theme. His arduous auditions called for singing, dancing, acting, and improvisation. He assembled a unique group of dancers that promised to portray believable, realistic businessmen and secretaries of the Sixth Avenue, glass-office building milieu. (Since it was 1968, there were no business*women* or male secretaries, any more than there were in the previous business musical, *How to Succeed in Business Without Really Trying.*)

Bennett didn't fully succeed. Chorus boys and girls tend to look like chorus boys and girls no matter what you do. Dancers are slim and, because it's a short-lived career, young. Singers are stiff and, because the staff was trying to add character types to the group, older. The boys and girls are good-looking, because producers believe that's what audiences want to see.

However, Bennett did create several extraordinary numbers that should have made musical theatre cognoscenti sit up and take notice: "Grapes of Roth," "She Likes Basketball," and "A Fact Can Be a Beautiful Thing."

For "She Likes Basketball," a chorus number had been planned. Basketball clothes had been ordered for the boys and cheerleader clothes for the girls. But Bennett's unerring instinct to avoid cliché dances designed solely for entertainment prevailed. Against the objections of his older collaborators, he staged the number for Jerry Orbach alone, using a rolled-up raincoat for a ball. It worked.

For "A Fact Can Be a Beautiful Thing" Bennett created a Christmas celebration among the bar patrons, featuring Orbach and Mercer, that was as much acting as dancing. He used bar props and nontechnical steps to create a dance that grew naturally out of the celebration.

But "Grapes of Roth" really told the story. Bennett opened a bar scene—unlisted in the script—with an intricate weave of patrons jammed like sardines into a space defined by light, smoking, passing drinks, and trolling for each other. It was tightly choreographed and set to music, a cartoon of a Third Avenue singles bar at happy hour.

Additionally, following on the fluidity that Oscar Hammerstein had written out and Jerome Robbins had physicalized, Bennett smoothed all the scene transitions and set changes over by creating a motif of dancing secretaries that bridged the gaps. Thus, he avoided the blackout-music-in-the-dark, thundering-scenery, lights-up approach of previous musicals, while at the same time translating the frantic energy of big business corridors into dance.

The whole show flowed like a river, an engineering of the structure of the musical that complimented the score precisely, and *Promises* was breaking ground there as well. The score, driven by unusual syncopations in odd meters, was written in the pop style of the music industry's latest hit songwriting team (Burt Bacharach and Hal David), marking the first time pop music had been used for a legitimate book musical on Broadway.

Bennett avoided classic show-stopping dance numbers until the show was in out-of-town tryouts. It was only then that he succumbed to the obvious need for something to beef up the first-act curtain, and hurriedly staged "Turkey Lurkey Time," an office party dance featuring Donna McKechnie, Baayork Lee, and Margo Sappington. (The first two dancers would return to Bennett musicals again and again.) Proving that he could stop the show if he wanted to, he learned an important lesson—the integration of dance into drama has to be compatible with, *but not at the expense of,* the entertaining sequences that audiences expect from a Broadway musical.

Bennett's next assignment was *Coco,* a dream of a production. Katherine Hepburn would play Coco Chanel in a new musical by Alan Jay Lerner, with music by André Previn. Bennett had the resources of designer Cecil Beaton and a large chorus of dancers and showgirls at his command.

But Murphy's law was operating in overdrive. Previn was a conductor and film scorer, comfortable with classical music and jazz. His composing simply wasn't up to creating an exciting Broadway score. Lerner, freed from the junior partner status he suffered under the tyrannical Frederick Loewe and without the theatrewise Moss Hart as a collaborator, was indulgent and unable to bring focus to the tepid story of an haute couture designer's comeback in late age. The concept—Coco would talk to actors on film to dramatize her past—was clumsy and untheatrical, invented in the mistaken belief that Hepburn was too old to play the youthful material.

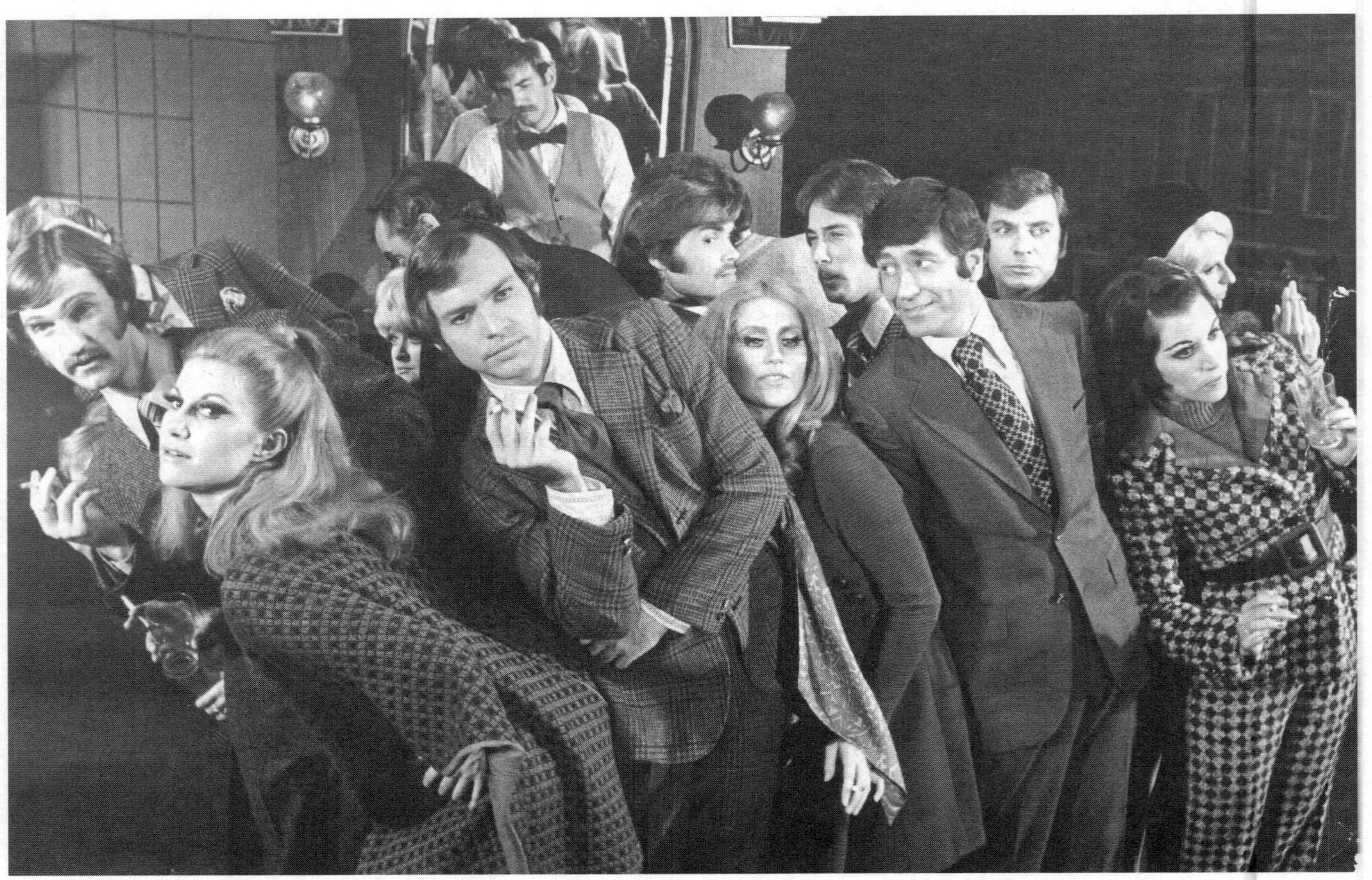

Happy hour in a Manhattan singles bar as choreographed by Michael Bennett for *Promises, Promises*
Photofest/Friedman-Abeles

Worst of all, this big, complicated musical had an inept, musically inexperienced director that Hepburn refused to fire because of ancient loyalties. And Hepburn herself, riveting on stage, lacked the singing and movement skills a musical lead requires.* The weight of the impending disaster fell on the young shoulders of Michael Bennett. Gradually Hepburn began to rely on him, and he attempted to pull the show together. Although nearly all his suggestions were implemented, he just didn't have the time or power to muscle *Coco* into shape.

He did contribute stunning "fashion" sequences that used a revolving stage, mirrors, blinding fast costume changes, and dozens of beautiful girls to dazzling effect. If the final product was a bit stodgy and ineffectual, it worked as an entertaining evening, with Hepburn's star shining bright and Bennett's wonderful staging. What Bennett learned was that a musical had to have a single iron hand behind it. His.

Before Bennett began directing, however, he accepted one more choreography job in 1970—*Company,* the new musical by Hal Prince and Stephen Sondheim. One example from Bennett's *Company* choreography will serve to show how successfully he incorporated story into his work. During "Side by Side by Side" there is a brief tap interlude. With the cast lined up by couples across the stage, with Bobby the Bachelor in the middle, one husband performs a simple four-count tap step—almost a mating call—and his wife answers with four additional tap beats. The next couple in line repeats the mating-call-and-answer routine, and so on down the line until it's Bobby's turn. But when Bobby executes the tap break, there is no partner to finish it. An ominous silence hangs heavily for the unfilled riff, and the others rush ahead to complete the number. After a second's wondering glance at the space around him, he catches up with his married friends. That brief tap routine is easy enough for the most unrhythmical actors to master—its place in tap vocabulary lies somewhere near the first lesson at your neighborhood sing-out-Louise dance academy. Yet in that one simple step lies the entire meaning of the show, a metaphor for the musical's dramatic intent. There is no better function of choreography in the theatre.

* When the cast complained that it was freezing in the theatre—her favorite temperature—she bought them all sweaters rather than allowing the heat to be turned on. When construction of a new office building next door broke the silence of a dramatic scene, she arranged for tea to be served to the construction workers at precisely that time every Wednesday matinée. A star is a star is a star.

Because of the fluidity of its set, staging, and song style, *Company* marked the first of Michael Bennett's "cinematic" musicals, a kind of staging developed by Jerome Robbins and then Harold Prince (who had observed Robbins develop the idea in *West Side Story* and *Fiddler,* which he produced). Cinematic staging furthered Hammerstein's concept of "continuous action" and owed much to modern film editing techniques, and marked the apex of the well-staged musical.

Bennett continued working with Prince and Sondheim. He codirected *Follies* (1971) with Prince, delivering some of the most brilliantly dramatic staging ever seen for his first "hot" musical. Bennett was more efficient than any choreographer before him at musical staging that dazzled, sparkled, and entertained, with the possible exception of Gower Champion in the period when he choreographed *Bye, Bye Birdie, Carnival,* and *Hello, Dolly!* Bennett used his talent in the service of the drama wherever possible, elevating the standard number to high art.

He needed all his talents to save *Seesaw* (1973). This big musical version of the two-character play *Two for the Seesaw* was sinking in Detroit under the guidance of a straight play director in way over his head and an experienced but uninspired choreographer. Bennett's reputation had reached its zenith in the Broadway community by then, and reputation is power. He was asked to take over as director when tryout performances were already underway, and he replaced half the chorus, the leading lady, some of the sets, and most of the staging. Probably no musical had undergone so many changes so quickly since the frantic 1920s. In a Herculean effort that drew on the choreographic talents of Tommy Tune and longtime assistants Bob Avian and Baayork Lee, Bennett turned a flop into a hit—not a big hit, and not a good one (it was little more than an old-fashioned musical with pseudocontemporary music by Cy Coleman), but a slick and amusing one.

With *Seesaw,* Bennett had turned a sow's ear into a silk purse, which only served to make him restless. Two young dancers, Tony Stevens and Michon Peacock, came to him with the idea for a meeting of dancers who would talk about their lives, and Bennett smelled subject matter that could return him to a "hot" milieu. One that he grew up in. One that would provide both drama and dance in equal parts.

• • •

At midnight on January 18, 1974, nineteen musical comedy dancers met in a rehearsal studio with director-choreographer Michael Bennett. They took a dance class, then sat and talked frankly and openly about their childhoods until noon the next day. It was a transforming emotional experience they would never forget. Three weeks later the discussions continued, this time covering their migration to New York and their dance careers. Thereafter, Bennett conducted individual interviews with other Broadway dancers, all of which were recorded. Bennett accumulated nearly thirty hours of taped conversations, and he found that the backgrounds of the dancers were dramatic and surprisingly consistent.

Bennett then directed a workshop at the New York Shakespeare Festival, a kind of exploratory rehearsal during which a musical might be created. He enlisted Nicholas Dante, a dancer who wanted to write and whose story that January night had been one of the most dramatic, to write the book. He hired Edward Kleban, a record producer who had written music and lyrics for several unproduced Broadway musicals, to write the lyrics, and Marvin Hamlisch, a one-time Broadway rehearsal pianist and dance arranger who had since won several Oscars for his film scores, to do the music. Bennett gathered a cast of dancers, many of whom had participated in the talk sessions.

The tapes were transcribed, and Dante turned the material into long monologues while Kleban and Hamlisch began to turn the larger ideas into songs. Simultaneously, Bennett and his assistant Bob Avian conducted rehearsals, during which the material was staged, altered, examined, and used to evolve additional ideas through a good deal of improvisational theatre work.

A hiatus followed. Bennett added James Kirkwood, a more experienced playwright and novelist, to the staff, and there was further consolidation of the material. With some cast changes, a second workshop was conducted under the same conditions, followed directly by a third six-week period officially labeled "rehearsals."

Finally, after sixteen months of work, Robin Wagner, Theoni Aldredge, and Tharon Musser were brought in to design the set, costumes, and lights. Public previews were given at the New York Shakespeare Festival's Newman Theatre, in the former Astor Library. Changes continued daily, even as nightly performances were hugely successful with audiences. Critics were invited, and on May 21, 1975 the musical opened off-Broadway to stunned audiences and rave reviews. It was the hottest ticket in town all summer.

On October 19, 1975, *A Chorus Line* opened on Broadway at the Shubert Theatre. Unlike any other opening-night performance before or since, this one had no effect on the show's future because *A Chorus Line* was already on its way to becoming the most successful musical in the history of the American theatre. Never had a show developed so organically from concept to performance. Never had so much experiment gone into the final product.*

A Chorus Line isn't just a great Broadway musical. It's a Broadway musical *about* Broadway musicals. It takes place at an audition, where a director-choreographer—intimidating, manipulating, driven, not unlike the great Broadway director-choreographers—is seeking four boys and four girls to be in the chorus of his next show. They have to dance, sing, and act. They have to expose their innermost secrets, as the director tries to find out who they really are. In doing so, the dancers tell the audience the unique life story of a dancer. The universal emotions encompassed by their yearning touched the hearts of audiences around the world.

The show's breathtaking emotionalism was based on the true lives of the dancers who inspired the story. There is a sincerity to the dialogue in *A Chorus Line* unequalled by any libretto before or since. *The New Yorker* labeled it *theatre vérité.* Its dramatic foundation is supported with more realism than any musical to date. It takes place "here and now" and is replete with the honesty expressed in that January meeting—a variation on group therapy or the old parlor game, "Truth." This sincerity is delivered directly to the audience, enabled by two devices.

First, *A Chorus Line* is a "hot" show as opposed to a "cold" one, a distinction Bennett uses to characterize presentational versus representational musicals. In the former, some aspect of the character's occupation allows singing and dancing. Thus, in musicals from *42nd Street* to *Funny Girl,* musical numbers are easy to motivate and can be performed directly to the audience. "Cold" (representational) musicals require the audience to accept ordinary people breaking into song and dance. Motivating a musical

* For a more complete history of this remarkable creative process, see *What They Did For Love* (New York: Bantam Books, 1989), a book which I bring to your attention because I wrote it.

sequence is more difficult in this case, and the smooth integration of music, song, and dance is more complicated. Although coming up with new angles for the old backstage story formula is not easy, Bennett returned again and again to "hot" plots (*Follies, Ballroom, Dreamgirls*) that allowed his musicals to dance.

Second, the "director" character spends most of the audition in the back of the theatre, heard by the audience as a disembodied voice. The dancers face this character and face the house also, delivering dialogue, songs, and dances directly to the audience.

The source of the show's slick virtuosity was Michael Bennett, a director-choreographer who had spent his life pursuing the total integration of techniques that make up the modern American musical. He alone was indispensable to the project, and no one else indelibly stamped his own creative personality on the show. Possibly no other director working, or indeed in the whole history of musical theatre directors, could have fashioned such a show. *A Chorus Line* was the culmination of Bennett's personal experience and of his lifelong desire to meld dance and theatre, as Jerome Robbins had done before him. Bennett had dropped out of high school to dance for Robbins in the international company of *West Side Story,* and he had keenly observed and understood the master's work.

Bennett drew on several advantages going in. Every actor would sing and dance, since all of the characters were Broadway gypsies. Using his voluminous files of musical veterans, Bennett assembled a cast of triple-threat performers. Those who had less acting experience could be brought up to standard by psychological manipulation, a controversial technique Bennett learned from Robbins in which the performer's facade and technique, are stripped away, and he is forced by the director to plunge directly into the emotional abyss of his character, especially where it intersects with the actor's own. This approach creates not the impression of reality, but reality itself, and dancers, used to both physical and emotional abuse, could easily be guided this way.

The stories were inner monologues in the Shakespearean soliloquy mode. Combined with the proposed framework—a Broadway audition for dancers—this emotional material could be acted, sung, and danced all at once. Bennett had in mind Jerome Robbins's setting of his ballet "Afternoon of a Faun" in a bare rehearsal studio. Bennett wanted total integration on a bare stage, a seamless show continuously propelled by musical techniques that could not be thwarted by the exigencies of sets, actors who didn't sing or dance, endings, or beginnings. He even had the Aristotelian entities of time and place on his side—very few musicals take place entirely in one place at one time.

Bennett was unafraid to attempt a musical on a bare stage—rare among directors. Only Peter Brook before him had such a vision of theatre as content first and foremost, having written that "[a]nything that diverts our attention from the emotional action is a mask, a counterfeit." Bennett's interest in this idea had nothing to do with his ability to create show-stopping dances—he knew he could visualize the dramatic content with staging, a technique which by then had become the dogma of Broadway's best choreographer-directors.

The theatre community, however, was reluctant to support this concept. In 1969, when Bennett had created the brilliantly integrated staging for *Promises,* the Tony award voters—supposedly knowledgeable members of the theatre community but in reality tradition-bound conservatives who had no idea what Jerome Robbins had wrought and preferred "bring on the girls" comedies—gave the choreography award to Joe Layton for the circusy *George M!,* which featured tap dancing and juggling in a vaudeville format.

In 1970 Bennett's incandescent staging of *Coco,* featuring the "all red" and "basic black" fashion sequences and a revolving turntable (not to mention the frustrating task of getting Hepburn to behave musically), lost the choreography award to Ron Field for *Applause,* which contained several slick, jazzy chorus boy-and-girl numbers. (Like Bennett, Field grappled with an unmusical lead in Lauren Bacall).

In 1971 Bennett lost a third time to Donald Saddler's ancient if enthusiastically performed tap dances for the revival of *No, No, Nanette.* That season Bennett had contributed the phenomenally well-integrated and brilliantly staged *Company.*

This encrusted conservatism on the part of even the Tony award voters (board members of various theatrical unions and guilds) goes back decades. If *The Music Man*'s bucolic style edged out the riveting *West Side Story* for best musical in 1958, an even more absurd event occurred following the 1959–60 season. *Gypsy* was blanked by more traditional musicals (*The Sound of Music* and *Fiorello!* tied for best musical), performers (Mary Martin in *The Sound of Music* over Ethel Merman, no recognition for Sandra Church as Gypsy and Jack Klugman as Herbie), and directors (George Abbott over

Jerome Robbins). *Gypsy*'s book—one of the best ever written for the musical theatre, by Arthur Laurents—was not nominated. Neither was its choreography, which featured the hysterical "You Gotta Have a Gimmick," the boys-growing-up montage, and the period vaudeville pastiches (including that centuries-old favorite, the dancing cow), all mixed in with fluid scene-to-scene staging and utter theatricality and realism in the simpler songs. Broadway's greatest musical director, Milton Rosenstock, whose brilliant work drove many pit musicians to loathe him, lost to *Sound of Music*'s Frederick Dvonch. Jo Mielziner's fluid and theatrical *Gypsy* sets lost to the old-fashioned work of Oliver Smith (*The Sound of Music*). The elegant but traditional and authentic 1880s costumes by Cecil Beaton for the flop *Saratoga* won over *Gypsy*'s perfect, humorous, exceedingly theatrical costumes by Raoul Pène du Bois. Incredibly, Jule Styne's all-hit score, certainly one of the five best ever written for a Broadway musical, wasn't even nominated.

While the other musicals that (last, great) season all deserve kudos—*Once Upon a Mattress, Fiorello!, The Sound of Music,* and even the rarely revived *Take Me Along* for its wonderful score—only *Gypsy* among them claims a place in the top pantheon of American musicals. Clearly, even within the theatre community itself, the many traditions of the pre-*Oklahoma!* theatre were still favored over the art and integration of the modern musical.

To their credit, neither Robbins nor Bennett ever succumbed to the temptation to stage a musical in the old-fashioned style just to win uneducated admiration. With devoted artistry, both pursued the fullest integration of direction and choreography, driven by content, to their last show.

• • •

Bennett continued to use the workshop process with several other musicals, two of which made it to Broadway. *Ballroom* (1978) was buoyed with several slick dance sequences in a variety of ballroom styles and weighted with a subtle antagonism on the critics' part toward Michael Bennett, on the heels of his gargantuan and over-publicized *Chorus Line* success. Unfortunately its setting, the Roseland Ballroom, led Bennett into dance sequences that failed to advance the plot or define the characters (as with *Coco*'s fashion sequences earlier in his career). A choreographer can usually get away with one plot-stopping, show-stopping number, but a series of them becomes dangerously antidramatic.

Dreamgirls (1981) returned Bennett to success, and his integrated staging reached epic proportions. The show moved continually (coincidentally, "move" is the first lyric). Its lighting towers crawled around the stage like androids, and its chorus was a continuous flux of characters.

Scandals became one of the most notorious still-born musicals in history when its subject matter, sex, was outdated overnight as AIDS suddenly swamped the sexual scene. Yet those who saw this workshop production praised it highly and were awed by Bennett's most erotic choreography and his attempt to push the subject matter into new (some would say tasteless) directions.

• • •

A Chorus Line closed on Saturday, April 28, 1990, fifteen years after opening on Broadway, after 6,137 performances, more than any other show in Broadway history. The show grossed $280,583,900 with a net income to the nonprofit Shakespeare Festival of $38,750,000 and an initial investment of less than $1 million; it had been seen by 6,642,400 theatregoers, a figure which undoubtedly includes duplicate visits by some and dozens of visits by mavens. *A Chorus Line* was subsequently staged in every major and minor theatre center in the civilized world from Las Vegas to Vienna. Since then almost every stock and community theatre, and every high school and college with a drama department, has attempted to perform it. Only the film version was a failure, a testament to (among other things) the show's quintessential theatricality. It was the first Broadway megahit since *Oklahoma!*. It reached an international audience, generated buckets of money, and affected young people who ordinarily didn't attend theatre.

But its huge commercial success, which has since been overshadowed by megamerchandized musicals playing larger theatres for higher ticket prices, pales in comparison to its artistic legacy, an endowment to the American musical theatre that will never be overtaken. Because of the ephemeral nature of theatre, the pristine clarity, overwhelming power, and the very *rightness* of the original cast in the original production will never be duplicated. Yet perhaps one of the show's greatest strengths is its ability to touch audiences through even the roughest productions.

A Chorus Line's legacy will ultimately depend on the use of its lessons by future generations in musical theatre. It is appropriate, therefore, to examine in detail what this extraordinary show has left us.

THE WORKSHOP

Michael Bennett invented the workshop process for the original production of *A Chorus Line.* He spent months with his cast and authors shaping the material, rehearsing it, rewriting it, and rehearsing again prior to public performances. This proved to be an artistically invaluable process.

The cost of a six-week workshop of *A Chorus Line* today would be less than $200,000 under the current Actor's Equity Association workshop code. Double or even quadruple that, and you still have less than five percent of the budget of a new Broadway musical. Sadly, today's workshop is not a creative process but a producer's event, a glorified backers' audition, often including moderate sets and costumes to hide dramatic deficiencies. Producers anxious to raise capital and get their show on the boards often overlook the enormous benefit of low-risk, pressure-free, artistic exploration.

ORIGINALITY

The vast majority of musicals are based on material from another medium. So was *A Chorus Line,* but the medium was real life. If American musical theatre is to continue its pursuit of serious themes that began with *Porgy and Bess* and *Show Boat,* if it is to be more than sets, costumes, jokes, chorus girls, hummable melodies, and happy endings, then serious playwrights have to be encouraged to shape librettos. Interestingly, *all* of Gilbert and Sullivan's ground-breaking works were original texts, not adaptations.

STAGING

Bennett's greatest contributions to the musical are the extraordinary cinematic fluidity of his staging; the fully integrated performer's technique of acting, singing, and dancing *all at the same time;* and the spectacle shaped with human beings rather than expensive sets. When Jerome Robbins staged *West Side Story* with dancers in the principal roles, he created a fluidity from scene to song to dance that is still the textbook structure of a great musical.

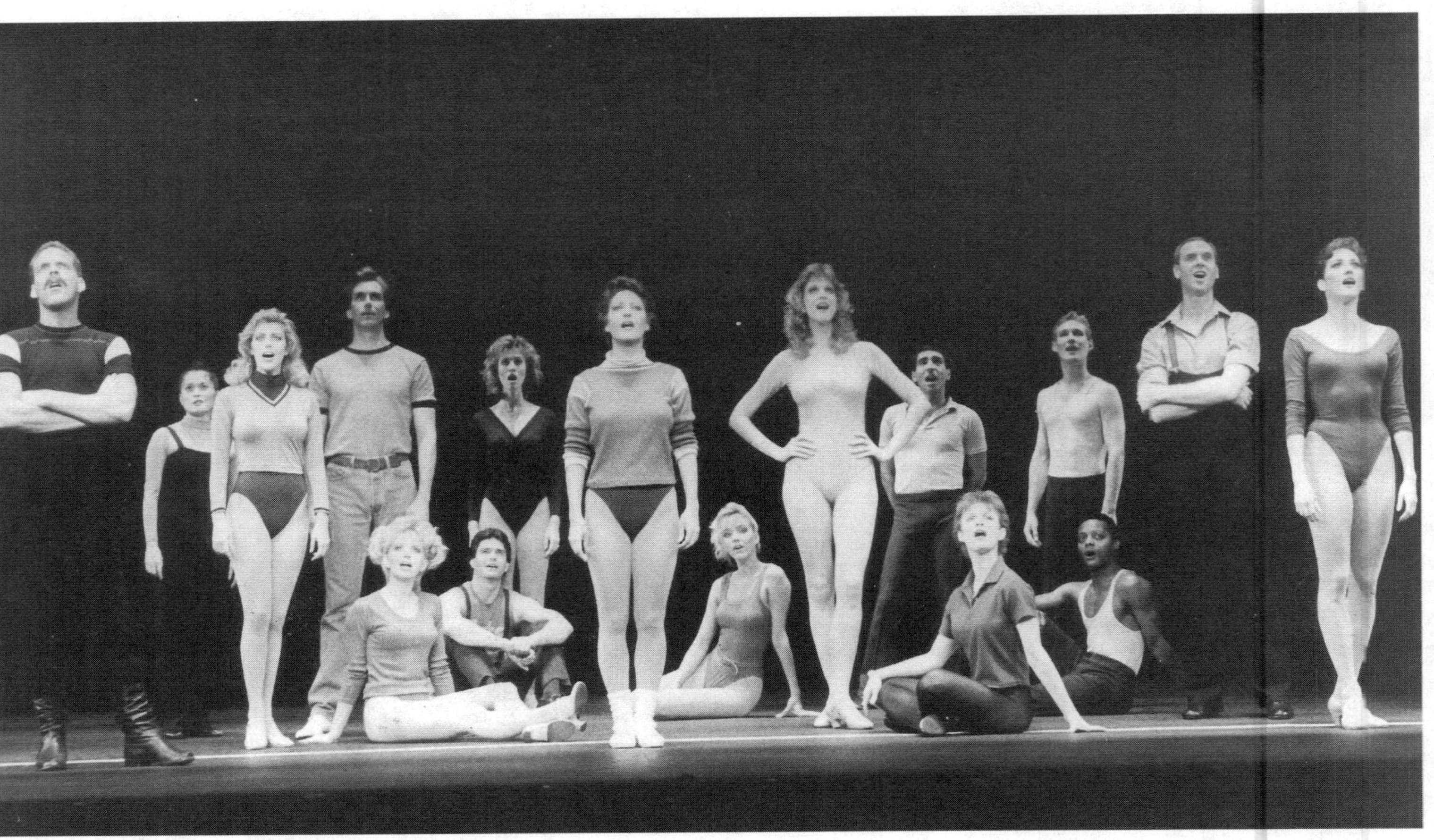

". . . and point me toward tomorrow . . ."

Photofest

By using *only* dancers for *A Chorus Line,* Bennett was able to go one step further. This was probably the ultimate step in the process of integration that is the hallmark of the craft of the American musical. Each idea is not acted *or* sung *or* danced, but acted *and* sung *and* danced. Although pure dance is featured in two numbers—in the opening and in Cassie's "The Music and the Mirror,"—every other moment of the show is specifically choreographed. (In a related idea, Marvin Hamlisch used underscoring far more extensively than any musical yet had, a technique that added dimension to the scenes as it had for decades in film.)

The "line," that amazing look that became the show's universal logo, is only one example of *A Chorus Line*'s kaleidoscopic array of content as spectacle, and how it is always superior to sets as spectacle. Musical as opera, operetta, or spectacle notwithstanding, the American musical's true greatness lies in the galvanic sweep, pulsing rhythm, and dancing visions that are only present when a score is written for more than singing, when it's written for action and dramatic content. Choreographers need to be more fully integrated into the writing and the early creative process.

ACTING

For a century musical comedy acting had been distinguished from dramatic acting by virtue of its broader strokes. But that style of acting had held the musical back from being treated seriously. Whether comedic or dramatic, all musicals benefit from a serious approach. The *Chorus Line* performances, those starkly real confessions told without cliché gestures, have helped to bury the old style, but not deeply enough.

SUCCESS

Most of the original cast and creators of *A Chorus Line* suffered in its aftermath. Bennett lived a chaotic and drug-hazed personal life and blamed success for his imbalance. Personal histories aside, the expanding American urge for a damn-the-ethics, headlong, conscience-free pursuit of material wealth is killing us and our art. Ironically, that is exactly how Bennett once described one of the themes of the show—his optimistic dancers are seeking happiness through the *process* of their lives, not the *result.*

The most famous chorus line of the modern musical
Photofest

Putting it together—the Las Vegas company in the glittering finale (with the author fifth from stage left)
Barbara Flinn

MANAGEMENT

Subsequent companies of *A Chorus Line* controlled by Bennett (there were two, running almost ten years each) and the show's performers (nearly 400 dancers played nineteen roles on Broadway and on tour during fifteen years) were all directly supervised by Bennett. He appeared again and again backstage, rehearsed casts prior to openings across the country, and hired and fired for every role. Programs for subsequent companies and national tours of Broadway plays and musicals invariably credit the original director, but in truth, until *A Chorus Line* the original directors and choreographers of hits seldom if ever returned to the theatre. Their work was left to be duplicated by stage managers while they went on to newer, more glamorous assignments. Gower Champion never returned to *Hello, Dolly!* nor Jerome Robbins to *Fiddler on the Roof,* though their shows each ran for a decade.

Additionally, the production values of *A Chorus Line* were maintained enthusiastically, with new clothes, new mirrors, and an unending supply of new shoes as needed. The tradition has been to skimp and save, putting more profits into the pockets of investors and producers and, once a show's reputation is established, favoring cost-saving over quality control.

MONEY

The extraordinary profits that accrued from the show did not go to the customary investors. They went to the New York Shakespeare Festival, a not-for-profit theatre that had sponsored the show from its inception. In the ensuing, highly profitable years, this gave producer Joseph Papp a handsome advantage in the ancient and never-enjoyable pursuit of raising money for art. Because today's musical is in dire straits commercially, more nonprofit theatres should attempt to mount musicals. But many theatre companies express a kind of reverse snobbism when confronted with commercial success: if it pleases too many people, it's not for them. This is utter nonsense, and there is no better example than *A Chorus Line,* whose artistic reputation shines extremely favorably on Papp's theatre. There is no more noble ambition than pursuing the art of the American musical, as it is the only performing art that has an American heritage. And there is no better way to support a not-for-profit theatre than with profits from a successful production.

• • •

If *A Chorus Line* leaves behind only these ideas, its legacy will be rich and valued. But it has left us with more than that. The dazzling images of that unique musical, and the wave of emotion we felt on first seeing it, must surely be etched in the hearts and minds of appreciative audiences for all time. The American musical began with *The Black Crook,* the drama that was saved with the insertion of dancers. By the time *A Chorus Line* was created around the dancers themselves, the Great White Way was paved with gold.

Part Three

THE GOLDEN AGE

PLAYBILL

BROADHURST THEATRE

Sixteen

Directors and Choreographers

I'm just a Broadway Baby . . .

Between *Show Boat* and *Oklahoma!* 308 musical productions opened on Broadway, an average of twenty per season. Many were descendants of the musical comedies of the 1920s. Many others, however, were descendants of the Princess musicals and *Show Boat.*

Between *Oklahoma!* and *A Chorus Line* the art of the American musical theatre was buffed to a razzle-dazzle. In those thirty-two seasons 449 musical productions opened on the Great White Way, an average of fourteen per season. The mainstream musical, in all its high-powered, newly integrated glory, roared from Broadway across America and even to London's West End, where American musicals could open with all-American casts.

Influences on this new art form—along with jazz, the only original native American contribution to the arts—came from a variety of sources.

But more than any other technique, *staging* expressed the rhythm and drive of the American musical.

• • •

Though known for his lyrics, W. S. Gilbert directed his comic operas, the results benefiting from his perfectionism and biting wit. No star was above being lashed with it. He used it to keep the company in line and allowed no extra "business," previously a hallmark of comedians. He gave the company specific gestures and exact blocking. He insisted autocratically on details of the onstage performance *and* the offstage demeanor of his casts. He was thus extremely instrumental in elevating the reputation of actresses from the level of prostitutes, with whom they were still synonymous in the mid-nineteenth century.

If Gilbert's plotting was often as absurd as that of earlier operettas, comic and romantic, his productions were models of great theatre, for Gilbert was the first modern stage director of the British musical theatre. More than half of Gilbert and Sullivan's success was due to the original productions, in which Gilbert made many demands—he insisted on realism, enunciation, and that actors stick to the script.

Gilbert was painstakingly prepared. He wrote, rewrote, and even staged his work well in advance, then taught it to his casts from a prompt book. (Sullivan, on the other hand, liked to write under the pressure of a deadline, relying as much on inspiration as groundwork. Some of his songs were delivered after rehearsals had gotten underway, and more than once the cast and his collaborator wondered if they would have them in time to sing on opening night.)

Gilbert's call for realistic scenery greatly influenced the English stage. For *H.M.S. Pinafore,* Gilbert visited Admiral Horatio Nelson's British sailing ship, the *Victory,* docked at Portsmouth harbor, sketched it, and put a wealth of detail on the stage. He had a naval supplier make the costumes. The costumes for *The Mikado* were genuine Japanese fabric. For *Ruddigore* he copied the British uniforms of 1812 exactly.

Gilbert carefully blocked all action in advance on a model, and insisted that the actors be precise and unwavering in their words and business. Above all, he demanded that they take their roles and actions seriously, making his satirical librettos all the funnier. (This solidified, if not invented, one of the comic actor's strongest maxims—if you laugh, the audience won't.) This theatre, then, was outstanding by any standards: the play was the thing, and performances supported it. There was little allowance for adjustments, and actors who inserted unauthorized business in their performances were fined. Nevertheless, Gilbert is said to have sanctioned a good many physical gags and topical interpolations in *The Mikado,* provided he saw and approved them first. He also allowed repetitions and encores during the play, a common practice at the time.

Gilbert wanted actors who could sing, not singers who could act, again emphasizing theatrical principals over musical ones. He demanded crisp enunciation, which was a boon to lyricists. He created the first production numbers in a musical comedy sense—the hornpipe in *Ruddigore* and the cachucha in *The Gondoliers,* followed by the minstrel scene and the drawing-room court procession in *Utopia.*

Gilbert and his producer established the first use of electricity in a London theatre auditorium when *Patience* moved to the Savoy in 1881. A year later it was used on the stage to illuminate the production of *Iolanthe.*

Arthur Seymour Sullivan, too, would rehearse the singers thoroughly (then return home from a day at the theatre and compose until dawn). Together they created the most exacting, entertaining, well-staged productions the musical theatre had yet witnessed.

• • •

The first well-directed theatrical productions in America were importations of authentic Gilbert and Sullivan (not to be confused with pirated American versions.) Before long, however, a host of American directors and choreographers outstripped their English counterparts.

The short, dapper, Julian Mitchell apprenticed with Charles Hoyt, playwright, actor, producer, and director, with whom he codirected *A Trip to Chinatown* in 1891, which held the record for the longest running musical for twenty-eight years. Mitchell went on to choreograph *The Pink Lady, Sunny,* and Florenz Ziegfeld's first *Follies.* Later he directed and choreographed the 1915 *Follies,* and he produced, directed, and choreographed *The Wizard of Oz, The Fortune Teller,* and Victor Herbert's *Babes in Toyland.* His must have been a career built on an outstanding visual sense (the musical theatre of his period was exceptionally visual), for in spite of the fact that he was nearly deaf and couldn't adequately hear the music in his shows, he was the first great, reigning director-choreographer of the musical theatre.

Ned Wayburn claims to have staged *six hundred productions* in New York and London, working for Marc Klaw and Abe Erlanger, the Shuberts, Ziegfeld (six editions of the *Follies,* and *Smiles* with Marilyn Miller and Fred and Adele Astaire), and Rodgers and Hart on *Poor Little Ritz Girl.* The tall, fat, multichinned, bespectacled man who usually wore a beret invented the famous Ziegfeld walk for showgirls who had to navigate steep and narrow steps in heels, hats, and awkward (if brief) costumes, and he was responsible for speeding up the ponderous productions.

• • •

In the beginning there was Busby Berkeley, who had no dance training at all—only imagination and ambition that led him to become one of the top dance directors of the musicals of the 1920s. He was born in a trunk in 1895; his father was the director of a touring repertory company, and his mother was an actress. When Berkeley's father died of influenza and his older brother of a heroin addiction, he learned the trade, touring with his mother from the age of eight to twelve. He was then sent to a military boarding school.

With the onset of World War I he enlisted in the army. He never saw action, but as an entertainment officer he turned a barn in France into a theatre and staged dramas, comedies, and musicals with soldiers. He continued mounting shows aboard ship even as he was sailing home.

When he returned home, he had no idea what he would do with his life. One day he was walking along Broadway with his mother, and they ran into a producer who thought he looked the part and gave him an actor's role in a tour. This led to a job as a sketch actor and assistant stage manager in *Hitchy Koo of 1923,* but the ever-ambitious Berkeley always looked for side jobs. He produced and directed amateur shows, and he directed in stock.

One day in Baltimore, with his own show dying, he learned the secret of show business. Visiting a successful play in town, he saw the villain tear the dress off the heroine, exposing one breast. He knew from then on what the public wanted. He hired eight dancing girls in see-through veils, and had his heroine expose *both* her breasts. His show turned into a hit, and he was swamped with offers to stage musicals up and down the East Coast. His work finally led to an offer to choreograph on Broadway.

He staged the musical numbers for *Holka Polka* (also known as *Spring in Autumn,* 1925), a Czech operetta refitted by Harry Ruby and Bert Kalmer and notable only for a father and daughter team who played the roles of a father and a daughter, and *Sweet Lady,* which closed out of town. But these musicals got him an agent, and his agent got him a respectable assignment with Richard Rodgers and Lorenz Hart. Berkeley staged the dances for *A Connecticut Yankee* in 1927, which ran for 421 performances, and he took his place among the top dance directors on Broadway. In 1928 he worked on five musicals: *Present Arms* with Rodgers and Hart; *The Earl Carroll Vanities* and *Good Boy* by Harry Ruby and Bert Kalmer; *Rainbow,* with a score by Vincent Youmans and Oscar Hammerstein II; and *Hello, Daddy,* with songs by Jimmy McHugh and Dorothy Fields. When he fixed—in one week—the dances for *Pleasure Bound* for J. J. Shubert and *The Wild Rose* for Arthur Hammerstein, he gained a reputation as a doctor for shows in trouble. He then choreographed *and* directed *A Night in Venice* (with The Three Stooges), *The Duchess of Chicago,* a flop, and *Broadway Nights,* a revue with Texas Guinan.

Berkeley, ambitious as ever, established the choreographer who ran the show when J. J. Shubert gave him a musical called *The Street Singer* to produce, direct, and choreograph. Although it failed, Berkeley's dances got raves. His chorus girls were noted for being "tireless, peppy, and pulchritudinous," the latter a compliment in the early days of the Broadway musical. In the hectic days before the 1929 stock market crash Berkeley worked with Sigmund Romberg (*Nina Rose*), Rudolf Friml (*The White Eagle*), Harold Arlen (*9:15 Revue*), Gertrude Lawrence (*International Revue*), and many others.

Hollywood beckoned when Samuel Goldwyn bought the stage musical *Whoopee,* starring Eddie Cantor, produced by Florenz Ziegfeld. Berkeley signed on to stage the dances, and in the spring of 1930, Broadway lost him. Once in Hollywood, he discovered that the film director was expected to photograph the musical sequences after Berkeley had staged them. He had never been behind a camera before, but nevertheless insisted that he shoot his own work. "Dances directed by" became his trademark, and his imaginative use of the camera virtually invented the great movie musical. In Hollywood he directed dances for *The Gold Diggers of 1933* (as well as *1935* and *1937*), *The Gold Diggers in Paris, Footlight Parade, Dames,* and, of course, the all-time backstage movie musical *42nd Street.* In the autumn of a tumultuous life, he directed the charming, no-chorus-girls, film musical *Take Me Out To the Ball Game* with Gene Kelly, Frank Sinatra, and Esther Williams. He returned to Broadway only twice—to direct and choreograph the 1944 Jule Styne-Sammy Cahn out-of-town flop *Glad To See You,* and later to work as a consultant, mostly for publicity purposes, on the 1971 revival of *No, No, Nanette,* starring old friend Ruby Keeler.

Berkeley was the son of a doting character-actress mother who never had a dance lesson in his life. He used women in musicals and films with spectacular success. Photographs of his Broadway productions evidence the virtuosic and spectacular staging that his later movies made famous. He also invented the little girl at the end of the revolving chorus line struggling to keep up, a comic image still popular in ice shows today. If Berkeley's stage images outstripped his limited dance vocabulary, he glorified the dancer (where Ziegfeld had only bothered with the showgirl) and integrated the spectacle with the chorus line.

• • •

Hassard Short was an English-born, one-time actor who directed over forty musicals on Broadway, including *Sunny, Three's a Crowd, The Band Wagon,* the all-black *Hot Mikado, As Thousands Cheer,* the first three Berlin-Harris *Music Box Revues,* Cole Porter's *Jubilee,* and *Between the Devil.* He directed several operetta imports, including *Fredericka* and *The Great Waltz.* With George S. Kaufman he codirected *Face the Music,* and with Oscar Hammerstein the 1946 Rodgers and Hammerstein revival of *Show Boat.* Short was the uncredited director of *Roberta,* and took over the Jerome Kern-Oscar Hammerstein *Very Warm For May* from Vincente Minnelli. He was always known for his innovative staging—for *Carmen Jones* he gave each scene a single-hue color palette. And he never went to Hollywood.

• • •

Early dances were entirely unconnected to the dramatic material. One of the most popular methods for adding dance to a musical was to hire prepackaged dancers and acts. Dance acts graduated from vaudeville to Broadway, where they were inserted not just in revues but in book musicals. In England at the dawn of the century, John Tiller ran a school that turned out lines of eight and sixteen precision girl dancers. Tiller wanted to satisfy his American clientele, and his choreography grew from ballet-based dance to the tap-and-kick line dancing that American shows prized. His numerous troupes were so popular that a "Tiller line" was itself a draw—indeed, a "chorus line" and a "Tiller line" were interchangeable phrases for some time.

Albertina Rasch, choreographer for *Rio Rita, The Band Wagon,* and *Lady in the Dark,* among dozens of other shows, brought a more legitimate ballet background to the theatre. By grafting European ballet onto the more vulgar American dances, she created a sensational style, and the "Albertina Rasch girls" were popular troupes throughout vaudeville and Broadway. Rasch's dances were not integrated into the shows, having descended from *The Black Crook.* When the plot slowed down, the dancers rushed on. Rausch recognized American talent, and—unlike Tiller, who looked for beautiful girls and then trained them—she found beauty in her girls' dancing ability.

Of Bobby Connolly, a press release said, "He treats the girls like sisters and he knows every Broadway show girl by her first, middle, or nick name. He even knows the real names of some." He choreographed *America's Sweetheart,* the *Ziegfeld Follies of 1931, Free for All, East Wind, Hot Cha!,* and *Take a Chance,* and he directed the *Follies of 1934.* Although he choreographed the operettas *Desert Song* and *New Moon,* Connolly was noted for tap dancing, having choreographed the musicals *Flying High, Follow Through, Funny Face,* and *Good News.*

Seymour Felix staged Rodgers and Hart's *Peggy-Ann* and *Simple Simon,* and may have been the first choreographer to worry that the dancer's customary bag of tricks didn't sit comfortably in a particular musical. For *Whoopee* he wanted the dances to look like they belonged, and often he wove them into the sets.

LeRoy Prinz broke up the traditional uniformity by giving different steps to different dancers, especially in the *Earl Carroll Vanities.* David Bennett choreographed André Charlot's *Revue of 1924* and *Rose Marie,* and he worked on *Sunny.* Englishman Edward Royce was the son of a dancer, comic, and director at London's Gaiety Theatre, and had been trained as a designer and a dancer. He choreographed musicals in London for Charles Frohman and Seymour Hicks, and in 1905 he began directing as well. He worked on many George Edwardes shows.

In the 1910s, Royce moved to New York, where he directed and

Fiddler on the Roof. There's no trick to the authentic bottle dance—a dancer has to leave the line if he drops his
Photofest

choreographed *Oh, Boy!; Leave it to Jane; Oh, Lady! Lady!; Going Up; Have a Heart;* and dozens more, making him the principal stager for the Princess musicals. In the 1920s Royce worked on *Sally* and the *Ziegfeld Follies.* A series of flops and health problems drove him to Australia for six years, where he resuscitated his career with a number of successful shows. In 1929 he returned to the States to work on several film assignments, and finally he went back to London to finish up a thirty-year career filled with an astounding number of musicals.

It was Robert Alton who bridged the generations from the twenties musicals to modern choreography. Alton's numerous credits for Broadway and Hollywood include *Hold Your Horses,* his 1933 début; *Life Begins at 8:40,* with a score by Harold Arlen, Ira Gershwin, and Yip Harburg; and the Cole Porter musicals *Anything Goes, You Never Know, Leave It To Me!,* and *DuBarry Was a Lady.* Alton worked with director Vincente Minnelli on *The Show Is On* and *Hooray For What.* He co-choreographed the *Ziegfeld Follies of 1936* with George Balanchine; *Thumbs Up!; Parade; Too Many Girls; Hellzapoppin'* (1940); Rodgers and Hart's *The Boys from Syracuse* and *Pal Joey;* Rodgers and Hammerstein's *Me and Juliet;* the film *There's No Business Like Show Business,* with songs by Irving Berlin; and the film *You Were Never Lovelier.* He was heavy on tap and eschewed the developing theatre dance style, but he put his traditional show-biz dancing at the service of his projects. John Martin wrote that *Pal Joey*'s dances were "nicely characterized and worked into the scheme of the whole . . . the dances are virtually inseparable from the dramatic action."

He was the first powerhouse choreographer, and he was very tough on dancers, whom he fired for adding weight or losing their spark during the run of a show. He was the first choreographer to hold brush-up rehearsals. This early Hollywood journalism unearthed by Richard Kislan for *Hoofing on Broadway* describes Alton:

> Some 300 hoofers, notified by Central Casting, answered his chorus call, but a lot of them didn't stay—just sneaked out when they saw the steps required. . . . Conclusive of his standards is that after the first day's rehearsal the chorus went on strike, saying in sulky astonishment, "This is specialty stuff! We aren't going to work for chorus wages. No movie director ever asked us to do these steps." Screen Actors' Guild officials, after

watching a routine, agreed, and ordered their salaries raised to that of specialty dancers.

• • •

In 1936, George Balanchine requested "Choreography by" rather than "Dances by" or "Dance Director" in the program for *On Your Toes,* the first time the phrase appeared on Broadway. He choreographed numerous shows, including *I Married An Angel, Babes in Arms, The Boys from Syracuse, Where's Charley?,* and *Song of Norway.* The dances of earlier choreographers were connected only obliquely to their books, usually through the lyrics or the costumes, but Balanchine, with his classic ballet background, wanted a plot for his dances. Some critics didn't even notice "Slaughter on Tenth Avenue" when they saw *On Your Toes,* but the *Herald Tribune* said it caused the most uproar among the audience.

One season after *Oklahoma!* twelve of the twenty-one new musicals featured some kind of ballet sequence. Richard Kislan has calculated that in the next three and a half years, seventy-two musicals were produced, forty-six of which featured ballet, and twenty-one of those were "dream ballets."

Walter Kerr described the early effect of show dancing as "a cold-blooded, calculating, haymaker thrust that is essentially concerned with keeping the entire production plunging onward," but he believed that the post-de Mille school was more emotional, sensitive, and expressive of character.

It was a long journey for the dancers. At first they only had to be great-looking. Later they had to tap. Then they had to dance, then be proficient in that most technical of all disciplines, ballet. Then they had to act, and then they had to sing.

Serious innovators like George Balanchine and Agnes de Mille integrated the tall (showgirls) and the short (ponies). Both choreographers temporarily pushed tap and earthier forms of dance right off the stage.

Yet no choreographer, no matter how successful, had a free hand. Agnes de Mille was forced to cut the powerful image of a dead soldier's body being returned to his wife from "Civil War Ballet" for *Bloomer Girl.* Her collaborators thought it was too dark. It took a number of decades for the choreographer-as-director to come about—power in the collaborative business of musical-making is not willingly given up—but the director who specializes in the musical goes back to the early twenties.

Like all the great talent that created the Hollywood movie musicals, Vincente Minnelli began in the theatre. He trouped with his family—the Minnelli Brothers Tent Theatre—until talkies put them out of business. When they settled down, he developed an interest in drawing and painting, which led to a job as a sign painter. Minnelli left home for Chicago with a portfolio of watercolors, and he got a job as an apprentice display designer at Marshall Field department store. Later, he worked as a photographer's assistant. Soon he talked his way into creating all the costumes for a local three-theatre chain that played one-hour stage shows in conjunction with films. When the chain expanded and moved their headquarters to New York, Minnelli found himself putting costumes together for a new unit every week that went out on the same bill with a film. This work led to an invitation to do sets and costumes for the 1932 *Vanities,* then costumes at Radio City Music Hall. Three weeks after his arrival at Radio City, art direction was added to Minnelli's duties. He was soon creating, producing, designing, and directing one show a month for the cavernous theatre.

In spite of their image today, the original Shubert brothers were a schlock operation. They consistently catered to the lowest common denominator with Americanized operettas, melodramas, and revues that fell far short of the Ziegfeld glamour. When the Shuberts wanted to upscale their operation, they hired young Vincente Minnelli to produce musical revues. He created, staged, and designed *At Home Abroad* for Bea Lillie, *The Ziegfeld Follies of 1935* (when the Shuberts rented the title from Ziegfeld's wife Billie Burke), and *The Show Is On,* again with Bea Lillie.

Minnelli's first trip to Hollywood was fruitless, and he spent months trying to get out of his contract with Paramount Studios. He returned to Broadway to direct and design *Hooray For What* (1937) starring Ed Wynn, and *Very Warm for May* (1939). But Arthur Freed asked him to try Hollywood again under Freed's auspice at MGM Studios, and Minnelli said yes. The brilliant Freed used him wisely, and Minnelli never returned to Broadway. His film career included direction of the musicals *Cabin in the Sky, Meet Me in St. Louis, The Ziegfeld Follies, The Pirate, An American in Paris, The Band Wagon, Gigi,* and *On a Clear Day You Can See Forever.*

Minnelli's work was based on the art director's eye—he may have been the only director-designer—and his small contribution to the stage musical consisted primarily of the elegant sets and costumes that he invented for songs in revues. Yet he integrated those sets and costumes well and used them economically—he hated Busby Berkeley's spectacles, with their overblown musical numbers unconnected to the plot. Minnelli's artistry really comes through in his film musicals, especially the final ballet for *An American in Paris,* and it set a standard that was actively followed by many directors and designers since.

• • •

In the film medium the director was already king, but prior to Rouben Mamoulian, stage directing was not considered a significant contribution. Florenz Ziegfeld's principal and highly prized director Julian Mitchell was actually thought of as his "stage manager." Musicals were often directed by whoever was in charge—thus, George M. Cohan staged many of his own, not so much because he considered himself a director per se, but because he wanted total control over the material. Sometimes he hired others to do chores as well, though without ever feeling he had given up that control. But Mamoulian changed all that with *Porgy and Bess, Oklahoma!, Carousel,* and *Lost in the Stars.*

Nothing after *Porgy* could have given him as much difficulty. "It is like breaking mountains of ice," he remarked of a rehearsal day. "The end of it leaves one completely exhausted and usually a little depressed. Everything seems awkward, disorganized, almost hopeless." In the end, it was anything but. To all his shows, he brought beautiful pictures in a theatrically impressionistic style (created out of larger choruses than the modern theatre could ever afford), realistic acting, and strong central ideas.

• • •

At various times a number of men have been called "the father of the modern American musical," notably Jerome Kern. Sometimes George Gershwin is included in this category among composers, who are often the first to be recognized because their music lives on and even grows through cast albums, revues, and multiple performances. Oscar Hammerstein is honored among the writers, George Abbott as a director, and Rodgers and Hammerstein as a powerhouse team of show writers and producers. George M. Cohan is often mentioned, depending on how far back you want to go. To give any

Rouben Mamoulian, the Moscow drama student who revolutionized the American musical with his productions of *Porgy and Bess* and *Oklahoma!*
Archive Photos/London Daily Express

one man credit is to misunderstand the very art of the American musical. Nevertheless . . .

Oscar Hammerstein II thought of himself as a librettist and lyricist, and posterity has proved his word. But as a young stage manager, Hammerstein had often been responsible for training understudies and replacements. He not only directed the actors in book scenes, but also taught the incoming dancers most of the simple dance steps; he did this without training but with, undoubtedly, the enthusiasm and naiveté of youth. He directed *The Gang's All Here* in 1931, for which he had cowritten the book—as in numerous other shows, though, he was not credited. By the time Hammerstein staged the gargantuan *Show Boat* he did so with expertise and experience. It is difficult even to confirm that he actually staged and directed *Show Boat.* Production stage manager Zeke Colvan, who had a Herculean job backstage keeping the huge production moving, was listed as director. In fact, it was Hammerstein who did most of the work that we think of today as directing.

It was *Show Boat* that launched the modern American musical, and Hammerstein who began to practice an idea he virtually invented and insisted on throughout his career, the idea of *continuous action.*

Hammerstein continued to direct for years after *Show Boat,* which included the doctoring of his friends' shows out of town. He tried many innovative staging ideas. One musical, *Free For All* (1931), did entirely without a chorus, which was unheard of at the time. Unfortunately, it was a flop.

Hammerstein's directing informed his work and arguably makes him the single most influential man in the history of the modern American musical. Following on the heels of George M. Cohan and the Guy Bolton-P. G. Wodehouse-Jerome Kern trio, Hammerstein's solid books and elegant lyrics form a body of work that serves as a crucial link between early and modern musicals. The craft of the modern musical started with Hammerstein's desire to explore important subjects, to write spare books that resounded with the dramatic intention of the story and characters. He sought to leave behind pure comedy, and, in particular, to eliminate blackouts and "in ones" in favor of continuous action. Thus, Hammerstein began streamlining the spotty staging of the period.

For *Music In the Air* Hammerstein experimented with transitory dialogue in rhyme that allowed the change from dialogue to song to flow more naturally. He also ensured that actors who were not singing continued their action during another performer's song. Even as he took less of a hand in directing, Hammerstein was purposely "staging" his musicals in his head as he wrote them, organizing a fluid, integrated show as he wrote. In later years, when other directors and choreographers staged his work, they undoubtedly found their job immensely easier because the show had already been schemed by an experienced director. And whether or not his initial staging was followed, all his scenes and songs benefit enormously from built-in action. Stephen Sondheim gave a famous lecture on lyrics at New York's 92nd Street YM-YWHA in the 1970s, in which he warned musical theatre composers that knowing what the characters were *saying* wasn't enough—a writer of theatre songs had to know what they were *doing,* something Sondheim learned in his talks with Hammerstein.

Hammerstein always wrote full stage directions into his texts, and when he carefully constructed *Allegro* and *South Pacific* to include continuous action, he made the single greatest contribution to the modern musical. Without this idea, the modern director-choreographer would never be able to create the fluid, cinematic locomotive of a musical that is today's ideal (if not the norm).

In 1946, Hammerstein's writing was represented on Broadway by *Oklahoma!* at the St. James Theatre; *Carousel* across the street at the Majestic; a *Desert Song* revival at City Center; an incoming *Carmen Jones* revival; and a *Show Boat* revival at the Ziegfeld. At the same time, he was represented as a producer with *Annie Get Your Gun* and the straight play *I Remember Mama.* Through all his success, he remained a kind and generous man who nurtured younger talents both personally and professionally, most notably Stephen Sondheim. Hammerstein's calm demeanor was notorious. It is said that an actor once sang a Hammerstein lyric incorrectly for seven straight performances, whereupon Hammerstein was overheard to say quietly, "I'm not very good-natured about this any more."

Hammerstein's famous musical writing lesson to the teenage Sondheim (following several hours in which he blitzed Sondheim's first manuscript) came in four exercises. Sondheim had to (1) write a musical based on a good play; (2) write a musical based on a weak play that had to be altered structurally; (3) write a musical based on a nontheatrical work, such as a novel or short story, that would require extensive editing, structuring, and invention; and finally (4) write an original musical. It was a course that any aspiring musical comedy writer would do well to follow. (Sondheim completed all four assignments in his ensuing college years, and the rest is history.)

• • •

George Abbott also began as a writer, but stuck with directing instead. A list of the musicals he directed is so long and impressive it's nearly impossible to digest: *Jumbo; On Your Toes; The Boys from Syracuse; Pal Joey; Best Foot Forward; On the Town; High Button Shoes; Where's Charley?; Call Me Madam; A Tree Grows in Brooklyn; Wonderful Town; Me and Juliet; The Pajama Game; Damn Yankees; Once Upon a Mattress; Fiorello!; Tenderloin; New Girl in Town; A Funny Thing Happened on the Way to the Forum; Fade Out, Fade In; Flora, The Red Menace; How Now Dow Jones;* and *Music Is.* As if that weren't enough, Abbott cowrote half a dozen of them, had an equally successful record in straight plays, and often functioned as a producer as well.

Characterized as a New England farmer, he was six feet six inches tall, stern, and had a resonant voice and commanding presence. His working method was inexpressive, unemotional, and authoritarian. Sondheim characterized his work as "totalitarian theatre."

Mr. Abbott, as he was called—the form of address tells us everything we need to know about the community's respect for him—was first and foremost a collaborator. He must have delighted in working with others, for he turned increasingly to musicals. And everyone wanted to work with him. His partners and associates became a who's who of the American theatre, from his first production in 1926 to his last in 1983.

Abbott's plays and musicals were never highly stylized. He directed in a straightforward, no-nonsense manner that allowed the writing and the performances to take center stage. His contribution to the American musical is not really marked by one individual production, nor by any particularly original approach. But his large body of work is a crucial link between the early musical comedies of the twenties and thirties and the modern American musical in its heyday. As a writer Abbott valued the material, whether his own or another person's—it was this dependence on dramatic content that helped raise the book, music, and lyrics to a more respectable level in the musical during its long gestation period.

Abbott was a direct descendant of the George M. Cohan "speed and plenty of it" school. The Abbott touch was often simplified as pacing, but there was more. As a rewriter, director, and collaborator first and foremost, he considered *construction* more important than prose. He wanted no waste, and insisted that each beat have the proper emphasis. He wanted not comedy or shtick on the stage, but utter truth most of all. He established that good theatre comedy flows not from an assemblage of gags, but from plot and character.

He gave line readings, which actors hate, ignored motivation and method, and limited exploration of actors' and characters' lives. Actors should "just say the lines and be in the right place at the right time," according to Abbott's method. In reality, he was demanding the essence of the later Method school: truth. He didn't teach it—he demanded it, and he had an outstanding ability to know when it was being delivered or not. He directed by staging a play logically and precisely, and disallowing anything phony. Abbott came into the theatre at a time when acting was still very artificial—focusing on performance and declamation—and thus he set the groundwork for the modern actor, who does not indicate, but is. Musicals, the natural home of performers, were the last art form to embrace this level of reality and truth, and benefited from it as much as straight plays. The new approach allowed musicals the freedom to become more serious, and raised their level of reality so that audiences could expect more than just entertainment—they could empathize with the characters.

Abbott's simplistic approach, however, can lead to simplistic theatre and would never have survived in the modern musical. One rare example was *New Girl in Town,* the musical version of Eugene O'Neill's *Anna Christie.* The play was laden with symbolism, metaphor, and depth, and it was not the right subject for a sentimental, formulaic, George Abbott musical comedy (though it may have worked as a musical drama). The Abbott approach was simply not appropriate to the material, and it failed.

Nonetheless, Abbott put musicals together more efficiently than they had ever been put together before. This efficiency in staging a production led directly to the high-tech directors and choreographers of the succeeding era. In fact, the vast majority of talent in the modern era trained directly with Mr. Abbott. He took an exceptional delight in new talent, and had the most extraordinary eye and ear for it ever seen in the American theatre. He directed the work of young composers Hugh Martin and Ralph Blane, Leonard Bernstein, Jule Styne, Frank Loesser, Jerry Ross and Richard Adler, John Kander and Fred Ebb, Jerry Bock and Sheldon Harnick, Bob

Merrill, and Stephen Sondheim; lyricists Betty Comden, Adolph Green, and Sammy Cahn; and performers Carol Burnett and Liza Minnelli. Abbott aided and abetted two of his assistant stage managers, whom he called "the boys," to become producers Harold S. Prince and Robert E. Griffith.

He stuck to his straightforward approach, but he was not afraid of originality in content—he was even enamored with it. He mounted the first musical based on a risqué subject—*Pal Joey*—without compromising or tacking on a happy ending. He was not afraid to insert the first major story ballet sequence in a musical ("Slaughter on Tenth Avenue" in *On Your Toes*), nor to bring in a classical choreographer to do it (George Balanchine). In fact, Abbott was one of the few nonchoreographing directors who was able to appreciate dance to its fullest extent. Without his assistance, the concept of the modern director-choreographer may never have emerged, because until choreographers demonstrated they could contribute dramatically they were unlikely to be entrusted with the whole show. He was more than willing to give up whole sections of his shows to talented choreographers, and he made room for major dance sequences in *Pal Joey, On the Town, High Button Shoes,* and *Pajama Game.* Abbott and Frank Loesser tailored *Where's Charley?* for the talents of Ray Bolger. The long dance sequences in these shows paved the way for the fully choreographed musicals of Jerome Robbins and Michael Bennett.

Understanding both the ensemble show and the star vehicle, he worked equitably with Gene Kelly, Ray Bolger, Ethel Merman, Shirley Booth, Rosalind Russell, John Raitt, Carol Burnett, Zero Mostel, and Liza Minnelli. Nor was he above working off-Broadway (*Once Upon a Mattress*).

Abbott was the director who gave the gift of authority to the modern director-choreographer, but he used it himself only to sharpen the material—never to shape it. He never superimposed his own vision, concept, or metaphor on the work. But his low profile, quiet authority, and gentlemanly demeanor were not his gifts to the eclectic group of talented newcomers who first practiced under his tutelage. Neither was his nonstylistic approach. What he gave them was an invaluable opportunity—experience at the highest level of the craft.

• • •

Not every good choreographer was cut in the Robbins-Bennett mold. Jerome Robbins and Michael Bennett were so dedicated to the idea of content over style that little of their work translated from show to show. There isn't a step in *West Side Story* that would make sense in *Fiddler on the Roof,* or vice versa. Each musical—in some cases each number in a musical—was unique. To achieve this, Robbins and Bennett often placed significant responsibility on their assistants because every choreographer is limited to his own body, which tends to fall into familiar and favorite patterns.* During his career, Robbins called upon Peter Gennaro and Bob Fosse, for example, while Bennett relied heavily on Bob Avian and Baayork Lee and often asked his dancers to contribute as well. Bennett enlisted Michael Peters when *Dreamgirls* required a more contemporary look than he and his associates had experience with. Robbins and Bennett pulled everything together—editing, arranging, rearranging, and encouraging.

But Agnes de Mille, Michael Kidd, Gower Champion, and Bob Fosse created dances out of a personal style that grew and expanded throughout their careers. This approach created shows indelibly stamped with their look.

• • •

Immediately following *Oklahoma!* American theatre choreographers, challenged by the astounding contribution of Agnes de Mille, poured fourth a body of work that will never be equaled. The American Dance Machine, a dance company founded by Lee Theodore, has tried to preserve these historic musical show dances, but the transitory and ephemeral nature of the theatre will for the most part deny future audiences a good look at these wonderful sequences. Not until 1978 was choreography even deemed suitable for copyrighting. Yet in 1959, Gwen Verdon had said:

> A choreographer is never afraid to move you around, while most directors have their mind on keeping you where you will be heard. . . . Choreographers have a greater sense of the visual, the composition of a scene, the look of a scene. You don't have to depend on words all the time.

The musical was becoming an increasingly visual medium, and choreographers were poised to capitalize on that.

* Similarly, Stephen Sondheim says that he prefers to compose *away* from the piano because the "fingers tend to fall into favorite patterns."

The legend goes that once in a rehearsal, choreographer Onna White took to shouting at the boy dancers that they were too weak, too effeminate. She berated them to butch it up. "Dance like you have some balls!" she shouted, whereupon a male dancer turned to the wings and lisped, "Props!" White's work was otherwise dismally uneventful. Her staging was appropriate but unremarkable, and her dances neither distracted from nor contributed to the musical.

Michael Kidd elevated male dancers to a new and respectable level by calling on their athleticism and gymnastic ability. His "Crapshooters Ballet" in *Guys and Dolls* featured only men and is surely one of the finest self-contained dance sequences in the musical theatre (fortunately captured for the film version). The dance has little to do with ballet and everything to do with crapshooting. Skyscraping jumps and freewheeling aerial somersaults exploded like fireworks in one of the most masculine dances ever created for a musical. (Kidd took masculine dancing to even greater heights when he choreographed the film *Seven Brides for Seven Brothers.*)

Kidd's "Sadie Hawkins Day Ballet" for *Li'l Abner* was filled with humor, as the girls of Dogpatch chased, caught, and married the boys in an exuberant, athletic romp. Michael Kidd was one of the first choreographers to combine gymnastics and tumbling with dance, and he liberated the men's chorus from both the refined, classical vocabulary of ballet and the limiting tap and soft-shoe routines on which almost all show dancing was based until then.

Gower Champion was already famous when he began to choreograph and direct because he had been a performer. In his early days he was half of America's top dance team, appearing with his wife Marge in several films (their most notable work being their two duets in MGM's 1951 *Show Boat*) and performing in swank nightclubs across the country. When Marge was laid up with an ankle injury, Gower staged the dances for *Lend an Ear,* a successful revue that earned him notice, and the die was cast. Once Champion directed and choreographed *Bye Bye Birdie,** he never went back to performing. He was the first director-choreographer to demand and receive over-the-title billing ("A Gower Champion Musical"). David Merrick, who produced many of his shows, called him the "Presbyterian Hitler."

* *Bye Bye Birdie* was the first show to have its choreography preserved in "Labanotation," a system for writing down dances which became obsolete with the invention of videotape.

Champion's ego was backed up with an eye for the spectacular. He used more dancers, more props, more costumes, and more sets for a single number than any other choreographer of the modern musical. He was a direct descendant of the Busby Berkeley school, and his early shows were filled with dancing. *Hello, Dolly!,* Champion's best show, virtually goes from one big number to the next. His patterns overshadow his steps, and his numbers didn't so much take place as build in ever-increasing tableaux. For *Carnival* he constructed an entire carnival in front of the audience, using animals and circus tricks.

Champion's vocabulary was rich enough when Marge assisted him—she had extensive dance training—but it grew shallow and limited as she withdrew to raise their children. Champion's first priority was maintaining his power, and without Marge he couldn't make proper use of (or was unable to identify) good assistants. He was seldom able to use dance with any originality after *Hello Dolly! The Happy Time* should have been an intimate, human musical, but he used the Busby Berkeley approach and nearly crushed it. *I Do! I Do!* was a two-character musical with the transcendent talents of Robert Preston and Mary Martin, so Champion was prohibited from overdoing it, but even then one or two numbers got away from the show. *Mack and Mabel* reunited him with *Dolly* writers Jerry Herman and Michael Stewart, but again Champion overburdened a very human story with too many musical sequences that slowed the plot. Jerome Robbins's "Mack Sennet Ballet" in *High Button Shoes* had brought the slapstick style of early silent comedies to the stage brilliantly, but Robbins used a plot for that legendary dance, and did it only once in the whole show. Champion attempted to do it half a dozen times, but he didn't have the ballet background Robbins brought to longer sequences. At the end of his life Champion rose from the ashes of *Prettybelle, Sugar, Rockabye Hamlet,* and *A Broadway Musical* to have his biggest hit in 1980, the stage version of *42nd Street.* He applied the Busby Berkeley style to an authentic Busby Berkeley story, reclaiming a place for the tradition of the early musical—long lines of girls, dancers rushing here and there, and props flying in and out. In truth, this creaky but splashy musical rode nostalgia more than originality into the hearts of matinée ladies, theatre parties, and expense accounts. Gower Champion died on the afternoon that *42nd Street* opened.

Frank Rich's obituary was effusive in its praise for Champion's old-fashioned musical comedy-making, but it doesn't go far enough—in his early musicals, Champion left a legacy of great if underestimated musical theatre. Rich wrote:

> For all the commercial and critical success Mr. Champion achieved during his lifetime, perhaps he was never fully appreciated on his own terms. That may be because he was an anachronism. He was no innovator, like Jerome Robbins or Michael Bennett.

Yes, he was every bit an innovator. He integrated sets and choreography in "The Telephone Hour" in *Birdie,* the carnival created from a bare stage for *Carnival*'s opening number, and the runway and staircase in *Hello Dolly!* He used props and choreography in new ways—the "Waiter's Gallop" in *Dolly,* and the unforgettable Robert Preston and Mary Martin playing the saxophone and violin in *I Do! I Do!* And Champion often used a complex tableau of dancers all doing different steps, as with "It Takes a Woman" in *Hello Dolly!*

Rich went on to say that Champion "never created his own distinctive choreographic style, like Bob Fosse" and that "he didn't try to tackle daring subjects, like Hal Prince." Nonsense. The look of a Champion show was as distinctive as that of any artist in the twentieth century. Sharp, clean, clever steps, Swiss-watch staging, and build-up from a single dancer to a roaring company in a gargantuan musical sequence ("Before the Parade Passes By") were his trademarks. Moreover, the drama of *Carnival,* the oddity of *Prettybelle,* and the pulsing rhythms of *Rockabye Hamlet* were certainly daring subjects.

"And yet," Rich continues, "Mr. Champion's body of work is as much a part of the history of the contemporary musical as that of his talented peers. By applying an unstoppable imagination, galvanizing enthusiasm and a taskmaster's professionalism to a series of unpretentious, empty-headed entertainments"—a rude stab at *Carnival, I Do! I Do!, Prettybelle,* and even *Hello Dolly!,* which is so entertaining that critics (though never audiences) sometimes overlook its Thornton Wilder heart, one of the warmest in theatre literature—"he almost single-handedly kept alive the fabled traditions of Broadway's most glittery and innocent past." At last a compliment for one of the most successful director-choreographers of the golden age.

• • •

When Marge and Gower Champion were headlining nightclubs, Bob Fosse and Mary Ann Niles introduced their act by saying, "You've heard of the Champions? We're the runners-up." Fosse's hoped-for film career as the next Gene Kelly (or at least Donald O'Connor) never really took off. He turned to choreography, successfully if reluctantly. When he got a chance to choreograph *The Pajama Game,* he stamped Broadway with an idiosyncratic, personal style, featuring tight, tiny moves; burlesque pelvic freedom; complex, intricate rhythms; and a floor-hugging, thigh-straining, low-center-of-gravity jazz dance that had been pioneered by Jack Cole.

In fact Cole, whose success in the theatre was erratic, became the single most influential choreographer of the modern age because of his nightclub and concert work featuring the Jack Cole dancers. He freed theatre choreography from too much reliance on ballet. He introduced sexuality into dancing, which coincidentally allowed character work and drama to flood forward. Cole was fascinated with Eastern dances, and he introduced "angularity," which pulled away from the classic ballet line just as the musical theatre needed a new vocabulary. His concept of "isolation" would be hugely useful when choreographers began dealing with eccentric, ethnic characters as writers looked further afield for subject matter. *Everyone* owes Cole a debt, including his own dancers Gwen Verdon, who subsequently influenced Fosse; Ron Lewis, who dominated Las Vegas choreography for years; and Ron Field, who started with the Brechtian dances of *Cabaret* and peaked with the slick Lauren Bacall vehicle *Applause.* Cole's influence reached a second generation of choreographers, such as Michael Bennett, Alan Johnson, and David Winters, who had grown up in the Cole atmosphere and took classes from Cole imitators, chiefly New York's most influential jazz dance teacher, known as Luigi.

Cole's shows, including *Allah Be Praised, Alive and Kicking, May Wine, Thumbs Up, Kean, Donnybrook,* and *Mata Hari,* were often credited for great dances in otherwise lackluster productions, though *Kismet* and *Man of La Mancha* succeeded and included brilliant dances. Cole's work can be seen in numerous films* because he was the creator of the first motion picture ensemble dance company for Columbia Pictures in 1944. But like all pio-

* These include *Moon Over Miami* (1941), *Kismet* (1944), *Cover Girl* (1944), *The Jolson Story* (1947), *The Merry Widow* (1952 and 1955), *Gentlemen Prefer Blondes* (1953), *There's No Business Like Show Business* (1954), *Let's Make Love* (1955), *Designing Woman* (1957), *Les Girls* (1957), and *Some Like It Hot* (1959).

neers, his true legacy is buried in the work of his dancers: Buzz Miller, Rod Alexander, Carol Haney, Matt Mattox. And Gwen Verdon.

Fosse had been a dancer who choreographed for himself; his choreographic vocabulary was personal and limited. He had to use invention and character because he had little formal training. As a result, he was an intensely individual and unique stylist. *Pippin* and *Chicago* are nearly identical, and by the time *Chicago* came around, audiences were a little weary of the slow-motion, dark, slithering, overtly erotic poses. His best work began with *Pajama Game* and *Damn Yankees,* two musicals adapted from novels and directed by George Abbott, with scores by Richard Adler and Jerry Ross. These shows were nearly identical in formula, and both featured fun subcultures (union pajama factory workers and an in-the-cellar baseball team); strong love stories set against unique plots (management versus workers, a Faustian tale of soul-selling); and choreography by the new-to-the-ranks Fosse, which is the contribution that really marked them as unique. Stylish, rhythmic, and funky ("beat") for the fifties, Fosse's vocabulary was a lighthearted version of the fierce, dark, Latin-influenced Cole. And it was sexy. "Steam Heat," a showstopper-within-a-show, featured Carol Haney and two boys in the most angular, ironic, dazzling, tongue-in-cheek specialty number that had yet been performed in a book show. Then Fosse had Gwen Verdon as Lola, the devil's tool, to work with in *Damn Yankees.*

Verdon grew up in Los Angeles, studied dance with Marge Champion's father, spent five years in Jack Cole's troupe, and achieved star status in *Can-Can.* Fosse was immoderately heterosexual and found in Verdon the perfect interpreter. Her sizzling charisma undoubtedly egged him on (eventually they were married). The come-hither choreography for "A Little Brains" and "Whatever Lola Wants" in *Damn Yankees* created the first (and last) female star dancer to reign on Broadway since Marilyn Miller.

In a further example of what sells popular culture and Broadway musicals, the original *Damn Yankees* logo featured Verdon in a baseball uniform. Despite outstanding reviews, ticket sales were lackluster. A month into the run the logo was changed to Verdon provocatively posed in a merry widow. The box office came alive, and the show eventually ran 1,019 performances and toured successfully.)

Fosse's work crystallized in *How to Succeed in Business Without Really Trying.* There his angular vocabulary supported the cartoonish show, and his clever theatre staging complimented the funniest book and best theatre songs he ever got to stage. He was not musical, but he was intelligent enough to change Frank Loesser's "A Secretary is Not a Toy" from 3/4 to 4/4 time when he couldn't find a way to stage it. To Loesser's credit, the composer liked the soft-shoe approach and rewrote the song for him. Fosse made his directorial debut with *Redhead,* and he truly arrived with *Sweet Charity,* both created for Verdon. He celebrated sexuality (offstage and on), an obsession that reached its apotheosis in *Pippin*'s sex ballet and in "Air Erotica" from the autobiographical film *All That Jazz.* Fosse celebrated sheer dancing with *Dancin'* (1978), consisting of twelve bookless musical theatre dances in the inimitable Fosse style. One-third of these fell flat, a third were entertaining, and a third were transcendental. *Dancin'* ran for 1,774 performances, a clear indication that audiences love American theatre dance.

Although the film version of *Charity* didn't fly, the "Rich Man's Frug" memorializes a good example of Fosse's group work. "There's Gotta Be Something Better Than This" demonstrates how brilliantly he worked with female jazz dancers, and "Big Spender" splashes his funky rhythms and eroticism all over the screen. Other examples of his best work are available on film, including the dazzling duet with Tommy Rall in *My Sister Eileen,* and "Steam Heat" in *Pajama Game,* the latter of which is probably the best nonbook dance number a show ever stopped for ("Before we get started, Gladys and the kids have been working up a little something they'd like you to see . . ."). Once Fosse became a hot film director with *Cabaret,* his work became increasingly personal, indulgent, and noncollaborative. He mounted his last stage musical, *Big Deal,* without a bookwriter, composer, lyricist, or producer looking over his shoulder. The value of an auteurist director-choreographer notwithstanding, *Big Deal's* failure is testimony to the necessity of collaboration.

Fosse's slouching, pigeon-toed posture became his personal style. He loved hats because he was balding, and he included them in several numbers. His love of props in general, particularly hats and canes, came from a love of vaudeville that pervaded all his work. He always gave the audience the old razzle-dazzle. Through Fosse, vaudeville illuminated the Broadway musical for the second time in its history (the first time was with George M. Cohan). In fact, Fosse was a throwback to the entertaining dance directors of the early 1920s musicals. He used bumps and grinds instead of high kicks and tap steps, and did set pieces—"Steam Heat," "Who's Got the Pain?" "If My Friends Could See Me Now"—in a slick, clean, fluid, sexy style. It was the purest jazz choreography in musical theatre. Were his shows integrated? Not always dramatically, but certainly stylistically. He was an artist who brought the whole show around to his personal vision.

Bob Fosse won the Oscar (*Cabaret*), the Emmy (*Liza with a Z*), and the Tony (*Pippin*) for directing in the same year, a triple-crown feat that will probably never be repeated. Only weeks later, he checked into a psychiatric clinic for "terrible depression." In the end, life for the hedonistic, self-destructive, drug-driven Fosse was difficult, but his shows were dazzling.

Agnes de Mille, Michael Kidd, Gower Champion, and Bob Fosse—with the ghosts of George Balanchine hanging over de Mille and Jack Cole over the others—are, with Jerome Robbins and Michael Bennett, the foundation of the modern American musical. Before their work, dancing in the musical theatre was at best entertaining, at worst simplistic, cheap, gaudy and seldom dramatic. American show dancing now ranks with ballet and modern dance as an art form in its own right. Its earliest contribution was sheer entertainment, of the highest intensity. By the golden age it helped to forward the story and defined the characters as much as the book, music, and lyrics did.

Interlude

Down the years there were a number of smaller achievements as well, and some shows and events also deserve to be singled out for a unique contribution.

Beggar's Holiday featured one of the earliest truly interracial casts, in 1946. Although nudity had long been featured in Florenz Ziegfeld's "Living Statues," the modern musical was more conservative. Donna McKechnie danced in only a slip in *Company* (1970), and eventually the entire cast let it all hang out in *Oh! Calcutta!* (1969). This pure sixties artifact, which now would seem quaint, featured an all-nude pas de deux choreographed by Margo Sappington which was both erotic and artistic, and it broke open barriers in both nudity and taste. *Grease* (1972), the fifties rock and roll musical, created a format for nostalgia. It was followed the very next season by two of the three living Andrews Sisters in *Over Here,* then by a legion of off-Broadway musicals that used or referred to songs from past eras. *Pippin* (1972) was the first show to use a television commercial, when its box office started dropping. The result was a four and a half year run. Now every musical needs television advertising, and advertising costs for a musical have skyrocketed. *The Wiz* (1975), a black pop-music version of *The Wizard of Oz,* received poor reviews when it opened, but the producer, Ken Harper, was a radio man. He pushed its most commercial song, "Ease on Down the Road," on rhythm-and-blues radio stations and created an audience for the show. It was the first time in years that a Broadway musical boasted a hit single, and practically the first time since *Tobacco Road* that a show reached a large audience in defiance of the critics. When it did, the ebullient, irreverent nature of the work, misunderstood and underappreciated by white conservative theatre critics, propelled it toward popular success.

But the two most noteworthy Broadway influences in the modern era were the introduction of the rock musical, and the reintroduction of the black musical.

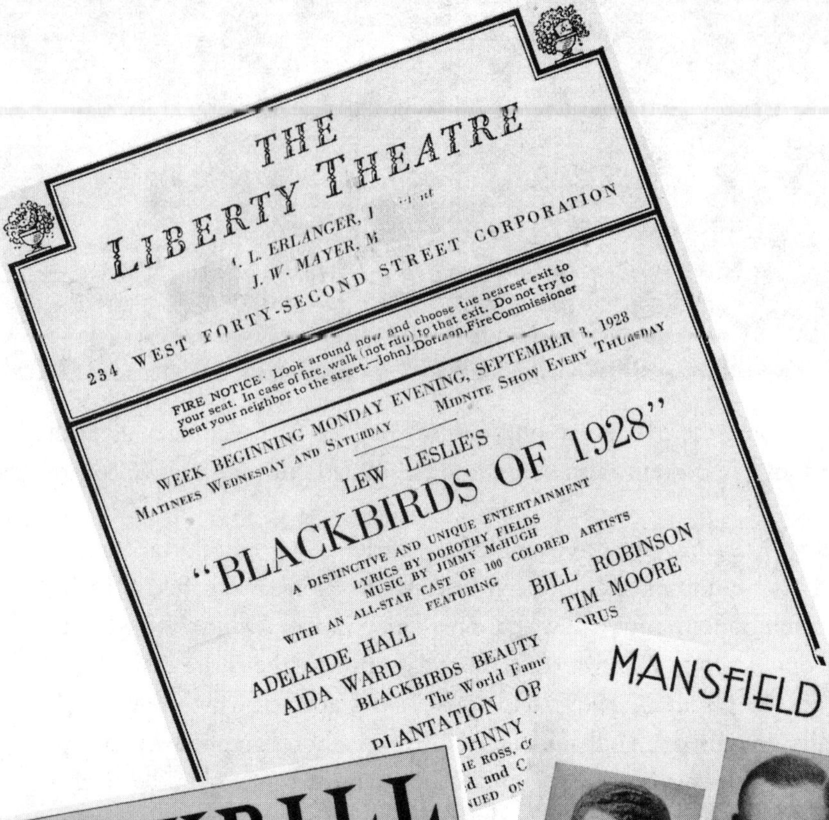

THE LIBERTY THEATRE

A. L. ERLANGER, P

J. W. MAYER, M

234 WEST FORTY-SECOND STREET CORPORATION

FIRE NOTICE: Look around now and choose the nearest exit to your seat. In case of fire, walk (not run) to that exit. Do not try to beat your neighbor to the street.—John J. Dorman, Fire Commissioner

WEEK BEGINNING MONDAY EVENING, SEPTEMBER 3, 1928

MATINEES WEDNESDAY AND SATURDAY — MIDNITE SHOW EVERY THURSDAY

LEW LESLIE'S

"BLACKBIRDS OF 1928"

A DISTINCTIVE AND UNIQUE ENTERTAINMENT

LYRICS BY DOROTHY FIELDS

MUSIC BY JIMMY McHUGH

WITH AN ALL-STAR CAST OF 100 COLORED ARTISTS

FEATURING

ADELAIDE HALL — BILL ROBINSON

AIDA WARD — TIM MOORE

BLACKBIRDS BEAUTY ORUS

The World Famo

PLANTATION OR

JOHNNY

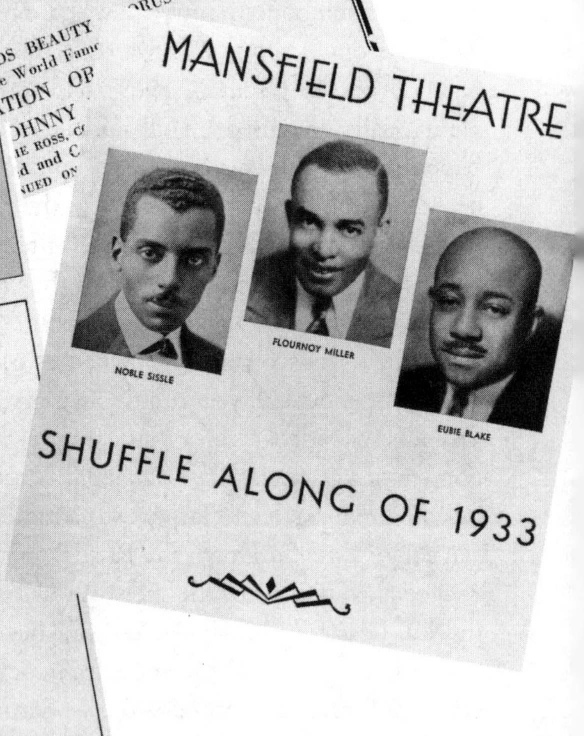

IE ROSS, C

d and C

NUED ON

MANSFIELD THEATRE

SHUFFLE ALONG OF 1933

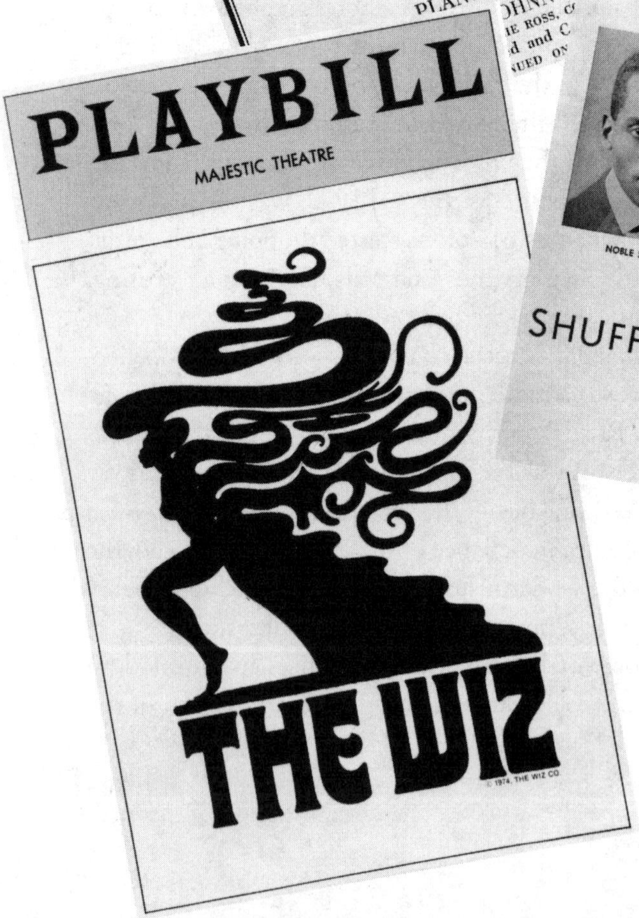

PLAYBILL

MAJESTIC THEATRE

Seventeen

The Black Musical

The original opening line of *Show Boat* was "Niggers all work on de Mississippi." It was later changed to "Darkies all work on de Mississippi." Then it was changed to "Colored folk work on de Mississippi." And in 1966 became "Here we all work on de Mississippi."

The constant struggle by revisionist productions to avoid insulting the sensibilities of a portion of the audience ("African-Americans work on de Mississippi?") places a spotlight on the humanity of Oscar Hammerstein II.

It was never the intention of *Show Boat*'s creators to slander African-Americans, and certainly not the Mississippi river workers that are sensitively portrayed in the musical, which includes one of the most beautiful, understanding, and heroic of all ballads ever written for the stage, "Ol' Man River."

"Ol' Man River" is about the ageless, inexorable, Mississippi River, but most of its lyrics refer to the backbreaking life of the Southern black, who "plants taters, plants cotton, and is soon forgotten," who gets "weary and sick of tryin', and tired of livin' and scared of dyin'." Nobody connected with *Show Boat,* least of all Hammerstein, could possibly be accused of indifference to American blacks. Just the opposite. The rest of the show's opening quatrain is "Niggers all work while de white folks play." *Show Boat* had come a long way from songs like "Paris is a Paradise for Coons," sung by Al Jolson in *La Belle Parée* fifteen years earlier, especially considering that Jerome Kern wrote that song too. It was not the producers' intention to shock the audience. "Nigger" was a common word in 1927. The opening line was meant to be real, not slanderous.

Florenz Ziegfeld, Jerome Kern, and Oscar Hammerstein, in fact, broke ground with *Show Boat*'s black and white chorus, since blacks and whites had not previously appeared on stage together. Until Ziegfeld booked Bert Williams for his *Follies,* black musical theatre was separate from white. And customs don't change overnight. *Show Boat*'s Queenie was played in blackface by Tess Gardella, a white performer who had made her "Aunt Jemima" character famous in vaudeville.

The Kern-Hammerstein musical introduced black history and society as a rich source for drama. Following *Porgy and Bess,* composer Harold Arlen, fascinated with blues music, chose no less than four black stories to musicalize—*Cabin in the Sky* (1940), *St. Louis Woman* (1946), *House of Flowers* (1954), and *Jamaica* (1957). They were white versions of the black experience, but they were nevertheless classy shows. Sammy Davis, Jr. played himself in *Mr. Wonderful* (1956). He was put into an amusing if trite backstage story, and given white costars to work with. His race wasn't a dramatic issue. In *Golden Boy* (1964), Davis's fame distracted from an intensely dramatic, jazz-scored story of a black boxer in love with a white woman (based on a play by Clifford Odets). The powerful *Purlie Victorious* and *Raisin in the Sun,* both written by black authors, were musicalized with some success. *Purlie*'s terrific score boosted it more than *Raisin*'s lackluster one. *Ain't Supposed to Die a Natural Death* (1971) and *Don't Play Us Cheap* (1972), both by Melvin Van Peebles, startled complacent white audiences with harsh, realistic descriptions of ghetto life. Spoken more than sung, the show's strong feelings expressed in ghetto language presaged the vogue for rap songs. *Dr. Jazz* (1975) started out as an honest book musical about the historical circumstances of whites usurping black jazz, but in a frantic attempt to save what the (white) producer thought was a flop, the creator and his concept were jettisoned. (That didn't help.) *Dreamgirls* (1980) transcribed the historically accurate problems of the black artist's attempts to break racial barriers and enter mainstream show business. *The Tap Dance Kid* (1983) suffered from increasing apathy toward the Broadway musical and an uneven production, its zippy dance numbers contrasting sharply with the serious eleven o'clock soliloquy. Yet the plot—the conflict between a child who wants to tap dance and a doctor father who wants his son to benefit from his own struggle—represents a serious problem for blacks, the exaggerated emphasis on sports and entertainment. A second stream of black musicals paralleled these—a line of shows far more controversial, if equally entertaining.

In 1898 on the roof garden of New York's Casino Theatre, E. E. Rice produced an afterpiece entitled "The Origin of the Cake Walk." It was the first show written and performed by blacks to play before a major white audience. The black book musical probably began with *A Trip to Coontown* that same year.

The 1920s and 1930s saw many black revues, like *Chocolate Dandies* and *Brown Buddies.* Editions of *Shuffle Along* were written by black songwriters Noble Sissle and Eubie Blake, but almost everything else was created by whites. In 1923, *Runnin' Wild* featured "The Charleston." Lew Leslie, a white producer with a background in vaudeville and nightclubs, produced *The Plantation Revue* in 1922, *Dixie to Broadway* in 1924, and *Blackbirds* in London in 1926. Two years later *Blackbirds* came to New York. It was a smash hit at 518 performances, the longest running black musical of the decade.

These black shows featured black talent—sometimes genuinely, sometimes with cruel caricature—for a white audience. The great tap dancer Bill "Bojangles" Robinson performed "Doin' the New Low Down" in *Blackbirds of 1928* and eventually—ignominiously, some would say—partnered Shirley Temple in Hollywood. Since the majority of these black shows were revues, they disappeared with the era.

In 1967, after a long run with Carol Channing, Ginger Rogers, Martha Raye, Betty Grable, and Dorothy Lamour, the all-white *Hello, Dolly!* was on its last legs when master showman David Merrick cast Pearl Bailey as Dolly Levi and, even more ingeniously, created the first all-black Broadway cast for a white musical since the black version of *The Mikado.* Bailey was as unique a performer as ever played legit theatre. She ad-libbed lines to the horse. She asked the audience if they wanted to see the title number all over again, then *did it* over again. She entered a scene as soon as her costume change was finished rather than waiting for her scripted entrance, and rapidly told the audience the plot of slow sections so they could "get on with it, honey, and see Pearl." Her run with the show coincided with enormous talent in all the other roles—exuberant Minnie Fays and Barnabys, honey-voiced Irenes, and dignified Corneliuses. The wild Cab

Calloway and the old black magic of Billy Daniels were her Vandergelders. And the show boasted an electric group of dancers.

The production sizzled, as if a lid kept on an entire community had burst open from the pressure. Talent shot out like lava from a volcano. And a new black audience that had seldom bothered with Broadway theatre—what did it have to say to them?—goosed the box office while white audiences rediscovered the show. *Hello Dolly!* was a hit all over again and launched a string of black musicals, including *The Wiz, Timbuckto* (a black version of *Kismet*), a black *Pal Joey,* and a black *Guys and Dolls.**

The revue format returned in a number of gospel celebrations led off by *Don't Bother Me I Can't Cope* and *Your Arms Too Short to Box With God. Bubbling Brown Sugar* (1976) began a second phase of resurrection for black revues, and audiences loved the various recreations of the Cotton Club era—*Eubie* (1978), *Ain't Misbehavin'* (1978), *Sophisticated Ladies* (1981), and *Black and Blue* (1989). Like the earliest revues, *Bubbling Brown Sugar* even had something of a story line, concerning a tour (the most popular excuse for a plot in the old days) of Harlem.

Broadway critic and historian Martin Gottfried refers to the all-black musical as a "sorry phenomenon" (and sums up *Porgy and Bess* as "inauthentic" and Hammerstein's *Carmen Jones* as a "racial gaffe"). This is a simplistic description of the genre. Perhaps Merrick's black *Dolly* wasn't a milestone in the nation's attempt to further integration or equality, but a return to the caricature of the black entertainer, with Aunt Jemima as Dolly Levi and twenty-four "Step 'n Fetchits" backing her up. On the other hand, *Dolly*'s characters are hardly authentic to begin with—they're musical comedy caricatures, and nobody performed them with more craft and talent than Pearl Bailey and black casts.

This slew of black musicals reached an ignominious peak in 1983 when the towering white Tommy Tune chose an all-black chorus for *My One and Only,* a very-revised version of the old George Gershwin musical *Funny Face.* Black male dancers were dressed in tuxedos and white gloves (they were lucky Tune didn't make them wear blackface and white lipstick), and they shuffled and bucked and winged their hearts out behind Tommy and Twiggy. This was a shabby use of the "Step 'n Fetchit" stereotype. Fortunately, in the same show the legendary black tap dancer Honi Coles got a duet with Tune.

*The Actor's Equity audition notice for the *all-black cast* of *Guys and Dolls* announced that "all calls will be conducted without regard to race, creed, color, or religion."

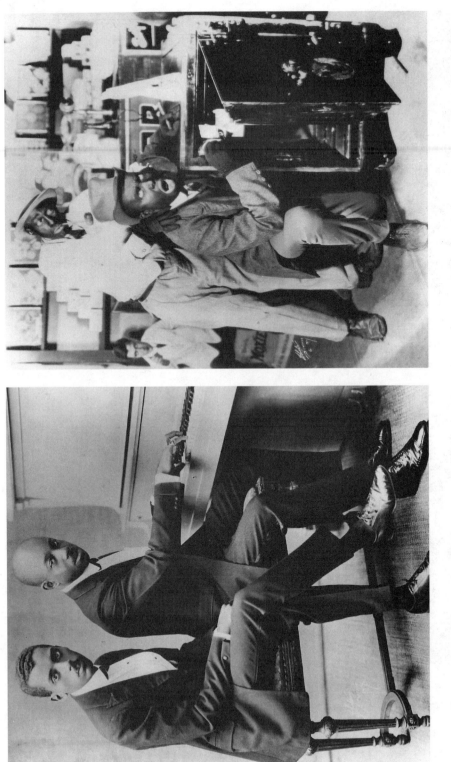

Eubie Blake and Noble Sissle, the writers of *Shuffle Along*
Museum of the City of New York

A sketch from *Shuffle Along*
Museum of the City of New York

Pearl Bailey put a distinctive stamp on the character Dolly Levi, and always lingered on the stairway with her radiant smile until applause redoubled
Museum of the City of New York

Dorothy and friends "ease on down" the yellow brick road
Photofest

The gawky, lead-footed Tune, dancing with all the grace of a flamingo taking off, got a lesson from the man once known as the black Fred Astaire, and audiences got to see great hoofing for one number in the second act.

As for the integration of white musicals, for some years every white musical had to have one black performer, often a maid (*Best Little Whorehouse in Texas*) or butler (*La Cage Aux Folles*) who could be relied on to stop the show with a second-act soul song or tap dance, or a few "black indignation" jokes.

These shows tread a dangerously thin line because their existence seems to affirm that the greatest talents of blacks lie in singing and tap dancing. They can be seen as exploitative, especially when white audiences stamp and clap and jive to black performers recreating an era of show business during which they could not be served in a restaurant or hotel near the theatre. Or they can be seen as celebratory, revealing a part of black history that was buried under the white rug.

The best of the genre is the musical that tells a story without stereotypes, and features both the talent and the true identity of its black characters. One of the earliest (and most obscure, since it never made Broadway) was a wonderful rhythm-and-blues version of *Othello* called *Catch My Soul.* In the Los Angeles of 1968, it preceded the acceptance of both black musicals and rock-and-roll musicals. The overwhelmingly white audience in the orchestra seats was confused, but the younger, black audience in the balcony was wildly enthusiastic. Jerry Lee Lewis (yes, "great balls of fire" Jerry Lee Lewis) played Iago to William Marshall's Othello, and both were brilliant. The huge Old Globe set and the overlapping styles of Haight-Ashbury and the Elizabethan era, the funky, crotchy music that drew on *Othello*'s raw themes of jealousy, racism, and erotica set the joint jumping. The producers never braved Broadway, but *Catch My Soul* ran in London for two years.

The breakthrough in theatre dance began with ethnic and character dance vocabularies. The use of the entire body in fluid movements, and especially the use of the pelvis, came from African dance brought here through the slave trade. The shift from European- to American-based musical idioms was due to black-based ragtime, minstrel-show music, rhythm and blues, and jazz. The second great stage of American music, rock and roll, was also based on black rhythm and blues, with a smidgen of spiritual music thrown in (as sung by black, not white, churches). The whole history of American music and dance is a history of white artists expropriating black art. A few more shows like *Porgy and Bess* and a few less like *My One and Only* won't redress that thievery, but it will go a small way toward paying for it.

Cheetah

PLAYBILL

the national magazine for theatregoers

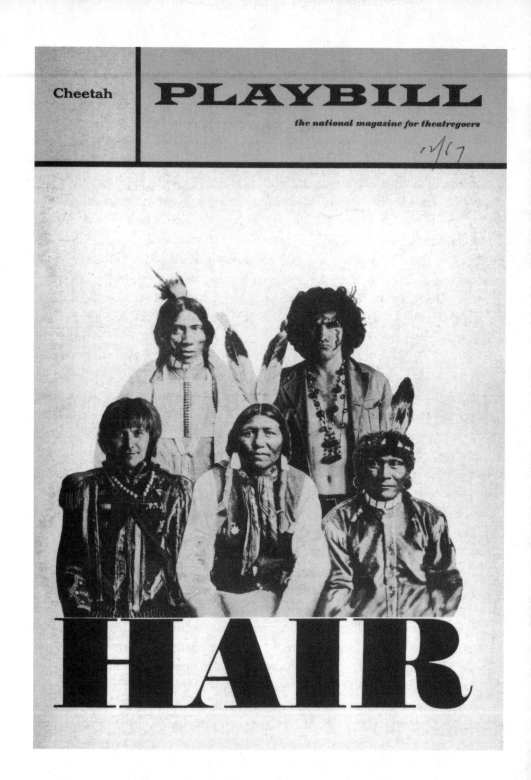

12/67

HAIR

Eighteen

The Rock Musical

Rock and roll began influencing popular music in the early 1950's, when black rhythm and blues first roiled white teenagers. An epic battle took place in the middle 1960's, when Dean Martin, tired of hearing the Beatles on his son's hi-fi said, "I'm gonna knock your little palies off the charts," then did so with his recording of "Everybody Loves Somebody Sometime." But if that week's battle was won, the war was lost, and popular American music would henceforth be divided into Before and After Chuck Berry. This pulled a once-substantial commercial rug out from under Broadway musicals. Theatre music was shortly consigned to the back bin of record shops. Nevertheless, the traditional score continued to dominate musicals for some time. When rock reared its noisy head, aged, conservative listeners clucked and slid deeper into red velvet seats. Although rock eventually made a place for itself on Broadway, the transition was not as quick as on the radio, and it took the turbulent sixties to breach the Great White Way.

Hello, Dolly! ran for seven years (1964–71), and was the last and best lighthearted musical with real impact. The Vietnam War was changing America, and in 1967 a nontraditional musical on that subject caused a sensation.

Followers of New York's avant-garde theatre scene were not surprised by *Hair.* It featured a truly contemporary score by Galt McDermott—wonderfully infectious melodies coupled not with theater lyrics but with tone poems of the hippie generation that bristled with originality. It was performed by a youthful, wildly talented, multiracial tribe of hippies. More than a few were bona fide would-be actors, but in the sixties the starving actor's lifestyle was not much different than that of the dropped-out generation.

Hair was not encumbered by staging in the traditional sense, but the show had a wonderful look to it. The cast sprawled about the stage throughout the show and executed numerous bits of shtick, a kind of in-your-face use of props that at once relied on and poked fun at traditional theatre. The loose-limbed gyrations that passed for choreography and a sprawling, messy, undisciplined use of the stage was in keeping with the obscure but heavily political anti-Vietnam plot. Nubile young men and women climbed off the stage to caress the audience, invited them to dance in the production, and took off their clothes in the last moments of the first act.

All this refreshing antitradition was the brainchild of Tom O'Horgan, who had developed his directorial style in the garrets and garages of the 1960s avant-garde theatre scene, which was shaped by the political hubbub caused by Vietnam, the social anarchy caused by the hippies, and the social consciousness encouraged by President John F. Kennedy.

The loose pamphlet that made up *Hair*'s libretto was ideally suited to O'Horgan's production, but unfortunately not for other shows. O'Horgan failed to realize that his directorial approach was really a *style,* and he did not express the content of other musicals well at all. Notwithstanding the concept musicals still to come, concepts are only attractive if they suit the drama. Subsequent O'Horgan-directed productions fared worse and worse.

Unfortunately for producers, the rock score that propelled *Hair*—the Fifth Dimension had a radio hit with the "Age of Aquarius" anthem—was not easy to duplicate. Singing self-contained pop songs with hand microphones isn't compatible with most scripted drama. And

Hair here, there, and everywhere
Museum of the City of New York

Mary Magdalene washes the feet of a rocking Jesus Christ
Photofest/Friedman-Abeles

pop rock music is only appropriate to certain settings. The attempt to couple it with a biblical story (*Jesus Christ Superstar*) or historical biography (*Evita*), for instance, creates a dichotomy that puts the drama in the back seat and makes the production more of a rock concert than theatre. When rock scores are hitched to nonrock milieux, the musical lumbers like a bicycle with mismatched wheels and the score falls between two idioms. Although rock's enormous influence affects all kinds of music and theatre, the true rock musical can only succeed if the *book* demands rock and roll.

Sometimes it does. *Grease* virtually required it. *Two Gentlemen of Verona* benefited from an infectious Galt McDermott score grafted onto John Guare's adaptation without transporting the period, and the show had a reasonable run. The creators simply said "the Elizabethans rocked" and got away with it. Off-Broadway's *Your Own Thing* was based on Shakespeare transposed to a brother/sister rock act lost in Manhattan, and it charmed its way into the hearts of large audiences and most critics. *Dreamgirls* was set in Motown.

But the ultimate pop score was written by popmeisters Burt Bacharach and Hal David. *Promises, Promises* took place in the present (1968), and thus the score was dramatically sound. It also reflected very well the frenetic pace of New York business, since Bacharach's principal stylistic mark was the quick change of meter (in one song alone he used 4/4, 3/4, 3/8, and 6/4 time signatures). *Promises*—tightly directed and choreographed by Robert Moore and Michael Bennett—may have been the last of the really slick musical comedy entertainments. It had great tunes, comic turns, an adultery plot featuring an age-old moral dilemma, and even brought on the girls when necessary, all within the modern musical framework. Call it high-tech Princess theatre.

But where *Promises* really broke ground—beyond the subtle Bennett staging that no one understood until years later—was in its sound system. Earl Carroll's infamous *Vanities* aside, voices in the theatre were originally heard hot off the vocal cords. You had to be quiet—no talking, like in front of the television—and the actors had to project their voices. The sound was real, and filled the great Broadway theatres. The music that floated up from the open pit was arranged specifically with this in mind. Orchestrators didn't double voice lines with horns, for example, and electronic musical instruments weren't yet in use. The musical director, not the sound engineer, balanced all the sounds, and voices that were too small moved to Hollywood. (Now you understand Ethel Merman's fame.) Since the lower registers of the male voice carried less, great baritones like Alfred Drake and John Raitt were much in demand.

When microphones came into general use they were laid along the footlights to pick up and enhance the voices. When smaller voices came along—Barbra Streisand in *Funny Girl*—they got personal microphones hidden in their costumes. (In Philadelphia Streisand picked up and broadcast local police calls until the system was ironed out.) In the latest episode of this transition, Michael Crawford conceals a microphone near his lips in his *Phantom of the Opera* mask, and the singers of *Smokey Joe's Cafe* (1995) and *Rent* (1996) wear headset microphones that put the transceiver in front of their lips, making them all look like telephone operators.

The 1968 production of *Promises* added a whole sound system. Burt Bacharach, who had come to Broadway on the heels of a number of gold records, brought the recording studio with him and installed it in the Shubert Theatre. He put back-up singers in the pit as if they were instruments, alleviating all that huffing and puffing dancers had been doing for generations when they had to swing into a vocal coda after a strenuous dance. He miked the onstage actors *and* the musicians and fed it all to the audience through speakers. On the way, the sound was mixed, balanced, and spiked by a sound engineer.

Let's stay away from the argument of whether Bacharach aided or harmed Broadway. Certainly he made the rock musical more palatable. Broadway audiences would never go for the volume of a rock concert, and they got their rock-and-roll muted. Ethal Merman herself couldn't be expected to compete with electric guitars and synthesizers. And microphones allowed fine actors whose singing couldn't be heard outside of their showers to perform major roles—Michael Crawford in *Phantom of the Opera,* Glenn Close in *Sunset Boulevard.* Sound amplification also encourages singers who *shouldn't* be heard outside of their showers—Anthony Quinn in a revival of *Zorba*, Tyne Daly in *Gypsy.*

Results vary wildly—a bad sound system makes you long for the old days, while a good one is hardly noticeable. The musical isn't as live as it once was, but audiences wouldn't stand for the old-fashioned way, so all musicals (and many plays) must have a sound system.

The introduction of electronic media makes possible a further technological intrusion into the suspense of live theatre. Some prerecording of voices takes place, so that in *The Act* for example, Liza Minnelli could sing and dance without wheezing, and Julie Andrews in *Victor, Victoria* could appear to hit high notes effortlessly eight times a week.

Lyricist Hal David combined with Michel LeGrand to write the execrable *Brainchild*, then beat a wise retreat from the Great White Way, but *Promises* was Bacharach's only Broadway score. Bacharach brought about the single most sudden and enormous change in the history of musical theatre, then returned to Hollywood.

Sam S.
Shubert
Theatre
PLAYBILL
a weekly magazine for theatregoers
STOP THE WORLD—
I WANT TO GET OFF

the weekly magazine for theatregoers
OLIVER!

Nineteen

THE ENGLISH MUSICAL

The English simply do not know how to do musicals. At least, that was the wisdom during Broadway's golden age, and there was some truth to the xenophobic statement. The principal difference between English and American musicals is in the choreography. The English never developed theatre dance, so their musicals are still laden with an ersatz combination of ballet, tap, and jazz. No English musical has ever developed a physical identity through its choreography, the way a Michael Kidd or Bob Fosse show did. Nor have any English musicals made use of content-based dance sequences, as Agnes de Mille, Jerome Robbins, and Michael Bennett did. English musicals also lacked the efficient staging that evolved through American choreographer-directors. English composers lacked the jazz influence that began in America with Irving Berlin, Jerome Kern, and George Gershwin and infused the Broadway score with a unique sound. Jazz is an American idiom, as is the musical itself. English musicals just don't *swing*.

Nevertheless, America was influenced by the European operetta via London. The Princess shows were inspired by the comic operas of Gilbert and Sullivan and the drawing-room musical comedy style of the George Edwardes shows—by the turn of the century the English musical stage was humming along.

The Black Crook went to London in 1872, six years after its American debut, but it was billed there as *opéra bouffe.* Twelve years later a "musical comedy drama" called *My Sweetheart* was imported from Broadway, where it had been a play with a few song specialties for the stars. More songs were added in London, and the show was more successful. In 1887 the West End mounted its first British musical, *Jack in the Box,* which had a successful run. It was variously labeled as a "musical comedy" and a "musical drama" in an attempt to leave no audience uninvited.

The West End also featured burlesque—not the American girlie shows, but rather a mix of songs and sketches, lavish costumes, an incoherent plot (if any), and broadly comic acting. The principal feature of these shows was a largely male audience that would come and go at will, eat, or even have sex, since the theatre was the Victorians' point of entry to illicit sexual liaisons. These entertainments were downscale compared to the Gilbert and Sullivan shows and the operettas imported from Europe, which reigned supreme on the West End.

Arthur Roberts was a short, wildly comedic entertainer with expressive hands and a funny walk due to a childhood illness. He toured music halls and pubs until he starred for George Edwardes in a musical at the Gaiety Theatre called *In Town* (apparently without ever bothering to read the script). When it became a hit, Roberts became England's first song-and-dance man—carefree, elegant, casual, P. G. Wodehouse's man-about-town. He set the pattern for the elegant leading role subsequently taken to great heights by England's Jack Buchanan and America's Fred Astaire. In photographs, the top-hatted, spats-wearing, cane-carrying entertainer is posed with the same cocky assurance as George M. Cohan.

Producer Edwardes, not knowing whether the show's success was due to Roberts or the format, covered his bets. He spent the next season at the Gaiety on comic operas and burlesques, but at the Prince of Wales Theatre he continued to experiment with the musical comedy format, producing *A Gaiety Girl* in 1893. This show had a stronger plot, an art-imitates-life story about chorus girls breaking into high society (some from the Gaiety actually had). It features a chorus girl who won't marry a guardsman, is accused of stealing (framed by a high-class lady), clears herself, and in due course falls into his arms. Act one takes place at a garden party, and act two on the French Riviera. *A Gaiety Girl* was a clear hit, assuring producers that "musical comedy," and not Arthur Roberts, was enough for audiences.

It toured America a year later, and was followed on the West End by *A Runaway Girl, A Country Girl, The Shop Girl, The Casino Girl, The Pearl Girl, The Quaker Girl, The Girl Behind the Counter, The Cherry Girl, The Girl Friend, The Girl from Kay's, The Girl from Utah, The Girl in the Taxi, The Girl on the Film,* and *The Girls of Gottenberg,* not to mention a number of belles, maids, and princesses. All featured cheery songs and plots of romantic misunderstanding and entanglement, suitably sorted out by the finale. Between 1894 and 1914 the "Gaiety girls" were to London what the Ziegfeld girls became to Broadway, and they surely influenced Guy Bolton, P. G. Wodehouse, and Jerome Kern in the creation of the Princess musicals. Eventually Edwardes was running three theatres and had at least two rivals producing the same format.

Just as in America, musical comedies ran on the West End side by side with lavish imported operettas, Anglicized by local comedians and composers. When World War II swept European shows off the boards, local actor-manager-author Oscar Asche created a show in the European operetta mode. *Chu Chin Chow* (1916) was based loosely on the *Arabian Nights* tales. It featured exotic settings, romantic melodies, and a romantic plot, and it was the first smash hit of the modern English musical stage, partially due to a tremendous advertising campaign on posters the likes of which London had never seen (and wouldn't again until Cameron Macintosh). *Chu Chin Chow* ran for 2,238 performances, longer than World War I.

The witty Noël Coward added to the musical stage's sense of pride with *Bitter Sweet* (1929), an operetta not influenced by Broadway in spite of Coward's transatlantic style and success. It was integrated and romantic, featured several great songs including "I'll See You Again," and ran for over 750 performances. In between *Chow* and *Bitter Sweet,* Gertrude Lawrence came across to star in *Oh, Kay!* (1926) and became the first English star to visit Broadway. In 1930 *Evergreen* was the first English musical built on a revolving stage, with a score by Americans Rodgers and Hart.

But the West End musical stage was subdued by two world wars and

Broadway imports and didn't keep up with advancing techniques in musical comedy. Between 1920 and 1980, Broadway held a virtual monopoly on the musical theatre. Critics and chroniclers of the West End admitted that English musicals had little history and no future.

With the arrival of the American production of *Oklahoma!* in 1947, according to English critic Sheridan Morley, "British producers and composers alike went into a state of prolonged and understandable shock, from which they only really began to emerge in the 1970s with the advent of Tim Rice and Andrew Lloyd Webber." Cast albums were not yet a big item, and travel was curtailed by cost and the war. Developments on America's musical stage came as something of a surprise and a shock to the English. When *Oklahoma!* opened at London's Drury Lane Theatre, it staggered unsuspecting audiences, critics, and theatregoers, and launched a British love affair with American musicals that swamped their local attempts. By the 1950s England's best theatre critic Kenneth Tynan was lambasting the West End musical technique. After the collapse of Noel Coward's *Cavalcade* (1931)—an operetta following *Bitter Sweet* which was beset by production problems and lost an unprecedented amount of money—and a poor production of his *After the Ball* (1955), Coward resolved to open his musicals on Broadway instead. Nevertheless, in between the *Gaiety Girl* era and the days of Andrew Lloyd Webber, a handful of unique English musicals did succeed.

The Boy Friend (1953) was a miniature period piece, a valentine to the *Gaiety Girl* musicals—not a lampoon, but a lovingly recreated spoof. It ran for over 2,000 performances and went to Broadway, where it played an affectionate season and introduced Julie Andrews to New York. Audiences who had seen the real thing forty years before were enthralled with this accurate and fresh production, and new audiences could experience its historical charm.

Salad Days (1953) was a musical about a tramp with a magic piano whose tunes made people dance. This was an odd show that baffled Americans and failed off-Broadway when it came over, but it ran even longer than *The Boy Friend,* and was in fact the West End's longest running musical during the 1950s.

Oliver (1960) suggested by the Charles Dickens novel, was the first really great British musical since *Bitter Sweet.* It grew out of a collaboration between director Peter Coe, designer Sean Kenny, and writer Lionel Bart while they were working on *Lock Up Your Daughters* (1959), a Mermaid Theatre adaptation of a Henry Fielding novel. England made the best Dickens films, and their theatre still bears the marks of the great Elizabethan dramas, which dealt with stories of great size and scope. Lionel Bart wrote a beautiful score, including the comic "You've Got To Pick a Pocket or Two"; the sublime "As Long As He Needs Me"; the hysterically funny, character-driven "Reviewing the Situation"; and the plaintive "Where Is Love?" It's a sort of classic comic version of the large novel, compacted intelligently, and its heart was evident in abundance. And America got to see some very impressive English acting. Clive Revell's Fagin was a towering comic achievement (and Ron Moody's West End original had been the performance of a lifetime), and Georgia Brown's Nancy was abetted by a big, rich voice.

But *Oliver*'s greatest significance to America was its set. Sean Kenny placed most of Victorian London on two enormous side-by-side revolves, scaffolded with wood. There was no dancing or even real musical comedy staging, but the dual turntables revolved to create place after place. The actors clamored around the set as they traveled from scene to scene, the concept of staging was newly defined, and Hammerstein's concept of continuous action was fully realized without a choreographer. *Oliver* boasted the first set to be applauded not just for its beauty but for its moves. And it rang the death knell for the stop-and-go musical, with its awkward "in one" transitions and slow scene changes. Subsequently this use of set would come to replace sound musical staging, and even good writing, in a new breed of spectacle musical (more about this later), but for *Oliver* the contribution *supported* the drama without becoming it.

Oliver also demonstrated the power of atmospheric music to Broadway. The second act opening, "Om Pah Pah," may be one of the show's lesser songs, but the smokey dive in which we first meet the villainous Bill Sykes was brought to wonderful musical life. It demonstrated how to take the comic character—once a staple of twenties and thirties Broadway musicals—and reinsert him successfully into a strong book musical. It urged Broadway designers to engineer their sets as well as paint them. It even gave an entrance to the leading lady at the top of a flight of stage-center stairs long before *Hello Dolly!*'s famous entrance, and made heart-tugging use of orphans without sacrificing sophistication. *Oliver* went on to become England's beloved chestnut, performed in every children's school, regularly revived, and representing the West End musical around the world.

Anthony Newley as a little chap

Photofest

Stop the World I Want to Get Off (1962) was written by Leslie Bricusse and Anthony Newley, and starred Newley. The score had an original sound of its own, and the melodies were taut and catchy. The ballad, "What Kind of Fool Am I?" became an international hit and one of the most recorded songs of all time. A little chap in clown whiteface represented everyman, and a Sean Kenny circus set was his world. A single actress played all the women in his life, an oboe stood in for his father-in-law, and the brisk, funny story of the self-centered schlemiel enchanted audiences. Not since the failure of *Allegro* fifteen years earlier had the theatre attempted such metaphor and theatrical devices. This presentational, symbolic musical did the job far more efficiently. Indeed, it was the life-cycle musical Oscar Hammerstein had envisioned.

It was followed by a nearly identical and even better sequel, *The Roar of the Greasepaint, The Smell of the Crowd,* which starred Norman Wisdom in England. The show flopped in the provinces and never arrived on the West End. David Merrick, who had presciently brought *Stop the World* to New York, brought the sequel over anyway. Merrick's production was helped by a rewrite and by Tony Bennett's recording of "Who Can I Turn To." Anthony Newley again starred as the underdog; Cyril Ritchard was brilliantly cast as the foppish Sir, representing the arrogant upper class; and the show succeeded on Broadway. Young black American singer Gilbert Price stopped the second act with a powerful song about "Feeling Good." Both musicals survived the transatlantic crossing because of the bravado of their nonrepresentational style and the success of their popular scores, but they owe most of their success to Newley's incandescent and original stage demeanor. He was a true star in the skin-tight role of a hapless little cockney desperately making his way through life, and one of the few (and last) male stars to grace Broadway in an original musical. As with Newley's equals Zero Mostel and Robert Morse, whose theatre-filling personae translated badly to film and television, only a precious few shows capitalized on this. Newley had to write his own material. Sadly, later generations of audiences could not understand what all the excitement was about, particularly when Sammy Davis, Jr. appeared in a miserably designed and directed revival of *Stop the World* in 1978.

Oh What a Lovely War (1963) was a savage antiwar satire and an attack on the officer class. Critic Sheridan Morley calls it the "most haunting evening in the musical theatre" he had ever seen. It was a product of Joan

Oliver. Neither the first nor the last use of orphans to tug at an audience's heartstrings
Photofest

The double turntables of Sean Kenny's *Oliver* set
Photofest/Alec Murray

Littlewood's off-West End, off-Stratford, avant-garde theatre, consisting of sketches and period songs, and it never traveled to America. Neither did . . .

Charlie Girl (1965) was crucified by the critics but subsequently ran for 2,202 performances, indicating that a gap between popular taste and critical opinion was always available to be exploited.

The Rocky Horror Show (1973) by Richard O'Brien was England's great rock musical, a burlesque of the *Frankenstein* story featuring a floor-shaking score and a transcendent, transsexual musical performance by Tim Curry. The faithful film version became perhaps the most successful cult movie of all time.

Many of these shows were unique fads like the American *Hair* and *Grease,* and with the exception of *Oliver* they have little to do with the ongoing state of the musical theatre, English or American. But in those years the English gave us Rex Harrison, Julie Andrews, and Stanley Holloway for *My Fair Lady,* without which that show would never have been the success it was. They gave us George Rose and Norman Wisdom for *Walking Happy,* P. G. Wodehouse for the Princess musicals, comedienne Bea Lillie (*High Spirits*), the iridescent Gertrude Lawrence (*Lady in the Dark, The King and I*), and the witty Noël Coward (*The Girl Who Came To Supper*). What they have given us lately is another story, and certainly not one for a golden age.

The

PLAYBILL®

for the Alvin Theatre

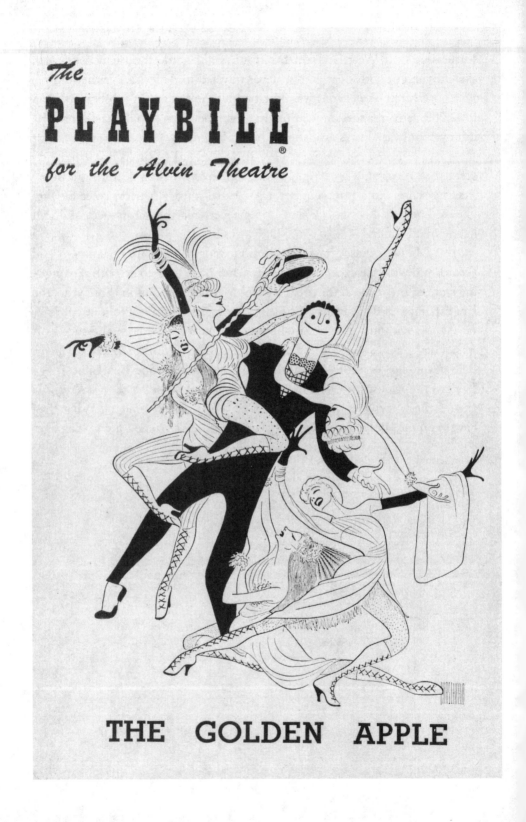

THE GOLDEN APPLE

Twenty

The Off-Broadway Musical

The American musical was in full swing before off-Broadway developed a rich and varied theatre. In the 1950s it was serious and dramatic, centering on José Quintero's direction of Eugene O'Neill revivals. The 1960s brought experimentation, in theatres like La Mama, with its political, avant-garde productions. The spectacle, dance, and orchestra that are so much a part of the Broadway musical are untenable in the small theatres and reduced budgets of off-Broadway, and very little has ever been done there that impacts on musicals. There are some extraordinary exceptions, however.

The New York Shakespeare Festival produced the original production of *Hair.* It had a jumbled book portraying the politics of the hippies and Vietnam, and it didn't have a score when James Rado and Jerome Ragni brought it to Joseph Papp. A youthful, talented cast and the infectious sixties pop music of Galt McDermott were added, and an unusual musical began to develop under the direction of Gerald Freedman.

But Freedman was a traditional and unimaginative director, and the production ran its course with little fanfare at the Public Theatre. Then a wealthy playboy with no theatrical experience saw the show and decided to reproduce it (angels rush in). He hired La Mama's most notable and radical director, Tom O'Horgan, and mounted it at the Cheetah nightclub on New York's West Side. There its reputation began to grow, but conservative Broadway producers and theatre owners remained uninterested. The producer, Michael Butler, raised additional money from rich friends and moved the show to Broadway's Brooks Atkinson Theatre, where it opened in 1968. Shortly after its brief nude scene was publicized in *Life* Magazine, the show caught on, and the rest is history. It ran for 1,750 performances and played successfully in cities throughout the world.

Hair was an unstructured, nontraditional musical that made a radical attack on the entrenched political and social institutions of the time, and as such it could never have been developed on Broadway. Its eventual success there was not based on its content or form, but on its value as a tourist attraction. It was the safest and most sanitized way to participate in the hippie phenomenon.

Hair caught the crest of a powerful grass-roots movement in the country, and crystallized in dramatic form the anger building over everything from the government's pursuit of an illegal and immoral war to the rigid social codes of the time. Moreover, it helped to *explain* that movement to the middle class. *Hair* made a good deal of the "peace and love" movement accessible to the "silent majority," many of whom were neither antagonistic to long hair and flamboyant dress nor supportive of the military-industrial complex that pursued a war the nation could not win. They simply didn't understand the other side. *Hair* explained it to them, and in its own small way aided the country in arresting the war machine. If the excesses of the hippies remained on the fringes (free love, orgies, drugs, eccentric dress), their ideas—a relaxation of the rigid social mores of the 1950s, a shifting of priorities from materialist to spiritual values—were annexed by mainstream culture and eventually found their way into the heart of America. *Hair* played a small part in achieving that change. Criticism of society's entrenched institutions, from the stage, hadn't been so severe since Aristophanes. *Hair* may be the most potent and successful use of drama as politics in musical theatre history.

The Broadway musical benefited as well. Contemporary music

began to influence theatre music. The nonstar ensemble musical flexed its muscles, later to be canonized by *Grease, A Chorus Line, Annie,* and *Cats.* Using the less expensive off-Broadway milieu to test the waters for an unusual show proved convenient. Thus *Hair* paved the way for another contemporary, ensemble, experimental musical fearful of opening directly on an increasingly conservative and expensive Broadway—*A Chorus Line.*

Most significant of all was the merchandising of *Hair.* Until 1968, hit Broadway musicals toured the country with one or two companies. They played the largest cities—San Francisco, Los Angeles, Chicago, Boston—for two months and the medium-sized cities for shorter runs. Then the bus-and-truck company was formed for one-night and split-week stands in the smallest towns of America. The *Hair* producers invented a new and more useful system. Local "tribes" were formed and productions of *Hair* were installed in theatres in a dozen American cities, there to run for up to a year. This not only reduced costs (transportation of equipment and per diem payments for actors), it generated larger attendance as local audiences discovered the show and told others about it. Profits for the big musicals have increased greatly from all the major cities with the advent of the sit-down companies that *Hair* promulgated.

The authentic off-Broadway musical, however, is a musical which couldn't, and shouldn't, be done in a larger theatre. Off-Broadway musicals at their best are utterly charming right where they are. *The Fantasticks* is the grandfather of them all. It opened in May of 1960 and is still running after all these years. This was the first musical written by Tom Jones and Harvey Schmidt, a clever adaptation of Edmond Rostand's *Les Romantiques.* It was an extraordinarily simple production perfectly in line with the slight fantasy, and it had a splendid romantic score that benefited from being played on piano and harp only. Its staging was very clever, highly theatrical, and inexpensively designed (proving necessity as the mother of invention), and has not been duplicated since.

The Fantasticks begot several other charmers, all of which did a service to the musical by providing great seats and low ticket prices and emphasizing the quality of the story and writing over production values (something the Broadway theatre of today should look at). *Your Own Thing* (1968) used rock music, albeit in an already dated bubble-gum style, to deliver Shakespeare's *Twelfth Night.* It was as slick as an off-Broadway musical can be, primarily because Michael Bennett silently helped out. *Dames At Sea*

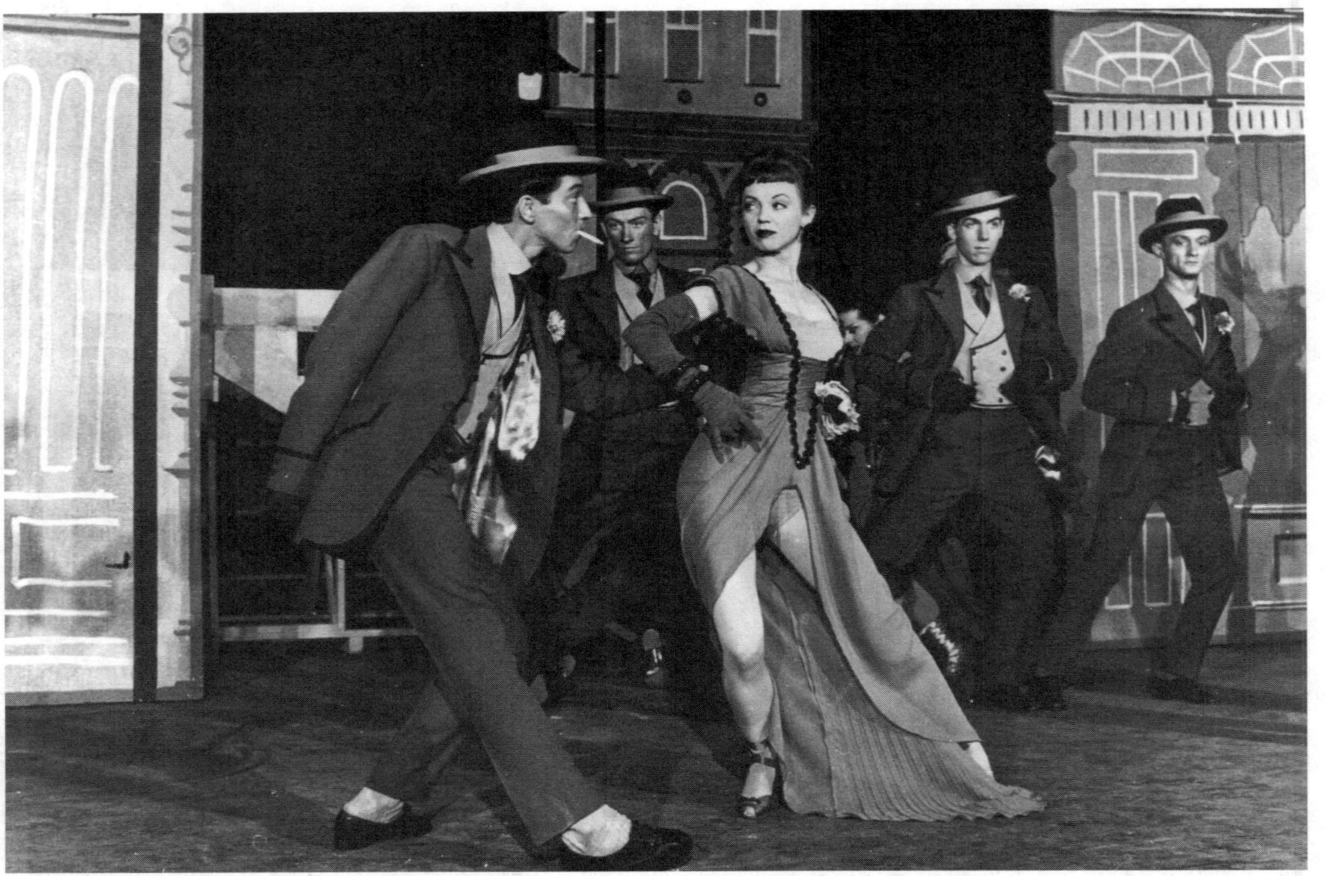

The opera ballet *The Golden Apple*
Museum of the City of New York/Fred Fehl

(1968) made a virtue of Bernadette Peters's cupie-pie lisp and delivered her to Broadway, and it spoofed early Hollywood film musicals. In fact, off-Broadway tends to carry spoofs better than uptown, since the big Broadway musical tends to crush lighthearted and casual attitudes.

You're a Good Man, Charlie Brown (1967) brought the *Peanuts* cartoon to life in good theatre for audiences young and old (that most valuable of all commodities). It was simple without being simplistic, tuneful but not complex; the utterly charming *Charlie Brown* should replace every awful children's theatre production of *Hansel and Gretel. Jacques Brel is Alive and Well and Living in Paris* (1968), the title now shortened because Jacques isn't, plunged audiences into an alien world with a combination of the unfamiliar French story-song (talk about dramatic possibilities in music) and New York's East Village basement cabaret scene. *Niteclub Confidential* (1985) played well in a cabaret, delivering the nonrock side of fifties music in a spoof of hard-boiled attitudes. The producers of *Little Shop of Horrors* (1982), which began off-off-Broadway, chose to move it off-Broadway and no further. They were aware that it was a slight spoof that benefited from a lively production whose raw exuberance might be lost in a larger theatre. It probably could have succeeded in a small Broadway theatre such as the Booth, the Plymouth, the Golden, or the Royale, as *Grease* had, but why take the chance in an increasingly expensive climate?

The most significant musical off-Broadway ever produced is its least known: *The Golden Apple* (1954). It's all song and dance, and its elegant and wonderful score (Streisand recorded "Lazy Afternoon") winds through Homer's *Iliad* and *Odyssey* in an American setting circa 1900. John Latouche wrote the libretto and Jerome Moross the music; their work far predated the sing-through musicals that got underway with *Jesus Christ Superstar.* It was a wholly Broadway score, but its sophisticated use of music took what Jerome Kern and George Gershwin had been doing and effectively returned it to musical comedy. The show moved uptown to the Alvin Theatre, but in spite of outstanding reviews (the critics were far easier on it than on *Show Boat* and *Porgy and Bess*), it ran only 125 performances. Too esoteric for the mob.

Today off-Broadway features fewer experimental plays and musicals and more of the safer, if equally important, productions intended to be commercial but unready and unwilling to face high expenses and Broadway's antipathy to serious drama, new faces, and unique concepts.

Anta Washington Square

PLAYBILL

the magazine for theatregoers

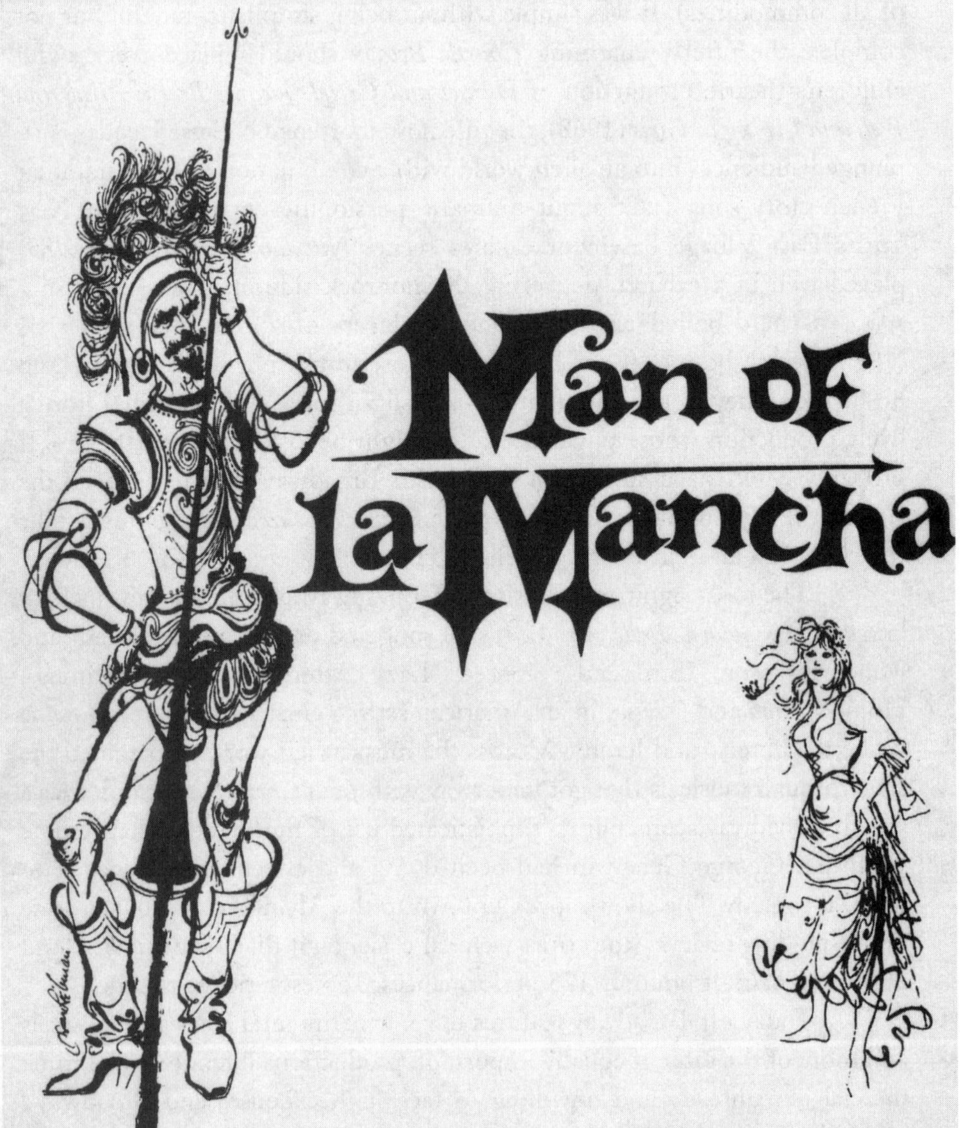

Twenty-One

Classics, Major and Minor

Not all productions redefined the form of the American musical. Some deserve mention as superbly crafted, mainstream entertainment, others for their unique if eccentric contributions.

Question: What American musical adaptation took on a great classic play (breaking a good rule—if it's not broken, don't fix it), featured a leading hero who could not sing, was written by American writers and staged by an American director handling subject matter that was quintessentially English, and didn't bother to include a romance? In short, which musical did just about everything wrong its creators could think of? You've probably got it by now—*My Fair Lady* (1956), one of the greatest works of art ever assembled for the Broadway musical stage, and at 2,717 performances one of the most popular.

My Fair Lady may be the most interesting musical ever produced on Broadway. A musical had never been built on a play like *Pygmalion.* It was

Shavian and polemic, and language was its strongest value. There seemed no place for songs or dances, and the ending was unsatisfying too. But sometimes the rules don't apply, or perhaps it depends on how you apply them.

Alan Jay Lerner was born in New York in 1918 to a wealthy family. He was educated in England, then at Choate and Harvard, where he contributed to two Hasty Pudding shows. Frederick "Fritz" Loewe was born in Berlin in 1904, the son of Edmund Loewe, a successful tenor who played *The Merry Widow*'s Prince Danilo in Berlin and on the first American tour. Loewe was something of a child prodigy on the piano, and he had an excellent European musical education. Both young and struggling, artistically if not financially (Irving Berlin notwithstanding, the vast majority of composers and lyricists of the golden age came from the upper classes), Lerner and Loewe met at the Lamb's Club and decided to do a rewrite of Loewe's musical *Great Lady,* which had had a twenty-performance run in 1938. It was revived in Detroit in 1942 as *Life of the Party,* which ran only nine weeks. (Lerner was wont to say, "If you went away for the weekend, you missed it.") Their next work, *What's Up?,* ran ninety-three performances in New York in 1943, and in 1945 *The Day Before Spring* ran 167 performances. *Spring* was not a success, but a $250,000 film sale to MGM Studios stabilized the team. (This was not by any means the last time Lerner's charm and upper-class connections helped him get money for his theatrical enterprises.) Then, three years after *Oklahoma!* had begun the golden age, Lerner and Loewe wrote the utterly charming *Brigadoon* (1947).

Everybody turned it down. Producer Cheryl Crawford picked it up, raised $175,000 at fifty-eight backer's auditions, and opened it to good reviews and excellent business. Loewe's growing skill is evident in the writing—in *The New York Times,* Brooks Atkinson wrote, "It is impossible to say where the music and dancing leave off and the story begins." Whereupon the team split up.

Lerner wrote *Love Life* (1948) with Kurt Weill. There is no original cast album due to a musician's union strike at the time, and it is by no means Lerner's best show, but it is his most unusual, following a married couple through 150 years in many different theatrical styles.

Lerner then joined the Arthur Freed unit at MGM, where he wrote the screenplay and lyrics for *Royal Wedding* (1951, music by Burton Lane). This show invented Fred Astaire's famous wall-and-ceiling dance, and includes the song with the longest title ever: "How Could You Believe Me

When I Said I Loved You When You Know I've Been a Liar All My Life." Then Lerner wrote the screenplay for *An American in Paris* (1951) around the Gershwin catalogue, for which he won an Academy Award. Lerner and Loewe eventually settled their differences and reteamed. In 1951 they wrote *Paint Your Wagon* for Broadway, a western musical with a sound score but a slight book and muddled structure.

In the meantime, an eccentric Romanian by the name of Gabriel Pascal secured, against all odds, the film rights to some George Bernard Shaw plays and asked Lerner—who was just finishing the film version of *Brigadoon*—to turn Shaw's *Pygmalion* into a stage musical. Lerner wasn't the first to be approached. Richard Rodgers and Oscar Hammerstein, Howard Dietz and Arthur Schwartz, Yip Harburg and Fred Saidy, Cole Porter, and Frank Loesser had all considered it and decided it couldn't be a musical. Lerner asked composer Harry Warren to work with him, but he shortly abandoned the idea. Some years later Lerner returned to the story of the professor who believes he can improve a cockney flower girl's life by improving her language, but he found that Pascal had died and legal rights to Shaw's play were in confusion. By this time Lerner had reconciled with Loewe, and the team went ahead without permission, a decision even more misguided than the original idea itself.

Eventually Lerner got the bank that controlled Shaw's estate to admit it couldn't make an artistic decision, and the court was petitioned to hire a literary agent as executor. Lerner and Loewe then promptly signed with that same agent, and he awarded them the rights over MGM. A New York judge found this entirely satisfactory.

While Lerner insists that Rex Harrison was the first choice to play Henry Higgins—he had played the role in London while Leslie Howard had played it in the film—many others remember that Noël Coward, John Gielgud, Michael Redgrave, and George Sanders were considered. Harrison said he couldn't sing, but the team, including director Moss Hart and producer Herman Levin, visited Harrison in London. Lerner's third wife found Harrison "opinionated, judgmental, very male and arrogant"—in other words, ideal for the character of Henry Higgins.

Indeed, Lerner and Loewe found that Harrison could not sustain a single note. They wrote the score accordingly, bringing the German *Sprechtgesang* (talk singing) to Broadway. Until then, patter songs, including those from the great Gilbert and Sullivan, had been without much melody.

But Loewe was a melodist (one of the finest ever) from the Viennese romantic school, and the songs that he and Lerner wrote for Higgins were musical as well as literate, combining the best of patter and melody.

The team hired twenty-year-old unknown Julie Andrews—marking the first time Liza would be played by an actress of the correct age—whom they had seen in the Broadway production of the English musical *The Boy Friend.* Lerner and Loewe extended the play's locations (to Ascot) and added the happy ending from the film (in the original play Liza doesn't return to Higgins at the final curtain). More importantly, they wrote some of the most effective character- and plot-oriented songs the American musical had ever heard. The budget for *My Fair Lady* was $400,000, the largest to date, and it was the first time a single investor had put up the entire amount—Columbia Records, in exchange for cast album rights.

Andrews had little real experience in professional productions, and hardly any as an actress. Eliza Doolittle is a difficult role that requires an actress who can play the cockney and the lady, sing, and hold her own against a luminous star. After a week or two of rehearsals, everyone wanted to replace her, and one Friday afternoon Rex Harrison loudly insisted that she be fired or he would not return the following Monday. Moss Hart spent the weekend alone with her in the theatre, and in one of the legendary makeovers of directing history, he coached, coaxed, gave her line readings, and explained her part beat by beat. On Monday she had it, and was on her way to brilliance.

In spite of an overlong first act (two songs and a ballet were eventually cut) and technical problems (the stagehands had to push double turntables around when they broke down), *My Fair Lady* did very well on opening night in New Haven. After a week it moved to Philadelphia for a month, by which time the box office advance was substantial and the anticipation enormous.

My Fair Lady opened on Broadway on March 15, 1956, was a smash hit, and subsequently ran for seven years. It crowned Harrison's career and made a star of Andrews. The cast album became the bestselling Columbia album of *any* kind to date (indicating how popular show music was in the mid-fifties), and the best-selling cast album of all time. The musical paved the way for plots revolving on something other than boy-girl romance.

Lerner had worried that he was out of touch with contemporary life.

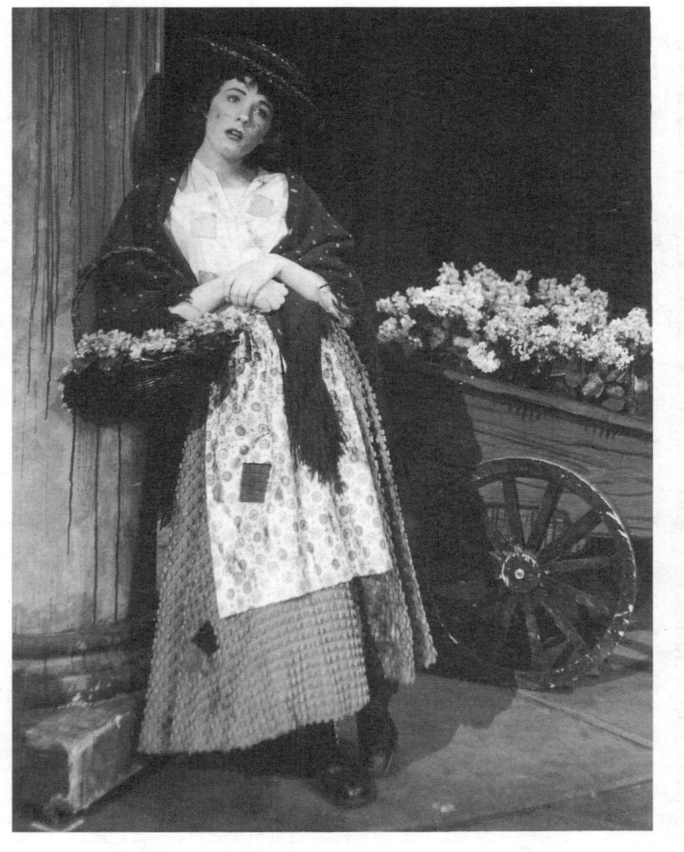

An Englishman and an Englishwoman give the crowning performances of the 1950s American musical play

Photofest

Photofest

He probably was. The era of rock-and-roll and television was beginning, and Lerner had grown up in a more romantic past, with an English education (Choate was modeled on Eton.) *My Fair Lady* has an old-school charm and brings the Viennese operetta style to a modern musical, reflecting Lerner and Loewe's background. Its originality comes from its partial talk-song score and a plot that, probably for the first time in a Broadway musical, does not feature an overt love story. Its utter tastefulness, from the direction to the designs (Cecil Beaton did the costumes, and Oliver Smith the sets) to the score, makes it a timeless masterpiece.

Fritz Loewe's music is an outstanding example of a dramatic, theatrical score. While Higgins's songs are patter-based, befitting a philology professor, Eliza's cockney number ("Wouldn't it be Loverly") is a lilting soft-shoe, in accordance with her coal-smudged charm. Her post-metamorphosis song ("I Could Have Danced All Night") is lyrical and romantic. Her father's two songs ("With a Little Bit of Luck" and "Get Me to the Church on Time") are music-hall ditties. "On the Street Where you Live" is a soaring ballad given to the love-sick Freddie. The celebration of success ("The Rain in Spain") is a fandango, and Higgins's capitulation ("I've Grown Accustomed to Her Face") is just the kind of theatre ballad that is best when done by an actor.

Unfortunately, the great success of *My Fair Lady* marked the beginning of the end of Lerner's ability to write hit shows, and although he continued to write outstanding lyrics, he never had that kind of success or clarity of vision again. Moss Hart had a lot to do with *My Fair Lady*'s success, as Lerner was often scattered in his concepts, excessive in his writing, and overly fantastic in his plots.

Four years later in 1960, *Camelot* had the largest box office advance in history, before it was even written. In tryout it ran four and a half hours, and even by Lerner's own account it was "humorless and heavy." Before the show reached New York, its multiple cuts and confused concept orientation gave Lerner a bleeding ulcer and Hart a heart attack. (Loewe had already experienced a heart attack, and he had learned the importance of taking things in stride. But he retired immediately after *Camelot*.)

Lerner was a poet who did not understand dramatic structure, and egotism prevented him from seeing his shortcoming. Although he had conceived and written *My Fair Lady*'s book with Moss Hart at his side (they had isolated themselves in a decrepit Atlantic City hotel and discussed it scene by scene), he wrote *Camelot* alone. Hart was hired to direct after the book was written, and the show was rushed into production on the incorrect assumption that it only needed the kind of tinkering that was done to *My Fair Lady.* In fact, *Camelot,* was not based on a solid play, but on a rambling, fantastic work of literature (*The Once and Future King* by T. H. White) that had a sequentially darkening plot of tridimensional love. Rehearsals brought more problems than solutions, and *Camelot* was nothing short of a disaster during its intensely scrutinized tryout in the brand-new 3,200 seat O'Keefe Centre in Toronto. While Hart was in the hospital, Lerner took over the direction of the show. (Not the first or the last time Lerner mistakenly believed he had abilities as a director.) When the show opened on Broadway it received disappointing reviews.

Three months after the opening, though, a miracle of coincidence took place. Hart had recovered from his illness, and reworked the show. Two songs were cut, and there was some rewriting. Coincidentally, Ed Sullivan wanted to do a segment on his popular Sunday night television show about the work of Lerner and Loewe. Julie Andrews, Richard Burton, and Robert Goulet did twenty minutes of highlights from *Camelot.* Due to the power of television in general and the Ed Sullivan show in particular, the next morning brought lines around the block at the box office. And those audiences saw the show that Moss Hart, genius of the American theatre, had finally found in Lerner's work.

In spite of numerous travails, multiple productions, star-driven tours, and an impoverished film version by Joshua Logan, *Camelot* became one of the musical theatre's most beloved shows. Jacqueline Kennedy even suggested that her assassinated husband's favorite song had been "Camelot." (apparently it wasn't, but she was a public relations genius).

Loewe retired to a sybaritic, jet-set life of girls and gambling, on yachts in the Riviera and in a palatial home in Palm Springs. Lerner soldiered on, but in spite of working with good composers—Burton Lane for *On a Clear Day You Can See Forever,* Leonard Bernstein for *1600 Pennsylvania Avenue,* and Charles Strouse for *Dance a Little Closer*—Lerner's career and personal life spiraled downward. He became wildly erratic because of an amphetamine addiction initiated by New York's famous Dr. Feelgood. *Gigi,* Lerner and Loewe's great film for which Loewe came out of retirement to write additional songs, wasn't impressive on the stage.

Lerner's books were often long, unmanageable, and conceptually unfocused, and his originals (like Hammerstein's) were weaker than his adaptations. *Coco* (music by André Previn) had virtually no drama, in spite of acting by Katherine Hepburn. Lerner's lucky number was thirteen, but *Dance a Little Closer,* an ill-conceived update of Robert Sherwood's antiwar satire *Idiot's Delight,* was his thirteenth and worst show, and marked the end of his career.

But Lerner never lost his fatal charm and zest for life. He had grown up in an unloving household and was educated away from home, and throughout his life he abandoned wives and collaborators without regret. His lyrics never limned true heartbreak, and his characters never reflected the middle or lower classes, or even the average audience member. But the English story in a musical only Americans could have created deserves the hands-across-the-sea award. Its fascination may also lie in the quaint, prefeminist notion that most men are happy to imagine themselves in the smug complacency of bachelorhood, while many women like to see themselves transformed like Cinderella into belles of the ball. In any case, *My Fair Lady* was the last great musical play, and the end of the Rodgers and Hammerstein era. The irascible, loquacious Henry Higgins remains a legend of the musical theatre.

• • •

Another great character came from *Man of La Mancha* (1965), about whom the following might be said:

> The principal character . . . sometimes behaves, with apparent impunity, in an uninhibited way which in real life would incur strong social disapproval or even severe legal penalties. The average member of the audience, identifying with such a character, may achieve a vicarious revenge on the social and political order within which he is compelled to live.

These words were written by K. Dover about the comedies of Aristophanes, but they are easily applied to several musical comedy roles, most notably Don Quixote. The character's first appearance on the musical comedy stage was in the unsuccessful 1889 version by Reginald De Koven and Harry B. Smith, about which Smith had said, "I doubt that a successful play, musical or otherwise, can be made of Don Quixote." But in the 1960s, *Man of La Mancha* ran for 2,328 performances. Audiences warmed to the romanticism of the epic sixteenth-century Spanish novel as interpreted through Dale Wasserman's libretto. Albert Marre managed a smooth production in which inquisition prisoners on a stark dungeon set by Howard Bay played out Cervantes's drama. After a yeoman's career supporting female stars, Richard Kiley combined fine acting and a great theatre voice into one of the most heart-tugging performances by a male in musical theatre history. Joan Diener's covered, operatic voice and shallow acting were not up to the role—later a number of women played Dulcinea/Aldonza better. She appeared in the show because Marre was married to her, and he always used her as his leading lady, to the detriment of his productions (including the potentially powerful *Cry For Us All* and the out-of-town disaster *Homer, Sweet Homer*).

When Mitch Leigh was invited to score Dale Wasserman's stage version of *Don Quixote,* he thought hard about what style he should compose in. He started, naturally enough, with the music of sixteenth-century Spain, but rejected it as dull and lifeless. He moved three centuries forward in the history of Spanish music and discovered flamenco, upon the intricate rhythms of which he based his score. The result was a highly successful and theatrical score, throbbing with the music of a Spanish culture that is, academically speaking, entirely inappropriate and incorrect.

Audiences did not hold Leigh's feet to the intellectual fire. It has survived performances by *Seahunt*'s Lloyd Bridges, *Star Trek*'s Leonard Nimoy (Mr. Spock), and translation into languages as remote as Japanese and Hebrew. The music seems rich in the ambience of Quixote as well as unique to the show, and it is emotionally powerful. Leigh's choice of style might seem obvious in retrospect, but it was brave, clever, and risky at the time.

Leigh tried several times again and suffered several failures: *Home, Sweet Homer* (1976) was based on the *Odyssey,* and *Sarava!* (1979) was based on the film *Doña Flor and Her Two Husbands.* But the score for *Cry for Us All,* based on a play called *Hogan's Goat* that received little attention and closed in less than a week, is a powerful combination of theatre music and Irish folk influences, and remains one of Leigh's strongest works.

• • •

Another great eponymous character appeared in *The Music Man* (1957), a one-of-a-kind musical that grew out of the unique Midwestern background

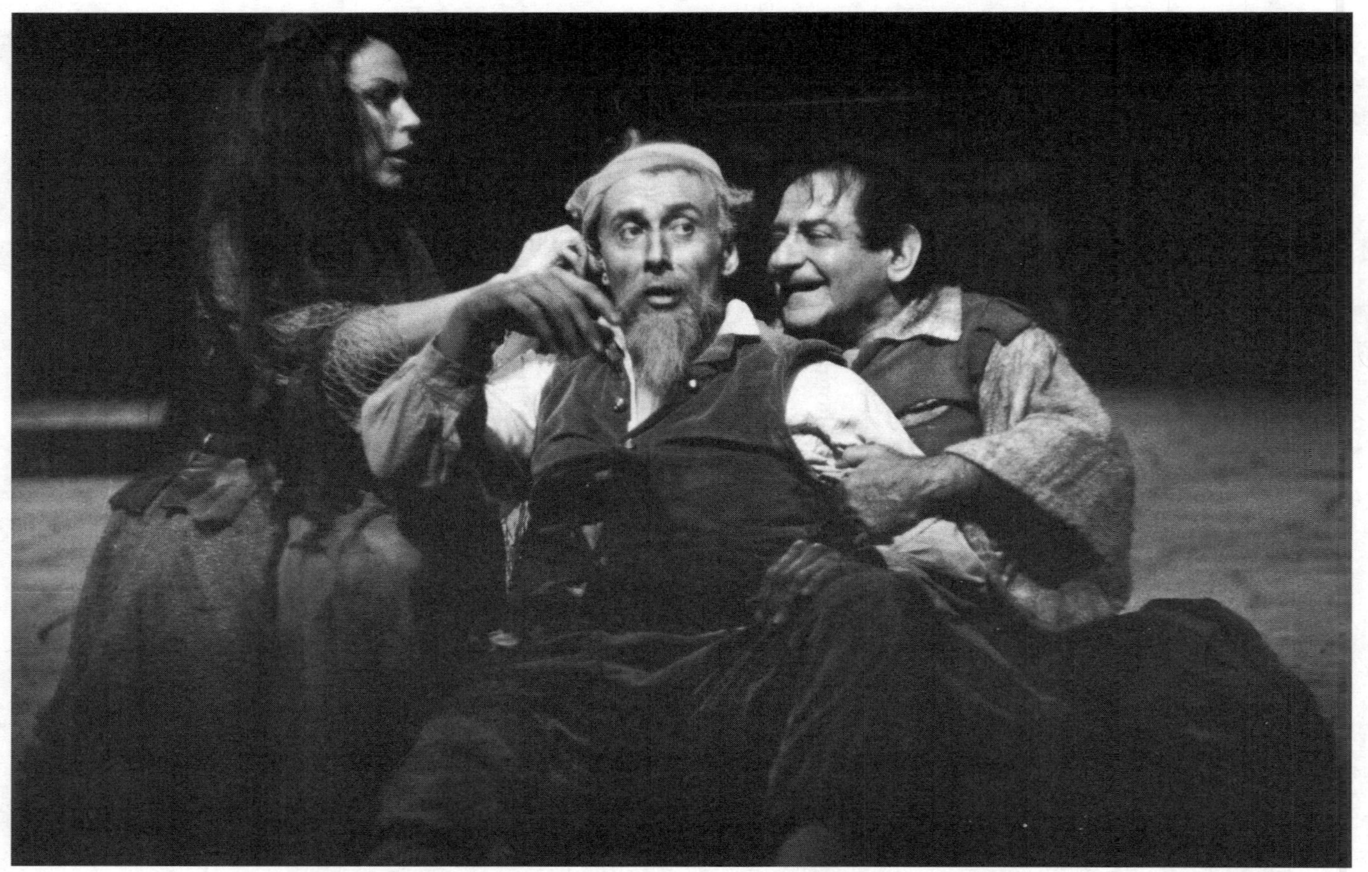

The dangerous business of tilting with windmills
Photofest/Bob Golby

of its creator, Meredith Wilson, who single-handedly wrote the book, music, and lyrics. This show stretched the form of the musical in a completely new direction, employing rhythms over melodies. The lead character is a fast-talking con man who has several monologues-in-syncopation that perfectly suit his character. Until *My Fair Lady* and *The Music Man*, the lead in a musical had to sing, or at least attempt to. Professor Henry Higgins and Professor Harold Hill (Rex Harrison and Robert Preston) didn't, couldn't, and probably shouldn't have. However, like their Gilbert and Sullivan antecedents, Higgins and Hill's songs satisfied a much more important tenet of the modern musical—they were dramatically appropriate. Hill's spiels and Higgins' musings served their characters far better than glorious melody could have.

Li'l Abner (1956) brought political satire back after a long hiatus. It featured a great score by primarily Hollywood songwriters Gene de Paul (music) and Johnny Mercer (lyrics), and it lambasted politicians. It was similar to *How to Succeed in Business Without Really Trying*, which satirized business, in that it entertained with wonderfully comic songs and sets, costumes, and choreography steeped in a cartoon style.

The musical *1776* opened in 1969 and boasted the most unusual subject ever conceived for a musical—the signing of the Declaration of Independence. With the help of librettist Peter Stone, Sherman Edwards dramatized it brilliantly (it would have worked as a straight play) and wrote a variety of spirited songs that were deeply embedded in the plot and characters. A collection of the theatre's best male actors brought the historical characters to life. The show was skillfully staged by Peter Hunt with (wisely) no choreography by Onna White. All of the action takes place in a chamber beautifully designed by Jo Mielziner (which did not resemble the real thing but reeked of Colonial style). This completely American musical should be required viewing for high school students. Additionally, "Mama, Look Sharp" ranks as one of the most plaintive antiwar ballads ever written.

Few theatregoers were unaware that the Declaration of Independence was successfully signed on July 4, but that didn't hurt a plot packed with the fascinating details of how Congress managed it. Suspense was encouraged in the form of a calendar, with pages coming ever closer to July 4 without consensus in sight. And to make that point even clearer, the yeas and nays were always visible on a roll call built into the set—a clever ruse, if historically inaccurate. At its heart, *1776* is a political dispute turned into outstanding musical drama.

Imperial Theatre

PLAYBILL

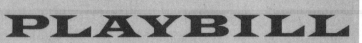

the magazine for theatregoers

Fiddler on the Roof

Twenty-Two

Bookwriters

Once, in an interview, Jerry Bock and I were asked the inevitable question: "What comes first, the words or the music?" Jerry's answer was, "The book."

—Sheldon Harnick

The idea that most musicals cannot sustain serious literary analysis is absurd. Too often critics use the dialogue—denuded of lyrics, music, dance, design, and acting—to claim that characters are shallow or ideas slim. Musicals are an impressionistic art form. They do not benefit from overly literal work. The "book" is the sum of all the content, not the dialogue alone. Music and dance in particular almost defy verbal articulation. Their ideas go straight to the heart.

At the core of every musical—good, bad, modern, old-fashioned, or even sung-through—is the book. It may feature a story with a beginning, middle, and end. It may only be a loose idea to support a revue, or an idea that isn't linear, a series of contemplations on a theme. The central ideas may even be expressed outside of the dialogue. Whatever it is, it's the responsibility of that unique specialist among inklings, the bookwriter—or librettist—for a musical.

• • •

Harry B. Smith was born in 1860 and became the earliest and most prolific bookwriter of all—he wrote over 120 operettas, comic operas, and musical comedies in a forty-five-year career. In 1899 he was represented by seven musicals, and in 1912 by six, though in the collaborative environment of that era he was often responsible for only some of the songs or a part of the book.

Smith loved books and was a rabid theatregoer. As an erudite and eager young man, he pursued careers as a clerk, actor, music critic, publisher of a weekly comic newspaper, and humor columnist until his freelance verses and essays led Fay Templeton to commission a libretto. Smith's book-writing career got underway when he and composer Reginald De Koven wrote what could be the first American comic operetta, *The Begum* (1887), which played with reasonable success in Philadelphia, New York, and the author's hometown of Chicago. Smith worked with all the best composers, including De Koven (*Don Quixote,* 1889 and *Robin Hood,* 1891), and Victor Herbert (*Sweethearts,* 1913). He collaborated with Irving Berlin on *Watch Your Step* in 1914 (with the thinnest of plots, this show demonstrated the confusion between revues and musical comedies of the period, some critics calling it one, some the other) and *Stop! Look! Listen!* in 1915. He teamed with Jerome Kern (*The Girl From Utah,* 1914 and *90 in the Shade,* 1915); Sigmund Romberg (*Princess Flavia,* 1925, adapted from the popular novel *The Prisoner of Zenda*); Ivan Caryll (*Papa's Darling,* 1914); and John Philip Sousa (*The Free Lance,* 1906). Smith also adapted French, English, and Viennese imports, depending on the reigning fashion, and provided a good deal of writing for Florenz Ziegfeld's shows as well.

The feverish pace of Smith's life led to utilitarian writing. After the successful flush of early operettas with De Koven, Smith did not contribute more than facile writing and rehashes of the traditional romantic scenes and comic routines of the form. Herbert's outstanding *Sweethearts* score is rich and diverse, but contemporary critics didn't believe the book or lyrics rose to the same level. Smith was also poorly reviewed for *Countess Maritza* (1926), though it is Emmerich Kallman's best score. In spite of the criticism, Smith's prodigious output was admired and his name became synonymous with the comic operettas of the period. He contributed many fine pieces of writing, particularly lyrics, and he was partly responsible for introducing slang to the stage as he adapted imports for American audiences. His work spanned two centuries and the various styles of the early American musical stage. With Victor Herbert he wrote *The Wizard of the Nile* set in Egypt, *The Idol's Eye* in India, *The Ameer* in Afghanistan, and *The Tattooed Man* in Persia. But Smith's sharp dialogue never left Broadway, and his line for *The Wizard of the Nile,* "Am I a wiz!" became popular slang.

Smith's last show was *Marching By* (1932), another in a long line of Shubert-produced, German operetta adaptations. It was a flop. By that time Smith's florid, romantic style was superseded by the musical comedies of the twenties, with their contemporary books and witty, sophisticated lyrics. Smith died a few years later.

• • •

Before settling on bookwriting, Herbert Fields choreographed two editions of the *Garrick Gaieties,* and acted in and directed several shows as well. His light, funny musicals were often successful and had substantial runs, especially the series of twenties musicals he wrote with Rodgers and Hart, including *Dearest Enemy* (1925) about the American Revolution; *The Girl Friend* (1926), a more contemporary show about a bicycle race and the hero's desire to win both it and a girl; *Peggy-Ann* (1926), which contained many clever and unusual dream sequences;* *A Connecticut Yankee* (1927), from the Mark Twain story; *Present Arms* (1928); *Chee-Chee* (1928 and 1932); and *America's Sweetheart* (1931), a satire on Hollywood.

Herbert Fields wrote *Hit the Deck* for Vincent Youmans in 1927. Herbert and his sister Dorothy wrote *Hello Daddy!* in 1928, with songs that featured Dorothy's lyrics and Jimmy McHugh's music. Herbert teamed with Cole Porter on *Fifty Million Frenchmen* (1929) and *The New Yorkers* (1930), the latter of which would have been far more successful but for the banks closing three days after it opened, marking the beginnings of the Great Depression.

For George and Ira Gershwin, Fields wrote the libretto for *Pardon My English* (1933), one of his few failures. For Cole Porter, Fields and Buddy DeSylva provided the books for *DuBarry Was a Lady* (1939) and *Panama Hattie* (1940). After that, Herbert and Dorothy Fields teamed up again and spent the rest of their careers writing in tandem. They provided Cole Porter with *Let's Face It!* (1941), *Something for the Boys* (1943), and *Mexican Hayride* (1944). They delved into operetta with *Up in Central Park*

* In one scene, Peggy-Ann talks to a fish that talks back. Alexander Woollcott likened the whimsy of this show to that of *Alice in Wonderland.*

(1945) for Sigmund Romberg's last show, but the team returned to their métier and wrote their most successful book, *Annie Get Your Gun* (1946, music and lyrics by Irving Berlin). They continued with *Arms and the Girl* (1950, music by Morton Gould), and *By the Beautiful Sea* (1954, Arthur Schwartz). Having firmly established themselves as the premiere bookwriters for the musical comedies of the 1940s, the Fields siblings ably bridged the gap to the deftly danced musicals ushered in next with *Redhead* for Gwen Verdon (1959) with composer Albert Hague (who later played the music teacher in the hit television show *Fame*). *Redhead* was Herbert Fields's last show, which he worked on with director-choreographer Bob Fosse—sadly, Fields died before rehearsals began. Thirteen of his shows ran more than 250 performances.

• • •

George Abbott was born in 1887 and lived more than a century. In 1912 he wrote his first play, *The Head of the Family,* a one-act for the Harvard Dramatic Club, and then concentrated on his career as an actor. He returned to writing in the mid-1920s with several collaborations, then scored his first major success with the play *Broadway* in 1926, written with Philip Dunning, which Abbott also directed. It was a fast-paced melodrama about gangsters and show business that took place in a nightclub. The show crackled with Broadway slang, and along with *Burlesque* (by Arthur Hopkins and George Manker Watters) and *The Royal Family* (by George S. Kaufman and Edna Ferber), *Broadway* was the hit of the season and an exemplar of 1920s Broadway theatre.

In 1935 Abbott added musicals to his hectic schedule and directed *Jumbo.* He was a frequent Rodgers and Hart collaborator and cowrote the libretto for their next show, *On Your Toes.* Abbott is known primarily as a director, but his writing included original works as well as adaptations, and his preferred method was that of collaboration with other bookwriters. Following the Cohan school, Abbott's structure and dialogue kept the musicals tight and swift and thus encouraged the developing form. Abbott's long career and strong influence on so many of the next generation's great talents makes him the principal bridge between the musicals of the 1920s and the fluid work of the director-choreographers of the 1950s and 1960s.

• • •

The brilliance of their lyrics and the longevity of their songs have overshadowed their other accomplishments, but Oscar Hammerstein II and Alan Jay Lerner usually provided their own books. Hammerstein provided dozens of scripts for both the operetta and musical theatre eras, where Lerner wrote solely for the latter but with a style influenced by the former. Lerner and Hammerstein are appreciated for the immense effort their books made to integrate song lyrics, using all sorts of techniques including rhymed couplets in dialogue (Hammerstein) and dialogue within song (Lerner). They constantly attempted to find new ways to smooth the transitions between book and lyrics. There is never a duplicated idea in their work—the emotional fabric of their scenes is so continuous that the drama never stops or doubles back on itself (as often happens in inept collaborations of song and scene). Together, Hammerstein and Lerner are responsible for the ultimate definition of the modern musical, in which each part makes its own contribution to the drama.

• • •

Howard Lindsay shifted from acting to directing. Then when he was assigned to direct the Cole Porter musical *Anything Goes* he was paired with Russel Crouse, and together they rewrote the Guy Bolton-P. G. Wodehouse libretto. The show's enormous success must have convinced them they were made for each other, and they wrote plays and musical librettos together for the next twenty-five years, including two of Ethel Merman's successes, *Red, Hot and Blue* and *Call Me Madam,* and the international triumph *The Sound of Music.*

Among Lindsay and Crouse's plays is the extremely long-running *Life with Father.* Their work moved away from the slam-bang school popularized by George Cohan and George Abbott and depended more on richness of character. Lindsay and Crouse brought the depth of playwriting to the musical, which is probably their greatest, if least understood, contribution. Both *Life with Father* and *The Sound of Music* show a balance between sentiment and treacle, a high-wire act that many authors can not perform.

• • •

Betty Comden and Adolph Green jumped frequently between Hollywood (screenplays for *The Barclays of Broadway, Singin' in the Rain, The Band Wagon,* and *It's Always Fair Weather*) and Broadway (librettos for *On the Town, Bells Are Ringing, Applause,* and *On the Twentieth Century)* as well as between books and lyrics. Their principal talent was comedy, which they had honed as nightclub performers, and their principal métier was show business, which they have pursued as a team longer than any other Broadway writers. They are reliable collaborators, and several shows with Jule Styne (including *Peter Pan* and *Hallelujah, Baby!*) mark them as pillars of the golden age, if not innovators.

• • •

Following the days in which musicals often had as many authors as chorus girls, and the period in which the musical's flow was smoothed over by double talents contributing book and lyrics, the era of the pure bookwriter arrived. Among the most successful was Joseph Stein, who began by providing sketches for the revue *Alive and Kicking* (1950), which featured choreography by Jack Cole and the dancing of Gwen Verdon. Stein cowrote *Plain and Fancy* (1955) and *The Body Beautiful* (1958), his first works with songwriters Jerry Bock and Sheldon Harnick.

Juno (1959) was Stein's adaptation of Sean O'Casey's *Juno and the Paycock,* and it only ran for two weeks. But *Take Me Along* (1959), which Stein cowrote and adapted from Eugene O'Neill's only comedy, was more successful. Then, in 1964, with Bock and Harnick's score, Stein painstakingly and exquisitely adapted the stories of Sholom Aleichem for *Fiddler on the Roof. Fiddler* ran until 1972 and became the longest running musical to date. Later, Stein wrote the equally sentimental *Zorba.*

Many successful bookwriters worked on adaptations, which require an understanding of the modern musical structure and a deft ability to integrate dialogue with lyrics. These include Joe Masteroff (*She Loves Me, Cabaret*) and Hugh Wheeler (*A Little Night Music, Sweeney Todd,* and the rewrite of the *Candide* book for Hal Prince's in-the-audience production.) Wheeler and Stein cowrote the *Irene* revival that attempted to follow the successful footprints of Ruby Keeler's *No, No, Nanette* revival, this time with Debbie Reynolds. With Reynolds's popularity and some tough doctoring by Gower Champion (after the original director, John Gielgud, discovered just how hard American musicals can be), it almost succeeded.

Zero Mostel and the mamas rehearse "Tradition" in *Fiddler on the Roof*
Photofest

• • •

Michael Stewart was a superb craftsman of the musical book, contributing ideas to his collaborators and deftly weaving extensive musical sequences in and out of his work. For example, the second act of *Hello, Dolly!* is dominated by song and dance as much as any book musical can be, yet it moves continually forward.

Like many of the young writers of the period, Stewart began with television (the Sid Caesar Show), summer shows, and revue sketches (*Shoestring Revue,* 1955). He jumped to Broadway when he teamed with Charles Strouse and Lee Adams to create the original musical *Bye Bye Birdie* (1960). He then adapted *Carnival* from the film *Lili*, *Hello, Dolly!* from the Thornton Wilder play *The Matchmaker*, and *Seesaw* from the two-character play *Two for the Seesaw.* He was unhappy with the results of *Seesaw*'s tumultuous out-of-town tryout and had his name taken off. Stewart then wrote the original *Mack and Mabel* from the true story of the infamous Mack Sennett and his silent film star Mabel Norman.

Stewart did the book and lyrics for *I love My Wife* and then formed a partnership with younger writer Mark Bramble for the second half of his long career. Together, Stewart and Bramble created *The Grand Tour*, based on S. N. Behrman's *Jacobowsky and the Colonel*; *Elizabeth the Queen* from Maxwell Anderson's play, *Barnum*, based on the notorious showman P. T. Barnum; *42nd Street*, from the famous movie musical, a production that probably reset the standards for mindless, entertaining, tap-dancing revivals of twenties musicals with contemporary showmanship; *Bring Back Birdie* (1981), a bad idea and a terrible flop driven by commercial motivations; and *Harrigan and Hart* (1985).

Stewart's last attempt was an adaptation of Robert Louis Stevenson's *Treasure Island* into *Pieces of Eight*, with a score by Jule Styne and lyricist Susan Birkenhead. It ran in England only. The decline visible in Stewart's final shows tells us more about the history of Broadway than the ability of authors like him who outlasted the golden age. Good, dramatic musicals had lost their way, their grip on the contemporary audience, and their commercial viability.

• • •

Adaptations are one thing and originals are another. Arthur Laurents may be the musical theatre's strongest original playwright. Though his *West Side Story* was a version of the age-old Romeo and Juliet story and *Gypsy* was adapted from published memoirs, *Anyone Can Whistle* (1964) and *Hallelujah, Baby!* (1967) were originals, and *Do I Hear a Waltz?* (1965) was taken from his own play. This remarkable output demonstrates a brilliant ear for dialogue. Laurents was once asked how he had researched the slang of the dangerous West Side gangs for his book, and he politely pointed out that he hadn't. The earthy ("Womb to tomb—sperm to worm"), snappy ("I know Tony like I know me"; "In, out, let's get crackin'") and wise ("You kids make this world stink") dialogue was invented. Books sometimes seemed to get away from him—the whimsical *Anyone Can Whistle* was ultimately unfocused with Laurents's hand in the direction, though choreographer Herb Ross provided memorable dances and Stephen Sondheim wrote one of his most charming scores. But *Hallelujah, Baby!* (1967) was another original; it was experimental and covered many time periods while the principals remained stationary, and its antiracist perspectives were serious.

In the able hands of Michael Stewart and Arthur Laurents, the book always disappeared effortlessly into the fabric of the show, and no modern bookwriters were more self-effacing in their work. There was room for substantial musical sequences, and Stewart and Laurents would give over the strongest emotional moments to the songwriters and the choreographer. As lyricists adapted whole paragraphs of their first drafts, they watched as some of their best writing become attached to other names. The overall structure of the shows, which in a musical could be equally credited to the writers and a strong director, was never compromised in a Stewart or Laurents musical, indicating the most confident knack for the rare art form since Oscar Hammerstein.

Peter Stone is a literate and intelligent writer who moves freely between media. He has contributed a number of books, including *Kean* (1961) from the play by Jean-Paul Sartre; *Skyscraper* (1965) from Elmer Rice's *Dream Girl; 1776* from a first draft by Sherman Edwards; *Two by Two* (1970) from Clifford Odets's *Flowering Peach; Sugar* (1972) from *Some Like It Hot,* by Billy Wilder and I. A. L. Diamond; *Woman of the Year* (1981) from the film by Ring Lardner, Jr. and Michael Kanin; *My One and Only* (1983), a new book for the Gershwin *Funny Face* songs that Stone took over out of town; and *The Will Rogers Follies* (1991), Stone's first original.

It's clear from this list that Stone's talents lie in the structure of the musical—all his adaptations take an already strong piece of material and integrate song and dance into it. In almost all of his musicals' song sequences, the music appears to belong—this kind of "belonging" is the most difficult and overlooked of musical theatre fundamentals.

Larry Gelbart began as a radio and television writer when comedy was king, and he stayed with this career through the milestone television series *M*A*S*H.* Gelbart wrote screenplays as well, including the award-winning *Oh, God!* starring George Burns. Gelbart's long career included plays and three Broadway musicals: *The Conquering Hero* (1961); *A Funny Thing Happened on the Way to the Forum* (1962), probably the funniest book ever written for the musical theatre and one of the few true farces; and *City of Angels* (1989), which featured Gelbart's cynical views of Hollywood.

City of Angels identifies Gelbart as an author inexperienced in the integration of the musical. Indeed, all of his books leave little room for musical sequences, though *Forum* establishes a standard of humor that writers everywhere aspire to.

• • •

Neil Simon, the most successful and prolific playwright of the modern era, claims he doesn't really like writing musicals, but that hasn't kept him from writing several. *Catch a Star!* (1955), a revue with sketches by Neil and his brother Danny, ran only three weeks. The musical adaptation of Patrick Dennis's novel *Little Me* was a vehicle for Sid Caesar, with whom Simon had begun his writing career by doing sketches for Caesar's television program.

Sweet Charity was based on a first draft by Bob Fosse, in turn based on an Italian film. *Promises, Promises* was adapted from the film *The Apartment. They're Playing Our Song* was an original story about a romance between a composer and a lyricist. *The Goodbye Girl* was from Simon's own successful, original screenplay.

Simon's librettos, like his plays, bristle with laughter. He is perpetually unwilling to do a straight adaptation, and always looks for a reason to musicalize and theatricalize a property. (He turned down *Sugar* because he thought the film version, *Some Like It Hot,* couldn't be improved.). In *Little Me* all the men in the heroine's life were to be played by the same actor. *Sweet Charity* was crafted for the special talents of Bob Fosse and Gwen Verdon, in a frame of vaudeville melodrama. *Promises, Promises* promised to leaven a good but earthbound film, then really took off when Simon hit upon the device of stopping the action for the principal character to talk to the audience.

They're Playing Our Song would work better as a two-character play—its dozen pop songs express neither plot nor character. The Broadway production was cluttered with a bizarre chorus jumping out from behind sofas for no apparent reason. *The Goodbye Girl*, too, needn't have been musicalized. But in Simon's earlier works he showed his skill at construction and adaptation—the art of not throwing out the baby with the bathwater—and at making room for the requisite songs and dances of the modern musical.

More than one outsider has tried his or her hand at the unique art of crafting a book for a musical. Truman Capote wrote the book *and* the lyrics for *House of Flowers* (1954). John O'Hara adapted his own stories into *Pal Joey.* James and William Goldman wrote *A Family Affair* (1962) with John Kander, before Kander teamed up with Fred Ebb. Both Goldmans found more success later—both went on to write novels and screenplays, and James wrote *Follies* with Stephen Sondheim. Lillian Hellman adapted Voltaire's *Candide.* Mel Brooks bridged his career from television to film with a book for a Broadway musical, *All American.*

Sometimes a playwright finds himself in the musical world by accident. George Furth submitted an evening of eleven one-act plays to Harold Prince, who asked Furth to get together with Stephen Sondheim and turn the work into *Company.* John Weidman had the same experience with Prince, who read his yet-to-be-produced play about East-West relations and again offered the collaboration of Sondheim; Weidman's play became *Pacific Overtures.*

Adaptations have come from plays, films, television dramas, novels, short stories, and the Bible, and good material tends to make the rounds. John Oxenford's English comedy *A Day Well Spent* became the nineteenth-century Viennese comedy by Johann Nestroy, *Einen Jux Will Er Sich Machen,* which became Thornton Wilder's *The Merchant of Yonkers* (1938), which Wilder rewrote as *The Matchmaker* (1955), the source for Michael Stewart's *Hello, Dolly!,* following which Tom Stoppard used the story for his play *On the Razzle.*

No matter what the source, the book of a musical is a complex crossword puzzle, requiring the skills of both a carpenter and a playwright. Bookwriting is often a thankless job, and more than one writer has been criticized for a "thin" book when all the poor fellow did was give over his strongest ideas to the lyricist.

The

PLAYBILL®

For the Mark Hellinger Theatre

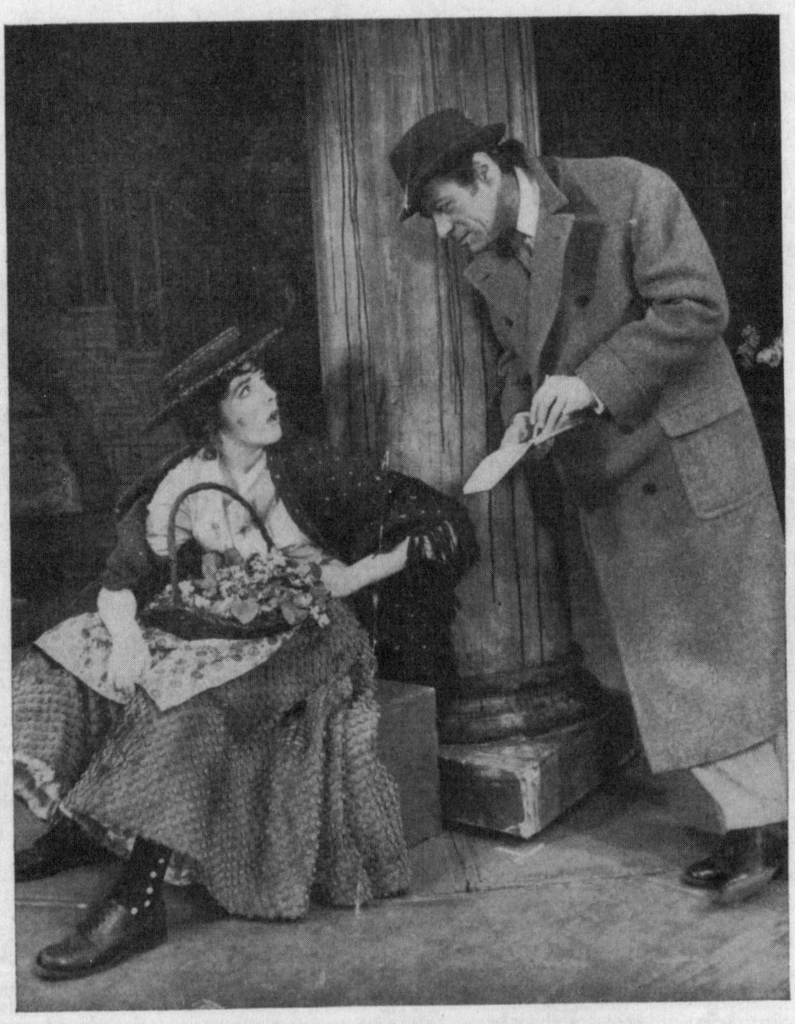

My Fair Lady

Twenty-Three

Lyrics

According to legend, Mrs. Oscar Hammerstein was at a party when she overheard someone say, "I just love Jerome Kern's 'Ol' Man River.'" Mrs. Hammerstein replied indignantly, "Jerome Kern did not write 'Ol' Man River.' My husband wrote 'Ol' Man River.' Jerome Kern wrote, *'Dum, dum, dum dum; dum, dum, dum, dum dum.'"*

A lyricist's notoriety is almost inversely proportional to the fame of his musical partner. This is not entirely due to the composer's ego. Great theatre lyrics, like great lighting designs, should not draw attention to themselves. They should fall on the ear with natural and effortless grace and express meaning clearly, without hard-to-follow convolutions or tricky rhymes. Audiences should be drawn to the expression of ideas by the characters, not by the cleverness of the words. Stephen Sondheim himself has expressed misgivings over some of his *West Side Story* lyrics, which may have been too clever for the characters. Maria, he claims retrospectively, wouldn't say "fizzy and funny and fine," or "It's alarming how charming I feel."

Perhaps not, but neat rhymes are a wonderful thing. There isn't a lover of musical theatre alive who hasn't marveled over the rhyming of "feminine" and "them in internal rhyme," from a chorus cut from "Bring on the Girls" by Sondheim. Nor one who hasn't cringed over false rhymes (also known as rock-and-roll rhymes), since words like "mine" and "time" can be made to seem to rhyme by slurring the words.

Rhymes that draw a laugh . . .

He: *You must meet my wife*
She: *Let me get my hat and my knife*

. . . inner rhymes that speed the words along . . .

Hobbies you pursue together
Savings you accrue together,
Looks like you misconstrue together

. . . tricky, hidden rhymes that tweak the ear . . .

What I am is winsome
radiant as in some dream come true

. . . alliterations that emphasize words . . .

From the pinch and the punch
to the paunch and the pouch and the pension

. . . and same word repetitions that re-emphasize words . . .

You hold her thinking "I'm not alone"
You're still alone

. . . all help to deliver clear ideas to an audience.

Nevertheless, impressive rhymes don't launch a show on a long run. Their purpose is to underscore the words for the ear, somewhat like underlining words on a page. Sometimes rhyming can clarify a word or phrase that might otherwise be difficult to understand ("personable" and "coercin' a bull").

The lyricist provides the composer with two initiating values—the general rhythm or cadence of the song, and its content. No member of the production team is more responsible for the musical's dramatic integrity than the lyricist.

Theatre lyrics are closer to dialogue than to poetry. They "come at you, and you hear them only once," as Sondheim explains. (As an example, Sondheim claims that for several years he thought Oscar Hammerstein's

"My Defenses Are Down" was "Mighty Fences Are Down.") Theatre lyrics are not pop lyrics, which rely on phrases and imagery alone. They must lie properly on the melody. (Another of Sondheim's self-lacerations is for the lyric "There's a place for us," in which, according to the way it's set to music, the most important word is "a.")

Lyrics should be simple, not packed, because there is so much else going on—character, sets, costumes, movement, and of course music, the richest and most emotional of all art forms. While pop singers can hold notes on consonants and closed vowels, it's difficult for theatre singers to be understood unless long notes coincide with open vowel sounds (though the personal microphone probably has decreased this problem).

Sheldon Harnick enumerates the requirements of a theatre lyric as:

(1) to continue the flow of the story,

(2) to provide insight into characters,

(3) to heighten climactic moments, and

(4) to enrich the feeling of time and place.

Sondheim adds two additional requirements:

(5) the actor must have something to act, and

(6) the actor must have something to do.

But the most curious thing about theatre lyrics is how the best lyrics suit a character neatly. "Once Upon a Time," a beautiful ballad written by Charles Strouse and Lee Adams for *All American,* improves musically when it is sung by a robust baritone, but loses its dramatic effect. The lyrics

Once upon a time
A girl with moonlight in her eyes
Put her hand in mine
And said she loved me so
But that was once upon a time
Very long ago . . .

. . . describe a romance in the character's past. The rich tones of a beautiful voice suggest someone too young to have that kind of hindsight. But when the number is sung in the unsteady tones of an older man or woman (Ray Bolger and Eileen Herlie in the original), the effect is heart-rending. This is one of the best examples (hear it on the cast album by Columbia) of the strength of the American musical as great theatre. Good theatre lyrics are written for a character, and it's far more important for the voice to represent that character than to ring out in dulcet tones.

In fact, the further removed a singing voice is from the normal human voice, the less effective it is in the theatrical context of a musical. Even the most operatic of scores—*Show Boat, Porgy and Bess, Candide,* and parts of *Most Happy Fella*—are less effective when great singing takes precedence over acting. Jule Styne once defined what the greatest female singers have in common: "They sing the lyrics, not the melody." The creators of those lyrics deserve a special place in the history of musical theatre.

• • •

Harry S. Smith provided his many books with lyrics of his own (for six thousand songs, he claimed), and he was the first American lyricist to be published in book form with *Stage Lyrics* (1900). Smith wrote lyrics for Florenz Ziegfeld's wife Anna Held when Ziegfeld produced *Papa's Wife,* which shows a keen sense of what would enable Held to hold the audience:

It seems one's dress is always changing;
For instance, a few years ago
Nobody seemed to mind my knees;
My stockings 'twas all right to show.
But then—my neck! It must be covered;
And now it's different, if you please;
For I can show my neck and shoulders,
But I must cover up my knees.

But why? What difference can it make?
I cannot see, although I try—
Whether one's frock is cut high below
Or cut below up high.

A lady dances in a ball-room;
She shows her shoulders and her arms
Only a bit of ribbon lies
Between the public and her charms.
A scandal if she showed her ankles!
A riot if she showed her knees!
But at the seaside in the summer,
Why, you can see them all you please.

One can only imagine the choreographic possibilities here, for Ziegfeld knew his audience and Smith knew the formulas. Smith created drinking songs:

O, it's will ye quaff with me, my lads,
And it's will ye quaff with me?
It is a draught of nut-brown ale
I offer unto ye . . .

Songs for dancing:

She did a little step or two
Swung her slipper like the pendulum of a clock
A gleam of silken shapeliness
A dozen chappies fainted from the shock
A fluttering of lingerie
A flash of lightning never was as quick
It caused a great sensation, did the pedal elevation
Of the five foot lady with the eight foot kick.

and comedy songs:

All the day and night
Raged the long, long fight,
All the day the cannon roared.
Many soldiers brave
Found a hero's grave
As the deadly hail outpoured

"Who'll blow up that wall?"
Then the General cried;
"It is a certain death," said he.
Then a small, pale man,
With a timid look,
Stood forth and said, "Take me."

For he was a married man
To certain death he swiftly ran
While all his comrades cheered,
No blowing up he feared,
For he was a married man.

The profusion of lyrics Smith turned out for new and existing musical entertainments from operettas to the *Ziegfeld Follies* were better than those of his contemporaries because he wrote *theatre lyrics*—in fact, he established them on the American stage. His lyrics have a dramatic function, providing a dance or an action for the singer to carry out, or a deepening of character.

• • •

To trace the beginnings of great theatre lyrics, though, we have to go back to London's Savoy Theatre, and to W. S. Gilbert.

In *Trial by Jury*'s "Judge's Song," Gilbert created what he has become particularly famous for—the autobiography of a comic character:

When I, good friends, was called to the bar,
I'd an appetite fresh and hearty,
But I was, as many barristers are,
An impecunious party.
I'd a swallow-tail coat of a beautiful blue—
A brief which I bought of a booby—
A couple of shirts and a collar or two,
And a ring that looked like a ruby!

In Westminster Hall I danced a dance,
Like a semi-despondent fury;

For I thought I should never hit on a chance
Of addressing a British jury—
But I soon got tired of third-class journeys,
And dinners of bread and water;
So I fell in love with a rich attorney's
Elderly, ugly daughter.

The rich attorney, he jumped with joy,
And replied to my fond professions:
"You shall reap the reward of your pluck, my boy
At the Bailey and Middlesex sessions.
You'll soon get used to her looks," said he,
"And a very nice girl you'll find her!
She may very well pass for forty-three
In the dusk with the light behind her!"

The rich attorney was good as his word;
The briefs came trooping gaily,
And every day my voice was heard
At the sessions of Ancient Bailey.
All thieves who could my fees afford
Relied on my orations,
And many a burglar I've restored
To his friends and his relations

At length I became as rich as the Gurneys—
An Incubus then I thought her,
So I threw over that rich attorney's
Elderly, ugly daughter.
The rich attorney my character high
Tried vainly to disparage—
And now, if you please, I'm ready to try
This breach of Promise of Marriage!

For now I am a judge!
(Chorus: And a good judge too)
Yes, now I am a judge

(And a good judge too)
Though all my law is fudge,
Yet I'll never, ever budge,
But I'll live and die a judge
(And a good judge too)

Gilbert also integrated the chorus well, and he did more than just bring on the girls. Generally his choruses were characters believably present (Jury, Pirates, Policemen), and they often echoed the last lines of the principal's song (as in gospel music) in order to underline the satire. Gilbert's extraordinary use of language in rhyme was sometimes erudite and sometimes invented ("crimes of heliogabalus" and "peculiarities parabolus").

H.M.S. Pinafore was eventually so popular that the words "Never!—What, never?—Hardly ever!" became a popular catch phrase of the day. *The Pirates of Penzance* also featured Gilbert's most famous autobiographical song for its modern major general.

I am the very model of the modern Major-General
I've information vegetable, animal and mineral
I know the kings of England, and I quote the fights historical
From Marathon to Waterloo, in order categorical
I'm very well acquainted too with matters mathematical
I understand equations, both simple and quadratical
About binomial theorem I'm teeming with a lot o' news
With many cheerful facts about the square of the hypotenuse

And *Iolanthe*'s "Nightmare Song" is still perhaps considered the best patter number ever.

If you want a receipt for that popular mystery,
Known to the world as a Heavy Dragoon,
Take all the remarkable people in history,
Tattle them off to a popular tune.
The pluck of Lord Nelson on board of the Victory—
Genius of Bismarck devising a plan;
The humour of Fielding (which sounds contradictory)—
Coolness of Paget about to trepan—

The science of Jullien, the eminent musico—
Wit of Macaulay, who wrote of Queen Anne—
The pathos of Pady, as rendered by Boucicault—
Style of the Bishop of Sodor and Man—
The dash of a D'Orsay, divested of quackery—
Narrative prose of Dickens and Thackeray—
Victor Emmanuel-peak-haunting Peveril—
Thomas Aquinas, and Doctor Sacheverell—
Tupper and Tennyson—Danile Defoe—
Anthony Trollope and Mr. Guizot!
Take of these elements all that is fusible,
Melt them all down in a pipkin or crucible,
Set them to simmer and take off the scum
And a Heavy Dragoon is the residuum!

"I Have a Little List" from Gilbert's *The Mikado* is the grandfather of all "list" songs.

As some day it may happen that a victim must be found,
I've got a little list—I've got a little list
Of society offenders who might well be underground,
And who never would be missed—who never would be missed
There's the pestilential nuisances who write for autographs
All people who have flabby hands and irritating laughs
All children who are up in dates, and floor you with 'em flat
All persons who in shaking hands, shake hands with you like that
And all third persons who on spoiling tête-à-têtes insist
They'd none of 'em be missed—they'd none of 'em be missed

Gilbert's gift was for words, not for plot. If the patter song harks back to the beginning of musical entertainments, it languished in anonymity until Gilbert and Sullivan raised it to perfection:

Then, if you plan it, he
Changes organity,
With an urbanity,
Full of Satanity,

Vexes humanity
With an inanity
Fatal to vanity—
Driving your foes to the verge of insanity!
Barring tautology,
In demonology,
'Lectro-biology,
Mystic nosology,
Spirit philology
High-class astrology,
Such is his knowledge, he
Isn't the man to require an apology!

Gilbert satirized the larger human foibles very effectively, allowing his body of work to transcend specific London characters of the time—Oscar Wilde, politicians, etc.—and to remain relevant today. One of Gilbert's early biographers likens him to Aristophanes, supported by critical writings in 1911 and 1927 in notable publications such as *Theatre Arts Monthly.* Gilbert was thinking of himself when he wrote the following (without Sullivan):

Other clowns make you laugh till you sink
When they tip you a wink;
With attitude antic
They render you frantic;
I don't. I compel you to think!

Gilbert's lyrics were nothing if not attention-getting, and they would remain so until Oscar Hammerstein, who became the standard for great theatre lyrics.

• • •

As part of the Princess musicals triumvirate, P. G. Wodehouse elevated lyrics from the silly, treacly sensibilities of early twentieth-century American musical comedy. Wodehouse was born in England in 1881 and surely became a Gilbert and Sullivan fan. His work strongly influenced modern Broadway musicals, lacing them with literate writing, clever

Oscar Hammerstein II, the father of the modern musical
Photofest

phrases and allusions, and rhymes which, however complex, never felt forced and always fell easily on the ear. Wodehouse's words, which he always wrote for existing melodies, sang easily, and if the style in which he wrote was limited by the shallow stories and silly characters of 1920s musicals, he nevertheless upgraded lyrics significantly from the standard of the period.

One incarnation of Jerome Kern's most enduring song demonstrates the difference between a lyric that rises to the melody and one that doesn't. In *Zip Goes a Million,* with a book by Guy Bolton and music by Kern, lyricist Buddy DeSylva took a shot at setting Kern's favorite trunk melody to words. The actor sang the following to a dollar "bill."

I found a friend, I want you to meet him.
You'll gladly greet him, I know
Though he's an old offender, he's tender,
To friend or to foe
To see him coming makes you glad,
Then to know he's leaving you makes you sad.
But great and small his worth proclaim,
And you'll know him when I tell his name:
He's Bill, Old Bill, who sticks to you until
You need him most.
He's willing to
Keep thrilling you,
By leaving your track and then
Hurrying back again.
In these hard times,
He's worth about three dimes, but still
I'm sure he can bring me happiness,
'Cause he's my old pal Bill

Fortunately *Zip Goes a Million* closed out of town. When Kern next pulled this same melody out of his trunk for *Show Boat,* he presented Oscar Hammerstein with the original Wodehouse lyric. Hammerstein liked it enough to keep it largely intact.

But long before *Show Boat* resurrected the great ballad, Wodehouse had been knocking audiences dead with comic songs ("Napoleon,"

"Cleopatterer"), quaint love songs ("Nesting Time in Flatbush," "Let's Build a Little Bungalow in Quogue"), and lyrics for dance numbers ("Dancing Time," "All the World is Dancing Mad"). His comic lyrics launched his career in London, where he provided lyrics for Seymour Hick's Aldwych Theatre for two pounds a week. Although Wodehouse's West End career was significant, he did most of his best work for Broadway:

My favorite Aunt Matilda
Found Oshkosh rather slow
It's going to be a painful tale, I know
She came to Greenwich Village
And took a studio
When she was eighty-three years old or so
She learned the ukulele
She breakfasted at Polly's
And what is worse she wrote free verse
And now she's in the Follies!

Wodehouse specialized in songs for star comics:

Napoleon, Napoleon
They thought him quite a joke
They'd take a glance at the little pill
With a line of chatter that they used to spill
But they couldn't faze Napoleon
When he started in to scrap
He was five foot high
But one tough guy
And I take after nap

And he wrote lyrics for prison valentines in "Dear Old Prison Days," "Put Me In My Little Cell," and:

When it's tulip, tulip, tulip time in Sing Sing
Oh it's there that I would be
There are gentle, gentle, gentle hearts in Sing Sing
Watching and yearning for me

Oh I wish I was back with a rock or two to crack
With my pals of the class of ninety nine
How I miss the peace and quiet
And the simple wholesome diet
Of that dear old fashioned prison of mine

Indeed, Wodehouse may have been the first and only lyricist to write so much about prison, a trait which came from his convoluted novel plots, many of which featured well-meaning burglars.

Wodehouse's career was filled with short stories, essays, and novels, but he always loved the theatre, both as a lyricist and a critic:

You want the best seats
We have plays of every kind
For all the shows in town
We have 'em
But upon all our lists you'll find
Not one bad 'un
All were praised by Archie Haddon
Plays with a bed scene, French farces that made the censor frown
Plays where wives behave as wives should never, never do
Also plays nice minded girls can take their mothers to
You want the best seats
We have 'em
For all the shows in town

Or he could simply write:

Go, little boat, serenely gliding
Over the silver water riding.
Nought but the stars I see,
Shining above
Flow, river, carry me
To him I love.

Go, little boat, serenely gliding
Love at the helm, your course is guiding.

Fair winds to hasten you
May fortune send,
Till I come safe to journey's end.

And the world he wrote about was ideal for the musical comedies of the 1920s. It lasted decades longer in his comic novels. In his memoirs, Wodehouse wonders if this world ever existed at all. Nevertheless, he was "frightfully fond of it anyway."

On the other side of the moon
Ever so far, beyond the last little star
There's a land I know where the good songs go
Where it's always afternoon
And snug in a haven of peace and rest
Lie the dear old songs that we love the best

It's a land of flowers
And April showers
With sunshine in between
With roses blowing
And rivers flowing
Mid rushes growing green
Where no one hurries
And no one worries
And life runs calm and slow
And I wish some day
I could find my way
To the land where the good songs go

In spite of his clever lyrics and literary background, Wodehouse was not one to upstage a magnificent Jerome Kern melody when he heard one. Together they created some of the loveliest songs of the early American musical:

Oh the rain
Comes a pitter, patter

And I'd like
To be safe in bed
Skies are weeping
While the world is sleeping
Trouble heaping
On our head
It is vain
To remain and chatter
And to wait
For a clearer sky
Helter skelter
I must fly for shelter
Till the clouds roll by

Wodehouse directly influenced the American musical through his literate songwriting, a significant departure from the florid, romantic lyrics of the operettas and a crucial link between the English Gilbert and the many witty American lyricists of the 1920s.

• • •

The transition of lyrics from something like poetry to something more like dialogue paralleled the general rise of lyrics as a more forceful contribution to the musical. Ira Gershwin's exquisite stanzas could never be mistaken for anything but clever dialogue in the guise of lyrics. Ira Gershwin bloomed somewhat later than his younger brother George (first writing under the name of Arthur Francis to avoid treading on his famous brother's name).

Considering George Gershwin's fame, Ira is the most overlooked lyricist in the history of the profession. Biographies of George and reviews of Gershwin shows often ignore Ira's essential, incandescent lyrics. He always accepted whatever jobs came along, and during the early stages of his career he was, like all other lyricists of twenties musicals, not concerned with the demands of the book, though he must have enjoyed writing for the better books demanded by the satires. Indeed, throughout the brothers' association, it was always George who chose the subject matter.

When *Porgy and Bess* came along, Ira rose to the occasion. In this case he was definitely a key to George's success, and his lyrics perfectly

The towering talents of the 1920s—George Gershwin, with Mrs. Mervyn LeRoy, Ira Gershwin, Dorothy Fields, and Jerome Kern
Archive Photos

Stephen Sondheim and James Lapine rehearse Bernadette Peters
Photofest

complimented George's often intricate (for a lyricist that means difficult) melodies. Perhaps his best song is the one that took him the longest to write, because at first he looked for too many rhymes; eventually he decided this would only cloud the forceful melody. Ira Gershwin, who always strove for simplicity, is the man who wrote:

I got rhythm
I got music
I got my man
Who could ask for anything more?

Gershwin may have limned love better than any lyricist before or since ("The Man I Love," "Looking for a Boy," "Boy! What Love Has Done to Me!" and "But Not For Me"). His words for Harold Arlen's music in the film *A Star is Born* is the out-and-out best unrequited love song ever written:

The night is bitter
The stars have lost their glitter
The winds grow colder
And suddenly you're older
And all because of the man that got away

He also wrote the definitive spoof on love songs:

Blah, blah, blah, blah, moon,
Blah, blah, blah, blah, above;
Blah, blah, blah, blah, croon,
Blah, blah, blah, blah, love.

Using vernacular frequently, Ira Gershwin and Dubose Heyward created "I Got Plenty o' Nuthin'," "There's a Boat Dat's Leavin' Soon for New York," and "It Ain't Necessarily So" for *Porgy and Bess.* Ira wrote the lyrics for what is probably the most difficult song to sing ever written—"Tschaikowsky," the tongue-twister for Danny Kaye about Russian composers (from *Lady in the Dark,* music by Kurt Weill). The refrain amply demonstrates Gershwin's ingenuity, strength in rhythm and rhyme, and capacity for research:

There's Malichevsky, Rubinstein, Arensky and Tschaikowsky,
Sapelnikoff, Dimitrieff, Tscherepnin, Kryjanowsky,
Godosky, Arteiboucheff, Moniuszko, Akimenko,
Solovieff, Prokofieff, Tiomkin, Korestchenko.
There's Glinka, Winkler, Bortniansky, Rebikoff, Ilyinsky,
There's Medtner, Balakireff, Zolotareff and Kvoschinsky.
And Sokoloff and Kopyloff, Dukelsky and Klenowsky,
And Shostakovitsch, Borodine, Gliere and Nowakofski.
There's Liadoff and Karganoff, Markievitch, Pantschenko
And Dargomyzski, Stcherbatcheff, Scriabine, Vassilenko,
Stravinsky, Rimsky-Korsakoff, Mussorgsky and Gretchaninoff
And Glazounoff and Caesar Cui, Kalinikoff, Rachmaninoff,
Stravinsky and Gretchaninoff,
Rumshinsky and Rachmaninoff,
I really have to stop, the subject has been dwelt upon enough!

Some of the Gershwin brothers' most popular songs throw light on that most difficult of categories, the song intended for a dancer. These were often written for Fred Astaire, and Ira had to fit his words to a complex syncopation and limited range melody. Songs in this category include "They Can't Take That Away From Me," "A Foggy Day (in London Town)," "Nice Work If You Can Get It," "Fascinating Rhythm," "Slap that Bass," "S'Wonderful," "They All Laughed," "Let's Call the Whole Thing Off," "Shall We Dance," and "(I'm dancing and) I Can't Be Bothered Now."

After George's premature death Ira amply demonstrated he could write great songs without the brother to whom he had been devoted. He wrote many wonderful songs with Kurt Weill ("My ship has sails that are made of silk"), Jerome Kern ("Long Ago and Far Away"), Harry Warren ("Shoes With Wings On"), Vernon Duke, Aaron Copeland, Arthur Schwartz, Burton Lane, and Harold Arlen. Ira's writing made him a popular collaborator and a pillar of the lyric theatre.

I'll hear words without music
All my life long
Hoping, praying
That what he's saying
Will turn to song.

• • •

E. Y. "Yip" Harburg sat next to Ira Gershwin in high school, and they collaborated on a column in the school paper. Harburg had a knack for standards—"April in Paris" (Did every young writer fall in love over there?) and "It's Only a Paper Moon"—possibly because he did his early lyrics for revues. He became one of the most socially conscious lyricists of the musical theatre, owing to a background of poverty, immigrant parents, a beloved older brother who died at the age of twenty-eight, and various odd jobs he had to take during the Depression. Harburg was also an early supporter of feminism ("It was good enough for Grandma, But it ain't good enough for me") and the civil rights of American blacks:

Free as the sun is free
That's how it's gotta be
Whatever is right for bumble bee
And River and Eagle
Is right for me
We gotta be free,
The Eagle and me.

Harburg wrote *Finian's Rainbow* with Burton Lane, which tells the story of a leprechaun chasing to America an Irishman who has stolen his pot of gold, and deftly includes an antiracist subplot. In a wildly comic finale to the first act, a Southern senator suddenly finds that he has become a black man. Finian's daughter provides the love interest ("Follow the fellow who follows the dream") and the leprechaun who wants his gold back provides the comic interest ("When I'm not near the girl I love, I love the girl I'm near").

Harburg wrote several Broadway scores, including *Hooray for What* (1937), *Bloomer Girl* (1944), and *Jamaica* (1957) with Harold Arlen; *Finian's Rainbow* (1947) with Burton Lane; *Flahooley* (1951) with Sammy Fain; *The Happiest Girl in the World* (1961), which Harburg adapted from Jacques Offenbach; and *Darling of the Day* (1968), a wonderful score for a failed show. However, he is best known for the songs he wrote with Harold Arlen for MGM's musical film *The Wizard of Oz:* "If I Only Had a Brain, "Follow the Yellow Brick Road," and of course:

Somewhere
Over the rainbow
Way up high
There's a land that I heard of
Once
*In a lullaby . . .**

If Yip Harburg is legendary for his whimsical work in *Finian's Rainbow* and *The Wizard of Oz*, his many socially conscious songs are his most significant contribution. The most famous of these was from the Depression revue *Americana* (1932), and it quickly became an anthem.

They used to tell me I was building a dream
And so I followed the mob
When there was earth to plough or guns to bear
I was always there

Right there on the job
They used to tell me I was building a dream
With peace and glory ahead
Why should I be standing in line
Just waiting for bread?

Once I built a railroad,
Made it run,
Made it race against time,
Once I built a railroad
Now it's done
Brother can you spare a dime?

Once in khaki suits
Gee, we looked swell
Full of Yankee Doodle-de-dum.
Half a million boots went sloggin' through Hell,
I was the kid with the drum

* "Over the Rainbow" was almost cut from the final film version because it "didn't advance the plot."

Say don't you remember,
They called me Al
It was Al all the time
Say, don't you remember
I'm your pal!
Buddy, can you spare a dime?

Not many lyricists followed Harburg's pithy style. When the Depression began to subside, the musical returned to romantic themes.

• • •

The first female lyricist of note was Dorothy Fields, who came to the theatre along with her brothers Joseph and Herbert, all against the advice of their famous father, Lew Fields of Weber and Fields. Like her literary contemporary Dorothy Parker, Fields's work was wry, if less cynical. Her contribution to the Depression ("I Can't Give You Anything But Love") was written for the Cotton Club revue *Hot Chocolates,* for which Fields and Jimmy McHugh wrote three editions. For other revues they wrote "On the Sunny Side of the Street" and "I'm in the Mood For Love." She was able to write colloquial slang throughout several generations without ever becoming old-fashioned or forced. Dorothy Fields's long career included collaborations with Jerome Kern, Sigmund Romberg, Harold Arlen, Arthur Schwartz, and finally Cy Coleman, with whom she wrote *Sweet Charity* (1966) and *Seesaw* (1973). Fields's career, probably more than that of any other writer, comfortably ranged from the musicals of the 1920s to the modern age. In those later years she was free to write outside the formula, and came up with one of Bob Fosse's most useful numbers:

The minute you walked in the joint
I could see you were a man of distinction
A real big spender
Good looking, so refined
Say, wouldn't you like to know what's goin' on in my mind?
So let me get right to the point
I don't pop my cork for every guy I see.

Hey! Big spender,
Spend a little time with me.

This contrasts nicely with Fields's earlier lyrics, such as:

We dance and sing, we steal a touch of spring
I dream of everything we two have known
And yet my dreams have shown
Perhaps I dream too much alone

• • •

Lorenz Hart was one of the incomparable manipulators of the English language. His words for popular songs and Broadway musicals (when they were one and the same) rank him among the great lyricists of all time. He wrote lyrics for "With a Song in My Heart," "Ten Cents a Dance," "Where or When," "My Funny Valentine," "The Lady is a Tramp," "Falling in Love with Love," "Bewitched, Bothered and Bewildered," and hundreds more. He wrote the lyrics for *Poor Little Ritz Girl* in 1920, and *The Garrick Gaities* and *Dearest Enemy* in 1925. In 1926 alone, he wrote *The Girl Friend,* a second *Garrick Gaieties, Peggy Ann, Lido Lady* (in London), and *Betsy.* After that, Hart averaged two productions a year for the remaining twenty years of his short, unhappy life, including *A Connecticut Yankee, Jumbo, On Your Toes, Babes in Arms, I'd Rather be Right, The Boys from Syracuse, Pal Joey* and *By Jupiter.*

But I always knew
I would live life through
With a song in my heart for you

In the early 1930s Hart went to Hollywood for two years, but he didn't like it very much.

His thoughts are seldom consecutive
He just can't write

I know a movie executive
Who's twice as bright.

Broadway was Hart's lifelong beat, and his heart was in the sophisticated frenzy of "Manhattan":

We'll bathe at Brighton
The fish you'll frighten
When you're in
Your bathing suit so thin
Will make the shell-fish grin
Fin to fin

And Hart wrote what is probably the most cynical and self-examining of love songs, a torcher for all time:

Bewitched, bothered and bewildered am I.

By 1943, Hart was too ill and unhappy to continue writing. He bowed gracefully out of the new era launched by his partner Richard Rodgers and Oscar Hammerstein with *Oklahoma!* At the premiere his praise for their work was effusive and genuine. He probably saw the success of *Oklahoma!* as something that might be available to him if he could get his act together, and he stayed sober long enough to write half a dozen witty new songs for a revival of *A Connecticut Yankee.* But once the work was done, Hart went on a drinking binge from which he never recovered. On opening night, he stood in the back of the Vanderbilt Theatre and began talking incoherently to the actors onstage. Rodgers had him carried home.

Two days later Hart turned up at the hospital with pneumonia, from which he slipped into a coma, and shortly thereafter died. The sadness of his life is belied in many of his lyrics, and only hinted at in some of his acerbic works.

Hart's personal problems undoubtedly included extreme discomfort with his homosexuality and the shadowy life he was forced to lead. Richard Rodgers's autobiography is consistently supportive of his partner, but Rodgers never mentions the subject, and even claims that he had no idea what Hart was doing when he disappeared for days into the dark bars of

Broadway. This demonstrates extraordinary naiveté, willful obtuseness, or tight-lipped puritanism. (Rodgers could be unemotional at times—when geniuses Hart and Oscar Hammerstein gave him lyrics, he was known to call them only "satisfactory." When Hammerstein was diagnosed with an ulcer, he said of Rodgers, "The bastard finally did it to me." Rodgers, nonetheless, once described Hammerstein as "the closest friend I had.")

Hart wrote more than a few songs about love, which no nightclub act would be complete without:

> *It seems we stood and talked like this before.*
> . . . .
> *But who knows where or when.*

Why was the man who could dazzle Broadway with a lyric so desperately melancholic and alcoholic?

> *"Without a dream in my heart, Without a love of my own."*

Richard Rodgers said that Hart was "never easy to work with, always drank too much, would do anything to avoid getting down to work, always loved staying out late and carousing until dawn." But Hart wrote so fast and so well that nothing about his work shows anything but skill and insight. He once arrived late to a chaotic rehearsal and, when pressed for a number, instantly wrote a great lyric on the back of a used envelope with a pencil borrowed from a chorus girl ("Zip" for *Pal Joey*).

Hart was a compulsive check-grabber. The world was his oyster. He was witty; he was swell; he was a giant.

> *And the words in my ears*
> *Will resound for the rest of my years*

• • •

In the depths of the Great Depression, who would have thought that the hedonistic lyrics and luxurious melodies of Cole Porter would have resonance? Perhaps Porter's songs, and Broadway musicals in general, lingered in the giddy, silly 1920s format precisely because of the Depression. Like the growing popularity of the movie experience during the same decade, musicals were a haven from reality for a few safe hours. ("When Rockefeller still can hoard enough money to let Max Gordon produce his shows, Anything goes.") Porter himself was insulated from life's vagaries and vulgarities. He grew up wealthy and privileged in the Midwest, became a popular student at Yale, and pretended most of his life to be above hard work. Well above it—the thirty-third floor of the Waldorf Towers, to be precise, where Porter spent the last half of his life. After Yale he went to Paris, where he studied serious music by day (he even wrote one serious piece, a ballet), and picked up the jazz rhythms of newer music in the clubs by night. Porter was influenced by poet Robert Browning as much as by W. S. Gilbert. He worked as hard as he played, and his life was an odd combination of the Midwestern Protestant work ethic and the upper-class idea that it was unseemly to work at all. Porter worked hard to create effortless lyrics and rolling melodies.

But it was a life lived in a dark shadow—a double life of homosexuality and cruel health. He was crippled by a riding accident and in pain from the age of forty-six until he died at seventy-three. This curse was balanced by an unfailing optimism that never deserted him, and a wealthy wife who hosted and organized his jet-set existence. (Although there were no jets in Porter's day, Porter would have loved the notion and found a rhyme for it.) His dual existence was probably what led to so many cynical, tortured, love songs:

It's the wrong time and the wrong place
Though your face is charming, it's the wrong face,
It's not her face but such a charming face
That it's all right with me.

Porter's music was often informed by the tango ("Night and Day," "Just One of Those Things," "I've Got You Under My Skin,") and was often longer and more sinuous than the average popular song ("Begin the Beguine"). His style was wildly naughty ("But In the Morning, No"), and probably reflected his own party-filled life. And no one ever put racier, more eyebrow-lifting lyrics to music than Cole Porter:

Love for sale
Appetizing young love for sale

Love that's fresh and still unspoiled
Love that's only slightly soiled
Love for sale

(That one was banned from the radio in the United States.) Porter was also the king of the "list song," featuring his characteristic clever rhymes, contemporary references, and comic metaphors:

You're the top!
You're an Arrow collar
You're the top!
You're a Coolidge dollar
You're the nimble tread of the feet of Fred Astaire
You're an O'Neill drama
You're Whistler's mama
You're Camembert
You're a rose
You're inferno's Dante
You're the nose
On the great Durante
I'm just in the way, as the French would say, "De Trop"
But if Baby, I'm the bottom
You're the top.

He wrote lascivious verses of tortured emotions ("Miss Otis Regrets"), bouncing refrains of cheerfulness ("Friendship," "It's De-Lovely," "Just One of Those Things"), paeans ("I Happen to Like New York," "I Love Paris"), show-biz anthems ("Be a Clown," "Another Opening, Another Show"). He wrote for stars like Mary Martin ("My Heart Belongs To Daddy, Da-da, Da-da-da, Da-da-da-Dad") and Ethel Merman (*Anything Goes; Red, Hot and Blue; DuBarry Was a Lady; Panama Hattie;* and *Something for the Boys*). Like Sondheim, Porter's direct lyric descendant, Porter had an ear for the unusual in the usual ("What Is This Thing Called Love?")

He was known for his clever, sophisticated lyrics, but his work also resounds with haunting melodies ("In the Still of the Night," "Night and Day," and "All Through the Night"). And his lyrics could be haunting as well:

Or will this dream of mine
Fade out of sight
Like the moon
Growing dim
On the rim
Of the hill
In the chill,
Still
Of the night?

Later, Porter worked harder to integrate his songs, and those from his later shows (*Kiss Me Kate, Can-Can, Silk Stockings*) are more effective in context. *Kiss Me Kate,* which opened in 1948, was Porter's greatest theatre score. Here he sacrificed pop song writing in favor of well-integrated songs that dazzled with their lyrics ("I've Come to Wive it Wealthily in Padua"). Still, he managed to sneak in a Porter classic.

According to the Kinsey report
Ev'ry average man you know
Much prefers to play his favorite sport
When the temperature is low
But when the thermometer goes way up
And the weather is sizzling hot
Mister Adam
For his madam
Is not
'Cause it's too, too, too darn hot

The great lingering image of Cole Porter is that of his crippled body being carried down to third-row-center seats to enjoy the opening night of one of his musicals, his crisp tuxedo and smiling face leading a pack of good friends, while colleagues paced and chewed their nails in the back. Ça, c'est l'amour.

• • •

Prior to the integration of songs into story, lyricists were less restricted by the content of the drama around them. Although pop music would continue to arise from the musical theatre well beyond *Oklahoma!,* the age of frivolous musical comedies gave us songs that were intended to be extrapolated.

In the early days the composer usually offered a melody and the lyricist looked for words to suit it. This practice was common because of the many adaptations of European operettas, to which American lyricists wrote English lyrics. Composers also found it easier to work with the complex syncopations of ragtime, jazz, and music for the dance craze without lyrics to hinder them.

With the ascendancy of songs that had to support character and story, words began to precede music. Richard Rodgers provided the melodies for Lorenz Hart, but Oscar Hammerstein provided the book and lyrics for Rodgers. No one trod the line between real sentiment and treacle more nimbly than Hammerstein, who set many lyrics about (and put great store in) the simple pleasures of life. Hammerstein was the opposite of Hart and Porter, and he purposely avoided many opportunities for rhymes, feeling that lyrics should be unassertive. He particularly avoided the common rhymes often heard in other songs because he felt that the audience would guess it before the character sang it. He loved, in fact, to keep his audience waiting for a rhyme until the end, as in the chorus of "Ol' Man River," which could, but doesn't, feature clever rhyme schemes. This is also appropriate for the character of an uneducated black laborer.

Hammerstein's favorite lyrics were simple and straightforward ("I'm in Love With a Wonderful Guy"), but they could rise to the level of superb poetry. The following lyrics were based on a real experience, and he set them to an existing tune by Jerome Kern:

I have seen a line of snow-white birds
Drawn across an evening sky.
I have seen divine, unspoken words
Shining in a lover's eye
I have seen moonlight on a mountaintop,
Silver and cool and still.
I have heard church bells faintly echoing
Over a distant hill.
Close enough to beauty I have been,
And, in all the whole wide land,
Here's the sweetest sight that I have seen—
One old couple walking hand in hand.

Hammerstein, however, could be clever when he wanted. ("No fat-bottomed, flabby-faced, pot-bellied, baggy-eyed bastard'll boss him around!")

It often took Hammerstein weeks to write a simple lyric to a tune Kern had written in an hour, and when he worked with Richard Rodgers he often labored for weeks over a lyric that Rodgers would then set in an hour. Hammerstein's painstaking professionalism came from an experience he had over the opening chorus of *The Desert Song* with Sigmund Romberg, a number intended for the mush-mouthed men's chorus to sing in the opening moments of the operetta while the audience was still arriving. (Writers subsequently helped to break this habit by taking their opening moments more seriously.) Upon hearing his intentionally tossed-off lyrics in the crisp consonants of the London company, Hammerstein was embarrassed and never again took any lyric half-seriously. To illustrate the importance of this, Hammerstein told Stephen Sondheim that the hair on the head of the Statue of Liberty is finished even though it was created before aviation, when no one would have been able to see it.

Out of my dreams and into your arms I long to fly
I will come as evening comes to woo a waiting sky
Out of my dreams and into the hush of falling shadows,
When the mist is low, and stars are breaking through,
Then out of my dream I'll go,
Into a dream with you.

Like all lyric writers, Hammerstein searched endlessly for a new way to sing "I love you." He wrote for several plots that forbade the hero and heroine from admitting their love until late in the second act, leading him to a number of "don't admit it" love songs ("If I Loved You," "Only Make Believe").

After Hammerstein's experience with Jerome Kern, who extended the thirty-two bar song into new and complex forms, he wrote the granddaddy of all soliloquies for *Carousel.* He also wrote the classic commencement anthem ("You'll Never Walk Alone") and the great paean to Paris ("The last time I saw Paris . . ."). A good deal of his simple honesty seems old hat today, especially when he writes about women:

A fellow needs a girl
To sit by his side

At the end of a weary day,
To sit by his side
And listen to him talk
And agree with the things he'll say.

Yet no one expressed romantic love more clearly than Hammerstein:

Some enchanted evening
You may see a stranger
You may see a stranger
Across a crowded room
And somehow you know,
You know even then,
That somewhere you'll see her
Again and again

South Pacific probably contains Hammerstein's best work ("You've got to be carefully taught, to hate your brothers . . ." "There is Nothing Like a Dame," "I'm Gonna Wash That Man Right Outta My Hair"). It also included this simple song sung by a minor character about the famous island that enchanted sailors during World War II. "Bali Ha'i" soon overshadowed almost every "wish" song ever written.

Bali Ha'i
May call you,
Any night,
Any day.
In your heart
You'll hear it call you:
"Come away,
Come away."

Bali Ha'i
Will whisper
On the wind
Of the sea:
"Here am I,

Your special island!
Come to me
Come to me."
Bali Ha'i, Bali Ha'i, Bali Ha'i

As great as the score for *South Pacific* was, Hammerstein wrote his most eloquent, American, homespun lyrics with Jerome Kern. A number of overtly operatic lyrics for *Show Boat* (including "You Are Love," and "Why Do I Love You") were greatly bolstered by the great American tone poem "Ol' Man River," and this great blues ballad:

Fish got to swim, birds got to fly,
I got to love one man till I die—
Can't help lovin' dat man of mine

With Kern he also wrote every nightclub singer's favorite words:

The music is sweet
The words are true
The song is you

This number starts with one of the great clichés in lyric writing, except that Hammerstein invented it in 1932:

I hear music when I look at you.

Hammerstein heard music everywhere he looked, and he set that music to words more gracefully, and with more clarity, than any wordsmith before or since.

• • •

Two of the most famous names in musical theatre are Betty Comden and Adolph Green. Their notoriety as a writing team began with *On the Town* and progressed to *Billion Dollar Baby; Wonderful Town; Two on the Aisle; Peter Pan; Bells are Ringing; Do Re Mi; Subways are for Sleeping; Fade Out, Fade In; Hallelujah, Baby!; Applause; On the Twentieth Century;* and *The Will Rogers*

Follies. This represents an extraordinarily fruitful career lasting more than five decades, but it never featured a truly great hit or a masterpiece after *On the Town.* (By contrast, their screenplays for the movie musicals *Singin' in the Rain* and *The Band Wagon* have immortalized them.)

Comedy was their strong suit, and with Jule Styne they wrote these raucous words for Judy Holliday:

I'm goin' back
Where I can be me
At the Bonjour Tristess Brassiere Company
They've got a great big switchboard there
Where it's just "hello, goodbye"
It may be dull
But there I can be
Just me, myself and I
A little modeling on the side
That's where I'll be
At the Bonjour Tristess Brassiere Company
And if anybody asks for Ella, Mella or Mom
Tell them that I'm goin' back where I come from
To the Bonjour Tristess Brassiere Company

They listed "One Hundred Easy Ways to Lose a Man" and turned varietyese into a song. Probably no lyricist in history, even Gilbert or Porter, mined the "lists" as successfully as they did. While the female cab driver in *On the Town* sings "Come Up To My Place" to the sailor, his part of the duet consists solely of what he wants to see on his single day in New York, wherein Comden and Green manage to list nineteen New York City landmarks. When the heroine of *Bells Are Ringing* is nervous about a party, she is advised to drop a name. The lyric consists of three dozen celebrity names in rhyme.

Their work reverberates with the "my dad has a barn" style of bouncy musical comedy that flourished in the 1920s and never completely gave up its grip on the musical stage.

• • •

Many examples of the more sophisticated creation of lyrics for a musical scene come from the work of Alan Jay Lerner. Since a musical score can only hold so many I-love-yous, writing the rest of the songs for an integrated modern musical is no mean feat for the lyricist. The best example of an exciting musical moment cleverly woven out of a scene is the exuberant "Rain in Spain" from *My Fair Lady*.

The plot includes a scene in which Liza is learning to speak proper English. The highest emotional moment is when she achieves her breakthrough, and that is the moment Alan Jay Lerner and Frederick Loewe musicalized. Their take on the subject, including the use of the line "I think she's got it!" as a lyric, focuses on Liza's elocutionary exercises, principally "The rain in Spain falls mainly on the plain," and in the bridge the marvelous "In Hartford, Hereford, and Hampshire, hurricanes hardly happen." They make the moment into a great celebration, turning the verbal exercise itself into a bolero and encouraging dance as well.

My Fair Lady (1955) and *Camelot* (1960) both featured stars who were not singers—Rex Harrison and Richard Burton. The score for *My Fair Lady* not only suited a nonsinger but, not coincidentally, suited the cerebral philologist Professor Higgins down to his argyles. Although comic patter songs were as old as Gilbert and Sullivan, until then they were written for comedy, not for character.

Right from the opening, Lerner captures the character's arrogance and his concerns, in words that owe much more to Gilbert and Sullivan than to operetta:

Why can't the English teach their children how to speak?
Norwegians learn Norwegian
The Greeks are taught their Greek
In France every Frenchman knows his language from "A" to "Zed"
The French never care what they do, actually, as long as they pronounce it properly
Arabians learn Arabian with the speed of summer lightning
The Hebrews learn it backwards which is absolutely fright'ning
But use proper English you're regarded as a freak
Why can't the English learn to speak?

The talk songs that Lerner and Loewe pioneered revolutionized the musical by extending the range of characters available for the starring roles.

When *The Music Man* came along two years later—Meredith Wilson had been working on the score for seven years—the audience was prepared to hear a leading man chatter his way through several monologues. Anything else would have been overly operatic, for Harold Hill, Henry Higgins, and King Arthur were not the kind of men who could believably break into full-voiced, lush melodies. Suddenly a wider range of musical material was available to exploit leading characters who didn't fit into the romantic mold. Meredith Wilson's *Music Man* score solidified this. From the salesmen's opening ("Rock Island") to the Iowan character ("Iowa Stubborn") to the ladies gossip ("Pick a Little, Talk a Little") to the soft shoes ("Marian the Librarian" and "The Sadder-but-Wiser Girl For Me") to the con man's con ("Trouble in River City"), the score wrapped Midwestern characters in a thick, utterly suitable musical blanket. It was as far from opera as you could get—and as close to good theatre.

Lerner's upper-class education led him to write often for intelligent characters, which he did with vocabulary rather than overtly clever rhymes:

But let a woman in your life
And your serenity is through!
She'll redecorate your home
From the cellar to the dome;
Then go on to the enthralling
Fun of overhauling
You.

If he always wrote in high style, he never let it interfere with his even greater characteristic, his poetic side, as in "They Call the Wind Maria," "If Ever I Would Leave You," "There But For You Go I," and:

A law was made a distant moon ago here
July and August cannot be too hot
And there's a legal limit to the snow here
In Camelot

After Frederick Loewe retired, Lerner wrote *On a Clear Day You Can See Forever* (1965), with music by Burton Lane—a charming musical with a rich score that ran only 280 performances. He also wrote *Coco* (1969) with André Previn; *Lolita, My Love* (1971), based on the provocative book by Vladimir Nabokov, with John Barry, which closed out of town; *Music!*

Music! (1974), a revue Lerner compiled as a tribute to the musical theatre he loved so much, which had a foreshortened run; *1600 Pennsylvania Avenue* (1976) with Leonard Bernstein, that ran only seven performances; *Carmelina* (1979), which ran for seventeen performances; and *Dance a Little Closer* (1983) with Charles Strouse, based on Robert Sherwood's *Idiot's Delight,* which closed on opening night.

The last shows of Lerner's career were fraught with problems and his last years with failure, but his lyrics always remained witty, clever, and sophisticated. He was once sued for divorce by one of his eight wives on the grounds of mental cruelty: she reported that he spent a week writing the words "loverly, loverly, loverly." He was a painstaking perfectionist, and as in all the best lyrics, there are no forced rhythms or rhymes—only the heart and soul of the characters.

• • •

Few women authored Broadway lyrics during the golden age (fewer still composed music), but Carolyn Leigh left a strong mark as one of those able to write in the sexy, sophisticated style of Lorenz Hart:

I've got your number
I know you inside out
You ain't no eagle scout
You're all at sea
Oh yes you brag a lot
Wave your own flag a lot
But you're unsure a lot
You're a lot like me
Oh, I've got your number
And what you're looking for
And what you're looking for
Just suits me fine
We'll break those rules a lot
We'll be damn fools a lot
But then why should we not
How could we not combine, when
I've got your number
And I've got the glow you've got

I've got your number
And baby, you know you've got mine

She could also write in a simpler style ("Pardon me miss, But I've never done this, With a real live girl"), as she did for *Peter Pan* ("I Gotta Crow" and "I'm Flying"). Although her lyrics for the musical *Smile* were replaced after she died, many people who heard the original score speak fondly of Leigh's satiric wit and humor.

• • •

The majority of lyricists worked hard to write songs that were intelligent and clever while owing their first allegiance to character, setting, and plot. But Tim Rice, writing for a far less particular theatre—rock and roll transported to the stage—seemed often not to care about these niceties. With lyrics like "Who could ever be fond of the back of beyond?" and nonsense like "I only want variety of society," and drivel like "What's new? Buenos Aires, I'm new—I wanna say I'm just a little stuck on you, You'll be on me too!" his shows are virtually illiterate. ("Take me in at your flood give me speed give me lights set me humming.") Phrases like "Shout me up with your blood" and "Wine me up with your nights" (which would sing "wind me up") sound plain dumb, and it's important to stay away from phrases like "watch me coming," unless you want the double meaning. Lyrics like "Let's get this show on the road" and rhymes like "They need to adore me, so Christian Dior me" or "That's what they call me, so Lauren Bacall me" are out of place in a story set in Argentina just after World War II.

Perhaps Rice's success lies in the fact that his shows are really staged rock concerts, and his lyrics nearly immaterial. Little effort is made to investigate character, reflect time or place, or even forward the plot.

• • •

In direct contrast to the vapid pop lyrics of Rice is Stephen Sondheim.

As pop music separated from show songs, theatre lyrics were freed to concentrate on specifics. More songs were particular to character, story, time, and place. Although the public still bought and listened to the great theatre scores, they did so with cast albums of entire shows, and fewer individual songs broke into the "top forty" or were part of the nightclub repertoire. Increasingly, the weakest songs in a show were generic, and the best were specific—just the opposite of the 1920s musicals.

Finally, a composer was lucky to write one or two songs for a show that had breakout capacity. Jule Styne wrote a rich score for Barbra Streisand in *Funny Girl,* but only "People" and "The Music That Makes Me Dance" have traveled beyond the show. In the case of Styne's seminal *Gypsy* for Ethel Merman, a towering musical achievement in which every song is remarkable, none of them really work out of context.

Sondheim, the most specific theatre lyricist of all, evolved from his *Gypsy* lyrics with Jule Styne into a composer-lyricist who was immediately at home on Broadway. When Judy Collins's version of Sondheim's "Send in the Clowns" actually got some radio play, the composer himself must have been startled. Sondheim's songs are as indigenous to his shows as Jerome Robbins's dance steps are to his. (All the rhyme examples at the beginning of this chapter are from Sondheim songs.)

Sondheim most appreciates the work of his mentor Oscar Hammerstein II, in particular the way Hammerstein wrote songs that grew out of the dramatic material organically, and disparages the work of Richard Rodgers's first collaborator Lorenz Hart. Yet Sondheim's work is more closely identified with Hart than with Hammerstein. Hart, along with Cole Porter, initiated the complicated rhymes, caustic wit, ambivalence, urban associations, and sophisticated language that Sondheim relies on. Hammerstein himself understood this. "I *believe* in wind and willow trees," he once said to Sondheim. "You don't." In fact, while Sondheim's songs are brilliantly integrated with the dramatic text, the lyrics are often so intricate and wordy that they draw attention to themselves over their sentiment.

Shorter and shorter phrases have characterized Sondheim's work since *Pacific Overtures,* in which he imitated haiku. Some songs seem virtually constipated. The tiny musical "dots" that begin *Sunday in the Park with George* (to reflect Georges Seurat's pointillist style) have threatened to overwhelm Sondheim's work. He's increasingly addicted to short phrases, cerebral ideas, and sophisticated vocabulary:

In view of her penchant
For something romantic

de Sade is too trenchant
And Dickens too frantic
And Stendhal would ruin
The plan of attack
As there isn't much blue in
The Red and the Black

This intellectualization and the lack of fundamental emotions in Sondheim's shows have denied him a larger audience, even while musical theatre mavens consider him the best composer-lyricist of the post-Hammerstein era.

Ambivalence:

You're always sorry
You're always grateful
You're always wondering what might have been
Then she walks in

and cynicism:

Someone to hold me too close
Someone to hurt me with love

often characterize Sondheim's work, which wouldn't hurt if he could embrace more universal ideas. But, true to his material and himself, he doesn't compromise.

• • •

As choreography, staging, and direction became increasingly dynamic, lyrics needed to support the new look. They needed to add activity to their other attributes. More and more choreographer-directors wanted to know exactly *what* was supposed to be happening on stage during a song. The great musical comedy sequence in the modern era kept the performers moving as well as the plot.

There is no greater example of integrated theatre lyrics than those written for *A Chorus Line,* and no better example of a *useful* lyric exists than "I Can Do That," in which a character tells the story of observing his sister in tap class and wanting to join in. As the character tells the story, he *acts it out.* The story is a song, the song is a dance.

These lyrics were the first and last created by Edward S. Kleban, a talented but blocked writer who earned his living as a record producer, wrote music and lyrics for a number of unproduced musical projects, taught young lyricists at the BMI Musical Theatre Workshop, and died prematurely.

Kleban's lyrics were character-specific. It was his genius to select from the dancer's stories those ideas that would best support a musical number, then turn them into lyrics. In addition to poring over the audiotapes, Kleban interviewed dancers on his own until he found subjects worth musicalizing. For the opening number, Kleban's collaborators were creating music and dances for an audition, but Kleban put their nerves, fears, hopes, and dreams into the lyrics. This gave the sequence an extra dimension that only theatre inner monologue can:

Who am I anyway?
Am I my resumé?
That is a picture of a person I don't know
What does he want from me?
What should I try to be?
So many faces all around, and here we go
I need this job
Oh God I need this show

He turned emotions into lyrics:

Everything was beautiful at the ballet
Raise your arms, and someone's always there
Yes, everything was beautiful at the ballet
I was pretty
I was happy
"I would love to"
At the ballet

To do this, he sometimes used comedy:

See I really couldn't sing

I could never really sing
What I couldn't do was sing
I have trouble with a note
It goes all around my throat
It's a terrifying thing

And sometimes he used pathos:

Play me the music
Give me a chance to come through
All I ever needed was the music
And the mirror
And the chance to dance for you

Even for the eleven o'clock spot, he was able to find an emotion universal enough for a hit, although "What I Did For Love" never achieved the popularity it would have in a musical written twenty years earlier. By 1975, America's taste in music was simply too far removed from Broadway theatre songs.

PLAYBILL

Jan. 20, 1958

a weekly magazine for theatregoers

Twenty-Four

Music

Guard against the natural tendency to make too frequent use of the sustaining pedal.

—George Gershwin on popular Broadway music

The golden age provided America with one of the great cultural chievements of the twentieth century—the musical comedy song. Ira Gershwin explained that music communicated an emotion to the heart, and lyrics an idea to the head. The song, he said, delivers an idea to the heart.

The early composers jotted down melodies in a notebook and pulled them up when they got an assignment. But the modern composer was more likely to be given a text—often including lyrics—and asked to create a musical fabric to suit it.

The question of musical ambience has always been one of the hardest for composers. Every great Broadway composer has a unique style of his own. You wouldn't confuse a Cole Porter song with a Leonard Bernstein one, or Lerner and Loewe with Kander and Ebb. Without asking songwriters to jeopardize what they do best, it is nevertheless necessary for the music to be specific to the setting. Unless the music supports the drama it isn't *theatre*—it's opera or concert music. On the other hand, good composers of film background music—the quintessence of scoring ambience—have often failed to write a good Broadway score. (*Merlin* and *How Now Dow Jones* by Elmer Bernstein; *Ballroom* by Billy Goldenberg; and *Baby* and *Big* by David Shire are five stultefyingly boring theatre scores by talented film composers.) Their music is simply too generic to give the musical a special identity. "What passes for sweet tunesmithery in a movie musical," wrote the acerbic critic John Simon on the occasion of the Broadway version of *Victor/Victoria* (music by Henry Mancini), "looks anemic on a Broadway stage." A multitude of young imitators of Stephen Sondheim—musical theatre writers' workshops are chock-a-block with them—have continually failed to write a decent Broadway score because they're imitating Sondheim's voice rather than offering their own.

Richard Rodgers wrote in a rich, romantic style, lush with lilting melodies and comfortable harmonies. Yet each of his scores successfully integrates an appropriate musical style as well. The title song of *Oklahoma!* is built on a hoedown rhythm. *Carousel* states its hurdy-gurdy, steam calliope origins right from the pantomime opening. *The King and I* is infused with Eastern harmonics. (But Rodgers didn't compromise his identity or the eight-tone scale. For *Pacific Overtures,* Stephen Sondheim strayed so far from Western music that he left most of his listeners behind.)

It is no coincidence that a majority of great Broadway musicals (three of the ten longest-running, and all three of the Pulitzer Prize-winners) take place in an American setting, for composers are most comfortable when they don't have to overreach for a compromise. Although great American musicals have been set in exotic locations, the full integration of music and lyrics with subject matter is easier in an American setting. Thus *Gypsy* is the quintessential American musical, its score the best of both Broadway pizazz and the raunch of vaudeville and burlesque. Without belittling offshore stories, it is fair to say that writers write best about what they know, and American composers usually work best with native subject matter. It would be hard to imagine Gershwin, for example, scoring a royal story set in Luxembourg as well as he did *Porgy and Bess.*

Now to the contrary: *My Fair Lady* (set in England), *The King and I* (Siam), and *Fiddler on the Roof* (Russia). There have been some fine scores for less successful offshore plots, such as *Can-Can* (set in Paris) by Cole Porter. *High Spirits* is set in Noël Coward's England in the twenties, but its

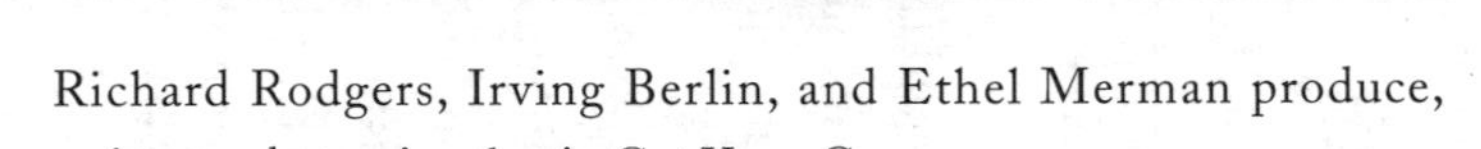

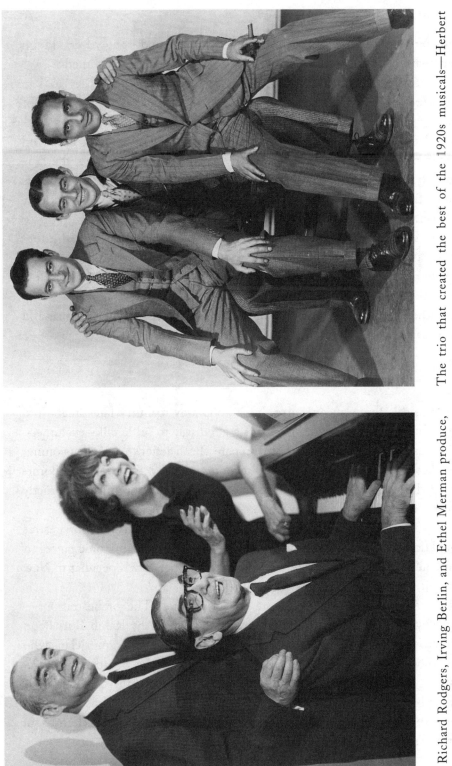

Richard Rodgers, Irving Berlin, and Ethel Merman produce, write, and star in *Annie Get Your Gun*
Photofest

The trio that created the best of the 1920s musicals—Herbert Fields (book) Richard Rodgers (music) and Lorenz Hart (lyrics)
Photofest

swinging-fifties, American pop score by Hollywood songwriters Hugh Martin and Timothy Blane (*Meet Me in St. Louis*) buoys this comedy.

Sometimes a compromise is reached before the composer goes to work. *Liliom,* set in Budapest, was moved to colonial New England for *Carousel.* Sometimes a production requires some identity other than its setting. *A Funny Thing Happened on the Way to the Forum* is not based on Roman music, whatever that is, but on vaudeville and burlesque, the dramatic style intended for that hilarious musical. The wonderful connection is that no two theatre styles in history were more related than Roman Comedy and American burlesque.

In the most productive years of the American musical, the formula was teased and tortured into a thousand different songs and dances by a hundred talented songwriters. Many good (and bad) musicals followed the pattern precisely, others stretched its barriers. The good musicals either followed the form or broke away from it with confidence and good reason.

• • •

Few musicals forgo an **overture**. It's a good way to hurry latecomers into their seats before the curtain rises. It's a good way to settle talky customers. It's a chance for the composer to prepare the listener's ear for upcoming melodies. The darkening of the auditorium and the white spotlight illuminating the maestro with his baton in the air can set the musical comedy lover's pulse racing. A great overture is foreplay.

The greatest overture of all is from *Gypsy.* Philharmonic orchestras would do well to consider it one of American's greatest symphonic pieces (if they could play it—playing show music in the proper zetz is peculiar to New York pit musicians). The first runner-up is *Funny Girl.*

An overture requires more than melodies. The orchestrations—*Gypsy* by Sid Ramin and Robert Ginzler, *Funny Girl* by Ralph Burns and Luther Henderson, both from scores by Jule Styne—and the musicians who play idiosyncratic show music so well are unique to the Broadway theatre. Listen to these two overtures on the original Broadway cast recordings, conducted by Milton Rosenstock. Then listen to the same overtures as recorded for the film versions. Clearly, something is missing—the heart and soul of the American musical theatre.

As the musical theatre grew more dramatic, writers and directors became restless with the overture. After all, nothing was really happening, and keeping the musical moving had become their creed. So Jack Cole choreographed an introduction to the characters for *Donnybrook*'s overture; *Baker Street* began with a scene introducing Sherlock Holmes, *then* played its overture; and *Superman* integrated its overture with cartoon bits. *Carousel* was conceived without an overture, but with a pantomime prologue that not only set the scene, but provided an important plot point. Harold Prince and Michael Bennett created an eerie, ghostly pageant for *Follies* as a prologue, which was less a collection of the upcoming songs than a foreboding piece of music on its own. Then for *A Chorus Line,* Bennett jettisoned the overture altogether. "Out of the darkness comes *A Chorus Line,*" he once joked, and indeed the lights come up and we're plunged into a world of thundering dancers already in motion.

No element of the musical theatre is more telling than **the opening number**. "If you start with the right opening," Sondheim quotes Hammerstein's teachings, "you can ride for 45 minutes on the telephone book. On the other hand, if you start off with a wrong one it's an uphill fight all the way." David Merrick always felt that he could judge a musical in the first ten minutes. Although George Abbott once wisely said, "I'd rather have a show start slow than end slow," nothing is more crippling than a bad opening number. Unless it's the wrong opening number.

When *A Funny Thing Happened on the Way to the Forum* tried out in Washington D.C., it nearly died. It was a comedy but audiences simply were not laughing. Producer Harold Prince was in trouble and brought in Jerome Robbins as a doctor.

(*Forum*'s star Zero Mostel, blacklisted during the McCarthy era, was gingerly canvassed about this, as his animosity toward Robbins, who had named names in order to protect his career, was well known. "We of the left," Mostel informed the producers when they asked his permission, "have no blacklist.")

The tryout of *Forum* opened with a clever and melodic Sondheim song, "Love is in the Air." A month before rehearsals had begun the writers felt something was wrong, and Sondheim crafted "Invocation" (*"Gods of the theater, smile on us . . ."*), but George Abbott didn't like it. (The song stayed in Sondheim's trunk until years later when he adapted it for his musical version of Aristophanes' *Frogs.*) When Robbins arrived, he pointed out that the show's principal dramatic value was not its plot. The plot was merely the springboard on which the style, a slavish devotion to broad humor, was propped. It was this humor that powered the musical.

"Comedy Tonight" was hurriedly written out of town, staged by Robbins, and inserted at the New York preview. Sondheim's claim that he works better under pressure was never better proved (unless perhaps with "Send in the Clowns" from *A Little Night Music,* or "I'm Still Here" from *Follies,* also out-of-town substitutions). "Comedy Tonight" became a classic, and probably no better opening song exists. Its greatest value is that it tells the audience what's going to happen. Lo and behold, everything else in the musical began getting laughs. Suddenly the audience was convulsed by Larry Gelbart and Burt Shevelove's book, one of the funniest ever written for the American musical theatre, and Stephen Sondheim's humorous songs.

Robbins worked with Jerry Bock, Sheldon Harnick, and producer Harold Prince to create another textbook opening for *Fiddler on the Roof.* "Tradition" limns the bonds that tie Tevye to his village and to the old ways. He introduces that tradition piece by piece, beginning with the fathers:

Who day and night must scramble for a living
Feed a wife and children
Say his daily prayers?
And who has the right as master of the house
To have the final word at home?

The mothers are next:

Who must know the way to make a proper home
A quiet home
A kosher home?
Who must raise a family and run the home
So Papa's free to read the holy book?

Then come the sons:

At three I started Hebrew school
At ten I learned a trade

I hear they picked a bride for me
I hope she's pretty

And finally the daughters are introduced:

And who does Mama teach
To mend and tend and fix?
Preparing me to marry
Whoever Papa picks
Tradition!

All of the family members are given their place in this society, which is based on enforced isolation from the outside world, poverty, and religion. The number is staged in flowing circular patterns, circles within circles representing the insular community.

A list of great opening numbers would be as long as a list of great musicals. Among the most unusual is "Rock Island" from *The Music Man.* Door-to-door salesmen riding a train to their next territory talk about their job, and about the notorious con man who is giving them a bad reputation. They talk in brisk, rhythmic sentences underscored primarily by the rhythm of the train they're riding. The effect is a cantata in syncopation that at once introduces the plot; paints the small town, turn-of-the-century ambience; warns us that we're in for a most unusual score; and introduces the principal character, who sits through the number with his back to the audience, quietly fleecing his colleagues at poker.

The opening segues directly into the song "Iowa Stubborn," a hymn to the warm but wary rural character that the music man will face in his next swindle—thus, the principal conflict and the leading man's obstacles are set up. Much as we are charmed by the character of Harold Hill, a con man can hardly be called a hero; he's probably the second antihero in musical theatre literature. Unlike pal Joey, however, in the end he learns his lesson and is reformed, by the love of a good woman, of course.

It's good practice to put a lot of information into the opening number. In the opening to *1776* we get ambience (*"It's hot as hell in Philadelphia"*); the principal conflict (*"Sit down, John!"*); John Adams's obsession (*"By God I have had this Congress!"*); his great heart (*"Oh, Abigail"*); and even a taste of the absurd political bickering that will characterize the nation's birth pangs (*"Someone ought to open up a window—No, no, too many flies!"*).

In the budding age of the director-choreographer, theatricality was a key as well. For *Carnival,* Gower Champion began with a quiet meadow and set up the entire carnival in choreographed pantomime (to "Love Makes the World Go 'Round"), leading to the carny folk introducing themselves in "Direct from Vienna." Mama Rose interrupts the opening of *Gypsy* when she enters from the rear of the auditorium shouting "Sing out, Louise!" as her daughter auditions for Uncle Jocko—there's no doubt who is the star of this show.

If the desires of the leading character are not spelled out in the opening, **the want song** is next. *West Side Story* contains a classic. Tony doesn't even *know* what he wants, but he's bursting with adolescent energy (reflected beautifully in the galloping rhythm) that he can't focus (demonstrated in the long, arching, yearning notes of the melody). He's just positive that "Something's Coming."

Fiddler's leading man tries to cope with the storms of change around him, most notably five strong-minded daughters praying that the town matchmaker will find them a match. Their desires are exploited in "Matchmaker, Matchmaker." All the king's son wants in *Pippin* is his "Corner of the Sky." And *The Music Man*'s Harold Hill will soon meet up with a woman who wants a man ("Goodnight, My Someone"). Since Harold is anything but a good catch, we're already on the edge of our seat. *Gypsy*'s Mama Rose sings, "Some people . . . but not me."

It was time for **the nine o'clock number**. In the vehicle musical, a star turn is best. Ethel Merman's "Some People" gives us her desires as well as her angry, driven character. In *Charity,* Gwen Verdon told us all about her nemesis—men—through "Charity's Soliloquy." "I Got Love" launched both Melba Moore and *Purlie.* Hear also *Funny Girl*'s "I'm the Greatest Star" and *South Pacific*'s "Cock-Eyed Optimist."

Before long the chorus should fill the stage. "Coffee Break" from *How to Succeed in Business Without Really Trying* allows a plethora of executives and secretaries to illuminate their angst. Jerry Herman combined the secondary character's wants with a chorus number by having all the men chime in with bachelor Horace Vandergelder, singing "It Takes a Woman." Throughout the rest of the evening a variety of songs and dances were necessary to the traditional musical.

Soliloquies. *Carousel*'s, conveniently called "Soliloquy," is the mother of them all. Billy agonizes over the news that he's going to be a father and all that fatherhood entails. We are touched by his suddenly discovered love for the unborn child even while we worry that he's going to do the wrong thing. (He does.) His thought process—from "my boy Bill" to "What if it's a she?" to "What can I do to support her?"—explains his justification for returning to a life of crime, so we feel sorry for him even as he does the stupid thing.

True soliloquies are inner monologues, also effective as eleven o'clock numbers when the leading character reaches a climactic turning point or decision. In *1776* John Adams, frustrated beyond anyone's patience that time is running out and he cannot get a majority of his congressional brethren to support independence, asks, *"Is anybody there? Does anybody care? Does anybody see what I see?"* in a stirring cry which only music could fully support.

Male chorus numbers. "There Is Nothing Like a Dame" from *South Pacific*. A stirring sound, and a chance for the women to change costumes. Its corollary is the female chorus number. The *Florodora* sextet was infamous, and many say caused the success of a show the critics disliked.

The show-within-the-show. "Honey Bun" in *South Pacific* is a USO show. "Let Me Entertain You" is *Gypsy*'s leitmotif, becoming in the end *Gypsy*'s striptease.

The list song. "You say tomato, and I say to-mah-to." Enumerating one's gifts ("I Can Cook Too" from *On the Town*) or reasons ("Why Do I Love You?") is dramatic, but the lyricist must be careful of overuse because, like "Ninety-Nine Bottles of Beer on the Wall," list songs basically go nowhere.

The song and dance. If you have Ray Bolger, use him. Frank Loesser's *Where's Charley?* boasts the classic "Once in Love With Amy." Swen Swenson stopped *Little Me* with "I've Got Your Number" because Bob Fosse set it as a male strip tease. Matt Mattox, one of Broadway's seminal jazz teachers, dazzled *Once Upon a Mattress* (an off-Broadway production with a charming score by Richard Rodgers's daughter Mary and lyricist Marshall Baer) with his "Very Soft Shoes." Ethel Merman sang seven numbers in *Gypsy,* but she can't dance, so "All I Need is the Girl" is for Tulsa, who demonstrates his new dance act.

The pure dance number. A favorite of choreographers. Self-contained dances tend to be less integrated, unless the leads can dance and the book demands it. Jerome Robbins set the standard with "The Mack Sennet Ballet" from *High Button Shoes* and "The Speakeasy" from *Billion Dollar Baby.* Bob Fosse scored twice, with "Rich Kid's Rag" in *Little Me* and "Rich Man's Frug" in *Sweet Charity.* Gower Champion's high point was the "Waiter's Gallop" in *Hello, Dolly!* Michael Kidd's "Crapshooters' Ballet" is a male classic. When the dance *is* the plot—the "Rape" in *Man of La Mancha*—dance is at its very best in the modern musical.

The barbershop quartet. Frank Loesser's "Standing on the Corner" from *The Most Happy Fella.* When properly staged, this number is done without staging. The quartet should be doing exactly what they say they are, and no more. In *The Music Man* Meredith Wilson actually turned the city fathers into a barbershop quartet, a style of music perfectly suited to the Midwest at the turn of the century, and the act was a neat metaphor for cooperation, a trait for which the four cantankerous councilmen had not previously been noted. Their best full number is "Lida Rose," but they have bits and pieces throughout, providing a recurrent motif.

The duet. Stands for dialogue and so easily advances the plot. *Fiddler*'s "Do You Love Me?" between Tevye and Golde, *Gigi*'s "I Remember It Well" (written for the film), and *All American*'s "Once Upon a Time" elevate comic dialogue. *West Side Story*'s Tony and Maria pledge "One Hand, One Heart." *Company*'s "Barcelona" broke the tradition of trading identical choruses, or even lines, for a much more intricate trading of dialogue within a long melody line. A good subcategory is the challenge duet—"There Once Was a Man" (*Pajama Game*) and "Anything You Can Do" (*Annie Get Your Gun*).

When dance is included, the classic vaudeville two-act is invoked. "Who's Got the Pain When They Do the Mambo?" coupled Eddie Phillips and Gwen Verdon. *Show Boat* gives Frank and Ellie two vaudeville turns.

Often in the first act the hero and heroine are not ready to admit they're falling in love—not to each other, anyway: "They Say That Falling in Love Is Wonderful" from *Annie Get Your Gun;* "We Could Make Believe" from *Show Boat;* "Wonder How It Feels" from *South Pacific;* and "People Will Say We're in Love" from *Oklahoma!*

The comic song. Not so easy. Funny music is hard to write, and if a lyricist was quick with jokes he'd be a bookwriter. Usually it's the underlying idea that scores. "Brush Up Your Shakespeare" from *Kiss Me Kate* gives two comic gangsters a chance to mangle the bard. "Gee, Officer Krupke" lets the

Jets imitate their elders in a burlesque of do-gooders. When a great clown gets his tongue around some lyrics, as in Bert Lahr's "If I Were King of the Forest" (from the film *The Wizard of Oz*), he can tickle the audience unmercifully.

If the musical has an intermission, it will require a **first-act finale.** Among its many powerful if incongruous numbers, *Hello, Dolly!* closes the first act with a parade. *Promises, Promises* ends the first act with an office party that conveniently turns into a rowdy dance. The most recent showstopper was "I'm Not Going" from *Dreamgirls*—the only trouble was that as the fat lady sang, the opera was over.

The unusual and clever. "I Believe in You" sounds like a perfectly straightforward love song (Hollywood stupidly straightened it out), but in fact Robert Morse sings it to himself in *How to Succeed*'s executive washroom mirror. "Pore Jud is Ded" gives the villain of *Oklahoma!* a somber and sympathetic look at his own funeral.

The flat-out showstopper. There's a framed letter on David Merrick's wall from Hal Prince in which Prince tells Merrick that his proposed new musical, *Hello, Dolly!*, looks very good in script form. "But get rid of that title number," he writes. He explains that Dolly Levi is hardly the kind of woman who would, or could afford to, patronize the Harmonium Gardens restaurant, and certainly the waiters wouldn't make such a fuss. The moral here is that good usually works. (Prince tried to get the letter back after the show opened.)

The talk song. George Bernard Shaw's *Pygmalion* so sparkles with language that no music, the theory went, could hope to equal it. But Alan Jay Lerner and Frederick Loewe gave the curmudgeonly philologist an expressive rap. It didn't hurt that their talent was as sparkling as Shaw's, but the key—in both *My Fair Lady* and *The Music Man*—was the neat fit of the character and the style within which the songs were written. Gwen Verdon also got her share of songs that verged on syncopated talking ("Herbie Fitch's Dilemma" from *Redhead*, and much of *Sweet Charity*) because her husky, quirky, honey-soaked but small voice had a limited range and lacked the strength to belt, the traditional style for dancers.

The eleven o'clock number. The star turn is virtually expected if the star is talented enough. Judy Holliday's greatest was "I'm Goin' Back" in *Bells Are Ringing*. Dolly Levi tells Ephraim "So Long, Dearie." Charity and the dancers perform "I'm a Brass Band." A supporting player can lead the chorus in a showstopper ("Sit Down, You're Rockin' the Boat," "Brotherhood of Man"). Best of all, the drama can reach a climax ("Promises, Promises," "Is Anybody There?") or the theme can be stated ("The Impossible Dream"). One way or another, the interior rhythm of the musical demands that the story's climax be musicalized.

The scene change song. These are no longer necessary, but before mechanized sets more than one songwriter used them to advantage. *My Fair Lady*'s "On the Street Where You Live," wouldn't be needed with today's high-tech set changes, but its loss would be a pity. Ruth Etting's "Love Me or Leave Me" from *Whoopee* is the best of a lovely breed, so exquisite that it became identified with her and not the show.

And of course, **the ballad.** There isn't much to say about these beyond the obvious, except that in its heyday, Broadway was awash in the best of the breed. Jule Styne's "People," Meredith Wilson's "Till There Was You," Lerner and Loewe's "If Ever I Would Leave You," and Lionel Bart's "As Long As He Needs Me." A lyricist really does his job when he gives this age-old formula a unique new twist. Martha Jefferson sings about how good a lover her husband Thomas is by telling us how well "He Plays the Violin." Forced to accommodate the unusual and specific texts of the *Chorus Line* stories, Marvin Hamlisch and Ed Kleban were increasingly frustrated that their score was not going to have a hit tune in it. Eventually they came up with the ballad "What I Did For Love," a love song to a life style, and conveniently placed it in the eleven o'clock spot. Michael Bennett went along grudgingly, since it was exactly the kind of generic book-slower that he assiduously avoided. But somewhere deep down in his show-biz soul, Bennett knew it was going to work. You have to give the audience something.

• • •

For *Guys and Dolls* (1950), director George S. Kaufman warned Frank Loesser, "If you reprise the songs, I'll reprise the jokes." But then, Kaufman was the most antimusical writer-director in the history of the American musical. He once told the composer of *Redhead* and *Plain and Fancy,* Albert Hague, that "music is a very expensive and unnecessary element in the musical theatre."

When the musical theatre lost its hold on the "top forty," it gained a firmer grip on the idea of the plot- and character-driven songs. Songs were cut if they didn't fit, didn't move the show forward, or didn't grow naturally out of the surrounding book ideas. There were still occasional breakthroughs—Barbra Streisand's recording of "People" helped push *Funny Girl.* And there were some failures—neither Steve Lawrence's nor Sammy Davis Jr.'s recordings of "I've Gotta Be Me" could save *Golden Rainbow* from a slow death. *Baker Street,* the Sherlock Holmes musical, almost got off the ground when Richard Burton recorded "A Married Man." (This was not because of his singing. He was having a well-publicized affair with Elizabeth Taylor at the time, and they were the most famous adulterous couple in the world. That's context, too.) Numerous recordings of "The Impossible Dream" can't replace its power in context. You just don't get goosebumps when Barry Manilow sings "What I Did For Love."

• • •

The premodern era of Broadway musicals was the heyday of the songwriter, and America's most successful writer of popular songs was musically illiterate, played rudimentary piano in one key only (F-sharp), and never wrote a musical that altered or improved the reigning format. Instead of creating original shows, Irving Berlin confined himself to original melodies, composing more than eight hundred of them in a Tin Pan Alley style that tolled the death knell for the European-influenced romantic operetta.

Berlin was born in Russia and emigrated to the United States as a child. After a stint as a fourteen-year-old chorus boy in a touring musical, a teenage apprenticeship as a singer in Bowery saloons and restaurants, a job plugging songs, some successful lyrics for other composers, and his first published song ("Marie from Sunny Italy"), Berlin wrote music and lyrics for "Alexander's Ragtime Band" at the age of twenty-three. This remarkable song, which altered American popular musical taste forever, popularized "ragtime" (without actually using ragtime meter), and launched the fast dance crazes—the Turkey Trot, Bunny Hug, Grizzly Bear, Castle Walk, Charleston, and Black Bottom—into American ballrooms and restaurants where popular music was played. Overnight, Berlin became one of Tin Pan Alley's most sought-after songwriters. In spite of many Broadway scores, he never really left Tin Pan Alley and his songs are nearly interchangeable among his shows.

Berlin's first full score was written for *Watch Your Step* (1914), featuring Irene and Vernon Castle. It was really a revue (the program read "Plot, if any, by Harry B. Smith"), and it was the first Broadway score to use ragtime, billed as "The First All-Syncopated Musical." (Scott Joplin had written a ragtime folk opera in 1911, *Treemonisha,* but it did not get produced in his lifetime.)

Berlin served in the American army in World War I, after which he wrote the all-soldier revue *Yip! Yip! Yaphank* (1918), which featured "Oh, How I Hate To Get Up in the Morning!" as well as the cakewalk "Mandy." Florenz Ziegfeld asked Berlin to write a *Follies* in 1919, for which Berlin created that producer's most enduring anthem, "A Pretty Girl is Like a Melody."

Berlin was anxious to highlight his songs more than Ziegfeld's girls, so he and George M. Cohan's old partner Sam Harris conceived small-scale revues for which they built the Music Box Theatre. They filled the venue with the lush but tasteful *Music Box Revues,* featuring extraordinarily inventive staging by Hassard Short and John Murray Anderson. Berlin's early book musicals include *The Cocoanuts* (1925), featuring the Marx Brothers, and *Betsy* (1926). In the 1930s Berlin followed the trend to more political stories with *Face the Music* (1932), which was about police and political corruption during the Depression; *As Thousands Cheer* (1933), a topical revue; and *Louisiana Purchase* (1940), also mildly political.

The Depression drove a number of great songwriters to Hollywood, and none was more successful in the new medium than Berlin, who wrote scores for Fred Astaire and Ginger Rogers (*Top Hat, Follow the Fleet,* and *Carefree*); Astaire and Bing Crosby (*Blue Skies* and *Holiday Inn*); Astaire and Judy Garland (*Easter Parade*); and Alice Fay (*On the Avenue* and *Alexander's Ragtime Band*). For World War II Berlin created a second successful all-soldier revue, *This Is the Army* (1942).

By the mid-1940s Berlin was unsure whether he could write songs under the constraints of the modern Broadway musical. When Richard Rodgers and Oscar Hammerstein invited him to score *Annie Get Your Gun* for Ethel Merman, he hesitated and promised only to think about it. "I don't know how to write western lyrics," he said. ("It's simple," Hammerstein encouraged, "you just drop all your g's.") But Berlin took the job in the end, insisted on composing four songs, and auditioned (despite his already legendary status) for the two titans of the new, modern musical theatre. In that version, Annie Oakley and Frank Butler are more show-business than

Western, so perhaps Rodgers and Hammerstein knew all along Berlin was the man for the job. In any event the result was a powerful Broadway score (including "There's No Business Like Show Business") with just a hint of its setting. It opened in 1946 and at 1,147 performances was Berlin's most successful show. Berlin then wrote *Call Me Madam* (1950) for Ethel Merman, and in the revival of *Annie Get Your Gun* she sang a new song, "An Old Fashioned Wedding."

In 1962 Berlin's last new musical, *Mr. President*, was fervently anticipated among theatre parties, and it boasted the largest box office advance to that time. However, it ran only 265 performances, primarily due to an old-fashioned simplicity and a cast that simply could not sing his songs (Nanette Fabray and Robert Ryan). It was also clear by that time that the integration of Berlin's songs into a musical was never his primary concern. As the sophistication of the musical theatre increased, his songs no longer seemed to fit.

Nevertheless, Berlin stayed on top for more than forty years. His was the voice of popular America because he wrote the songs with which Fred Astaire dazzled filmgoers ("Blue Skies," "Top Hat, White Tie and Tails," "Easter Parade," "Heat Wave"); songs that transcended his forgotten shows ("Play a Simple Melody," "Say It With Music," "What'll I Do," "Alone," "Let's Have Another Cup of Coffee," "Shaking the Blues Away," "Lazy"); and the song that Kate Smith introduced in 1939, "God Bless America." Yet Berlin's greatest influence was his first hit song, "Alexander's Ragtime Band." The musical stage followed that lead, and for decades composers wrote syncopated, foot-tapping rhythms to which chorus boys and girls—and hopefully everyone else as the sheet music sold—could dance.

• • •

Vincent Youmans, runner-up to George Gershwin during the musically roaring 1920s, was born the same year as Gershwin and had a tragically short career, retiring at the age of thirty-five due to poor health. Youmans was from a wealthy family, but he became a song-plugger and rehearsal pianist until his friend Gershwin got him a job writing the songs for *Two Little Girls in Blue* for producer Alex Aarons. Shortly after turning in the score, with lyrics by Ira Gershwin, Aarons sold the show to another producer, Abe Erlanger, but Aarons warned the neophyte songwriters to stay away from rehearsals lest it be discovered how young they were. Director Ned

Wayburn liked the score, and the show opened in 1921 to a healthy 135 performances, launching both careers.

Youmans then wrote *Wildflower* (1923) with Oscar Hammerstein II and Otto Harbach, and *No, No, Nanette* (1925) with Irving Caesar and Otto Harbach. The latter included "Tea for Two," and "I Want To Be Happy," the quintessential twenties songs. *No, No, Nanette* underwent many out-of-town travails (more even than the 1971 revival) but came in a hit, with 321 performances, many tours, and a London production that ran even longer. (The sequel, *Yes, Yes, Yvette,* was not written by Youmans and quickly failed.) Youmans also wrote *Hit the Deck* (1927) with Herbert Fields, which ran 352 performances.

His most ambitious show was *Rainbow* (1928) with Hammerstein and Laurence Stallings, and dances by Busby Berkeley. It was a sweeping American musical in the tradition of *Show Boat,* with a full-blooded romantic score. The critics favored it in spite of a production dogged with misfortune. Audiences were uninterested, however, and the show collapsed after thirty performances.

Youmans's work didn't survive the 1920s. The 1930s brought *Smiles* (1930), which disappeared at once in spite of Fred and Adele Astaire; *Through the Years* (1932), another flop; and *Take a Chance* (1932). This last show was a hit, and though his final score was only a partial one (with Richard Whiting and Herb Nacio Brown), his number for Ethel Merman "Eadie Was a Lady" brought down the house nightly.

One of Youmans's obstacles may very well have been that he was difficult to work with. He wrote seven scores with nine different lyricists for six producers, rarely collaborating with the same partners more than once. He was always unhappy with his lack of control and attempted to produce his own shows. Even then, things seemed to go wrong—people quit or were fired, and trouble dogged his work. Youmans died after a twelve-year invalidism, and his biography was aptly titled *Days To Be Happy, Years To Be Sad.* His songs were not unique, but they capture the essence of America in the 1920s.

One way to secure a good score is to appropriate one. *The Great Waltz* (1934) was a lavish and expensive operetta (by Moss Hart) that used a fictional biography but the real music of Johann Strauss and son. It was the first Broadway musical to fit lyrics to classical music, which brings us to the career of Robert Wright and George Forrest. They put lyrics to the music of deceased composers Edvard Grieg for *Song of Norway,* Victor Herbert for

Gypsy Lady, Aleksandr Borodin for *Kismet,* and Sergei Rachmaninoff for *Anya. Magdalena,* which they wrote with Heitor Villa-Lobos, failed (in no small part because it was produced by Edwin Lester, who did more damage to musical theatre *outside* Broadway than anyone else did *on* Broadway). Wright and Forrest's *Kean,* featuring Alfred Drake as the famous rakish actor, boasts a strong score all their own.

• • •

One of the great songwriters to ambitiously push the envelope of the American musical was Frank Loesser. He wrote lyrics under contract to Paramount and Universal Studios for hundreds of songs, many of which became standards—"Two Sleepy People" with Hoagy Carmichael; "See What the Boys in the Backroom Will Have" with Frederick Hollander for Marlene Dietrich; and "I Don't Want to Walk Without You" with Jule Styne. He wrote music and lyrics for "Spring Will Be a Little Late This Year," "Slow Boat to China," and "Baby It's Cold Outside," all for forgettable films (though "Baby" won an Academy award for best song). When Loesser turned to Broadway, his very first show succeeded. *Where's Charley?* (1948) was based on the farce *Charley's Aunt,* with Ray Bolger in the role of a student disguising himself as his own aunt. His second show, *Guys and Dolls* (1950), established him as one of the finest musical comedy writers ever and became one of the best and most beloved American musicals Broadway ever produced.

With a book by Jo Swerling and Abe Burrows, directed by George Kaufman, with dazzling, stylized choreography by Michael Kidd, *Guys and Dolls* put on the musical stage a theatrical version of unique characters created by Damon Runyon. Runyon was a journalist and short-story writer who spent so much time in Depression-era Times Square that when he died his ashes were scattered over it from a plane. From "Fugue for Tinhorns" to "Luck Be a Lady," the show rang with the brashness and rhythm of Runyon's world. Loesser used Runyon's colorful slang to craft a score of solid hits ("I'll Know," "If I Were a Bell"), comic songs ("Bushel and a Peck," "Adelaide's Lament") and driving Broadway anthems ("Guys and Dolls"). But more to the point, he wrote songs that worked brilliantly on two levels—as popular standards (not since Berlin's *Annie Get Your Gun* had a show featured so many hits), and as integrated, character-driven, plot-related book songs. The

"Fugue" is a wonderful cantata of counterpoint, using the crazy names for racehorses that Loesser learned about when Jule Styne took him to the Hollywood Park racetrack. For his next show, Loesser reached much further.

He took several years to write the book, music, and lyrics for *The Most Happy Fella* (1956), an ambitious musical play. In addition to his ear for a hit ("Standing on the Corner") he crafted much more complex melodies and longer musical sequences, and he cast opera star Robert Weede as an older, Italian, Napa Valley winemaker with a young mail-order bride to sing them. The large, emotional story had tragic dimensions, and Loesser's work rose to the occasion. A good production of this show (no easy feat) certainly has the power to move audiences today. The entire score was recorded and released on a three-record set, a first for a Broadway musical.

The next musical play Loesser attempted was *Greenwillow* (1960), based on a bucolic folk tale in the whimsical nature of *Brigadoon.* It didn't have the larger-than-life characters from which *Fella* had benefited, and it was his least successful musical. It has a lovely score, however, rooted in the folk-song style, which was recorded and years later became one of the most highly prized original cast albums among failed productions.

Loesser reunited with Abe Burrows and created a score for one of the funniest books ever written for a Broadway musical. *How to Succeed in Business Without Really Trying* (1961) won them all the Pulitzer Prize. Loesser's score was as funny as the book, even as funny as Robert Morse's star-making comic performance, not an easy job for a songwriter. *How to Succeed* and *Guys and Dolls* have long stood the test of time. (In theory if not in fact. In 1974 *Where's Charley?* was bludgeoned by an inept revival at Circle in the Square Theatre, starring everybody's favorite tap dancer, Raúl Julia. In 1995 a revival of *How to Succeed* lost all that comic musical's uniqueness with an aimless production.)

What pulled *Guys and Dolls* and *How to Succeed* together so seamlessly was the choreography of Michael Kidd and the musical staging of Bob Fosse, respectively. Kidd's masculine (oh, how we need him now) dances, blowzy nightclub routines, and caricatures gave the right physicality to Runyon's characters, just as Loesser had put the right music into their big and brassy hearts. Fosse's angular, syncopated, high-precision dancing—pure Fosse before his bump-and-grind period—gave *How to Succeed* a satiric physicality, matching the cartoonish tone of the material.

Unfortunately, Loesser and Fosse's next collaboration—*Pleasures and Palaces* (1965)—collapsed out of town, proving that in the musical theatre even the most talented of artists can misfire. Sadly, Loesser died a few years after that. In addition to giving Broadway five wonderful shows, he encouraged many young Broadway songwriters through his music publishing company, and coproduced the risky and unusual *The Music Man.* If *Guys and Dolls* and *How to Succeed* are Loesser's most commercial and successful scores, his *Happy Fella* stretched the ever-growing formula for American musicals beyond its boundaries. Loesser's great shows will be consistently rediscovered if inconsistently revived.

• • •

The preeminent Broadway songwriting team of the golden age was Jerry Bock and Sheldon Harnick, whose first show, *The Body Beautiful* (1958) failed, but whose second a year later won the Pulitzer Prize. *Fiorello!,* about New York City mayor Fiorello La Guardia, ran for 796 performances and contained the best examples of political satire since *Of Thee I Sing:* "Politics and Poker," in which Harnick deftly weaves the subject and the game in one of the best examples of scene and song ever written; "The Bum Won," which demonstrates for all time how to use recitative without ponderous writing; and "Little Tin Box," the hysterical explanation of how city officials, on meager salaries, managed such luxuries as a private yacht, a Rolls Royce, and mistresses:

I went without my lunches
And it mounted up your honor, bit by bit
(Up your honor bit by bit!)
It's just a . . .
Little tin box
A little tin box
That a little tin key unlocks

In 1960, Bock and Harnick followed with *Tenderloin* (1960), directed by George Abbott, book by Abbott and Jerome Weidman, produced by Robert Griffith and Harold Prince. The show continued their interest in politics—a minister battles a corrupt policeman in an attempt to clean up the worst district of late-nineteenth-century New York. It didn't have the theatrical excitement of *Fiorello!* but Bock and Harnick's score was prized. Harnick, like Lorenz Hart and E. Y. Harburg before him, is a direct descendant of W. S. Gilbert in his clever, intelligent use of language, while his intensely character-driven lyrics fully exploit the text. These two raucous musical comedy scores were followed with the team's first ambitious jump. For *She Loves Me* (1963) they created a long, romantic score sung almost entirely by individuals, often as inner thoughts, in an intimate musical adaptation of the romantic comedy *Parfumerie* by Miklos Laszlo and the Ernst Lubitsch film *The Shop Around the Corner.* Echoes of operetta, however, are overshadowed by Harnick's outstandingly clever lyrics and Bock's music, always alive with ideas as rich as the text itself. Here the character of Ilona, who has never been inside a library, sings about her first experiences there:

"Let me tell you, you've never seen anything like that library. So many books. So much marble. So quiet."

And suddenly all of my confidence dribbled away with a pitiful plop
My head was beginning to swim and my forehead was covered with cold perspiration
I started to reach for a book and my hand automatically came to a stop
I don't know how long I stood frozen, a victim of panic and mortification
Oh how I wanted to flee
When a kindly voice, a gentle voice
Whispered, "pardon me"
And there was this dear, sweet, clearly respectable, thickly bespectacled man
Who stood by my side and quietly said to me
"Ma'am, don't mean to intrude, but I was just wondering, are you in need of some help?"
I said no, yes, I am
The next thing I know I'm sipping hot chocolate and telling my troubles to Paul
Whose tender brown eyes kept sending compassionate looks
A trip to the library
Has made a new girl of me
For suddenly I can see
The magic of books
I have to admit that in the back of my mind I was praying he wouldn't get fresh

And all of the while I was wondering why an illiterate girl should attrac-
thim
Then all of a sudden he said that I couldn't go wrong with the way of all
flesh
Of course it's a novel but I didn't know or I certainly wouldn't have
smacked him
But he gave me a smile that I couldn't resist
And I knew at once how much I liked this optometrist
You know what this dear, sweet, slightly bespectacled gentlemen said to
me next?
He said he could solve this problem of mine
I said, "How?"
He said if I'd like he'd willingly read to me some of his favorite things
I said, "When?"
He said, "Now."
His novel approach seemed highly suspicious and possibly dangerous
too
I told myself wait, think, dare you go up to his flat?
What happens if things go wrong?
It's obvious he's quite strong
He read to me all night long
Now how about that?
It's hard to believe how truly domestic and happily hopeful I feel
I picture my Paul there reading aloud as I cook
As long as he's there to read
There's quite a good chance indeed
A chance that I'll never need
To open a book
Unlike someone else, someone I dimly recall
I know he'll only have eyes for me, my optometrist Paul

In 1964 Bock and Harnick, teaming up with bookwriter Joseph Stein and director Jerome Robbins, took another great step in their extraordinary career when they scored *Fiddler on the Roof.* Bock's music was characteristically original, melodic, and theatrical, this time with underpinnings of Jewish music. Harnick's lyrics were clever (*"If I were a rich man, Dai-dle, dee-dle, dai-dle, dig-guh, dig-guh, dee-dle, dai-dle, dum"*) and soaring:

Wonder of wonder, miracle of miracles
God took a Daniel once again
Stood by his side and miracle of miracles
Walked him through the lion's den

Harnick knew how to touch the audience's heart:

When did she get to be a beauty?
When did he grow to be so tall?
Wasn't it yesterday when they were small . . .

Bock and Harnick followed *Fiddler* with another experiment, three one-act musicals under the title *The Apple Tree* (1966), all charming and funny, with a tuneful score. The show was brilliantly directed by Mike Nichols and starred the wildly talented and eccentric Barbara Harris. Then they returned to a Jewish story with *The Rothschilds* (1970), a production complicated by changing directors and structural problems, but wonderfully evocative of the epic story of the banking family. The show ran for 505 performances but was financially unsuccessful, and it took its place among the near-great American musicals. The *Sturm und Drang* of Broadway musical production took its toll on Bock and, like Frederick Loewe before him, he retired from the fray. Harnick went on to write with others—*Rex* (1976), music by Richard Rodgers—but the business of Broadway in the 1970s was increasingly difficult, and he moved on to other songwriting arenas, including a set of English lyrics for Peter Brook's splendid theatrical production of *Carmen*.

But his humanity:

In my own lifetime
I want to see the fighting cease
In my own lifetime
I want to see my sons enjoy the fruits of peace
While I'm still here I want to know beyond a doubt
That no one can lock us in, or lock us out
We have climbed higher
Much higher than I thought we'd climb
It's a long journey

And even though the end's in sight
There's not much time
I want to know we haven't built on sand
In my own lifetime

and wit:

We danced in a trance
And I dreamed of romance
Till the strings of my heart
Seemed to be knotted
And even the palms seemed to be potted
The Boston Beguine
Was casting its spell
And I was drunk with love
*And cheap Muscatel**

. . . have been missing ever since. Bock and Harnick created as varied a group of musicals as any writers ever have, all scored with the kind of theatrical writing that best exemplifies the golden age of Broadway songwriters after the integration of the musical.

• • •

Charles Strouse and Lee Adams burst upon the scene fresh from a summer camp with *Bye Bye Birdie* (1960), which was also Michael Stewart's first libretto and Gower Champion's first direction. This lighthearted love story is set in the teenage rock-and-roll world—an Elvis Presley character (hysterically lampooned by Dick Gautier) visits teenagers in a small town prior to going into the army. The combination made *Bye Bye Birdie* the all-time champion of high school, college, and summer stock productions. (This financial success encouraged an ill-advised sequel, *Bring Back Birdie,* that flopped in 1981.) The score included "Put On a Happy Face," which became one of pop music's most enduring anthems, but it also featured hard-to-

* From "The Boston Beguine," *New Faces of '52,* words and music by Sheldon Harnick.

write satires on rock that were at once funny and tuneful ("Honestly Sincere," "One Last Kiss"). In "The Telephone Hour," the writers created a rousing montage of teenage gossip in a canonical style that exemplifies the best of chorus writing for theatre.

Two more wonderful scores for *All American* (1962) and *It's a Bird . . . It's a Plane . . . It's Superman!* (1966) fared less well, but the recordings are effervescent. Strouse and Adams hit it big again with *Applause* (1970), created for Lauren Bacall out of the witty, bitchy, theatre film *All About Eve,* but the stage version isn't nearly as acidic—the score is pallid, and the story doesn't benefit from being updated. Strouse's erratic success in the middle of his career included the hugely successful family musical *Annie,* as well as a number of flops—*A Broadway Musical* (1978), with lyrics by Lee Adams; *Charley and Algernon* (1980), with lyrics by David Rogers; *Dance a Little Closer* (1983), by Alan Jay Lerner; and *Rags* (1986), with Stephen Schwartz. Strouse has worked with other lyricists as well as provided his own lyrics, while Adams takes more time away from the musical world. For one of this team's best examples of musical theatre writing, listen to the soundtrack for the film *The Night They Raided Minsky's,* a rousing recreation of burlesque:

Take ten terrific girls
And only nine costumes
And you're cooking up something grand
Mix in some amber lights
And elegant scenery
Then stir in a fine jazz band
Then add some funny men
And pepper with laughter
It's tart and tasty I know
Then serve it piping hot
And what you got?
A Burlesque show!

A surprising number of theatre writers speak of Adams as their favorite lyricist—surprising because Adams lacked a significant body of work or the popular success of so many others. Adams's charm masks both skill and talent:

Take off the gloomy mask of tragedy
It's not your style
You'll look so good that you'll be glad ya de-
cided to smile

• • •

The central figure in American "serious" music was Leonard Bernstein, the composer who brought the legacy of Aaron Copeland's robust American folk concertos and George Gershwin's jazz-based ambitions into the modern American musical. Bernstein had time in his multifaceted career to write only five Broadway musicals: *On the Town, Wonderful Town, West Side Story, Candide,* and *1600 Pennsylvania Avenue.* (As an example of how the business had changed, consider that Jerome Kern once wrote five in a season.) All but the last were successful, and quite possibly *1600* only lacked a talented director-choreographer to focus its sprawling, ever-changing concept.

On the Town's reputation has been upstaged by *West Side Story.* But a careful listen to the score will revive another of its great strengths. With *On the Town,* the American musical comedy song began to benefit from a composer with lofty ambitions, as it hadn't since the untimely death of George Gershwin. The show's dance music is original and was created by the composer. Even its musical comedy songs, written by Betty Comden and Adolph Green, are special.

With *Candide,* Bernstein had the opportunity to write his most ebullient "light" opera. He pulled out all the stops for Barbara Cook's "Glitter and Be Gay," but the entire score resounds with some of his best (if most lighthearted) work, and the overture is often heard in concert. Unfortunately, the original production was cumbersome and unfocused. It's an American musical that has been looking ever since for the perfect solution, only to find bits and pieces here and there.

• • •

Kurt Weill once said, "There is only good music and bad music." If there was ever a composer who took seriousness to an extreme, who bridged opera and musical comedy more than anyone and refused to acknowledge any difference between serious and light music, it was Weill. In Berlin in 1928 he wrote *The*

Threepenny Opera with Bertolt Brecht, using the John Gay story that had begun the whole idea of using musical theatre for political satires (they eventually had to leave Nazi Germany for those beliefs). Weill and Brecht fashioned a raucous version in which Weill's original music held down the often pedantic and dogmatic writing of Brecht. They called it a *Zeitoper*, or popular opera written to reflect the spirit of the times. It opened on Broadway in 1933, where it closed after twelve performances. However, the 1954 off-Broadway production at the Theatre DeLys ran for ninety-five performances. It settled in again the following season, when it ran for 2,611 performances, finally establishing the musical as one of the most original ever created. Already Weill had written *Happy End* (1929) and *Mahagonny* (1929) to follow it, though neither has yet found a definitive Broadway production. Even revivals of *The Threepenny Opera* have been flawed and unsuccessful.

In a 1940 *New York Sun* interview, Weill found the Metropolitan Opera and its world to be a musty vestige of a bygone age. He looked to Broadway for new opera, and found a lively scene there. His shows were dramatic, but his music wasn't, and he rejected the notion of flavoring his songs with an idiom that could have reflected his libretto in favor of his unique grafting of American jazz and European operetta. This reduced the theatrical effectiveness of the music, though at the same time it freed him to write his best work, which was very great indeed.

Hence, Weill's scores have become more successful than his productions, and the posthumous revue *Berlin to Broadway with Kurt Weill* (1972) is his best show. It rings with his great songs ("Mack the Knife," "Surabuya Johnny," "September Song," "My Ship," "Speak Low," "Lost in the Stars") and four great theatre voices as well (on the original cast album).

Still, his catalog rings with wonderfully experimental shows that he wrote with some of America's most talented writers, as well as melodic music.

In 1936, he created *Johnny Johnson* with Paul Green for the left-wing Group Theatre. It's really a play with music, an antiwar farce allegory.

Knickerbocker Holiday (1938, with Maxwell Anderson), is a fairly dark political satire with a complex interwoven score, from which only the more standard "September Song" survives.

Lady in the Dark (1941), features some of Ira Gershwin's cleverest lyrics, and a literate Moss Hart libretto that was topical at the time—it concerned the Freudian psychology of dreams. All the complex musical sequences were the dreams of Liza (played by Gertrude Lawrence) except for the haunting "My Ship," the first provocative notes of which Weill used repeatedly to denote something that Liza couldn't remember. Liza comes to believe these notes would unlock her memory and lead to a resolution of her emotional problems. Finally, when the song is remembered and sung in full, it acts as the final clue to a mystery, providing musical and dramatic resolution. Seldom had a song been used so intrinsically before. It's time for a sumptuous revival, with the dreams in vivid colors and reality in shades of brown and gray.

One Touch of Venus (1943) featured Mary Martin and two Agnes de Mille ballets. If its Galatea story—a statue comes to life and entrances a young man—was the stuff of simple-minded musical comedy, its form and literate writing (book by S. J. Perleman, lyrics by Ogden Nash) were strictly those of the modern musical. Weill's "That's Him" and "Speak Low" have become cabaret stalwarts.

Firebrand of Florence (1945, lyrics by Ira Gershwin) flopped, mostly for its book, a ponderous romance featuring sixteenth-century artist-metal-worker Benvenuto Cellini.

Street Scene (1947) was a dark but powerful drama on which Weill built his idea of the American opera. He integrated the music and used long song forms. Its single set makes it inexpensive for a thoughtful revival of its strong book by Elmer Rice and poetic lyrics by Langston Hughes. However, it was weaker when produced as opera than as theatre, relying on much recitative and opera singers with a mélange of accents.

Love Life (1948) featured the lyrics of Alan Jay Lerner. Without Loewe, Lerner's grand ambitions led to elegant overwriting and unfocused concepts. If it takes a modern marriage a few years to show the strain, this one took from 1791 to 1948. Like *Allegro,* it's an example of how hard it is to integrate theatricality (in this case vaudeville and minstrel-show turns), allegory, a Greek chorus for musical numbers, and powerful drama.

Lost in the Stars (1949) with book and lyrics by Maxwell Anderson, was Weill's most ambitious musical, adapted from the South African novel *Cry, the Beloved Country,* by Alan Paton. The book-heavy musical and a Greek chorus sunk a stirring score.

Weill died before *Stars* closed, at the early age of fifty. He only did fifteen years of Broadway shows, but his unique songs were kept alive by his wife Lotte Lenya and cabaret singers everywhere.

• • •

A theatre maven was raving over the 1989 revival of *Gypsy* starring Tyne Daly. He waxed rhapsodic over that great show—the raw power of a good old-fashioned musical; a solid book and unique story (from the memoirs of stripper Gypsy Rose Lee, though in truth much fictionalized); superb writing; classy, precise choreography and fluid staging; a concept (the vaudeville musical); strong performances all around; one of the theatre's really great scores; telling and clever Sondheim lyrics; Tyne Daly's experienced actor's approach to the musical theatre's King Lear of roles. Finally he stopped, exhausted. After a beat, he delivered the coup de grâce. "Of course," he said in a small voice, "she can't sing it."

If Kurt Weill had been a round peg in the square hole of Broadway, Jule Styne fit it perfectly. He was born Jules Stein in London in 1905, and became much more than one of the greatest composers of the golden age of Broadway—he *is* the golden age of Broadway. In a short list of composers whose work bespoke the mood of their generation, from Sigmund Romberg at the turn of the century to Jerome Kern to George Gershwin, Jule Styne personifies the last great era in the American theatre. His hot music was hotter than anyone else's, his ballads more lilting, his comedy numbers funnier. If music is more a matter of pure talent than any other art form, Styne was almost mystically gifted.

His most famous score, written for Ethel Merman, has defeated all others, including Rosalind Russell, Angela Lansbury, Tyne Daly, and Bette Midler. He had an instinctive understanding of the developing American musical, encouraged not least through a lifelong friendship with Jerome Robbins. Styne was a thick-skinned collaborator who wasn't overly attached to any one song, and he often wrote two or three for many spots in a show. He was obsessively dedicated to his musicals. (On the afternoon that *Gypsy* opened, he went out and bought stools for the trumpet players, anxious that they shouldn't be muffled too deep in the pit). His personality was kinetic, and he was known to shout "Hello!" at a telephone even as he reached for it. Styne was a diminutive giant of a musician with a Runyonesque attraction for tall chorus girls, and he was an exuberant storyteller.

He began writing songs for movies, including "Three Coins in a Fountain" (Academy award), "Time After Time," and "It's Magic." Then he tackled Broadway. He wrote music for *Glad To See You* (1945), which closed after a pre-Broadway tryout in Philadelphia and Boston; *High Button Shoes* (1947); *Gentlemen Prefer Blondes* (1949), which was revised and revived as *Lorelei—Gentlemen Still Prefer Blondes* for a much older Carol Channing in

1974; *Two on the Aisle* (1951); *Hazel Flagg* (1953); *Bells Are Ringing* (1956); *Gypsy* (1959); *Do Re Mi* (1960); *Subways Are For Sleeping* (1961); *Funny Girl* (1964); *Fade Out, Fade In* (1964); *Hallelujah, Baby!* (1967); *Darling of the Day* (1968); *Look to the Lillies* (1970); *Prettybelle* (1971), whose pre-Broadway tryout closed in Boston); *Sugar* (1972); *Bar Mitzvah Boy* (1978) on London's West End; *One Night Stand* (1980); *Pieces of Eight* (1985) in London; and *The Red Shoes* (1993).

To give credit where it's hardly necessary, Styne also contributed songs to *Michael Todd's Peep Show* (1950), *Wake Up Darling* (1956), and *Say, Darling* (1958). He wrote half the score of *Peter Pan* (1954); music for stage versions of Nathaniel West's *Miss Lonelyhearts* (1957); and Tony Richardson's controversial, compelling production of *Arturo Ui* (1963). He produced *Make a Wish* (1951); the 1952 revival of *Pal Joey* with Harold Lang, which gave the musical the recognition it deserved; and Sammy Davis Jr.'s first Broadway musical, *Mr. Wonderful* (1956). And he directed the musical *Something More* (1964).

In twenty-seven seasons between 1945 and 1967, after which he seems to have lost his way, Styne wrote twelve Broadway musicals. In those years he had only one bona fide flop, which was his first Broadway attempt. Five of his shows ran almost a full season, and six were clear hits. But the remarkable thing about this career isn't the number of hit shows, nor the number of classics. (*Gentlemen Prefer Blondes, Bells Are Ringing, Gypsy, Peter Pan,* and *Funny Girl* are still revived.) It's the quality of the scores, now only familiar to cast album collectors. *High Button Shoes* contained "Papa, Won't You Dance With Me"; *Two on the Aisle* was ideal for the outlandish talents of Bert Lahr and Dolores Grey; *Hazel Flagg* was a strong dance score for Helen Gallagher; *Do Re Mi* contained "Make Someone Happy," and was tailored for the comic talents of Phil Silvers; *Fade Out, Fade In* was created for Carol Burnett; and *Hallelujah, Baby!* was tailored for black entertainers, a truly great score in search of a show.

Darling of the Day was a flop, and Styne never got back on track. However, except for the fact that its leading man, Vincent Price, can't sing at all, it's a wonderfully entertaining score. *Prettybelle* contains some very nice ballads and comes close to being a successful attempt to write contemporary pop. His stretch from *Peter Pan* to *Gypsy* to *Hallelujah, Baby!* is the single most remarkable range ever for a Broadway composer.

Even Styne's bad scores have their highlights. *Sugar,* the show that should have been, is based on the classic farce film *Some Like It Hot.* It's a story that couldn't be funnier, and boasted a richly comic performance by one of Broadway's greatest clown actors, Robert Morse. It was beleaguered with enormous problems out of town, including an ugly and unworkable set that had to be replaced entirely; a rambling structure that had to be completely made over; uneven casting (a fey Cyril Ritchard in the dirty-old-man role of Joe E. Brown, and a pretty but talentless "discovery" in the Marilyn Monroe role); and plenty of backstage bickering and blaming. Director Gower Champion never understood the nature or potential of the material. He spent weeks in rehearsal attempting to create his customary Busby Berkeley numbers and avoiding the comedy. In the end, however, the Jule Styne-Bob Merrill songs "The Beauty That Drives Men Mad" (Robert Morse and Tony Roberts in their drag entrance) and "Beautiful Through and Through" (Morse in a cocktail dress keeping Cyril Ritchard in the mood) provided outstanding comic material for Morse. "People in My Life" comes close to Styne's classic "People" from *Funny Girl.* It was replaced with "It's Always Love" for Tony Roberts, then reinserted for Larry Kert, but the moment never worked. The creators never understood their own musical. You can't stop a farce for a realistic love ballad.

But Styne demonstrated how to write a great Broadway score in *Sugar, High Button Shoes* (his first), and almost everything in between. He tailored his music for the stars. He often told a story about *Bells Are Ringing,* during which he protested the casting of Sydney Chaplin, whose vocal range was limited to three notes. Styne banged out those lone notes on the piano, over and over, screaming to his collaborators, "These are the only notes he can sing! How can I write a song just on these three notes!" Then he caught himself listening, played the three notes again, and composed "Just in Time." It's no coincidence that Ethel Merman's greatest performance came in *Gypsy* and Barbra Streisand's in *Funny Girl.* After his experience as a child prodigy at the piano and a bandleader in Chicago, Styne was a vocal coach to Hollywood starlets and knew the female singing voice better than anyone. He also tailored his music for the story, drawing on the time and place, whether it was Neverland, burlesque ("Let Me Entertain You"), or the ghetto ("Smile, Smile").

Styne wrote fine, original, sometimes transcendent melodies. He wrote them in an accessible style that he had honed in his early songwriting days, when he and Sammy Cahn turned out songs for Frank Sinatra. He disdained the complicated rhythms and sophisticated harmonics of Leonard

Bernstein and Stephen Sondheim. Any overly tricky rhythm or vamp pattern wouldn't have appealed to him. It would have interfered with the solid driving rhythm that characterized his writing, and Broadway at its zingiest. His music virtually rippled with the mood of the Great White Way during its golden age. He is the inheritor of the Manhattan melodies that George M. Cohan begot, infused with the jazz era.

His greatest musical moment was "Rose's Turn," Mama's complex, multituned soliloquy from *Gypsy.* Styne was a songwriter by trade, so it's unlikely he would have created that kind of intricate, intense monologue on his own. But he was working with Arthur Laurents, an experienced librettist dedicated to the dramatic musical, and the most sophisticated and knowing lyricist of Styne's era.

• • •

John Kander and Fred Ebb began with *Flora, the Red Menace* (1965), starring eighteen-year-old Liza Minnelli. The musical was unsuccessful, but Kander and Ebb were noted for their strong theatre songs, and wrote the scores for *Cabaret* (1966), *Zorba* (1968), *The Happy Time* (1968), *70 Girls 70* (1971), *The Act* (1978), *Woman of the Year* (1981), *The Rink* (1984), and *Kiss of the Spider Woman* (1993). This inconsistent body of work demonstrates the harsh nature of Broadway, in which the score is at the mercy of the director and choreographer (*70 Girls 70* was staged without inspiration, and its charming score was not heard after thirty-five performances) as well as the star (Liza Minnelli was woefully miscast in *The Rink,* and having to write *Woman of the Year* for the voice of Lauren Bacall must have been a trial).

But Kander and Ebb also demonstrate the nature of good theatre music. The score for *Zorba* was never praised enough. Their humor and charm ("No Boom-Boom") and their romanticism ("The Butterfly," "The House at the End of the Road") attest to a superior talent for music and lyrics that *dramatize.* Unfortunately their close relationship with Liza Minnelli and their skill at creating slick, show-bizzy numbers have too often led them to write songs like their super-successful "New York, New York," which grew from a flop film musical to a hit Sinatra tune and became that city's anthem. Their writing for *The Act* (in which their songs were little more than a nightclub act for Minnelli) and *The Rink* (a clumsy and cold libretto that rambles on and on about less and less) revealed little content and reinforced the slickest but shallowest aspect of their talent. The result doesn't service the drama, because the drama didn't inspire the music. While an individual song might survive and even score well in a Kander and Ebb revue (*Two By Five* and *The World Goes Round*), shallow content and generic razzle-dazzle don't fly in good musical theatre. Special material for nightclub acts has its own requirements, but drama isn't one of them.

• • •

Off-Broadway's introduction of new talent was its greatest contribution to the American musical. On the heels of their success with *The Fantasticks,* Tom Jones and Harvey Schmidt moved up to Broadway, where they adapted *The Rainmaker* into *110 in the Shade* (1963) and *The Fourposter* into *I Do! I Do!* (1966), both fine musicals with lovely scores. When they left the arena of adaptation and created original books (*Celebration, Philemon,* and *Ratfink*), they lost the power of a good story and disappeared from the Broadway scene.

Jerry Herman also started off-Broadway with *I Feel Wonderful,* a college revue that ran for two months, and two cabaret revues, *Nightcap* and *Parade.* He moved to Broadway with the music and lyrics for *Milk and Honey,* which many believe to be his best score, then became a moneymaker with *Hello, Dolly!*

Here was a case of the Broadway coincidences falling in the songwriter's favor. Herman's style is popular, unique, and simplistic, favoring a bouncy, cakewalk-and-polka sound that is enormously useful to choreographers who look to tempo over content. Gower Champion was perfect for *Hello, Dolly!* and Herman's score was perfect for Champion.

After *Dolly,* Herman's scores remained consistent but rose and fell with the productions. His songs entertained audiences, but his peppy style was self-contained and never grew out of the drama. *Mame* was Herman's *Dolly* follow up, and included another title song with legions of male dancers celebrating the leading lady in a formula that became *de rigueur* for a few unfortunate years. *Mame* was a hit, but dropping all the songs wouldn't hurt a bit. It's a great play to which Herman added little.

The problem with Herman's music is that it's more generic and less dramatic than it might be. Like George Cohan, Herman created a popular, hummable style of his own, but he succeeds only when a light, entertaining story happens to match it. *The Madwoman of Chaillot* was a delicate fantasy that had a producer with an abysmal track record for big musicals (Alexander Cohen) and three successive directors who attempted to sort out the problems. Herman turned it into *Hello, Madwoman.* Sadly, Angela Lansbury's greatest stage impersonation prior to Mrs. Lovett was buried under a lumbering, misguided adaptation.

Herman's score for *Mack and Mabel,* on the other hand, is precisely right for a story set in Hollywood's silent movie era (magnificently reinforced by Philip Lang's orchestrations). In this case it wasn't the appropriateness of the score that sunk it, but Gower Champion's misguided production, which was stylistically based on Mack Sennett's films but disregarded a potent, tragic love story. Champion's Busby Berkeley musical numbers were dwarfed by a gargantuan and ever-present sound stage. When the set is "larger" than the actors, the show is in trouble.

Finally, there's *La Cage Aux Folles.* This curious musical pretended to deliver to Broadway audiences a sober story of gay relationships, couched in a wild farce featuring flamboyant characters. The original French film trod that line beautifully. When it became a Jerry Herman musical, however, it lost both the farce and the realism, and came across as a cotton-candy drag show, successful as a tourist attraction. Never for a moment did the audience need to be uncomfortable, for the casting and the performances clearly implied that sex would not be an important component of the show. Even the matinée ladies must have gone home relieved and full of pride that they could applaud this story of forbidden love.

• • •

Stephen Sondheim was the lyricist who put "Rose's Turn" together from the songs that he and Jule Styne had written. He wrote music and lyrics for *A Funny Thing Happened on the Way to the Forum* and *Anyone Can Whistle,* and then reached his full personal stride with *Company.* That score was driving ("Another Hundred People"), melodic ("Sorry-Grateful"), emotional ("Being Alive") and witty ("You Could Drive a Person Crazy"). It resonated with the urban environment it took place in, using tricky rhythmic vamps ("The Little Things You Do Together"), dripping sarcasm ("The Ladies Who Lunch"), and jangly chords (Cmaj7 9/6; Am7/sus/c).

Sondheim began to use complex song forms ("Barcelona") that few Broadway songwriters bothered with, beyond Jerome Kern, George Gershwin, Leonard Bernstein, and Kurt Weill.

Company featured a unique title song that limned the central theme. Best of all, it was rooted in American rhythms and Broadway zetz (though this was overlooked because it's rare for Sondheim). It got your feet tapping, your mind humming, and your heart pounding. On its own, *Company* stands as a wonderful representation of the best that Broadway offers, and at the same time it strikes out in new dimensions.

But it wasn't on its own. It was coupled with a tight, funny series of sketches transcribing various clichés about modern relationships. The plot concerns five couples and the three girlfriends of a central bachelor figure, who wanders through the show wondering if he's missing something he's constantly being offered but hasn't yet embraced—commitment. The show was mounted in a steel-and-glass elevator unit set by the brilliant designer Boris Aronson, and every number was exquisitely staged by Michael Bennett.

Bennett worked with one dancer and thirteen klutzes, but he made huge sections of the show dance. He did this not just for the sexy, jazzy, second act solo for prima jazz dancer Donna McKechnie ("Tick Tock"), but for all the numbers that featured more than one voice. Two inspired numbers are the title song and the second-act opener "Side by Side by Side," which seems to go on and on and on, building and building, getting laughs, nailing the theme of the show in one simple tap routine. The song makes fun of the show-bizzy formula choreography popularized by Ed Sullivan, yet effectively uses that kind of choreography at the same time.

The show was pulled together by the protean producer-director Harold Prince. The insertion of numbers into the book was startlingly nontraditional. There is no plot—each scene is a self-contained riff on a male-female relationship—and few characters sing their own feelings until Bachelor Bob's ambivalent eleven o'clock number. Many of the songs are comments on the action of other characters, leading to an ensemble performance that keeps the stage busier than legions of chorus boys and girls can in big musicals.

Curiously, this is also typical of pre-Princess musical comedy, in that songs written as popular music were performed directly to the audience more than acted in the context of the drama. Because musical theatre grew out of musical comedy, which grew out of vaudeville, this will always be the case. But presentational songs will always be a barrier to complete involvement. And therein lies the failure of this spectacular show to become one of America's beloved musicals.

Company disallows emotional involvement because of the way the songs are structured—the songs comment upon, rather than grow out of, the scenes. As with Bertolt Brecht's *Verfremdungseffekt* (alienation effect), the audience is time and again disrupted from its willing suspension of disbelief and reminded that they are an audience.

Company's ambivalence—in the end, the audience has to decide whether marriage is worthwhile—is perfectly justified, especially for a revue disguised as a musical. The show examines specific themes intently, from several points of view, but without making a final judgment. (However, Bobby's failure to appear at his friend's surprise party indicates that he is no longer going to be satisfied with being an observer/catalyst in the couple's relationship, and may find a life of his own.) Mass audiences simply are uncomfortable with this kind of theatre. Their first choice is a happy ending and their second is at least a clear one. Life as transcribed by drama is more successful with audiences when it is black and white, as against the grey shades of real life. Audiences go *into* the theatre to get *out* of life for a couple of hours. The most commercially successful musicals avoid reality, or translate it to another time or place that allows comfortable displacement. Anything else is art, and, as Sondheim himself proposes in *Sunday in the Park with George,* art doesn't sell.

Thus we can postulate that "concept" musicals will never be the most commercially successful shows. The audience wants to be involved in the drama, not lectured to. They might admire Brecht's *The Threepenny Opera,* but they'll turn out in droves for the romantic, sentimental *Phantom of the Opera.*

Company's lyrics consistently fall into the presentational category more than the representational. Instead of inner monologues or musicalized dialogue, these songs are mostly set pieces that tell us something. Thus, Michael Bennett could use a good-old fashioned show-business flash-act approach to the staging. This turned a dark story—none of the relationships is healthy—into a wildly entertaining musical, carrying the material into the hearts of the audience. On opening night, they stopped the show cold with thunderous applause after four musical numbers. Although Bobby draws positive conclusions from his observations (*"Alone is alone, not alive*"), they're framed in Sondheim's typically ambivalent attitude:

Somebody hold me too close
Somebody hurt me too deep
Somebody sit in my chair and ruin my sleep
And make me aware
Of being alive

That song was a last-minute out-of-town replacement for an even more pessimistic one ("Happily Ever After"). The fact is that *Company*'s creators all had a problem with significant one-on-one relationships, an inability to embrace romanticism without reservation, and a ready scalpel for heterosexual love. This astoundingly original, electrically entertaining musical was successful—it drew rave reviews from every critic except the muddleheaded Clive Barnes, and earned a profit—but it never achieved the worldwide acceptance that characterizes a smash hit. It ran through knowledgeable theatregoers then ran out of steam and closed after 706 performances, a dismal showing for the period if you consider its state-of-the-art craft; thundering originality; clever, tuneful score; and reasonable cost.

The team—Harold Prince, Stephen Sondheim, Boris Aronson, and Michael Bennett—immediately coalesced around a new book, *Follies,* by James Goldman. The only thing really wrong with *Follies* is the inability of its creators to understand that they did not fail. The show only ran for 522 performances during the 1971–72 season and lost nearly all its capitalization. This, along with the collapse of the tour, has compelled analysis and even rewrites ever since. But the author's attempt to lighten the book for the London version (along with the inability of the London producer and director to duplicate such a masterpiece) led to an inferior production.

The original was one of the shining *tours de force* of the musical theatre. It holds a fond place in the hearts of theatre lovers who saw it. On closing night, the ovations for *each number* were deafening and extended the show by an hour.

Two things mitigated against the universal acceptance of *Follies* from the beginning. One was the plot. It doesn't have one. This confused critics, who complained about the book, which was conceptually wonderful, literate, charming, and technically sound. What it didn't have, never intended to have, was a linear rising line of dramatic action.

Alumni of the *Weissman Follies* (read Ziegfeld) hold a reunion in their grand old theatre, now scheduled for demolition. They hash over their past, and we see how the hopes and dreams they held for their lives have soured since. They are shadowed by metaphysical and literal ghosts of themselves much of the time. The finale is a long, spectacular sequence in which the principals perform numbers in Ziegfeld fashion that are keyed thematically to their failures and frustrations. Finally the long night ends, and as the dawn comes up and the wrecker's ball demolishes the theatre, they put their personas back together and stagger out into the morning.

Follies is not unlike the off-Broadway play *The Boys in the Band,* a *Walpurgisnacht* of misgivings, a minuet of conflicts, a dream-like cantata of the things one doesn't say in daytime, all in one hellish and claustrophobic night. But it isn't a story.

That should have been all right. More than one great musical has been a revue disguised as a musical, including *Company, Man of La Mancha,* and *A Chorus Line.* This useful form is a series of scenes and songs sketched *around* a particular theme. The revue format is disguised with a simple ruse—it uses a framework device that gives the material an excuse for its presentation. The device stands in for story structure. In *Company,* a bachelor is part of the life of each couple, providing continuity between what are essentially seven vignettes on relationships. In *Man of La Mancha,* author Miguel Cervantes has to defend himself before a band of cutthroats and thieves with whom he is thrown in jail. He does so by entertaining them with episodes from the wacky misadventures of Don Quixote. In *A Chorus Line,* the dancers are auditioning for a new musical. The director interviews them, a device which allows them to tell their individual stories.

But critics were confused by the complexity of *Follies.* The Tony award for best musical went to the frothy *Two Gentlemen of Verona,* a now-forgotten ersatz musical with a pop-rock score. *Verona* also won best book (William Shakespeare by way of John Guare). *Follies* won for best score, direction, and choreography, as well as for sets, costumes, and lights.

And then the audiences turned on it as well. The subject matter was too dark, the themes too close to real, as the aging actors and actresses (Dorothy Collins, Gene Nelson, Alexis Smith, Yvonne DeCarlo, and others) struggled to taste the old glory in an eerie parallel of the show's very themes. The combination turned audiences off. They rejected it all as too dreary, and the American musical theatre, to its eternal loss, took a decisive turn away from serious drama.

By 1971 the modern musical began to stumble as the musical theatre returned to mass entertainment. The masses don't like dreary. They don't like pessimism, in which Stephen Sondheim is steeped, and they don't like dark ideas that are too close to home. They don't like to think, which is necessary for a show based on ideas rather than events. They don't even like to give up the traditional intermission, which revues disguised as musicals must do because they don't have a first-act plot climax to suspend. (Attempts by summer stock producers to put an intermission into *Man of La Mancha, A Chorus Line,* and *Follies* have been hurtful and annoying.)

They especially don't like seeing themselves on stage, and by 1971 the average age of the Broadway theatregoer was perilously close to the age of both the *Follies* cast and the characters they brilliantly portrayed. Ruby Keeler's success in the revival of *No, No, Nanette* that same year had her tap dancing like a kid, not angst-ridden like an adult. Early twentieth-century immigrant audiences liked to see themselves in comic caricatures; late twentieth-century Americans don't pay to see the shadows in their lives.

Audiences like hope and optimism, a happy tune and happy children, Christmas trees and faithful dogs. Five years later they got what they deserved.

Part Four

END OF AN ERA

The Broadhurst Theatre
PLAYBILL
the magazine for theatregoers
KELLY

YBILL
ALVIN THEATRE
Annie

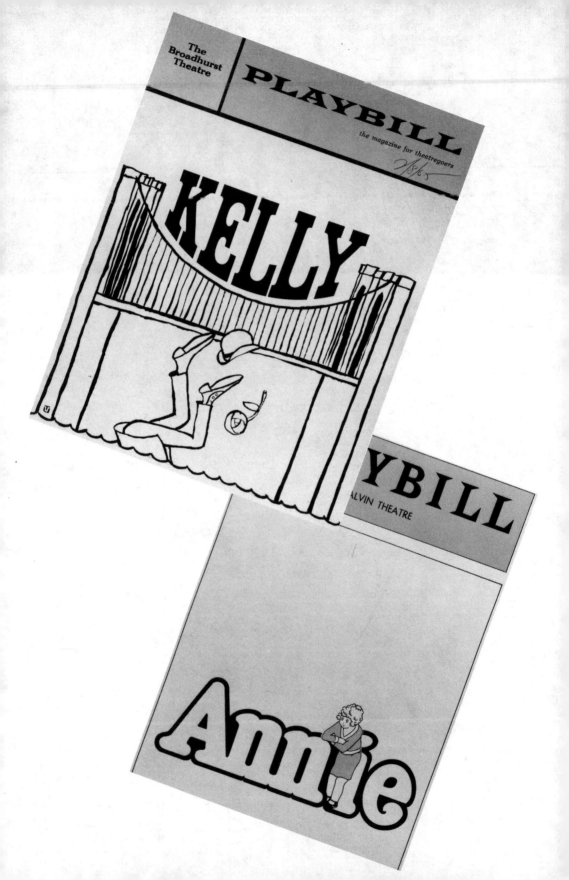

Twenty-Five

Decline and Fall

Broadway is a rat race.

—Jule Styne

To be precise, the end began at eight o'clock on April 21, 1977 when *Annie* opened at the Alvin Theatre on West Fifty-second Street. *Annie* was written in 1972—book by Thomas Meehan, music by Charles Strouse, lyrics and direction by Martin Charnin—and after two and a half unsuccessful years of auditions for Broadway producers, it tried out with the Goodspeed Opera House, a summer stock operation in East Haddam, Connecticut. The world premiere was inauspicious. Boston's Elliot Norton liked the show but felt that "at the moment, *Annie* is more than a little cumbersome." The reviewer from the Middletown, Connecticut newspaper hated the first act, but stayed to like the second, while the *Christian Science Monitor* felt the second act "almost sinks the show." Another local paper felt, "Not even Daddy Warbucks can save Little Orphan *Annie* this time." *Greenwich Time* liked the show, especially the girl playing Annie (she was fired three days later), Reid Shelton (before he shaved his head for the role), and the dog. The *New Haven Register* gave it a rave, the *Hartford Courant* a pan ("almost nothing works"), and *New Era* thought it had possibilities. Walter Kerr wrote a wildly misguided review claiming the show was "ideologically treacherous," apparently because it made war profiteering appear virtuous, and little Annie failed to take Daddy Warbucks to task for this.

Mike Nichols took over as producer. They moved the show to the Kennedy Center in Washington, D.C., where there were multiple problems, then limped onto Broadway behind pessimistic rumors. There the show's reviews were mostly favorable, and *Annie* became a smash hit.

What happened—which had never happened before but has happened several times since—is that *Annie* arrived at the tail end of a disastrous Broadway musical season. The 1976–77 season had opened with a disco-style, all-black revival of *Guys and Dolls,* confusing caricature with stereotype. Then the Goodspeed Opera House brought in a revival of *Going Up,* confusing summer stock with Broadway. *Oh! Calcutta* moved to the Edison Theatre from off-Broadway, confusing Seventh Avenue with Ninth Avenue. There followed a lumpish operatic revival of *Porgy and Bess;* a solid original, *The Robber Bridegroom,* that simply didn't have Broadway direction and choreography or money behind it and could have run longer off-Broadway; a version of *Twelfth Night* called *Music Is,* directed by the eighty-nine-year-old George Abbott (no one younger evidenced any talent); a black gospel meeting called *Your Arm's Too Short To Box With God;* a revival of *Fiddler on the Roof* in which Zero Mostel tortured his fellow cast members with antics that alternately bemused, confused, and convulsed the audience; a collection of South African dances called *Ipi-Tombi;* Betty Comden and Adolph Green's nightclub act; Debbie Reynolds's nightclub act; an ice show with brilliant choreography by John Curry; and the nostalgic spectacle *Beatlemania.*

There were only two interesting productions that season. *Side by Side by Sondheim* was an English import that featured three actors, two pianos, and a sardonic narrator. The songs had been wildly entertaining to the English just as Noël Coward is to us, but impossibly shallow if you'd spent the last ten years hearing them with orchestrations and seeing them in full drama. And there was an unimaginative but solid revival of Kurt Weill's idiosyncratic *Happy End,* starring a singing Meryl Streep.

Not a single musical had impressed critics or audiences. The critics were suffering from a cranky reputation, audiences from musical comedy withdrawal. Then, with only weeks to go before the Tony eligibility cutoff, two simpleminded, unpretentious, uncontroversial musicals came in.

I Love My Wife should have run off-Broadway. It was cheaply and sloppily staged, and featured a quartet of musicians bouncing around on stage and four energetic, if insufficiently musical, actors. It was set against the already waning sexual liberation movement, and featured Cy Coleman's pastiche score from 1960s rock and barrelhouse polka to country-western and ragtime. Critics chose to focus on the musical's good-heartedness, and eight years after the film *Bob and Carol and Ted and Alice,* whose plot it shamelessly cribbed, they appreciated its sit-com approach to wife-swapping. *I Love My Wife* was strictly for the bridge-and-tunnel crowd. It closed out an 872-performance run with its sole claim to immortality: the Smothers Brothers took over the leading roles. (They were charming and surprisingly adept).

And *Annie. Annie* was a great idea—an optimistic family musical—and little else. The tuneful score is hummable but exceedingly simplistic and thin. The lyrics are abysmal ("Tomorrow is only a day away"—no kidding). The book is loony and mawkish, and the staging old-fashioned and uninspired. The one comic bit—when Daddy Warbucks picks up the smallest of the orphans and she remains curled in a ball—is a direct steal from *The King and I.* Each of the actors was playing in a style all his/her own, virtually ignoring the others, from the scenery-chewing Miss Hannigan (Dorothy Loudon) to the realistic Daddy Warbucks (Reid Shelton) to the big-voiced, broadly-acted Annie (Andrea McArdle) to the vaudeville routines of Rooster and Lily (Bob Fitch and Barbara Erwin) to Laurie Beechman belting in an inappropriate rock style from her oft-highlighted position in the chorus. Not only was *Annie* very old-fashioned musical comedy, it wasn't even *good* old-fashioned musical comedy. *Annie*'s overture, for example, doesn't compare to the overture from the same composer's *All American.*

During the golden age, hodgepodge musicals like *Annie,* which suffered so much tsuris out of town, came in and died if they came in at all. But something happened in the late 1970s to change that. The competition was so reduced that audiences and critics had little material for comparison. The musical's one good song was replayed several times during the show, and it became popular without any pop coverage. The orphans were endearing. Families took their children. The best seats were fifteen dollars. The Tony awards, which had gone to *A Chorus Line* the previous season with enthusiasm, went to *Annie* and *I Love My Wife* in lieu of anything else. *Annie* won for book and choreography, while *Wife* won for directing. *Annie*'s wan score won the Tony, beating out the tuneful and original *Godspell,* which had appeared on Broadway after a hugely successful off-Broadway run, and the revival of Kurt Weill's *Happy End,* making its first major Broadway attempt with the haunting "Surabaya Johnny." The score for *1600 Pennsylvania Avenue,* written by Leonard Bernstein and Alan Jay Lerner, was a superior piece of songwriting within an ineffectual stage show, and it wasn't even nominated. *Annie* became a nationwide hit.

It seems curmudgeonly to deride a national treasure like *Annie,* but as the art of the musical diminishes and bad work substitutes for good, the end is surely near—for bad work cannot perpetuate itself for long.

• • •

There have always been flops, of course. In 1926 *Hoopla* closed out of town at intermission. One long wall of Joe Allen's restaurant is devoted to the posters of musicals that lost their entire investment in a quick overnight fold. The tradition began with *Kelly* (1965), an infamous megadisaster about a man who jumped off the Brooklyn Bridge and lived; it was the first musical to lose $650,000 in one night. Since then many others have been added, including *Breakfast at Tiffany's; Bring Back Birdie; Come Summer; A Doll's Life; Fig Leaves Are Falling; Georgy; Got Tu Go Disco; Here's Where I Belong; Home Sweet Homer; I'm Solomon; La Strada; Lolita, My Love; Mata Hari* (which flopped on and off-Broadway); *Miss Moffat; Nefertiti; Onward Victoria; Rags; Rosa; Spotlight; The Three Musketeers; Via Galactica;* and many others.

Most of these washouts had a good deal going against them from the get-go. There is often a misunderstanding of what kind of material benefits from musical treatment. Were Leon Uris's *Exodus,* the biography of Marilyn Monroe, or James Clavell's *Shogun* really good ideas for musicals? The success of a musical depends on its *justification.* What can song and dance bring to the story and characters that mere words can not? Sometimes inexperience does a show in. *Carrie* was put together by a German producer, Hollywood songwriters, an English director, and a television choreographer.

The Broadway musical is such a strange beast that the best of ideas and intentions can go wrong (*Merrily We Roll Along*). Conversely, the worst can go right. Who would have thought that the signing of the Declaration of Independence would make a rich, funny, original, even suspenseful musical? Answer: Sherman Edwards, a songwriter and history teacher.

There's always something new to learn—*On the Town, The Music*

Man, 1776, Hair, and *Grease* were written by first-timers. And there is something old to learn. While the Broadway establishment thought that reviving *No, No, Nanette* was a terrible idea, two outsiders, Harry Rigby and Cyma Rubin, did not. It not only succeeded, but launched the modern craze for revivals.

Sometimes a show is that close. *Working* was based on the book by Studs Turkel, who had interviewed hundreds of Americans across the country about their jobs. Terkel's material was powerful, transcribing the many hidden dreams and frustrations of us all. And it was delivered by a strikingly talented cast. In a way, *Working* was similar to *A Chorus Line,* but better—it was a collection of inner monologues by a variety of characters on a central theme. And *Working* was surely a far more universal subject. But the show didn't succeed. So what went wrong?

Let's examine what it lacked. *A Chorus Line* had framed the material, providing a time and place (the audition). *A Chorus Line* had suspense—everyone was auditioning for a job. The stories were in chronological order, subtly becoming a story with a rising line of dramatic action: a dancer's life. And *A Chorus Line* was brilliantly staged.

Working didn't have a framework, suspense, or staging. Its content, score, and performances were superior to many successful musicals, but it didn't *look* or *feel* like a good musical. Stephen Schwartz as director was inexperienced and indulgent. *Working* lacked the drive and focus of a good production. And no one there knew how to impose the modern musical theatre technique that would have delivered that excellent material to the audience in an effective and entertaining way. *Working* also lacked the single essential ingredient of theatre—character. Each of the talented cast members had ideas to present, but not personalities. They were faceless. It is possible to do a show without a book, but you can't do one without characters.

In these waning days, the modern musical formula also became as much a burden as an asset. Unless it was handled with exceptional originality or talent, modern musical theatre could suddenly, easily look like hoary musical comedy. Repeated adherence to this formula very nearly put an end to the musical by boring its audience to death. Indeed, the clichés of the musical's structure motivate many otherwise astute theatregoers to conclude that they "don't like musicals much."

Generic musical comedy scores can kill a show. Richard Maltby and David Shire's score for *Baby* surprised everyone when it failed because they had written so many successful songs, as demonstrated in their tuneful off-Broadway revue *Starting Here, Starting Now.* Many of the songs in *Baby* were melodic and fun, but they had no dramatic resonance in a show that took place Anywhere and featured Anyone. (It didn't help that the book featured three couples and repeated each issue three times, in the most predictable structure ever perpetrated on an audience. Also, the staging was dull and the physical production was cheap.)

If a good song can hurt a show by failing to express a plot point or deepen a character, so can a dance. A knowledgeable audience groans when they hear lines like "Let's rehearse the court dance!" (*Merlin*), or "Okay, everybody, let's run through the hobo number!" (*My Favorite Year*), whereupon a zippy chorus appears with plastic smiles and coordinated clothes.

Some stars can't sing. This hurts the score, and producers must face the fact that people come to see the stars. As soon as they leave, so does the show. Stars often cause problems with the book as well. Jackie Gleason turned Eugene O'Neill's *Ah, Wilderness!,* a charming story about an adolescent named Richard, into *Take Me Along,* a musical about Uncle Sid, overweighting the libretto toward a supporting character. Shelly Winters turned a story about the young Marx brothers—all five were incandescent onstage—into a story about the Marx Brothers' mother. Liza Minnelli forced *The Rink* to be as much about a daughter as a mother, around whom the story should have revolved.

On the other hand, sometimes you really need a star, and a good actor isn't enough to carry the show. Major roles require major actors. That doesn't necessarily mean they are talented or skilled. Some human beings are larger than life and fill the stage, projecting their role to the last balcony. You can't take your eyes off them. Gwen Verdon really couldn't sing much at all, and by the time *Chicago* rolled around, even her incendiary dancing ability was subdued. In fact, a younger Chita Rivera blew her away. But a funny thing happened—Verdon was mesmerizing anyway. Rivera can't carry a show. Neither could Helen Gallagher (*Hazel Flagg*), though both Gallagher and Rivera could stop one in a supporting role. John Cullum—brilliant in "Molasses to Rum" in *1776*—gets the "close but no cigar" award for *Shenandoah* and *On the Twentieth Century.* In the former, you wished for John Raitt, not because he's any more talented than Cullum but because he had charisma. In *Twentieth Century* Cullum fell short of *owning* the show, something the role should have allowed, as it had for John Barrymore in the film. And Madeleine Kahn stared off into space as if uncertain of her next line. Thus a young Kevin Kline stole the show with a secondary role. (Once

Kahn was gone, replacement Judy Kaye demonstrated some of the possibilities that had been left uncovered.)

Sometimes you need both talent and charisma. If the principal character requires virtually all the important songs (*Cyrano*) and you go with an inexperienced singer (Christopher Plummer) it might not matter how well he delivers the material (very)—the show simply isn't going to lift off the ground when it needs to. *Ballroom* boasted two wonderful character actors as its leads, Dorothy Loudon and Vincent Gardenia, but neither was a singer. *Ballroom* had virtually no singers in a musical that had a romantic score.

The musical traditionally provided roles for great entertainers. Broadway, having been upstaged by film and television, no longer has the high profile that put a musical's lead on the international map and launched a career. If you can get a star, he or she is probably from Hollywood and wants to go home before your investors can recoup.

The musical theatre doesn't have to be as star-driven as producers think. Among the ten longest-running Broadway musicals, three were created without stars at all, and the others have transcended theirs. Audiences might enter the theatre because of a favorite personality, but they leave it happy because of the show.

The days of Alfred Drake, John Raitt, Mary Martin, Ethel Merman, and Gwen Verdon are over, and with them disappeared a popular category of musical—the vehicle. And drawing power. There are no replacements—young actors don't have the opportunity to hone their talent because musicals from summer stock to Broadway are now very limited in number.

The loss of so many talented young artists to AIDS is the single greatest catastrophe that has ever visited the cultural scene. It is impossible to calculate the number of writers, producers, directors, choreographers, designers, and musical theatre performers whose careers have been foreshortened by the disease.

Michael Bennett died at forty-five, an age when George Abbott had only completed the first ten years of a fifty-year span of directing musicals. Gower Champion died of a rare blood disease a few years earlier, and, Bob Fosse died from the cumulative effects of drugs, alcohol, cigarettes, and hyperactivity. Their species—great modern musical theatre director-choreographers—has disappeared entirely in the space of a single generation.

Bad work, tired formulas, no stars, no writers, and the AIDS crisis have all helped to cripple the American musical theatre. And money. *South Pacific* cost $180,000 to produce in 1949. (Having raised $225,000, producers Richard Rodgers, Oscar Hammerstein, and Leland Hayward made their first payback to their investors at the Broadway premiere.) *The King and I* cost $360,000 in 1951. In 1956 *My Fair Lady* cost $401,000.

In 1975, *A Chorus Line*'s workshop, off-Broadway run, and move to Broadway cost $1,145,000. *Jerome Robbins' Broadway*—a compilation of thirty years of great musical numbers and an historical affidavit of unparalleled importance—was capitalized in 1989 for nearly $7 million. *Phantom of the Opera* (1986) capitalized at $8 million. Andrew Lloyd Webber's investors spent $12 million to open *Sunset Boulevard* in Los Angeles.

Under the conditions of the Princess Theatre days, at the beginning of the century, investments could be recouped in four to eight weeks. In 1956 *My Fair Lady* cost $46,000 a week to run and had a capacity gross of $68,000, allowing it to pay off its investment in twenty-five weeks. *Phantom of the Opera* incurred $375,000 in expenses each week, requiring sixty-five sold-out weeks to pay off. *Jerome Robbins' Broadway,* with a large cast, had weekly costs of $400,000 and needed at least a year to break even, which it never did.

You don't have to be an accountant. Capitalization for a Broadway musical has skyrocketed. Weekly costs have risen significantly, both on Broadway and on the road. At the same time, film investment has only improved. In the late 1960s and the 1970s, investment in film became a good tax shelter due to a probusiness government. The average studio film cost $36 million in 1994. Walt Disney spends half that, and independent films cost much less. A good genre knock-off can easily be made for $500,000 to $5,000,000 today.

The principal difference between film and theatre is that the film industry is capital-intensive. Once the film is finished, the costs decrease considerably and you've got a permanent asset on your hands. Theatre, on the other hand, is a labor-intensive business. The payroll has to be met for *every performance,* and once it isn't the asset disappears entirely.

The Broadway musical is now a huge gamble, and that has painted the art into a conservative corner, inhospitable to serious drama. It is becoming increasingly inhospitable to serious musical theatre. The 1991 Tony award for best musical went to *The Will Rogers Follies,* a no-brainer.

Show Boat, Porgy and Bess, Oklahoma!, West Side Story, and *A Chorus Line* are all stunning artistic achievements and each show represents a major leap forward in the history of the modern American musical theatre. Every one of them was preceded by a chorus of disapproval from investors (many had trouble raising money), critics (only *A Chorus Line* was unanimously well-reviewed), and Broadway naysayers. Not one smelled good to the community. Not one had a healthy box office advance, even though each was sponsored by a major figure in the New York theatre community (Florenz Ziegfeld; the Theatre Guild; the Theatre Guild; Harold Prince and Robert Griffith; and Joseph Papp, respectively). These shows were written by star composers (Jerome Kern; George Gershwin; Richard Rodgers; Leonard Bernstein; and Marvin Hamlisch) and were directed by experienced hands (Oscar Hammerstein; Rouben Mamoulian; Mamoulian; Jerome Robbins; and Michael Bennett). Each show was the latest project of successful, established professionals with the highest of reputations. Yet each had a downbeat story, and each was untraditional for the period.

In other words, all of the great leaps in the art form occurred in spite of *and virtually because of* the fact that they were risks. In the increasingly conservative climate of the Broadway musical, risk-taking is *verboten.* Not a single hit musical since Michael Bennett's *Dreamgirls* has grappled with the boundaries of the technique of the musical. Few American musicals since *A Chorus Line* have dealt with serious subjects.

During the 1927–28 Broadway season there were 264 productions, forty-six of which were new musicals. In the 1975–76 season, there were sixty-two productions, sixteen of them new musicals. During the 1992–93 season, Broadway mounted thirty-three productions, and nine of them were new musicals. In the 1994–95 season, there were only two new musicals out of twenty-nine productions, though the 1995–96 season brought seven new tuners and four revivals.

The narrower the breadth of an art form, the less movement can take place. Hit musicals provided Broadway with fresh capital and satisfied audiences. Marginal musicals provided Broadway with writers, directors, choreographers, designers, performers, fresh ideas, and individual, specific achievements.

Higher costs and fewer shows have impacted the theatre all across America in much the same way. In particular, cities that once saw four musicals per season now see one every two years. Subscriptions that used to support a marginal musical between two hits have disappeared, and the marginal musical, if it exists at all, doesn't tour.

Even down the ladder, there are fewer summer stock productions. Many of the famous summer theatres that once produced ten musicals in ten weeks have turned their theatres over to concert bookings, if they haven't closed their doors entirely. It isn't possible to present the same old chestnuts every year. Unless new musicals enter the literature regularly, summer stock has nothing to produce.

The most damaging effect of these changes is the disappearance of the apprentice system that every art form needs to continue to grow. Where once a young choreographer like Michael Bennett could gain experience by staging half a dozen musicals in summer stock, now few such operations exist. Once young dancers could work for a dozen choreographers in the choruses of a dozen Broadway musicals, and there's no better firsthand experience than watching a new musical being put together from the chorus. If an artist can't work at his chosen form, he can't add to it. An artist doesn't learn anything by waiting on tables. The musical comedy actor-singer-dancer, that wonderful American phenomenon, will disappear if young performers can't gain experience by performing roles in the classic musicals.

The younger generation of aspiring writers, directors, choreographers, actors, composers, lyricists, producers, and designers did not grow up with Broadway and Forty-second Street as their mecca, the way Moss Hart did. Consequently, its unlikely that they will participate in the next *My Fair Lady.* Today's young talent heads for Hollywood. An apprenticeship on the stage has been replaced with a childhood in front of the television.

This is not to say that the theatre could or should compete with the money Hollywood has to offer. But the theatre has offered something else, a *process* that is far more satisfying, a community of intellectuals, a "happy band of brothers" in pursuit of artistic success—not a good table at the best restaurant. The theatre offered an opportunity for an artist to become skilled. Acting is not learned from short, repetitive takes in front of a camera, but from complete performances in front of an audience.

The pool of talent that was responsible for the golden age of the Broadway musical is gone, and it hasn't been replaced. Soon there won't be a large professional class of actors or artists, only a tiny group of Broadway musicals for the upper class. The musical theatre will never die—it's as old as the human race—but perhaps Broadway will be supplanted by more amateur theatre activity in communities around the country. That situation is, in fact, far more normal. Only in the twentieth century, and only in the most developed countries, has the professional theatre become a practical business proposition.

Throughout its history the theatre has seldom been professional or commercial. The twentieth century has given the Western world a theatre lucrative enough to support a community, which in turn could devote itself entirely to theatre. But the Greek and Roman theatres that started it all were occasional festivals. Traveling players during the Middle Ages and the Renaissance eked out an impecunious and precarious living. The great Renaissance theatre employed artisans with other skills, a lucky few supported by the undependable largess of a royal patron. The companies of Shakespeare and Molière went in and out of solvency—only the principals ever earned much—and the benefit was born out of the sudden need of the actor.

By the eighteenth century the business of city playhouses and touring productions was established, but it was wildly precarious. During America's golden age of musicals, when jazz dancing boomed and Broadway was awash in sensationally talented singer-dancer-actors, London's West End dancers required day jobs because the minimum wage was so low.

Ticket prices have risen sharply over the years. During the first half of the twentieth century, the top ticket price was $1.50 (capacity gross was ten thousand to fifteen thousand dollars at most theatres). You could see *The Black Crook* for as little as five cents, or a penny an hour, if you didn't want the best seats. By 1956, the best seats for *My Fair Lady* were $6.00. *Hello, Dolly!* opened with a top ticket price of $9.90. (Scalpers collected $25.00)

When *A Chorus Line* opened in 1975 the top price was $15.00, and the average price was $9.86. When it closed fifteen years later, the top ticket price was $50.00, and the number of top-priced seats was increased to include the majority of the theatre. The average ticket price during Broadway's 1992–93 season was $41.71, with the best seats for musicals costing $65.00. The mid-1990s *Show Boat* revival charged $75.00 for most seats.

Consider that a first-run film at a premium theatre costs $8.00, a videotape can be rented for under $4.00, the best seats at a Yankees game go for $17.00, and a full day at Disneyland runs about $30.00.

When the musical theatre appealed to the American middle class, a varied, successful, professional theatre, and a great one, became possible. Now that ticket prices are prohibitively high, the commercial theatre is only for the élite. The middle class has no theatre left to attend. Although the average American probably doesn't care—there are plenty of films and television programs—the theatre has been irrevocably hurt.

The worst effect of high ticket prices is the elimination of the best and brightest of the theatre audience—students, teachers, artists, and plain theatre lovers.

If ticket prices have risen so dramatically to cope with the increasing cost, why does it also take longer to recoup the initial investment? Probably because many running costs—television advertising, union salaries—have increased faster than inflation. When a producer must tell an investor that he'll get his money back *if* the show runs at capacity for a year and a half (which only a fraction of musicals do), the investor is going to start thinking wistfully of a bank deposit. In fact, the average investor is long gone from Broadway, and a small group of theatre owners, wealthy corporations, and extremely wealthy individuals now put up the money—another trend that inhibits quality and experimentation.

Walk-in business, once a bulwark of the marginal shows, is virtually nonexistent. At current prices, few people are willing to take the chance. Fewer still are willing to pay good money to sit in the far reaches of the balcony.

There's also significant competition from film, television, radio, recordings, and the emerging digital media, none of which existed when George M. Cohan took Broadway by storm and the American musical began to pick up steam. *Oklahoma!* played to twelve million people in its legendary run. Rodgers and Hammerstein's television musical *Cinderella* was seen by 107 million viewers during its single broadcast. A recent poll demonstrated that while film, video, television, compact disks, and even museums are experiencing consistent *increases* in audience size, audiences for theatre and dance are *decreasing*.

Producers have also disappeared, a number of whom contributed to the golden age. Cy Feuer and Ernest Martin ably managed *Can-Can, Guys and Dolls,* and *How to Succeed in Business Without Really Trying.* Saint Subber, with unerring taste, brought Cole Porter to *Kiss Me Kate.* Stuart Ostrow put his faith and his money behind two oddballs that turned out to be *1776* and *Pippin.*

Two producers left an indelible mark. The reckless and extravagant Florenz Ziegfeld was followed by the Machiavellian, penny-pinching David Merrick. Merrick was the most successful theatrical producer in the history of the commercial, professional theatre, the impetus behind dozens of musicals. He was legendary for erratic behavior throughout his career, as Ziegfeld had been. The instability and anger of Merrick's last active years were exacerbated by age, cocaine, and a stroke, but his behavior in his personal and professional lives had always been destructive. He was probably manic-depressive, certainly paranoid, and often messianic. Such is the Broadway musical that these characteristics fueled as well as hindered his work.

Sadly, beneath Merrick's erratic and off-putting antics lurked a man with a Dickensian childhood who most of all had missed, and failed to ever understand, the simple love that children have a right to. But he was enamored with talent and all that came with it—he loved the theatre and was more devoted to it than any producer since. His Herculean efforts to produce Broadway musicals—and keep them afloat—began with the tasteful and charming *Fanny,* moved through the musical comedy *Destry Rides Again,* peaked when *Hello, Dolly!* became the longest running Broadway musical to that time, and ended with an elephant of a hit, *42nd Street.* It included such gems as *Carnival, Gypsy, I Do! I Do!* and *Promises, Promises* in addition to numerous straight plays. In one season alone (1963–64) David Merrick had nine new productions open, three of them musicals. It's unlikely that any producer will ever mount such a body of work again.

There's an enormous difference between counting pennies and cutting corners. Merrick could close a show with blinding swiftness, preferring not to throw good money after bad, but he never intentionally made a financial decision that undercut an artistic one. Many of today's Broadway producers don't make this distinction.

• • •

Twenty-five years ago the rising costs and increasing conservatism of Broadway began to force regional theatres to play a larger part in the development of new plays and the presentation of serious drama. The result benefited both new plays and regional theatre. Now musicals are in the same predicament, and regional theatres face the same responsibility.

But the resources needed to mount new (or revive old) Broadway musicals are simply not available to regional theatres in the United States. Contributions to the arts are shrinking. The financial needs of a musical are much greater than those for a play. The artistic directors of regional theatres, who didn't grow up on Broadway musicals, are often not equipped to develop and direct them. Finally, there is enmity at many regional theatres towards anything that smacks of the commercial.

In the May 21, 1990 issue of *The New Republic,* Robert Brustein, artistic director of the American Repertory Theatre in Cambridge, Massachusetts, publicly chastised the Yale Repertory Theatre and the Center Theatre Group in Los Angeles for presenting August Wilson's *The Piano Lesson* on Broadway, as well as Lloyd Richards for directing productions of it outside the nonprofit theatre he ran. Indeed, Brustein is a constant critic of nonprofit theatres that involve themselves in commercial theatre.

But the gulf between commercial and nonprofit theatre is a hoax, given lip-service by regional theatre directors fearful of Broadway's shadow. There isn't any substantive artistic difference between theatre for profit and theatre not for profit—there is only good theatre and bad theatre.

The involvement of the Yale Rep in *The Piano Lesson* on Broadway was an extremely healthy interaction that augers better theatre on Broadway and better theatre at Yale. The play won a Pulitzer Prize and brought a black playwright to national attention, reflecting well on the Yale Rep. Potential profits allow the theatre to thrive; the New York Shakespeare Festival has sponsored numerous new works with its profits from *A Chorus Line.*

It is axiomatic that new and existing regional theatres are going to need a great deal more money if they are to pursue the past, present, and future of the American musical theatre. It will probably have to come from the private sector. In an age when funding for health and public education have been drastically curtailed, we cannot expect Washington to figure out how to fund the arts. The forces of conservatism have long opposed the liberal arts, for fear of both the prurient and critical nature of drama.

According to a 1992 Harris poll conducted on behalf of the American Council on the Arts, the public still favors supporting the arts by a clear majority. Curiously, however, younger people expressed far more support for public arts funding than their elders—78 percent of 18- to 29-year-olds were in favor, as were 64 percent of 30- to 49-year-olds. Among subjects over the age of fifty, a majority (54 percent) opposed public funding for the arts. These figures may bode well for the future if the younger generations continue to believe that the arts are important to the quality of life, and that the community needs to support the arts through public and private grants. However, the poll may also reflect people's tendency to become more conservative as they age. As the baby boomers get older, America might be in for a decrease in support for the arts.

Even when adequate funding is available, the American musical has not been easy to produce outside of Broadway. Consider Los Angeles, for example, where the money, talent, and the audience all exist. In 1938, Edwin Lester created the Los Angeles Civic Light Opera (LACLO). He presented musical comedy, beginning with two-week engagements of four shows each season. By the 1960s, LACLO's subscription guaranteed full houses for an eight-week run of each production. When he opened another theatre in San Francisco, his shows were able to play nearly six months of successful West Coast engagements.

But these were not Lester's shows. They were national touring companies fresh from Broadway, completely created and cast in New York. He merely booked them.

When a Broadway producer had a hot show, he made money by sending companies on the road. Because Lester could offer a presold six-month run, every producer wanted his blessing and booking, in return for which Lester was able to make certain demands. He often insisted on the original cast, which enabled local theatre lovers to see the great musicals in near-perfect, original productions.

What Los Angeles audiences never quite realized is that they were seeing Broadway shows, although the programs stated the they were presented by the Los Angeles Civic Light Opera. These shows had nothing to do with LACLO in any creative sense—in fact, many of them played there *in spite of* Edwin Lester. His own taste—most seasons included one locally produced musical—was extremely conservative. His idea of the contemporary American musical theatre stopped with the Bavarian *Waltzspiels* he adored. Lester didn't want the exuberant new entertainments, but they were the big hits his audiences had read about in national magazines.

As the American musical theatre took on a more American tone, Lester was increasingly uncomfortable. He refused the original *Sweet Charity* as too risqué and attempted to impose restrictions on other shows, sometimes trying to tone down the hot brass sections and augment the violins, in a vain attempt to stem the tide of the bolder, brassier musicals of the golden age. For the most part, New York composers and directors held fast.

On one occasion Lester complained about the orchestrations for a Jule Styne score. They were too brassy, too hot. In conversation with several experienced, New York musical theatre people, he stated that the worst overtures he'd ever heard were for Styne's shows *Funny Girl* and *Gypsy.* A profound silence greeted the remark. This was beyond a matter of taste—these two overtures are the finest American musical theatre overtures ever written.

Broadway touring companies continued to increase the success of Lester's seasons until it was the largest in the nation, with 270,000 subscribers. LACLO became a cornerstone of the philanthropic drive to build the Los Angeles Music Center. Meanwhile, Lester's own shows continued to be disastrous. He was fond of remounting cobwebbed operettas like *Naughty Marietta, The Vagabond King, The Gypsy Baron,* and *Rosalinda.* Worse yet, he occasionally attempted to produce original shows. His flops included *Gypsy Lady, Magdalena, At the Grand, Dumas and Son!* and *1491.* Only two homegrown shows ever gained attention for LACLO. *Kismet,* an Arabian nights musical with a funny if old-fashioned book, did well in New York. (This was partly because a newspaper strike diluted the effect of weak reviews.) Lester also produced *Peter Pan,* but it was created entirely by New York theatre people for Mary Martin—Lester simply booked its tryout in Los Angeles. In thirty-eight years, Lester was never able to personally produce a really successful musical.

When the Dorothy Chandler Pavilion was opened in 1965, LACLO and Edwin Lester finally had the home they desired—offices, rehearsal and backstage space, and a new theatre. But the theatre had been designed for the aesthetics of opera and operetta, with chandeliers and red carpeting adorning a vast space. It is an inhospitable auditorium for musical theatre. The subsequent decline and collapse of LACLO was attributed to the lack of product coming out of New York, which is certainly a factor, but there are three other reasons. Lester had helped create the wrong auditorium; Lester's organization was incapable of producing its own shows; and New York producers were able to avoid him as other theatres in Los Angeles were refurbished. A director of the Shubert Organization once said that the Shubert Theatre in Los Angeles was built, in part, to avoid having to deal with Edwin Lester when presenting musicals on the West Coast.

Following Edwin Lester's reign at LACLO, New York theatre producers Cy Feuer and Ernest Martin stepped in to keep the organization on its feet. Their credentials were impeccable, but they too were from an era long past. They moved local musical theatre only one generation forward into their own days of *Bells Are Ringing* and *Wonderful Town.* Their productions continued to erode LACLO's subscription base, which shrunk by nearly eighty percent over the years. To put this in perspective: during the time that greater Los Angeles grew more rapidly than any city in the United States, LACLO lost its audience faster than any theatre in the country. In the 1980s the Los Angeles Music Center rejected the tenancy of LACLO altogether.

Three companies in Southern California then attempted to take up the mantle. The University of California at Los Angeles sponsored a company that attempted two musicals in repertory at the Doolittle Theatre, *Leave It To Jane* and *The Boys From Syracuse,* which failed resoundingly. Neither of their shows evidenced any talent for the craft of the musical, and both were chosen from an early, giddy, silly time in the history of American musicals.

The Long Beach Civic Light Opera catered to a local crowd, and only musical comedy mavens trekked out to see their productions, which were principally tired packages. Typically, a cast of actors, all of whom had played their roles before, would be thrown together by a stage manager or assistant choreographer from the original production. The show would be rehearsed in two weeks and performed on rented sets built for much smaller theatres, using rented costumes that had long since lost their luster. Three consecutive managements could not avoid bankruptcy.

The California Music Theatre at the Pasadena Civic Center, originally housed in a barn it couldn't fill, was a descendant of Edwin Lester's LACLO (he held an honorary position on the Board), and it was the first theatre company in decades created to produce musicals. Their first season of four productions included three operettas. Each show suffered from the same "my dad has a barn, let's put on a show" mentality. They had a "loud is good, big is better" approach to acting, often featuring long, straight lines of chorus boys and girls who would throw their hands in the air on the final notes. This approach, with its bright colors, bright voices, and bright make-up, revived a kind of musical comedy that never really existed but seems to be the norm in community theatre. Numbers were performed with all the gusto of Debbie Reynolds and Carelton Carpenter in "Abadaba Honeymoon." The trouble with this form of delivery is that the American musical comedy had given way to American musical theatre half a century earlier. Reviewers consistently criticized the company's hoary performing and staging until it collapsed.

The Los Angeles Opera even tried its hand at musicals with a production of *Oklahoma!* In 1990, tickets cost $115.00 per seat, plus a $3.50 charge for the privilege of purchasing each one and $4.00 for parking, for a total of $241.00 per couple. These prices clearly indicate that the Los

Angeles Opera is intended for the financial elite of the city. The decision to mount *Oklahoma!* blatantly catered to conservative audiences left over from the LACLO era. What's more, there was no intellectual rationale for the traditional production. The musical is set in 1907, and Agnes de Mille herself would have found its 1940s style arcane by 1990.

These theatres defend themselves with the same argument that Edwin Lester had used—that they are giving audiences what they want. But this becomes a self-fulfilling prophecy, as it did for Lester. By ignoring the last two generations in Broadway musical theatre, his productions grew decrepit with age and when his supply of New York shows dwindled so did his audiences.

French film director Robert Bresson said, "It is not my job to give the audience what they want. It is my job to make the audience want what I give them." Delivering operettas as if they were musical theatre, and staging shows with a kind of Busby Berkeley enthusiasm but no real understanding of what the American musical theatre has become, may satisfy a small, undiscerning audience but will severely limit the life of any new company.

• • •

Lately the recording industry has conspired to sabotage the American musical as well. When *Oklahoma!* was recorded for Decca Records, the vogue for original cast albums came about and the musical theatre capitalized on that particular subsidiary right. On a well-recorded album, a good deal of the spontaneity and liveliness of a great musical can be heard. In Broadway's heyday, audiences often came to the theatre already knowing the score. Show tunes occupy only a tiny, fanatic corner of the market, but the availability of old recordings has maintained an awareness of musical theatre. They are the immortal footprints of the musicals that played Broadway.

Hundreds of these recordings exist. Typically the cast and orchestra would report to the studio on their first day off following the official Broadway opening, and in a single marathon day they would record the score. After weeks of rehearsals and preview performances, the actors were capable of vocal performances imbued with all the dramatic fervor of the live show. The album producer tried to capture something of that feeling of live theatre, and many of the best recording producers succeeded (notably, Goddard Lieberson at Columbia Records).

It has lately become popular to re-record the well-known scores under controlled studio conditions. The theory behind these studio productions is to capture the music under optimum conditions, using operatic voices unencumbered by the need to act, dance, or meet the requirements of the role. The new recordings focus solely on musical values to the exclusion of dramatic ones, and the result is to eviscerate the very heart and soul of the great musical scores.

This trend began with Leonard Bernstein's recording of *West Side Story,* with Kiri Ti Kanawa as Maria and José Carreras as Tony. Bernstein was well aware that outside of the United States his score is taken as serious music and produced in opera houses, and he hoped to focus the attention of serious music fans in America as well. But he created an operatic version of the score, and reduced it to notes—glorious notes, but without meaning. In particular, the casting of José Carreras, with his Spanish accent, as Tony, a white American teenager, leads to ludicrous renditions of "Something's Coming," "Maria" and "One Hand, One Heart" as if they were sung by Bernardo (who has no accent at all in this version!). The musical's ethnic roots—much of the score is a contrast between American jazz and Puerto Rican rhythms—are severely contradicted.

Carreras and Kanawa next recorded *South Pacific.* Miscasting reached its apotheosis when Kanawa sang "He's a Cultured Frenchman," and Carreras answered in a thick Spanish accent. The liner notes to the *South Pacific* recording point out that the "world class London Symphony Orchestra is surely superior to the normal Broadway pit orchestra." This presumptuous canard overlooks the magnificent, versatile, New York pick-up musicians who specialize in Broadway shows. The new recordings do benefit from larger orchestras, and Bernstein's New York pick-up orchestra for *West Side Story* must have been a special treat for the maestro. But there's not a horn player in a symphony orchestra anywhere in the world who can duplicate what Dick Parry did for the overtures on the original *Gypsy* and *Funny Girl* cast albums. The London Symphony Orchestra plays all the notes right, but "it don't mean a thing, 'cause it ain't got that swing."

The new *South Pacific* does boast two outstanding cuts from jazz stylist Sarah Vaughan. She delivers "Bali Ha'i" in a rendition that almost makes the whole album worth owning, chewing the words ("Bali Huyuyh") and "glissing" the intervals in her distinct style. There's nothing wrong with pop vocalists covering show tunes (though let's hope Jim Nabors will not follow up his recording of *Man of La Mancha*). Richard Rodgers's lush *South Pacific* score benefits from Kanawa's rich voice. But listen to Mary Martin and you'll hear something much better, a voice that effervesces with cockeyed optimism.

Also missing is the special verve of that unique institution, the Broadway chorus. In the re-recording of *West Side Story,* you can't tell the Jets from the Sharks (it's the same men's chorus). In *South Pacific*'s original cast recording, the chorus holds on to their notes like a sailor clinging to the mast in a high sea. That's what gives the great "Dames" song reality. The new recording features a chorus that sings more properly, but they're not supposed to be a professional men's chorus—they're Seabees.

Recently trunks full of original music and orchestrations from the shows of the twenties and thirties (long thought lost) were found in a New Jersey warehouse. This discovery justified the first really full recording of *Show Boat* (Frederica Von Stade, Teresa Stratas), so full that it contained six numbers eliminated by Kern and Hammerstein. But this operatic recording, including dialogue, was done without any dramatic rehearsal by singers inexperienced in acting. There is an all-white chorus for both black and white parts because the black singers walked out rather than sing the "nigger" lyric. If the glorious music is well-served, the drama is not at all.

A new *My Fair Lady* is the worst of these re-recordings. Kanawa sings the ultimate English role as if she struggled to learn both parts, the cockney and the upper class, and English wasn't her native language. She makes the percussive "Show Me!" into four or five syllables, and enunciates her lyrics too carefully. Jeremy Irons's wavering tenor plays against Kanawa's robust mezzo as if they were mother and son. His voice is far too thin and immature to play the irascible bachelor Henry Higgins. He tries to sing more of the role, but the score was created for a nonsinger and he gets no mileage out of his crooning, and he loses the opportunity to act. In a radio interview he bragged about his full week of rehearsal. Would he have dared Richard III on a week's rehearsal?

Producers of these ill-begotten albums believe they are preserving great scores. No one has ever claimed that all musical comedy stars had terrific voices. Richard Rodgers used to cringe when he heard Gertrude Lawrence wobble off key as Anna in *The King and I.* But it is the raw vitality of character that makes these historic original cast albums sing with the drama and comedy of theatre.

• • •

The American musical arrived at its most effective form in the 1940s, 1950s, and 1960s. Not coincidentally the commercial Broadway theatre was at its healthiest, with a large, knowledgeable, and appreciative audience, reasonable ticket prices, and hundreds of young artists aspiring to contribute. Tyrone Guthrie called Broadway in the 1950s the greatest experimental theatre in the world.

Conservative attitudes have steadily eroded the production of new musicals. But numbers only tell a fraction of the story. The shift of the largest song market away from show tunes toward rock music has eroded the American musical's popularity base. Thirteen- to eighteen-year-olds have become the largest and most sought-after market for leisure activity, curtailing media like the theatre and emphasizing escapist entertainment, such as cartoon-style movies. Even the increasingly hostile and difficult environment of our urban centers has affected audience habits. It's much easier to watch television than to face traffic, parking, restaurant prices, and marginal neighborhoods.

Our American heritage includes only two native art forms—jazz and musical theatre. Jazz is preserved in numerous legendary recordings, and is still practiced in its optimum form. But the musical theatre, evanescent and ephemeral, is rapidly disappearing. And you can't go home again.

Unfortunately, the creators of *Annie,* the show which begot the downfall, tried. During the 1989–90 season, Martin Charnin, Charles Strouse, and Thomas Meehan went back to *Annie* and attempted to mount a sequel titled *Annie Warbucks.* Not a bad idea—a revival with a twist. But they lacked the two crucial ingredients of their earlier success: luck and Mike Nichols. The show collapsed during tryouts. It was reworked and remounted for the road and collapsed again. It was reworked yet again and mounted off-Broadway, where lower ticket prices might attract a family audience. It closed again, having created only one legendary record: it's the musical that flopped more times than any other in history.

It hardly mattered to Broadway. By that time theatre owners had found an alternative source of income, and big Broadway musical theatres no longer stood empty. In the 1980s the Nederlander Organization sold the Mark Hellinger Theatre to a religious organization. The rest were inhabited by the latest evolutionary wave in the musical theatre, the English poperetta.

PLAYBILL®
MAJESTIC THEATRE

PLAYBILL®
WINTER GARDEN THEATRE
CATS

PLAYBILL®
THE BROADWAY THEATRE
Les Misérables

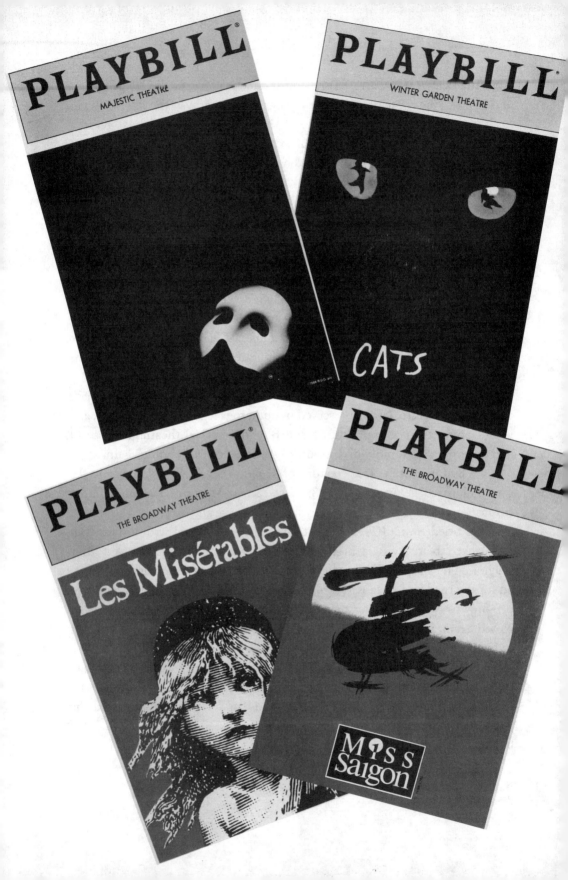

Twenty-Six

INTO THE WOODS

The party's over . . .

Producer George Abbott always had a soft spot for energetic young theatre lovers, and when Harold Prince offered to work for him for nothing, he started Prince as an office boy. Prince became assistant stage manager on Abbott's *Touch and Go* and *Call Me Madam.* When Prince left for the Korean War, Abbott promised he'd have a job when he returned, and was as good as his word. Prince returned to civilian life as the assistant stage manager on *Wonderful Town.*

Abbott never attempted to keep his assistants in their place. When Robert E. Griffith, another Abbott stage manager, and Prince came to him with a property they wanted to produce as a musical—the novel *7½ Cents* by Richard Bissell—he agreed to coauthor and direct, and even invested some of his own money. *The Pajama Game,* scored by newcomers Richard Adler and Jerry Ross, was a success, and at the age of twenty-six Harold Prince began a long and productive career.

Since that first musical, Prince's influence on the American musical theatre has been enormous. Between 1954 and 1993 he produced and/or directed twenty-nine new American musicals. He worked with George Abbott on nine musicals and with Jerome Robbins on three, an ideal apprenticeship that couldn't be duplicated today. When he began directing on his own, he did not incorporate Abbott's reliance on romance, comedy, and formula but made great use of his mentor's efficiency and pacing. He developed an interest in the seriousness of the musical that Jerome Robbins always showed, but he wasn't a choreographer and used choreography as little as possible. Prince replaced the fluidity of dance with elaborate set designs.

Prince directed four successive shows that had brief runs—*Family Affair, Baker Street, Superman,* and *She Loves Me*—then hit the bull's eye. With *Cabaret* (book by Joe Masteroff, music and lyrics by John Kander and Fred Ebb, choreography by Ron Field) Prince created a commercial success that left an indelible mark on the art of the musical. Prince married the performance style of Bertolt Brecht and Kurt Weill in their German period with the modern musical, and irrevocably broke the romantic tradition of the American musical to which even masterpieces like *My Fair Lady, West Side Story,* and *Fiddler on the Roof* had adhered. Instead of a realistic or representational set, Boris Aronson created a black box and used harsh lighting and distorted pieces to give the show a look based on German expressionism. The Kit Kat Club stood in for decadent Weimar Germany, and act two opened with a high-kicking chorus line metamorphosing into goose-stepping Nazis, echoing Germany's transition in the 1930s.

Prince used cabaret songs to comment upon, rather than further, the action. Freed from the realistic, representational style of acting that book songs need to be performed in, these numbers engaged the audience via a more presentational, vaudeville style. Oscar Hammerstein had pioneered the device in *Allegro,* but Prince avoided the usual problems associated with commentary songs by putting real characters in his Greek chorus.

This use of music as commentary was copied often in subsequent shows by Prince and others, and by Bob Fosse in the dark vaudeville *Chicago;* the technique has also appeared in a multitude of flop musicals, and it seems almost tired today. *Miss Saigon* features a *Cabaret*-derived master of ceremonies called the "engineer." But imitation is the sincerest form of flattery, and *Cabaret* legitimized an alternative use of song in musical theatre that gave future creators a wider range of options in structuring their story musically.

The following season Prince and his team, with Joseph Stein as librettist, musicalized the novel/film *Zorba the Greek.* Both *Zorba* and *Cabaret* have young and old lovers, sad endings, and literary sources. Both used frameworks—the Kit Kat Club and a Greek bouzouki circle. *Zorba*'s story was more representational, and the score was warmer and more romantic, befitting a more life-affirming story. *Zorba* is not as notorious for originality, but it was emotionally richer than *Cabaret.*

Prince then set to work on musicalizing a collection of plays about marriage by George Furth, using the commentary song technique he had pioneered in *Cabaret.* And with that, the "concept musical," first devised by Oscar Hammerstein for *Allegro* and strongly associated with Prince today, was off and running.

A "musical with a concept" is a wonderful show to behold. But a "concept musical" can be a dangerous thing, especially when it puts the concept ahead of the story. Hammerstein's idea of "continuous action" was more possible than ever—a single set with projections, set pieces moving smoothly on and off, no scenes-in-one, no curtains, no stops or starts, lots of light and staging, and a choreographer to direct or collaborate with a director. The result was the streamlined musical. Beginning with *Cabaret* and climaxing with *Company,* Prince expanded the use of musical sequences in musical theatre.

It's all very well for the creators of *Company* to claim they had produced an optimistic show because it embraced the institution of marriage in the end. But *Company* dissects five dysfunctional marriages and three demanding girlfriends in sarcastic, cynical, even bitter terms. After two hours of that, you can't reverse the mood of the evening with a last-minute "Oh well, it's better than nothing." Consequently the modern theatre's most original and contemporary musical did not become a smash hit, but it turned a reasonable profit. After that Prince surely had his greatest disappointment with *Follies.*

By this time the tastes of the American audience had begun to reject the most innovative work of the theatre community, especially when it was applied to serious themes. Serious drama began to disappear from Broadway, where it had reigned for almost four decades. And serious musicals were supplanted by extravaganzas.

But Prince soldiered on with unusual musicals, collaborating almost exclusively with his long-time friend from the Ivy league, Stephen

Sondheim, the man who was virtually hounded as the hope of the American musical. Their next show was *A Little Night Music,* which should be an operetta or light opera in the Mozart mode. But it was produced in 1973, and Prince, Sondheim, and librettist Hugh Wheeler were reluctant to risk the specter of "opera" on Broadway. To some extent the creators must have known that *Night Music* was an operetta, because they readily accepted Sondheim's suggestion for a title, a direct translation of Wolfgang Mozart's *Eine kleine Nachtmusik,* and they crafted an overture of pure vocalese. It's a musical that cries out for more complete scoring. Wheeler's book, based on the Ingmar Bergman film *Smiles of a Summer Night,* is sound, bright, and witty but never rises to the extravagant style of the piece, which is established at once by Sondheim's wickedly intricate, inordinately erudite, bitingly funny lyrics and effervescent, complex melodies all written in 3/4 meter.* The material gave Sondheim his first chance to demonstrate his extraordinary talent, and the opportunity to write for witty, intelligent, sophisticated characters in many complex song forms. Although *A Little Night Music* is readily accepted as a fine piece of work, it will be more comfortable with itself and will have the impact of great music theatre when it is recreated as an all-sung operetta.

In Harold Prince's book of theatrical memoirs, *Contradictions,* he claims that *A Little Night Music* as "mostly about making a hit." However, it is clear that his taste and that of the audience had grown quite far apart since the days of *Pajama Game.* Imagine thinking that a Viennese operetta set in Sweden about a "romantic chateau weekend" was just what Broadway wanted in 1973, with the 1971 revival of *No, No, Nanette,* starring the grandmotherly Ruby Keeler, still running.

One noteworthy production element was the staging, which was stiff and awkward, though it benefited from fluid panels that moved like shower doors across the stage. This was due to the fact that Michael Bennett had gone on to projects of his own after *Company* and *Follies,* and Prince, traumatized from having worked with a talented choreographer with an ego as big as his own, hired Patricia Birch, a choreographer whose lackluster career was based on the avoidance of having to make up choreography. The clumsy waltzing and lugubrious staging of *Night Music* began a transition for

* In 1946 Jerome Kern had suggested to Columbia Studios that he write the score for *Centennial Summer* entirely in 3/4 meter. His idea was rejected.

the modern musical away from the fluid staging created by Jerome Robbins, Michael Bennett, Gower Champion, and Bob Fosse, and back toward a time of stodgy, static pictures.

In the original musical *Candide,* Leonard Bernstein's great score was undercut by Lillian Hellman's didactic version of the story and Tyrone Guthrie's overproduced and opera-oriented production. When Prince resuscitated the show in 1973, he replaced Hellman's book with one by Hugh Wheeler that was more faithful to the comic spirit of Voltaire. Taking his clue from Candide's long journey, Prince staged the show to be played throughout the audience, with performers racing past spectators from one playing area to another. This "environmental" use of theatre (from the avant-garde experiments of off-Broadway theatre in the 1960s) created exuberant staging without any choreography at all.

Bernstein's score could have benefited from a larger orchestra and better singers—necessary compromises were struck for the production—but at least it had been returned to the theatre stage comfortably.

After the *Candide* revival, Prince began to take himself and his concepts too seriously. They began to overwhelm his material, and the production as well. In *Pacific Overtures,* Stephen Sondheim's score was sabotaged by one of the most ambitious and crippling production concepts ever to be not thought out. Amid Boris Aronson's breathtakingly beautiful set, Prince staged a Japanese Noh-theatre version of John Weidman's book about Western influences on Eastern culture (via Commodore Perry's exploration of Japan). The show's kabuki make-up and a declamatory acting style prevented the actors from being expressive. Also, there were not enough Asians with musical comedy experience to go around. Mako, in the leading role, spoke and sang in a garbled and almost unintelligible voice, and the rest of the cast was lackluster but adequate. But what really killed the show was the lack of flesh-and-blood characters, which had been replaced with representative ideas. And Prince used an all-Asian cast, which undercut the theme of the work and denied songs like "Please Hello," (an hysterical Gilbert and Sullivan sequence featuring American, British, Dutch, Russian, and French admirals) the cross-cultural variety they deserved. Prince almost bankrupted himself by supporting the show financially, then complained that Western audiences didn't take to it. The style of *Pacific Overtures* stood in the way of communication, the very essence of theatre.

Next, Betty Comden, Adolph Green, and Cy Coleman adapted the comic play and hysterical film *Twentieth Century,* and Prince chose a comic operetta style. He was moving further away from the techniques inherited from Jerome Robbins, the ones that had made the American musical theatre the great, streamlined art form that it was. The original was a farce. The new production delivered an uncomic operetta.

Stephen Sondheim followed the same operatic instincts for different reasons (Sondheim sought musical grandeur, Prince wanted decorative grandeur), and Sondheim's next project was to musicalize almost all of *Sweeney Todd,* a bloody Victorian melodrama. It was staged within a gargantuan and realistic factory set that was coldly Brechtian. The metaphor Prince tried to establish with this production—the destructive force of the industrial revolution—was an intellectual conceit that crushed the melodrama, and the cavernous factory set obliterated the director's most useful tool—focus. The complex lyrics couldn't be heard. Actors couldn't get their laughs. They could hardly get the audience's attention.

In *Sweeney Todd,* as in so many Prince shows from *Cabaret* onward, Prince had figures observing action that they were not realistically privy to. This device is a staging corollary to the commentary song, and by then it was overused and in most cases amounted to directorial diddling.

For Sondheim, *Sweeney Todd* was meant to be fun in the way that a horror film is, including suspense and moments of great horror relieved by the nervous laughter of farce. Prince ignored this entertaining and commercial approach, overburdening the material with his own feelings about man's inhumanity to man. Too often Prince's concepts overwhelm the material. This makes for musicals everyone talks about with awe, but which nonetheless leave the audience out in the cold.

Prince entirely failed to use the entertaining values of the music hall tradition that resonated in the *Sweeney Todd* material, once again rejecting a choreographic contribution in order to feature his own work. Brilliant performances—notably those of Angela Lansbury and Len Cariou—couldn't warm up the audience, not because of the material but because of the production. Sondheim and Prince were essentially working on two different shows. Sondheim's Gothic horror, B-movie, musical ambitions did not intersect with Prince's industrial-age metaphor. Later the enforced intimacy of off-Broadway generated a second, more successful look at the material, which may be Sondheim's greatest effort to date. Musical theatre, opera, or whatever it is, *Sweeney Todd* is a stunning score and a huge achievement, but it has yet to be given a really entertaining production.

Intellectual analysis completely replaced common sense and dramatic tenets in *Merrily We Roll Along,* the next and last, Sondheim-Prince collaboration. Once again, Prince chose a concept that refuted communication and distracted from, rather than supported, the material. The story spanned thirty years, but the roles were all played by young actors. In casting the show this way, Prince thought that "the audience would be less apt to identify with the characters and thus not be put off by the seriousness of the material," but audiences *want* to identify with characters. Nor did the vitality of the youthful cast make up for the experienced hands a Broadway audience expects to be in. *Merrily* smacked of amateurism, especially because the actors started out by playing their older counterparts. (The action runs backwards chronologically, as in the original play by George Kaufman and Moss Hart.) The show previewed on Broadway—producers at the time were attempting to save money by forgoing out-of-town tryouts, arguably the equivalent of artistic suicide—during which all the costumes were jettisoned for sweatshirts bearing the character's names, perhaps the single most desperate act ever seen during the sinking of a musical. The damage was complete. This may have worked off-Broadway—or better, in someone's dad's barn—but not at the Alvin Theatre.

Another mistake with *Merrily* was recasting the time frame from the original, 1931 to 1918, to Prince's own, 1980 to 1950, and changing the main characters to a composer and lyricist. The musical smacked of autobiography, and if there's anything an audience cares about less than a show about whiny rich people, it's a whole show *by* rich people about whiny rich people. The bitchy and self-aggrandizing book by George Furth and Prince's "hey kids, let's put on a show" concept combined to make the show a big whine, and audiences don't like that. Most people *would* sell their souls—they just don't get any offers.

Prince had become disenchanted with the time-consuming business of raising money, and investors had become disenchanted with the money-consuming business of serious, innovative, concept-oriented theatre, especially when it misfired, so Prince abandoned producing in favor of directorial assignments. His first real commercial success since *Cabaret* came about when he undertook to stage the rock musical *Evita.* There Prince worked for the first time with England's up-and-coming theatre composer of the postmodern age, Andrew Lloyd Webber. The current form of the mainstream musical is almost entirely due to the influence of these two men.

• • •

The mass-merchandising of art for the sake of commerce has caused a decline in the quality of American culture, and there is no clearer signpost than the rise to fame and fortune of Andrew Lloyd Webber, who has created scarce melodies for abysmal librettos and expensive, dismally choreographed extravaganzas.

Today's audiences favor the worlds of antiquity, futurism, and fantasy, where right and wrong are clearly delineated, where evil is easily identifiable and always defeated, and where nothing lurks to remind us that we are comporting ourselves in an uncivilized fashion. The real world—overloaded with pollutants, disrupted by religious wars and uncontrollable crime, led by corrupt politicians, divided by political animosity, and splintered by economic warfare—is of little interest to Broadway theatregoers. The presentation of a world gone sane has made Andrew Lloyd Webber a multimillionaire.

Lloyd Webber is unquestionably a skilled craftsman, manipulating theatre technique in precise, complex, extraordinary detail, but he has not shown much original creativity. He depends heavily on the tricks of composing, using the fundamental and simplistic ideas of each category—thus, *The New Yorker* labeled *Phantom of the Opera* "pop schlock." A "blues" number sounds like all blues numbers; a "tap" number sounds like all tap numbers; the country-and-western song in *Joseph and the Amazing Technicolor Dreamcoat* ("One More Angel") sounds like "Happy Trails" without copying it precisely; and *Phantom of the Opera* imitates Giacomo Puccini.*

When Sondheim writes pastiche, he does so for dramatic effect. *Follies* includes takeoffs on American composers of the period. It's a *Follies* as if written by Friml and Romberg ("One More Kiss"); Irving Berlin ("Beautiful Girls"); DeSylva, Brown, and Henderson ("Broadway Baby"); Jerome Kern ("Loveland"); Harold Arlen ("Losing my Mind"); and Cole

* With respect to *Phantom of the Opera,* Dan Sullivan of the *Los Angeles Times* wrote "Lloyd Webber's score is . . . rife with the usual borrowings, those from Puccini being not inappropriate in this case perhaps. But there's a really offensive one in the opening phrase . . . of 'The Music of the Night.' It doesn't take a master tune detective to identify the strain as Lerner and Loewe's 'Come to Me, Bend to Me' from *Brigadoon.*"

Porter ("The Story of Lucy and Jessie"). Because these composers all were, or could have been, contributors to the Ziegfeld shows, it's a brilliant panorama of the period. Andrew Lloyd Webber doesn't bother with dramatic justifications—he quotes from a wide range of musical sources, often anachronistically.

With generic music that is not appropriate to the period, the director is confronted with two options. Either he dramatizes the content, in which case the music and drama are in conflict, or he mimics the music. *Joseph and the Amazing Technicolor Dreamcoat* works best as a musical vaudeville, encompassing as it does a wide range of musical styles from Elvis Presley to French *chansons,* from singing cowboys to bubble gum rock. *Joseph* was originally written as a cantata for a boy's choir, a story told by narrative lyrics, not acted out—it is entertaining but never dramatic. Directors of *Jesus Christ Superstar* tend to avoid the glitzy approach of the original Broadway production (directed by Tom O'Horgan) and stage the music in a medieval setting. Glitz makes fun of the show's powerful story, but the medieval approach gives audiences an awkward picture of biblical figures rocking and rolling in their robes and sandals.

Poperetta fits neatly into Andrew Lloyd Webber's desire for continuous musical events. The strength of this concept is that the division between the reality of book scenes and the more theatrical level of song and dance do not conflict. There's no need to craft the transitions, over which Hammerstein labored so mightily in creating his continuous-action musicals, because the entire musical stays in the surreal world of music.

The danger is that the bookless musical fails to use dialogue and dance to further ideas they could better communicate. It falls short of the "total theatre" idea that began with Richard Wagner, painstakingly developed through the twentieth century, and culminated in *West Side Story* and *A Chorus Line.* Sung-through shows lack the integration that makes the American musical the great and original art form that it is. Artists like Lloyd Webber and Prince attempt to make the musical all music, harking back to an older, simpler form of theatre that lacked integration. But the through-music form requires that all ideas, even small or not very emotional ones, be communicated via lyrics, and awkward moments arise when actors passionately sing ideas not worthy of musicalization.

In 1949 Oscar Hammerstein II turned away from operetta, saying:

The show-within-the-faux opera
Clive Barda

"One Day More" of the revolution in *Les Misérables*
Photofest/Joan Marcus

> If a character is calling up an airport and trying to reserve two seats on a plane and asking how much they are and what time the plane leaves, this is not good lyric or musical material. In grand opera, however, this would be sung in recitative or incorporated into an actual aria. I do not believe the American public will ever accept this kind of convention in its own language. When composers and librettists try to write what they call American operas and include the singing of passages like these, they are really not writing American operas at all. They are writing European operas governed by European traditions. That is one reason why such efforts have never been successful.

Until now. But Hammerstein was proved wrong. The form didn't begin with Andrew Lloyd Webber. The original *Porgy and Bess* was written to be entirely sung. The more obscure but wonderfully experimental *The Golden Apple* is through-sung, and features a lead character portrayed entirely through dance. And Hammerstein was incorrect in predicting that audiences wouldn't accept it. But his instinct to musicalize only sections which could sustain heightened theatricality was appropriate, and marks a fundamental distinction between good musical theatre and operetta.

Furthermore, poperetta composers prefer "legit" voices, a style of singing rooted in the formal, operatic tones of sopranos and tenors. But the natural voice bridges the gap between drama and music, making drama of the music and allowing actors to make smooth transitions between song and dialogue. Ethel Merman, Mary Martin, Gwen Verdon, and Betty Buckley don't shift gears when they sing. The pure legit sound, which almost always has a tessiturra in the upper register, is not really natural and draws the audience away from the drama. Giorgio Tossi's performance in a *Most Happy Fella* revival wasn't human enough. The drama of *1776* was stronger for William Daniels's shaky, earthy, realistic voice.

Dialogue interludes move the plot forward with quicker momentum. This kind of dialogue, however, needs careful construction. If it's too verbal, too long, or too realistic it throws the musical into the wrong gear and contrasts awkwardly with the songs. The integration of scene, song, and dance cannot be solely one of fluid staging. Dialogue has to match the lyrics in dialect, period, brevity, and—most ephemeral of all—theatricality.

The marriage of Harold Prince and Andrew Lloyd Webber for

Evita was made in theatre heaven. *Evita* allowed Prince to avoid the acting and dance sequences that were his weakness.

Prince had previously used a metaphor to underscore the content of a script, but he began to invert their importance, attempting to make the metaphor—his concept—the principal dramatic value, which would be supported by the story. For *Evita,* Prince attempted to stage Evita Perón's rise to power as an example of the manipulating techniques and effects of the news media. But *Evita* as a sung-through piece just doesn't have the depth to make important distinctions. Except for the narration of the Che Guevara character, there's no clear thought in the show that defines the inherent danger of fascism. With *Evita,* Prince's transition to auteur-director was complete. The material was inadequate as drama, and as such made a better vehicle for the director's point of view.

To present fascism as show-biz in order to manipulate the audience is an awkward and ultimately unworkable concept, one more of Prince's increasing overintellectualizations. Fascism isn't show business. It is a brutal, inhumane, and corrupt form of government that doesn't deserve glorification. Eva Perón wasn't Judy Garland.

After *Evita,* Lloyd Webber chose a book of poetry by the late T. S. Eliot for musicalization. *Cats* is an undisguised revue. Its pamphlet of a book is vague and hard to identify. The plot is hardly forwarded by song after song bearing the same information ("I'm a cat") in different musical idioms. When Grizabela eventually descends to the "heaviside layer," we wonder why (because she's the one with the best voice). Theatre dance could have made the show immensely more exciting. A choreographer like Jerome Robbins or Michael Bennett would have created a unique, individualized vocabulary that stood for the movement of cats. A stylized choreographer like Bob Fosse or Michael Kidd would have imposed his own vocabulary on the show. (In fact, Fosse's graceful, erotic, feline work might have been well-placed in *Cats.*) The English choreographer Gillian Lynne used the tap, modern, and ballet vocabularies that the American musical gave up in the 1940s, and she staged the numbers like the musical pastiches they are, denying the show a style of its own.

Cats marked the beginning of the megamusical, wherein spectacle not only superseded but *replaced* drama. Its gargantuan environment by John Napier was a breathtaking achievement. The roof of the theatre had to be torn open so that Grizabela could have the most dramatic exit Broadway had ever witnessed (with the help of a crane). It dwarfed even *Follies* in its use of the historic Winter Garden Theatre. Its lack of action, redundant songs, and pop-rock music caused many theatregoers (especially older ones) to walk out, but its awesome set, surround-sound, and energetic cast convinced many people that they'd got their money's worth.

With the success of *Jesus Christ Superstar, Evita,* and *Cats,* English poperetta traveled to every corner of the theatre world and began to influence local theatre.

• • •

Hard on the heels of *Irma la Douce* the French provided the international musical theatre scene with a second hit. *Les Misérables,* based on Victor Hugo's novel, was first performed at a small theatre on the outskirts of Paris. There it was seen by Cameron Macintosh, an English impresario who had masterminded the international merchandising of the spectacle-on-steroids musicals. Macintosh coaxed *Cats* director Trevor Nunn into staging it and, after much expansion and translation of lyrics—there is no dialogue—the show was booked for ten weeks at London's Royal Court Theatre, where Nunn was artistic director.

The 1985 opening of *Les Misérables* in London received poor reviews, which is significant for two reasons. First, the critics were neither devastatingly correct nor wildly mistaken. They were misled. The show marked the apex of a movement in the musical theatre that had crept up on fans and critics surreptitiously. This extravagant style was seen in America with *Sweeney Todd* and had been encouraged by Harold Prince, but it really flourished on the West End. The English had no previous history of great musical theatre to get in its way, no superstar choreographers to stage musicals. In addition, English theatre has a four-hundred-year history of pageantry, and English directors are comfortable with the grand designs and opera staging.

But *Les Misérables,* for all its nobility, lacked musical theatre craft. The opening was the dullest seen on a musical stage in years. Hunched chorus men sing about how tough it is on the chain gang. The drab subject matter, drab sets, and drab costumes are appropriate, but the lack of invention is not. The chorus stands in two straight lines on a bare stage, the melody and the lyrics are dull.

Then the character of Jean Valjean is introduced, looking much too well-fed to have been in prison for nineteen years. He is turned into a good man by an act of kindness, and the scene changes to eight years later. In the blink of a light cue he's a successful factory owner and local mayor. How he got there from penniless bum in a class-conscious society, with the aid of two silver candlesticks, we don't know, but if we're going to cover Hugo's 1,200 pages in three hours, we'll have to move quickly.

As the show develops, nothing is left unsung, no matter how trivial. But most of it isn't trivial. The story concerns revolution, morality, and the true nature of mankind, and if anything we begin to wish the stage could hold a revolution. It doesn't. The show builds to the night before the most important battle, and then—again in the blink of a light cue—a student leader tells us that the battle is lost, and women, children and fathers should go home and not waste their life on a lost cause.

Just when you get comfortable with the operatic milieu, and don't mind another aria sung downstage center on the knees facing the audience, two supporting comedians enter and a little vaudeville is thrown in. The innkeeper and his wife burlesque their roles in a vaudeville style reminiscent of Rooster and Hannigan on "Easy Street" in *Annie,* another cast in which every actor seems independent of every other. (Good American musicals and plays do not feature a hodgepodge of acting styles, devoted as they are to ensemble work, but this is accepted on the English stage.) Mr. and Mrs. Innkeeper chew the scenery, and the villain Javert plays his role in the style of classical ballet pantomime, with big gestures and lots of body follow-through. The young lovers are simple and realistic, and Jean Valjean, with constantly clouded brow, is almost Brando-like in his intensity. The chorus is always a group, with no individual characteristics. All the poor people are hunched over and walk with a limp; all the prostitutes sing to the audience with thrusting breasts; all the soldiers swagger; and the student revolutionaries shake their long locks heroically. This is known as "indicating," a technique that is indigenous to operetta but is considered bad acting in a musical.

In the second phase of Prince's directing career, he developed a Brechtian approach to theatre and the commentary score. This powerful theatrical style used in a musical, however, didn't draw the kind of audiences commercial theatre needed, and gradually Prince turned to the third style of his career—the poperetta.

Unfortunately, Prince's desire to operatize musical theatre denuded it of the drama and staging that characterized the golden age. He admits to using dance less in order to maintain control of the show, since he's not a choreographer, and has become enormously dependent on set design as a substitute. Prince's work—primarily with the great Boris Aronson—continued to integrate set design as a further useful technique for the musical. Lacking Jerome Robbins's ability to choreograph and stage musical numbers, Prince leaned on his sets to provide the movement, and the result—amplified by English director Trevor Nunn with his productions of *Cats* and *Les Misérables*—has been to exaggerate the production elements at the expense of the drama. Thus, Prince, Lloyd Webber, and Trevor Nunn have seduced the American musical away from its greatest strength—the integration of all the techniques of the theatre—in favor of opera. The next Prince/Lloyd Weber production was just that.

With *Phantom of the Opera,* Lloyd Webber moved away from rock and pop to a more legitimate "serious" music, and capitalized on his ability to manufacture a few soaring melody lines on a super-romantic story. Prince got to do the "opera" he'd dreamed about.

By then the tenets of opera were in full flower on musical stages throughout the world, and Broadway was just another stop on the tour. *Miss Saigon,* a poperetta from the French writers and English producer that brought in *Les Misérables,* opened in 1991. It's based on *Madame Butterfly* (a short story by John Luther Long, 1898, a drama by Long and David Belasco, 1900, and an opera by Puccini, 1906) reset against the American involvement in Vietnam. Elaborate sets feature the famous helicopter landing and a towering statue of Ho Chi Minh. It is possibly the worst-crafted musical ever to succeed on Broadway.

The music is banal to the point of tunelessness, like some kind of *Forbidden Broadway* take-off on a Jacques Brel chanson, and endlessly repetitive, an ersatz combination of recitative, French pop, and occasional Asian tonalities. The English lyrics are shallow, feature incredibly dull rhymes, and don't lie with the music well, since they're translations of the French. After the doomed love affair there's a scene change and the Ho Chi Minh re-education ballet marches downstage (using back-flips and martial arts that have no connection to Communist soldiers). It takes most of this scene to figure out that it's three years later and the Americans have left. In an arrangement that allows the big scenic moment to take place in the second act, the fall of

Saigon and the American retreat (in the helicopter) are done in flashback, long after that most dramatic part of the story has passed chronologically. This leaves the first act with a hole of enormous proportions.

There isn't any thematic material on the central issue of the clash of cultures. There's nothing on the politics of Americans in Vietnam, a theme not necessary but certainly relevant and almost unavoidable. There isn't anything on the heroine's religion, though there is a tantalizing hint in the set design—surely it's an integral part of her culture and motivation. Considering the abundance of time devoted to Asian prostitutes in their underwear, there should have been ample opportunity for material deeper than "The American Dream," a Busby Berkeley number featuring the narrator's fornication with a Cadillac.

The characters are drawn in such caricature that "The Engineer" steals the show with an overwritten and narrative role unrelated to the basic love story. The American lieutenant in particular starts off as a naïve young soldier who refuses the gift of a prostitute from his boss, then beds the virgin whore, falls in love with her, disappears without explanation (because that scene has also been moved to the second act), falls in love with and marries an American woman (offstage), and finally wonders about his "Butterfly" and returns to Vietnam with his wife in tow. From each of these moments to the next there is no transition or character motivation, no inner thoughts or emotions to propel the action, just the booming noise of pseudo-music. Curiously, the singular piece of effective theatre is a song called "The Dust of Life," backed up not by scenery or staging, but a *film documentary* of the despised and deserted children of American servicemen and Vietnamese girls. Still, there is enough melodrama to affect an audience. By the time Butterfly commits suicide (offstage) in order to give her little boy the chance to go to America, only the stone-hearted aren't crying.

Miss Saigon's international success clearly reminds us that melodrama and spectacle are commercial. Unfortunately, it also spotlights the collapse of good writing, directing, and choreographing, once essential parts of the musical theatre.

Andrew Lloyd Webber mounted two pre-Broadway productions of *Sunset Boulevard* (London and Los Angeles), thereby circumventing the critical drubbing that was becoming normal for his New York shows. He spent more money than had ever been spent to create a musical. His music failed to support the time or place or characters and succeeded only when its Gothic pop sound came from the grotesqueries of Norma Desmond, the

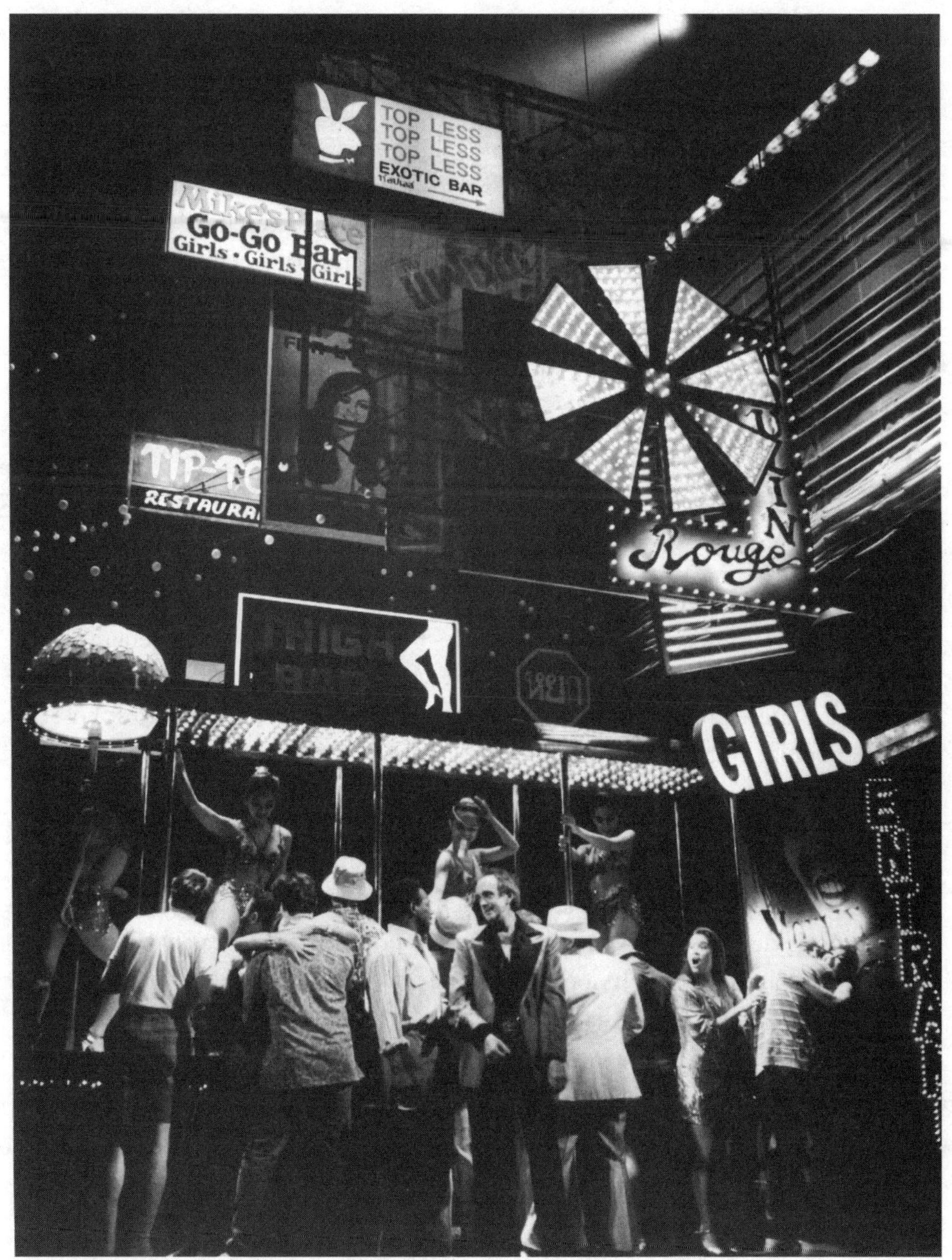

The "engineer" (Jonathan Pryce) takes us on a tour of Saigon nightspots in *Miss Saigon*
Photofest/Michael LePoer Trench/Joan Marcus

washed-up silent screen star. Patti Lupone couldn't act her and Glenn Close couldn't sing her, a clue to how difficult it is to cast a musical today, but Betty Buckley succeeded at both. Once again Lloyd Webber couldn't get a libretto of any quality. (Of *Phantom*'s libretto, *Time* had said, "Charles Hart's lyrics . . . oscillate between the banal and the impenetrable.") Its mediocrity stands out glaringly when compared to the scintillating witticisms of the original film by Billy Wilder. The chorus numbers were tuneless and without direction, returning us to the chorus behavior of the early musical comedy.

Given the technology of sound processing, there is no longer much of a distinction between good and bad singers. Glenn Close's tiny monotone can sound nearly the same as George Hearn's great musical theatre voice. And given the operatic approach to rendering characters, there's no longer much of a difference between good and bad acting either.

Cats, Les Misérables, Phantom of the Opera, Miss Saigon, and *Sunset Boulevard* did not receive good reviews, especially in the United States. Nevertheless, these productions are the biggest hits of the newest generation of musicals in England and America. There are several reasons for this. First, critics are increasingly out of step with popular opinion and mass response. Mass popular culture has moved to the center of the stage because it has the largest group of consumers, while art has moved out to the fringes. Second, there will always be a hit musical on Broadway, and if the critics can't find one the audience will. Big musicals are more and more like the circus. You don't need critics to weigh this year's pachyderms. Third, producer Cameron Macintosh demonstrated that audiences respond better to easily digestible publicity than to essays. In a nutshell, one good photo on the cover of *Time* magazine beats a pan inside.

The success of poperettas has had a significant impact on the American musical (and has generated some antagonism). "All singing, no talking, no dancing" has become the preferred form, and spectacle the preferred package. But dramatist Wilson Mizner once said that "people beat scenery." This moves dangerously close to denying the most important lesson a century of musical theatre has taught us—that the form should serve the content. Wall-to-wall music and set designs that are impressive on their own but overshadow the drama have undercut the story in favor of the experience, a further example of the musical theatre as circus, in which technique takes center stage.

England's *Chu Chin Chow* in 1916 was probably the first time audiences left humming the scenery instead of the songs. (The working model of the set raised the money for the show.) Until then costumes and girls and stars had reigned.

Spectacle, then, was not a new idea when Kenneth Tynan wrote the following about a big West End musical:

> [T]here are distinct signs that sets are now taking over. They swoop down on the actors and snatch them aloft; four motor-driven towers prowl the stage, converging menacingly on any performer who threatens to hog the limelight; and whenever the human element looks like gaining control, they collapse on it in a mass of flaming timber. In short they let the cast know who's boss.

Although you may have guessed *Cats, Dreamgirls,* or *Les Misérables,* Tynan was writing about Lionel Bart's *Blitz!* in 1962. Sheridan Morley, an English critic who can hardly be accused of an American bias, writes:

> The big musical hits of the current British theatre are not in fact about anything very much: *Cats* is certainly a superlative celebration of the poems of T. S. Eliot and *Starlight Express* a hugely commercial roller disco, but neither has a plot which would occupy more than the back of a matchbook. That is why they work so well: they ask nothing of their audience beyond attendance on a certain night. No language problems for tourists, no demands of a shared heritage or education, no cultural barriers to be stormed. And that, I fear, is the way ahead: if a musical is to earn back the initial investment, it now needs to be an event rather than a plot with songs, and therefore the less a show is actually about, the better its chances of crossing the Atlantic in either direction. It is not purely an English problem: as the scores of Sondheim have become more and more specialized, less and less of them have gone from Broadway to the West End. What we now send each other are the easy spectaculars. New York gets *Starlight Express* and London gets *42nd Street.* The fact that we could learn vastly

> more about America from *Merrily We Roll Along* or *Follies* or even *Dreamgirls* and they could learn vastly more about us from *Blood Brothers* or *The Hired Man,* is, alas, irrelevant to the men who do the financial estimates.

This emphasis on the look of a musical has included the staging, which is still emphasized by American choreographers. In *The New York Times,* critic Frank Rich raved about *Grand Hotel* (1990), with lengthy, glowing admiration for Tommy Tune's slick staging. But on the second page of his review, he briefly mentioned that the book, music, lyrics, and performances were all poor ("showmanship untethered to content"). Thus did Rich inadvertently give legitimacy to the new American musical—it has a mediocre book, music, lyrics, and performances, but staging and scene design are outstanding. This kind of theatre, Rich aptly observes, "impresses the audience without engaging it."

In the last twenty years the American musical has replaced drama with spectacle (which has happened with American movies as well). This trend has often signaled the decline of great civilizations. In the dawn of drama, the Greeks had a superb literature, nowhere better expressed than in their theatre. The Romans, too busy with wars and politics to read, replaced literature with spectacle.

In addition to the poperetta, the West End has exported another style of entertainment. English director Mike Ockrent has refashioned two old musical comedies there that were also accepted on Broadway, both considerably rewritten. *Me and My Girl* was originally a British music-hall musical. In 1984, ace comedian Robert Lindsay impressed audiences with his bag of tricks. *Crazy for You* (1992), based on the Gershwins' rip-roaring 1930 musical *Girl Crazy,* was little more than a cobbled book with songs inserted willy-nilly. Both shows featured repetitive tap-dancing and took irrelevance to new heights.

Thus, by the mid-1990s an English invasion had returned the American musical stage to the 1920s: operettas and silly musical comedies.

• • •

While Harold Prince followed Andrew Lloyd Webber into poperetta, Stephen Sondheim stuck to his intellectual guns. Sondheim is the most respected writer of the American musical score. His recently floundering career demonstrates that musicals are a collaborative art form. Musicals need strong books, wise direction, and brilliant staging, little of which Sondheim musicals have been able to manage lately. Nevertheless, he has pursued his art relentlessly and become the father of the American post-modern musical.

After Sondheim and Prince separated, Sondheim wrote scores for two pretentious, turgid, wandering books with no second acts by James Lapine, who also directed without intelligence or choreography. *Sunday in the Park with George* and *Into the Woods* are only interesting as examples of Sondheim's technical skills. On stage they're bloodless, meandering, and without the central concepts that were so strong in his earlier shows. Lapine plays into Sondheim's predilection for academic, intellectual themes. In his famous lecture on lyrics, Sondheim extols the composer who knows what is going to happen onstage during his songs, on the grounds that songs are obligated to fill a dramatic function. Yet since *Follies* Sondheim's wonderful scores have been increasingly cerebral. For *Sunday in the Park,* Sondheim's most personal score, the first act does contain songs that illustrate the passion of the artistic personality, an arcane but emotionally charged subject. The second act wanders off into an obscure discussion by a grandson whose art is significantly less brilliant. *Into the Woods* attempts to tell human truths through fairy tale characters—shallow possibilities at best—and gets lost, again in the second act, with a convoluted plot of too many stories and a dearth of new ideas. Neither of these musicals has any physical or narrative drive whatsoever.

Assassins, done off-Broadway with a book by *Pacific Overtures* librettist John Weidman, was a song-and-sketch revue about presidential hit-persons. In it Sondheim abandoned narrative altogether, and wrote on a theme. His ability to get to basic truths in song, coupled with a talented bookwriter doing the same in sketch, created a way-off-Broadway musical evening that lacked only an audience. *Assassins* painted itself into a commercial corner with both the subject matter (Americans like to hear the gory details of murder but not the psychology of it) and the lack of Broadway slickness. And its underlying theme—that everyone is searching for his five minutes of glory—may not warrant a full-length musical. Nevertheless, this work of art will probably be discussed and remounted for years in an attempt to find a place in the increasingly anti-artistic business of the Broadway musical.

The promise of the Prince-Sondheim collaboration that began so fruitfully with *Company* ended in the ashes of *Merrily We Roll Along.* Prince's intellectual concepts sunk *Pacific Overtures, Sweeney Todd,* and *Merrily,* just as Lapine's weak books and lackluster direction underwhelmed *Sunday in the Park with George* and *Into the Woods.* Consequently, five of Sondheim's most brilliant scores were not delivered to the public in a palatable form. Cast albums aside, it's over for a theatre composer if the show closes.

• • •

While Broadway was awash in English and French poperettas, slapdash revivals, and esoteric Sondheim, the modern American musical suffered a paucity of product, imagination, and craft. In the twenty years since A Chorus Line, only eleven original, American musicals have won the Tony award. Only forty-six nominees out of a minimum of eighty were actually original American musicals. All the rest of the nominees were revues, revivals, or imports. Since 1980 six British musicals have won the Tony award for best musical. Often there were no viable American entries at all. In 1987 three of the four nominees for best musical were English. All four nominees for best director of a musical were English. Only four times in the twenty years since *A Chorus Line* has the best musical also had the best choreography. One year the choreography category had to be eliminated altogether.

Since 1976, when *A Chorus Line* beat out the respectable *Chicago, Pacific Overtures,* and *Bubbling Brown Sugar* for the Antoinette Perry award for best musical, fifteen American musicals have won tainted honors. *Ain't Misbehavin'* (1978) and *Jerome Robbins' Broadway* (1989) were both revues. *Annie* dates its style as well as its story to 1933. In 1979 *Sweeney Todd* competed against three original American musicals—the last strong, if not remarkable, field. And *42nd Street* (1981) is hardly a new musical.

Nine (1982) has long been forgotten. Incredibly, it won over *Dreamgirls,* a triumph of the drummingly inane and pseudo-intellectual over the only post-*Chorus Line* musical to be well-staged. Honest musicals about black characters tend to be less appreciated than exploitative black musicals featuring gospel and tap dancing. In 1984 *La Cage Aux Folles* made gay theatre safe and silly for the masses. It beat out *Sunday in the Park with George* and *The Tap Dance Kid,* which aimed at something significant within the traditional book musical comedy, and fell only a bit short. In 1985 *Big River,* an original American musical, tried out in regional theatre and never left its amateur roots behind. But by then there was no such thing as competition, and the English didn't have an entry that year. In 1986 Broadway got *The Mystery of Edwin Drood* by way of Charles Dickens and the New York Shakespeare Festival. Actually, but for bumpy spots—no opening number, generic choreography, lackadaisical pacing, uneven performances, and an insignificant score—it was a crowd-pleaser and a charming idea. Four years later another original American musical won an undeserved Tony.

The gimmick behind *City of Angels* was a strong one. The creator of a hard-boiled detective is hired by a Hollywood producer to turn his books into a screenplay. We see the writer dealing with Hollywood—the ham-handedness of the producer, the seductive charms of money and loose women—while the pulp plot is played out—the detective deals with similar threats to his integrity and testicles. A couple of very neat tricks are derived from this theatrical device: The writer and his creation get to argue, and two levels of reality alternately move forward—one in black and white and the other in color.

But the inept execution of this clever idea illustrates the depths to which the American musical had sunk by then. The libretto is extraordinarily cumbersome. In spite of the occasional snappy pulp patter and the Humphrey Bogart style with which it's delivered, the scenes are either rehashes of black mask novel clichés—a collection of standard plot twists, complete with broken-down shamus, lovestruck secretary, devious blonde, and all the other clichés of the genre right down to the Asian coroner and the Mexican detective—or Hollywood-bashing scenes between two natural antagonists, a writer and a producer.

Instead of two plots moving forward simultaneously, we get one plot endlessly repeated and agonized over in the other. Instead of insight into the process of collaboration, we get Larry Gelbart's gripes about his Hollywood work being ruined by others. We laugh when the producer says, "Writers. All they can think of is words, words, words!" but films are about images, not words, and good screenplays are not literary works but blueprints for films.

There was no staging at all. A choreographer was listed, but there was hardly a dance step in the show. Though the director tried to move actors from one set to another gracefully, he seldom succeeded.

The Cy Coleman score is ersatz music. A 1940s vocal group scats some of the overture and appears here and there to no useful dramatic purpose, and most of the songs sound like improvs in search of a melody.

Most appalling of all is the total lack of understanding of the purpose of music in a musical by a large collection of theatre professionals. Gelbart's libretto simply isn't a musical book. Cutting all the singing wouldn't harm the show in the least (and might actually help). The songs stop the slow-moving plot dead in its ponderous tracks, and while they're being sung nothing happens physically. David Zippel's lyrics—wordy, heavily rhymed, and not at all in the same style as the book—are actually about *less* than the dialogue.

In 1991 Broadway saw yet another *Follies,* this one named for *Will Rogers,* at the opposite end of the musical theatre spectrum from the great Prince-Sondheim collaboration twenty years earlier.

If there is a single practitioner of the streamlined American musical left on Broadway, it's Tommy Tune. But Tune's career—*The Club, The Best Little Whorehouse in Texas, A Day in Hollywood/A Night in the Ukraine, Nine, My One and Only, Grand Hotel, The Will Rogers Follies, The Best Little Whorehouse Goes Public,* and the revival of *Grease*—is virtually a metaphor for the dying light of the modern Broadway musical, and for the near-complete absence of real talent the Broadway musical community now suffers. Most of Tune's productions have been reminiscent of the silly musicals of the 1920s. He brings on the girls, and boys-as-girls, encouraging the idea that all male dancers are giddy and effeminate, in fey choreography.

Tune's work does feature both choreography and staging, something the Sondheim musicals and the poperettas eschew. But the staging becomes the substance. The songs and sketches that make up *The Will Rogers Follies* are instantly forgettable; the score for *Grand Hotel* had to be doctored; and the songs for *Nine,* his musical version of the Fellini film *8½,* are academic, unmelodic, lyrically stupid and don't augment the film at all.

Tune's choreographic vocabulary seldom stretches beyond the entertaining tap dance that is his foundation. He uses props and sets the way Gower Champion did, and like the British, relies instead on a choreographic vocabulary built around show biz clichés. Tune's *Follies* dragged us back to the age when for a musical's best features were patty-cake dancing and naked derrières.

Yet most new musicals don't bother with staging at all. In 1992 the Tony for best book and score went to *Falsettos,* an off-Broadway oratorio bereft of ideas, featuring instead ersatz emotion delivered in endlessly repetitive, derivative, generic, ambient songs with lyrics that rise from empty-headedness to vague indications of meaning. *Falsettos* purports to be about the new nuclear family, but isn't really about anything, much less anything homosexual, though its writing and staging is drenched in faux/fey-musical comedy. James Lapine directed in the footsteps of Hal Prince. He shuns choreography, thinking that good taste will allow him to create stage pictures, and out of the actor's improvisations (read desperation) will come movement. The result is that the actors, saving themselves, appear to be moving, but the movement is aimless and nearly always presentational rather than representational.

In 1993, *Kiss of the Spider Woman* arrived, another *Evita*-like homage to strong women by men. A curious runner-up that year—and a far more significant production to the future of musical theatre—was *Tommy,* a stage musical version of the twenty-five-year-old concept album by Pete Townshend and The Who about a deaf, mute, blind young man who becomes a genius at playing pinball. The album, called a rock opera, was a song cycle, lacking a narrative structure. *Tommy*'s re-creators structured a story line, and set up a nice back story using pantomime and slide projections to accompany the overture, but their plot peters out in the second act and has no ending. Moreover, a story is the beginning, not the end, of the transfer of a group of songs to the theatre. The characters remain caricatures, the action is often unclear, and the intellectual themes are tantalizingly out of reach. Only one new song was created to fill these enormous gaps. There is no dialogue, and so little real "playwriting" in the lyrics that the production was as shallow as an action film.

Moreover, each production element in *Tommy* boasts its own unconnected raison d'être. The costumes are solidly period, 1940–63, with the exception of Tommy, who is always in contemporary white. The sets are stark modern pieces in front of huge, rapidly changing slide projections of realistic photography, a media-smitten 1990s approach that upstages the live action. The choreography is 1970s jazz dance. The music is snug in 1960s rock. This disparate grouping of elements—each admirably executed on its own—creates a cacophonous theatrical mélange that bars the audience from embracing Tommy's plight. The music, orchestrated with guitar, drums, and three synthesizers, has no variety in emotion or volume, just the glass-shattering din of rock and roll from curtain up to curtain down, disallowing the actor-singers any nuances. (Composer Pete Townshend said he regrets his own substantial hearing loss, caused by years of rock and roll performances.)

Tommy was also softened for Broadway. In this version, Young Tommy doesn't sleep with the Acid Queen—who is here only a Gypsy. Uncle Ernie's molestation isn't too clear either, and Tommy happily embraces his parents in the end. According to director Des McAnuff, this version is "more about redemption than revolution." The production supplies its own jumble of vivid, colorful, LSD-like images to mask its lack of content. Audiences can now experience hallucinations here and in music videos without the disturbing side effects of doing drugs. Thus pop culture has invaded Broadway—as it has every other art form—with its noncontroversial approach and substitution of style for content.

• • •

Louis Malle's film of André Gregory's production of David Mamet's adaptation of Anton Chekhov's *Uncle Vanya,* titled *Uncle Vanya on 42nd Street* (1994), is a wonderful metaphor limning the near-complete dissociation of serious art from contemporary entertainment, particularly in musicals. This production of *Uncle Vanya* was so devoted to the emotional action of the play that it was done without sets, costumes, lighting, or blocking—the actors sit in chairs around tables handling a few nondescript props and talking quietly for a close camera. Dialogue is performed by actors who are so devoted to the principles of method acting that it's less Wallace Shawn as Uncle Vanya than Uncle Vanya as Wallace Shawn.

Close camera work allows the actors to do virtually nothing but *be.* They do this with a craft so polished, creating a level of reality so high, that the audience must be drawn into the drama. Certainly there is no other reason to admire this minimalist film of an ultraminimalist production of a play devoted almost entirely to emotional ideas. These superb actors perform the piece in front of a couple of friends of Shawn's, in a theatre building that is condemned and crumbling around them.

And in the ultimate irony, they're in the New Amsterdam Theatre, once a masterpiece of theatrical architecture hosting the great musical revues of Florenz Ziegfeld during Manhattan's gilded age of production. The building was purchased by the Walt Disney Company for use in their ever-expanding entertainment empire of animation and *faux* life experiences. If Disney's imagineers are loyal to the original designs—i.e., hamstrung enough by historical preservationists—they will recreate a near-real experience, which will be just like going to the theatre. As much as riding the bobsled in the Magic Kingdom is like visiting the Matterhorn. Disney has already mounted *Beauty and the Beast* on Broadway as part of a campaign that has included film, television, toys, games, dolls, t-shirts, and lunch boxes. It's a cartoon on stage—even the human characters are caricatures. Disney's *Beauty and The Beast* is to musical theatre what animation is to real life. The libretto is barely a jot more than the screenplay. Hardly any attempt has been made to deepen the emotional action or explore the characters. The new songs fall far short of the originals because ace lyricist Howard Ashman died and hackmeister Tim Rice filled in, and because the shallow libretto doesn't impel any strong new ideas.

The actors who play these larger-than-life characters do score well in the time-honored tradition once known as mugging. Terrence Mann is less successful in his attempt to bring a full characterization to the Beast. Mann is unable to sing his first-act closing number effectively, either because of all his makeup or because he doesn't have the voice for it. When he is supposed to turn into the young, handsome prince he turns instead into a forty-year-old character actor (no surprise for people familiar with his outstanding performances in other musicals). That he did so spinning above the stage floor seemingly unaided was, for the purposes of spectacle, satisfying enough.

Tom Bosley's television acting is utterly swamped by the production, and one wonders why the star of *Fiorello!* who surely has banked a fortune as the *Happy Days* television Dad, needs to return to the American theatre in a tiny role with one forgettable and dramatically unnecessary song.

Undoubtedly Disney will soon discover that by replacing the human performers with "animatronic" robots, they'll be able to eliminate a multitude of salaries and union rules and run live stage versions of their eighty-four-minute animated films continuously at the New Amsterdam theatre.

In the meantime, in that dusty, crumbling theatre, hidden from the full regalia of modern society by a thin collapsing wall, eight actors pursue their arcane craft on a Chekov play—unrewarded, unrecognized, unappreciated, and under the shadow of the wrecking ball. That's American theatre in the 1990s.

In 1994, *Beauty and the Beast* lost the award for best musical to *Passion,* the Stephen Sondheim-James Lapine musical that had a short run. English directors won in both play and musical directing categories. (This was no surprise, since three out of four nominees in both categories were English.) The English even won in the category of best revival, and best director of a revival, for an American classic when the English National Theatre mounted a new production of *Carousel.* Ironically, the English now mount our golden age musicals with more enthusiasm than we do.

• • •

A light, however dim, shines at the end of the tunnel. Four original American musicals were still playing Broadway to healthy houses by the end of the 1995–96 season. More significant, two of them were traditional musical comedies, two broke new ground, and the latter were welcomed far more warmly.

Big, a big musical comedy based on the film about a twelve-year-old who gets his wish to become an adult, only provided evidence that a talent for crafting traditional musical comedy no longer exists. Endless rewrites and out-of-town travails didn't produce the witty book and lyrics or sparkling score that might have rescued a weak idea. In their place was a poverty of entertainment. Director Mike Ockrent and choreographer Susan Strohman brought all the zest of their *Crazy for You* revival to a new musical—which is to say that energy, however repetitive, cannot replace content any more than spectacle can.

The current spectacle of a beloved, luminous, talented megastar will not save *Victor, Victoria* from obscurity either, when Julie Andrews leaves the cast. This film adaptation, with score by Henry Mancini and Frank Wildhorn, book and direction by Blake Edwards, only proves the adage that Hollywood doesn't understand Broadway, for the attempt to insert musical numbers into the sex farce was utterly clumsy.

On the other hand, *Rent* and *Bring on Da Noise, Bring on Da Funk,* both of which began off-Broadway and clearly were generated from an artist's heart instead of a businessman's ledger, were rewarded by critics and audiences as well as with Tony awards. *Rent,* all-sung, falls into the category of poperetta yet eschews spectacle to concentrate the considerable talents of its cast and writer on a relevant, contemporary translation of *Scènes de La Vie Bohème. Funk,* all-danced, highlights the jaw-dropping terpsichorean talents of Savion Glover, not just a descendent but an actual extension of the exhilarating history of Bill Robinson, Fred Astaire, Honi Coles, the

Nicholas Brothers and Hines, Hines, and Dad. Glover uses his great skills to a greater purpose, staging a history, in tap dance, of African-Americans, from lynchings to the upstaging of Bojangles by Shirley Temple. The breathtaking journey is only marred by two rap singers who constantly insist on getting between the dancers and their audience, and would be better off consigned to the pit with the other supporting musicians.

Neither of these two young, daring musicals is uneven, but both are unfinished. *Rent*'s composer Jonathan Larson died hours after the dress rehearsal, leaving his progeny abandoned at a crucial stage in the off-Broadway musical's development, and Glover's director failed to encourage enough breadth of subject, attitude, and humor in the short entertainment.

Yet both musicals represent the best of American musical theatre craft by astonishingly young talents. Broadway's coronation of these two musicals bodes well for its precarious future. After two decades of domination by heavy-handed entertainment without substance, style, or sense, perhaps the American musical theatre will still be here tomorrow—alive and well and shining.

PLAYBILL

PALACE THEATRE

Finale Ultimo

The song is ended, but as the songwriter wrote,
"The melody lingers on"

In the great theatre film *All About Eve,* the theatre director is questioned on his motives for going to Hollywood to make a picture. He responds:

> Listen, junior, and learn. Want to know what the Theatre is? A flea circus. Also opera. Also rodeos, carnivals, ballets, Indian tribal dances, Punch and Judy, a one-man band—all Theatre. Wherever there's magic and make-believe and an audience—there's Theatre. Donald Duck, Ibsen and The Lone Ranger, Sarah Bernhardt, Poodles Hanneford, Lunt and Fontaine, Betty Grable—Tex the Wild Horse and Eleanora Duse. You don't understand them all, you don't like them all—why should you? The Theatre's for everybody—you included, but not exclusively—so don't approve or disapprove. It may not be your Theatre, but it's Theatre for somebody, somewhere.

Okay. It isn't my intention to give musical theatre such a narrow definition that only *West Side Story* and *A Chorus Line* fit it comfortably. Musicals without dialogue (*The Golden Apple*) or dance (*1776*) can be equally brilliant. All musicals deserve glorious sets, whether the brilliant simplicity of the periactoids of *A Chorus Line* or the extravagance of *Jumbo.*

And it's narrow-minded to insist that musicals follow a set pattern, no matter how well established or useful. Comic opera, operetta, extravaganzas, spectacles, revues, musical comedies, musical dramas, musical plays, plays with music, revues disguised as musicals, rock operas, and poperettas should all exist side by side in the cultural pantheon.

But the true glory of the American musical was the integration of music, lyrics, dialogue, design, acting, direction, and choreography, and their subjugation to the drama. Synergy—wherein the whole is greater than the sum of the parts—was the result. It took almost a century for the theatre to arrive at that formula. Today it's no longer practiced, either in the breach or the observance, and a great art form has passed.

We can only hope that another solidifies to take its place, for the musical's form cannot—as with any art—be expected to remain stationary. From *The Black Crook* to George M. Cohan, from Bolton, Wodehouse and Kern, to Kern and Hammerstein, to Rodgers and Hammerstein, to Jerome Robbins, from Robbins to Michael Bennett, the musical theatre moves on. Americans sent the world products from McDonald's to musicals. Now our hegemony is over—our economy, our products, our military posturing, and our very national character are going to change, and so is the musical. Art is always the earliest harbinger of significant cultural, political, and sociological changes.

What to say? Such a glorious history. Ethel Merman stood down center and belted out "I Got Rhythm," and America's hair stood on end. Mary Martin cooed "My Heart Belongs to Daddy," and we fell in love. Gwen Verdon wiggled her hips and rasped out "Whatever Lola Wants," and our temperature rose. The Jets and the Sharks joined together to carry Tony's body to the grave, and we cried.

Musical audiences became almost Pavlovian. The house lights went out (or should have, to keep the audience from talking through the overture), the spotlight hit the back of the conductor's head, he raised his baton, and already we were transcendently happy. The chorus kids came on, and we knew the star was changing into her most glittering costume. The eleven o'clock title number was just around the corner.

A thousand and one nights we sat in the dark and watched the singing and the dancing, the costumes and the comedy, the bits, the shtick, the turns, the specialties. We watched it turn from low entertainment to high art, from giddy silliness to compelling drama to cathartic tragedy. From wing and drop and in-one and scene-song-dance, to a driving rhythm machine that flew from opening to closing like a sleek rocket. We saw it always bathed in the brightest of lights, sparkling like a jewel in the moonlight. It represented our dreams, our hopes, our joys, and our sorrows. We were Americans, and it was the voice of America for over a century.

And now it's silent.

Anyway, it was loverly.

BLACKOUT

PLAYBILL®

GERSHWIN THEATRE

SINGIN' IN THE RAIN℠

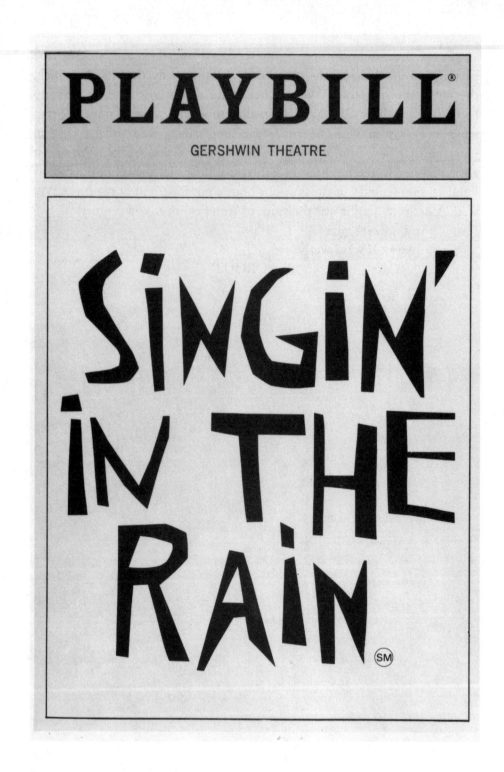

On its own, Hollywood has produced a treasure trove of outstanding original American film musicals. From *42nd Street* to the Fred Astaire-Ginger Rogers series to the Arthur Freed unit at MGM, the art and craft of the American musical was practiced as well in the movies as it was on the stage, primarily by people with a Broadway background who expanded their creativity by embracing what the art of film could do.

With the advent of sound in 1926, films embraced the theatre community and the studios brought New York stage talent to Hollywood by the trainload. Broadway songwriters (Comden and Green; Lerner and Loewe; DeSylva, Brown, and Henderson), Broadway directors (Busby Berkeley, Vincente Minnelli, Rouben Mamoulian), and Broadway choreographers (Busby Berkeley, Gene Kelly, Michael Kidd) created those wonderful movies, and in them you can see the dancing, hear the songs, and discover the golden age of Broadway in bits and pieces. Arthur Freed, Jr., the lyricist-turned-producer and principal architect of Hollywood's golden age of film musicals, always credited Oscar Hammerstein II with pioneering the integrated musical on stage, and attempted to emulate him on screen. See particularly *Singin' in the Rain* (an all-time favorite for most fans); *An American in Paris* (a pretty close second, climaxing with an extraordinary piece of original film ballet); the unique *Invitation to the Dance;* the romantic and beautifully scored *Gigi;* and the robust *Seven Brides for Seven Brothers.*

But Hollywood also translated many Broadway musicals into film, sometimes faithfully, sometimes not. The first talkie, *The Jazz Singer,* was a musical based on a Broadway production, and from then on Hollywood looked east for material. Because of the ephemeral nature of the stage, film versions of stage musicals are often the only way to get an idea of the original Broadway production. For that reason, we ought not judge them too harshly. Don't expect to be transported—they're only movies. Even the best films have been bowdlerized in Hollywood, making, for example, Rodgers and Hammerstein's many tragic/heroic stories seem like fairy tales.

Herewith a list of Broadway musicals to be found on the screen and what can be gleaned from them. Most of these can be rented, but many are only available from the most devoted and obscure video stores. It would be better to find a revival house with musical taste, since the small screen is not kind to musicals.

• • •

ANNIE (COLUMBIA, 1982)

Proof positive the show wasn't so good to begin with.

ANNIE GET YOUR GUN (MGM, 1950)

Howard Keel is stiff and Betty Hutton chews the scenery, but there's a lot still there, including most of the fabulous Berlin score. Unfortunately, Berlin's estate owns the film, and doesn't want you to see it. If they did, Indians and women would complain.

ANYTHING GOES

In 1936 Paramount replaced most of the Cole Porter songs. In 1956 Paramount replaced the story. Hollywood should try again, without replacing anything.

ARE YOU WITH IT? (UNIVERSAL, 1948)

Except for Donald O'Connor in the film, neither the stage nor film versions is interesting.

***BABES IN ARMS* (MGM, 1939)**

First teaming of Mickey Rooney and Judy Garland, with only three of Rodgers and Hart's songs. Same story—the original "let's put on a show!" plot—with a Hollywood ending—the show is a hit.

BABES IN TOYLAND

Laurel and Hardy for Hal Roach in 1934; Disney in 1961; neither remotely faithful.

***THE BAND WAGON* (MGM, 1953)**

Nothing like the stage revue, but on its own one of the best Hollywood musicals ever made, an original story and screenplay by Betty Comden and Adolph Green based on the Dietz and Schwartz catalogue.

***THE BELLE OF NEW YORK* (MGM, 1952)**

A brand new score for this 1897 story, and Fred Astaire, make a silk purse out of a sow.

***BELLS ARE RINGING* (MGM, 1960)**

Still there: most of the score and story, Judy Holliday's great performance. Dean Martin is better than was Sydney Chaplin. Unwisely replaces dancing with dialogue.

***BEST FOOT FORWARD* (MGM, 1943)**

Good college musical fairly resembling the show.

***BITTER SWEET* (BRITISH, 1933)**

Noël Coward is reputed to have cried on seeing the film, and not out of joy. Some of his songs remain, though not "If Love Were All."

***THE BOYS FROM SYRACUSE* (UNIVERSAL, 1940)**

Butchered the Rodgers and Hart score, but film technique at least allowed one actor for each of the two sets of twins.

***THE BOHEMIAN GIRL* (HAL ROACH, 1936)**

This early British musical (1843) was an American success on stage, but not as a Laurel and Hardy comedy on screen.

***THE BOY FRIEND* (MGM, 1971)**

Now more a satire of music hall in the provinces than a valentine to the Gaiety Girl musicals, it was a disaster at the time. Faithlessness aside, it's worth watching Ken Russell's hallucinogenic mind embrace Busby Berkeley.

BRIGADOON (MGM, 1954)

A lot of the music and plot are there, and Gene Kelly is charming. It's set-bound, but Broadwayites never complain about that.

BYE BYE BIRDIE (COLUMBIA, 1963)

Missing the Gower Champion dances and theatricality, but otherwise a wonderful film that's semi-faithful to the story and songs of the original. The title song is not from the show, but written for the talents of a young Swedish bombshell with one name.

CABARET (ABC, 1972)

Though greatly changed from the Hal Prince-Ron Field stage version, this is Bob Fosse's incandescent contribution to film musicals. Realizing that book songs no longer worked on screen by 1972, he cut them, keeping only the cabaret numbers and a beer-hall sing-a-long. (In his biography of Fosse, Martin Gottfried credits Fosse with the fascinating idea of relating the cabaret numbers to the dramatic action, but that was in fact an integral part of the original Hal Prince concept.) Capturing the decadence in high cinematic style, and going back to the Christopher Isherwood original for a fuller story, it won the Oscar for best picture.

CABIN IN THE SKY (MGM, 1943)

It is noble that Hollywood made a black musical at all, but there are too many interpolations to the John LaTouche-Vernon Duke score.

CALL ME MADAM (TWENTIETH CENTURY FOX, 1953)

One of the first film musicals that Hollywood didn't bungle, with Ethel Merman intact and in toto, as is the wonderful Berlin score. If it seems stagy for a film, that's good news for Broadway fans who want their musicals remembered, not "opened up."

CALL ME MISTER (TWENTIETH CENTURY FOX, 1951)

Three songs and some of the story.

CAMELOT (WARNER BROTHERS, 1967)

Sumptuous costume melodrama, this film has its fans and detractors. Vanessa Redgrave is less a queen than a peasant, and Richard Harris will never be Richard Burton, but the score, production values, and classic tale shine through.

CAN-CAN (TWENTIETH CENTURY FOX, 1960)

Some Porter substitutions, Frank Sinatra's New Jersey Frenchman and Shirley MacLaine's Brooklynese strain credibility.

CARMEN JONES (TWENTIETH CENTURY FOX, 1954)

A good way to see Hammerstein's unusual experiment in opera.

CAROUSEL (TWENTIETH CENTURY FOX, 1956)

Extremely faithful, including Agnes de Mille's ballet. Gets the four handkerchief award for not tacking on a happy ending.

THE CAT AND THE FIDDLE (MGM, 1934)

The songs by Jerome Kern and Oscar Hammerstein made the cut, but the book was nixed by the Hayes office.

THE CHOCOLATE SOLDIER (MGM, 1941)

When George Bernard Shaw asked too much money for the film rights to *Soldier*'s story (his play *Arms and the Man*) from Louis B. Mayer, Shaw said, "I fear we two will never understand each other. You're an idealist, you see, whereas I'm only a businessman." Mayer bought Molnar's play *The Guardsman* instead and substituted the story. The Oscar Strauss score was mostly lost.

A CHORUS LINE (EMBASSY/POLYGRAM, 1985)

The worst film of a great Broadway musical. Ever.

THE COCOANUTS (PARAMOUNT, 1929)

The Marx Brothers' first talkie. Most of the score was cut, and one Berlin tune was added. Funny film, though.

A CONNECTICUT YANKEE IN KING ARTHUR'S COURT (PARAMOUNT, 1948)

Without the Rodgers and Hart songs, because MGM owned them. Leave it to the lawyers.

DAMN YANKEES (WARNER BROTHERS, 1958)

We're awfully lucky to have this one, featuring George Abbott's direction, Bob Fosse's choreography, and the entire Broadway original cast except Stephen Douglass. Tab Hunter's plenty good enough. Hollywood cut the sentimental numbers ("Near To You" and "A Man Doesn't Know") and censored the best comic song ("The Game"), but Gwen Verdon's "Whatever Lola Wants" and Ray Walston's "Those Were the Good Old Days," are 1950s musical numbers hot off the stage. The choicest bit: Fosse himself dancing with Verdon in "Who's Got The Pain?"

THE DESERT SONG

1929 at Warner Brothers, with much of the score; 1943, updated to Nazi's; 1953 with Kathryn Grayson and Gordon MacRae, a time when the heroic Red Shadow couldn't be red, so became El Khobar. Part of the score, and some intrusions.

DUBARRY WAS A LADY (MGM, 1943)

You'd think a film with Red Skelton, Lucille Ball, Gene Kelly, and Zero Mostel couldn't be boring. Wrong. Every songwriter in Arthur Freed's stable tried to fix Cole Porter. Hollywood saved Cole Porter's "Friendship" and "Madame, I Love Your Crêpes Suzette" but little else of the score or humor. But dig the Brothers Dorsey and Buddy Rich on drums.

FANNY (1954)

Harold Rome's score is used as background music only.

FIDDLER ON THE ROOF (UNITED ARTISTS, 1971)

The exquisite theatricality of Broadway's greatest musical is missing, and Topol's Tevye is humorless, heartless, and heavy, and Anatevka is peopled with Hollywood's idea of Jews. But the story and score are intact.

FIFTY MILLION FRENCHMEN (WARNER BROTHERS, 1931)

Six Cole Porter songs made it, as well as Broadway stars William Gaxton and Helen Broderick, to which were added comics Olsen and Johnson, but little else.

FINIAN'S RAINBOW (WARNER BROTHERS, 1968)

Compare the picnic number to Fosse's in *Pajama Game* and you'll understand musical staging. The score and story are almost intact, though "Old Devil Moon" doesn't survive the 1960s pop vocalization of Petula Clark. Grandfatherly Astaire is a charmer.

THE FIREFLY (MGM, 1937)

New book and lyrics to the Rudolf Friml score, and the hit song, "The Donkey Serenade," isn't from the show.

FLOWER DRUM SONG (UI/RODGERS AND HAMMERSTEIN, 1961)

Not politically correct in today's climate. Rodgers's brush with jazzy music ("Grant Avenue," "I Enjoy Being a Girl") without leaving romanticism behind ("Love Look Away") is mostly there on the screen in a limping, but somehow transfixing, film.

FLYING HIGH (MGM, 1931)

This one lost all but the title song and Bert Lahr.

FOLLOW THRU (PARAMOUNT, 1930)

Jack Haley recreated his Broadway role. Otherwise not much.

FUNNY FACE (PARAMOUNT, 1957)

A new plot and only some of the Gershwin songs, but catch Audrey Hepburn dancing in the cellar.

FUNNY GIRL (COLUMBIA, 1968)

A perfect combination of remaining faithful and making changes, this one is actually better on the screen thanks to William Wyler and Herb Ross's direction of the musical numbers and Barbra Streisand's one great performance before she became a movie star. Jule Styne didn't write "My Man," but he wrote "The Music That Makes Me Dance," a soaring ballad overshadowed by the popular success of "People."

A FUNNY THING HAPPENED ON THE WAY TO THE FORUM (BRITISH, 1966)

Wrongheadedly directed in a quirky jump-cut style. Only shards of the original humor and score remain.

THE GAY DIVORCÉE (RKO, 1934)

Hollywood ruled out the word "divorce" in the title. The film kept only Porter's "Night and Day," but Astaire and Rogers, in their first real vehicle (after being introduced in *Flying Down to Rio*) introduced their charisma, and Hermes Pan and Fred Astaire, as choreographers, introduced to the film musical dances that told as much about the characters' relationships as the screenplay.

GENTLEMEN PREFER BLONDES (TWENTIETH CENTURY FOX, 1953)

Some great Jack Cole numbers. Interpolations dulled the score, but it still retains the Jule Styne-Leo Robin "Diamonds Are a Girl's Best Friend," "Bye, Bye, Baby," and "I'm Just a Little Girl from Little Rock," here done by Marilyn Monroe and Jane Russell, who were never better. We complain if Hollywood alters Broadway and fails, but don't give them enough credit when they alter Broadway and succeed. Here it is.

GIRL CRAZY

Ignore the 1932 RKO version, and MGM's *When the Boys Meet the Girls* in 1965. But the 1943 MGM version has most of the songs and no interpolations, with the story and characters pretty close. Mickey Rooney and Judy Garland do the Gershwins justice.

GOLDEN DAWN (WARNER BROTHERS, 1930)

As bad as the original operetta.

GOOD NEWS (MGM, 1930 AND 1947)

The second version used more of the score. If June Allyson and Peter Lawford are your idea of musical comedy stars, this one's for you.

THE GREAT WALTZ (MGM 1938)

Oscar Hammerstein II wrote new lyrics to Johann Strauss's music, and amid sumptuous old Vienna sets tells the odd story of professional jealousy between Strauss, Sr. and Strauss, Jr. Fathers and sons who are in the same business should see it.

GREASE (PARAMOUNT, 1978)

Adds disco Bee Gees to the original 1950s score. Much is in place, but played straight it's a Frankie and Annette film instead of a farcical spoof. This successful film has, unfortunately, almost totally obscured the hilarious original stage version, so that high schools (and Broadway revivals) now perform this charmer by taking the fifties seriously!

GUYS AND DOLLS (GOLDWYN, 1955)

Very faithful. Marlon Brando's attempt at versatility. "A" for effort, and dig those Michael Kidd dances.

GYPSY (WARNER BROTHERS, 1962)

Ethel Merman was diagnosed as too big for the screen and Rosalind Russell is too small for the part. But it's worthwhile for substantial sections that recall the original, and far better than the "faithful" television ho-hummer with out-of-her-schmata-league Bette Midler.

GYPSY LOVE (ON BROADWAY, 1911)

This became *The Rogue Song* (MGM, 1930) with a lavish production and an altered score, directed by Lionel Barrymore.

HAIR (UNITED ARTISTS, 1979)

Its Broadway success won't make any sense, but the score and the 1960s are there.

HEAD'S UP (PARAMOUNT, 1930)

Kept only two songs.

HELLO, DOLLY! (TWENTIETH CENTURY FOX, 1969)

Gower Champion refused to direct the film version because he thought it wouldn't translate. He was proved right. Fast forward to Louis Armstrong.

HELLZAPOPPIN' (UNIVERSAL, 1942)

Olsen and Johnson are hilarious, as they must have been in the stage revue. A wonderful record of a certain kind of committed comic zaniness that hasn't been done well since *Saturday Night Live* replaced Carol Burnett in the national consciousness.

The dance at the gym, film version
Archive Photos

Robert Preston leads the Iowa youth in "76 Trombones" in the film version of *The Music Man*
Archive Photos

HIGH BUTTON SHOES

Supposedly there's a kinescope of this production. If you spot a copy, call me.

HIGHER AND HIGHER (RKO, 1943)

A complete rewrite of the story and Rodgers and Hart's songs for Frank Sinatra's first film.

HIT THE DECK (RKO, 1930)

Failed. Worked as *Follow the Fleet* (1936) with Fred Astaire, Ginger Rogers, and lots of great Irving Berlin numbers instead of the original Vincent Youmans score. Failed again in 1954 (CinemaScope) with a conglomeration of songs and a third plot cribbed from *On the Town.*

HOLD EVERYTHING (WARNER BROTHERS, 1930)

Warner dumped the DeSylva, Brown, and Henderson score and rewrote the story.

HOW TO SUCCEED IN BUSINESS WITHOUT REALLY TRYING (UNITED ARTISTS, 1967)

Some of the Pulitzer-Prize-winning book and score is in place, but Bob Fosse's work is only imitated, and Robert Morse on the screen will only make you wonder what all the shouting was about.

I MARRIED AN ANGEL (MGM, 1942)

Nearly unrecognizable from the Rodgers and Hart musical.

IRENE (RKO, 1940)

Not much is there except "Alice Blue Gown."

IRMA LA DOUCE (UNITED ARTISTS, 1963)

No longer a musical, and you'll only hear that joyful score in the background. But the story and comedy work well.

JESUS CHRIST SUPERSTAR (UNIVERSAL, 1973)

Nothing could help, least of all a film.

JUMBO (MGM, 1962)

Not the stage extravaganza, but worthwhile for Jimmy Durante's "What elephant?"

KNICKERBOCKER HOLIDAY (UNITED ARTISTS, 1944)

"September Song" remains, but not much else of the original music or politics.

THE KING AND I (TWENTIETH CENTURY FOX, 1956)

Hollywood's consistent faithfulness to Rodgers and Hammerstein was the luckiest thing that ever happened to the American musical. Reprising his discovery role, Yul Brynner demonstrates why he became a star in this sumptuous, musical film.

KISMET (MGM, 1955)

How could they leave out "Was I Wazir? I Was!"—the score's only comic song? Otherwise it's all there.

KISS ME KATE (MGM, 1953)

This gem is a faithful adaptation with terrific dances, comedy, and Cole Porter. Bob Fosse, Tommy Rall, and Bobby Van are centerpieces in the golden age of dance.

LADY, BE GOOD (MGM, 1941)

Three Gershwin songs but otherwise no relation to the original.

LADY IN THE DARK (PARAMOUNT, 1944)

If 1940s Hollywood feared Cole Porter, it ran from Kurt Weill. Too bad, because the songs-as-dream-sequences would work well on film.

LET'S FACE IT (PARAMOUNT, 1943)

A rewritten story and all but two Cole Porter songs.

LI'L ABNER (PARAMOUNT, 1959)

Very faithful, including the performances, the score, and Michael Kidd's great "Sadie Hawkins Day" ballet.

LITTLE JOHNNY JONES (1928)

This version cut all but two George Cohan songs. See instead James Cagney in *Yankee Doodle Dandy.*

A LITTLE NIGHT MUSIC (AUSTRIA, 1977)

Jealous wives will be glad to hear Elizabeth Taylor sing. Like the original, this film was directed by Harold Prince and only demonstrates why film musical translations of stage properties are so hard. See Ingmar Bergman's film of Mozart's *The Magic Flute* instead.

LITTLE SHOP OF HORRORS (WARNER BROTHERS, 1986)

Sometimes being faithful can be a mistake. This one is leaden on the screen, and the whole point of the story is undercut by a happy Hollywood ending.

LOST IN THE STARS (1974)

A photographed stage production from an aborted venture into special event films by one of those Hollywood impresarios with more money than brains.

LOUISIANA PURCHASE (PARAMOUNT, 1941)

All but three songs were dropped from Irving Berlin's 444-performance hit.

MADEMOISELLE MODISTE

Retitled *Kiss Me Again* (Warner Brothers, 1931) after the 1903 Victor Herbert hit song.

MAME (WARNER BROTHERS, 1974)

Hello, Dolly! didn't translate to film, and this one was a second-rate *Dolly* with an aging and unmusical Lucille Ball. In spite of the original show's crafty execution and the transcendent Angela Lansbury, the Lawrence and Lee play and Roz Russell film of it remains better.

MANHATTAN MARY

Became *Follow the Leader* (Paramount, 1930), with Ed Wynn, Ginger Rogers, and Ethel Merman.

MAN OF LA MANCHA (UNITED ARTISTS, 1972)

Why Hollywood would let Peter O'Toole sing again after *Goodbye Mr. Chips* is a mystery. The essential theatricality of the stage incarnation of Don Quixote went unreplaced. Avoid this one or you'll misunderstand a theatrical masterpiece.

MAYTIME (MGM, 1937)

A new plot, but Jeanette MacDonald and Nelson Eddy sing Sigmund Romberg.

THE MERRY WIDOW

MGM tried this one three times: a silent version in 1925, Maurice Chevalier and Jeanette MacDonald for Ernest Lubitsch in 1934, and Fernando Lamas and Lana Turner in 1952. The Lubitsch touch takes it.

MURDER AT THE VANITIES (PARAMOUNT, 1934)

More murder, less *Vanities.*

MUSIC IN THE AIR (FOX, 1934)

Only six Kern-Hammerstein songs made it, but two of them were "I've Told Every Little Star" and "The Song is You."

THE MUSIC MAN (WARNER BROTHERS, 1962)

Great musical theatre on film. Theatrical and cinematic, it's the best argument for being faithful to the original and using the original star.

MY FAIR LADY (CBS, 1964)

The friends-of-Broadway award goes to this one. Jack Warner and George Cukor are faithful to the material while juicing it up with everything Hollywood did well in the old days. Rex Harrison insisted on singing live, not lip-synching, and his legendary performance benefits. Audrey Hepburn had the lady down fine, but couldn't quite get the hang of the Cockney lass. Oscar for best picture.

NAUGHTY MARIETTA (MGM, 1935)

The first film to team Jeanette MacDonald and Nelson Eddy retained five hit songs and jettisoned the rest.

NEW FACES (1954)

Leonard Sillman's only film of his series, it will give you a good idea of the foundations of the second great age of the revue: material and talent. Note Eartha Kitt and Paul Lynde.

NEW MOON (MGM, 1930 AND 1940)

Lawrence Tibbett and Grace Moore, then Jeanette MacDonald and Nelson Eddy. A different story and setting, some of the score, no "The."

NO, NO, NANETTE

Warner Brothers in 1930, and RKO in 1940. Both muffed the musical numbers. In 1950 Warner used its property for *Tea for Two* with Doris Day, rewriting the plot and stuffing it with song chestnuts by Vincent Youmans and others.

OKLAHOMA! (RODGERS AND HAMMERSTEIN, 1955)

Produced by its creators, it was the most expensive film made to that date, costing 7 million 1954 dollars. It was also the first movie in "Todd-AO," a new sixty-five millimeter process, and stereophonic sound. Rodgers and Hammerstein, Agnes de Mille, and even those bucolic sets are exquisitely represented. Catch Rod Steiger singing.

OLIVER! (COLUMBIA, 1968)

Without Sean Kenny's stunning set, you can't imagine how great the show was. But it works, so rent it for the kids.

ON A CLEAR DAY YOU CAN SEE FOREVER (PARAMOUNT, 1970)

From the Hollywood period in which only Barbra Streisand could star in a musical. For her fans and Jack Nicholson trivia buffs only.

ON THE TOWN (MGM, 1949)

First film musical to attempt some location work, but Hollywood dropped the score by Leonard Bernstein, Betty Comden, and Adolph Green, *and* the Jerome Robbins choreography! (The Hollywood studios owned music publishing companies and could make more money by inserting their own songs. Thus Broadway scores often got dumped for financial, not artistic, reasons.)

ON YOUR TOES (WARNER BROTHERS, 1939)

The Rodgers and Hart, Abbott and Balanchine classic was originally conceived as a Fred Astaire film! But after Ray Bolger wowed Broadway, Eddie Albert played the rewritten part. Oops.

ONE TOUCH OF VENUS (UNIVERSAL, 1948)

Great Kurt Weill music and Ogden Nash lyrics were replaced with mush.

PAINT YOUR WAGON (PARAMOUNT, 1969)

Little relation to the original. It was "adapted by" Paddy Chayefsky (stolen from *Jules and Jim*). Alan Jay Lerner produced, and Lerner's biographer claims that Lerner did most of the writing and rewriting. Half the lovely Lerner and Loewe songs were replaced with lesser songs by Lerner and André Previn. The supporting comic actors are wonderful, the "Maria" sequence is brilliant, and the singing of Clint Eastwood and Lee Marvin is hysterical.

PARIS (1928)

Hollywood's homogenization machine dropped Cole Porter's score, afraid of its sophistication.

PAJAMA GAME (WARNER BROTHERS, 1957)

An outstanding film. Bob Fosse's stuff and the score are intact, and Janis Paige added to the Broadway cast of John Raitt, Eddie Foy, Jr., and Carol Haney. Accurate filming of "Steam Heat" is worth its weight in tap shoes.

PAL JOEY (COLUMBIA, 1957)

Remade for singer Frank Sinatra instead of dancer Gene Kelly, and Hollywood cowardly sanitized the real dirt, but the Rodgers and Hart song additions are actually better than the original.

PANAMA HATTIE (MGM, 1942)

Once again, Cole Porter lost out to lesser writers.

PETER PAN (NBC, 1959)

A television film of Jerome Robbins's stage production, featuring originals Mary Martin and Cyril Ritchard. No child should be without the videotape.

PORGY AND BESS (COLUMBIA, 1959)

Sidney Poitier, Dorothy Dandridge, Pearl Bailey, Brock Peters, Diahann Carroll, and Sammy Davis, Jr. as Sportin' Life. Just now the film can only be seen at the Library of Congress.

PRESENT ARMS

This became *Leathernecking* (RKO, 1930), dropped all but two of the Rodgers and Hart songs, and added some by others.

PRINCESS CHARMING (BRITISH, 1935)

Ruritanian operetta. To Hollywood's credit, in the 1930s and 1940s they even bought and made *bad* musicals.

RAINBOW

Became *Song of the West* (Warner Brothers, 1930). The stage version was a noble failure, the film just a failure.

THE RAMBLERS

Became *The Cuckoos* (RKO, 1930). Lots of laughs.

RED, HOT AND BLUE! (PARAMOUNT, 1949)

Only the title remains the same. Frank Loesser wrote a new score to replace Cole Porter's. Those were the days.

RIO RITA

RKO released it in 1929 with Tierney's score, MGM in 1942 with Abbott and Costello instead.

ROBERTA (RKO, 1935)

Also *Lovely To Look At* (MGM, 1952). Neither is, but in fact the stage show was also poor. Yes, a musical could succeed on one song before Andrew Lloyd Webber: "Smoke Gets in Your Eyes."

ROCKY HORROR PICTURE SHOW (TWENTIETH CENTURY FOX, 1975)

Faithful to the original, and the most successful cult film of all time. It illustrates what off-Broadway did best in its heyday. (In fact, its roots are in London and Los Angeles, and it was scuttled in New York by producers who put it in the wrong theatre).

ROSALIE (MGM, 1937)

After decades of being ignored, Cole Porter replaced George Gershwin and Sigmund Romberg.

ROSE-MARIE

MGM tried three times, and none was faithful. The 1928 silent version featured a new plot. The 1936 version was a vehicle for Jeanette MacDonald and Nelson Eddy. For the 1954 version, the first film in CinemaScope, Mervyn LeRoy used bits and pieces. But dig Bert Lahr singing "The Mountie That Never Got His Man," and Busby Berkeley's extravaganzas.

SALLY (WARNER BROTHERS, 1930)

With Marilyn Miller. A lavish Hollywood film, but unfaithful to the show.

SALLY, IRENE AND MARY (TWENTIETH CENTURY FOX, 1938)

No relation to the original.

1776 (COLUMBIA, 1972)

The film is stagey, but the stage version is well worth remembering. This one features the entire original cast except Betty Buckley as Mrs. Jefferson, so it's missing the greatest female voice on the American musical stage since Ethel Merman and Barbara Cook.

SHOW BOAT

The first attempt by Universal in 1929—in the midst of the talkie revolution—resulted in a half-silent, half-talkie film that departed from the stage work, added interpolations, featured a tacked-on prologue of the Broadway performers singing songs, and is apparently lost. But in 1936, Universal made a long and faithful version with Irene Dunne (who followed Norma Terris in the role of Magnolia during the show's first post-Broadway tour), Allan Jones, Helen Morgan, Paul Robeson, Charles Winninger, and Hattie McDaniel, one of the most extraordinary casts ever assembled for a musical film. MGM and Arthur Freed made a glamorous Technicolor hodgepodge in 1951, with surges of power due to Howard Keel and William Warfield singing Jerome Kern's great score. The rest of the production, except the cinematography, features a lack of faithfulness to the period; a truncated story; a mean-spirited Parthy; and a complete ignorance of the mood, style, and ambience of the true showboats of theatrical history. The second version remains the best.

SILK STOCKINGS (MGM, 1957)

An altered story but much of Porter, and no interpolations, with Fred Astaire and Cyd Charisse chemistry. Peter Lorre, Jules Munshin, and Joseph Buloff make a hysterical trio of supporting comics.

SOMETHING FOR THE BOYS (TWENTIETH CENTURY FOX, 1944)

Only Cole Porter's title song remains.

SONG OF NORWAY (ABC, 1970)

Operettas were already old hat when the stage show appeared in 1944, so a quarter of a century later was not a good time for the film version. The subject of a critical massacre and audience apathy, for good reason.

SONG OF THE FLAME (WARNER BROTHERS, 1930)

This didn't save much of Gershwin's music, but as it was his least remarkable work, no one complained.

THE SOUND OF MUSIC (TWENTIETH CENTURY FOX, 1965)

Best film musical for the handkerchief-and-saccharine set. It's Julie Andrews's "I told you so" for not getting to play Eliza in *My Fair Lady.* Slightly altered without damage from the stage, and probably the last of the great and faithful Hollywood versions of Broadway musicals. The film won the Oscar for best picture.

SOUTH PACIFIC (1958)

The producers of the film cowardly dropped the anti-bigotry song "Carefully Taught" so as not to insult the racists in their audience. Otherwise it's a good and faithful version, though a color-filter gimmick destroyed the cinematography. Hollywood's consistent snubbing of Mary Martin is their greatest shame. (They thought she was too old; twenty-five years later, they let a forty-year-old Barbra Streisand play an eighteen-year old *Yentl.* Go figure.)

SPRING IS HERE (FIRST NATIONAL, 1930)

Contains some of the original Rodgers and Hart, and some interpolations, with a new story.

THE STUDENT PRINCE

MGM did a silent version in 1926, and a talkie in 1954 with Mario Lanza's voice but not his face.

STRIKE UP THE BAND (MGM, 1940)

No relation to the original—only the title song was used.

SUNNY

Warner Brothers, 1930, with Marilyn Miller; RKO, 1941. The Kern-Hammerstein "Who?" made the transition, but nothing else.

SWEET ADELINE (WARNER, 1934)

The plot and songs were fairly faithful to the Kern-Hammerstein musical, and you can hear the beauties that Jerome Kern wrote for Helen Morgan.

SWEET CHARITY (UNIVERSAL, 1969)

Evidence that the better the stage show, the less effective the film. But Bob Fosse's choreography, and hints of his strong cinema style to come, are intact, as is the elevator scene, one of the funniest in a musical.

SWEETHEARTS (MGM, 1938)

Dorothy Parker wrote the new book, and Robert Wright and George Forrest wrote new lyrics. It's the best (and only color) Jeanette MacDonald-Nelson Eddy film.

THIS IS THE ARMY (WARNER BROTHERS, 1943)

All the right Irving Berlin stuff.

TOO MANY GIRLS (RKO, 1940)

Looks like a play, and remains faithful to the plot and songs. George Abbott directed. Lucille Ball and Desi Arnaz met.

TOP BANANA (UNITED ARTISTS, 1953)

A film of the Phil Silvers stage show shot from the audience of the Winter Garden Theatre exists. Due to legal complications, it hardly ever surfaces.

THE UNSINKABLE MOLLY BROWN (MGM, 1964)

Faithful and charming, with a mild Debbie Reynolds instead of the spicy stage star Tammy Grimes.

UP IN CENTRAL PARK (U-I, 1948)

Since the show featured some of Sigmund Romberg's best songs, Hollywood naturally dropped them.

THE VAGABOND KING

The 1930 version with Dennis King is reputedly close to the stage version, but it was lost. Paramount did a dull remake in 1956.

VERY WARM FOR MAY

Became *Broadway Rhythm* (MGM, 1943), with a new story and new songs by a cacophony of composers, with only the Kern-Hammerstein "All the Things You Are" remaining.

THE WALTZ DREAM

Became *The Smiling Lieutenant* (Paramount, 1931) under Ernest Lubitsch.

WEST SIDE STORY (UNITED ARTISTS, 1961)

The best film record of a stage musical ever made. The film maintains the original's impressionistic style, while adding just enough realism to be a movie. Though Jerome Robbins had to be thrown off the set for his annoying perfectionism, his dances are all there, and two tiny changes in structure are barely noticeable improvements (the boys are added to "America"; "Cool" and "Gee, Officer Krupke" switch places). Richard Beymer was crucified for his performance (but Pat Boone was worse in summer stock). It won the Oscar for best picture.

WHERE'S CHARLEY? (WARNER BROTHERS, 1952)

The film was withdrawn from the market by Frank Loesser's widow because she thought it could hurt his reputation. It's not great work but it can't hurt anybody, and the songs and Ray Bolger are a delight.

WHOOPEE (GOLDWYN, 1930)

Busby Berkeley's first Hollywood assignment starred Eddie Cantor singing "Makin' Whoopee" and (the new) "My Baby Just Cares for Me." The rest of the score was dropped. Berkeley was hired as a choreographer, but insisted on photographing the dances himself, launching his career and Hollywood musicals on the right track.

THE WIZARD OF OZ (MGM, 1939)

Really a Hollywood original (which launched the Arthur Freed unit at MGM), but in 1903 there had been a lavish and successful Broadway musical version of Frank Baum's story.

THE WIZ (UNIVERSAL, 1978)

Starring Diana Ross. Dorothy doesn't work as a thirty-year-old. But you could have guessed that.

WONDER BAR (WARNER BROTHERS, 1934)

Not the musical, but Al Jolson, Al Dubin, and Harry Warren songs, and some fascinating and bizarre musical sequences by Busby Berkeley.

YOKEL BOY (REPUBLIC, 1942)

Not the original story, and not the songs either. Sometimes you wonder why Hollywood bothers with the title.

• • •

Broadway has done even worse by Hollywood than Hollywood has done by Broadway. So far, most attempts to translate original film musicals to the stage—*Hans Christian Andersen* (London, 1971), *Gigi* (1973), *Seven Brides for Seven Brothers* (1982), *Singin' in the Rain* (1985), *Meet Me in St. Louis* (1989)—have been awful. The David Merrick-Gower Champion success with *42nd Street* stands as the only financially (if not artistically) successful film-to-stage translation of a musical.

ANYTHING GOES (from *Anything Goes*, words and music by Cole Porter) Administered by Warner Chappell. All Rights Reserved. Used by Permission.

AT THE BALLET (from "A Chorus Line"), music by Marvin Hamlisch, lyrics by Edward Kleban. Largo Music Inc. o/b/o American Compass Music Corp. and Wren Music Corp. Used by Permission. All Rights Reserved.

THE AUDITION (from "A Chorus Line"), music by Marvin Hamlisch, lyrics by Edward Kleban. Largo Music Inc. o/b/o American Compass Music Corp. and Wren Music Corp. Used by Permission. All Rights Reserved.

BALI HA'I (Rodgers, Hammerstein II)
Copyright © 1949 by Richard Rodgers and Oscar Hammerstein II
Copyright Renewed. WILLIAMSON MUSIC owner of publication and allied rights throughout the world.
International Copyright Secured. Used by Permission.

BEING ALIVE by Stephen Sondheim © 1970 Range Road Music Inc., Quartet Music Inc., and Rilting Music Inc. All rights administered by Herald Square Music Inc. Used by permission. All rights reserved.

BIG SPENDER (from *Sweet Charity*, music by Cy Coleman, lyrics by Dorothy Fields) Administered by Warner Chappell. All Rights Reserved. Used by Permission.

BLAH, BLAH, BLAH (from *Delicious*, Music by George Gershwin, Lyrics by Ira Gershwin)
Administered by Warner Chappell. All Rights Reserved. Used by Permission.

BOSTON BEGUINE (words and music by Sheldon Harnick)
Adminstered by Warner Chappell. All Rights Reserved. Used by Permission.
Thanks to A.P. Watt Ltd. And the trustess of the Wodehouse Estate for permission to quote from *Bring on the Girls* by P.G. Wodehouse and Guy Bolton.

BROTHER, CAN YOU SPARE A DIME? (from *Americana*, Music by Jay Gorney, lyrics by E.Y. Harburg)
Administered by Warner Chappell. All Rights Reserved. Used by Permission

CAMELOT (from *Camelot*, music by Frederick Loewe, lyrics by Alan Jay)
Administered by Warner Chappell. All Rights Reserved. Used by Permission

CAN'T HELP LOVIN' DAT MAN written by Jerome Kern and Oscar Hammerstein. Copyright © 1927 PolyGram International Publishing Inc. Copyright renewed. Used By Permission. All Rights Reserved.

THE EAGLE AND ME (from *Bloomer Girl*, music by Harold Arlen, lyrics by E.Y. Harburg)
Administered by Warner Chappell. All Rights Reserved. Used by Permission

A FELLOW NEEDS A GIRL (Rodgers, Hammerstein II)
Copyright © 1947 by Richard Rodgers and Oscar Hammerstein II
Copyright Renewed. WILLIAMSON MUSIC owner of publication and allied rights throughout the world.
International Copyright Secured. Used by Permission.

I DREAM TOO MUCH written by Jerome Kern and Dorothy Fields. Copyright © 1935 PolyGram International Publishing, Inc. (And as designated by co-publisher). Copyright Renewed. Used By Permission. All Rights Reserved.

I GOT RHYTHM (from *Girl Crazy*, Music by George Gershwin, lyrics by Ira Gershwin)
Administered by Warner Chappell. All Rights Reserved. Used by Permission.

I'M AN ORDINARY MAN (from *My Fair Lady*, music by Frederick Loewe, lyrics by Alan Jay Lerner)
Administered by Warner Chappell. All Rights Reserved. Used by Permission.

I'M GOIN' BACK (from *Bells Are Ringing*, music by Jule Styne, lyrics by Betty Comden and Adolph Green)
Administered by Warner Chappell. All Rights Reserved. Used byPermission.

IN MY OWN LIFETIME by Jery Bock, Sheldon Harnick © 1970 Appletree Music Corp. Used by permission. All rights reserved.

IN THE STILL OF THE NIGHT (from *Rosalie*, words and music by Cole Porter) Administered by Warner Chappell. All Rights Reserved. Used by Permission.

IT'S ALL RIGHT WITH ME (from *Can-Can*, words and music by Cole Porter) Administered by Warner Chappell. All Rights Reserved. Used by Permission.

IT WAS GOOD ENOUGH FOR GRANDMA (from *Bloomer Girl*, music by Harold Arlen, lyrics by E.Y. Harburg)
Administered by Warner Chappell. All Rights Reserved. Used by Permission.

LIFE UPON THE WICKED STAGE written by Jerome Ken and Oscar Hammerstein II. Copyright 1927 PolyGram International Publishing, Inc.

MANHATTAN by Righard Rodgers, Lorenz Hart © 1925 Edward B. Marks Music Company and Piedmont Music Company. Copyright renewed. Used by permission. All rights reserved.

SORRY-GRATEFUL by Stephen Sondheim © 1970 Range Road Music Inc., Quartet Music Inc., and Rilting Music Inc. All rights administered by Herald Square Music Inc. Used by permission. All rights reserved.

YOU COULD DRIVE A PERSON CRAZY by Stephen Sondheim © 1970 Range Road Music Inc., Quartet Music Inc., and Rilting Music Inc. All rights administered by Herald Square Music Inc. Used by permission. All rights reserved.

Several people were kind enough to peruse the original manuscript and brought issues to my attention: to Ken Bloom, David Goldman, Barry Kleinbort, Edward Strauss, and Jim Volz I owe a great debt.

Thanks also to Paul Newman for the use of his outstanding collection of theatre programs, John Wilson White for his photography, Kristin Johnson, curator of the Goodspeed Opera House Library of the Musical Theatre, and Marc Jacobs and Marguerite Lavin of the Museum of the City of New York.

As usual, my wife Barbara scrutinized every word and let me know when she found some wanting.

• • •

I also owe a debt to the authors whose books provided so much information on the people and the shows of the American Musical.

Abbott, George. *"Mister Abbott."* New York: Random House, 1963.

Alpert, Hollis. *The Story of "Porgy and Bess."* New York: Knopf, 1990.

Atkinson, Brooks. *Broadway.* New York: Macmillan, 1970.

Bloom, Ken. *American Song: The Complete Musical Theatre Companion.* New York: Schirmer Books, 1996.

———. *Broadway.* New York: Facts on File, 1991.

Bordman, Gerald. *American Musical Revue.* New York: Oxford University Press, 1985.

———. *American Musical Theatre, A Chronicle.* New York: Oxford University Press, 1978.

———. *American Operetta from "HMS Pinafore" to "Sweeney Todd."* New York: Oxford University Press, 1981.

———. *Jerome Kern: His Life and Music.* New York: Oxford University Press, 1980.

———. *Days To Be Happy, Years To Be Sad: The Life & Music of Vincent Youmans.* New York: Oxford University Press, 1982.

Brissenden, Alan. *Shakespeare and the Dance.* New Jersey: Humanities Press, 1981.

Brockett, Oscar G. *The Theatre, An Introduction.* New York: Holt, Rinehard and Winston, 1964.

Corio, Ann. *This Was Burlesque.* New York: Grosset & Dunlap, 1968.

Crawford, Cheryl. *One Naked Individual.* New York: Bobbs Merrill, 1977.

Davis, Lee. *Bolton & Wodehouse & Kern: The Men Who Made Musical Comedy.* New York: James H. Heineman, 1993.

Davis, Lorrie, with Rachel Gallagher. *Letting Down My Hair.* New York: Arthur Fields, 1973.

deMille, Agnes. *Dance to the Piper.* Boston: Little, Brown & Company, 1951.

Dickinson, Patric. *Aristophanes: Plays.* London: Oxford University Press, 1970.

Dietz, Howard. *Dancing in the Dark.* New York: Quadrangle, 1974.

Dover, K.J. *Aristophanic Comedy.* Berkeley: University of California, 1972.

Engel, Lehman. *American Musical Theatre: A Consideration.* New York: Macmillan, 1967.

———. *Their Words Are Music: The Great Theatre Lyricists and Their Lyrics.* New York: Crown, 1975.

Ewen, David. *George Gershwin: His Journey to Greatness.* New Jersey: Prentice Hall, 1970.

———. *The World of Jerome Kern.* New York: Henry Holt and Company,

1960.

Fordin, Hugh. *Getting to Know Him.* New York: Random House, 1977.

Freedland, Michael. *Irving Berlin.* New York: Stein & Day, 1974.

———. *Jerome Kern.* New York: Stein & Day, 1978.

Gänzl, Kurt. *The Encyclopedia of Musical Theatre.* New York: Schirmer Books, 1994.

Gay, John. *The Beggar's Opera.* New York. The Heritage Press, 1937.

Gershwin, Ira. *Lyrics on Several Occasions.* New York: Viking, 1973.

Gilbert, Douglas. *American Vaudeville, Its Life and Times.* New York: Dover Publications, 1940.

Giordano, Gus. *Anthology of American Jazz Dance.* Illinois: Orion, 1975.

Goldberg, Isaac. *The Story of Gilbert & Sullivan.* New York: Crown, 1935.

Gottfried, Martinl. *All His Jazz.* New York: Bantam Books, 1990.

———. *Broadway Musicals.* New York: Harry N. Abrams, 1979.

Green, Stanley, *Broadway Musicals, Show by Show.* Milwaukee: Hal Leonard, 1987.

———. *Ring Bells, Sing Songs: Broadway Musicals of the Thirties. New York: Arlington House, 1971.*

———. *The World of Musical Comedy.* New York: Grosset & Dunlap, 1960.

Guernsey, Otis L. Jr., ed. *Playwrights, Lyricists, Composers on Theatre.* New York: Dodd, Mead & Company, 1974.

Hammerstein II, Oscar. *Lyrics.* New York: Simon & Schuster, 1949.

Hart, Dorothy and Robert Kimall. *The Complete Lyrics of Lorenz Hart.* New York: Knopf, 1986.

Higham, Charles. *Ziegfeld.* Chicago: Henry Regnery, 1972.

Hirsch, Foster. *Harold Prince and the American Musical Theatre.* Cambridge: Cambridge University Press, 1989.

Jablonski, Edward. *The Encyclopedia of American Music.* New York: Doubleday, 1981.

———. *Gershwin.* New York: Doubleday, 1987.

———.and Lawrence D. Stewart. *The Gershwin Years.* New York: Doubleday, 1958.

Laurents, Arthur, Leonard Bernstein, and Stephen Sondheim. *West Side Story.* New York: Random House, 1956.

Kimball, Robert and Brendan Gill. *Cole.* New York: Holt, Rinehard & Winston, 1973.

———. and Alfred Simon. *The Gershwins.* New York: Atheneum, 1973.

Kislan, Richard. *Hoofing on Broadway.* New York: Prentice Hall, 1987.

Krueger, Miles. *"Show Boat," The Story of a Classic American Musical.* New York: Da Capo, 1977.

Laufe, Abe. *Broadway's Greatest Musicals.* New York: Funk & Wagnalls, 1973.

Lees, Gene. *Inventing Champagne, The Worlds Of Lerner and Loewe.* New York: St. Martin's, 1990.

Lerner, Alan Jay. *The Musical Theatre: A Celebration.* New York: McGraw, 1986.

———. *The Street Where I Lived.* New York: Norton, 1978.

McCabe, John. George M. Cohan: T*he Man Who Owned Broadway.* New York: Doubleday, 1973.

Mordden, Ethan. *Better Foot Forward.* New York: Grossman, 1976.

———. *Broadway Babies.* New York: Oxford University Press, 1983.

———. *Rodgers and Hammerstein.* New York: Harry N. Abrams, 1992.

Morley, Sheridan. *Spread a Little Happiness: The First One Hundred Years of the British Musical.* London: Thames and Hudson, 1987.

Nagler, A.M. *A Source Book in Theatrical History.* New York: Dover Publications, 1952.

Payne, Charles. *American Ballet Theatre.* New York: Knopf, 1978.

Peyser, Joan. *Leonard Bernstein.* New York: Bantam, 1982.

Prince, Harold. *Contradictions: Notes on Twenty Six Years in the Theatre.* New York: Dodd, Mead & Company, 1974.

Roberts, Vera Mowry. *On Stage, a History of Theatre.* New York: Harper & Row, 1952.

Rodgers, Richard. *Musical Stages.* New York: Random House, 1975.

Rosenberg, Deena. *Fascinating Rhythm: The Collaboration of George and Ira Gershwin.* New York: Dutton, 1991.

Sanders, R. *The Days Grow Short, The Life and Music of Kurt Weill.* New York: Holt, Rinehart and Winston, 1980.

Smith, Harry B. *First Nights and First Editions.* Boston: Little, Brown and Company, 1931.

———. *Stage Lyrics.* New York: R.H. Russell, 1900.

Sobel, Bernard. Burleycue. New York: Farrar & Rinehart, 1931.

Stevenson, Isabel. *The Tony Award.* New York: Crown, 1989.

Sullivan, Herbert and Newman Flowers. *Sir Arthur Sullivan: His Life, Letters and Diaries.* London: Cassell & Company, 1927.

Traubner, Richard. *Operetta: A Theatrical History.* New York: Doubleday, 1983.

Wilk, Max. *They're Playing Our Song.* New York: Atheneum, 1973.

———. *OK! The Story of "Oklahoma!"* New York: Grove Press, 1993.

Wodehouse, P.G., and Guy Bolton, *Bring on the Girls.* New York: Simon & Schuster, 1953.

Zadan, Craig. *Sondheim and Company.* New York: Avon, 1974.

About the Author

Denny Martin Flinn grew up in San Francisco, then journeyed to New York City, where he spent twenty years in the American musical theatre as a dancer, choreographer, and director before turning to writing. Following his performances as Greg and Zach in the international touring company of *A Chorus Line,* he wrote *What They Did for Love,* the story of the making of that musical. He is also the author of the mystery novels *San Francisco Kills* and *Killer Finish,* the Star Trek novel *The Fearful Summons,* and co-screenwriter of *Star Trek VI: The Undiscovered Country.* He and his family live in Los Angeles.